From Java to C#

PEARSON
Education

We work with leading authors to develop the
strongest educational materials in computing,
bringing cutting-edge thinking and best learning
practice to a global market.

Under a range of well-known imprints, including
Addison Wesley, we craft high quality print and
electronic publications which help readers to
understand and apply their content, whether
studying or at work.

To find out more about the complete range of our
publishing, please visit us on the World Wide Web at:
www.pearsoneduc.co.uk

From Java to C#

Glenn W. Rowe

ADDISON-WESLEY

An imprint of **Pearson Education**

Harlow, England • London • New York • Boston • San Francisco • Toronto
Sydney • Tokyo • Singapore • Hong Kong • Seoul • Taipei • New Delhi
Cape Town • Madrid • Mexico City • Amsterdam • Munich • Paris • Milan

Pearson Education Limited
Edinburgh Gate
Harlow
Essex CM20 2JE
England

and Associated Companies around the world

Visit us on the World Wide Web at:
www.pearsoned.co.uk

———————————

First published 2004

© Pearson Education Limited 2004

ISBN 0 321 15572 6

British Library Cataloguing-in-Publication Data
A catalogue record for this book can be obtained from the British Library.

Library of Congress Cataloging-in-Publication Data
Rowe, Glenn (Glenn W.)
    From Java to C# / by Glenn W. Rowe.
        p. cm.
    Includes index.
    ISBN 0-321-15572-6
     1. Java (Compuer program language) 2. C# (Computer program language) I. Title.

  QA76.783.J38R69 2004
  005.13'3--dc22

                            2004040997

10 9 8 7 6 5 4 3 2
08 07 06 05 04

Typeset in 10/12pt Caslon by 30
Printed and bound in Great Britain by Henry Ling Ltd., at the Dorset Press,
Dorchester, Dorset

The publisher's policy is to use paper manufactured from sustainable forests.

Contents

Preface   xiii

Acknowledgements   xv

1   Introduction to C# and .NET   1

1.1   What are C# and .NET?   1
1.2   Writing your first C# program – using the command line   3
1.3   Writing your first C# program – using Visual Studio .NET   6
Summary   9
Exercises   10

2   Classes and objects   11

2.1   Object-oriented programming   11
2.2   Why 'objects first'?   11
2.3   The object-oriented idea: encapsulation   13
    2.3.1   Encapsulation   14
    2.3.2   Example: an `Employee` class   15
    2.3.3   Properties in C#   19
2.4   Case study: an adventure game   21
Summary   27
Exercises   27

3   Data, expressions and statements   29

3.1   Primitive data types   29
    3.1.1   Integer types   29
    3.1.2   Data type conversion   31
3.2   Data overflow and the `checked` keyword   32
3.3   Floating-point types   33
3.4   The decimal type   35
3.5   The `bool` (Boolean) type   36
3.6   The `char` (character) type   36
3.7   Strings   38
3.8   String formatting   40
3.9   Regular expressions   42

3.10 Implicit type conversions 44
3.11 Explicit type conversions – casting 45
3.12 Operators 47
    3.12.1 Increment and decrement 50
    3.12.2 Bitwise operators 52
    3.12.3 Logical operators 54
    3.12.4 Bit shift operators 54
    3.12.5 Equality testing operators 55
    3.12.6 Comparison operators 55
    3.12.7 Assignment operator 56
    3.12.8 Convenience assignment operators 56
    3.12.9 The conditional operator ?: 57
3.13 Operator associativity 58
3.14 Operator precedence 59
3.15 Conditional statements 61
    3.15.1 The if...else statement 61
    3.15.2 The switch statement 63
3.16 Loops 66
    3.16.1 The while loop 66
    3.16.2 The do...while loop 67
    3.16.3 The for loop 68
3.17 The break and continue statements 71
3.18 The goto statement 72
Summary 75
Exercises 75

4 Inside C# objects 81

4.1 Value and reference types 81
4.2 Passing by value and passing by reference 86
4.3 The ref keyword 88
4.4 The out keyword 91
4.5 Arrays 93
    4.5.1 Arrays of reference types 94
    4.5.2 Bounds checking 95
    4.5.3 Array initialization 96
4.6 The foreach loop 97
4.7 Multidimensional arrays 98
    4.7.1 Rectangular arrays 98
    4.7.2 Jagged arrays 101
    4.7.3 The foreach loop with jagged arrays 102
    4.7.4 The null row problem 103
    4.7.5 Passing arrays to methods 104
    4.7.6 The params keyword 106
4.8 Enumerations 108

4.9	Variable scope	112
	4.9.1 Local variables	112
	4.9.2 Method parameters	115
	4.9.3 Class data fields	115
4.10	Memory management in variable declarations	117
	4.10.1 The program stack	120
	4.10.2 The program heap	120
4.11	Garbage collection and the managed heap	126
4.12	Structs	127
	Summary	130
	Exercises	131

5   C# classes – advanced features   137

5.1	Constructors	137
5.2	Method overloading	142
5.3	The static keyword	144
	5.3.1 Static data fields	144
	5.3.2 Static methods	146
	5.3.3 Static constructors	147
5.4	The const keyword	149
5.5	The readonly keyword	150
5.6	Method implementation	151
5.7	The this keyword	151
5.8	Operator overloading	153
	5.8.1 Overloading comparison operators	157
	5.8.2 Overloading ++ and --	157
	5.8.3 Overloading assignment operators	157
	5.8.4 The true and false operators	158
	5.8.5 Overloading && and ||	159
	5.8.6 General rules for operator overloading	161
5.9	Casting	162
5.10	Indexers	167
5.11	Namespaces	170
	5.11.1 Defining a namespace	170
	5.11.2 The using statement	172
5.12	Case study: the adventure game	174
	Summary	191
	Exercises	192

6   Inheritance   195

6.1	The concept of inheritance	195
6.2	Syntax for inheritance	196
6.3	Accessing base class data from a derived class	198

6.4	Inheriting methods	200
6.5	Constructors and inheritance	201
6.6	Name hiding	202
6.7	Polymorphism	203
6.8	Virtual methods	204
6.9	Polymorphism and method parameters	207
6.10	Versioning	207
6.11	Inheriting static methods	209
6.12	The `Object` class	211
	6.12.1 The `ToString()` method	211
	6.12.2 The `Equals()` and `ReferenceEquals()` methods	212
6.13	Boxing and unboxing	216
6.14	Structs and inheritance	218
6.15	The `is` operator	220
6.16	The `as` operator	221
6.17	Sealed classes and methods	222
6.18	Abstract classes	224
6.19	Interfaces	227
6.20	Case study: the adventure game	231
	6.20.1 Using inheritance	231
	6.20.2 Adding new commands	236
	6.20.3 Rules of combat	237
	6.20.4 `Item` classes	238
	6.20.5 `Character` classes	247
	6.20.6 The `Room` class	256
	6.20.7 The `Adventure` class – initialization and command handling	260
	Summary	278
	Exercises	278

7 Exceptions 281

7.1	Encountering exceptions	281
7.2	Handling exceptions	283
7.3	Exceptions and inheritance	286
7.4	Throwing exceptions	288
7.5	Data carried by exceptions	289
7.6	User-defined exceptions	290
7.7	When to use exceptions	292
	Summary	293
	Exercises	293

8 Events and delegates 295

8.1 Events 295
8.2 Events in Java 295
8.3 Delegates 296
8.4 Multicast delegates 301
8.5 Handling events 303
8.6 Threads 307
  8.6.1 Threads in Java 307
  8.6.2 Threads in C# 308
  8.6.3 Uses of threads 311
Summary 311
Exercises 311

9 GUI programming with Windows Forms 313

9.1 Using the .NET libraries 313
9.2 Writing GUI code in C# – the choice of environment 313
9.3 Windows code in Visual Studio .NET 315
9.4 Console versus Windows programs 317
9.5 The structure of a Windows program 318
9.6 Editing a Windows Form 318
9.7 Building a first GUI program from scratch 320
9.8 Adding an event handler 321
9.9 Layouts: anchors and docks 322
9.10 Using the MSDN documentation 324
9.11 A simple calculator in Windows Forms 326
9.12 Error handling and the `ErrorProvider` control 331
9.13 Checkboxes and radio buttons 335
9.14 Menus 342
9.15 Dialogs, status bars and toolbars 348
  9.15.1 Dialogs 348
  9.15.2 Status bars 350
  9.15.3 Toolbars 351
9.16 Example: a Notepad clone 354
9.17 Other controls 367
Summary 368
Exercises 368

10 Graphics 371

10.1 Graphics: Java versus .NET 371
10.2 Vector graphics 373
  10.2.1 Colo(u)rs 373
  10.2.2 Drawing shapes – the `Pen` class 374

		10.2.3	Filling shapes – the `Brush` classes	376
		10.2.4	Brushes as pens	384
	10.3	The `GraphicsPath`		385
	10.4	Filling shapes		387
	10.5	Transformations and the `Matrix` class		391
		10.5.1	Translation	393
		10.5.2	Rotations	396
		10.5.3	Scaling	398
		10.5.4	Shearing	398
	10.6	Fonts and drawing strings		400
	10.7	Raster graphics		404
		10.7.1	Displaying an image from a disk file	404
		10.7.2	Drawing on an image	405
	10.8	Mouse events		407
		10.8.1	Mouse events example: checkers game	410
		10.8.2	Other mouse events	417
	10.9	Keyboard events		418
	10.10	Animation – threads revisited		421
	10.11	Case study: the adventure game graphical interface		428
		10.11.1	The interface to the game	429
		10.11.2	Class design	430
		10.11.3	The GUI code	431
		10.11.4	`AdventureForm` – initialization	431
		10.11.5	Non-rectangular buttons	441
		10.11.6	Drawing the map	447
		10.11.7	Displaying the player's statistics	451
		10.11.8	Event handlers	454
	Summary			465
	Exercises			466

11 Databases

469

	11.1	The basics		469
	11.2	SQL		473
		11.2.1	Data types	474
		11.2.2	Inserting a new record	475
		11.2.3	Queries	476
		11.2.4	Joins	478
		11.2.5	Updates	482
		11.2.6	Deleting records	482
	11.3	Driving databases from C#		483
	11.4	ODBC drivers		484
	11.5	Connecting to a database from C#		484
	11.6	Accessing other databases from C# – MySQL example		487

11.7   SQL Server and the `SqlClient` namespace   490
11.8   Running SQL commands   491
        11.8.1   Querying   492
        11.8.2   Non-queries   496
        11.8.3   Prepared statements   497
11.9   `DataSets`   500
11.10   Databases and Windows Forms: `DataGrids`   504
11.11   More with `DataGrids` and `DataSets`   511
11.12   Case study: the adventure game   525
        11.12.1 Building a database for the adventure game   525
        11.12.2 Writing the C# code   527
Summary   535
Exercises   535

12   XML   537

12.1   Introduction   537
12.2   Simple XML   538
12.3   Using XML   541
12.4   Reading XML: `XMLTextReader`   543
12.5   Document Type Definitions – validating XML files   550
        12.5.1   Writing DTDs   551
        12.5.2   DOCTYPE statements   553
        12.5.3   Using a validating parser   554
12.6   The Document Object Model   558
12.7   Searching an XML tree with XPath   562
12.8   Editing and writing XML   566
        12.8.1   `XmlTextWriter`   567
        12.8.2   Writing XML using `XmlDocument`   568
12.9   Transforming XML – XSLT   578
12.10   XML documentation in C# code   585
12.11   Case study: saving and loading the adventure game   589
        12.11.1 DTD for the Adventure XML file   589
        12.11.2 C# code for saving the game as XML   590
        12.11.3 C# code for loading a saved game   594
Summary   599
Exercises   600

13   Web pages and the Internet   603

13.1   Generating web pages   603
13.2   ASP .NET and C#   604
        13.2.1   How it works   607
13.3   Web controls   610

13.4	Web controls and databases	610
13.5	Case study: an on-line scores list for the adventure game	611
	13.5.1 The `DataGrid` web control	612
	13.5.2 Customizing a `DataGrid`	614
13.6	Graphics on web pages	619
13.7	Interactive web pages	622
13.8	Case study: an item editor for the adventure game	623
	13.8.1 The interface	624
	13.8.2 The ASP .NET code	625
	13.8.3 Validation of data	630
	13.8.4 Interactive data display	631
	13.8.5 Templates	632
	13.8.6 C# code for item editor	634
13.9	Web services	647
	13.9.1 Writing a web service in C#	648
	13.9.2 Consuming a web service	651
13.10	Accessing the Internet	654
	13.10.1 Downloading files	654
Summary		659
Exercises		659
Index		662

Preface

This book provides a comprehensive introduction to the C# programming language introduced by Microsoft with the first official release in February 2002. C# is part of a much larger project called .NET, which provides a vast library of classes allowing software developers to create applications to meet almost any need in the industrial and research areas.

A prospective reader of this book will no doubt want to know what is expected of him or her. As the title implies, this book is written primarily for readers who have some (but not necessarily a lot of) programming experience using Java, such as might be gained from an introductory programming course. At the moment, Java is a very popular language in such courses at colleges and universities worldwide, due to its clean structure and relatively shallow learning curve.

However, readers who have some experience with object-oriented programming in other languages such as C++ should also be able to follow the book, as although in the early chapters there are numerous comparisons with Java, the material on C# itself does not actually depend on the reader understanding Java code specifically.

Those of you who have glanced at the table of contents will notice that the later chapters in the book deal with topics such as graphics, databases and so on, and may wonder if they will be able to understand the material in them. This book assumes no prior knowledge of any of these topics, so you should be confident that the material here will be accessible. Most introductory courses are taught using only programs that produce textual output, since dealing with graphical interfaces involves concepts that beginners find rather daunting.

If you are looking at this book in a bookshop or library, you may well have noticed a large number of other books on C#, .NET and their relationship with the topics in the later chapters of this book. You may also notice that many of these books are quite large, with many of them having in excess of 1000 pages. If you deduce from this that there is a lot more to .NET than what is contained in the book you are holding, you are quite right.

This fact means that when writing the book, I had to decide what parts of C# and .NET were the most suitable for a reader with a modest programming background. The book's early chapters (up to Chapter 8) provide a fairly thorough and complete coverage of C# as a stand-alone language. All programs developed up to Chapter 8 are textual programs, meaning that all interaction with them is done via the Windows console. C# is a considerably bigger language than Java, even without considering the .NET libraries, so a complete coverage does take some time to complete.

Beginning with Chapter 9, the book becomes more of a tour of the main features of .NET and how C# can use these features. There is much more that could be said about each of the topics in Chapters 9 through 13 (as indeed, much *has* been said, since many of those 1000+ page books are devoted entirely to an expansion of what is in one of the chapters in this book). There are also several topics upon which this book does not touch at all.

In selecting the topics from .NET to cover, I have tried to heed the current demands of industry and research to determine what is most popular and commonly used. Graphical interfaces and graphics are common to almost all programs these days, so they form the foundation chapters (9 and 10). Almost as commonly used are databases, so Chapter 11 is devoted to them. XML is now very widely used to transmit information between clients and servers, and also forms the core of much of .NET's way of doing things, so we have a chapter on that. Finally, one can hardly consider a computing book complete without some coverage of the Internet, so C#'s role in producing and accessing web pages is described in the final chapter.

In these later chapters, the approach becomes less formal and more illustrative, since each topic covered in this part of the book is much too big for a thorough treatment. I have tried to set the scene in each case by describing the basics and then provide some paths into the more advanced areas by giving several progressively more detailed examples.

In order to show how many of the topics in the book can work together in a substantial program, I have developed a major case study (an adventure game) progressively over several chapters in the book. The adventure game makes its first appearance in Chapter 2 as a collection of skeleton classes and is progressively enhanced and developed until by the end of the book it is a full program with a graphical interface, a database for storing the initial data used in the game, a saved game file using XML, and a web interface for editing the contents of the database.

The book is meant to be approached by reading the chapters in order, since most chapters make references to preceding ones. Readers anxious to learn about a particular feature of C# or .NET may, however, dive in at the appropriate point and then refer back to earlier chapters as required.

Finally, a brief note on some of the aspects of C# and .NET that are *not* included in the book.

The only feature of C# itself that is not covered is *unsafe code*. Unsafe code allows programmers direct access to specific memory locations by means of *pointers*, which will be a foreign concept to Java programmers (although painfully familiar to C or C++ veterans). The idea of direct memory access is counter to the philosophy of programming which is encouraged by both Java and C#, and is certainly not needed for any of the examples we develop in the book.

There are many areas of the .NET libraries that are not covered at all. Although these are quite useful in many areas, they are not likely to be encountered by programmers taking their first steps in the .NET landscape and can safely be left to a more advanced book or course.

Although the accepted development environment for writing C# and .NET applications is Visual Studio .NET, I made a conscious decision not to rely on this package for the examples in this book. This is for two main reasons. First, the book is aimed mainly at a student audience and students are notoriously short of funds. Visual Studio .NET, although very useful, is also quite expensive. Most of the sample code in the book can therefore be entered in an ordinary text editor such as Notepad, and compiled using a command line, if required.

The second reason is that, although Visual Studio's code generation facilities can be quite useful, they also tend to generate far more code than is needed to get a program up and running. This makes the code harder to understand and maintain. It is better at least to see how to build code from scratch when you are learning a new system and if you then decide you want to use the automated project generation in Visual Studio, you will have a solid understanding of the underlying code.

Just as this book was going to press, version 1.5 of Java was released in beta. It contains many enhancements to the basic Java language which were not present in version 1.4, so that some statements about Java's capabilities in the book are no longer valid for version 1.5. For example, Java 1.5 now supports the enum keyword, variable-length argument lists in methods, formatted input and output, a rough equivalent to C#'s 'foreach' loop and several other features.

Acknowledgements

In addition to several anonymous referees who provided many useful suggestions and corrections, I would also like to acknowledge the comments and suggestions of many past and present students at the University of Dundee, especially Jonathan Bowyer, Allan McCulloch, Callum Urquhart, Simon Barber, Iain Milne, Iain Wilkie and Graham Cannell. Since the book is intended primarily for students, their input has been particularly valuable.

Finally, a special vote of thanks to the staff at Pearson Education, particularly Kate Brewin and Owen Knight, who provided friendly advice and help over the entire course of the writing and production of this book.

Glenn W. Rowe

Introduction to C# and .NET 1

1.1 ■ What are C# and .NET?

This introductory session is placed at the start of Chapter 1 rather than in the book's preface, since most readers (the author included) probably don't read book prefaces. As the book's title suggests, this book is written for students who have a working knowledge of Java and wish to use that knowledge to learn something about Microsoft's C# language and the associated .NET libraries.

First, we need to get straight exactly what C# and .NET are. C# is a new computer language devised by Microsoft. The structure of the language is strongly reminiscent of Java (even though no mention of Java is made in C#'s language reference manual!) and is obviously inspired by Java. .NET is a very large library of classes and methods that may be used in C# programs (and indeed in programs written in several other languages as well). .NET also provides an underlying *framework* which allows programs using the .NET libraries to run. In a sense, .NET can be thought of as analogous to the Java Virtual Machine, which must be running on a computer before any Java programs can be run on that computer. But .NET combines this framework with the vast collection of libraries that may be used within C# programs. In this sense, .NET is analogous to the many Java packages (such as the Java AWT, Swing, Java 3D and so on) that are available for use in Java programs.

One of Java's main selling points is that it is *platform independent*, meaning that a Java program can be written on one platform such as Windows and then ported directly to any other platform running a Java Virtual Machine, such as Linux, UNIX or the Macintosh. The amazing thing about Java is that this platform independence really does work. The author has written substantial applications in Java that have run without modification on other operating systems without any significant problems.

At the time of writing, the full .NET framework is available only on later versions of Windows (Windows 2000, XP and later), so it is not yet platform independent. However, a third-party effort is being made to produce an open-source (essentially, free) version of .NET and C# that is runnable on Windows and Linux. The Mono project (see www.go-mono.com) is making good progress towards its goal, although at the time of writing, not all the libraries in the commercial version of .NET have been written in Mono.

One interesting feature of .NET is that although it is not officially *platform*-independent, it is currently *language*-independent. This means that different parts of a program may be written in different .NET-compliant languages and linked together into the final executable file. This is achieved by .NET's *Common Language Runtime*, or CLR, which is a program similar in spirit to Java's Virtual Machine, in that it runs code compiled from any of the .NET languages. Unlike the JVM, however, the CLR (at least Microsoft's version of it) only runs on Windows at present.

The main .NET languages in the first release of .NET are C#, Visual Basic .NET and managed C++. Browsing through the documentation that is available for .NET (the Microsoft Developer's Network or MSDN documentation) reveals that almost all classes and methods have examples provided in C# and Visual Basic .NET and sometimes C++ as well. C# and Visual Basic .NET have equal power when it comes to using the .NET libraries. The main difference between C# and Visual Basic .NET is that C# is a more versatile language with more powerful innate language features, so it is better suited for writing programs that require implementation of more sophisticated algorithms.

The approach to learning C# and .NET we will take in this book is to begin by concentrating on the C# language on its own first and only later adding in some of the main .NET libraries to get some idea of what can be achieved using the full .NET system. Readers with a year's experience of Java will find that C# as a language has a much richer repertoire of operators and data structures than Java, which some programmers regard as a mixed blessing. Probably the best approach to C# is to get an idea of what's available and then form your own personal programming style which will tend to use certain techniques for writing code rather than others that are equally valid, and could be favoured by a different programmer's style.

The book is reasonably complete in its description of the basic syntax and operation of C# on its own. Such a comprehensive cover of the vast .NET libraries, however, is simply not possible in a book of this size. We have therefore tried to include chapters on the more important and commonly used features of .NET such as Windows Forms for creating graphical interfaces, graphics libraries for drawing images, databases, XML and ASP .NET for the creation of interactive web sites. Even within these broad areas however we cannot explore any of these topics fully. These later chapters of the book should therefore be used as introductions to topics rather than comprehensive reference manuals.

In Java programming, once a student progresses beyond the basics of writing textual programs and starts to use the Java libraries such as Swing, the Java AWT and so on, it is essential to become conversant with the Java documentation. Similarly, when using .NET it is vital to become familiar with the MSDN documentation. MSDN is included as part of the Visual Studio .NET package, but is also freely available (for consultation, not download) on Microsoft's MSDN web site, at msdn.microsoft.com. The MSDN documentation contains many sections, only some of which are directly concerned with C# and .NET, but it is worth a browse through the top levels of the full site to see what is available.

Finally before we begin, a word on what is expected of the reader and how this expectation affects the structure of the book.

The book's title states that it takes the reader 'from Java to C#'. This means that we will assume that readers have taken the equivalent of a single-year introductory programming course using Java as the language. Since most introductory Java courses restrict themselves to the basics of classes and objects (hopefully done in an objects-first fashion!), and do not progress beyond textual programs, that is essentially what this book also assumes. In particular, we will not be assuming that the reader has written graphical user interface (GUI) programs in Java or made any significant use of most of the Java packages beyond perhaps some usage of classes in the standard `java.lang` package such as `String` for representing text strings.

In the early chapters of the book, where we will describe the fundamentals of C#'s syntax and operators, we will be pointing out similarities and differences between C#'s way of doing things and methods you may have learned in Java. Readers will find that much of C# at this level is very similar to Java, which should hopefully ease the learning process.

In later chapters, where we consider some of the .NET libraries, comparisons with Java will be much scarcer. The reason for this is that we are not assuming that readers have had much experience with using Java beyond writing textual programs that make minimal use of the various Java packages, so drawing comparisons between .NET libraries and packages in Java would serve no useful purpose.

Enough introductory remarks. It is time to dive in and see what C# code looks like!

1.2 ■ Writing your first C# program – using the command line

Although we haven't yet introduced any of C#'s features officially, readers with some experience of Java programming shouldn't have any difficulty in understanding how a simple C# program works.

We'll begin with the traditional 'Hello world'-type program since an essential first step in learning how to use any new programming language is to discover how to compile and run the simplest possible program.

The most popular development environment for C# and .NET programs is Microsoft's Visual Studio .NET, but although this package is very powerful and useful, it is also quite expensive, so we cannot assume that all readers of this book will have access to it. Fortunately, it is possible to write most C# and .NET programs without using Visual Studio, since Microsoft provides the .NET Framework Software Development Kit (SDK) as a free download from their web site. At the time of writing, the SDK is at version 1.1 and is available from http://www.microsoft.com/downloads/details.aspx?FamilyID=9b3a2ca6-3647-4070-9f41-a333c6b9181d&DisplayLang=en. The file size is 108 MB, so it's a non-trivial download. (If you find that the web link above no longer works, a search of Microsoft's Download Center for .NET Framework Software Development Kit should locate the new link.)

The SDK includes a command line C# compiler and all the .NET libraries required to run all the examples in this book. All that is missing is the graphical environment in which the code can be written, so you will need to use a separate editor to write your code. A program as simple as Notepad can be used for this, although there are many other free text editors available on the web.

The simplest possible C# program that produces some output is:

```
public class FirstProgram
{
  public static void Main(string[] args)
  {
    System.Console.WriteLine("This is a lot like Java!");
  }
}
```

This code was written using Windows Notepad, but any text editor could have been used. The program is stored in the file `FirstProgram.cs`. For convenience, we have used the class name to create the filename, but unlike Java, this is not essential in C#. We could have named the file `FirstTry.cs` (or anything else, as long as it has a `.cs` extension) without changing the class name.

To compile this program using the command-line C# compiler, we first need to find the compiler program, which is harder than it sounds. If you have installed Visual Studio .NET, one of the files that it installs is called `csc.exe`, which is the C# compiler (the acronym 'csc' stands for C-Sharp Compiler). It is actually buried deep in the Windows directory in a folder that depends on the version of the .NET Framework SDK you have installed.

If Windows has been installed on your C drive, the location of `csc.exe` is C:\Windows\Microsoft.NET\Framework\v1.0.3705\csc.exe. Note that the last directory listed in this path (v1.0.3705) contains the version number of the release of .NET that you have installed, and was correct for the first official release of .NET in February 2002. If you are using a later version, the name of this directory will be different. The current version at the time of writing is version 1.1, and the last directory is called v1.1.4322. If all else fails, use the Search facility in Windows Explorer to locate the compiler.

Once we've found the C# compiler, we can compile the above program with the command (which should all be on one line):

```
C:\Windows\Microsoft.NET\Framework\v1.1.4322\csc
   FirstProgram.cs
```

Alternatively, if you get tired of typing out the entire pathname of the compiler each time, you can add the compiler's directory to your PATH variable. The exact procedure for doing this varies slightly with different versions of Windows. Under Windows XP, the procedure is as follows.

Find the 'My Computer' icon on the desktop and right-click it. Select 'Properties' from the popup menu – this should display the 'System Properties' box. In this box, select the 'Advanced' tab and then click the 'Environment Variables' button. In the 'System variables' list, find the 'Path' variable, select it and then click 'Edit'. Add the directory containing the compiler:

```
C:\Windows\Microsoft.NET\Framework\v1.0.3705
```

to the end of the Path, separating it from the preceding directory with a semi-colon. Then click OK enough times to close all the dialog boxes. If you now open a new Console Window and move to the directory containing FirstProgram.cs, you should be able to compile it with the command:

```
csc FirstProgram.cs
```

After compilation, run the dir command to list the files in the directory. You should see FirstProgram.exe listed. If you run this program, the output should be:

```
This is a lot like Java!
```

As the output suggests, this simple C# program should remind you strongly of the first Java program you ever wrote. Like Java, C# is a *pure object-oriented* language, which means that *all* code must be contained within a class. Like Java, one class must contain an *entry point* – a method which tells the program where to start. In Java, this method must have the signature public static void main(String[] args). As we can see from the above example, the only difference in C# is that 'Main' must be spelled with an uppercase 'M', and 'string' with a lowercase 's'.

The output line is also reminiscent of Java's System.out.println(). In C#, however, System is a *namespace*, which is roughly analogous to a package in Java. Since most C# programs make use of one or more methods in the System namespace, it can get tedious having to type out System in front of each method call. C# defines the using keyword which allows namespaces that will be used frequently within a program to be declared at the top of the file, thus avoiding the need to prefix each method call with the namespace name. This is similar to the import statement in Java.

We could therefore rewrite the FirstProgram.cs file as follows:

```
using System;

public class FirstProgram
{
  public static void Main(string[] args)
  {
    Console.WriteLine("This is a lot like Java!");
  }
}
```

1.3 ■ Writing your first C# program – using Visual Studio .NET

The command-line compiler has the advantage of being free, as it is available as part of the .NET Software Development Kit (SDK), so if you are on a limited budget (or just don't want to buy Visual Studio .NET), you can manage perfectly well with it. All the examples given in this book have been written in such a way that they can be compiled and run without using Visual Studio .NET (which is often an advantage in that in many cases, hand-written code is significantly shorter and easier to understand). However, Visual Studio .NET *is* an exceptionally powerful and useful development environment, so even if you don't have it, it is worth knowing a bit about how it can be used, since many other books rely heavily on it for their examples.

We'll begin by showing how to type in, compile and run the FirstProgram example from the previous section. Since it is possible to customize Visual Studio .NET's menus and toolbars in a number of ways, the instructions for building and running a program may vary from one setup to another. The instructions in this section will use the default menu settings.

The first step after starting Visual Studio .NET is the creation of a new *project*. Visual Studio .NET has followed the corporate trend in redefining the English language by inventing new (and in this author's opinion, inaccurate) meanings for existing words. A *solution* is a container that can hold several *projects*, each of which can represent one portion or aspect of the overall solution. To start out, we will need only a single project in a solution, and if we tell Visual Studio .NET to create a new project, it will create the encompassing solution automatically.

To create a new project, select the File menu, then submenu New, and submenu Project. We are then confronted with the dialog shown in Figure 1.1.

Select 'Visual C# Projects' in the left panel, and 'Console Application' in the right. We name our project 'FirstProgram' and assign it a location using the boxes at the bottom of the dialog. Click OK and wait for Visual Studio .NET to create the project and its associated solution. When this process is complete, there should be a box in the main Visual Studio .NET window labelled 'Solution Explorer'. If this isn't visible, open the View menu and select 'Solution Explorer'. Listed in the Solution Explorer are the files associated with the project. Files with a .cs extension are C# source code files; files with other extensions contain other information relevant to the maintenance of the project, but not immediately useful to us at the moment.

Before we proceed to enter some code into Visual Studio .NET, it's worth taking a look at the directory in which the project was created. We can do this in Windows Explorer. We will find several files other than those listed in Solution Explorer, such as FirstProgram.csproj, which contains information about the structure of the project, and FirstProgram.sln, which contains more information about the overall solution itself. These files are all managed by Visual Studio .NET and it is usually a bad idea to modify them your-

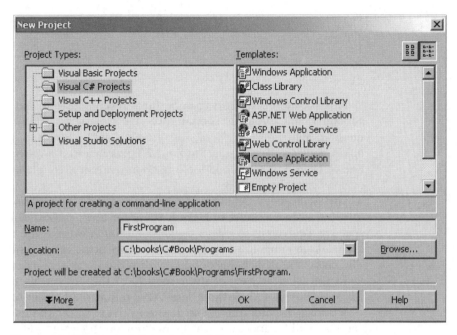

Figure 1.1 New Project dialog in Visual Studio .NET

self. However, if you want to copy a project you are working on to a different computer, make sure you include *all* the files and directories from the project directory, since they are all required for Visual Studio .NET to open the project on the other computer.

We can now return to Visual Studio .NET and have a look at the code in the file Class1.cs, which is shown here.

```
1. using System;
2.
3. namespace FirstProgram
4. {
5.    /// <summary>
6.    /// Summary description for Class1.
7.    /// </summary>
8.    class Class1
9.    {
10.       /// <summary>
11.       /// The main entry point for the application.
12.       /// </summary>
13.       [STAThread]
14.       static void Main(string[] args)
15.       {
16.          //
```

```
17.         // TODO: Add code to start application here
18.         //
19.     }
20.   }
21. }
```

This skeleton code bears a superficial resemblance to the command-line version in the previous section. We see a class definition and a `Main()` method, and the `using System` statement at the top of the file. The main differences are that Visual Studio .NET has inserted a `namespace` block at line 3, there are some odd-looking comments in a couple of places, and a curious entry on line 13.

The namespace definition isn't required for a simple program such as this, but it doesn't hurt to leave it there for now. You can think of a namespace as equivalent to a Java package, although without the restriction that the package name must match the directory structure in which it is stored. The class `Class1` is being defined within the `FirstProgram` namespace.

To get a better view of the structure of the project, go to the Solution Explorer box and click the 'Class View' tab at the bottom of the box. This view shows the hierarchical structure of the solution and its enclosed project. Open all layers in the tree by clicking on the little squares with a + sign inside them. The top level (root) of the tree is the solution itself. Underneath this is the `FirstProgram` namespace, whose icon is a pair of empty braces: `{ }`. Underneath the namespace is class `Class1`, and inside that is the `Main()` method, and another entry labelled 'Bases and Interfaces' which we will leave for now.

If you haven't used this sort of interface for viewing the structure of your code before, it is worth spending a while experimenting with it to see how it works. The entries in the Solution Explorer and Class View are dynamic, meaning that they automatically update whenever you change the code. To see how this works, try changing the name of the class from `Class1` to `FirstProgram` directly in the code window. You will see the Class View update to reflect the change.

After changing the name of the class, it is a good idea to change the name of the file in which the code is stored to keep things consistent. To do this, go back to Solution Explorer, right-click on the `Class1.cs` file, select 'Rename' and change the name of the file to `FirstProgram.cs`. You can check that the filename has taken effect by looking in Windows Explorer.

Before we add any code to the `FirstProgram` class, try compiling and running the program as it stands. To compile the program, select the Build menu, and then 'Build solution'. After a brief pause, you should see some text printed in the 'Output' box at the bottom of the Visual Studio .NET window. The last line of this text, assuming there were no warnings or errors during compilation, should say: '`Build: 1 succeeded, 0 failed, 0 skipped`'.

Since compiling and running the program will be frequent operations during the development of the code, you will probably find it more convenient to use keyboard shortcuts to do them. In the Build menu, any commands that have keyboard shortcuts have them displayed on the menu. For 'Build solution' the default keyboard shortcut is Ctrl + Shift + B.

If you have used an earlier version of Visual Studio (or one of its sub-programs such as Visual Basic or Visual C++) and prefer the keyboard shortcuts in that version, you can change the shortcuts by opening the Tools menu and selecting the Options command. In the Options dialog, select the Environment folder in the left panel, and then select Keyboard. From the 'Keyboard mapping scheme' drop-down list, select the keyboard map you want. You can also customize the keyboard map by selecting individual commands and specifying keystrokes for them.

To run the program, select the Debug menu, then 'Start without debugging' (default keystroke: Ctrl + F5). A console window will appear and the message 'Press any key to continue' is printed. This message is not produced by your program, but rather indicates that the program has finished and that the console window can be closed by hitting any key. Since we haven't added any code to the program, it hasn't produced any output.

To complete the program, add the line:

```
Console.WriteLine("This is a lot like Java!");
```

to the `Main()` method (replace the comments on lines 16 to 18 with this code), and compile and run the program to produce the output.

Finally, a note on the other features mentioned above. The unusual comments on lines 5 to 7 and 10 to 12 are special comments that allow Visual Studio .NET to produce XML documentation for your code. XML is used a lot in .NET for the transmission and storage of hierarchical information, and is rapidly becoming a standard method of information representation on the web. Visual Studio .NET can also produce HTML web page documentation from these special comments. We will consider them in more detail in Chapter 12, but for now, remember that any comment beginning with three slashes (///) rather than the usual two, is a comment that will produce XML documentation.

■ Summary

This introductory chapter has introduced you to C# and .NET and described how to write a simple C# program, both by using a simple text editor and command-line compiler statement and by using Visual Studio .NET.

Exercises

1.1 Search the web for articles that compare C# and Java. At this stage you may not be able fully to appreciate the comparisons being made since you do not yet know much about C# or .NET, but it is worth storing these articles for future reference as you proceed through the book.

1.2 Visit Microsoft's web site (www.microsoft.com) and search it for information on .NET and C#. This is worth doing every so often to see if new releases have come out or if service packs are available that correct bugs in earlier versions.

1.3 Search the web for sites that provide tutorials on C# and .NET. Sites such as these are often invaluable when you are trying to understand how to do some particular task, so it is worth building up a list of these sites in your Favourites menu in your web browser.

1.4 Use the MSDN documentation (either from the MSDN web site or locally if it is installed on your computer) to find out what methods (in addition to `WriteLine()` that we used in the example in this chapter) are available in the `Console` class. See if you can figure out how to read a line of text from the console window and print it out. Thus modify the simple program given in this chapter so that it asks the user for their name and then prints a message such as (assuming the user's name is Glenn):

```
Hello Glenn! Welcome to C#.
```

1.5 To get a feel for how similar C# and Java are, try writing, inside the `Main()` method in the example program given in this chapter, some simple code using Java syntax and run the result through the C# compiler. Take note of which language features of Java are accepted in C# and which are not. Try things such as declarations of primitive variable types such as `int` and `float`, loops (`for` and `while`), `if` statements, simple arithmetic operations and so on. Use the `string` data type to store text strings (instead of Java's `String`) and `Console.WriteLine()` and `Console.Write()` to produce output to the console window. Avoid using any other method calls, since these are usually different in C#.

Classes and objects 2

2.1 ■ Object-oriented programming

Readers of this book should already have met classes and objects while learning Java – indeed, it is impossible to write a Java program without using the keyword `class` at least once. Even so, various books and courses introducing object-oriented programming take different approaches to the subject.

At present, there are two main opinions as to how an object-oriented language such as Java or C# should be taught. The 'old school' believes that classes and objects are in some sense an 'advanced' or 'difficult' topic and can only be tackled after an initial grounding in variable declarations, arithmetic expressions, and control statements such as `if`, `while` and `for`. The 'new' or 'objects-first' school (to which this book belongs) believes that classes are a more natural way of thinking about program design and that it makes much more sense to build the learning of an object-oriented language around the concept of the class from the outset.

Since this book specified only that readers should be familiar with Java, and not necessarily be the product of a particular school of object-oriented thought, we'll begin this chapter with a quick review of the ideas behind classes and objects. After that, we'll see how C# represents classes and objects by considering a specific example.

2.2 ■ Why 'objects first'?

Until relatively recently, most introductory programming courses taught programming using a *procedural language*. In the 1980s and early 1990s, the most popular (amongst tutors, at any rate) teaching languages were Pascal, Modula-2 and C. All of these procedural languages evolved from, or were at least influenced by, earlier languages which ultimately can trace their ancestry back to assembly language, which required programs to be written at the level of moving bytes of data between memory locations and performing primitive operations such as addition or multiplication.

Although a procedural language such as Pascal is a 'high-level' language, in that the programmer need not understand anything about the set of machine instructions used by any particular processor, the idea behind a procedural language is that a program should be written as a sequence of actions or instructions which should be executed in a particular order. This is, after all, how a computer operates – it is provided with a sequence of primitive instructions and executes each one in a linear fashion (on a single-processor machine). Higher-level procedural languages simply defined higher-level instructions which were transformed into lower-level instructions by the compiler.

Writing a program in a procedural language therefore requires the programmer to analyze the project as a sequence of instructions. The 'proper' way of designing a procedural program was usually taken to be *top-down design*, in which the structure of the program is viewed hierarchically. At the top, or root, of the design is an overall 'instruction' which corresponds to the entire program. On the next level, this single master instruction is analyzed to determine several sub-instructions, and each of these sub-instructions is studied to find sub-sub-instructions within it, and so on until we find a level at which the instructions are simple enough not to require subdivision. Each of these simple instructions is then coded as a *function* or *procedure* within the program. Higher-level instructions are built up by calling lower-level functions to execute each sub-instruction required.

For example, suppose we are writing a car racing game. At the top level, the instruction would be just that: run a car racing game from start to finish. On the next level, this overall goal could be broken into sub-instructions such as 'offer to load previous game', 'start new game', 'select model of car', 'select racing track', 'start race', 'handle joystick signals' and so on. Each of these instructions must again be analyzed to see if it can be broken down further or is simple enough to be coded using a single function.

The procedural model has been used with a good deal of success for many years, and many millions of lines of code have been written in procedural languages. There are some widely recognized problems with procedural languages, however.

Experienced programmers often find that dealing with large procedural programs is difficult because there is just one large structure describing the whole program. Logical sub-units within a large program are difficult to isolate, which can hinder debugging and maintenance. Libraries of procedural code consist of large collections of individual functions with little or no internal structure, which makes it more difficult to reuse existing code in new projects.

At the other end of the scale, there is some evidence that students find procedural programming languages harder to learn than object-oriented ones, although the results are far from conclusive. However, since this book is primarily aimed at students rather than professional programmers, let us examine why this might be so.

A procedural language emphasizes *actions* as the central feature of a program. Looking back at the car racing example above, we see that all the instructions listed are commands to do something, rather than descriptions of static objects. However, if you think about how most people view the world, you will probably come to the conclusion that *objects* are more central to people's ways of perceiving the general scene around them than what those objects are doing. In terms of grammar, a noun is much easier to visualize than a verb – in fact, it is almost impossible to visualize an action without also visualizing an object that is carrying out that action. For example, try visualizing the concept of 'running' without thinking of an object, such as a person or dog, doing the running. However, it is simple to visualize a dog or person without associating any particular action to them.

It stands to reason, therefore, that a programming system that emphasizes actions above objects might be harder to learn than one that does the opposite. This is, of course, where object-oriented languages make their grand entrance.

Like most things in technology, the origins of object-oriented programming extend back a lot further than you might think. The object-oriented idea began in the early 1960s with the work of Ole-Johan Dahl and Kristen Nygaard in Norway. In 1965, the first compiler for the Simula I language was produced, and this is usually regarded as the first object-oriented language. The Smalltalk language was developed in the 1970s, but object-orientation (OO) had to wait until the 1980s with the creation of C++ by Bjarne Stroustrup before it began to be widely used. Other OO languages such as Eiffel were invented around the same time, but it wasn't until the introduction of Java in the 1990s that C++ had any major competition. With the entrance of .NET in 2002, two more major players in the OO game have appeared: Visual Basic .NET is now fully object-oriented, and C# is a new language that looks set to rival both C++ and Java in popularity.

2.3 ■ The object-oriented idea: encapsulation

If we trace the production of a computer program back to its origins, we must ultimately come to a description, in a human language such as English, of the problem the program is meant to solve, or the system which it is meant to simulate or represent. This *specification* of a program can be as simple (and vague) as 'write a program which will predict the state of the world economy over the next year'. It can also be a highly detailed, lengthy document describing every nuance of the finished product.

Once we have a detailed description of what the finished program should contain, the next stage is the production of an *object-oriented design*. Such a design is a set of *classes* which encapsulate the features and actions listed in the formal specification. Many formal design methods have been proposed and used in the past, although currently UML (unified modelling language) seems to be the dominant system used by professional designers.

The production of both specification and design documents is a major field in its own right, and we will not dwell on it here. These formal methods are required for large-scale programming projects, particularly if they involve teams of engineers. We won't be using any of these formal methods in this book, however, as it is certainly possible to produce good small-scale designs with a bit of thought and some common sense.

The main idea behind any object-oriented design, as mentioned above, is the creation of a set of classes that logically and consistently portrays the problem specification. Candidates for classes can be found by reading through the specification and identifying the key nouns used to describe the central concepts. Once we have identified the classes, we need to determine what properties each class will have and how the classes will interact with each other in the running program.

Each property of a class is represented by a *data field* within the class, and each action by a *method* (sometimes called a *function*). If your English grammar is up to the task, just as we can think of a class as a noun in the specification document, so can we think of the properties or data fields as adjectives that describe the noun, and the methods as verbs that describe actions that the class can do or have done to it.

This book assumes that readers have come across these concepts before in their initial study of Java, since it is not possible to write a Java program without creating at least one class. As such, we won't dwell on the process of analyzing a specification and building an object-oriented design. We will instead concentrate on how classes can be written in C#.

2.3.1 ☐ Encapsulation

The idea of creating classes to represent the items within an object-oriented design and protecting the data fields within each class from external code is called *encapsulation*. Encapsulation is one of the three central concepts of object-oriented programming, and is certainly the most important. The other two concepts, *inheritance* and *polymorphism*, are not needed to write simple OO programs, so we will deal with them later.

The principle of encapsulation states that once we have identified the classes that are to be used in our design, each class should contain a number of properties (data fields) which should be *private*, or inaccessible to any other class, except as specified by user-defined accessor *methods*. In Java and C#, the keyword `private` is used to define private data fields. There is no separate Java language construct for implementing accessor methods (as opposed to any other kind of method), although it is conventional to prefix a method name with 'get' if it is meant to retrieve a particular data field, or 'set' if it is meant to write a new value to a particular field. We will see that in C# there *is* a specific language feature (the *property*) that enforces accessor methods and thus allows encapsulation to be implemented in a more natural way.

Key point

Encapsulation requires that the data fields within each class are private, and that access to them is only allowed through accessor methods.

The terms *class* and *object* have precise meanings in the OO context. A *class* is a definition of a *data type*, and an *object* is a particular instance of that type. For example, if we have defined a class named `Car` to represent a car, then `Car` becomes a new data type in our program. We can use the name of the class to declare an *object*, or particular instance of a car, by giving an ordinary variable declaration statement, such as:

```
Car myCar;
```

Here, `myCar` is an object or variable which is an instance of the `Car` data type. (Technically, as in Java, a declaration such as this creates a *reference* to an object, so that the creation of the object itself requires using the `new` operator, but more on this later.)

Key point

A *class* is a data type and an *object* is an instance of a class.

We can now see an example of a simple object-oriented program in C#.

2.3.2 ☐ Example: an `Employee` class

We'll consider a specific example to illustrate how to write a class in C#. We will develop a class that represents an employee of some company or organization.

At this stage in the book, we will just dive in and present a complete C# class. Readers should find most of the code is very similar to Java. Those features that are specific to C# will be mentioned briefly following the code listing, but we will explain all these features of C# in detail later in the book. The goal at this stage is to get a feel for how C# represents classes and implements encapsulation.

Here's the code for the `Employee` class:

```
 1. using System;
 2.
 3. /// <summary>
 4. /// A single employee in a company
 5. /// </summary>
 6. public class Employee
 7. {
 8.     /// <summary>
 9.     /// Employee's name
10.     /// </summary>
11.     private string name;
12.     /// <summary>
13.     /// Employee's yearly salary (before deductions)
14.     /// </summary>
15.     private decimal salary;
16.     /// <summary>
17.     /// Employee's position within the company
18.     /// </summary>
19.     private PositionTitle position;
20.
```

```
21.    public enum PositionTitle
22.    {
23.       ManagingDirector = 0,
24.       Director = 1,
25.       Accountant = 2,
26.       Programmer = 3
27.    }
28.
29.    // Name property
30.    public string Name
31.    {
32.       get
33.       {
34.          return name;
35.       }
36.       set
37.       {
38.          name = value;
39.       }
40.    }
41.
42.    // Salary property
43.    public decimal Salary
44.    {
45.       get
46.       {
47.          return salary;
48.       }
49.       set
50.       {
51.          if (value <= 0.0M)
52.          {
53.             Console.WriteLine("Error: salary must be positive");
54.          }
55.          else
56.          {
57.             salary = value;
58.          }
59.       }
60.    }
61.
62.    // Position property
63.    public PositionTitle Position
64.    {
65.       get
66.       {
```

```
67.         return position;
68.       }
69.       set
70.       {
71.         position = value;
72.       }
73.     }
74.
75.
76.     public override string ToString()
77.       {
78.         return Name + " (" + Position + ")" + ": £" + Salary;
79.       }
80.   }
```

Before we describe the contents of this class, a few notes about the use of comments in this book are in order. In the `Employee` class shown above, we have added comments before the data field declarations and method definitions. The judicious use of comments in code is, of course, good programming practice and is to be encouraged in all code that you write. For this reason, in this example we have included the comments so you can see how they look in a C# program.

For most of the code in this book, however, we will not include the comments as part of the listing, since all examples in the book are fully explained by the text that follows them, and including comments within the code as well would duplicate the explanation and increase the size of some already rather lengthy code listings. The code that may be downloaded from the book's web site, however, *does* have a full set of comments embedded within it, since that code does not have the accompanying text to explain it. Remember that the purpose of comments is to explain in a concise manner what a section of code is doing when there is no other source of information, and as such, comments should always be included in 'live' code that is actually being used to develop a software project.

The three data fields of an `Employee` are declared on lines 11, 15 and 19. The employee's name is stored in a `string`, which is similar to the Java `String` class. The word 'string' (all lowercase letters) is a keyword in C++, however, and may not be used for variable or method names.

The salary is stored as a `decimal`, which is a special floating-point numerical data type especially suited to storing currency values. Finally, the employee's position within the company is stored as a `PositionTitle` variable. `PositionTitle` is not a built-in data type or a class – rather it is defined on lines 21 to 27 as an `enum` (enumeration) type. Readers who have done some C or C++ programming may have used an `enum` in those languages, but the C# `enum` is considerably more sophisticated. We shall study the full syntax of `enum` in Chapter 4. All we need to know now is that an `enum` provides a way of associating a set of labels with `int` values. This has the advantage of making code easier to read, since we can use the actual name of the employee's position as a value rather than some abstract quantity such as 0 or 1. However, the enum also allows the compiler to do type-checking in variable assignments, thus preventing us from assigning an illegal value to a PositionTitle variable.

Before we consider the remainder of the Employee class, let us write a preliminary version of the CompanyDemo class which we can use to create an Employee object and test it. The code for CompanyDemo is:

```
1. using System;
2.
3. /// <summary>
4. /// Controlling class for the Companies program.
5. /// </summary>
6. class CompanyDemo
7. {
8.     /// <summary>
9.     /// The main entry point for the application.
10.    /// </summary>
11.    [STAThread]
12.    static void Main(string[] args)
13.    {
14.      Employee employee1 = new Employee();
15.      employee1.Name = "Glenn Rowe";
16.      employee1.Position =
17.        Employee.PositionTitle.ManagingDirector;
18.      employee1.Salary = 1000000M;
19.      Console.WriteLine(employee1.ToString());
20.    }
21. }
```

In the early stages of code development, especially if we are learning a new language, it is useful to have a class which can be used to test the other classes as they are being written. It is important to test code by compiling and running it as often as possible.

As with Java, every C# program must contain one class with an *entry point*, that is, a method which can be used to start the program. In Java, that method must be called main(), while in C# it is called Main() (with a capital 'M'). The signature of the Main() method must always be as shown on line 12 of the CompanyDemo listing above (although an int return type is also allowed). The args parameter allows command-line arguments to be passed to the program.

On line 14, we declare and create a new Employee object. As in Java, creating an object is a two-stage process. First, the *reference* to the object is declared (the variable employee1 on line 14), then the object itself must be created. The creation of a new object can only be done by using the new operator, which reserves the memory required for that object and calls a *constructor* to initialize the data fields. The `Employee` class above does not contain any user-defined constructors (yet), since we don't want to cloud the issue with too many concepts at once. Most readers will probably be familiar with constructors from their study of Java – in most cases, C# constructors work the same way as those in Java.

Line 14 therefore calls a default constructor which is generated by the compiler, and which does nothing more than initialize the data fields in the new `Employee` object to default values (an empty string for `name`, and zero values for the other two data fields).

Lines 15 through 18 initialize the three data fields in `employee1`. At first glance, you might think everything is obvious, but if you look more closely, you will notice that something appears to be wrong. The three data fields defined in the `Employee` class were `name`, `position` and `salary` – all spelled with lowercase letters. The corresponding terms in lines 15 to 18 are all capitalized (and besides, the original data fields were all declared as `private`, and so shouldn't be accessible from outside the `Employee` class anyway).

However, there is no error here. We are not accessing the data fields in `Employee` directly – we are using *properties* to set these values. The C# property has no direct counterpart in Java, but it is central to C#'s way of implementing encapsulation, and thus of defining classes properly. We will therefore explain properties here, ahead of all the other language features in C#.

2.3.3   ☐ **Properties in C#**

Recall that the idea behind encapsulation is to control access to the private data fields within a class. The class should decide whether or not another class can read or write a data field. In the case of writing a new value to a data field, the class should be able to check that the new value is valid. C# provides the *property* mechanism which allows this to be done in a formal, controlled way.

Look at lines 30 to 40 in the `Employee` class above. Here, a property called `Name` (with a capital 'N') is defined which controls access to the `name` (with a small 'n') data field. A property must contain an *accessibility modifier* (in this case, `public`), a data type (`string`) and a label (`Name`).

A property contains at least one and possibly two *accessors*: a `get` and/or a `set`. The `get` accessor controls read access to the property, and the `set` accessor controls write access. Each accessor acts like a method, one of which (`get`) returns a value that must match the data type specified for the property, and the other of which (`set`) is passed a value of that same data type.

With the `Name` property, the `get` accessor simply returns the current value of `name` (which is a `string`, so the data type is correct). This is the class's way of allowing read access to the `name` data field. To obtain the `name` of an `Employee` in external code, we use the property label `Name` instead of the actual bare data field `name`. An example of this is given in the `ToString()` method on lines 76 to 79 of `Employee`. This method returns a `string` that contains the information stored in the three data fields. Note that Name is the first component of the string that is returned on line 78. This reference to Name calls the get accessor in the Name property on line 32, which returns the name data field. (Since the ToString() method is actually part of the Employee class, it is allowed direct access to name, but it is safer to go via the property route even within the same class.)

Now return to the CompanyDemo class and look at line 15, where a value is specified for the name of employee1. Notice that the Name property is used on the left side of the assignment statement. In this case, since we are attempting to *set* the value of a property, the set accessor of that property is called. The code for the set accessor of the Name property is on lines 36 to 39 of the Employee class.

The set accessor is passed a value whose type must match the data type of the property. The keyword value represents this value within the set accessor's scope. On line 38, we assign value to name to set the name of the employee.

A property's set accessor is called whenever a value is assigned to a property. Line 15 in the CompanyDemo shows this happening to the Name property. The string "Glenn Rowe" is assigned to the property Name. This calls the set accessor on line 36 in Employee, with "Glenn Rowe" being passed in as value. Line 38 then assigns "Glenn Rowe" to name.

The other two properties work in much the same way for the salary and position variables. The set accessor for the salary illustrates how a check can be made on value to ensure it is valid. On line 51, a check is made that the salary is positive, and only if value passes this test is it assigned to salary. (A better way of handling this would be to throw an exception if valid fails the test. We cover exceptions in Chapter 7.) The 'M' after the constant value being assigned to the salary specifies that the number should be interpreted as a decimal.

Either of these accessors can be omitted from a property (but at least one of them must be present). If we decided, for example, that the Name property cannot be changed, we could simply omit the set accessor. Then any statement such as

```
employee1.Name = "Susan Jones";
```

would not compile, since write access is denied to Name.

The final method, ToString(), on line 76 simply returns a string containing the information about the employee. (The override keyword on line 76 has to do with inheritance, which we consider in Chapter 6.)

Key point

C# provides *properties* with get and set accessors to implement the principle of encapsulation.

Although encapsulation in C# could be implemented the same way as in Java, by providing separate methods for each 'get' and 'set' operation, the C# property is a much neater way of doing it, and is recommended for all interaction with class data fields.

2.4 ■ Case study: an adventure game

Throughout this book we will be developing an extended case study consisting of an adventure game written in C#. In certain chapters, we will be expanding the game to illustrate the features of C# introduced since the previous version of the game.

For the uninitiated, an adventure game is one in which the player takes the role of a hero who explores various locations in a fantasy world, usually with the objective of completing some quest. The player may be required to solve puzzles, fight monsters and evil-doers, and collect treasure at the various locations in the game.

The computer plays the role of a 'gamesmaster', in that all details of the locations in the fantasy world are stored within the program. The computer also determines what challenges the player must face at each location, and provides appropriate responses to the player's actions.

One of the first adventure games was a standard part of the UNIX operating system back in the 1960s, and was simply called 'adventure'. It was a text-only game, played by typing in commands at a text prompt. The computer would respond with a textual statement giving the result of the user's command.

As the reader is no doubt aware, adventure games have progressed since those early days. Current adventure games provide immersive three-dimensional graphics, realistic animation and multi-channel sound. Although the final result of the case study in this book won't be quite as impressive as the games available from the leading games companies, we hope to introduce a reasonable amount of sophistication into the finished product.

We need to begin with something a bit less ambitious, however, since so far all we have covered of the C# language is a description of how C# implements encapsulation using classes and properties. Even at this early stage, we can sketch out the general form of an adventure game and build the beginnings of some of the classes that will be needed.

In planning a more involved project, it is useful to sketch out a *class diagram* to illustrate what classes are to be defined, what properties they contain, and how they relate to each other. The creation of class diagrams is one part of a more general field known as object-oriented design or OOD. We won't have space to go into OOD in any depth in this book, but we will occasionally make use of the class diagrams that might come out of such an analysis. A proper analysis of a software project involves a number of stages, such as the production of a formal *requirements document* (a list of conditions that the finished program should fulfil), *use cases* (a list of the various ways a user can interact with a program) and so on, but we will not go into these except in an informal way, since our main goal is to produce a working program that illustrates the features of C#.

The simplest type of adventure game would consist of a single player, a number of locations and a number of items that may be found at these locations. The player should be able to move between locations and pick up and drop items at each location. We will add more features, such as other *non-player characters* (NPCs – characters that are controlled by the computer and may be friendly or hostile), specialized item types and so on, at a later stage.

To build a class diagram, we need to propose some *class candidates* – objects which we need to represent as classes within the program. For each class that we accept, we need to provide *properties* and *methods*.

From the brief description of the first stage of the game given above, a number of class candidates should be fairly obvious. A Player class will represent the character controlled by the person playing the game. A Room class can be used to represent the various locations, and an Item class can represent items that may be found at the locations or carried by the player. Finally, we will need an overall class to control the running of the game. We will call this class Adventure, and this is where the Main() method will go.

A class diagram illustrating the structure of the program is shown in Figure 2.1.

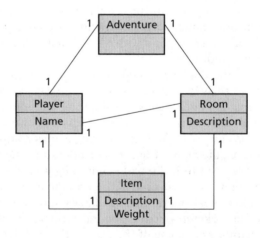

Figure 2.1 Class diagram for the first version of the adventure game case study

At this stage in the development of the program, we will restrict the game to a single location, and restrict that location and the player to holding a single item. In Figure 2.1, this is indicated by the number 1 labelling the ends of the lines connecting the various classes. For example, the line connecting the Adventure class with Player has a 1 on each end, indicating that a single Adventure object contains one Player. Note that only those data fields that are of a primitive type (single numbers or strings) are contained within the box representing a class. If one class (such as Adventure) contains an instance of another class (such as Player), this is indicated by a line connecting the two classes.

The restriction of Adventure to a single Room and of Room and Player to a single Item is because we have not yet covered those data structures required for storing arrays or lists of objects. When we study arrays in Chapter 4, we will modify the game to allow it to cope with several locations, each containing several items.

Let us now have a look at the code for the four classes. We begin with the simplest class: Item.

```
public class Item
{
   private string description;
   private int weight;

   public string Description
   {
      get
      { return description; }
      set
      { description =  value; }
   }

   public int Weight
   {
      get
      { return weight; }
      set
      { weight = value; }
   }

   public override string ToString()
   {
      string itemInfo = description;
      itemInfo += ": (" + weight + ")";
      return itemInfo;
   }
}
```

We have added a couple of data fields to Item, providing each item with a description and a weight. (The weight will be useful if we wish to restrict the total weight our player can carry.) There is a property provided for each of these data fields, and we have added a ToString() method which constructs a string showing the values of these two fields.

Next, we consider Room:

```
public class Room
{
   private string description;
   private Item locationItem;

   public string Description
   {
     get
     { return description; }
     set
     { description =  value; }
   }

   public Item LocationItem
   {
     get
     { return locationItem; }
     set
     { locationItem = value; }
   }

   public override string ToString()
   {
     string locationInfo = description;
     if (LocationItem != null)
       locationInfo += "\nContains: " +
         LocationItem.ToString();
     else
       locationInfo += "\nThe room is empty.";
     return locationInfo;
   }
}
```

Room contains a string for its description, and a single Item field allows one item to be stored within a Room. Properties are provided for accessing these fields. The ToString() method first adds description to the output string. It then tests LocationItem to see if it is null. If it is, this means that the location does not contain an Item, so we add the message 'The room is empty.' to the output and return. If LocationItem is not null, we call its ToString() method to add the Item's data to the output for the Room.

The Player class is much the same as Room:

```
public class Player
{
  private string name;
  private Item playerItem;

  public string Name
  {
    get
    { return name; }
    set
    { name = value; }
  }

  public Item PlayerItem
  {
    get
    { return playerItem; }
    set
    { playerItem = value; }
  }

  public override string ToString()
  {
    string playerInfo = "Name: " + name;
    if (PlayerItem != null)
      playerInfo += "\nCarrying: " + PlayerItem.ToString();
    else
      playerInfo += "\nNot carrying anything.";
    return playerInfo;
  }
}
```

Instead of Room's description, Player has a name, but otherwise the code is identical to that of Room.

Finally, the Adventure class ties everything together and provides a Main() method to start the program:

```
using System;

public class Adventure
{
  private Player gamePlayer;
  private Room room;

  public void Initialize()
  {
    gamePlayer = new Player();
    gamePlayer.Name = "Wibble the Wizard";
```

```
        room = new Room();
        room.Description = "A magic laboratory.";
        Item crystalBall = new Item();
        crystalBall.Description = "A crystal ball";
        crystalBall.Weight = 10;
        room.LocationItem = crystalBall;
    }

    public void PlayGame()
    {
        Console.WriteLine("Welcome to Adventure!");
        Console.WriteLine("\nPlayer:\n" + gamePlayer.ToString());
        Console.WriteLine("\nLocation:\n" + room.ToString());
        Console.WriteLine();
    }

    public static void Main(string[] args)
    {
        Adventure adventure = new Adventure();
        adventure.Initialize();
        adventure.PlayGame();
    }
}
```

The `Main()` method creates an `Adventure` object and then calls `Initialize()`. This method creates the `Player` and gives it a name, but does not assign anything to `PlayerItem`, since we are starting the `Player` off with an empty backpack. Next, `Initialize()` creates the `Room` and gives it a description, then it creates an `Item` and assigns it to `room`.

The `PlayGame()` method simply tests that the `Player`, `Room` and `Item` were all constructed properly by calling `ToString()` for the `Player` and `room`. The output is:

```
Welcome to Adventure!

Player:
Name: Wibble the Wizard
Not carrying anything.

Location:
A magic laboratory.
Contains: A crystal ball: (10)
```

Note that the `PlayGame()` method tests *all* the code we have written so far, since it demonstrates that all the classes have been used, and calls all the `ToString()` methods (recall that the `ToString()` method in `Item` is called from `ToString()` in `Room`). It is important to continually test code as you write it in order to avoid long lists of error messages when you compile a program and complex errors when you run it. In fact, during the development of the program as shown here, the code should have been tested many times even before reaching this point. The author's personal preference is to compile the program almost as often as after each line of code is added or changed. With a proper development environment, all files can be saved and compiled with a single keystroke, so it takes little effort to do this, and can save hours of debugging time later on.

At this stage, although the program does not present us with a playable game, the basic framework has been laid down. We have the core classes that will be needed throughout the various versions of the game and although the classes will undergo quite a few modifications, the underlying structure of the object-oriented design will not change.

■ Summary

In this chapter, we have reviewed the main ideas behind object-oriented programming. The central concept is that of *encapsulation*, in which the data fields and methods describing an entity are grouped together in a *class*. Access to data fields (either to *get* (read) or *set* (write) their values) is controlled by *interface methods*. In Java, each interface method must be written as a separate method within the class. In C#, a *property* may be defined for each data field where external access is needed. The property has a `get` and a `set` section, where the corresponding access may be provided.

We presented the first version of the extended case study that appears over the course of the book: an adventure game. This first version defines an initial set of classes and provides some skeleton code for them.

Exercises

2.1 Think of some everyday objects such as a car, a clock, a television and so on and list properties that are associated with each object. For example, a car's properties could include the make, model, colour, price, registration number and so on. When you have made a list of properties for an object, examine the lists to see which properties could be grouped together into classes. For example, some of the properties of a clock could include hour, minute and second, which could be grouped together into a `Time` class. The `Clock` class could then include an instance of `Time` as well as other data fields that are based on primitive data types. Using your class definitions, draw a simple class diagram similar to that in this chapter for the adventure game.

2.2 Using your class diagram for one of the everyday objects in Exercise 2.1, write out some C# classes that implement the classes identified in the diagram. For each property in each class, declare a variable within the class and provide a C# property with `get` and `set` accessors to allow reading and writing of the variable. Some of the variables will be primitive data types such as `int` or `float`, but others could be instances of other classes you have defined. For example, a `Clock` class could have an instance of a `Time` class to represent the clock's current time.

2.3   Add a `ToString()` method to each class from Exercise 2.2 so that you can display the values of the variables in that class. Use the `ToString()` methods in the adventure game classes as models.

2.4   Using the `Adventure` class for the adventure game in this chapter as a model, write a `Main()` method that creates an object from each of the classes you wrote in Exercises 2.2 and 2.3 and then calls the `ToString()` method from each object so that you can get a printout on screen of the values of each object's properties.

2.5   Do some research on the web to discover some more information on the differences between procedural and object-oriented programming methods. Include in your research an investigation into the history of the two methods. Your research may try to answer the following questions: When and where did they originate? What were the first procedural and object-oriented languages? What are the most popular methods and languages in research and industry at the moment? What sort of developments in programming methods are predicted for the future?

Data, expressions and statements

3

In Chapter 2, we introduced the concept of a class and showed how encapsulation can be implemented in C#. In the 'objects-first' approach taken by this book, it is important to be comfortable with the idea that the first step in writing an object-oriented program is the identification of the classes which are to be used. It is not necessary to worry about how the code within each method of a class will be written at this stage – what is important is the creation of the overall structure of the program.

Once we have identified the classes and created their skeleton structures, of course, we then *do* have to write the code within each method. This chapter will guide you through the nuts and bolts of C#: what primitive data types are provided, what sorts of arithmetic and logical expressions can be constructed, and what sorts of statements, such as conditionals and loops, the language provides.

Although at this level C# and Java are very similar, there are enough subtle differences that it would pay you to read this chapter carefully even if you are an experienced Java programmer. It is very easy to write code that is correct in Java but will not work properly in C# because you have overlooked one of these little variations.

3.1 ■ Primitive data types

C# provides 13 'primitive' data types: eight integer types, two floating-point types, a Boolean type, a character type and an odd beast called the decimal type. At this stage, we will regard these primitive types as bare values, in the same way as primitive types in Java. We will see, however, that C# primitives actually have a more complex side, but we must delay an exploration of this until we have studied inheritance in Chapter 6.

3.1.1 □ Integer types

The integer types may be grouped according to the range of values that they can store. The smallest integer types can store 8 bits (one byte), which means that they can store 256 different values. There are two of these 8-bit types: `byte`, which stores *unsigned* integer values between 0 and 255, and `sbyte`, where the first bit is used to indicate a sign (the 's' in `sbyte` stands for 'signed'). Since the sign bit leaves only 7 bits for storing the numerical value, an `sbyte` can store values in the range –128 to +127.

The remaining integer data types all come in pairs of one signed and one unsigned type. The 2-byte types are the `short` (for signed values) and the `ushort` (for unsigned values). At the 4-byte level we have the ordinary `int` (signed) and `uint` (unsigned). Finally, at the 8-byte level we have the `long` (signed) and `ulong` (unsigned).

Notice the difference in the naming convention between the byte-sized integers, where the *unsigned* version gets the common name (`byte`), and the other three sizes where the *signed* version gets the common name (`short`, `int` and `long`).

A summary of the integer types, their sizes and ranges is given in the table.

Data type	Size (bytes)	Value range
byte	1	0 to 255
sbyte	1	−128 to 127
short	2	−32768 to 32767
ushort	2	0 to 65535
int	4	−2147483648 to 2147483647
uint	4	0 to 4294967295
long	8	−9223372036854775808 to 9223372036854775807
ulong	8	0 to 18446744073709551615

C# vs Java

The `byte` data type in C# is *unsigned*, while the `byte` in Java is *signed*. This means that the range of a Java `byte` is −128 to 127, which is the same as the `sbyte` in C#.

The C# compiler will attempt to match the type of a constant integer value with its context. For example, consider the assignment:

```
int x = 2147483647;
```

This assigns the maximum value for an `int` to the `int` variable `x`. In this case, the constant 2147483647 is interpreted as an `int`. However, suppose we make `x` a `long`:

```
long x = 2147483647;
```

Now the constant value is interpreted as a `long`.

C# vs Java

The Java compiler is not quite as adaptable. Any constant integer value is interpreted as an `int`, so that a statement such as

```
long x = 9223372036854775807;    // Won't compile in Java
```

will result in a compiler error stating that the integer value is too large. In Java, you must force a constant to be `long` by adding an 'L' after the value:

```
long x = 9223372036854775807L;    // Will compile
```

In C#, an integer constant can be forced into a particular type by appending a 'U' to make it unsigned, an 'L' to make it `long`, or a combined 'UL' to make it `ulong`. The actual value of the constant must, of course, match the data type we are attempting to force on it. Thus,

```
ulong x = 42UL;
```

would be fine, but

```
ulong y = -42UL;
```

would not, since a negative number cannot be unsigned.

3.1.2 ☐ Data type conversion

C# will convert any integer value to an `int` unless that value is outside the range of the `int` data type. This can give rise to some perplexing compiler errors. For example, the following code looks perfectly fine:

```
short x = 42;
short y = x + 1;
```

The compiler, however, complains that we 'Cannot implicitly convert type "int" to "short". The problem is that although x was declared as a `short`, the '1' in the expression x + 1 on the second line is taken as an `int` constant, which forces the result of the addition to be an `int`, not a `short`. Since an `int` has a greater range than a `short`, there is the possibility that the `int` value won't fit into a `short` variable, so the compiler complains that we can't implicitly assign an `int` to a `short`.

However, if we try making y a `long` instead, there is no problem:

```
short x = 42;
long y = x + 1;
```

We see that the C# compiler will automatically convert an `int` to a `long`. Conversions from a type (such as `int`) with a greater range to a type (such as `short`) with a smaller range are possible in C#, but require the use of *casts*, which we will consider later.

The C# compiler will automatically convert any data type to another data type if the second data type can absorb the first data type without any loss of data. Thus, since an `int` can contain any `short` value, converting from `short` to `int` is automatic, but the reverse conversion, from `int` to `short`, is not, since not all `int` values will fit into a `short`.

Note that the compiler does not work out the actual values of the variables involved – it simply applies the rules blindly according to the data types.

Key point

The C# compiler will automatically convert a numerical data type to a more general type if required by an assignment operation.

3.2 ■ Data overflow and the `checked` keyword

If we try to assign a value to an integer type outside the range of that type, we can get some rather odd results. For example, consider the code:

```
int x = 2147483647;
int y = x + 1;
Console.WriteLine("x = " + x + "; x + 1 = " + y);
```

The first `int` is initialized to the maximum value for an `int`, and then `y` is initialized to one more than this. The third line prints out the values:

```
x = 2147483647; x + 1 = -2147483648
```

Obviously the second value is not correct, because we have exceeded the range of the `int` data type. (To understand why we get the actual value we do, we would need to analyze the binary representation of an `int`, but we won't get into that now.) Clearly, no bounds checking is occurring here and, since no errors were flagged up at either compilation or during the running of the program, this sort of error could have serious consequences if the overflow happened at some point deep within a complex calculation. We may or may not spot the fact that the final answer is wrong, and if we did spot it, it could take a lot of effort to find out where the bug lies.

Fortunately, C# offers a solution to this problem with the `checked` keyword. Any code enclosed within a `checked` block is checked for overflow when the program runs. We can therefore rewrite the above code as:

```
int x = 2147483647;
int y;
checked
{
    y = x + 1;
}
Console.WriteLine("x = " + x + "; x + 1 = " + y);
```

This code will compile without errors, since `checked` only catches overflows at runtime. When we run the program, we get an error message stating:

```
Unhandled Exception: System.OverflowException:
Arithmetic operation resulted in an overflow.
```

The line number in the source code producing the error is also given.

Clearly, if we have a lot of areas in the code which are prone to overflow, it can be tedious having to enclose all these areas in `checked` blocks, so the C# compiler has a command switch that allows us to enable overflow checking for the entire project. If we are using the command-line version of the compiler (the `csc` command), global checking can be enabled by adding the option `/checked` in the command line. If we are using Visual Studio .NET, checking can be enabled by selecting the View menu, then 'Solution Explorer'. This should display the Solution Explorer within the Visual Studio .NET window. Right-click on the project node within Solution Explorer and select Properties from the popup menu. Within the Properties dialog box, open the 'Configuration Properties' folder and then select the 'Build' item. Finally, set 'Check for Arithmetic Overflow/Underflow' to 'true'.

If we enable global overflow checking, we can remove the `checked` block from the code above and run it again. We should still get the error message since now the entire program acts as if it were enclosed with a `checked` block. (If global checking is enabled and for some reason we want some portion of the code *not* to be checked, there is an `unchecked` keyword which can be used in the same way as the `checked` keyword above to define blocks of code where overflow checking should *not* take place.)

Key point

Overflow checking can be enabled in C# by enclosing code within a `checked` block. Checking can be enabled for an entire project by setting the `/checked` option in the command line for the compiler. There is no analogous feature in Java.

3.3 ■ Floating-point types

C# provides two traditional floating-point data types: `float` and `double`. These two types are the same as the corresponding types in Java, but it will still be worth summarizing their properties (see table below).

Data type	Size (bytes)	Value range	Significant figures
float	4	$\pm 1.5 \times 10^{-45}$ to $\pm 3.4 \times 10^{38}$	7
double	8	$\pm 5.0 \times 10^{-324}$ to $\pm 1.7 \times 10^{308}$	15 or 16

Floating-point constants are always assumed to be `doubles` by the C# compiler. This can cause unexpected compilation errors, with statements such as:

```
float x;
x = 3.14;        // Will not compile
```

producing an error that 'Literal of type double cannot be implicitly converted to type "float"; use an "F" suffix to create a literal of this type.' The error message also provides the solution: use an 'F' suffix after the 3.14 to specify that the constant is a `float` rather than a `double`:

```
float x;
x = 3.14F;       // 3.14 is now a float
```

This problem and its solution are common to both C# and Java.

Another common problem with both the `float` and `double` types is *round-off error*. These two data types store their values in binary form, not decimal. This is achieved by separating the value into two parts: a *mantissa* (fractional part) and an *exponent*. In decimal form a number such as 0.345×10^{45} has a mantissa of 0.345 and an exponent of 45. To store this number as a `float`, it must be converted to binary, which involves calculating a mantissa (a fractional binary value) and an exponent that is a power of 2 rather than 10. Not all decimal numbers can be converted to binary exactly, given the limited number of bits available, so when the binary representation is converted back to decimal, the result may not be exactly equal to the original decimal value.

To see this effect, consider the simple loop shown:

```
float x;
for (x = 1.0F; x < 2.0F; x += 0.01F)
    Console.WriteLine(x);
```

We declare x as a `float`, and use the loop to print out the values 1.0, 1.01, 1.02, ... up to 1.99. At least those are the values that *should* be printed if all the arithmetic is done exactly. In fact, what we see looks correct up to 1.52, but the next line shows the value 1.529999 instead of 1.53. This is the result of cumulative rounding errors introduced over the preceding 52 additions, since the value of 0.01 is not represented precisely in binary.

The `double` type has greater accuracy, but does not eliminate this problem – in fact, in the above example it actually makes things worse. If we declare x as a `double` instead of a `float`, the very first value after 1.0 that is printed is 1.00999999977648 rather than 1.01. Why does the lower precision `float` give better results than the higher precision `double`?

The answer is that it actually doesn't – it just appears to since the binary value is rounded off to produce the decimal output. A `float` can hold only 7 significant (decimal) figures, so if we take the 1.00999999977648 produced by the `double` arithmetic and round it off to these 7 figures, we do indeed get 1.01. The `float` gets the exact answer in this case, but for many other calculations it will not.

3.4 ■ The decimal type

C# introduces a new data type that provides a solution to the round-off error problems inherent in the `float` and `double` data types. The `decimal` type uses 16 bytes, twice that of a `double`, and provides up to 28 significant figures of accuracy. A `decimal` is, as its name implies, stored in *decimal* rather than binary form, so that a number like 345.12389123 is stored as the integer 34512389123 and an extra value indicating where the decimal point should be inserted (in this case, after the third digit). Since integers do not suffer from round-off error (any integer value within the range of one of the integer data types is always represented exactly), the `decimal` type always represents its values precisely.

The main drawbacks of the `decimal` are that it uses up a lot of memory (twice as much as a `double`) and due to the method by which it stores its value, the range of values that it can store is much more limited than either of the traditional floating-point data types (see table below).

Data type	Size (bytes)	Value range	Significant figures
decimal	16	$\pm 1.0 \times 10^{-28}$ to $\pm 7.9 \times 10^{28}$	28

A common use of the `decimal` is in currency calculations where absolute accuracy is often required, and the range of values is more limited than in many other scientific calculations. If we use only two decimal places (to represent pence or cents, for example), we still have 26 significant figures that can be used for the pounds or dollars part of the amount. Such a value is many orders of magnitude larger than the fortunes of even the wealthiest software company executives.

Key point

A `decimal` allows a floating-point value to be represented exactly, without round-off error. It is frequently used to represent currency amounts.

A floating-point number can be specified as `decimal` by adding an 'M' (for 'money'?) as a suffix. For example, we can rewrite the simple loop above using a `decimal` as:

```
decimal d;
for (d = 1.0M; d < 2.0M; d += 0.01M)
  Console.WriteLine(d);
```

In this case, all values are printed exactly, with no round-off error.

3.5 ■ The `bool` (Boolean) type

C# provides a dedicated Boolean data type `bool` for representing `true` and `false` values. The `bool` type is the *only* data type which may be allowed to represent a conditional value within statements such as `if`, and as a termination condition within loops such as `for` and `while`. A `bool` may not be converted into any other data type.

Comparison operators such as `==`, `>`, `<` and so on all return `bool` values as results.

C# vs Java

The C# `bool` type is equivalent to Java's `boolean` type.

Readers who have used C or C++ where any numerical zero value is interpreted as `false` and any non-zero value as `true` should note that attempting to use an `int` or `float` in place of a `bool` in C# will *not* work – the compiler will generate an error (the same is true in Java, so Java programmers should already be used to this behaviour).

3.6 ■ The `char` (character) type

The final primitive data type available in C# is the `char`, which is used for storing single characters.

Older character data types in languages such as C and C++ only required a single byte, since the only character sets that were widely recognized were those that were restricted to the characters used in English text. The most commonly used character set was the ASCII set, which consists of 128 standard single-byte codes representing the characters on a standard English-language keyboard. The other 128 characters available in a one-byte character type were used for various symbols depending on the application. Some systems used a set of simple graphics characters, while other systems used mathematical symbols or non-English alphabets.

Now that computer use has spread to most areas of the world, an expanded character set is needed, so that symbols from most human languages, along with other specialist symbols, can be represented. The Unicode system uses two-byte characters, which allows for 65,536 different characters. The first 128 Unicode characters are identical to the 128 standard ASCII characters. The other Unicode symbols are used for non-English alphabets such as Greek, Arabic, Hebrew and Cyrillic (Russian). Several thousand Chinese and Japanese characters are also represented, along with technical symbols from areas such as mathematics, music and astronomy.

The official web site for the Unicode system is www.unicode.org, which also contains tables listing all the symbols currently in use, and news about the addition of further symbols to the standard.

Of course, in order for us to make use of all these Unicode characters, we must have access to a font that contains them. Most of the standard Windows textual fonts such as Times New Roman and Arial contain the more common international alphabets, but special fonts are needed for many Asian languages such as Chinese. Under Windows, you can check to see which characters a given font supports by using the charmap program, which can be run from a command prompt (in a console window) or using the Run command in the Start menu by typing the command 'charmap'.

A `char` constant can be specified by enclosing a character within single quotes, as in:

```
char capA = 'A';
```

There are several special characters that are represented by using the backslash (\) as an *escape* character, indicating that the character following the backslash should be interpreted in a special way. All *whitespace* characters except the single blank are represented as escaped characters. (A whitespace character is one that doesn't produce a visible mark on the screen, but which moves the cursor along a certain distance. Typical whitespace characters are the tab, backspace, newline and carriage return.)

The escaped characters are shown in the following table:

Character	Escape sequence
Single quote	\ '
Double quote	\ "
Backslash	\ \
Null	\ 0
Alert	\ a
Backspace	\ b
Form feed	\ f
Newline	\ n
Carriage return	\ r
Tab	\ t
Vertical tab	\ v

The escaped double quote is not really needed, since the double quote character " may be used on its own as a character constant, as in:

```
char doubleQuote = '"';
```

The non-printing characters (from Null to Vertical tab in the table above) will not produce the same effect in all situations, so some experimentation may be needed to see what they do in your particular application. In particular, in some applications, it is necessary to combine a carriage return with a newline to move the cursor to the beginning of the next line.

If the font supports it, any Unicode character may be used in a `char` constant by using the four-digit escaped Unicode notation. The code for any character can be obtained from the Unicode web site given above, or from the `charmap` program under Windows. The code must be in hexadecimal.

For example, if we look up the code for 'A' in `charmap`, we find it has a hex value of 41 (65 in decimal). We can then assign a `char` variable the value 'A' using Unicode notation:

```
char capA = '\u0041';
```

Note that if we use Unicode notation, the numerical code *must* always contain 4 digits, even if the first couple of digits are 0. If we try:

```
char capA = '\u41';   // Won't compile
```

we will get a compiler error of 'Unrecognized escape sequence'.

Alternatively, we can use a pure hex number without the leading zeros:

```
char hexA = '\x41';
```

or a decimal integer, if we use an explicit cast to convert it to a `char` (we'll consider casting later in this chapter):

```
char decA = (char)65;
```

Note that in the latter case, we don't need quotes around the value.

3.7 ■ Strings

Although C#, like Java, contains a special class for handling strings, it makes sense to consider strings at this point since they are treated almost like primitive data types in C#.

The `String` class is part of the `System` namespace (just like `Console`), but it is more usual to use the `string` (lowercase 's') C# keyword to declare a string variable, as it is just an alias for the `String` class and is easier to use, since no reference to the `System` namespace (or `using` statement) is required.

A `string` can be initialized to a constant value by enclosing the text in double quotes, as in:

```
string text = "This is a C# string.";
```

The `Console.WriteLine()` method takes a `string` as a parameter, so a `string` can be written to the console as follows:

```
Console.WriteLine(text);
```

The `String` class contains a number of methods that allow strings to be compared and combined, or which allow various other searches and extraction operations to be done. You should browse through the MSDN documentation for `String` to see what is available – most of the methods have code examples provided so you can see what they do. We will use some of these methods in sample programs throughout the book as well.

It is also possible to join (concatenate) two or more strings using the + operator. For example, we can write:

```
string start = "This is the start,";
string end = " and this is the end.";
string sentence = start + end;
Console.WriteLine(sentence);
```

This produces the output:

```
This is the start, and this is the end.
```

The += operator, which we will meet below for arithmetic operations, may also be used to join a new string onto the end of an existing one. For example, this code has the same effect as the previous example:

```
string start = "This is the start,";
string end = " and this is the end.";
string sentence = start;
sentence += end;
Console.WriteLine(sentence);
```

The + and += operators also allow numerical data types to be appended to strings without any special method calls or casting. For example, we could say:

```
int meaning = 42;
string result = "The meaning of the universe is " + meaning;
```

This produces the text 'The meaning of the universe is 42' in result.

An important point about string variables is that they are *immutable*, meaning that once a string object has been created and initialized, it cannot be changed. This may seem silly, since in the last example it appears that we have changed sentence by appending end onto it. In fact, any operator or method that seems to be changing an existing string object is creating a brand new string with the new value. Thus, the statement sentence += end actually produces a brand new string containing sentence joined onto end and then sets sentence to refer to this new string.

Special characters such as newlines and tabs can be inserted into a string by using the backslash character \ as an *escape* character. For example, if we wanted to write two lines of text, we could say:

```
string twoLines = "The first line\nand the second line";
```

The \n is a newline character and separates the string into two lines. A tab can be inserted using \t. To insert a backslash as a character in its own right, write a double backslash, as is commonly used in specifying a full path to a file name:

```
string fileName = "C:\\Windows\\System32\\AFile.exe";
```

Since specifying full file paths is fairly common in programs, C# provides a shorthand way of writing a string which allows a backslash to be treated as an ordinary character and not as an escape character. If the string is prefixed with the @ character, all backslashes are treated as regular text. Thus the file path above could be written as:

```
string fileName = @"C:\Windows\System32\AFile.exe";
```

3.8 ■ String formatting

The `Console.WriteLine()` method, as we have already seen, takes a single `string` as its parameter. For most uses of this method, this is all we need to know, since we can build up a `string` from other strings, the `ToString()` methods of any objects, and numerical values can be appended to `strings` with the + and += operators.

However, in some cases, more precise control over the format of a `string` is needed, and C# provides a rich vocabulary of formatting syntax. A complete description of string formatting can be found in the MSDN documentation under 'string formatting', but a few examples will be useful here.

First, we can describe the *placeholder* syntax in the `Console.WriteLine()` and `Console.Write()` methods (C programmers will find this reminiscent of placeholders in C's `printf()` function). Rather than creating a single `string` for display in `WriteLine()`, we can use a series of numeric indexes embedded within constant text and then list the variables whose values we wish inserted at the indexed places. For example:

```
int x = 45;
double pi = 3.14159, absZero = -273.15;
Console.WriteLine("The value is {0} and pi is {1}", x, pi);
```

Here we have defined a few numerical values and then printed two of them. The `WriteLine()` call contains three parameters: the first is a `string` that contains a couple of placeholders, and the remaining two parameters are the values that are to be inserted into the places indicated.

A placeholder in `WriteLine()` is an integer enclosed within braces, such as {0} and {1}. As we will see in a minute, a placeholder can contain information on the type and formatting of the output as well, but the bare placeholders used here cause each value to be printed in its default format. The output from this line is:

```
The value is 45 and pi is 3.14159
```

There are a large number of different formatting options, so we'll consider just a few of them here to give an idea of what's possible. Here are a few more `WriteLine()` calls using various formatting codes:

```
Console.WriteLine(
    "The value is {0:d7} and pi is {1:f3}", x, pi);
Console.WriteLine(
    "You owe me {0:c} and absolute zero is {1:e3}",
    x, absZero);
Console.WriteLine();
Console.WriteLine("It is now " + DateTime.Now);
Console.WriteLine("Today's date: " +
    DateTime.Now.ToString("M"));
Console.WriteLine("The time now is " +
    DateTime.Now.ToString("T"));
```

Using the variables defined above, the output from this code is:

```
The value is 0000045 and pi is 3.142
You owe me £45.00 and absolute zero is -2.732e+002

It is now 23/04/2003 17:40:49
Today's date: 23 April
The time now is 17:40:49
```

A formatting code has the form of a single letter followed by a one- or two-digit integer. The letter determines the general format of the output and the number determines the precision. For example, 'd7' indicates decimal format with seven digits displayed. If the number being formatted is less than seven digits, leading zeros are inserted to make up the space. The 'f3' code indicates floating point with three decimal places displayed. If the number contains more than three places, it is rounded to three.

The 'c' code indicates currency, so the output will depend on the currency settings on your computer. Since I live in Scotland, currency is displayed using the pound sign (£), but in North America, for example, the dollar sign would be used. The currency code does allow a precision value as well – omitting it as we have done here means that just whole pounds are displayed, without any pence.

The 'e3' code uses exponential format with the precision value indicating how many digits to use in the exponent.

After printing a blank line (produced by calling `WriteLine()` with no parameters), we illustrate a few ways of printing the date and time. `DateTime` is actually a `struct` (which we will consider later, but it is similar to a `class` in some ways) which contains properties giving the day, month, year, hour, minute and second of a given date and time. Its `Now` property returns a `DateTime` containing the date and time when the property was called (so its accuracy depends on the computer's clock). The first `WriteLine()` just displays `DateTime.Now` in its default form, which will depend on the settings for date and time you have installed on your computer. In Britain, we use the day/month/year notation while in the USA the notation is month/day/year.

There are many ways of formatting dates and times – see the documentation for the `DateTime` structure for details. A couple are shown in the sample code above.

Rather than using placeholders in the `WriteLine()` string, we have used `DateTime`'s `ToString()` method, but with a parameter. The value of the parameter determines the format used to display the date and time. An 'M' means that only the day and the month should be displayed, while 'T' displays only the time (without the date). Explore the documentation for more details.

3.9 ■ Regular expressions

For completeness in our discussion of strings, we will include here a brief description of C#'s facilities for handling *regular expressions*. A regular expression is a definition of a set of possible string patterns that can match part or all of another string, and is most commonly used in code that must search through some text for a particular string pattern.

Regular expressions make use of many special characters to define the string pattern to be matched. We will restrict this discussion to fairly basic patterns, since a full treatment is a subject in its own right. The MSDN documentation has a more complete description of regular expressions, and there are many other sources in textbooks and on the web.

A regular expression is just a string itself, but the string contains a 'code' that specifies the pattern that should be matched in the source text. In a regular expression, an alphanumeric character (a letter or a number) matches itself, but most punctuation and other symbols have special meanings. The most common of these symbols are the asterisk *, the plus sign + and the question mark ?.

An asterisk means that any number (from zero upwards) of the immediately preceding character or regular expression may occur. For example, if we wanted to search for all numbers that are powers of 10 in a list of numbers, we would like to match 1, 10, 100, 1000, and so on. The regular expression that would match this is `10*`, since the 1 will match a single occurrence of the digit '1' and the * after the 0 indicates that we accept zero or more '0' characters.

The + symbol is similar to * except that it matches one or more (rather than zero or more) occurrences. The ? symbol matches exactly 0 or 1 occurrence of the preceding character. Thus, `10+` matches 10, 100, 1000, ... but not just 1 on its own. The expression `10?` matches only 1 and 10.

Another useful expression is that for specifying a range or set of characters that can be matched. The range of characters is placed inside square brackets. For example, the expression `b[eaiu]d` matches the words 'bed', 'bad', 'bid' and 'bud'. The set of characters inside the brackets acts as a unit for the purposes of the quantifier characters *, + and ?, so we can say `b[eaiu]*d`, which matches any string that begins with a 'b', ends with a 'd' and contains any number of e, a, i or u in between, such as 'bd', 'bed', or 'beauiauiueeed'.

A range of characters can be specified by giving the first and last character separated by a hyphen, as in [a-z], which matches any lowercase letter or [a-zA-Z], which matches any upper- or lowercase letter. Thus a string of length at least one character that contains nothing but letters can be specified by [a-zA-Z]+.

Finally, a useful pair of symbols is ^ which indicates that the string must begin with the pattern, and $ which indicates that the string must end with the pattern. For example, ^[0-9]+$ means that the string must begin with a number and end with a number. (The pattern [0-9]+ on its own would match a string that contained a sequence of numbers anywhere within it.)

There are many other symbols and rules that can be used in regular expressions, but these should be enough to get you started.

A regular expression can be defined and used to match other strings by using C#'s Regex class. In the simplest case, a Regex object can be created by passing the regular expression string as the parameter in the constructor, and then the IsMatch() method used to match against the target string. For example, the following code reads in a string and then tests first to see if the string consists only of numerical characters and, if so, whether it is a power of 10:

```
Console.Write("Enter a number: ");
string number = Console.ReadLine();
string regExp = "^[0-9]+$";
Regex numberExp = new Regex(regExp);
if (numberExp.IsMatch(number))
{
    Console.WriteLine("That is a number");
    string power10 = "^10*$";
    Regex power10Exp = new Regex(power10);
    if (power10Exp.IsMatch(number))
        Console.WriteLine(" -- and it's a power of 10");
}
else
    Console.WriteLine("That is not a number");
```

After reading the string into number, we construct regExp to test if the string contains only numbers. A Regex is created using this pattern, and then IsMatch() is used to test number to see if it matches this pattern. If it does, the string is tested again, this time against the expression ^10*$ which identifies powers of 10.

Regex has many other methods which allow various types of matching between regular expressions and strings, so consult the documentation for details and some more examples.

C# vs Java

As of version 1.4, Java also provides support for regular expressions.

3.10 ■ Implicit type conversions

We mentioned above when discussing the integer data types that C# will perform several implicit data conversions (in assignment statements, for example) automatically, provided that the conversion does not lose any data.

For example, we can write:

```
short smallInt = 234;
int largerInt = smallInt;
```

Since the int type can hold all values within the range of a short, this implicit conversion cannot lose any data, so it is performed automatically by the compiler.

This general rule applies to implicit type conversions between all pairs of C# data types – if the range of the data type of the source variable (that is, the variable that is to be converted) fits inside the range of the destination variable, the conversion will be done, otherwise, the compiler will flag an error. This rule also allows integer types to be converted to floating-point types implicitly.

Key point

Implicit type conversions can only be used to convert a less general data type into a more general one.

The complete list of implicit data conversions performed by the C# compiler is shown in Table 3.1. We have included a 'conversion' from a data type to itself in the table even though technically no conversion takes place so that you may use the table to see which data types may be assigned automatically to which other data types.

Table 3.1 The C# compiler will implicitly convert a data type listed in the first column to any other data type marked with an 'x' on that row

	byte	sbyte	short	ushort	int	uint	long	ulong	float	double	decimal	bool	char
byte	x		x	x	x	x	x	x	x	x	x		
sbyte		x	x		x		x		x	x	x		
short			x		x		x		x	x	x		
ushort				x	x	x	x	x	x	x	x		
int					x		x		x	x	x		
uint						x	x	x	x	x	x		
long							x		x	x	x		
ulong								x	x	x	x		
float									x	x			
double										x			
decimal											x		
bool												x	
char			x	x	x	x	x	x	x	x			x

Most of these conversions are straightforward applications of the rule given above. For example, a `float` will be converted to a `double` but not a `decimal`, since the range of `float` values fits within the range of `double` values, but not within the range of `decimal` values.

However, if the rule for implicit conversion is that no data should be lost in the conversion, some of these conversions may give cause for concern. For example, the compiler will convert a `long` to a `float`, even though a `float` can store only 7 significant figures while a `long` can store up to 19 digits, so for large `long` values, some precision will be lost, although the value stored in the `float` will be a correctly rounded copy of the `long`.

Conversely, although the `decimal` type's range is less than that of a `float`, an implicit conversion from `decimal` to `float` is *not* allowed by the compiler, presumably because the whole point of using a `decimal` is to eliminate round-off error.

3.11 ■ Explicit type conversions – casting

In some cases where the compiler will not implicitly convert data from one type to another, we can still force it to do so by applying an explicit conversion, commonly called a *cast*. To apply a cast to a variable, simply place the data type (within parentheses) to which the variable is to be converted in front of the variable name.

For example, to convert a `long` to an `int` (something that cannot be done implicitly, since data could be lost if the value of the `long` is outside the range of an `int`), we can write:

```
long x = 1234;
int y = (int)x;
```

Any numeric data type can be cast into any other numeric data type, even if the conversion actually *will* cause data to be lost. This is always a danger with an explicit cast, so you should use them sparingly and with care, and only do so if there is no other way around the problem.

Key point

An explicit cast can be used to force one data type into another, but data could be lost in the process.

For example, we can modify the earlier example by setting the initial `long` variable x to a value outside the range of an `int`:

```
long x = 12345678900;
int y = (int)x;
```

This code will still compile without errors, but since the value stored in x won't fit into an `int`, what actually does get stored in y? The answer is −539222988. The problem is that to convert a `long` to an `int`, the four high-order bytes in the `long` are simply discarded. This is fine if they are all filled with zeros, which will be true if the value stored in the `long` is within the range of an `int`, as it was in the first example. But if the value is too large, data will be lost and no warning of this will be given by the compiler.

Fortunately, the `checked` feature described earlier can be used to detect overflow problems when an incorrect cast is used. We can put the offending statement within a `checked` block as before:

```
long x;
int y;
checked
{
    x = 12345678900;
    y = (int)x;
}
```

This code will still compile, but a runtime error will be generated by the cast statement.

The `checked` keyword can also be used locally by using parentheses rather than braces to enclose the operation that is to be checked for overflow:

```
long x = 12345678900;
int y = checked((int)x);
```

Key point

The `checked` keyword can be used to detect overflows when an explicit cast is used.

Casts may be used to convert floating-point values to integers, but this results in the fractional part of the `float` or `double` being lost. For example:

```
double x = 3.1415;
int y = (int)x;
```

Here, y will contain the value 3.

For the purposes of casting, a `char` is considered to be a numerical data type with a value given by the Unicode value for the character. In this context, a `char` is essentially the same as a `ushort`, since it contains 2 bytes and is unsigned. For example, we can write:

```
float x = 65.723423F;
char c = (char)x;
```

Here, the cast truncates x to produce a `ushort` integer (65), which is then stored in the `char`. If printed out, c has the value 'A', since the Unicode (or ASCII) for 'A' is 65.

Finally, remember that the `bool` type can *never* take part in a cast with a numeric type, in either direction. The `bool` is not considered to be a numeric type – its possible values are always just `true` and `false`, which have no numeric value.

Key point

`bool` can never be cast into another data type.

The last word on casting is to use common sense – if you attempt to cast one variable into another, make sure that the destination variable can handle the value you are forcing onto it. If in doubt, enclose the cast in a `checked` block to catch any overflows.

3.12 ■ Operators

Programming novices often get confused by operators, since many introductory courses and textbooks tend to treat individual operators as distinct topics.

In fact, a more unified approach to operators should reduce the confusion. An *operator* is a symbol or keyword which can be applied to one or more *operands* to produce a *result*. For example, the + operator takes two numeric operands, and produces a result which is the sum of these two numbers.

An operator can be classified according to the number of operands it requires. In C# (and Java), all operators require at least one operand, and none accepts more than three. An operator that takes a single operand is called a *unary* operator. The minus sign can be used as a unary operator whose purpose is to reverse the sign of a numeric quantity. For example:

```
int x = 34;
int y = -x;
```

The – operator here has x as its single operand, and returns the value –34 as its result.

Operators taking two operands are called *binary*, and an operator (there is only one in C# and Java) taking three operands is called *ternary*.

Key point

An operator takes one, two or three operands and always returns a result.

C#'s operator set is almost identical to that of Java, so readers should be familiar with most of their functions. It will still be helpful to list the properties of the operators available in C#. Since C# is strict in its type-checking, it is important to remember that certain operators accept only certain types of operands. Table 3.2 lists the C# operators, giving the number of operands each one takes, the types of valid operands and return values, and a brief description of what the operator does. For the purposes of this table, a 'Numeric' operand is any of the numeric primitive data types (including char), and an 'Integer' operand is any of the integer primitive types (again including char).

Table 3.2 C# operators

Symbol	No. of operands	Operand type	Return type	Effect
+	1	Numeric	Numeric	Returns value
−	1	Numeric	Numeric	Negation
+	2	Numeric	Numeric	Addition
+	2	string/any	string	String concatenation
−	2	Numeric	Numeric	Subtraction
*	2	Numeric	Numeric	Multiplication
/	2	Numeric	Numeric	Division
%	2	Numeric	Numeric	Modulus
++	1	Numeric	Numeric	Increment
−−	1	Numeric	Numeric	Decrement
&	2	Integer, bool	Integer, bool	Bitwise AND
|	2	Integer, bool	Integer, bool	Bitwise OR
^	2	Integer, bool	Integer, bool	Bitwise XOR
~	1	Integer, bool	Integer, bool	Bitwise NOT
&&	2	bool	bool	Logical AND
||	2	bool	bool	Logical OR
!	1	bool	bool	Logical NOT
<<	2	Integer	Integer	Bit shift left
>>	2	Integer	Integer	Bit shift right
==	2	All	bool	Equality test
!=	2	All	bool	Inequality test
>	2	Numeric	bool	Greater than
<	2	Numeric	bool	Less than
>=	2	Numeric	bool	Greater or equal to
<=	2	Numeric	bool	Less or equal to
=	2	All	Type assigned	Assignment
+= −= *= /= %= &= |= ^= <<= >>=	2	As first part of operator	Type assigned	Combination of first operation and assignment
? :	3	bool /all/all	All	Conditional operator

Table 3.2 lists all the operators that may be used with primitive data types. There are several other operators that are used only with compound data types such as classes or arrays. We will meet these when we study the associated data types.

Although many of the operators have obvious effects, a few comments about how some of them work may be helpful.

The effect of some of the operators depends on their context. For example, the + operator can occur as a unary operator, in which case it has no effect other than to return the value of its operand. That is, the following code will give the same result whether or not we use the + operator in front of x:

```
int x = 34;
int y = +x;
```

Used as a binary operator where both its parameters are numeric, the + operator adds together the two numbers and returns the sum as a result. Although this seems straightforward enough, there are a few things to beware of even here. If the two numeric parameters are of different types, such as an int and a float, the operand whose data type has the smaller range of values will be implicitly converted into the other operand type before the addition is performed, and the result will also be an instance of the data type with the larger range. Thus adding an int to a float will result in a float sum, and so on.

There is, however, an exception to this rule: adding two integers will always produce an int if both the operands have data types that are shorter than int (that is, they are char, byte, sbyte, short or ushort). For example, adding together two shorts will produce an int result. This can produce some unexpected compiler errors, as in the following code:

```
short x = 34, y = 56;
short z = x + y;
```

The compiler will complain that we 'Cannot implicitly convert type "int" to "short", because even though x and y are both shorts, the value returned by the + operator as their sum is an int and we cannot assign an int directly to another short, z in this case. We can, of course, force the issue by casting the result of the sum:

```
short x = 34, y = 56;
short z = (short)(x + y);
```

Key point

Adding two short integers always returns an int result.

Finally, the + operator can be used as a string concatenation operator if at least one of its operands is of type `string`. Any other primitive data type can be inserted into a `string` by joining it to an existing string using the + operator. This is handy for constructing strings for output in `WriteLine()` calls. For example:

```
int x = 42;
string message = "The value of x is " + x;
Console.WriteLine(message);
```

Before leaving integer arithmetic, we must mention the 'integer division pit-fall' which can still bite even experienced programmers. Remember that any arithmetic operator will always return an integer result if both its operands are integers. For addition, subtraction and multiplication this is not a problem, since the results of these operations are always integers anyway, but for division this can cause serious bugs. For example:

```
int x = 3, y = 4;
int z = x / y;
Console.WriteLine("z = " + z);
```

The output will be 'z = 0' since the division in the second line will truncate the result to the integer portion, discarding any fractional part. There is nothing in the C# language that can prevent us from making such an error, since we are not exceeding any ranges of data types or dividing by zero or doing any other illegal operation. In some cases, we just have to be careful!

Key point

Division of two integers always returns an integer result. Any fractional part in the quotient is discarded.

The modulus operator `%` applies to numeric data types, and returns the *remainder* after its left operand is divided by its right. For example, the expression `53 % 7` will return a value of 4 since 53 divided by 7 gives 7 with a remainder of 4. Note that the modulus operator also works with `float` and `double` operands, so that for example, `5.5 % 2.2` returns `1.1`, since 5.5 is 2*2.2 + 1.1.

3.12.1 ☐ Increment and decrement

The increment (++) and decrement (--) operators often give rise to confusion because they can be used in two ways: as a *prefix* (coming before their operand) or as a *suffix* (after the operand). In both cases, the effect each operator has on its operand is the same; what differs is the return value of the operator. The ++ operator always adds 1 to its operand, and the -- operator always subtracts 1. If the return value from the operator is ignored, then there is no difference between the prefix and suffix versions. For example, the following code results in both x and y storing the value 43:

```
int x = 42;
int y;
x++;
y = x;
```

This code does exactly the same thing:

```
int x = 42;
int y;
++x;
y = x;
```

However, the next two examples do *not* produce the same result. The first example results in y being 42 and x being 43:

```
int x = 42;
int y = x++;
```

The second example results in both x and y being 43:

```
int x = 42;
int y = ++x;
```

Why the difference? Many books attempt to explain the ++ operator by stating that in the suffix form, it doesn't have any effect on its operand until after the enclosing statement has finished. Besides being confusing (when, exactly, *does* the value of x get changed in this case?), it is also untrue.

The ++ and -- operators are just like any other operator – they have an effect on their operand *and* return a value, and both of these things happen at the time the operator is applied, not after other operations within the same statement.[1] In the *suffix* form of the ++ operator, the return value is the value of the operand *before* the 1 is added. In the *prefix* form, the return value is the value of the operand *after* the 1 is added. Therefore, in the first example above, where y = x++, x has the value 42 before the ++ operator is applied, so the result of the operation is to increase x to 43 and return 42. In the second example, where y = ++x, the ++ operator increases x to 43 and returns the value *after* the operation, so it returns 43.

---

[1] In C and C++, it has to be admitted that this statement is not always true, since these languages have a bizarre behaviour with respect to these operators, and the actual point at which the value of x gets changed varies between compilers. It is actually unsafe to attempt to modify a variable more than once within a single statement in C and C++. C# (and Java) behaves somewhat more sensibly.

Key point

The prefix form returns the value of its operand *after* the operation; the suffix form returns the value of its operand *before* the operation.

Both the increment and decrement operators may be applied to all numerical types, including floating-point types.

3.12.2 ☐ Bitwise operators

The three bitwise operators &, | and ^ apply the AND, OR and XOR (exclusive OR) operations to each corresponding pair of bits in their two-integer or bool operands. The unary bitwise NOT operator ~ inverts each bit in its operand.

In binary bitwise operators, because the two operands are compared on a bit-by-bit basis, they must be the same size in memory. If we attempt to apply a bitwise operator to integer operands of different sizes, the smaller operand is implicitly converted into the larger data type before the operator is applied. The extra bytes added in the conversion are all filled with zeros if the number is zero or positive, and with ones if the number is negative.

Let us quickly review what each of these operators does. A bit, of course, can have only two values: 0 or 1. The AND operator applied to two individual bits returns a value of 1 only if both its operand bits are 1, and 0 otherwise. The OR operator returns 1 if either of its operands is 1, and 0 only if both operands are zero. The XOR operator returns 1 only if exactly one of its operands is 1 and the other is 0. XOR returns 0 if both operands have the same value.

To predict the result of any of the bitwise operators, we need to convert their operands into binary and then apply the operation to each pair of bits separately. For example, consider the line:

```
byte x = 3 & 5;
```

To predict the value of x, we can write out 3 and 5 in the binary form, as single bytes:

```
    3 = 00000011
    5 = 00000101
3 & 5 = 00000001
```

We can see that the result of the bitwise AND is 1.

Similarly, a bitwise OR gives a value of 00000111 or 7, and an XOR gives 00000110 or 6.

One common use of bitwise operators is to provide a way of storing information in compact form. For example, if we have a number of binary properties (properties which have only two possible values, such as 'yes' and 'no') to set in a program, we can store the values of eight such properties within a single byte, rather than declaring eight separate variables. We can then select the value of a single property by doing a bitwise AND with a constant containing a 1 bit at the location occupied by that property. For example, the following code snippet shows four properties that might be set in a computer game:

```
1.    const byte Light = 1;
2.    const byte Sound = 2;
3.    const byte Shadow = 4;
4.    const byte Animation = 8;
5.
6.    byte Properties = 0;
7.    Properties = (byte)(Properties | Light);
8.    Properties = (byte)(Properties | Shadow);
9.
10.   if ((Properties & Light) == Light)
11.   {
12.      Console.WriteLine("Lights are on.");
13.   }
```

The four properties are declared using the const keyword, which we shall consider in more detail in Chapter 5. For now, it is enough to realize that they define a 'variable' as a constant, which means that its value cannot be changed after initialization.

Each of the four properties is assigned to a single bit within a byte variable. The Light property gets the least significant bit, Sound the next bit, and so on. The Properties variable will store the current settings of all four of these properties (it could store up to eight properties since it has 8 bits available). When it is declared on line 6, it is set to 0, which turns off all the properties. On lines 7 and 8 we turn on the Light and Shadow properties by using the bitwise OR to change the corresponding bits to 1.

We can use the bitwise AND operator to test if a property is set as shown on line 10 (note that we need to cast the result into a byte since any binary operator operating on small integers returns an int result). By doing a bitwise AND between Properties and one of the constant property bytes, in this case Light, we mask out all the bits except the one we are interested in.

```
     Properties = 00000101
          Light = 00000001
Properties & Light = 00000001
```

We can see that the result of the Properties & Light operation will be equal to Light only if the Light property has been switched on – it will be zero otherwise.

Obviously this program is a bit of an overkill for only eight properties, but in a larger application where there are a lot of binary properties to store it could result in a significant space saving.

3.12.3 ☐ **Logical operators**

The three logical operators are && (AND), || (OR) and ! (NOT). They all take only `bool` operands and return a `bool` result. The && operator returns `true` only if both its operands are `true`, the || operator returns `true` if either of its operands is `true`, and the ! operator returns the opposite of its single operand. Their most common use is within the `if` statement or as part of the Boolean expression used to determine when to terminate a loop. For example:

```
int x = 42, y = 63;
if (x > 0 && y > 0)
{
    // Perform some actions
}
```

If the operands of && or || are formed from comparison expressions as in this example, note that each operand must be a complete expression. For example, if we wanted to check that x was greater than 0 and less than 10, we must say

```
if (x > 0 && x < 10) // Correct
```

rather than

```
if (x > 0 && < 10) // Wrong!
```

In other words, we cannot just translate an informal English expression into computer code – each operand must be a well-defined `bool` value.

The && and || operators only evaluate enough of their operands to determine what the result will be. For example, since the && operator returns `false` if either of its operands is false, if the left operand of && is false, the right operand is not evaluated at all, since its value can have no effect on the result of the && operation. Similarly, since the || operator returns `true` if either of its operands is true, if the left operand is true, the right operand is never evaluated.

Although this behaviour is more efficient, it can have an unexpected side effect if the programmer is relying on the operator evaluating both its operands. For example, in the expression

```
x > 0 || ++y < 12
```

if x actually is greater than zero, then the ++y operation never gets performed, which could have consequences for later code.

3.12.4 ☐ **Bit shift operators**

The bit shift operators << and >> are basically quick ways of multiplying or dividing an integer by a power of 2. The left shift operator << shifts its left operand to the left by the number of bits given in its right operand. The empty bits opened up by the shift are filled in with zeros. For example:

```
int x = 42;
int y = 42 << 3;
```

The value of y is 42 shifted to the left by 3 bits, which is 42 * 8 = 336. In binary, 42 is 101010, so shifting to the left by 3 bits gives 101010000.

Similarly, shifting to the right divides by a power of 2. The empty spaces on the left that are opened up by the shift are filled in with whatever bit was originally in the leftmost place. For a positive integer, this value will always be 0, but for negative numbers it will be 1.

Remember that integer division rules will be applied so that any fractional part will be truncated:

```
int x = 42;
int y = 42 >> 3;
```

In this case, the value of y is 5. In binary, shifting 101010 to the right by 3 bits gives 101, with the rightmost '010' in the original binary number being lost.

If the number to be shifted is negative, we cannot predict the result by simply multiplying or dividing by a power of 2, since negative integers are stored using *two's complement*. We don't want to get into the details of two's complement here, but if you know the notation you may wish to work out what effect the shift operators will have on negative numbers.

3.12.5 ☐ Equality testing operators

The tests for equality == and inequality != may be applied to all primitive data types. They both return a bool result, and may therefore be used as operands for the logical operators.

These operators hold no surprises for integer or decimal data types, but should be used with care when comparing floats or doubles due to the fact that these two data types are prone to round-off errors as we saw earlier. Remember that two floats must be *exactly* equal in order for the == operator to return true. If one float has a value of 1.53 and another has a value of 1.529999, they will not be seen as equal. When comparing floating-point numbers it is safer to test if they both lie within a small interval, rather than checking precise equality. For example, we might say:

```
if (x > y - 0.000001 && x < y + 0.000001)
```

rather than

```
if (x == y)
```

3.12.6 ☐ Comparison operators

The four comparison operators <, >, <= and >= may be applied to any numeric types. They are all binary operators and all return a bool result. The numeric data types need not be the same for the two operands, but if they differ, the less general data type is implicitly converted into the more general one before the comparison is made.

3.12.7 ☐ Assignment operator

The main assignment operator is the single equals sign =. Assignments of primitive data types follow the rules for implicit conversion given above. If the value on the right of the = operator is of a less general data type than the variable on the left, an implicit conversion will take place before the assignment is made. If the value on the right is *more* general than the variable on the left (and no explicit cast is specified), a compiler error will occur. For example, the following code is correct:

```
int x = 42;
long y;
y = x;        // Implicit conversion from int to long
```

but reversing the roles of x and y produces an error:

```
long x = 42;
int y;
y = x;        // Can't convert long to int
```

The compiler will not accept this even though the value stored in x (42) will fit into an int variable. In order for this code to compile, a cast is necessary:

```
long x = 42;
int y;
y = (int)x;
```

Apart from type conversion problems, the assignment operator produces no surprises when applied to primitive data types, since it always copies the value on the right into the variable on the left. After the assignment, the two variables go their separate ways without interfering with each other. We will see that when we consider objects, this is not the case, but more on that later.

Incidentally, we mentioned earlier that all operators in C# return a result, and it may not be obvious what is returned from an assignment operation.

In fact, an assignment operator always returns the value that it assigns. This fact means that assignment operations can be *chained*, as in:

```
int x, y, z;
z = y = x = 42;
```

We'll explore this chained statement in more depth later when we consider the associativity of operators.

3.12.8 ☐ Convenience assignment operators

There are ten convenience assignment operators listed in the table above: +=, -= and so on. Each of them is a combination of another operator with the regular assignment operator =. Taking the += operator as an example, the code:

```
int x = 42;
x += 12;
```

is equivalent to:

```
int x = 42;
x = x + 12;
```

That is, the += operator is just a shorter way of writing something that could be written with the other more basic operators. For simple expressions such as those in the example here, it is a matter of personal taste which way we write them. The convenience operators become most useful when the variable involved has a long name, or is a complex chain of class data fields or array indexes. In these cases, using a convenience operator can save a lot of typing and make the code more readable.

All the convenience operators return the value of their left operand *after* the operation. In the code above, for example, the expression x += 12 returns 54, since the value of x after 12 is added to 42 is 54.

3.12.9 ☐ **The conditional operator ? :**

The final operator we shall consider at this point is the only *ternary* operator in C#. It is essentially a shorthand version of an if...else statement. A conditional expression takes three operands. The first must be a bool expression. If this expression evaluates to true, the second operand is evaluated and its value is returned by the conditional operator, completing the operation. In this case, the third operand is not evaluated at all.

If the bool expression evaluates to false, the second operand is ignored and the third operand is evaluated and returned.

Key point

The ?: operator is equivalent to an if ... else statement.

The general form of the conditional operator is therefore:

```
(bool expression) ? (if true) : (if false)
```

For example:

```
int x = 42;
int y = (x > 0) ? (x + 3) : (x - 3);
```

The first operand is x > 0, which in this case returns true, so the second operand x + 3 is evaluated and the result (45) is returned and assigned to y. If the first operand had been x < 0, this would return false with x = 42, so the conditional operator would evaluate its third operand x - 3, and return a value of 39 which would then be assigned to y.

The second and third operands can return any data type, but of course they must match the context in which the conditional operator is used. For example, if y had been declared as a short in the example above, a compiler error would occur because we are attempting to assign an int to a short.

Conditional expressions can be nested, so that either the second or third operand (or both) could be another conditional expression. Although this can be useful in some situations, it is not recommended as it makes the code hard to understand.

The use of the conditional expression is really a matter of personal taste, since the same effect can be obtained using an `if...else` statement. Some programmers find the conditional expression hard to understand and never use it, but you should be familiar with it so that you can recognize it in other people's code.

3.13 ■ Operator associativity

If a given binary operator occurs more than once within an expression, we need to know the operator's *associativity* to predict the final value of the expression. For example, take the statement:

```
int x = 34 - 5 - 2;
```

To determine the value of x, we need to know which subtraction is done first. If it is the first one, as in:

```
int x = (34 - 5) - 2;
```

the answer will be 27, but if it is the second, as in:

```
int x = 34 - (5 - 2);
```

the answer will be 31.

If a sequence of identical operators is evaluated left-to-right, the operator is said to be *left-associative*, and if the evaluation proceeds from right-to-left, the operator is *right-associative.*

The subtraction operator is left-associative, so that the value assigned to x above is 27. All operators except assignment operators are in fact left-associative, so the rules are quite easy to remember.

Key point

All assignment operators are right-associative. All other binary operators are left-associative.

Assignment operators, including the ordinary = operator and all the convenience forms such as +=, are right-associative. It is often not realized that the associativity of the assignment operators matters, but if we take a closer look at what happens in an assignment, we will see that it is important.

Consider the simple assignment:

```
x = 42;
```

We stated earlier that all operators do two things: use their operands to perform a calculation and *return a result*. The fact that the assignment operator returns a result is often forgotten, since in many programs this return value is never used. In the simple assignment above, for example, the result of the assignment is that the = operator returns the value that it assigns to x, in this case 42, but this returned value is not used and is lost after the statement finishes.

Now suppose we have two assignments in the same statement:

```
y = x = 42;
```

Since the assignment operator is right-associative, the rightmost operator is evaluated first, resulting in 42 being assigned to x. That is, the statement is equivalent to:

```
y = (x = 42);
```

The operation within the parentheses returns the value 42 after the assignment to x is done, so when the second = operator gets its turn to run, its right operand is 42, and y thus gets the value 42 assigned to it. Note that the right operand of y is *not* x: it is the returned value of the first assignment. If the = operator had been defined so that it did not return a value, it could only be used once in any single expression, and expressions such as y = x = 42 would not compile.

The convenience operators such as += work the same way. It is perfectly legal to write code such as:

```
y = x = 42;
y -= x += 5;
```

In the second line, the += operator runs first, resulting in x becoming 47. The += operator then returns 47 as its result, and this is used as the right operand of the -= operator, so that the final value of y is –5.

3.14 ■ Operator precedence

As we have seen above, when several instances of the *same* operator occur in the same expression, the *associativity* rules are used to find the order in which they are evaluated. When several *different* operators occur together in an expression, we need to use the rules of *operator precedence* to find the order in which they are applied.

The simplest example of operator precedence is probably familiar to the reader from high school algebra. In any expression containing a combination of addition, subtraction, multiplication and division, the multiplications and divisions are done first, followed by the additions and subtractions. For example:

```
x = 3 + 4 * 7 - 8 / 2;
```

The * and / operators have a higher precedence than + and –, so they are done first. To find which of * and / is done first, we resort to the associativity rules, since these two operators have equal precedence. As they are left-associative, the * is done first, then the /.

Similarly, + and – have equal precedence so we use the associativity rules to find that the + is done first since it occurs to the left of the –. The final order of the four operations can therefore be shown by inserting parentheses:

```
x = (3 + (4 * 7)) - (8 / 2);
```

The precedences of the operators we have met so far are shown in Table 3.3.

Table 3.3 Operator precedence

Type	Operators
Unary	( ) ++ -- + – ! ~ casts
Multiply/Divide	* /
Add/Subtract	+ – (as binary operators)
Bit shift	<< >>
Comparison	< > <= >=
Equality	== !=
Bitwise AND	&
Bitwise OR		
Bitwise XOR	^
Logical AND	&&
Logical OR	||
Ternary	? :
Assignment	= += –=, etc

If you find the precedences hard to remember, it is best to enclose operations within parentheses if you want to ensure that they are done in the correct order. Doing this also makes the code easier to read.

Key point

Use parentheses to make the order of operations explicit if you cannot remember the precedence rules.

For example, in the expression (assuming all variables are `int`s):

```
if (x & y == w | z + 2) ...
```

it can be difficult to determine whether the expression will compile, and if it does, what it will do. Referring to the precedence table above, we see that the order in which the compiler will attempt to run the operations is:

1. `z + 2`

2. `y == w`

3. `x & (y == w)`

4. `(x & (y == w)) | (z + 2)`

If we study this list of operations, we find that the expression will not compile, since in step 3, we are attempting to apply the `&` operator to a combination of a `bool` operand and an `int` (the `y == w` operation returns a `bool`).

What the programmer probably intended is that the `==` operator be run last, which can be made explicit using parentheses:

```
if ((x & y) == (w | z + 2)) ...
```

3.15 ■ Conditional statements

C# provides the same two conditional statements as Java: `if...else` and `switch`.

3.15.1 ☐ The `if...else` statement

The `if...else` statement in C# is identical to its counterpart in Java. The general structure of the statement is:

```
if (condition)
{
   statements if value is true
}
[else
{
   statements if value is false
}]
```

The text in italics in the structure is, of course, not actual C# code but a description of what must be placed at that location. The square brackets around the `else` clause indicate that it is optional – it is perfectly legal to have an `if` statement without a following `else` clause. (It is, of course, *not* legal to have an `else` without an `if` preceding it.)

The 'condition' can be any expression that returns a `bool` value. Typical conditions are formed from expressions using the equality or comparison operators such as `==` and `>`, but `bool` variables may also be used. Anyone who has programmed in C or C++ should remember that numerical values are *not* allowed as conditions in `if` statements in C# – the condition *must* be a `bool` value.

If only a single statement is to be included within the body of an if statement the enclosing braces are not required. That is, we can say:

```
if (x > 7)
    y = x;
x += 3;
```

Here, the y = x statement would be run only if x > 7, but the x += 3 statement will always be run.

Although this code is legal, the author prefers using braces for all if statements because it avoids a common error. Frequently it is discovered while debugging or modifying existing code that an extra line needs to be inserted into the body of an if statement, and it is very easy to forget that braces must also be inserted. For example, we might modify the code above as follows:

```
if (x > 7)
    y = x;
    z = x + 1;
x += 3;
```

The intention is that the extra z = x + 1 statement should only be run if x > 7 (hence the reason for indenting this statement), but when the program is run we find that it is *always* executed, regardless of the value of x. The problem is that we forgot to insert the braces:

```
if (x > 7)
{
    y = x;
    z = x + 1;
}
x += 3;
```

Although indenting the original code makes it look to a human observer that there are two statements within the if statement, we must remember that indentation of code means nothing to a compiler – we could write the entire program on a single line without even putting in any line breaks between statements and it would still compile properly.

The else clause can be chained with further if statements to allow one possibility to be selected from several choices. For example, we may say:

```
1. if (x > 7)
2. {
3.     y = x;
4.     z = x + 1;
5. }
6. else if (y < 0)
7. {
8.     y = -x;
9. }
```

```
10. else
11. {
12.    x += 3;
13. }
14. z = 3 * x;
```

In this example, lines 3 and 4 are run if x > 7, after which the program jumps to line 14. Line 8 is run only if x > 7 is *false* and y < 0 is *true*. Again, control passes to line 14 after line 8.

Finally, if both x > 7 is false *and* y < 0 is false, line 12 will be run. An else without an if immediately after it is a catchall clause which will always be run if none of the preceding if statements was executed.

3.15.2 ☐ **The switch statement**

The switch statement in C# is similar to Java's switch statement, but there are a couple of differences which need to be noted.

The general structure of the switch statement is:

```
switch (integer or string value)
{
  case constant1:
    statements
    break;
  case constant2:
    statements
    break;
  ...other cases
  default:
    statements
    break;
}
```

The 'integer or string value' that serves as the parameter to a switch can be any variable or expression that returns an integer value (of any of the C# integer types, including char) or a string. The body of the switch acts like a series of if...else statements. The first case statement tests if the value of the switch's parameter is equal to constant1. If so, the statements immediately following this first case statement are executed. When the break statement is reached, control passes out of the switch statement and resumes with the first statement following the end of the switch.

If the first case does not produce a match between the value and constant1, the next case statement is tested. This process continues until either a match is found, or a default statement is encountered (if there is one). The default acts like a catchall else clause – if control reaches a default, then its statements will be run.

As an example, consider the following code:

```
int x = 42;
switch (x)
{
  case 41:
    Console.WriteLine("x = 41");
    break;
  case 42:
    Console.WriteLine("x = 42");
    break;
  case 43:
    Console.WriteLine("x = 43");
    break;
  default:
    Console.WriteLine("x is something else");
    break;
}
```

Since x is assigned the value 42 at the start, only the case 42 clause will be activated. If x had been assigned 57, the default clause would be run.

Readers familiar with the Java switch statement may already have spotted a difference between the Java and C# forms. In Java, the parameter of a switch must be an integer – it cannot be a String. In C#, a string *is* allowed as a parameter, something which experienced programmers will greatly appreciate.

C# vs Java

In C#, a string may be used as the test variable; in Java, only an integer value may be used.

The second difference between Java and C# is a bit more subtle. The Java switch statement allows 'fall-through', which means that if the statements following one of the cases don't end with a break, all the statements in the following case will also be run, regardless of whether the value passed into the switch matches the constant value the second case statement is trying to match. For example, if we take the previous C# example (which is also valid in Java if we replace Console.WriteLine by System.out.println), and left out the break in the case 42 clause, we would get:

```
int x = 42;
switch (x)
{
  case 41:
    Console.WriteLine("x = 41");
    break;
```

```
case 42:
  Console.WriteLine("x = 42");
  // break omitted: valid in Java, but not in C#
case 43:
  Console.WriteLine("x = 43");
  break;
default:
  Console.WriteLine("x is something else");
  break;
}
```

In Java (if we use `System.out.println` to print things), the output from this code would now be:

```
x = 42
x = 43
```

In C#, the above code would not compile, as C# requires that each non-empty `case` clause *must* end with a `break` (or a `goto` – see section 3.18 on `goto` below). The 'non-empty' qualification means that several `case` statements *can* be grouped together so that they all execute the same code. For example, we could alter the earlier example:

```
int x = 42;
switch (x)
{
  case 41:
  case 42:
  case 43:
    Console.WriteLine("41 <= x <= 43");
    break;
  default:
    Console.WriteLine("x is something else");
    break;
}
```

In this case, if `x` had any of the values 41, 42 or 43, the output would be:

```
41 <= x <= 43
```

Key point

Any non-empty `case` clause must end with a `break`.

The final point to remember about the `switch` statement is that the parameters used in each `case` clause must be constants, not variables or expressions containing variables. In the examples so far, we have used literal values such as 42 as `case` parameters, but we may also define a symbol to represent a constant using the `const` keyword:

```
const int FirstValue = 41;
int x = 42;
switch (x)
{
  case FirstValue:
    Console.WriteLine("x = " + FirstValue);
    break;
  case FirstValue + 1:
    Console.WriteLine("x = " + (FirstValue + 1));
    break;
  case FirstValue + 2:
    Console.WriteLine("x = " + (FirstValue + 2));
    break;
  default:
    Console.WriteLine("x is something else");
    break;
}
```

This example illustrates the use of a `const` as a `case` parameter, but it also shows that expressions are allowed as `case` parameters provided that all operands within the expression are constants.

Key point

The parameter in a `case` clause must be a constant.

3.16 ■ Loops

C# provides the same three loops as Java (`while` `do...while`, and `for`), but adds an extra loop species: the `foreach` loop.

3.16.1 □ The `while` loop

The simplest type of loop is the `while` loop, which has the general form:

```
while (condition)
{
  statements
}
```

As with the `if` statement, the 'condition' must be either a `bool` value or an expression that returns a `bool` result. Any other data type will not be accepted as a condition.

The first time the loop is encountered during the running of a program, the condition is evaluated and, if it is true, the statements within the loop are executed. Then, the condition is evaluated again and if it is still true, the statements are executed again, and so on until the condition becomes false. The following loop prints out the squares of the numbers from 1 to 10:

```
int x = 1;
while (x <= 10)
{
   Console.WriteLine(x + " squared is " + (x*x));
   x++;
}
```

Three things should always be remembered when using a `while` loop. First, make sure that whatever variable is to be used in the termination condition is properly initialized before the loop starts – in this case we've set x to 1 just before the loop.

Second, make sure the termination condition will eventually be reached. In the above example it is easy to forget the `x++` statement at the end of the loop's statements. If we had omitted this statement, the value of x would never change, meaning that the condition x `<=` 10 would always be true. This would cause an *infinite loop*. In this situation, the presence of an infinite loop would be obvious as soon as the program starts running, since an endless stream of '1 squared is 1' lines would appear in the console window. However, in more complex programs, especially if the loop doesn't produce any visible output, an infinite loop can cause a program to lock up for no apparent reason. Since the loop is also absorbing virtually 100 per cent of the processor's attention, it can be difficult to get the computer's attention long enough to kill the program. Despite C#'s many built-in features that help prevent you from making obscure errors, there really is no safeguard against infinite loops apart from careful programming.

Finally, remember that the condition will always be tested at least once, even if the statements within the loop are never run. This can be important if the expression used as the testing condition alters some of its variables (which in general isn't a good idea). Also remember that the last time the loop is run, the condition must return `false`. Therefore, the values of any variables changed within the loop will *not* necessarily be the same as they were during the last iteration of the loop. In the example above, the value of x after the loop finishes will be 11, not 10, since the condition x `<=` 10 must be false in order for the loop to finish.

3.16.2 ☐ The do...while loop

The `do...while` loop is basically an inverted `while` loop: whereas the `while` loop tests its condition first and only enters the loop body if that condition is true, the `do...while` loop always executes the statements within the loop *first*, then tests the condition to see if another iteration is required. Its form is:

```
do
{
   statements
} while (condition);
```

Apart from this difference, it is the same as the `while` loop. We could rewrite the above table of squares example as follows:

```
int x = 1;
do
{
   Console.WriteLine(x + " squared is " + (x*x));
   x++;
} while (x <= 10);
```

3.16.3 ☐ The `for` loop

As you might have noticed in the examples above for the `while` and `do...while` loops, two common steps that are required in the use of a loop are initializing the loop condition before the loop is run for the first time and changing the value of some variable or expression after each iteration. Using a `while` loop requires us to do this using separate statements outside or within the loop. Since these operations are so common, a special type of loop which incorporates them into the syntax of the loop itself would be useful. Enter the `for` loop.

The general structure of a `for` loop is:

```
for (initialization; condition; update)
{
   statements
}
```

The first line of a `for` loop contains three components. The first of these is an expression that is always performed before the loop itself starts – the *initialization expression*. This expression is performed only once, no matter how many times the statements within the loop are executed. Its main purpose is to initialize the variable that is to be used as the loop counter, although in practice, any expression can be placed here, provided that it assigns or changes the value of a variable. We'll explain this in a bit more detail below after we've looked at an example of a `for` loop.

The second component is the termination condition for the loop. This condition must satisfy the same restrictions as the condition in a `while` loop: it must return a `bool` value. As with the `while` loop, this condition is checked before the loop is run for the first time, so it will always be evaluated at least once, even if it returns `false` and the statements of the loop are never executed.

The final component is the *update expression*. This expression is evaluated *after* each loop iteration, and so will only be run if the loop's statements are executed. After the update expression is run, the condition is checked again, and if it is still true, the statements within the loop are executed again.

The order in which the four components of a `for` loop are run is then:

1. Initialization

2. Test Condition. If false, exit loop

3. Statements

4. Update Expression

5. Test Condition. If false, exit loop

6. Statements

7. Update Expression

8. Test Condition. If false, exit loop

9. Etc…

The only natural exit point for a `for` loop is therefore if the condition is false. The table of squares example above can be written using a `for` loop:

```
int x;
for (x = 1; x <= 10; x++)
{
   Console.WriteLine(x + " squared is " + (x*x));
}
```

In fact, we can condense the code even further, as `for` loops allow variables to be declared as part of the initialization component:

```
for (int x = 1; x <= 10; x++)
{
   Console.WriteLine(x + " squared is " + (x*x));
}
```

The *scope* of x is restricted to the `for` loop and the statements it contains, that is, we cannot use x in any statements before or after the loop since it is not defined at those points. This is fine if we just wish to use x as a kind of dummy parameter for counting the iterations within the loop. (We will treat the subject of variable scope in more depth once we have covered classes and objects in more detail in Chapter 4.)

There is one other feature unique to `for` loops in both Java and C#, although it is not often used. The update expression (the third component in the loop's first line) may contain a list of expressions separated by commas rather than just a single expression as we've seen in the examples above. For example, suppose we wanted to calculate the sum of squares of the integers between 1 and 10 and print it out after the table of squares. We could do it the traditional way, of course:

```
int sum = 0;
for (int x = 1; x <= 10; x++)
{
```

```
    Console.WriteLine(x + " squared is " + (x*x));
    sum += x*x;
}
Console.WriteLine("Sum of squares = " + sum);
```

However, we can also do it this way:

```
int sum = 0;
for (int x = 1; x <= 10; sum += x*x, x++)
{
    Console.WriteLine(x + " squared is " + (x*x));
}
Console.WriteLine("Sum of squares = " + sum);
```

Notice that we've moved the sum += x*x from a statement of its own in the body of the loop to one of the expressions in the update component of the for statement itself.

The curious thing is that this is the *only* place where a comma-separated list of expressions is allowed in C# (and in Java). If we tried placing the statement

```
sum += x*x, x++;    // Not allowed in Java or C#
```

as a line on its own, it will be rejected by the compiler.

As an aside to C and C++ programmers, this behaviour is quite different from that of the comma operator in those languages. In C++, the statement above *would* be acceptable on its own, and would simply evaluate the two separate expressions from left to right. In fact, the comma operator returns the value of the right-hand expression, so in C++ we can even use it in an assignment statement:

```
int result = sum += x*x, x++;    // Works only in C, C++
```

Beware that this is *not* allowed in either Java or C#.

Although it is not recommended in most cases, it is legal to omit any or all of the three components in the definition of a for loop. The effect of doing this varies, depending on how much code you have at other places in and around the loop.

If we omit the initialization component, nothing disastrous will occur providing we have initialized things before the loop starts, just as we did for the while loop.

Omitting the loop termination condition is much more entertaining, as this causes an infinite loop – the compiler interprets no termination condition as a permanent 'true' condition. This is not something that should be encouraged, unless you have other ways of stopping the loop, such as using a break somewhere within the body of the loop (see below).

Finally, omitting the update expression could cause an infinite loop if no other provision is made for changing the variables used in the termination condition. However, if we update these variables within the body of the loop in the same way as we did for the while loop earlier, everything should still work correctly.

3.17 ■ The `break` and `continue` statements

We have met the `break` statement when studying the `switch` statement, but it may also be used for breaking out of loops before the termination condition is reached. For example, the following code asks the user to enter a number and then prints out the square of that number. The loop will continue until the user enters a negative number:

```
1. do
2. {
3.    Console.Write("Enter a number (< 0 to quit): ");
4.    string number = Console.ReadLine();
5.    int x = int.Parse(number);
6.    if (x < 0)
7.    {
8.       break;
9.    }
10.   Console.WriteLine(x + " squared is " + x*x);
11. } while (true);
```

Line 4 reads in the number as a `string` and line 5 converts the `string` to an `int`. (It should be noted that this program is very fragile, in that it has no checks that the string entered by the user is actually an integer. We have omitted the error checking to save space.)

The `if` statement on line 6 tests if the number is negative and, if so, a `break` terminates the loop. Otherwise, the number and its square are printed out on line 10.

Note that the loop itself is a potentially infinite one, since the termination condition on line 11 is always true. However, since the program always pauses on line 4 to wait for the user to enter a number, it won't lock up the machine.

The `break` statement will only break out of the actual loop in which it is found. If it occurs within the inner loop of a nested loop, it will return control to the outer loop, rather than breaking out of all the loops entirely. The only quick way of breaking out of a deeply nested loop right back to the surface is to use the much maligned `goto` statement, which we will mention later.

The `continue` statement is a bit like `break`, except that instead of breaking out of the loop entirely, it skips the remainder of the statements in the loop body *for the current iteration only*. For example, the following program asks the user to enter two integers and then prints out their integer quotient. If the user enters a negative number for the numerator, the `break` statement stops the loop, but if the user enters a zero for the denominator, an error message is printed and the `continue` on line 17 causes the remainder of that loop iteration to be skipped, but the loop itself starts again with the next iteration.

```
1.  do
2.  {
3.     Console.Write("Enter the numerator (< 0 to quit): ");
4.     string numString = Console.ReadLine();
5.     int numerator = int.Parse(numString);
6.     if (numerator < 0)
7.     {
8.        break;
9.     }
10.    Console.Write("Enter the denominator: ");
11.    string denomString = Console.ReadLine();
12.    int denominator = int.Parse(denomString);
13.    if (denominator == 0)
14.    {
15.       Console.WriteLine(
16.         "Error: denominator cannot be zero.");
17.       continue;
18.    }
19.    Console.WriteLine(numerator + " / "
20.      + denominator + " = " + numerator / denominator);
21. } while (true);
```

The final loop type, foreach, can only be used with compound data types such as arrays and other collections, so we must defer its description until we have considered these data types.

3.18 ■ The goto statement

Despite the bad press that the goto statement tends to get, it actually can be useful in some situations. Unlike Java, which does define goto as a reserved word but doesn't actually implement it, C# provides two types of goto statement. One type may be used to redirect the program within a switch statement, while the other may be used to transfer control to a labelled statement anywhere within the same method.

The use of goto in a switch statement effectively provides a way of getting around the prohibition of fall-through that we discussed earlier. The syntax for a goto within a switch is:

```
goto case case-label;
```

Its effect is to redirect the program to the case clause with the given label. For example:

```
int x;
Console.Write("Enter x: ");
x = int.Parse(Console.ReadLine());
switch (x)
```

```
{
   case 1:
     Console.WriteLine("case 1");
     break;
   case 2:
     Console.WriteLine("case 2, then case 1");
     goto case 1;
   case 3:
     Console.WriteLine("case 3, then default");
     goto default;
   default:
     Console.WriteLine("default");
     break;
}
```

Here we read in a value for x from the console and use it as the parameter in a switch. If x is 1, only the line in the case 1 clause is printed. If x is 2, the line in the case 2 clause is printed, then control is directed to the case 1 clause, so two lines are printed. Note that since goto is an unconditional jump in the code, there is no need for a break statement in a case clause that ends with a goto.

The case 3 clause shows that it is also possible to use goto to redirect control to the default clause.

The other use of goto is more conventional, in that it can be used to redirect program flow anywhere within a method. The warnings that you may have heard about misuse of the general goto statement are well-founded, in that it should only be used in cases where it really is the best option. It is very easy to rely on a goto to patch up some bad logic in the program. In most cases, a goto can be avoided by using a conditional statement such as if or switch.

Probably the most common (proper) use of a general goto is to break out of a nested loop. As we saw earlier when we considered nested loops, the break statement will break the program only out of the innermost loop, so if we find ourselves deep within a nested loop and want to break out of all layers of the loop, we would need a series of break statements at each level, which can be difficult to program. In such a case, using a goto makes a lot more sense.

Using a goto requires the definition of a *label* somewhere within the scope of the goto. The scope of a goto is restricted to code within the same method as the goto statement. Further, a goto cannot redirect the program to the inside of a loop or conditional statement, unless the goto itself is also within that statement. A couple of examples should clarify this.

The first example shows a legitimate use of goto:

```
void TestGeneral()
{
   for (int i = 1; i < 10; i++)
```

```
    {
        for (int k = 1; k < 10; k++)
        {
            if (k * i % 5 == 0)
            {
                goto Breakout;
            }
            Console.WriteLine(i + " * " + k + " = " + i*k);
        }
    }
    Breakout:
        Console.WriteLine("Loops finished.");
}
```

The `TestGeneral()` method contains a nested loop which iterates over two integer variables. In the inner loop, if the product `k * i` is evenly divisible by 5, the program is redirected to the `Breakout` label, which is defined after the loops. The output from this method is:

```
1 * 1 = 1
1 * 2 = 2
1 * 3 = 3
1 * 4 = 4
Loops finished.
```

An illegal use of `goto` would be an attempt to redirect the program from the outer loop into the inner loop, bypassing the setup statements in the inner loop:

```
for (int i = 1; i < 10; i++)
{
    if (i % 5 == 0)
    {
        goto InnerLoop;
    }
    for (int k = 1; k < 10; k++)
    {
        InnerLoop:
            Console.WriteLine(i + " * " + k + " = " + i*k);
    }
}
```

This loop attempts to jump into the inner loop whenever `i` is divisible by 5. The compiler will not allow this, since the `InnerLoop` label is not within the scope of the `goto` statement. Allowing a jump such as this would skip the declaration and initialization of `k`, so the `WriteLine()` statement would not have a valid variable to use.

Similar restrictions apply to jumping from one loop to another loop that does not contain the first loop, and to jumping into the interior of a conditional statement.

■ Summary

In this chapter, we have explored the basics of C#, including the built-in data types and basic statements and expressions. Much of this material should be familiar to Java programmers, but C# does have enough differences from Java that it is worth making sure you are familiar with these basics before moving on.

Exercises

3.1 Which of the following code fragments will cause *compilation* errors, and why? (Each fragment should be taken in isolation.) For any statements that *do* compile without errors, can you see any *runtime* errors that might occur?

(a) `sbyte number = 643;`

(b) `sbyte number = (sbyte)643;`

(c) `short x = 643;`
    `sbyte number = (sbyte)x;`

(d) `sbyte number = 42;`
    `short x = number;`

(e) `sbyte number = 42;`
    `short x = number + 1;`

(f) `sbyte number = 42;`
    `int x = number + 1;`

(g) `byte number = 255;`
    `sbyte snumber = number;`

(h) `byte number = 255;`
    `number = number + 1;`

3.2 The following code causes an infinite loop when run. Why? (Note that the compiler produces a warning about this code.)

```
for (byte i = 0; i < 1000; i++)
{
    Console.WriteLine(i);
}
```

3.3 How could the infinite loop in the previous exercise be prevented without changing the data type of `i`? The solution will cause the program to crash (unless the exception is handled – see Chapter 7) at which value of `i`?

3.4 As stated in the text, the code fragment below will not compile:

```
float x;
x = 3.14;
```

However, the following code *does* compile:

```
float x;
x = 3;
```

Why?

3.5 As an illustration of round-off error, write a program which calculates the area of a square with a side length of 100 units by subdividing the square into a grid of one million smaller squares, each of side length 0.1, calculating the area of each of these smaller squares and adding them all up to produce the total area. Use `floats` for all your calculations and compare the area obtained by just squaring 100 to that obtained by adding up the million small squares. Repeat the calculation using `doubles` instead of `floats`. Does this make things better or worse?

3.6 Repeat the previous exercise using `decimals` instead of `floats` or `doubles`. Does the `decimal` live up to its claim of eliminating round-off error?

3.7 Write a program using a `decimal` variable to keep track of the user's bank balance. The program should simply use a loop to request the amount to be added to the balance at each point, with a positive value being used for deposits and a negative value for withdrawals. After each transaction, print out the new balance and then request the amount for the next transaction. The program should quit when the user enters a zero amount for a transaction. (Obviously this program has limited use without the ability to store the amount on disk between runs of the program, but we can add this later when we learn about using files.)

3.8 Suppose the following code is run, and the user enters 1 on the first iteration and 40 on the second. For each operator in the code, state whether it is a unary or binary operator, find the value(s) of its operand(s) and the value that the operator returns after the operation. Remember that not all return values are used in the program.

```
int x, y, z;
z = y = x = 42;
while (x != 0)
{
    Console.WriteLine("The current value of x is " + x);
    Console.Write("Please enter the new value (0 to quit): ");
    x = int.Parse(Console.ReadLine());
    if (x > y)
    {
        z = -x;
        y += 2 * z;
    }
    else
    {
        z = x + 2 * y - z;
        y -= 3 * x;
    }
    Console.WriteLine("y = " + y + "; z = " + z);
}
```

3.9 Suppose we have declared three `int`s named `x`, `y` and `z`. The initial values are `x = 17` and `y = 3`. What value does `z` have after each of the statements below?

(a) `z = x / y;`

(b) `z = y / x;`

(c) `z = x % y;`

(d) `z = y % x;`

3.10 A common programming practice is to use the `++` or `--` operator to change the value of a loop variable within a `while` loop, but to do so as part of another statement. What will be printed to the console in each of the following code fragments?

(a)
```
int x = 0;
while (x < 5)
{
    int y = 2 * x++;
    Console.WriteLine("x = " + x + "; y = " + y);
}
```

(b)
```
int x = 0;
while (x < 5)
{
    int y = 2 * ++x;
    Console.WriteLine("x = " + x + "; y = " + y);
}
```

3.11 Consider again the `byte` parameters defined in the text to illustrate bitwise operators:

```
const byte Light = 1;
const byte Sound = 2;
const byte Shadow = 4;
const byte Animation = 8;

byte Properties = 0;
Properties = (byte)(Properties | Light);
Properties = (byte)(Properties | Shadow);
```

(a) Write a method with the prototype:

```
byte OffBit(byte properties, byte parameter)
```

which will switch off the `parameter` in `properties` and return the result. For example, if `parameter` is `Light` in the above code, `OffBit()` will set the `Light` bit to zero no matter what its original value in `properties` is.

(b) Write a method with the prototype:

```
byte InvertBit(byte properties, byte parameter)
```

using bitwise operators that will invert the specific value given by `parameter` in `properties` while leaving the others unchanged, and return the modified value of `properties`. For example, the method could turn `Light` off (change the bit corresponding to `Light` in `Properties` to a 0) if it is on, and vice versa, but leave the values of the other three parameters as they were.

(c) Why does the following code produce a compilation error?

```
byte x = 5;
byte y = !x;
```

3.12 In each of the following cases, is anything printed to the console?

(a)
```
int x = 2, y = 2, z = 4;
if (x == y || z == x && z == y)
{
    Console.WriteLine("Got here");
}
```

(b)
```
int x = 2, y = 2, z = 4;
if ((x == y || z == x) && z == y)
{
    Console.WriteLine("Got here");
}
```

(c)
```
int x = 2, y = 2, z = 4;
if (x == y || (z == x && z == y))
{
    Console.WriteLine("Got here");
}
```

3.13 Why would the following code give a compilation error?

```
int x = 2, y = 2, z = 4;
if (x == y || z = x && z == y)
{
    Console.WriteLine("Got here");
}
```

3.14 Given the declarations:

```
int x = 16, y = -16;
```

what value is returned by each of the following operations?

(a) x << 2

(b) x >> 2

(c) x << 40 (try this one in a program to check it – can you explain the result?)

(d) y << 2

(e) y >> 2

(f) y >> 10 (try this one and the next in a program and try to explain the result)

(g) y >> 40

3.15 Given the declaration:

```
int x = 5;
```

what value does x have after each of the statements below? In each case, assume that x has the value 5 before the statement is run, so that each statement should be treated in isolation.

(a) x *= 10

(b) x /= 10

(c) x <<= 3

(d) x >>= 3

(e) x |= 3

(f) x &= 3

3.16 Given the declaration:

```
int x, y = 20;
```

the following code fragment is run:

```
x = int.Parse(Console.ReadLine());
int z = (2 * x == y) ? x + y : x - y;
```

What value is assigned to z if x is (a) 10 and (b) 60?

3.17 For each of the following, determine if the code will compile and, if so, what is printed to the console. In each case, assume that the code is properly contained within a method. Carefully consider the return types of the operators and the associativity and precedence rules to work out your answers. Check your answers by compiling and running the code in a test class.

(a) ```
int x = 3 & 7 | 12;
Console.WriteLine(x);
```

(b) ```
int a = 1, b = 2, c = 3;
bool x = a > b && c > a;
Console.WriteLine(x);
```

(c) ```
int a = 1, b = 2, c = 3;
bool x = a > b & c > a;
Console.WriteLine(x);
```

(d) ```
int a = 1, b = 2, c = 3;
bool x = a > (b & c) > a;
Console.WriteLine(x);
```

(e) ```
int a = 1, b = 2, c = 3;
bool x = (a > b & c) > a;
Console.WriteLine(x);
```

3.18 The following code was intended to produce a table of squares of the integers from 0 to 9, but what is actually printed?

```
int i;
for (i = 0; i < 10; i++);
{
    Console.WriteLine(i + " * " + i + " = " + i*i);
}
```

(Hint: examine the code *very* carefully and note that although the code compiles without errors, a warning of a 'possible mistaken null statement' is given.)
```

3.19 Convert the following `if` statement into a `switch` statement, assuming that a and b are `int`s that have been properly declared and given values elsewhere in the program. Use a as the parameter in the `switch` statement.

```
if (a == 1)
{
    Console.WriteLine("a is 1");
}
else if (a == 0 && b < 0)
{
    Console.WriteLine("a is zero & b is negative");
}
else
{
    Console.WriteLine("something else has happened");
}
```

3.20 Write a `while` loop, a `do...while` loop and a `for` loop, each of which prints out a table of squares of the integers from 1 to 10.

3.21 What is printed by the following nested `for` loops?

```
for (int i = 0; i < 10; i++)
{
    for (int j = 0; j < 10; j++)
    {
        if (i * j > 50) break;
        Console.Write(i * j + " ");
    }
    Console.WriteLine();
}
```

3.22 If the `break` is replaced by `continue` in the code in the previous exercise, show that the output remains the same. Which version of the program would take longer to run?

3.23 Write a version of the program in either of the preceding two exercises that uses `goto` in place of `break` or `continue`.

Inside C# objects **4**

In Chapter 2, we saw how the basic idea of object-oriented programming, the concept of encapsulation, is implemented in C#. In Chapter 3, we saw how primitive data types and basic control statements are written. In this chapter, we shall bridge the gap between the lower-level data types and statements and the overall class structure of an object-oriented program. We will examine how objects are stored in memory, how the individual methods within a class can be defined and used, and how the primitive data types we met in the previous chapter are related to classes in the .NET library.

It is probably at this level that C# differs most strongly from Java. Java's handling of classes and objects is deliberately stripped-down, whereas C# has reintroduced many of the alternative methods for doing things that may be more familiar to C++ programmers than those brought up on Java.

4.1 ■ Value and reference types

In Chapter 3, we met the primitive data types provided by C#. These data types may be used to declare variables without any prior preparation on our part – they are predefined by the language.

In Chapter 2, we saw that we could also create *objects* by using a user-defined *class* such as `Employee` to declare a variable.

The distinction between these two types of variable declarations should be familiar to anyone with some experience in Java, but it is important to understand the differences between these two types, both in Java and C#.

The primitive data types we met in Chapter 3 are known as *value* types, while all other data types (with the exception of the `struct` and `enum`, which we shall meet later in this chapter) are *reference* types. What's the difference?

In order to answer this question, we need to understand something about how variables are stored in memory. Computer memory may be thought of as a one-dimensional line of individual locations, rather like a very long street with individual houses on it. In computer memory, each 'house' is a single byte (8 bits), and just like a house has a number on it to identify it (for the postman to deliver letters, among other things), each byte in a computer's memory also has an *address*. The address of a byte is needed for much the same reason as the address on a house: the operating system and the programs it runs must have some way of finding individual bytes so that data can be stored there and recalled later when it is needed.

The address of a byte is just an integer, with each byte receiving an address one greater than the byte before it. The address is usually written in hexadecimal, simply because it is easier for computers to handle hexadecimal numbers than ordinary decimal ones. However, it is probably easier for you to think in decimal (if you *do* find it easier to think in hexadecimal, you probably should get out more), so if you want to visualize memory locations in the following discussion, just think of ordinary decimal integers.

Now that we've got a simplified view of computer memory fixed in our minds, let's get back to what happens when variables are declared. We will start with a simple declaration such as:

```
int x;
```

When the compiler encounters this declaration, it must first determine how much memory the variable x requires. It does this by looking up the data type (int) and finding out from its definition that an int takes 4 bytes. Next, it consults the operating system to find an available contiguous block of 4 bytes that can be used to store memory for a new program. The operating system will find such a block (unless all the memory is being used for other programs, in which case the compiler will stop with an error message) and reserve it for the variable x. The compiler will link x with the memory that has been allocated to it, so that each time some data is assigned to x as in:

```
x = 42;
```

the program will know exactly where to go in memory and store 42 at that location.

All the primitive data types work the same way. Any variable declared from a primitive type will have a memory location directly linked to it, and any data that gets assigned to such a variable will be stored at that location.

This probably all seems rather obvious, but there is a subtlety in here which must be appreciated. Suppose we write the following:

```
int x, y;
x = 42;
y = x;
x++;
```

What are the values of x and y after this code has run? You probably answered that x is 43 and y is 42, and you would be right. The reason is that, for value variables, the assignment operator = *copies* the data from its right operand to its left operand. Thus the line y = x copies the data stored in x (42) to the location where y is stored. After this assignment, there are two distinct copies of the 42 data, one at location x, and one at location y. This means that the expression x++ then operates *only* on the data stored at location x, leaving the value of y unchanged. Obvious, right?

Well, maybe not.

Let's now go back to the Employee class we introduced in Chapter 2. We can try doing much the same thing with two Employee objects as we just tried with two ints:

```
Employee x, y;
x.Salary = 42;
y = x;
x.Salary++;
```

If we insert this code into the `Main()` method of the `CompanyDemo` class that we defined in Chapter 2 and try to compile it (you are urged to try this yourself), we find that the code will not even compile. The error reported is: 'Use of unassigned local variable "x" and the line causing the problem is the second one, where we attempt to assign 42 to `x.Salary`.

We can solve the problem by inserting a line after the declaration, so that the code now looks like this:

```
Employee e1, e2;
e1 = new Employee();
e1.Salary = 42;
e2 = e1;
e1.Salary++;
```

Notice that we didn't have to do this when we were declaring `int`s – we could just declare an `int` and then assign a value to it in the very next step. Why the difference with an `Employee`?

In principle, we might think that the compiler could treat an `Employee` object in exactly the same way as an `int`. Since the definition of the `Employee` class is provided, the compiler should be able to work out by looking at the primitive data fields within the class how much memory is needed to store all the data fields for an `Employee`, reserve that memory and then simply associate `x` with that memory. (In fact, if you declare an object in C++, that's what happens, more or less.)

The point is that declaring an object from a class is treated in a fundamentally different way in C# (and Java) from declaring a variable from a primitive data type. A declaration such as:

```
Employee e1;
```

creates a *reference* to an `Employee` object, but doesn't actually create the object itself. So what's a reference?

A reference is essentially the address of the memory location at which the object can be found. A declaration such as `Employee e1` therefore states that `e1` will hold the *address* of an `Employee` object, but it does *not* do anything more than that. In particular, it doesn't actually allocate any memory for the `Employee` object, or assign any values to the data fields within the object. It is up to us (the programmers) to do that in the code.

Until we actually create the object, the reference itself is assigned the special value `null` by the compiler. The keyword `null` is a symbol that indicates an uninitialized reference. Any attempt to read data from a `null` reference while the program is running will cause an error, and it is a pretty safe bet that before you do too much programming in C#, you will encounter this error. In fact, from your Java experience, you may remember the 'NullPointerException' which is Java's error message in the same situation.

The C# compiler attempts to help you avoid null reference errors by insisting that any reference is initialized before it is used. This is the origin of the 'unassigned local variable' error we got above when we tried to assign a salary to e1 immediately after declaring it – we hadn't actually created an Employee object, so it didn't make any sense trying to assign a value to its Salary property.

To create the Employee object, we need the line

```
e1 = new Employee();
```

The new operator (for it is actually an operator) takes a single operand on its right, which must be the name of a class. The class name in this case is followed by a pair of empty parentheses, which indicates that a constructor is being called, but we'll get to that in Chapter 5 when we examine constructors in detail. We haven't provided any explicit constructor in the Employee class yet, so all that happens is a set of default actions provided by the new operator.

So what does new do? Basically, it duplicates the steps that are done automatically for value variables when they are declared. That is, it will first determine how much space is needed for an Employee object to be created. Then it will ask the operating system for that much memory. Since we haven't provided an explicit constructor, it will then initialize all the data fields in the Employee object to default values. (The default value of any numeric data field is 0, a bool is set to false, and a char to 0.)

Finally, since new is an operator, it will return a value, which is the reference to the location in memory that was allocated to the new object. Thus the statement

```
e1 = new Employee();
```

results in e1 being assigned to the location in memory occupied by the new Employee object.

The important point to remember about all this is that e1 itself contains only the *reference* to another location in memory, while an int variable such as x in the example above refers directly to the data stored in memory. Why is this so important?

To answer this, let's go back to the original bit of code, except this time we'll add a couple of output lines:

```
Employee e1, e2;
e1 = new Employee();
e1.Salary = 42;
e2 = e1;
e1.Salary++;
Console.WriteLine("e1 salary = " + e1.Salary);
Console.WriteLine("e2 salary = " + e2.Salary);
```

If we run this code, we get the output:

```
e1 salary = 43;
e2 salary = 43;
```

In other words, the `Salary` of *both* employees has been changed by the increment of e1's salary. This result may or may not surprise you, depending on how closely you've been following the argument above. If it does surprise you, it is probably because you think the expression e2 = e1 should be doing the same thing as the y = x expression in the example with `int`s earlier. Obviously, it isn't, but why?

We declare two `Employees`, call the `new` operator to create a new object for e1, and then set the salary for e1 to be 42. So far, so good. But what does the next line, e2 = e1, do?

Remember that e1 and e2 are *references* to `Employee` objects. What is happening in the expression e2 = e1 is that the *reference* stored in e1 is copied into e2, *not* the object that e1 is referring to. The effect of this is that both e1 and e2 now refer to the same location in memory. That is, they are two different *aliases* for the *same* object. In other words, although we have two references, we only have one object for them to refer to.

The effect of this is that after the assignment e2 = e1, we can use either e1 or e2 to refer to the object that was created with the `new` operator on the second line. When we increase the salary with the e1.Salary++ expression, we are changing the salary of the single `Employee` object. Whether we use e1 or e2 to refer to it doesn't matter since they both refer to the same object anyway. We could equally as well have said e2.Salary++ instead of e1.Salary++; the effect would be the same. It is for this reason that the two output lines produce the same result, since they are both accessing exactly the same object.

This is a subtle point, but a very important one, since failing to recognize the difference between value and reference data types can lead to some serious bugs.

Key point

A value variable refers directly to the data it represents. A reference variable contains the address of the location in memory where the object is stored.

Key point

An assignment of one value variable to another copies the actual data between the variables. An assignment of one reference variable to another only copies the reference (memory address) between the variables. The object to which that reference refers is *not* copied.

4.2 ■ Passing by value and passing by reference

Now that we've seen the fundamental difference between value and reference variables in C#, we need to examine what happens when these variables are passed as parameters to methods.

We shall begin by trying a few experiments in code. Consider the following method:

```
void IntValue(int arg)
{
   arg++;
}
```

The method takes a single `int` parameter and increments its value. We now call this method using the code:

```
int x = 42;
IntValue(x);
Console.WriteLine("x = " + x);
```

We find that the output is:

```
x = 42
```

That is, the value of x is not changed by the method call. The reason is that x is being *passed by value* to the method, which means that the value of x, in this case 42, is copied into the parameter `arg` within the function. The parameter `arg` becomes a new variable which is independent of x, so that any changes made to `arg` do not affect x.

Now let's try something similar with a reference variable like an `Employee` object:

```
void EmployeeValue(Employee e)
{
   e.Salary += 1000;
}
```

We will call this method with the code:

```
Employee employee = new Employee();
employee.Salary = 5000;
EmployeeValue(employee);
Console.WriteLine("Salary is " + employee.Salary);
```

In this case, the output is:

```
Salary is 6000
```

Note that this time, a change that we made to the method's parameter e *does* make a difference to one of the data fields in the original `employee` object. Does this mean that reference variables are passed to methods in a different way than value variables? Not really.

Remember that a declaration such as

```
Employee e;
```

actually declares only a reference to an `Employee` and does not create an `Employee` object. When we call the `EmployeeValue()` method, we pass it the `employee` reference variable as a parameter. This variable contains only the reference to the actual `Employee` object that was created with the `new` operator. When the `EmployeeValue()` method starts up, the parameter e is created and receives a copy of the reference stored in the original `employee` variable. We therefore have two references (e and `employee`) that both refer to the same `Employee` object. In other words, it is the same situation as we had when we used the assignment operator to assign one `Employee` reference to another.

Essentially what is happening when we pass a reference variable to a method in this way is that we are passing the reference itself by value, since the reference does get copied in the calling process. However, many books and articles still call this sort of parameter passing as passing by reference, since any changes made to the actual object within the method are permanent, and do affect the original object in the code that called the method. Others argue from the purist standpoint, claiming that since the reference is getting copied when the method is called, we are really passing by value.

Key point

Passing a primitive variable by value creates a copy of the data held in the variable, but passing an object by value copies only the reference to the object. Any changes made to a reference variable within a method affect the original object.

In Java, these arguments were largely pointless, since this is the only way objects can be passed into methods. As long as we understand what is happening, it doesn't really matter whether we think of the process as passing by value or passing by reference. In C#, however, the situation becomes a bit more complicated since C# offers other ways of passing parameters to methods.

Before we dive into these new methods, let us do one more experiment that should drive home what is actually happening when we pass a reference into a method. Suppose we modify the `EmployeeValue()` method above by adding an extra line:

```
void EmployeeNewValue(Employee e)
{
   e = new Employee();
   e.Salary = 6000;
}
```

We now call this method with the code:

```
Employee employee = new Employee();
employee.Salary = 5000;
EmployeeNewValue(employee);
Console.WriteLine("Salary is " + employee.Salary);
```

This time, the output is:

```
Salary is 5000
```

The reason for this is that after copying the reference stored in `employee` into the method's parameter `e`, we immediately overwrite this reference by creating a new `Employee` object in the method and storing *its* reference in `e` instead. That is, we now have two separate `Employee` objects, with the `employee` reference referring to the first one and `e` referring to the second. In this case, we set the salary of the second object to 6000, which of course does not affect the salary of the original object.

Everything we have tried with parameter passing so far in C# would work the same way in Java. Now, however, we are ready to introduce a couple of features that are unique to C#.

4.3 ■ The `ref` keyword

One shortcoming of Java is that all primitive data types can only be passed by value. This means that there is no way of sending an `int`, say, as a parameter to a method and allowing the method to alter the `int` in a way that will be seen in the original code that called the method. (Java does provide *wrapper classes* such as `Integer` which allow primitive data types to be wrapped up within a class and then passed by reference, but there is no way of passing a bare `int` by reference.)

Some programmers argue that is a good thing, since there is a school of thought that states that methods should never have *side effects*. That is, the only way a method should be able to change any data in the code that called it is by returning a value which the calling code may or may not decide to use. There is merit in this argument, since many bugs have been caused in languages such as C++ (which does allow primitive data types to be passed by reference) by methods that alter the values of parameters without letting the programmer know this is happening.

However, Java's policy of prohibiting passing by reference does seem overly restrictive in many cases, so the ability to do it in C# is welcome.

To pass a parameter by reference in C#, we need to add the `ref` keyword before the parameter in the method declaration *and* in the parameter list when that method is called. For example, if we return to our `IntValue()` method above, we can rewrite it to pass by reference:

```
void IntRef(ref int arg)
{
  arg++;
}
```

We can now call this new method with the code:

```
int x = 42;
IntRef(ref x);
Console.WriteLine("x = " + x);
```

The output this time is:

```
x = 43
```

so that now, the `IntRef()` method's increment statement results in a change to x.

The introduction of the `ref` keyword means that rather than creating a copy of x when it is passed to `IntRef()` as a parameter, the `arg` variable within the method becomes a reference to the same memory location as that occupied by x, so that any changes to `arg` are also changes to x.

Note that we must put a `ref` before the x when we call `IntRef()`. This is mainly a safety feature in C#, as it forces the programmer to realize that a parameter is being passed by reference and therefore that the method could change its value permanently. If this may cause a problem, the programmer should check the documentation for the `IntRef()` method to ensure that any side effects will not cause a bug to appear.

This safety feature is not optional – it is enforced by the compiler. If we tried to call `IntRef()` without the `ref` keyword, as in:

```
IntRef(x);      // Will not compile
```

the compiler will complain that it cannot convert 'int' to 'ref int'. In other words, a 'ref int' is treated as a data type distinct from just 'int'.

Key point

The `ref` keyword passes any data type by reference. The `ref` keyword must be present both in the method definition and in a call to the method.

Now let's try passing an `Employee` by reference using `ref`. We rewrite `EmployeeValue()` from before:

```
void EmployeeRef(ref Employee e)
{
  e.Salary += 1000;
}
```

We can call this new method with the code:

```
Employee employee = new Employee();
employee.Salary = 5000;
EmployeeRef(ref employee);
Console.WriteLine("Salary is " + employee.Salary);
```

Running this code produces the output:

```
Salary is 6000
```

Nothing appears to have changed from the earlier version using `EmployeeValue()`. Does this mean that the `employee` object is being passed the same way in both cases? Not at all.

To see that there really is a difference, we will rewrite the second `Employee` example above, to produce a new version of `EmployeeNewValue()`:

```
void EmployeeNewRef(ref Employee e)
{
  e = new Employee();
  e.Salary = 6000;
}
```

We now call this method with the code:

```
Employee employee = new Employee();
employee.Salary = 5000;
EmployeeNewRef(ref employee);
Console.WriteLine("Salary is " + employee.Salary);
```

This time, the output is:

```
Salary is 6000
```

So here there *is* a difference. What's going on?

In the old `EmployeeNewValue()` method, remember that the `Employee` parameter `e` within the method was a separate reference to the original `Employee` object, and that this came about because the reference (memory address) stored in `employee` was copied into `e` when the method was called. That is, the variable `employee` was actually being passed by *value*, since it was being copied into a new variable when the method was called.

This time, we are passing the variable `employee` by *reference* into the method, which means that it is *not* being copied into `e`. Rather, both `e` and `employee` become references to the same data, and that data in this case is the memory address of the actual `Employee` object. Therefore, when we change that address within the method by creating a new `Employee` object and setting `e` to refer to it, we are also changing what the original `employee` reference refers to.

The net effect of calling `EmployeeNewRef()` is that both `employee` and `e` refer to the new `Employee` object created within the method, and that there are no longer any references to the original `Employee` object created before the method was called. The latter point is important, since it shows that using `ref` can have serious consequences if you're not certain what you're doing. It is very easy to lose a reference to an object completely if that reference is reassigned within a method.

4.4 ■ The `out` keyword

As we've seen earlier, the C# compiler requires that a variable be initialized before its value is used in an expression. For example:

```
void TestInit()
{
   int x, y;
   y = x;
}
```

The compiler reports an error due to the 'Use of unassigned local variable "x" in the expression `y = x`. This is sensible, since in most cases, there is no logical reason to use a variable before it has been assigned a value.

There is one situation, however, where the ability to use an uninitialized variable would be quite useful. Consider the following method:

```
void TestUninitArg(ref int arg)
{
   arg = 42;
}
```

The method expects an `int` parameter passed by reference, which it then assigns a value. Clearly the whole point of passing the parameter by reference is to assign it a value that will remain in place after the method finishes. Since whatever value is passed into the method gets overwritten by the `arg = 42` expression, there wouldn't seem to be any need to initialize the parameter that is passed to the method.

However, if we attempt to call the method using the code:

```
int x;
TestUninitArg(ref x);
```

the compiler again reports the error 'Use of unassigned local variable "x" when we attempt to call the method.

We could get around this error by just assigning any old value to x, as in:

```
int x = 0;
TestUninitArg(ref x);
```

but this is a clumsy way of doing things, since the value assigned to x is never used for anything other than avoiding a compiler error message.

C# comes to the rescue with the `out` keyword. We can now write:

```
void TestUninitArg(out int arg)
{
   arg = 42;
}
```

where we have replaced `ref` by `out` in the parameter list. We can call this function using the code:

```
int x;
TestUninitArg(out x);
```

That is, the `out` keyword works in much the same way as `ref`, except that it allows the variable that is passed as a parameter to be uninitialized. Any variable passed using `out` is passed by reference, so any assigned value, such as the `arg = 42` in the `TestUninitArg()` method, will affect the original variable, in this case `x`.

Key point

The `out` keyword allows an uninitialized variable to be passed by reference to a method.

The only condition imposed on an `out` variable is that it *must* have a value assigned to it within the method in which it is a parameter, and this assignment must occur before the variable is used for anything else.

For example, if we tried the following:

```
void TestUninitArg(out int arg)
{
   int number = arg + 3;
   arg = 42;
}
```

we would get a compiler error, since we have attempted to use the value of `arg` before it has been assigned one. Note that this error will occur even if we *do* provide a value for the parameter before it is passed into the method, that is, if we try to call this new version of `TestUninitArg()` using the following code:

```
int x = 99;
TestUninitArg(out x);
```

the compiler will still report an error inside the method from attempting to use `arg` before it has been assigned a value. Whenever a variable is passed as an `out` parameter, its value is not relevant, since the compiler requires that the parameter be assigned a new value within the method. We cannot, therefore, pass a variable using `out` and expect to be able to use its value before overwriting it with a new value. If we want to do that, we can just use `ref`.

4.5 ■ Arrays

We have left the consideration of arrays until now since C# treats an array as a reference object in much the same way as Java. We therefore needed a better understanding of value and reference types before arrays could be treated properly.

First, a quick refresher as to the definition and purpose of an array. An array is a set of elements, all of the same data type, which are stored together under a single variable name, such as `IntArray`. Individual elements within the array can be accessed by using a *subscript* after the array name. In C#, as in Java and C++, the array subscript begins at 0 for the first element in the array. The first element in `IntArray` is therefore written as `IntArray[0]`. If the array contains 10 elements, the last element is written as `IntArray[9]`.

Arrays are the natural choice for a data type when we wish to store a block of related data types, such as the average temperatures for all the days in August, or the marks scored by the students in a class. In the absence of the array data structure, we would need to declare a separate variable for each data element we wanted to store, which for larger data sets would rapidly get cumbersome to type and difficult to read.

As in Java, the declaration and creation of an array requires several steps. First, we need to declare the array object and then we need to create array elements. To create an array of 10 `int`s, for example, we can write:

```
int[] IntArray;
IntArray = new int[10];
```

The first line declares the array object `IntArray`, but at this stage we have not specified how many elements are to be in the array, nor allocated any memory for these elements. The second line states that an array of 10 `int`s is to be allocated using the `new` operator, and the location of these elements (actually, the location of the first element in the array) is to be stored in the `IntArray` reference variable.

It is more usual to combine these two steps into a single statement:

```
int[] IntArray = new int[10];
```

but the effect of this statement is the same as the two given earlier.

We can see the reference nature of an array from this two-step process, as it mirrors the declaration and creation steps for an object such as the declaration of an `Employee` that we looked at earlier. As an aside to C++ programmers, we *cannot* declare an array and specify its size in a single expression, such as:

```
int IntArray[10];   // Works in C++ but not in C#
```

Java programmers may remember that Java allows arrays to be declared in two ways:

```
int[] IntArray;      // Legal in Java and C#
int IntArray[];      // Legal in Java but NOT in C#
```

Java allows us to put the brackets either after the data type or after the variable name, but C# allows only the first type of declaration.

The example with which we began this section, where we created an array of 10 ints, is an array of value variables. As such, each int in the array is initialized with the default value for an int, which is 0. We do not need to provide initial values for each array element and can, if we wish, use these elements in other expressions straightaway. To show this, we can write out the contents of the array:

```
int[] IntArray;
IntArray = new int[10];
for (int i = 0; i < IntArray.Length; i++)
   Console.Write(IntArray[i] + " ");
```

The output is:

```
0 0 0 0 0 0 0 0 0 0
```

We have specified the upper limit of the array indexes by using the quantity IntArray.Length. As the array is a built-in data type in C#, there are a number of properties that are available automatically for any array object. The Length property returns an int stating how many elements are in the array. Note that Length does *not* return the index of the last element in the array – the last element will always have a value one less than Length, since array indexes start at zero.

Key point

The elements of an array of value types are created by the new operator, and can be used immediately.

4.5.1 ☐ Arrays of reference types

The syntax for declaring an array of objects is very similar to that for an array of value types:

```
Employee[] EmployeeList = new Employee[10];
```

There is a subtle difference between an array of reference types and the earlier array of value types, however. An array of value types such as int is ready for use after its memory has been allocated with the new operator. However, when we create an array of reference types, as in the array of Employees, the new operator only creates an array of references – it does *not* create the objects they refer to. Remember that when we created a single Employee we had to do it in two stages. First declare the reference:

```
Employee employee;
```

Second, create the actual `Employee` object for the reference to refer to:

```
employee = new Employee();
```

When we create an array of 10 employees using the `new Employee[10]` expression, we are only doing the first of these two steps: we are creating an array of 10 references, each of which needs to have an `Employee` object created for it to refer to. To complete the creation of the `Employee` array, therefore, we need a loop which handles this creation process:

```
Employee[] EmployeeList = new Employee[10];
for (int i = 0; i < EmployeeList.Length; i++)
{
    EmployeeList[i] = new Employee();
}
```

Notice the difference in the two uses of the `new` operator here. If `new` is used with square brackets `[]` after the class name, it is creating an *array of references*, but is *not* creating any actual objects. In this case, the `new` operator returns a reference to the first element in the array. If it is used with parentheses `()`, it is creating a *single* object and returning a reference (memory address) to that one object.

Key point

Each element within an array of reference types must be created separately using the `new` operator.

4.5.2 □ Bounds checking

Like Java, C# provides bounds checking on array indexes, meaning that a runtime error will be generated if an array index is outside the bounds of the array. For example, suppose we made a mistake in specifying the upper bound of the `for` loop in the last example:

```
Employee[] EmployeeList = new Employee[10];
for (int i = 0; i <= EmployeeList.Length; i++)
{
    EmployeeList[i] = new Employee();
}
```

This code would still compile, but when we run it, we get the following error: 'Unhandled Exception: System.IndexOutOfRangeException: Index was outside the bounds of the array'. The line number on which the error occurred is also generated. We will see in Chapter 7 how to handle exceptions more gracefully than simply letting the program crash, but the point is that over- or understepping the bounds of an array does not slip through a C# program unnoticed, as it could in C++.

4.5.3 ☐ **Array initialization**

In the examples above, we have seen that the elements in an array of value types are all initialized to their default values when they are created with the new operator, but that arrays of reference types must be initialized separately after the creation of the references themselves.

C# provides another way of initializing both types of array through the use of *initialization lists*. For example, if we wish to initialize an array of ints to the integers from 1 to 10, we can write:

```
int[] numbers = { 1, 2, 3, 4, 5, 6, 7, 8, 9, 10 };
```

The initialization list is a comma-separated list of constants whose data type must be the same as that of the array elements. The list is enclosed in braces and terminated with a semi-colon.

Notice that the length of the array is never explicitly stated – the compiler will infer it from the number of elements in the list, and the size of the array then becomes accessible through the Length parameter of the array. For the numbers array, numbers.Length would return the value 10.

We can initialize arrays of references in the same way, providing we have a way of specifying a value for each reference to refer to. The simplest example of this is probably an array of strings, since the string data type is a built-in C# reference type. We can therefore create an array of strings as follows:

```
string[] sentence =
  { "We", "will", "consider", "the", "string" };
```

This produces an array of strings with five elements, each of which is already initialized to a string value.

We can generate arrays of any reference type using an initialization list if we use the new operator to generate each element in the list. For example, we could create an array of Employees this way:

```
Employee[] empArray =
  { new Employee(), new Employee(), new Employee() };
```

This generates an array of three Employee references and initializes each reference by giving it an Employee object to refer to. Obviously this is not as efficient a way of initializing a large array as simply using a for loop, but once we learn how to use constructors in Chapter 5, we can combine the use of new with a user-defined constructor to produce Employee objects with different initial values for each of their data fields. In that case, the initialization list is often a more compact method of creating a reference array.

The examples of initialization above refer only to the declaration of an array. If we want to reassign a predeclared array later in the program, the required code is slightly different.

For example, if we take the numbers array above, it may be *declared* as we have already stated:

```
int[] numbers = { 1, 2, 3, 4, 5, 6, 7, 8, 9, 10 };
```

However, if we want to reassign `numbers` to a completely new array with different values and a different length, we have to use the `new` operator to do this:

```
numbers = new int[] { 12, 13, 14, 15 };
```

Just saying

```
numbers = { 12, 13, 14, 15 };   // Won't compile
```

won't work, since this way of assigning values to an array only applies when the array is being declared.

4.6 ■ The `foreach` loop

We mentioned in Chapter 3 when considering the various types of loop available in C# that there was a fourth type of loop in addition to those available in Java. This is the `foreach` loop, which is only usable with certain compound data types (technically, a `foreach` loop can be used with any class that implements the `IEnumerable` interface, which will make more sense after we have studied interfaces in Chapter 6) of which the array is the simplest example.

The `foreach` loop can be used to iterate through each element in an array, provided that the array elements are treated as 'read-only' objects. Any attempt to assign a value to an array element within a `foreach` loop will generate a compiler error. For example, we may print out all the values in an array:

```
int[] numbers = { 1, 2, 3, 4, 5 };
foreach (int element in numbers)
{
   Console.Write(element + " ");
}
```

The syntax of the `foreach` loop should be fairly obvious from this example. We must specify a loop index whose data type matches the type of the elements in the array. In this case we have specified the loop index to be an `int` named `element`. Following the declaration of the loop index is the keyword `in`, and after that is the name of the array. The definition of a `foreach` loop can almost be read in ordinary English if the variable names are chosen sensibly: 'For each element in the array numbers...'.

The body of the loop will then be executed once for each element in the array. The output of the loop above is therefore:

```
1 2 3 4 5
```

The restriction on `element` that it is used as a read-only variable means that we cannot use a `foreach` loop to change the data in the array. For example, if we wanted to add 1 to each array element, we might try:

```
int[] numbers = { 1, 2, 3, 4, 5 };
foreach (int element in numbers)
{
    element++;    // Won't compile: element is read-only
}
```

The `element++` expression attempts to change the value of `element` however, and is not allowed by the compiler. The reason for this restriction is that the value of `element` is used by the loop to determine how far through the iteration cycle it has gone. If we changed the value of the loop index, the loop itself will get confused. If we do want to change the values of the array elements, we will need to use a standard `for` loop to iterate over the elements.

Key point

A `foreach` loop cannot be used to change the values of the object over which it is iterating.

4.7 ■ Multidimensional arrays

The arrays we've seen above are all *one-dimensional* arrays, in that they only have a single subscript or index. In many situations it would be convenient to define arrays with two or more indexes. C# supports two types of multidimensional arrays: the *rectangular* array and the *jagged* array. In what follows, we will discuss mainly two-dimensional arrays, although the principles apply to arrays with any number of dimensions.

4.7.1 □ Rectangular arrays

A rectangular two-dimensional array can be used to represent any data that can be laid out in a grid pattern, such as the cells in a spreadsheet, the squares in a crossword puzzle, and so on. The distinguishing feature of a rectangular array is that all rows have the same length.

A simple example is a two-dimensional array in which we can keep track of the positions of chess pieces on a chessboard. A chessboard consists of 64 squares arranged in an 8-by-8 pattern. In chess jargon, the horizontal rows on the board are known as *ranks* and the vertical columns as *files*. At the start of a game, the bottom two ranks are occupied by white pieces and the top two ranks by black pieces, with the middle four ranks being empty.

To store the locations of the pieces on the board, we could define a two-dimensional rectangular array of `strings` with eight rows and eight columns. The syntax for doing this is:

```
string[,] Chessboard = new string[8,8];
```

We can then populate the array by providing a description of what piece sits on each square. One way of doing this which allows us to see how to refer to individual elements within a two-dimensional array is as follows:

```
Chessboard[0,0] = "White rook";
Chessboard[0,1] = "White knight";
Chessboard[0,2] = "White bishop";
// and so on
```

Rectangular arrays can also be declared using initialization lists, just as we did for one-dimensional arrays. Since this method does not explicitly state the dimensions of the array, we must write the initialization list in a way that allows the compiler to figure out these dimensions. This is done by enclosing the set of values that initialize each row within braces, and then to enclose the whole set of rows within an outer set of braces. For example, a complete initialization for the starting position on a chessboard could be written as:

```
string[,] Chessboard =
{
  {
    "White rook", "White knight", "White bishop",
    "White queen", "White king", "White bishop",
    "White knight", "White rook"
  },
  {
    "White pawn", "White pawn", "White pawn",
    "White pawn", "White pawn", "White pawn",
    "White pawn", "White pawn"
  },
  {
    "Empty", "Empty", "Empty",
    "Empty", "Empty", "Empty",
    "Empty", "Empty"
  },
  // Remaining rows in similar fashion
};
```

Remember that merely declaring an array of reference types does *not* create the objects to which each array element refers. We still need to create a separate object for each element in the array. In the chessboard example, we did this by setting each element to a constant `string` value. For most reference data types, however, we will need to use the `new` operator to create the objects.

For example, suppose we have a company that had a number of divisions, and each division could hire up to five employees. We could then represent the employees within the company as a two-dimensional rectangular array of `Employee` references:

```
const int NumberOfDivisions = 4;
const int MaxEmployeesPerDivision = 5;
Employee[,] EmployeeList =
    new Employee[NumberOfDivisions, MaxEmployeesPerDivision];
```

This code merely allocates 20 (5*4) `Employee` references, but does not create any `Employee` objects. To do that, the easiest way is to use a nested `for` loop:

```
for (int d = 0; d < NumberOfDivisions; d++)
{
    for (int e = 0; e < MaxEmployeesPerDivision; e++)
    {
        EmployeeList[d, e] = new Employee();
    }
}
```

Multidimensional arrays may be iterated using a `foreach` loop in much the same way as one-dimensional arrays. For two or more dimensions, the `foreach` loop acts as a set of `for` loops nested to the same level as the number of dimensions in the array.

With two or more dimensions, there could be some uncertainty as to the order in which the elements will be visited within the loop. The rule is that the *rightmost* index is iterated first, with the other indexes from right to left iterated in that order. For example, we could use a `foreach` loop to list the pieces on a chessboard by saying:

```
foreach (string square in Chessboard)
{
    Console.WriteLine(square);
}
```

This loop is equivalent to writing a nested `for` loop where the second array index is iterated by the inner loop and the first index by the outer:

```
for (int row = 0; row < 8; row++)
{
    for (int col = 0; col < 8; col++)
    {
        Console.WriteLine(Chessboard[row, col]);
    }
}
```

The output from either of these loops begins:

```
White rook
White knight
White bishop
White queen
...
```

Clearly the `foreach` loop is much easier to write, although it imposes the usual restriction that the array elements are read-only objects within the loop.

4.7.2 ☐ Jagged arrays

In many cases, a rectangular array wastes space since the rows of data that we wish to store are not all the same length. To deal with such cases, C# provides the second type of multidimensional array, the *jagged* or *orthogonal* array.

As a simple example, suppose we wish to store the list of final marks for several classes taught in a computing department at a university. The numbers of students enrolled in each course will vary, so if we were to store the data in a rectangular array, we would need to declare the array so that the length of each row was at least as large as the largest class. Since many universities have first-year classes with several hundred students and higher-year classes with only 15 or 20 students, this would obviously waste a lot of memory.

A better solution is to declare a jagged array to store the data:

```
const uint NumberOfCourses = 10;
uint[][] Marks = new uint[NumberOfCourses][];
```

We use two separate pairs of brackets after the data type to indicate that we are declaring a jagged array rather than a rectangular array. The allocation of the array using the new operator specifies *only* the number of rows that the array is to contain – the empty pair of brackets at the end is there to tell the new operator that it is creating a set of rows in a jagged array and not a one-dimensional array of uints. (To create higher-dimensional arrays, just add extra pairs of brackets.)

It is not only unnecessary to specify the lengths of the rows in the declaration of a jagged array, it is also prohibited by the compiler. That is, if we tried to say:

```
const uint NumberOfCourses = 5;
uint[][] Marks = new uint[NumberOfCourses][50];
```

we would get a compiler error of 'Incorrectly structured array initializer'. The point is, of course, that if we could specify both the number of rows and the length of each row when we declare the array, we should be using a rectangular array and not a jagged array.

Having declared the array, we now need to construct each row in the array and fill it with data. There are two ways we can do this: we can use the new operator again to allocate the elements within each row, or we can use an initialization list for each row to specify implicitly the size of the row and the data that should be stored there.

Using the first method, we can write:

```
Marks[0] = new uint[250];   // First year course
Marks[1] = new uint[175];   // A second year course
Marks[2] = new uint[100];   // Another second year course
Marks[3] = new uint[25];    // A third year course
Marks[4] = new uint[10];    // A harder third year course
```

We have allocated space for each row in the array according to how many students are enrolled in each course. In this way, the compiler reserves exactly the right amount of memory for each row of data with no wasted space.

The second method allows us to set up an initialization list for each row. This is usually sensible only if the amount of data is small enough to type in without too much effort. For the classes in the `Marks` array, it is feasible for courses 3 and 4 but probably too much work for the other courses. If we used an initialization list to create row 4 in the array, we could replace the code above with:

```
Marks[0] = new uint[250];   // First year course
Marks[1] = new uint[175];   // A second year course
Marks[2] = new uint[100];   // Another second year course
Marks[3] = new uint[25];    // A third year course
Marks[4] =
   new uint[] { 57, 63, 21, 45, 90, 23, 77, 28, 95, 0 };
```

The syntax for the initialization list may look a bit odd, but the easiest way to remember it is to realize that it is dynamically creating a one-dimensional array of `uint`s which is to be attached as row 4 within the `Marks` two-dimensional array. Thus the 'new `uint[]`' part states that we are creating a one-dimensional array of `unit`s, and the elements in braces provide the raw data that is placed in that array.

4.7.3 ☐ The `foreach` loop with jagged arrays

The `foreach` loop *cannot* be used directly on a jagged array to iterate over all elements in all rows of the array. The reason is that a `foreach` loop can only look one layer deep into the structure over which the iteration is taking place, so if we try to use `foreach` on the `Marks` array, for example, it will see each row of that array as the elements, and not the individual `uint`s within each row. We can use a nested `foreach` to access the elements of each row. For example:

```
uint[][] numbers = new uint[3][];
numbers[0] = new uint[] { 1, 2, 3 };
numbers[1] = new uint[] { 4 };
numbers[2] = new uint[] { 5, 6, 7, 8, 9 };

foreach (uint[] x in numbers)
{
   foreach (uint y in x)
   {
      Console.Write(y + " ");
   }
}
```

The outer `foreach` loop treats each of the three rows in the `numbers` jagged array, and the inner loop iterates over each element within each row. The output is therefore:

```
1 2 3 4 5 6 7 8 9
```

Had we attempted to iterate over the entire jagged array with a single `foreach` we would get a compiler error:

```
foreach (uint x in numbers)   // Won't compile
{
   Console.Write(x + " ");
}
```

The first line produces the error: 'Cannot convert type "uint[]" to "uint" since the elements within `numbers` are the individual rows, each of which is a one-dimensional array of `uint`.

Key point

A `foreach` loop cannot be used to iterate over a jagged array.

4.7.4 ☐ The null row problem

We have seen that the C# compiler checks that variables have been assigned values before they are used for the first time, but these checks do not extend to jagged arrays. This means that it is possible for one or more rows in a jagged array to remain uninitialized when the program is run. In the previous example we could change the number of rows in the array but neglect to provide the additional initialization lists to create the extra rows:

```
uint[][] numbers = new uint[5][];      // 5 rows
numbers[0] = new uint[] { 1, 2, 3 };
numbers[1] = new uint[] { 4 };
numbers[2] = new uint[] { 5, 6, 7, 8, 9 };
// Rows 3 and 4 are null
```

Because we have not provided any initialization for rows 3 and 4 they will remain `null`. This will not be a problem unless we try to access these rows before creating them, as could happen if we tried to list all the elements in the array using the nested `foreach` loops above. In this case, the outer loop would still include rows 3 and 4 as values of x, but when the inner loop attempted to access the elements of these rows, a runtime error will occur due to an attempt to read from a null reference.

Higher dimensions

It is worth giving one more example of a jagged array with more than two dimensions to see how the syntax generalizes to higher dimensions. We can declare a three-dimensional jagged array as follows:

```
uint[][][] threeDims = new uint[3][][];
```

We need three pairs of brackets after the data type on the left. For the `new` operator on the right, we must specify the size of the first dimension *only*. Jagged arrays must be created gradually from the top down, so we cannot try to specify the first two dimensions in the declaration:

```
uint[][][] threeDims = new uint[3][5][]; // Not allowed!
```

We can now create the next layer, remembering that the size of each dimension can be different at the next level:

```
numbers[0] = new uint[3][];
numbers[1] = new uint[5][];
numbers[2] = new uint[27][];
```

Finally, for each of these elements, we can create the bottom level:

```
numbers[0][0] = new uint[55];
numbers[0][1] = new uint[3];
// etc.
```

Remember also that if the array's elements are reference variables, we must also create an object for each reference to refer to, just as we did earlier.

4.7.5 ☐ Passing arrays to methods

An array acts in much the same way as any other reference variable when passed to a method as a parameter. The array name acts as the reference to the main body of the array, and the individual elements of the array act like data fields within a class. This means that if we pass an array by value to a method, changes we make to the elements of that array will affect the original array elements, but we cannot redefine the original array to refer to a new block of memory. That is, we can define a method which accepts an array by value:

```
void PassArrayValue(int[] IntArray)
{
    for(int i = 0; i < IntArray.Length; i++)
    {
        IntArray[i]++;
    }
}
```

We can call this method with the following code:

```
int[] TestArray = { 1, 2, 3, 4, 5 };
PassArrayValue(TestArray);
foreach (int element in TestArray)
{
    Console.Write(element + " ");
}
```

The `PassArrayValue()` method will add 1 to each of the array elements, so the output will be:

```
2 3 4 5 6
```

However, if the method tried to reassign the array itself to a new object, with a different number of elements, we will find that the change will not be reflected in the code that called it:

```
void PassArrayValue(int[] IntArray)
{
    for(int i = 0; i < IntArray.Length; i++)
    {
        IntArray = new int[] { 11, 12, 13 };
    }
}
```

If we call this method with the same code as above, the output will now be:

```
1 2 3 4 5
```

The reason here is the same as it was in our original example of passing objects by value: passing `TestArray` to the method creates a copy of the `TestArray` reference and that copy is stored in `IntArray`. At this point, just after the method is called, both `TestArray` and `IntArray` contain references to the *same* array, so anything we do to the array elements via `IntArray` (inside the method) will be reflected in the array referred to by `TestArray` back in the calling code.

However, if we reassign `IntArray` within the method to refer to a brand new array, we break the link with the original `TestArray`, and anything further we do using `IntArray` has no effect on `TestArray`.

If we want to allow the method to assign a new array to `TestArray`, we need to pass `TestArray` by reference to the method:

```
void PassArrayRef(ref int[] IntArray)
{
    for(int i = 0; i < IntArray.Length; i++)
    {
        IntArray = new int[] { 11, 12, 13 };
    }
}
```

We can now call this with the test code:

```
int[] TestArray  = { 1, 2, 3, 4, 5 };
Console.Write("Before method call: ");
foreach (int element in TestArray)
{
   Console.Write(element + " ");
}
Console.WriteLine();
PassArrayRef(ref TestArray);
Console.Write("After method call: ");
foreach (int element in TestArray)
{
   Console.Write(element + " ");
}
```

Now that we are passing the array reference `TestArray` itself by reference, we can reassign it to a new array within the method. The output from the test code is now:

```
Before method call: 1 2 3 4 5
After method call: 11 12 13
```

4.7.6 ☐ The `params` keyword

C# provides one other way of passing an array to a method that has no counterpart in Java. Using the keyword `params` we may pass a variable number of individual (non-array) parameters to a method when calling that method. In the method definition, this list of individual parameters is grouped together into a single array. For example:

```
void PassParams(params int[] ParamsArray)
{
   Console.WriteLine("PassParams was passed " +
     ParamsArray.Length + " parameters.");
   foreach (int element in ParamsArray)
   {
     Console.Write(element + " ");
   }
}
```

We can call this method with the test code:

```
PassParams(1, 2, 3);
```

or with the code:

```
PassParams(2, 3, 4, 5, 6, 7, 8, 9);
```

or even with no parameters at all:

```
PassParams();
```

Using the first call, the output from `PassParams()` is:

```
PassParams was passed 3 parameters.
1 2 3
```

From the second, we get:

```
PassParams was passed 8 parameters.
2 3 4 5 6 7 8 9
```

and from the last:

```
PassParams was passed 0 parameters.
```

The `params` keyword allows a method to be called with any number of parameters which are merged into a single array within the method. There are a couple of restrictions on its use however.

The first condition is a purely practical one. Only one `params` array is permitted within any single method's parameter list, and that `params` array must be the last parameter in the list. That is, we can add extra parameters to the `PassParams()` method above provided they are inserted before the `params` array:

```
void PassParams(Employee e, int f,
  params int[] ParamsArray)
{
  // other code
}
```

Changing the placement of the `params` array will cause a compiler error:

```
// Won't compile: params not last parameter
void PassParams(Employee e, params int[] ParamsArray,
  int f)
{
  // other code
}
```

This restriction is because the compiler could not tell where the `ParamsArray` parameter list ended and the ordinary variables began. If the `params` list is at the end, then all other parameters can be matched first and everything that is left over must belong to the `params` array.

The restriction to a single `params` array is for a similar reason. If we had two or more `params` arrays we couldn't tell where one stopped and the next one started.

The final restriction is that any parameters passed as part of a `params` array must be passed by value: we cannot use the `ref` or `out` keywords with `params`. However, this means that any group of reference variables that are passed together as a `params` list can still have their internal data fields modified within the method. For example:

```
void PassArrayParams(params int[][] ParamsArray)
{
   Console.WriteLine("PassArrayParams was passed " +
      ParamsArray.Length + " parameters.");
   ParamsArray[0][0] = 5555;
}
```

Here we define a `params` list that contains `int[]` arrays as its elements. Although each individual array must be passed by value as it is part of a `params` list, the elements within each array may still be altered, which is what we do within the method. We can now call this method with the code:

```
int[] array1 = { 1, 2, 3 };
int[] array2 = { 4, 5, 6, 7 };
PassArrayParams(array1, array2);
foreach (int element in array1)
   Console.Write(element + " ");
```

We pass two arrays as parameters to `PassArrayParams()`, so that within the method, `array1` gets mapped to `ParamsArray[0]` and `array2` to `ParamsArray[1]`. When we set `ParamsArray[0][0]` to 5555 within the method, this should change the contents of `array1` to { 5555, 2, 3 }. This is verified by the output from the test code:

```
PassArrayParams was passed 2 parameters.
5555 2 3
```

The method says it has been passed two parameters rather than seven since it counts the arrays `array1` and `array2` as the individual parameters and doesn't look inside them.

4.8 ■ Enumerations

One principle of good programming is that programs should use meaningful names for all variables and constants. In particular, we should not use 'bare' numbers such as 12 or 127 in statements, since it is very difficult to figure out what these numbers represent when reading over a code listing.

C# provides the `const` for defining names for single constants, which is described in more detail in Chapter 5. However, frequently we have a number of related constants so it would be more convenient if we could group them together under a common heading.

The *enumeration* allows us to do just that. C and C++ programmers may be familiar with the `enum` in those languages, but Java has no equivalent. As in C, C# defines `enum` as a keyword that allows us to create a list of related constants. As an example, we can return to the `Employee` class that was introduced in Chapter 2. The code (minus the comments) is reproduced here for convenience, with a `Main()` method added at the end so the class can be run as a complete program for illustration.

```
1.  using System;
2.
3.  public class Employee
4.  {
5.      private string name;
6.      private decimal salary;
7.      private PositionTitle position;
8.
9.      public enum PositionTitle
10.     {
11.        ManagingDirector = 0,
12.        Director = 1,
13.        Accountant = 2,
14.        Programmer = 3
15.     }
16.
17.     public string Name
18.     {
19.        get
20.        {
21.           return name;
22.        }
23.        set
24.        {
25.           name = value;
26.        }
27.     }
28.
29.     public decimal Salary
30.     {
31.        get
32.        {
33.           return salary;
34.        }
35.        set
36.        {
37.           if (value <= 0.0M)
38.           {
39.              Console.WriteLine("Error: salary must be positive");
40.           }
41.           else
42.           {
```

```
43.              salary = value;
44.          }
45.       }
46.   }
47.
48.   public PositionTitle Position
49.   {
50.      get
51.      {
52.         return position;
53.      }
54.      set
55.      {
56.         position = value;
57.      }
58.   }
59.
60.
61.   public override string ToString()
62.   {
63.      return Name + " (" + Position + ")" + ": £" + Salary;
64.   }
65.
66.   public static void Main(string[] args)
67.   {
68.      Employee employee = new Employee();
69.      employee.Name = "Tess Trueheart";
70.      employee.Position = PositionTitle.Director;
71.      employee.Salary = 40000;
72.      Console.WriteLine(employee.ToString());
73.   }
74. }
```

An enum is defined on lines 9 to 15, where we have defined several job titles. The enum provides a way of associating meaningful names with integer values so that the names can be used within the program.

An enum effectively defines a new data type which can be used to declare variables and define method parameters. We've used the PositionTitle type to declare a data field on line 7 and a property referring to this data field on line 48.

The value of using an enum instead of a bare (and usually meaningless) number can be seen on line 70, where we assign a position to a new employee. The employee's Position property is assigned a value by using the Director field from PositionTitle. Note that we must always prefix a specific field from an enum with the name of the enum type (PositionTitle in this case). If we wished to refer to the PositionTitle enumeration from outside the `Employee` class (assuming the `enum` itself is declared as `public`), the class name would also need to form part of the prefix. For example, if `employee` had been declared in a different class, we would need to say:

```
employee.Position = Employee.PositionTitle.Director;
```

to assign a `Position`.

In the code above, we have assigned specific values to each field in `PositionTitle` (lines 11 to 14), but in fact this is not always required. If we had omitted the numerical assignments, as in:

```
public enum PositionTitle
{
   ManagingDirector,
   Director,
   Accountant,
   Programmer
}
```

then the compiler will provide numerical values for the fields, starting at zero by default. If we want the `enum`'s fields to have consecutive values that start at a different value, we need to give the value only for the first field. So if we wanted `PositionTitle`'s fields to begin at 10 instead of zero, we could say:

```
public enum PositionTitle
{
   ManagingDirector = 10,
   Director,
   Accountant,
   Programmer
}
```

The values assigned to individual fields in an `enum` need not be consecutive or even unique. For example, we could define an `enum` where the fields have the names of the months and the value attached to each field is the number of days in that month:

```
public enum MonthDays
{
   Jan = 31, Feb = 28, Mar = 31, Apr = 30,
   May = 31, Jun = 30, Jul = 31, Aug = 31,
   Sep = 30, Oct = 31, Nov = 30, Dec = 31
}
```

As can be seen in `Employee`'s `ToString()` method (line 61), an `enum` field can be included as part of a `string`. The value that is included in the `string` is the name of the field and *not* the numerical value. The output from the above program is thus:

```
Tess Trueheart (Director): £40000
```

If we do need the numerical value of an `enum` variable, we can put an `(int)` cast in front of it. Changing line 63 to:

```
return Name + " (" + (int)Position + ")" +
    ": £" + Salary;
```

results in the following output:

```
Tess Trueheart (1): £40000
```

Although an `enum` can provide names that are easier to read, we must remember to include this `(int)` cast whenever an `enum` field is used in a situation (such as an array index) where a numerical value is required.

An `enum` variable is a value type, so it behaves like a C# primitive type when passed to and from methods.

4.9 ■ Variable scope

Readers with some programming experience in Java should be familiar with the concept of the *scope* of a variable – the fact that a given variable only exists in certain sections of a program. Any attempt to use a variable outside its scope will be flagged as an error by the compiler.

In order to avoid these compiler errors and make proper use of variable declarations, it is important to understand the rules for scoping imposed by C#. First, we need to distinguish between two main types of variables: local variables and class data fields.

4.9.1 □ Local variables

Any variable in a C# program that is not a class data field must be some sort of *local variable*. Such variables include things like method parameters, variables declared within methods, and return values from methods. These variables all have a limited life-span. Some of them endure for the duration of a method call; others exist only within an internal statement or loop. We'll explore the rules for declaring and using these local variables here.

The simplest type of local variable is one that is declared on its own within a method, such as `locVar` in the method `LocalTest1()`:

```
void LocalTest1()
{
    // preceding code
    int locVar;
    locVar = 42;
    // following code
}
```

The scope of locVar begins at its point of declaration and extends to the end of the method. In this example, it would be an error to refer to locVar in any of the 'preceding code', but legal to refer to it in the 'following code'.

In fact, this sort of local variable is just a special case of a more general rule. Any *compound statement* in C# can contain its own set of local variables, where the scope of a variable within a compound statement extends from the point of declaration of the variable to the end of the compound statement.

A compound statement is any set of statements enclosed between braces. The body of a method is just one example of a compound statement. The bodies of loops and if statements are also compound statements, and can therefore contain their own local variables. For example:

```
1. void LocalTest2()
2. {
3.    int locVar = 42;
4.    if (locVar == 42)
5.    {
6.       int tempVar = 1;
7.       locVar += tempVar;
8.    }
9.    else
10.   {
11.      int elseVar = 3;
12.      locVar += elseVar;
13.   }
14. }
```

This time, LocalTest2() contains three separate scopes. The first scope covers the entire body of the method. The variable locVar is in this scope and since it is declared right at the start of the scope, it is in scope for the entire method.

The second scope consists of the body of the if statement and covers only lines 6 and 7. The variable tempVar exists only within this scope so that it is an error to attempt to use it in the else block or anywhere else within LocalTest2() that is outside the braces enclosing the body of the if statement. Similarly, the third scope covers lines 11 and 12 and is restricted to the body of the else clause.

The if and else scopes are *nested* inside the overall method scope, so that any variables declared in the method scope are also valid within the two inner scopes. Any variables declared inside a nested scope must have different names from all variables declared in the enclosing scope. For example, we might try this:

```
void LocalTest3()
{
   int locVar = 42;
   if (locVar == 42)
```

```
    {
        int tempVar = 1;
        int locVar = 12;       // Cannot duplicate variable name
        locVar += tempVar;
    }
}
```

This generates a compiler error because we have attempted to declare a variable `locVar` inside the `if` statement that has the same name as a variable in the enclosing scope. However, it *is* legal to have two variables with the same name provided that they exist in non-overlapping scopes. For example, we could rewrite `LocalTest2()` and use the same name for the two inner variables, one within the `if` statement and the other within the `else` clause:

```
void LocalTest4()
{
    int locVar = 42;
    if (locVar == 42)
    {
        int tempVar = 1;
        locVar += tempVar;
    }
    else
    {
        int tempVar = 3;
        locVar += tempVar;
    }
}
```

Here there is no confusion for the compiler since by the time we have reached the `else` clause, the `tempVar` declared in the `if` statement has fallen out of scope and no longer exists.

The `for` loop also allows a variable to be declared within its first line:

```
for (int i = 0; i < 10; i++)
{
    Console.WriteLine("Array element " + i +
        " has value " + array[i]);
}
```

The variable `i` is declared within the opening line of the `for` statement, and its scope extends through the rest of that line (so that we can refer to it in the termination condition `i < 10` and the update expression `i++`) and also throughout the body of the loop (so we can use `i` to refer to an array index within the loop). However, any attempt to use `i` outside the loop will cause a compiler error:

```
for (int i = 0; i < 10; i++)
{
  Console.WriteLine("Array element " + i +
    " has value " + array[i]);
}
Console.WriteLine("Final value of i = " + i);   //Error
```

The final `WriteLine()` statement attempts to access i after it has fallen out of scope.

4.9.2 ☐ Method parameters

Method parameters act in much the same way as other local variables. Their scope begins when the method is called and lasts until the method finishes. The only real difference between method parameters and other types of local variables is that parameters must be initialized by values passed into the method.

Reference parameters (those prefixed by either the `ref` or `out` keyword) work in a special way, however, and we will consider these in more detail below when we discuss the *stack* and *heap* in memory management.

4.9.3 ☐ Class data fields

A class data field is a variable that is declared as a member field of a class. In the `Employee` class, for example, we have declared data fields such as `name` (a `string`) and `salary` (a `decimal`). Whenever a new `Employee` object is created, it gets its own copies of all data fields declared within the `Employee` class. The scope of a class data field covers all methods within that class. We could add a method to the `Employee` class that prints out the employee's name:

```
public void PrintName()
{
  Console.WriteLine("Employee's name: " + name);
}
```

Since `PrintName()` is a member of the `Employee` class, we can access the `name` data field directly, without having to go through a property or other method, even if `name` itself is declared as `private`.

Class data fields do not follow the same scoping rules as local variables, primarily because it is legal to declare a local variable that has the same name as a class data field (although it is usually not good programming practice to do so, since although the compiler can figure out which variable we are referring to, humans often can't). Within the `Employee` class, for example, we could modify the `PrintName()` method to use a local `string` called name, which has the same name as the class data field:

```
public void PrintName()
{
   string name = "Employee's name: ";
   Console.WriteLine(name + this.name);
}
```

The local variable name is said to *override* the class data field name because it essentially eclipses it within the method. As this example shows, though, it is still possible to access the class data field by using the this keyword, which we will describe in more detail in Chapter 5. For now, all we need to know about it is that it refers to the Employee object that called the method. So we might call PrintName() in the following context:

```
Employee director = new Employee();
director.Name = "Otis P. Filigree";
director.PrintName();
```

Within PrintName(), this refers to the director object that called the method, so this.name would have the value "Otis P. Filigree", while the unadorned name variable would contain the string Employee's name:. The output from the PrintName() method would therefore be as expected:

```
Employee's name: Otis P. Filigree
```

The reason why this facility of C# can be so confusing to human readers of code is that if no local variable with the same name as a class data field exists within a method, then it is legal to refer to the class data field without putting a 'this.' in front of it. That is, in the original version of PrintName():

```
public void PrintName()
{
   Console.WriteLine("Employee's name: " + name);
}
```

the name variable is actually the same as this.name since no local variable called name has been declared.

If we know that a programmer is in the habit of overriding class data fields with local variables having the same name, then in a long method it can be difficult to tell whether a variable without a this in front of it refers to a local variable or class data field. To make things even more confusing, the local variable that overrides a class data field need not even be the same data type. We could, for example, have declared the local name variable in PrintName() to be an int, while the class data field name is a string. Hopefully it should be obvious from these examples that overriding a class data field with a local variable of the same name is not good programming practice and should be avoided if at all possible.

4.10 ■ Memory management in variable declarations

We have already seen that variables can be divided into two main types: *value* variables and *reference* variables. The memory space required for a value variable is allocated at the same time as the variable itself is declared, as in:

```
int x;
```

This declaration allocates the 4 bytes required for an int and sets up the variable x ready for use.

The declaration of a reference variable, on the other hand, only allocates memory for the *address* of the actual object to which the variable refers. A declaration such as:

```
Employee director;
```

allocates enough memory (typically 4 bytes since most memory addresses fit into an int) to store a memory address, but does not allocate any memory for the Employee object to which the director variable can ultimately refer. The creation of the object requires the new operator:

```
director = new Employee();
```

For a complete understanding of how these two types of variables work, we need to investigate how the CLR (Common Language Runtime, introduced in Chapter 1) manages the computer's memory as a program is run.

The lifetimes of both types of variables, value and reference, are governed by the scope rules we have just described. Since all variables must be declared either in the Main() method with which all C# programs must start, or in one of the methods called by Main(), all variables have a limited scope. Those variables whose scope lasts until the end of the Main() method will exist as long as the program is running, while others will have a more transient lifetime.

To try to uncover some pattern in the existence of variables, we need to make a crucial observation. Suppose we have a simple class called StackDemo (the significance of the name will become apparent shortly), defined as follows:

```
1.  class StackDemo
2.  {
3.    int x, y;
4.
5.    public void Init()
6.    {
7.      string input;
8.      Console.Write("Enter x: ");
9.      input = Console.ReadLine();
10.     char firstChar = input[0];
11.     if (Char.IsNumber(firstChar))
```

```
12.      {
13.          int tempX = int.Parse(input);
14.          x = tempX;
15.      }
16.      Console.Write("Enter y: ");
17.      input = Console.ReadLine();
18.      firstChar = input[0];
19.      if (Char.IsNumber(firstChar))
20.      {
21.          int tempY = int.Parse(input);
22.          y = tempY;
23.      }
24.   }
25.
26.   public void SwapXY()
27.   {
28.      int temp = x;
29.      x = y;
30.      y = temp;
31.   }
32.
33.   public override string ToString()
34.   {
35.      return "x = " + x + "; y = " + y;
36.   }
37.
38.   static void Main(string[] args)
39.   {
40.      StackDemo demo = new StackDemo();
41.      demo.Init();
42.      demo.SwapXY();
43.      Console.WriteLine(demo.ToString());
44.   }
45. }
```

Starting in `Main()`, let's follow through the program as it runs and see which variables are defined at each point. As `Main()` starts on line 40, the first variable to be declared is `demo`, which will remain in existence until the end of `Main()` and hence the end of the program. The variable list after line 40 is therefore:

demo

Leaving aside the call to `new StackDemo()` for now (this is an important step, but we'll get to it in a minute), the next thing that happens is a call to `Init()` on line 41. Looking at the code for `Init()` on lines 5 to 24, we see that a local variable `input` is declared on line 7, so we now have the variable list:

```
demo input
```

The job of `Init()` is to read in two values for the `int`s x and y. We have introduced a crude check that the user has actually typed in a number (this could be done better by handling exceptions – see Chapter 7). After we read in and store the value entered by the user on lines 8 and 9, we extract the first character in the string on line 10. For this, we introduce a new local variable, `firstChar`, so our variable list now looks like:

```
demo input firstChar
```

On line 11, the `if` statement uses the library method `IsNumber()` to test if `firstChar` is one of the digits from 0 to 9. If it is, `IsNumber()` returns `true`, and the statements inside the `if` will be executed.

The body of the `if` introduces a new scope, and within that scope, we declare the variable `tempX`. After line 13, the variable list is now:

```
demo input firstChar tempX
```

After the `if` finishes on line 15, its scope expires, and therefore `tempX` disappears as well, so the list contracts to:

```
demo input firstChar
```

When the value for y is read in, the process repeats itself, with the variable list first expanding to:

```
demo input firstChar tempY
```

and then contracting back after the second `if` statement's scope ends:

```
demo input firstChar
```

When the `Init()` method finishes on line 24, its scope ends as well, which means that all variables created within that scope disappear. This means that we lose `firstChar` and `input`, so the variable list is now back to:

```
demo
```

We are now back in `Main()` about to call the `SwapXY()` method which swaps the values of x and y. Going into this method (lines 26 to 31), we create a local variable `temp`, so the variable list is now:

```
demo temp
```

When the method finishes, its scope ends and `temp` disappears, so we are back to:

```
demo
```

The final call to `ToString()` on line 43 doesn't create any more variables, so the program itself gracefully ends and `demo` expires at the end.

4.10.1 ☐ **The program stack**

The key point to notice about all of this is that each time a variable is added to the list it always gets added at the right-hand end of the list, never in the middle. Similarly, whenever a variable goes out of scope and gets deleted from the list, it is always the rightmost variable that gets deleted first. Another way of saying this is that it is a *last in, first out* system. If you have learned some elementary data structures in your programming career, you will recognize this as the definition of a *stack*.

We don't need to go into any detail about the nature of a stack other than to note that it is a linear data structure (its elements can be stored in a one-dimensional array, for example). To add, or *push*, data onto a stack we always add it to one end, and to remove, or *pop*, data from the stack, we always remove the data from the same end to which it was added. Only that one end of the stack is ever accessible – other data buried in the middle cannot be reached until enough elements have been removed from the end for them to become exposed.

This is in fact just how local variables are stored in memory. A block of memory is reserved as a program stack when the program starts, and variables are added to or removed from the stack as the program runs, in exactly the way outlined in the example above. This makes memory management particularly easy and efficient for the CLR, since all it has to keep track of is the memory location where the last variable was added to the stack. Items are always added or removed at that point. The only thing that can ever go wrong with the stack (in principle) is that the amount of memory allocated to it can fill up, resulting in a stack overflow error. This sort of error is quite common in incorrectly written recursive programs, where an infinite chain of method calls results in an infinite number (or at least as many as can be created before the machine runs out of memory) of local variables being created.

4.10.2 ☐ **The program heap**

Memory management would be particularly simple if all variables were local, value variables, since the stack is all we would need to look after them. The picture is complicated by the arrival of reference variables, however. To see why this is the case, we need to examine exactly what happens when a reference variable is declared and used.

Let us consider a new class called `HeapDemo`, which we will build up gradually. We will include this class in the same project as the `Employee` class so that we can create `Employee` objects within it:

```
class HeapDemo
{
  static void Main(string[] args)
  {
    Employee director;
    director = new Employee();
  }
}
```

All that `Main()` does so far is to declare an `Employee` reference variable called `director` and then create an `Employee` object for it to refer to. The declaration of `director`, as we've seen above, will take place on the stack, but `director` is only a reference. The actual `Employee` object itself is created with the `new` operator on the next line. This requires that more memory is allocated somewhere, and that the address of this memory is loaded into `director`. Where is the object itself actually created? Can it be placed on the stack too?

To see why this might be a problem, let's change the `HeapDemo` class a bit:

```
class HeapDemo
{
   Employee director;

   public void Init()
   {
      director = new Employee();
      director.Name = "Neumann K. Glottis";
      director.Salary = 60000;
      director.Position = Employee.PositionTitle.Director;
   }

   static void Main(string[] args)
   {
      HeapDemo demo = new HeapDemo();
      demo.Init();
      Console.WriteLine(demo.director.ToString());
   }
}
```

We've now made `director` a class data field rather than a local variable within `Main()`. We create a new `HeapDemo` object in `Main()` and then call `Init()` to create `director`. Since `demo` is declared within `Main()` its scope runs for the duration of the program, and since `director` is now a class data field, it will exist as long as the object that contains it (`demo`) exists, which in this case is also the entire program.

But now look at what happens inside the `Init()` method. We create the `Employee` object inside the method and assign its data fields. If this new object were placed on the stack in the same way as a local variable, its scope would be limited to the scope of the `Init()` method, which means that the object would be deleted when the `Init()` method finished. If that happened, the attempt to call the `ToString()` method for `director` in the last line of `Main()` would fail, since the object to which `director` refers would no longer exist. However, if we run this program, it works perfectly and produces the output:

```
Neumann K. Glottis (Director): £60000
```

Obviously objects created with the new operator are not placed on the stack. In fact, there is a separate area of memory called the *heap* which is used for all objects created using new. Anything created on the heap is exempt from the scoping rules we saw earlier – once created, it will remain in existence until it is no longer needed. (In fact, in C++, objects created with new remained in existence even after they were needed, which is a serious problem in that language. Java and C# both have *automatic garbage collection* which cleans up unwanted objects, but more on that later in this chapter.)

The heap, as its name implies, is a rather less orderly arrangement of memory than the stack. The reason for this is that there is no way to predict the order in which objects are added to or deleted from the heap. Each time the new operator is used, a block of memory is allocated on the heap for the object that is being created. The object must be retained until all references to it from within the program are removed. As we have seen in examples earlier in this chapter, it is possible for a single object to have several references pointing at it, so the object itself cannot be deleted until all these references to it are removed. The order in which references to objects are broken is not an orderly process like it is for variables created on the stack, so the CLR has to do a lot more work to keep the heap in order.

To get a better feel for how the stack and heap work together, we'll return to a couple of examples we did earlier in this chapter when discussing passing by value and reference. Recall the sample method which takes an Employee as a parameter and increases the salary:

```
void EmployeeValue(Employee e)
{
   e.Salary += 1000;
}
```

We called this method with the code:

```
Employee employee;
employee = new Employee();
employee.Salary = 5000;
EmployeeValue(employee);
Console.WriteLine("Salary is " + employee.Salary);
```

Let us trace the stack and heap with the aid of some diagrams as this code runs. First, we declare a reference to an Employee object, which gets placed on the stack (Figure 4.1).

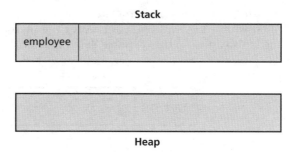

Figure 4.1 State of the stack and heap after the declaration of a reference to an Employee object. The reference at this point is still null

Next, we use new to allocate some memory on the heap for a new Employee object, and load the address of this object into the employee variable (Figure 4.2).

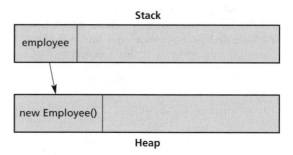

Figure 4.2 State of the stack and heap after the creation of the Employee object

After setting the salary to 5000, we call EmployeeValue() and pass the employee reference as a parameter to this method. Within EmployeeValue(), the employee reference gets copied into the local method parameter e, which is placed on the stack. Since the value of e is a copy of the value of employee, both e and employee refer to the same Employee object on the heap (Figure 4.3).

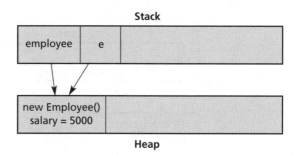

Figure 4.3 State of the stack and heap after copying the employee reference into the e reference

Using the e reference, the salary of the Employee object is increased by 1000 within EmployeeValue(). After the method ends, the scope containing e also ends, so this variable gets removed from the stack (Figure 4.4).

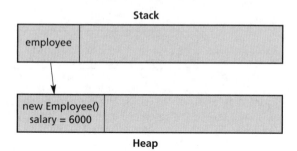

Figure 4.4 State of the stack and heap after the method EmployeeValue() has finished

We can see that the net result is that the object referred to by employee has had its salary changed to 6000, which is what is printed out in the last line.

Now let us see what happens when the employee reference variable is itself passed by reference to a method. The example we did earlier to illustrate this situation used the method EmployeeNewRef():

```
void EmployeeNewRef(ref Employee e)
{
    e = new Employee();
    e.Salary = 6000;
}
```

This method was called with the code:

```
Employee employee = new Employee();
employee.Salary = 5000;
EmployeeNewRef(ref employee);
Console.WriteLine("Salary is " + employee.Salary);
```

The situation after the employee reference has been declared and allocated to a new Employee object (and its salary set to 5000) is the same as in the previous example (Figure 4.5).

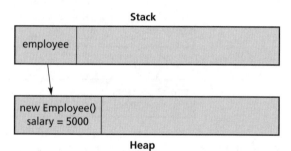

Figure 4.5 State of the stack and heap after the declaration of the reference and creation of the Employee object

This time, the `employee` reference is passed to `EmployeeNewRef()` *by reference* using the `ref` keyword. This means that the parameter `e` within the method refers to `employee` itself, and not to the actual `new Employee()` object on the heap. The situation after the method call starts to look as shown in Figure 4.6.

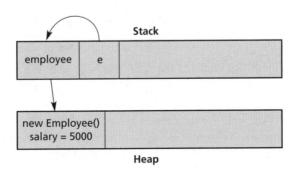

Figure 4.6 State of the stack and heap after `employee` is passed by reference to `EmployeeNewRef()`

When we run the code inside `EmployeeNewRef()`, the first line assigns a new `Employee` object to `e`, but since `e` is a reference to `employee`, this results in `employee` being assigned to the new object on the heap (Figure 4.7).

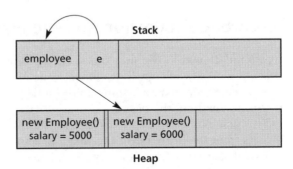

Figure 4.7 State of the stack and heap after `employee` is assigned to a new object inside `EmployeeNewRef()`

After the `EmployeeNewRef()` method ends, the `e` variable falls out of scope and is deleted from the stack, but the heap remains unaltered, so we end up with the situation shown in Figure 4.8.

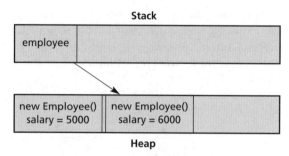

Figure 4.8 State of the stack and heap after the method `EmployeeNewRef()` has finished

The `employee` reference has been reassigned to a new area on the heap, and the original `Employee` object is still there, but has no references pointing to it. Memory on the heap that cannot be reached by any references currently active within the program are marked as 'garbage' by the CLR, and the next time the garbage collector runs, it will free up this memory by deleting the `Employee` object. (In C++, which has no garbage collector, this situation would be a *memory leak*, since in C++ it is the programmer's responsibility to delete any unused memory 'by hand'. Java and C# both have automatic garbage collection, however, so this problem should not occur in those languages.)

4.11 ■ Garbage collection and the managed heap

As we mentioned in the previous section, C# provides *automatic garbage collection*. We won't go into complete details of how garbage collection works here since there are some quite subtle points involved, but it's important to understand the basics.

The first point to keep clear is that the garbage collector only deletes objects from the heap, never the stack. Because of the way the stack works, any variable that is stored on it must still be in scope, so the only way a variable should ever be deleted from the stack is when the scope to which it belongs ends.

As we implied earlier, the garbage collector keeps track of which objects on the heap still have one or more active references pointing at them. The bottom line is that any object on the heap which cannot be reached by a reference variable that is currently in scope will be marked for deletion. In the last example above, the first `Employee` object is such an object.

You might be worried that such a mechanism would delete data that you will need later in the program, but if you think about it, that cannot happen. The only way we can access an object on the heap is if we know its memory address, and the only place we can store that address is in a reference variable. Once all the references to a given object have been deleted or reassigned, there is no record anywhere in the program to the memory address of that object, so there is no way we could ever retrieve it again even if we wanted to. There is therefore no risk in deleting it from the heap.

Besides deleting unreferenced objects, the C# garbage collector also *manages* the heap. As we noted earlier, there is no requirement that memory be allocated in an organized fashion on the heap – all that is needed is that a block of memory of the right size is found somewhere on the heap and allocated for a new object. Heaps that work by simply keeping a list of which blocks of memory are available and allocating the first block they find to new objects are called *unmanaged heaps*. After a program has been running for a while, such heaps usually become fragmented, with allocated and unallocated blocks of memory scattered all over the heap area. Searching such heaps in an attempt to find a suitable location to allocate a new object can be time-consuming, thus slowing down a program.

The *managed heap* used by the CLR not only contains a garbage collector but a 'trash compactor'. Each time the garbage collector runs, it also compresses the remaining objects to one end of the heap's memory area, so that there are no gaps between objects. Although this compacting procedure takes time, experiments with running programs show that there is a significant performance gain over an unmanaged heap, since the search time for allocating new memory is reduced by more than the extra time required to run the compactor.

Since the compactor actually moves objects in memory, it also has to update all the references that point at these objects. All of this happens invisibly from the programmer's point of view – a reference variable may actually change the physical memory location that it stores, but as far as we are concerned, we can still be confident that it will always refer to the same object in the heap, no matter where that object may be.

4.12 ■ Structs

We've seen that C# provides a selection of primitive data types such as int, float and so on, all of which are value variables, and the class data structure which allows the programmer to create reference data types. From the sections in this chapter, we've also seen that value and reference data types each have their own pros and cons when it comes to program efficiency.

A value variable is handled more efficiently in memory, since it is created on the stack when it is declared and simply popped off the stack when its scope expires. No complicated memory management or garbage collection is required. This very simplicity, however, restricts the areas in a program where value variables can be used.

A reference variable requires a separate object to be allocated on the heap, which is more costly in time since it takes processing power to manage the heap and perform garbage collection. Reference variables, however, can be created at any time and are not constrained by the scope in which they are allocated. They remain in existence as long as at least one reference points to them.

So far, all the value variables we've seen are primitive data types capable of representing a single numerical quantity or Boolean value. In Java, this is the end of the story – we can have either primitive value data types similar to those we have studied in C#, or we can have reference data types (objects) created from classes. C#, however, provides an extra data type: the `struct`.

A `struct` is a compound data type similar in many ways to a `class`, but it is intrinsically a *value* data type. The main reason `struct`s exist is to provide a simple alternative to the `class`, efficient in their use of memory, when we merely wish to group several primitive data types together. Since a `struct` is a value type, it behaves in the same way as the primitive value types we've studied before. In particular, a `struct` variable can be declared without the use of the `new` operator, is allocated on the stack, and exists only for the duration of the scope in which it is defined.

Key point

A `struct` is a value data type which is allocated on the stack, not the heap.

A `struct` is declared in much the same way as a `class`, simply by replacing the `class` keyword with `struct`. Although a `struct` is allowed to be as complex as we like, with many data fields and methods, building a `struct` with that level of complexity really defeats its purpose. If we want such a complex data type, we should be using a `class` instead.

As a simple example of a `struct`, suppose we want a relatively simple data type for storing the dimensions and location of a simple geometric figure, such as a rectangle. To specify the location and size of a rectangle (assuming it is oriented with its sides parallel to the horizontal and vertical axes), all we need are its length (vertical size), width (horizontal size), and coordinates of its upper left corner. If we are thinking of displaying the rectangle on a computer display, all these values will be non-negative integers, so we can use the `uint` data type to represent them. A suitable `struct` declaration for a rectangle would be:

```
struct Rectangle
{
    public uint Length;
    public uint Width;
    public uint CornerX, CornerY;
}
```

We have declared all the data fields as `public` since the purpose of a `struct` is just to group together a few related variables for convenience in handling, rather than to form a class as part of a grand object-oriented design.

We could, of course, equally well declare a class for rectangles by just replacing struct by class, so what is the point of introducing the struct just because it is a value variable? The main differences between a class and a struct come in how it is declared and passed as a parameter to a method.

First, let's consider a simple declaration:

```
Rectangle box;
box.Length = 20;
box.Width = 10;
box.CornerX = 100;
box.CornerY = 240;
```

Notice the absence of the new operation. The first line declares a Rectangle object *and* allocates the memory for all of its data fields. However, a simple declaration such as this does *not* initialize the data fields with the box object. This means that we cannot use any of the data fields in box until we assign values to them, as we have done here. For example, if we tried:

```
Rectangle box;
uint boxWidth = box.Width;
```

we would get a compilation error, since the declaration has not initialized the Width field in the box object.

Key point

An object can be created from a struct without using the new operator, but its data fields must be initialized before they can be used.

We can initialize all the data fields in a struct by using the new operator, just as with a class. The following will compile without errors:

```
Rectangle box = new Rectangle();
uint boxWidth = box.Width;
```

Despite the similarity in appearance to the allocation of a class object, the use of new for initializing a struct object does not use the heap at all. The sequence of events is as follows.

The declaration Rectangle box creates the box object *and* allocates memory for all its data fields, but does *not* initialize these fields. Calling new Rectangle() does *not* allocate any further memory since box has already been allocated on the stack. All it does is initialize all the data fields to their default values (zero for all numerical data types).

When we assign one struct to another, or pass a struct to a method, a full copy of the struct's data fields is made. This is in contrast to an object declared from a class, where an assignment only copies the reference from one variable to the other. For example, suppose we expand the code above by introducing a second Rectangle and do an assignment, as in:

```
Rectangle box;
box.Length = 20;
box.Width = 10;
box.CornerX = 100;
box.CornerY = 240;
Rectangle otherBox;
otherBox = box;
box.Length = 500;
Console.WriteLine(otherBox.Length);
```

As we've seen in our earlier examples using classes, if `Rectangle` had been defined as a class instead of a struct, the final line would write out the value 500, since the assignment of `box` to `otherBox` would make the two variables refer to the same object on the heap. Since `Rectangle` is a struct, however, the assignment statement *copies* all the data fields from `box` into the corresponding data fields in `otherBox`, making the two objects completely separate entities, independent of each other. When we change `box`'s `Length` to 500, this doesn't affect the `Length` of `otherBox`, so the final line prints out the value 20.

The same logic applies if we pass a struct to a method – the parameter within the method receives a complete copy of the struct that was passed in, and any changes made to this copy within the method are lost when the method ends.

The main advantage of structs is that they are faster to allocate and de-allocate, since they avoid the managed heap. However, the fact that structs are copied in full when passed to methods can cause quite a performance hit if a struct contains a lot of data fields, or if many method calls are made. If the struct is not changed within the method, we can avoid the copying by passing the struct as a `ref` parameter.

Before we leave structs, it is worth pointing out that all the 'primitive' data types in C# are actually structs themselves. The simple names such as `int`, `float` and so on for such primitive types are actually aliases for the full struct name. For example, an `int` is an alias for `System.Int32`, a `float` is an alias for `System.Single` and so on. In practice, you should never need to know the actual struct name for the primitive data types, but looking up the primitive name in the C# documentation will tell you its `System` struct equivalent.

■ Summary

In this chapter, we have taken a deeper look at how C# stores and handles variables and objects. We have also introduced a few more language features such as arrays, enumerations and structs.

It is important to understand the methods by which C# handles data in order to avoid obscure bugs and runtime errors. However, Java programmers should find that C#'s methods for many of these things are essentially the same as those of Java.

Exercises

4.1 Trace in detail what happens in memory when each of the following code fragments is run. You should consider each operation separately, and display the final values of all variables. You may find it helpful to draw a diagram to display each variable and its current value as a specific location in memory.

(a)
```
int a, b;
a = b = 55;
a += 33;
```

(b)
```
void AddNumber(int x)
{
    x += 33;
}

int a = 55;
AddNumber(a);
```

(c)
```
void AddRefNumber(ref int x)
{
    x += 33;
}

int a = 55;
AddNumber(ref a);
```

(d)
```
int ReturnNumber(int x)
{
    return x += 33;
}

int a = 55;
a = ReturnNumber(a);
```

(e)
```
void OutNumber(out int x)
{
    x = 55;
}

int a;
OutNumber(a);
```

4.2 Repeat the previous exercise for the following code fragments, involving reference variables. Use the same `Employee` class that was used in the chapter for examples. In this exercise, make sure you distinguish between memory allocated on the stack and on the heap.

(a)
```
Employee a, b;
a = new Employee();
b = a;
```

(b)
```
Employee a, b;
a = new Employee();
b = new Employee();
```

```
        b = a;
        a.Salary = 6000;
```

(c)
```
    Employee a, b;
        b = a = new Employee();
        a.Salary = 6000;
```

(d)
```
    void NewSalary(Employee x)
        {
            x.Salary = 6000;
        }

        Employee a = new Employee();
        NewSalary(a);
```

(e)
```
    void NewSalary(Employee x)
        {
            x = new Employee();
            x.Salary = 6000;
        }

        Employee a = new Employee();
        NewSalary(a);
```

(f)
```
    void NewRefSalary(ref Employee x)
        {
            x.Salary = 6000;
        }

        Employee a = new Employee();
        NewRefSalary(ref a);
```

(g)
```
    void NewRefSalary(ref Employee x)
        {
            x = new Employee();
            x.Salary = 6000;
        }

        Employee a = new Employee();
        NewSalary(ref a);
```

4.3 Why does the following method produce a compilation error?

```
    void OutNumber(out int x)
    {
        x += 55;
    }
```

4.4 Write a C# program that calculates the squares of the integers from 1 to 20 and stores the results in an array. Use a `foreach` loop to print out the results to the console.

4.5 Extend the previous exercise to use a multidimensional rectangular array to store the squares and cubes of the numbers from 1 to 20. Use both a nested `for` loop and a `foreach` loop to print out the results.

4.6 Read the documentation on the `Split()` method in the `String` class and write a program which reads a `string` typed in by the user at a console prompt, then splits up the string into separate words (adjacent words are assumed to be separated by a blank) to create an array of `strings`, each element of which is one word from the original string. Use a `foreach` loop to print out these words, one per line.

4.7 Extend the previous exercise so that the program reads in any number of lines from the console, splits up each line into separate words, and then stores the resulting array as a distinct row in a single jagged array of `strings`. The program should stop reading text when the user types in the word 'quit' on a line by itself. Have a look at the documentation for the methods available in the `String` class to see how to detect when 'quit' is entered.

Print out all the text entered as a single paragraph. At the end of the printout, display the total number of words that have been entered.

4.8 Write a class called `Planet` which is to represent a planet in the solar system. The class should contain a few properties that store some data on the planet, such as its mass, distance from the Sun and so on.

Write another class called `SolarSystem` which contains an array of nine `Planets`. Define an `enum` within this class to list the names of the planets in our solar system, and use this `enum` to define the array elements of the planet array, and thus store some data on the planets. Print out the data in a neat format to the console.

(If you're not into astronomy, just invent some numbers to store. If you want some real data, try http://www.jpl.nasa.gov/solar_system/planets/planets_index.html.)

4.9 For this exercise, assume that we have a class called `ScopeTest` with data fields defined as follows.

```csharp
public class ScopeTest
{
    private int a, b, c;

    void Init()
    {
        a = 1;
        b = 2;
        c = 3;
    }

    // Scopes() method inserted here

    public static void Main(string[] args)
    {
        ScopeTest test = new ScopeTest();
        test.Init();
        int x = 12;
        test.Scopes(x);
    }
}
```

For each question, determine if the `Scopes()` method will compile. If so, state what is printed by the output statement. If not, state what the problem is. You should try each of these methods in a real program to verify your answers.

(a)
```
void Scopes(int x)
{
    a = x;
    Console.WriteLine(a);
}
```

(b)
```
void Scopes(int a)
{
    this.a = a;
    Console.WriteLine(a + ", " + this.a);
}
```

(c)
```
void Scopes(int b)
{
    a = b;
    Console.WriteLine(a + ", " + b);
}
```

(d)
```
void Scopes(int x)
{
    int x;
    a = x;
    Console.WriteLine(a + ", " + x);
}
```

(e)
```
void Scopes(int x)
{
    if (x < b)
    {
        int a = 2 * b;
    }
    else
    {
        a = 3 * b;
    }
    Console.WriteLine(a);
}
```

(f)
```
void Scopes(int x)
{
    if (x < b)
    {
        int a = 2 * b;
    }
    else
```

```
        {
           int a = 3 * b;
        }
        Console.WriteLine(a);
    }
(g) void Scopes(int x)
    {
        if (x < b)
        {
           int a = 2 * b;
        }
        else
        {
           int a = 3 * b;
        }
        Console.WriteLine(this.a);
    }
```

C# classes – advanced features

5

So far, we have seen how to create classes and objects in C# and how to populate these classes with data fields and methods. In principle, we now know enough to be able to write pretty well any console (text-only) application in C#. However, the language contains many more specialized features which allow the programmer to write more sophisticated and usable code. We'll examine these features in this chapter.

5.1 ■ Constructors

Constructors will no doubt be familiar to Java programmers as specialized methods which allow the initialization of data fields when an object is created using the `new` operator. Although C#, like Java, provides default initializations for all class data fields even if we don't write any constructors ourselves, these default values are not usually the ones we want.

To illustrate the use of a constructor, let's return to the `Employee` class that we first introduced in Chapter 2. We reproduce that portion of the class that defined the data fields here:

```
public class Employee
{
   private string name;
   private decimal salary;
   private PositionTitle position;

   public enum PositionTitle
   {
      ManagingDirector = 0,
      Director = 1,
      Accountant = 2,
      Programmer = 3
   }

   // Properties and methods defined here
}
```

When we used this class to declare an `Employee` object in the `HeapDemo` example in the last chapter, we had to write a method called `Init()` to initialize the data fields of an `Employee` after we created it. As a reminder, here is the `HeapDemo` class in full again:

```
1.    class HeapDemo
2.    {
3.       Employee director;
4.
5.       public void Init()
6.       {
7.          director = new Employee();
8.          director.Name = "Neumann K. Glottis";
9.          director.Salary = 60000;
10.         director.Position = Employee.PositionTitle.Director;
11.      }
12.
13.      static void Main(string[] args)
14.      {
15.      HeapDemo demo = new HeapDemo();
16.      demo.Init();
17.      Console.WriteLine(demo.director.ToString());
18.      }
19.   }
```

The `Employee` is created and initialized in the `Init()` method. In fact, if we don't write a constructor explicitly, the compiler will create one for us, and it is this constructor which is actually being called in the `new Employee()` statement in the `Init()` function. This constructor simply initializes all data fields to be either `null` (if they are reference data fields) or zero (if they are numeric data fields). Thus if we delete lines 8 through 10 in the `HeapDemo` class so that we rely on the initializations of the default constructor, we find that the `name` is set to the empty string, `salary` is set to zero and `position` is set to zero, which from the `enum` listing the various possible values of position, means `ManagingDirector`.

To add a constructor to `Employee`, we need to know the syntax rules. First, a constructor *always* has the same name as the class in which it is found. Second, a constructor *never* has a return type (not even `void`). Apart from these two rules, a constructor is built in just the same way as an ordinary method.

Key point

A constructor's name is always the same as the class in which it is found, and it never has a return type.

Now let us add a constructor to `Employee` that initializes all three data fields to constant values. The code may be inserted anywhere within the `Employee` class, but it is conventional to keep the constructor near the beginning of the class so it is easy to find. The code looks like this:

```
public Employee()
{
  Name = "A. N. Employee";
  Salary = 10000;
  Position = PositionTitle.Programmer;
}
```

We provide default values for the three data fields (using the properties that we defined back in Chapter 2). If we now modify the `HeapDemo` class by omitting the assignment statements from the `Init()` method, we get:

```
class HeapDemo
{
  Employee director;

  public void Init()
  {
  director = new Employee();
  }

  static void Main(string[] args)
  {
    HeapDemo demo = new HeapDemo();
    demo.Init();
    Console.WriteLine(demo.director.ToString());
  }
}
```

The call to `new Employee()` in `Init()` calls the constructor automatically, and results in the newly created `Employee` object having its data fields initialized according to the code within the constructor. The output from the `WriteLine` at the end is:

```
A. N. Employee (Programmer): £10000
```

demonstrating that the constructor is doing its job by initializing the data fields of `director`.

Although the ability to specify the default values for an object's data fields is handy, it's not as flexible as it could be. Ideally, we would like to be able to specify the initial values separately for each object we create. This is easily done if we add some parameters to the constructor. For example, we can change the constructor above so that it has three parameters, as follows:

```
public Employee(string e, decimal s, PositionTitle p)
{
  Name = e;
  Salary = s;
  Position = p;
}
```

We can now change the `Init()` method in `HeapDemo` above to use this new constructor:

```
public void Init()
{
    director = new Employee("William Wibble", 40000,
        Employee.PositionTitle.Accountant);
}
```

We call the three-parameter constructor by adding the parameters as part of the `new` operation. We need to specify the `PositionTitle` parameter by prefixing it with `Employee`, since `PositionTitle` is an `enum` contained within the `Employee` class and is not known to the `HeapDemo` class.

Although we introduced the three-parameter constructor by replacing the zero-parameter constructor we defined originally, we did not need to do this. C#, like Java, allows more than one constructor to be present within a single class, provided that the parameter lists are different in each constructor. We could therefore write the `Employee` class with both constructors present:

```
public class Employee
{
    private string name;
    private decimal salary;
    private PositionTitle position;

    public enum PositionTitle
    {
        ManagingDirector = 0,
        Director = 1,
        Accountant = 2,
        Programmer = 3
    }

    // Zero-parameter constructor
    public Employee()
    {
        Name = "A. N. Employee";
        Salary = 10000;
        Position = PositionTitle.Programmer;
    }

    // Three-parameter constructor
    public Employee(string e, decimal s, PositionTitle p)
    {
        Name = e;
        Salary = s;
```

```
        Position = p;
    }


    // Other properties and methods
}
```

The compiler can always tell which constructor should be called by matching up the parameters in a new expression with the list of constructors available in the class. This is a special case of *method overloading* which we will consider later in this chapter.

Key point

A class may have any number of constructors provided that they all have different parameter lists.

One final point should be made. If we don't write *any* explicit constructors for a class, the compiler will provide a single, default constructor which takes no parameters and initializes all data fields to null or zero, as we mentioned above. However, if we provide *any* constructors ourselves, this default constructor is no longer provided by the compiler. This means that if we deleted the zero-parameter constructor in Employee but retained the three-parameter constructor, then an object declaration of the form

```
Employee drone = new Employee();
```

would no longer compile, since the only constructor available is one requiring three parameters. However, if we deleted *both* constructors from Employee then the declaration *would* compile, since the compiler would supply a default constructor with no parameters. This is a common error, since it is easy to write a class without any explicit constructors and test it with declarations such as this, and then add an explicit constructor later, which causes the earlier object declarations to break. This behaviour is the same as in Java.

Key point

Adding any explicit constructors to a class removes the default constructor provided by the compiler.

We will return to constructors after we have studied inheritance.

5.2 ■ Method overloading

We pointed out in the section on constructors that it is legal in C# to have more than one constructor provided that the parameter lists are different in all constructors. This is a special case of *method overloading*.

Java programmers will be familiar with the idea that it is possible to define several methods with the same name, all within the same class. The only condition that is imposed is that the *signatures* of all versions of an overloaded method must be different.

The signature of a method is defined as the method's name combined with its parameter list. The return type of a method is specifically excluded from the signature, since values returned from methods are not always used in code.

> **Key point**
>
> A method's *signature* is its name plus its parameter list.

Since by definition, an overloaded version of a method has the same name as the original version of that method, this condition amounts to the requirement that the parameter lists in all overloaded versions of a method must be different. This provides the clue that allows the compiler to tell which version of an overloaded method is to be called.

> **Key point**
>
> Two overloaded methods must have different parameter lists. Two methods that differ only in their return types are *not* allowed.

Although it is possible to create overloaded methods that do completely different things, this isn't good programming practice. Typically, we would define overloaded versions of a method if there were a single action that could be done in different ways depending on the types of parameters being used.

As an example, suppose we were writing a class to represent a bank account. Such a class would have a data field for the account's balance, and methods for depositing and withdrawing money. Some banks provide accounts where withdrawal is free if done in one way (such as visiting the bank in person) but incurs a charge if done another way (such as using a teller machine from a rival bank). In this case, the action in both cases is the same (withdrawing cash), but the parameters required differ in the two cases. In the first case (no fee), only the withdrawal amount is needed, while in the second case, we must provide both the withdrawal amount and the fee to be charged.

We might design the class as follows:

```
1. public class Account
2. {
3.    public decimal balance;
4.
5.    // Constructors and properties omitted...
6.
7.    public bool Withdraw(decimal amount)
8.    {
9.       if(Balance >= amount)
10.       {
11.          Balance -= amount;
12.       }
13.       else
14.       {
15.          Console.WriteLine("Not enough funds.");
16.          return false;
17.       }
18.       return true;
19.    }
20.
21.    public bool Withdraw(decimal amount, decimal fee)
22.    {
23.       if(Balance >= amount + fee)
24.       {
25.          Balance -= amount + fee;
26.       }
27.       else
28.       {
29.          Console.WriteLine("Not enough funds.");
30.          return false;
31.       }
32.       return true;
33.    }
34. }
```

Only those parts of the Account class involving the overloaded methods are shown. There would also be a property called Balance allowing access to the balance data field.

The first version of Withdraw() (line 7) contains a single parameter and would be called to withdraw funds when no fee is involved. The overloaded version (line 21) would be called when a fee is to be charged.

These two methods could be called using code such as this:

```
Account myAccount = new Account(1000);
myAccount.Withdraw(50);
myAccount.Withdraw(50, 1.50);
```

The first line assumes that there is a constructor that takes a single parameter and initializes the `balance` to that value. The second line calls the single-parameter version of `Withdraw()` and the last line calls the two-parameter version. The compiler sorts out which method to call by examining the number and types of the parameters being passed to the method.

Because C# implicitly converts some numeric data types into other types if required, we need to be careful in using overloaded methods if the only difference between two methods is in the type of numeric data being passed as parameters. For example, suppose we added another overloaded method to the `Account` class above which took a single `int` as a parameter:

```
public bool Withdraw(int amount)
{
  // code goes here
}
```

If we now make the method call:

```
myAccount.Withdraw(50);
```

which `Withdraw()` method will be called – the one with a `decimal` parameter or the one with an `int` parameter?

It turns out that the `int` version will be used, since the value 50 is actually an `int` constant, so it most closely matches the overloaded method with an `int` parameter.

In the original example, where we had only the two overloaded versions of `Withdraw()`, the call to `myAccount.Withdraw(50)` called the version with a `decimal` parameter because C#'s implicit conversion rules (see Chapter 3) will convert an `int` to a `decimal` if required.

However, if we tried things the other way round, that is, we deleted the version of `Withdraw()` that takes a `decimal` parameter and kept the version that takes an `int`, and then tried the method call:

```
myAccount.Withdraw(50M);
```

we get the compiler error 'The best overloaded method match for Withdraw(int) has some invalid arguments'. The compiler is trying to tell us there is a version of `Withdraw()` that takes an `int` parameter, but the method call we are trying to make doesn't match this version, and all the other versions of `Withdraw()` produce a worse match. This is because C# will not implicitly convert a `decimal` to an `int` because of possible loss of precision.

5.3 ■ The static keyword

5.3.1 □ Static data fields

Like Java, C# supports static data fields and methods within classes. To understand the difference between static and ordinary (non-static) class members (sometimes called *instance* members, for a reason we shall spell out below), we need to consider again what happens when a new object is created.

As we've seen, the creation of an object in C# requires two steps. First, we declare the reference variable and then we use the `new` operator to allocate memory for this reference to refer to. The memory allocation step reserves space for a copy of all *ordinary* (non-static) data fields which can then be used by the new object.

Ordinary data fields are thus associated with specific instances of a class – each object gets its own copy of each data field, and the values assigned to one object's data fields are independent of those assigned to any other object's data fields. This is the reason these data fields are called *instance* fields – they are associated with particular instances of the class.

A *static* data field, however, does *not* get copied to each object – there is only a single copy that is associated with the *class* itself and not with any one object created from that class. A static field may be declared by inserting the keyword `static` immediately after the accessibility keyword (`public`, `private`, etc) in the data field declaration. For example, if we wished to define an interest rate for all accounts that were created using the `Account` class above, we could add a static decimal field to the class:

```
public static decimal interestRate = 4.2M;
```

The most common use of static fields is in the definition of constant parameters such as the interest rate which are the same for all objects created from a given class. For example, the `Math` class (available in the default `System` namespace, which also contains the `Console` class we have been using for output to the screen) contains two static fields: a `double` called `PI` which contains the ratio of a circle's circumference to its diameter (3.14159...) and another `double` called `E` which contains the base of natural logarithms (2.718...). Many other classes in the various .NET libraries make use of static fields to store parameters and constants.

Since a `static` field is not associated with any specific object, how do we refer to it from outside the class (assuming that it is a `public` variable)? We simply prefix the name of the static variable with the name of the *class* (rather than a specific object) that contains it. For example, if we wished to calculate the area of a circle with a radius given by the `double` quantity `radius`, we could write:

```
double area = Math.PI * radius * radius;
```

Similarly, if we wanted to calculate how much interest would be paid on a certain amount of money using the interest rate defined in the `Account` class above, we could write:

```
double interest = money * Account.interestRate / 100M;
```

Key point

Static fields require the *class* name in front of the variable name, while instance fields require the *object* (instance) name in front of the variable.

We could write this statement inside any method within any class, since `interestRate` was declared as a `public` data field. Of course, if we had declared `interestRate` as `private` and `static`, we could only use it within the `Account` class, just like any other `private` data field. If we use a static field within the same class, we do not need to add the class name before the variable name. For example, if we added a method to the `Account` class to calculate the interest payable on the `balance` of an account, we could write (within the `Account` class):

```
public decimal Interest()
{
    return balance * interestRate / 100M;
}
```

5.3.2 ☐ Static methods

It is also possible to define methods which are static. Like static data fields, a static method is called without any reference to a specific instance of the class. As such, a static method can only refer to static data fields, since any other data field in a class must be associated with a particular instance of that class.

For example, we could add a method which calculates the simple interest on a given amount of money (the *principal*) over a given period of time. Assuming simple interest (that is, the interest is paid only on the original amount of money, so that there is no 'interest on the interest'), the formula for calculating the interest is:

interest = (principal) * (number of years) * (interest rate / 100)

The method for calculating this is then:

```
public static decimal TotalInterest(decimal years,
  decimal principal)
{
    return years * principal * (interestRate / 100M);
}
```

In this method, `interestRate` is the static data field we introduced above. There is no reference to any of the instance data fields in this method, since a static method has no connection to any particular instance of the class.

Since this static method is public, we can call it from any other class in our program. The syntax for calling a public static method is to prefix the method call with the class name:

```
Console.WriteLine("Interest over 5 years on £50 is: £" +
    Account.TotalInterest(5, 50));
```

Now suppose we tried to write a version of `TotalInterest()` that calculated the interest on the present balance within a particular account:

```
public static decimal BalanceInterest(decimal years)
{
   return years * balance * (interestRate / 100M);
}
```

We get the compiler error: 'An object reference is required for the non-static field, method, or property Account.balance'. The compiler is saying that we cannot refer directly to an instance variable (`balance`) within a static method. Since this calculation refers to an instance variable, it would make more sense just to remove the `static` keyword from its definition, and make it an ordinary instance method instead.

A C# property can also be declared as `static`. In this case, the property is used as an accessor for a `static` data field. Other than that, it is identical to the properties we met in Chapter 2. A property for `interestRate` could be defined as follows:

```
public static decimal InterestRate
{
   get
   {
      return interestRate;
   }
   set
   {
      interestRate = value;
   }
}
```

5.3.3 ☐ Static constructors

We have seen that `static` variables can be initialized when they are declared within the class, but there are situations in which the initial value of a `static` variable cannot be hard-coded with a constant value. In the `Account` class, for example, the interest rate on a bank account changes periodically so rather than having to edit the code and recompile the program each time the rate changes, it would make more sense to allow the user to enter the rate (or to read the current value from some external source such as the Internet or a database) each time the program runs. Since we have not yet covered methods whereby data can be obtained from external sources other than the keyboard, we will add a facility that requests the interest rate from the user each time the program starts.

Key point

A static constructor may initialize static variables only.

We could, of course, simply add another method to the `Account` class which does this, and then call the method from `Main()`. However a neater way of doing it is to use a *static constructor* for the `Account` class. A static constructor is just like an ordinary constructor except that it is declared as `static` and must obey the main rule of static methods, namely that it can only refer to static variables.

A static constructor, however, is *always* called each time a program containing the class in which the constructor is written starts, whether or not the program declares any instances of that class. Since no object declarations are required to call a static constructor, it cannot accept any parameters, since there is no way they could be passed to the constructor. Consequently, only one static constructor can be defined for each class.

We can declare a static constructor for the `Account` class which requests the current interest rate from the user:

```
static Account()
{
   Console.Write("Enter interest rate: ");
   interestRate = Decimal.Parse(Console.ReadLine());
   Console.WriteLine("Interest rate set to " + interestRate);
}
```

This constructor will always be run whenever any program containing the `Account` class is run, even if there is no code in the `Main()` method at all.

What happens if several classes in the same program have static constructors? In which order are they called? In fact, we can't rely on any particular ordering for static constructor calls, and we can't specify this in the code. All we can be sure of is that static constructors are called *after* any default values have been allocated to static variables, but *before* any instances of the class have been created and *before* any other static methods are accessed. This means that all static constructors should be independent of each other, in that no static constructor should rely on a variable initialization that is done in a different static constructor in another class.

In the `Account` class example, this means that the value read into `interestRate` within the static constructor will override the default value of 4.2% that was assigned when `interestRate` was declared. It also means that we can rely on the user being asked for the current interest rate before any `Account` objects have been created.

C# vs Java

The static constructor in C# performs much the same role as the stand-alone `static` block in Java.

5.4 ■ The const **keyword**

C# provides two keywords that allow us to create objects that cannot be changed after initialization: const and readonly.

The const keyword is the most restrictive. An object declared as const must be initialized at the same time that it is declared. It is not even permitted to defer the initialization to a constructor. Thus, we can create a const integer as in the following class:

```
class Test
{
   public const int number = 345;

   static void Main(string[] args)
   {
      Console.WriteLine("const number = " + number);
   }
}
```

Leaving a const declaration uninitialized is a compiler error. We cannot say, for example:

```
const int number;
```

All const data fields are also implicitly static, so that there is only a single instance of them in any given class. This is sensible, since if a value is really constant, there is no point in creating a separate copy for each object. Bizarrely, however, it is illegal to explicity state that a const parameter is static. The following declaration produces the compiler error 'The constant "Test.number " cannot be marked static'.

```
static const int number = 345;
```

Since a const object is also static, if we wish to refer to it outside the class, we need to prefix the const parameter's name with the name of its enclosing *class*, not the name of an instance of that class. For example, since number in the class Test above is declared as public, we can refer to it from any other class using the notation Test.number.

Key point

A const value may be initialized only when it is declared, and is implicitly static.

C# vs Java

The const keyword is roughly equivalent to Java's final keyword, although in Java it is permissible to declare a final parameter as static as well.

5.5 ■ The `readonly` keyword

C# allows a less restrictive type of constant data field using the `readonly` keyword, which has no equivalent in Java. A `readonly` data field can be either a static field or an instance field, but it may be initialized either where it is declared or in one or more of the class constructors. Once it is assigned a value in one of these locations, the 'read-only' nature of the parameter comes into effect, since it cannot be changed in any other class method.

Key point

A `readonly` parameter may be initialized at its declaration or in a constructor, and cannot be changed thereafter.

A static `readonly` field is useful if we wish to do some calculations to determine its value, which is not possible with a `const` field, since it must be initialized where it is declared. For example, we could have declared the `interestRate` in the `Account` class above as `static` and `readonly`:

```
public static readonly int interestRate;
```

The static constructor given above could then be used to read in an initial value for `interestRate`, and this value then becomes constant throughout the rest of the program.

Apart from the ability to assign an initial value to a `static readonly` quantity within a constructor, such a quantity is the same as a `const` parameter.

Since the account number of a bank account should remain constant once it is assigned, but is different for each account, an `accountNumber` field is a good candidate for an instance field that is `readonly`. We could declare it thus:

```
public readonly int accountNumber;
```

Notice that making an instance `readonly` parameter public does not really violate the principle of encapsulation, since it is impossible to change the value of `accountNumber` after it has been initialized, so there is no possibility of an external class modifying `accountNumber` in any way.

We could then initialize `accountNumber` in the usual way within a constructor:

```
public Account(int number, int bal)
{
   accountNumber = number;
   Balance = bal;
}
```

After this constructor is run, no further changes to `accountNumber` are allowed.

5.6 ■ Method implementation

It is worth taking a closer look at how instance and static methods are implemented in running code. A static method is the easier of the two to understand, since it has no dependence on any instance of a class. When a static method is called, its parameters are passed to it (either by value or reference, depending on how the parameters are declared) and the method just carries on and does its job.

An instance method is a bit more devious, however, so let's consider a specific example. Suppose we declare an `Account` object and then call its `Withdraw()` method:

```
Account myMoney = new Account(1000);
myMoney.Withdraw(50);
```

We create an `Account` called `myMoney` and initialize it by depositing £1000 in it. Next, we wish to withdraw £50, so we call the `Withdraw()` method. But the only parameter passed to `Withdraw()` is the amount we wish to withdraw, so how does the `Withdraw()` method know which `Account` object to withdraw the money from? If you glance back at the code for the `Withdraw()` method given earlier, you will see that it makes use of the `Balance` property defined in the `Account` class, but how does it know which `Account` object this `Balance` property is associated with?

The answer is that the object that calls an instance method *also* gets passed to that method as an extra, hidden parameter. It is almost as if we were making a method call of the form:

```
Withdraw(myMoney, 50);
```

where the `Withdraw()` method accepts an `Account` as its first parameter and a `decimal` as its second parameter. Within the `Withdraw()` method, any reference to a property or data field of the `Account` class is implicitly prefixed with this hidden object. Thus the reference to `Balance` is effectively rewritten to `myMoney.Balance` within the method.

5.7 ■ The `this` keyword

Although we know we can access the instance data fields of this hidden parameter directly, since these data fields are part of the same class that contains the method, we might wonder if there is any way of referring directly to this hidden object itself. In other words, if we call `Withdraw()` in a statement such as

```
myMoney.Withdraw(50);
```

is there any way of obtaining a reference to `myMoney` within the code of the `Withdraw()` method?

In fact, there is, and it makes use of a new keyword in C#: the `this` keyword. The meaning of `this` in C# is the same as in Java: it is a reference to the object which called the instance method.

Recall the original code we wrote for `Withdraw()`:

```
public bool Withdraw(decimal amount)
{
   if(Balance >= amount)
   {
      Balance -= amount;
   }
   else
   {
      Console.WriteLine("Not enough funds.");
      return false;
   }
   return true;
}
```

We have used the property `Balance` to access the private instance data field `balance`. We could also have bypassed the property by just writing `balance` instead of `Balance` in both places where it occurs, since by default, a class method has direct access to all class data fields. We can make this fact absolutely explicit in the code by prefixing each occurrence of `balance` with `this`, as in:

```
public bool Withdraw(decimal amount)
{
   if(this.balance >= amount)
   {
      this.balance -= amount;
   }
   else
   {
      Console.WriteLine("Not enough funds.");
      return false;
   }
   return true;
}
```

This particular use of `this` is not that common since it is redundant, although at times it can help to make code more readable since it labels a variable as an instance data field, as opposed to just a local variable within the method. The `this` keyword is more often used as a parameter in a method call where we need to pass a reference to the current object to a method in another class. We will see some examples of this usage later in the book.

5.8 ◼ Operator overloading

We've seen earlier in this chapter that we may overload a method by defining several methods with the same name, provided that each method with that name has a different parameter list. It is also possible to overload many of C#'s operators in a similar way.

We saw in Chapter 3 that operators in C# are defined so that they take a specific number of operands (1, 2 or 3) and that in most cases, there are restrictions on the data types that these operands can have. For example, the * operator is always a binary operator that requires two numeric data types as its operands, and always produces the product of these two numbers as its result. Similarly, the && operator requires two `bool` operands and returns a `bool` result.

None of these operators has any built-in definition when used with a class, so that if we tried, for example, to add together two instances of a user-defined class, we would get a compiler error:

```
Test obj1, obj2;
obj1 = new Test();
obj2 = new Test();
Test obj3 = obj1 + obj2;    // Error: + not defined for Test
```

Here, `Test` can be any user-defined class, such as the one used when discussing the `const` keyword earlier in this chapter.

Before we dive into the rules for operator overloading in C#, it is worth considering where such a feature would be used. Although C# allows you to overload operators so that the last line in the example above would work in some user-defined way, it should be obvious that we could achieve the same goal by simply defining a method called `add()` that takes two `Test` parameters and returns a `Test` result:

```
public static Test add(Test obj1, Test obj2)
{ ... }
```

We could then replace the last line above with:

```
Test obj3 = add(obj1, obj2);
```

Apart from the definition of the `add()` method (which as we will see, we need to write anyway if we want to overload the + operator), there is scarcely more typing using the second method.

In fact, all operator overloads *could* be implemented equally well by using ordinary methods. It is for this reason, in fact, that operator overloading is not allowed in Java – the designers of the language saw it as an unnecessary extra, so in line with Java's philosophy of keeping things simple, they left it out. Except in a few cases, it is probably better to use an ordinary method instead of an overloaded operator in C# as well, because it usually makes the code clearer for human readers. It is possible, for example, to choose a method name that tells the reader more about what the method does than can be implied through the use of an operator. You may well find that after the novelty of being able to overload operators wears off, you hardly ever use the feature.

Having said that, there are some cases where operator overloading is quite convenient. Many mathematical quantities such as vectors and matrices have definitions of things such as addition and multiplication, and it is handy to be able to use simple operators for these actions in computer code as well as on paper.

Let us now have a look at the rules for operator overloading in C#. If your only prior programming experience is with Java, these techniques will be new to you, but if you have studied C++, you should be aware that C# places many more restrictions on operator overloading than does C++, so you should take note of the rules below with particular care. For the benefit of C++ users, we will point out the differences as they arise.

To avoid requiring the reader to learn about mathematical quantities such as vectors, we will use an artificially simple class for demonstrating operator overloading, but once the fundamentals are understood, applying them to 'real' mathematical objects should be straightforward. We will use a class called `OverloadTest`, defined as follows:

```
class OverloadTest
{
   private int x, y;

   public OverloadTest(int nX, int nY)
   {
      x = nX;
      y = nY;
   }

   public OverloadTest(OverloadTest original)
   {
      x = original.x;
      y = original.y;
   }

   public string ToString()
   {
      return "x = " + x + "; y = " + y;
   }
}
```

The class contains two `int` data fields and a constructor for initializing them. We have added a second constructor which creates a new `OverloadTest` object by copying an existing object called `original`. (We'll see why we need this second constructor in a minute.) We've also added a `ToString()` method which allows the values of `x` and `y` to be printed to the screen.

We can now add an overloaded + operator to this class:

```
public static OverloadTest operator+(
   OverloadTest left, OverloadTest right)
{
   OverloadTest result = new OverloadTest(left);
   result.x += right.x;
   result.y += right.y;
   return result;
}
```

Before we consider the details of what our new + operator does, we should examine the structure of this method since it contains the essentials of most overloaded operators in C#.

First, all overloaded operators in C# *must* be declared as `static`, meaning that the operator is associated with the class as a whole and not with a particular instance of that class. This is different from the way overloaded operators are implemented in C++, where an overloaded + operator, for example, is an *instance* method and takes only a single parameter, which represents the right-hand operand of the + operator. The left-hand operand is provided by the object that calls the operator method.

Key point

Overloaded operators are always `static`.

Second, the name of an overloaded operator method always starts with the C# keyword `operator` and ends with the actual operator symbol that we wish to overload. (This syntax is the same in C++.) This is the only case where operator symbols may be used within method names.

Third, the overloaded form of an operator must contain the correct number of parameters. For a binary operator such as +, the `operator+()` method must specify two parameters, the first of which is the left-hand operand (called `left` in the example above) and the second of which is the right-hand operand (called `right`). If we attempt to define `operator+()` with either fewer or greater than two parameters, we will get a compiler error.

Key point

The number of operands cannot be changed by overloading an operator.

Fourth, `operator+()` *must* return something (i.e. it cannot be `void`). This enforces the rule mentioned in Chapter 3 that all operators must return something after they perform their operation. (This is different from C++, where we are allowed to define an overloaded operator that returns nothing.) There is no restriction on the data type that an operator can return, however, so we could, if we wanted, define `operator+()` so that it returned an `int` or `bool`, although in this case it wouldn't make sense to do so.

Key point

An overloaded operator must return a value.

Now we can consider what our overloaded + operator actually does. We have defined it so that if we add two `OverloadTest` objects together, the result is a third `OverloadTest` object whose x field is the sum of the x fields of the two operands, and similarly for its y field. That is, if we have declared two `OverloadTest` objects called `obj1` and `obj2`, then `obj1 + obj2` should give a third object, `obj3`, where `obj3.x = obj1.x + obj2.x` and `obj3.y = obj1.y + obj2.y`.

Referring back to the definition of `operator+()` above, we can now see how this is done. We first create the third `OverloadTest` object called `result` which will store the result of the operation. We do this by using the second constructor defined above, which creates a copy of an existing `OverloadTest` object. In this case, we initialize `result` so that it is a copy of the left-hand operand of the + operator.

The next two lines add the x and y fields of the right-hand operand to the corresponding fields in `result`. Finally, we return the completed `result`.

Having done the work of creating the new operator, using it is very simple. We can add a `Main()` method to the `OverloadTest` class to demonstrate:

```
static void Main(string[] args)
{
    OverloadTest obj1 = new OverloadTest(1, 2);
    OverloadTest obj2 = new OverloadTest(3, 4);
    OverloadTest sum = obj1 + obj2;
    Console.WriteLine(sum.toString());
}
```

We create two `OverloadTest` objects using the first constructor and then call the overloaded + operator to add them together and produce the third `OverloadTest` object called `sum`, which is then printed to the console using the `toString()` method defined in the class above. The result is:

```
x = 4; y = 6
```

as expected.

Most C# operators can be overloaded in a similar way (see Table 5.1 on page 163), but there are a few operators that require special consideration.

5.8.1 ☐ **Overloading comparison operators**

C# supports six comparison operators: ==, !=, <, >, <=, >=. For the purposes of operator overloading, these operators must be considered in pairs, as the C# compiler will only permit one operator from a pair to be overloaded if the other operator in the same pair is also overloaded. For example, if we overload the == (equality test) operator, we must also overload the != operator. In a similar way, we must consider < and > together, and also <= and >=. All six of these operators must also return a `bool` value.

Key point

Comparison operators must be overloaded in pairs.

5.8.2 ☐ **Overloading ++ and −−**

When applied to primitive numerical data types, the ++ and −− operators may be used as either prefix, as in ++x, or postfix, as in x++, operators. Although the effect of the operator on its operand is the same in both cases, the return values differ depending on the relative position of operator and operand.

Both these operators can be overloaded in the usual way, but it is not possible to distinguish between the prefix and postfix forms when overloading them. Thus, if we provided an overloaded ++ operator for `OverloadTest` and applied it to an instance of this class called `obj1`, the two expressions ++obj1 and obj1++ would produce identical results, both in terms of the effect they had on `obj1` itself and of the value they returned. (This is in contrast to C++, where it is possible to define distinct prefix and postfix overloads of both operators.)

Key point

Overloads of ++ and −− do not distinguish between prefix and postfix forms.

5.8.3 ☐ **Overloading assignment operators**

One of the banes of C++ students is the overloaded = (assignment) operator, as in C++ this operator is required in order to produce a proper, or *deep* copy of any object containing dynamically allocated memory. Since C#, like Java, treats all objects as references, this problem does not arise, so C# does not allow the = operator to be overloaded at all.

The numerous 'convenience' assignment operators such as +=, however, *can* be overloaded, but only indirectly, by overloading their corresponding binary arithmetic operators. For example, if we provide an overloaded + operator (as in the `OverloadTest` class above), then an overload for the += operator is also provided automatically (without us needing to write a separate method for it). Writing the statement

```
obj1 += obj2;
```

is equivalent to saying:

```
obj1 = obj1 + obj2;
```

where the sum is performed using the overloaded + operator. It is not possible to provide a separate overload for the += operator by writing a specific method for it – only an implicit overload is available as provided by the explicit overload of the + operator. The same rule applies to all the other combination assignment operators such as -=, *=, and so on.

5.8.4 ☐ The `true` and `false` operators

We have met `true` and `false` as C# keywords earlier, where they were defined as the two possible values of a `bool` variable. Somewhat bizarrely, it may seem, C# also allows us to treat `true` and `false` as unary operators, but only if we define our own overloaded versions of them.

Like the comparison operators above, the `true` and `false` operators must always be overloaded as a pair. As a simple example, let us add overloaded versions of these operators to the `OverloadTest` class above.

```
public static bool operator true(OverloadTest operand)
{
    return operand.x > operand.y;
}

public static bool operator false(OverloadTest operand)
{
    return !(operand.x > operand.y);
}
```

We have chosen arbitrarily to define an `OverloadTest` object to be 'true' if its x value is greater than its y value, and 'false' otherwise. Notice that `true` as an operator can actually return either the `true` or `false` Boolean value, as can the `false` operator. Here we have just taken the return value of the `false` operator to be the opposite of that of the `true` operator.

How do we actually use these overloaded operators? The `true` operator is the most useful, as it allows us to use an unadorned `OverloadTest` object as a test value in any statement requiring a `bool` value, such as `if`, `while`, `for` and so on. For example, we could say:

```
OverloadTest obj2 = new OverloadTest(30, 4);
if (obj2)
{
Console.WriteLine("obj2 is true");
} else {
Console.WriteLine("obj2 is false");
}
```

The call to the `true` operator is deduced by the compiler from the context in which `obj2` is found. Since it is the condition within an `if` statement, a `bool` value is required, so the `OverloadTest` class is searched to see if an overload of `true` has been defined.

Using an unadorned object as a loop or conditional statement parameter always calls the `true` operator, however, so why do we need an overloaded `false` as well? The answer is rather subtle and arises when we attempt to overload the `&&` and `||` operators.

5.8.5   ☐ Overloading `&&` and `||`

C# does *not* allow us to overload the logical comparison operators `&&` and `||` directly, but it is possible to overload them indirectly. To understand the rationale behind this, we must first examine how these two operators are evaluated when both their operands are `bool`s.

Considering the `&&` operator first, if we are given an expression such as:

```
x && y
```

where `x` and `y` are both `bool` variables, how is the expression evaluated? First, we evaluate `x`. If `x` is `false`, then we can return immediately, without even examining `y`. The return value of the operator in this case is just `x`, since `x` is `false`.

If `x` is `true`, however, we then must examine `y`. If `y` is also `true`, then we return `true`, but if `y` is `false`, we return `false`. In other words, if `x` is `true`, we return `y`. We can write the operation as an `if` statement:

```
if (x == false)
{
   return x;
} else {
   return y;
}
```

C# generalizes this to allow the `&&` operator to be applied to any user-defined data type as follows. The operation `obj1 && obj2` (where both `obj1` and `obj2` are of the same class, say `OverloadTest`) returns a result that is of the same data type as the operands, and whose value is determined by the following:

```
if (OverloadTest.false(obj1))
{
   return obj1;
} else {
   return OverloadTest.&(obj1, obj2);
}
```

Here `OverloadTest.false()` is the overloaded `false` operator within the `OverloadTest` class, and `OverloadTest.&()` is the overloaded `&` (bitwise AND) operator. Clearly this definition reduces to the previous one if both `obj1` and `obj2` are `bool`, since `x & y` will always return `y` if `x` is `true`.

A similar line of reasoning shows that the expression `x || y` is equivalent to the following `if` statement:

```
if (x == true)
{
  return x;
} else {
  return y;
}
```

When the `||` operator is applied to user-defined types, as in `obj1 || obj2`, the result is defined to be:

```
if (OverloadTest.true(obj1))
{
  return obj1;
} else {
  return OverloadTest.|(obj1, obj2);
}
```

where `OverloadTest.|()` is the overloaded bitwise OR operator. Again, we can see that this reduces to the built-in definition for `bool` operands, since `x | y` always returns `y` if `x` is `false`.

In order to define overloaded versions of `&&` and `||`, therefore, we need a total of four overloaded operators: `true`, `false`, `&` and `|`. We can add overloaded versions of `&` and `|` to `OverloadTest` as follows:

```
public static OverloadTest operator&(
  OverloadTest left, OverloadTest right)
{
  OverloadTest result = new OverloadTest(left);
  result.x &= right.x;
  result.y &= right.y;
  return result;
}

public static OverloadTest operator|(
  OverloadTest left, OverloadTest right)
{
  OverloadTest result = new OverloadTest(left);
  result.x |= right.x;
  result.y |= right.y;
  return result;
}
```

These definitions simply apply the corresponding bitwise operators to the two `int` data fields of an `OverloadTest` object. Combining these definitions with the overloaded versions of `true` and `false` given earlier, we can now use both the `&&` and `||` with `OverloadTest` objects:

```
OverloadTest obj1 = new OverloadTest(3, 1);
OverloadTest obj2 = new OverloadTest(3, 4);
if (obj1 && obj2)
{
   Console.WriteLine("obj1 && obj2 is true");
}
```

It is worth tracing the steps followed when the `if (obj1 && obj2)` expression is evaluated. First, we apply the algorithm given above to work out `obj1 && obj2`. The algorithm tells us first to evaluate `OverloadTest.false(obj1)`. Looking up the definition of the overloaded `false` operator in the `OverloadTest` class, we find that it returns the `bool` value `false`, since `obj1.x > obj1.y`. We must then calculate `OverloadTest.&(obj1, obj2)`, so we examine the overloaded `&` operator. This operator produces a new `OverloadTest` object whose `x` and `y` fields are calculated by applying the bitwise AND operation to the corresponding fields in `obj1` and `obj2`. The result can be calculated by comparing a few bits, and we find that the `result` object contains fields `result.x = 3` and `result.y = 0`.

This means that the `if (obj1 && obj2)` expression has now reduced to `if (result)`, so we now must use the overloaded `true` operator to determine if `result` is `true` or `false`. We find that `result` is `true`, since `result.x > result.y`, so the message 'obj1 && obj2 is true' is printed.

Clearly there is a lot going on here, so the moral of the story is that if we really do wish to overload `&&` or `||`, we need to think through the algorithms quite carefully.

5.8.6 ☐ General rules for operator overloading

We conclude our discussion of operator overloading by summarizing the rules under which it may be done.

First, all overloaded operators require that at least one of the operands be of the class or struct in which the operator is defined. This means, for example, that we cannot overload an operator such as + where both its operands are built-in data types such as `int`s. In other words, we can only overload operators within user-defined classes or structs.

Second, we cannot change the syntax, precedence or associativity of an operator when overloading it. This means, for example, that a binary operator must always be binary, that the relative precedence (see Table 3.3 in Chapter 3 for operator precedences) of the operators cannot be altered, and that the left-to-right or right-to-left order of evaluation of a sequence of operators cannot be changed.

These rules are absolute, and are enforced by the compiler. There are other rules which, although not enforced by the compiler, are still good ones to follow in order to make code easier to understand. Wherever possible, an overloaded operator should have a meaning that is clear from the type of operator being overloaded. For example, the > operator should always compare its two operands and return true if the left operand is in some sense greater than the right operand. Exactly how the comparison is done will depend on the data type being compared. For example, for objects containing string data, it could be an alphabetical comparison, while for a class representing points in three-dimensional space, the comparison could be done by calculating the distance of a point from the origin. However, the > operator should always produce some sort of comparison of a quantity calculated from the data fields of the class in which it is defined.

Key point

Use overloaded operators sparingly and make sure they have a sensible meaning.

To summarize, Table 5.1 shows all operators that may be overloaded in C#. Note that some operators are overloadable directly by defining a static method as we have done above, but others are only overloadable indirectly, such as the && and || operators, the generalized assignment operators such as += and so on. An entry of 'yes' in the 'Overloadable?' column means that the operator can be overloaded directly by means of defining a method, while 'indirectly' means that no such function may be defined, but that an indirect method exists of overloading that operator.

Table 3.2, Chapter 3, gives the meanings of the operators.

5.9 ■ Casting

We have seen in Chapter 3 that C# will implicitly convert from one primitive data type to another if no data will be lost in the process. For example, in the following code, an int is implicitly converted to a long since all ints can be represented as longs without loss of information.

```
int x = 1234;
long y = x;
```

We also saw in Chapter 3 that if we wish to reverse the process by assigning a long quantity to an int variable, the compiler will not do this implicitly, since a long variable could contain data that will not fit into an int. We can force the compiler to do the conversion by explicitly *casting* the long into an int:

```
long y = 1234;
int x = (long)y;
```

Table 5.1 Rules for overloading operators

Symbol	No. of operands	Overloadable?	Notes
+	1	Yes	
−	1	Yes	
+	2	Yes	
−	2	Yes	
*	2	Yes	
/	2	Yes	
%	2	Yes	
++	1	Yes	Only one overload allowed for
−−	1	Yes	both prefix and postfix forms
&	2	Yes	
|	2	Yes	
^	2	Yes	
~	1	Yes	
&&	2	Indirectly	Requires overloads of `true`,
||	2	Indirectly	`false`, `&` and `|`
!	1	Yes	
<<	2	Yes	
>>	2	Yes	
==	2	Yes	Must be overloaded as
!=	2	Yes	a pair
>	2	Yes	Must be overloaded as
<	2	Yes	a pair
>=	2	Yes	Must be overloaded as
<=	2	Yes	a pair
=	2	No	
+= −=			
*= /=			Uses overload of
%= &=	2	Indirectly	corresponding binary
|= ^=			operator
<<=			
>>=			
true	1	Yes	Must be overloaded
false	1	Yes	as a pair

If the value of y lies within the range that can be represented as an `int`, all is well, but if y lies outside this range, the value of x will not be valid. We have also seen that these errors can be caught by enclosing the code within a `checked` block.

These two examples illustrate *implicit* and *explicit* casting respectively. An implicit cast is performed without any visible indication that a data conversion is taking place, while an explicit cast requires the data type to be stated within parentheses.

In addition to these built-in casts, C# allows programmers to define their own casts. These user-defined casts are another form of operator overloading, since they are defined as static methods using the `operator` keyword. A cast may be defined which converts any data type into any other data type, provided at least one of the two types is a user-defined class or struct. Although there is complete freedom in how the cast may be defined, it is of course good practice to provide a sensible conversion wherever possible.

The ability to create user-defined casts will be new to Java programmers, as no such feature exists in that language. It is possible, of course, simply to define a Java method within class A that returns an object that is an instance of class B, but this sort of conversion requires an explicit method call (and could of course be done in C# as well).

C++ programmers may be aware that C++ does provide the ability to define a cast from a user-defined data type to any other data type (user-defined or built-in), although this is an obscure feature of C++ and is not widely used. It is important not to confuse this sort of user-defined cast with casts implemented using one of C++'s four built-in casting operators (`static _cast`, `const_cast`, `dynamic_cast` and `reinterpret_cast`).

In C#, casts may be defined as either `implicit` or `explicit` (both of which are C# keywords). A cast declared as `implicit` may be used in a similar way to the first example above (without specifying the name of the destination data type). An `explicit` cast must provide the destination data type, as we did in the second example above. An `implicit` cast may also be used in explicit form.

As a simple example of a cast definition, consider the following class:

```csharp
using System;

class CastTest
{
    private int number;

    public CastTest(int n)
    {
        number = n;
    }

    public static implicit operator int (CastTest obj)
    {
        return obj.number;
    }

    static void Main(string[] args)
    {
        CastTest castTest = new CastTest(42);
        int castNumber = castTest;
        Console.WriteLine("CastTest cast to int: " + castNumber);
    }
}
```

We have defined an `implicit` cast within the `CastTest` class that casts a `CastTest` object to an `int` by returning the object's `number` field. The form of a cast definition is similar to that of an ordinary overloaded operator, except that instead of the operator symbol following the keyword `operator`, we insert the name of the *destination* data type. The *source* data type makes up the single parameter of the method.

The keyword `implicit` has been placed before the `operator` keyword. This keyword (or `explicit`) is required in a user-defined cast – leaving it out causes a compiler error.

We can see how this cast is used by examining `Main()`. We create a `CastTest` object by calling the constructor in the usual way. In the next line, we declare an `int` and initialize it by assigning the `castTest` object to it directly, without any visible method call. This sort of assignment is only possible if a cast has been defined in the *source* class.

If we had declared the cast to be `explicit` instead of `implicit`, the second line in `Main()` would need to be written:

```
int castNumber = (int)castTest;
```

Leaving the `(int)` off causes a compiler error.

Key point

An implicit cast is not visible in code; an explicit cast requires the data type to be explicitly stated.

For straightforward casting such as this, the main difference between `implicit` and `explicit` is in the level of security afforded. Declaring a cast to be `explicit` forces the programmer to remember that a cast is actually taking place, and can help prevent runtime errors caused by unexpected data transformations. For example, suppose we added a cast from `CastTest` to `byte` to the `CastTest` class:

```
public static implicit operator byte (CastTest obj)
{
    return (byte)obj.number;
}
```

We have made the cast `implicit` despite the fact that we need an explicit cast (from `int` to `byte`) in the `return` statement, since a conversion from `int` to `byte` can lose data. If we now change the code in `Main()` to:

```
static void Main(string[] args)
{
    CastTest castTest = new CastTest(999);
    byte castNumber = castTest;
    Console.WriteLine("CastTest cast to byte: " + castNumber);
}
```

we find that the output becomes:

```
CastTest cast to byte: 231
```

The problem, of course, is that 999 is too big to represent in a byte so the explicit cast from int to byte within the user-defined cast lost some of the bits from the int and gave an incorrect value for the byte. Since the cast is implicit, this problem is not obvious if we only had access to the code within Main().

If we remember from Chapter 3 that C# provides the checked keyword to catch data overflows, we might think we can catch the error by enclosing the code in Main() within a checked block, as follows:

```
static void Main(string[] args)
{
  checked
  {
    CastTest castTest = new CastTest(999);
    byte castNumber = castTest;
    Console.WriteLine("CastTest cast to byte: " + castNumber);
  }
}
```

If we try this, we find that we get the same output as before (231) and no error message. The problem is that the overflow does not happen within Main(), but actually within the user-defined cast itself, where we attempt to convert an int into a byte. Thus to fix the problem, we need to enclose the code in the cast within a checked block:

```
public static implicit operator byte (CastTest obj)
{
  byte returnByte = 0;
  checked
  {
    returnByte = (byte)obj.number;
  }
  return returnByte;
}
```

Attempting to run the code in Main() (with or without the checked block in Main()) now produces a runtime error.

In fact, the implicit cast from CastTest to byte is an example of bad program design. All the built-in *implicit* casts in C# will *never* give rise to loss of data or result in data overflow, and any user-defined implicit cast should obey the same rule. Since the number field in CastTest was declared as an int, we should not attempt to define an implicit cast which converts this value to any data type, such as byte, where any data could be lost. The fact that an explicit cast within the byte cast method was required to convert number from an int to a byte should have been a warning that we weren't doing things properly. Any cast that could result in data loss should always be made explicit.

Key point

An implicit cast should *never* cause data to be lost.

Another common misuse of casts occurs when we use them to extract only a part of the data from a given object. For example, if the `CastTest` class contained several data fields instead of the single `number` field above, we could still define the cast to `int` that we have shown above. However, this is not a sensible cast, since we are ignoring all the other data in a given `CastTest` object. If we really want to extract just the value of `number`, we should define a property with a `get` clause to do this, as this makes it explicit that we are extracting a single data field from a larger object.

One final note about casting: the compiler can be quite clever in working out pathways in an attempt to cast one data type into another. For example, if we had only the cast to `int` in `CastTest` above, we could still write:

```
CastTest castObj = new CastTest(42);
long longValue = castObj;
```

Although we have not defined a cast from `CastTest` to `long`, this code would still compile, since the compiler has figured out that there *is* an implicit cast from `CastTest` to `int`, and C# itself provides an implicit cast from `int` to `long`, so an implicit cast from `CastTest` to `long` is allowed.

Provided we have followed the guideline above that no implicit cast can ever give rise to an error, these implied paths discovered by the compiler should never cause any problems. If we are at all uncertain that an implicit cast should be allowed under any specific situation, we should make the cast explicit, since this will prevent the compiler from applying it unless we give our express permission in the code.

5.10 ■ Indexers

Those whose only prior programming experience is Java will know the square bracket notation `[]` only in the context of specifying an array index. C++ programmers may be aware that in C++, the `[]` notation is actually regarded as an operator that can be overloaded, usually to provide a check that the value being specified as an array index is within the bounds of the array.

It can be seen by examining the table of overloadable operators in C#, earlier in this chapter, that `[]` is not one of the operators listed. The reason for this is that C# provides a different method by which this symbol can be effectively overloaded: the *indexer*.

Key point

An indexer effectively overloads the [ ] notation.

Syntactically, an indexer looks very similar to a property, which we met first back in Chapter 2 as a way of ensuring encapsulation of data within a C# class. We will illustrate with a class containing a simple indexer. A full explanation follows the class listing.

```
1. using System;
2.
3. public class IndexerTest
4. {
5.     private int[] square;
6.
7.     public IndexerTest(int size)
8.     {
9.         square = new int[size];
10.        for (int i = 0; i < square.Length; i++)
11.        {
12.            square[i] = i * i;
13.        }
14.     }
15.
16.    public int this [int index]
17.    {
18.        get
19.        {
20.            if (index >= 0 && index < square.Length)
21.            {
22.                return square[index];
23.            }
24.            throw new IndexOutOfRangeException(
25.                "Array index " + index + " out of bounds.");
26.        }
27.        set
28.        {
29.            if (index >= 0 && index < square.Length)
30.            {
31.                square[index] = value;
32.                return;
33.            }
34.            throw new IndexOutOfRangeException(
35.                "Array index " + index + " out of bounds.");
36.        }
37.    }
38.
39.    public static void Main(string[] argv)
40.    {
41.        IndexerTest test = new IndexerTest(10);
42.        for (int i = 0; i < 10; i++)
```

```
43.        {
44.            Console.WriteLine("Square of " + i + " = " + test[i]);
45.        }
46.    }
47. }
```

The `IndexerTest` class contains an `int` array called `square` (line 5). The size of the array is specified in the constructor (lines 7 through 14), and the array is initialized with a value that is the square of its index.

Lines 16 through 37 define the indexer for this class. The declaration of the indexer on line 16 is similar to a property declaration, except that the name of the indexer is always `this`, and an additional parameter (enclosed in square brackets, not parentheses) must be provided. We have used an `int` here, but this parameter can be of any data type, as we will see below.

An indexer contains `get` and/or `set` accessors, just like a property. Let us consider the `get` accessor.

We have written the indexer so that it accesses the individual array elements of the `square` array. On line 20 we test to see if `index` is within the bounds of the array and, if so, return the corresponding element from `square`. Otherwise we *throw* an *exception*. (We will consider exceptions in Chapter 7.) This is a way of allowing a program that encounters an error condition to handle it gracefully rather than simply crashing.

The `set` accessor on lines 27 to 36 works in a similar way. We again check the value of `index` and if it is valid, we assign a value to the corresponding element of `square`, otherwise we throw an exception.

The code in `Main()` shows how the indexer is used in practice. Within the `for` loop, we use the `get` section of the indexer to retrieve the elements of `square` and print them out.

Key point

An indexer can use any data type as an index.

To illustrate that indexers can take any data type as a parameter, we will add a second indexer to `IndexerTest` that allows us to refer to elements in `square` by using a string to spell out the index number, rather than an `int` as we did above. We add a `static` string array after line 5:

```
public static string[] number =
    {
        "zero", "one", "two", "three", "four",
        "five", "six", "seven", "eight", "nine"
    };
```

We can now add the second indexer to the class (it can go anywhere, but we will insert it following the constructor on line 15):

```
public int this [string index]
{
  get
  {
    for (int i = 0;
         (i < number.Length) && (i < square.Length);
         i++)
    {
      if (index.Equals(number[i]))
      {
        return square[i];
      }
    }
    throw new IndexOutOfRangeException(
      "Array index " + index + " too large.");
  }
}
```

We have provided only a get accessor, since the set accessor is very similar. We use a loop to run through the number array, comparing each entry with the index string that was passed in as the parameter to the indexer. We need to stop the loop after reaching the end of either number or square, whichever is shorter. If we find a match, we return the corresponding element from square, otherwise we throw an exception.

We can produce the same output as in the previous version of the program by replacing line 44 in the listing above with:

```
Console.WriteLine("Square of " + i + " = " + test[number[i]]);
```

That is, we use a string as an indexer parameter instead of an int. Obviously this is a cumbersome way of specifying an array index, but the example should illustrate the power of the indexer. Arrays in C# have effectively been generalized so that any data type may be used as the index into the array.

Although the examples above used an indexer to provide an interface with an actual array data field within the class, there is no need for this to be the case. We could equally well have declared 10 separate data fields in IndexerTest and then used a switch or if…else statement to return the field corresponding to the indexer parameter.

5.11 ■ Namespaces

5.11.1 □ Defining a namespace

A namespace in C# is roughly analogous to a package in Java, in that it provides a kind of higher-level organization inside which new classes and structs can be defined. Unlike the Java package however, a C# namespace does not impose any restrictions on the directory structure in which files within certain namespaces must reside.

A namespace simply defines a new scope level within a C# program. Only user-defined data structures such as classes and structs may be created inside a namespace. We are not allowed to create stand-alone data fields or methods, so it is not correct to regard a namespace as a kind of 'super-class'.

The motivation for the namespace concept comes from larger programming projects, since it provides a way for several classes with the same name to co-exist. Suppose that you are working on your own part of a large software project. You need a way of defining your class names so that you can be sure they won't clash with class names chosen by others working on different areas of the same project. If you have been assigned a unique namespace inside which all your classes are placed, you can work securely in the knowledge that your class names cannot conflict with the names of any other classes being written by others working on the same project.

A namespace is easily defined – we simply use the namespace keyword followed by the name of the namespace:

```
namespace NamespaceTest
{
  public class Class1
  {
    public Class1()
    {
    }
  }
}
```

The class Class1 now resides within NamespaceTest, so it is safe to define another class, also named Class1, that lives in a different namespace:

```
namespace OtherNamespace
{
  public class Class1
  {
    public Class1()
    {
    }
  }
}
```

We can even define a third version of Class1 that doesn't belong to any namespace and have it co-exist happily with the other two versions of Class1 above:

```
public class Class1
{
  public Class1()
  {
  }
}
```

To refer to any of these versions of Class1, we need to specify the namespace (if any) to which the particular version of the class belongs. For example, if we wanted to define an instance of each of the three versions of Class1 in a Main() method in some other class, we could say:

```
public static void Main(string[] args)
{
  NamespaceTest.Class1 testClass =
    new NamespaceTest.Class1();
  OtherNamespace.Class1 otherClass =
    new OtherNamespace.Class1();
  Class1 lonelyClass =
    new Class1();
}
```

A class that resides within a namespace must be preceded by the namespace, while a class that is not associated with a namespace appears on its own in the usual way.

To add more classes or structs to a given namespace we can simply include them in the same file within the single namespace scope, or we can write each class in a separate file, but just enclose the class definition within its own namespace wrapper.

5.11.2 ☐ The using statement

Having to add the namespace qualifier in front of all occurrences of every class that resides within that namespace can become very tedious when typing out code, and also makes the code harder to read. For this reason, C# provides the using statement. For example, if we had a namespace called Transport that contained three classes named Car, Boat and Airplane, we could refer to these classes by inserting a using Transport statement at the start of a file:

```
using Transport;
public class TestTransport
{
  public static void Main(string[] args)
  {
    Car astonMartin = new Car();
    Boat qe2 = new Boat();
    Airplane concorde = new Airplane();
  }
}
```

Key point

The using statement allows a class to be referenced without its namespace prefix.

Note that the `using` statement occurs outside the class. If we did not have this `using` statement, we would need to write `Main()` as:

```
public class TestTransport
{
  public static void Main(string[] args)
  {
    Transport.Car astonMartin = new Transport.Car();
    Transport.Boat qe2 = new Transport.Boat();
    Transport.Airplane concorde = new Transport.Airplane();
  }
}
```

We can have more than one `using` statement within a file, but we need to be a bit careful if two namespaces contain classes with the same name. Attempting to 'use' both namespaces at the same time will cause a compiler error if we refer to a class name that is common to both namespaces. In that case, we need to prefix the class name with the namespace name, even if the `using` statement is present for that namespace.

Key point

Beware of classes with the same name in two different namespaces when including several `using` statements.

Namespaces can be nested, although this is rarely done except in large projects. We might, for example, define namespaces inside the `Transport` namespace above, called `LandTransport` and `WaterTransport`:

```
namespace Transport
{
  namespace LandTransport
  {
    public class Bicycle
    {
      // class definition
    }

    public class Tricycle
    {
      // class definition
    }
  }

  namespace WaterTransport
  {
    // classes such as Sailboat, Rowboat, etc
  }
}
```

To refer to `Bicycle`, we would need to write:

```
Transport.LandTransport.Bicycle
```

or else include the statement

```
using Transport.LandTransport;
```

at the top of the file.

A variant of the `using` statement allows us to define an *alias* for a namespace name. For example, instead of having to write out `Transport.LandTransport` every time we wanted to refer to classes within the nested namespace, we could define an alias and then use that alias to refer to the nested namespace:

```
using Land = Transport.LandTransport;
```

Now we can use the alias to declare objects:

```
Land.Bicycle bike = new Land.Bicycle();
```

One final note: if you have used Visual Studio .NET to add a C# class to a project, you will find that the 'Add class' dialog insists that any new class must belong to a namespace, which might lead you to believe that all classes have to be defined inside a namespace. This is not true, as we've seen with most of the examples in the book so far – it is perfectly legal for classes to exist on their own, outside of any namespace.

Key point

Classes need not be embedded within a namespace.

5.12 ■ Case study: the adventure game

We have now covered enough of C# to return to our adventure game that we started back in Chapter 2. The first version of the game sketched out the main classes that would be used in the game, but provided no real functionality. In this second version, we won't add to the number of classes, but we will expand the game in several ways.

First, we will write the code in such a way that the game can contain any number of locations, that each location can contain an arbitrary number of items, and that the player can carry an arbitrary number of items, up to a weight limit.

We will also add a command-line interface that recognizes several commands:

■ `look`: prints a description of the current location and lists the items it contains;
■ `status`: prints the player's name and lists the items in the player's backpack;

- move <direction>: attempts to move in the direction specified. The direction can be one of north, east, south, west, up or down, but not all directions will work for every room, since only certain exits will be specified for each location;
- take <list of items>: for each word in the <list of items>, a search is made of the items in the current location's contents. If an item whose description contains that word is found, it is added to the player's inventory, provided there is space in the player's backpack;
- drop <list of items>: essentially the take command in reverse – for each item in the list it will search the player's inventory and, if a matching item is found, it will move it to the contents of the current location, if there is enough space in the room;
- quit: quits the game;
- help: prints a list of available commands.

Although implementing all these features does require a fair bit of coding, it should be noted that the underlying object-oriented structure of the game has not changed much at all. The only difference is that instead of the game containing only a single location, and each location being allowed only a single item, we have introduced arrays of locations and items to allow several of each type to be present.

The main purpose of this second version of the game is to illustrate some of the features of the C# language that have been introduced in the last three chapters. The code will not, of course, contain *all* the features we have discussed, since many of them are not needed.

Let us examine each of the four classes (Item, Room, Player and Adventure) that we introduced in the first version to see how they have been modified. (To save space, we have removed the comments in the versions of the classes printed in the book, but the original code, downloadable from the book's web site, contains comments for each method.) First, let us look at Item:

```
1. public class Item
2. {
3.    private string description;
4.    private int weight;
5.
6.    public Item(string description, int weight)
7.    {
8.       Description = description;
9.       Weight = weight;
10.   }
11.
12.   public string Description
13.   {
14.      get
15.      { return description; }
```

```
16.      set
17.      { description =  value; }
18.   }
19.
20.   public int Weight
21.   {
22.      get
23.      { return weight; }
24.      set
25.      { weight = value; }
26.   }
27.
28.   public override string ToString()
29.   {
30.      string itemInfo = description;
31.      itemInfo += ": (" + weight + ")";
32.      return itemInfo;
33.   }
34.
35.   public bool MatchesDescription(string itemDesc)
36.   {
37.      string thisLower = this.Description.ToLower();
38.      string otherLower = itemDesc.ToLower();
39.      if (thisLower.IndexOf(otherLower) != -1)
40.         return true;
41.      return false;
42.   }
43. }
```

Item contains the same two data fields as before, but we have now added a constructor (line 6). The properties and ToString() method are the same as before. We have added a new method called MatchesDescription() (line 35) which allows an Item to compare its description with a search string. This method is used in the take and drop commands.

This method makes use of a couple of methods that are defined in the System.String class (for which the string data type is an alias). Although we haven't yet considered any of the .NET library classes in detail, it is a good habit to have a look at the documentation from time to time to see if some methods exist that will serve our purposes, rather than assuming we have to write everything from scratch.

Before we consider the method in more detail, let us consider its main purpose. Suppose a particular location has Items in it that have descriptions such as 'crystal ball', 'dusty tome' and 'magic wand'. We would like to be able to match these items by typing only enough text to make the identification unique. Thus we would like to be able to type just 'ball' to match 'crystal ball'. The match should also not depend on the case, so typing 'BALL' or 'Ball' should also produce a match.

Now let us return to `MatchesDescription()`. The parameter `itemDesc` is the word typed in as part of the `take` command ('ball' in our example above). We want to compare this with the `description` field for the current `Item`. To ensure a case-independent comparison, we convert both `description` and `itemDesc` to lower-case using the `ToLower()` method in the `String` class. This produces the two `strings` `thisLower` and `otherLower`, respectively. (Full details of what this method does can be found in the documentation for the .NET classes.)

Once we have eliminated any of the case differences between the two strings, we need to see if `otherLower` forms a substring within `thisLower`. Another of the library methods in the `String` class can do this. `IndexOf()` returns the index of its parameter `string` within the `string` that calls the method. If the parameter is not found within the main `string`, the method returns -1, otherwise it returns the location within the main `string` of the first character of the search `string`. In this case, once we know whether or not the search string is within the main string, we don't care *where* it is, so we only need to check whether `IndexOf()` returns -1 (line 39).

Now let us consider `Room`:

```
1. using System.Collections;
2.
3. public class Room
4. {
5.    private string description;
6.    private ArrayList itemList;
7.    private Room[] exits;
8.    public enum Direction
9.    {
10.      North, East, South, West, Up, Down
11.    }
12.    public string[] directionNames =
13.      { "north", "east", "south", "west", "up", "down" };
14.
15.    public Room()
16.    {
17.      description = "";
18.      itemList = null;
19.      exits = null;
20.    }
21.
22.    public Room(string description)
23.    {
24.      description = description;
25.      itemList = new ArrayList();
26.      exits = new Room[6];
27.    }
28.
```

```
29.    public void SetExit(Direction dir, Room loc)
30.    {
31.      exits[(int)dir] = loc;
32.    }
33.
34.    public Room HasExit(Direction dir)
35.    {
36.      return exits[(int)dir];
37.    }
38.
39.    public Room FindExit(string dirString)
40.    {
41.      for (int i = 0; i < directionNames.Length; i++)
42.      {
43.        if (dirString.Equals(directionNames[i]))
44.          return HasExit((Direction)i);
45.      }
46.      return null;
47.    }
48.
49.    public void AddItem(Item newItem)
50.    {
51.      itemList.Add(newItem);
52.    }
53.
54.    public Item RemoveItem(string itemDesc)
55.    {
56.      Item removedItem = FindItem(itemDesc);
57.      if (removedItem != null)
58.      {
59.        itemList.Remove(removedItem);
60.      }
61.      return removedItem;
62.    }
63.
64.    public Item FindItem(string itemDesc)
65.    {
66.      foreach (Item item in itemList)
67.      {
68.        if (item.MatchesDescription(itemDesc))
69.        {
70.          return item;
71.        }
72.      }
73.      return null;
74.    }
```

```
75.
76.    public string Description
77.    {
78.      get
79.      { return description; }
80.      set
81.      { description =  value; }
82.    }
83.
84.    public ArrayList ItemList
85.    {
86.      get
87.      { return itemList; }
88.      set
89.      { itemList = value; }
90.    }
91.
92.    private ArrayList ExitsToString()
93.    {
94.      ArrayList exitStrings = new ArrayList();
95.      for (int i = 0; i < exits.Length; i++)
96.      {
97.        if (exits[i] != null)
98.        {
99.          exitStrings.Add(directionNames[i]);
100.       }
101.     }
102.     return exitStrings;
103.   }
104.
105.   public override string ToString()
106.   {
107.     string locationInfo = "\n=========================";
108.     locationInfo += "\nYou are in the " + description + "\n";
109.
110.     // Print exits
111.     ArrayList exitStrings = ExitsToString();
112.     if (exitStrings.Count == 0)
113.     {
114.       locationInfo += "\nThere are no exits from this room.";
115.     }
116.     else if (exitStrings.Count == 1)
117.     {
118.       locationInfo += "\nThere is one exit " + exitStrings[0];
119.     }
120.     else
```

```
121.     {
122.       locationInfo += "\nThere are " + exitStrings.Count +
123.         " exits: ";
124.       foreach (string exit in exitStrings)
125.       {
126.         locationInfo += exit + " ";
127.       }
128.     }
129.
130.     // Print contents
131.     if (itemList.Count != 0)
132.     {
133.       locationInfo += "\nContains:\n";
134.       foreach (Item item in itemList)
135.       {
136.         locationInfo += item.ToString() + "\n";
137.       }
138.     }
139.     else
140.       locationInfo += "\nThere are no items here.";
141.
142.     locationInfo += "\n=========================";
143.     return locationInfo;
144.   }
145. }
```

Since we want the location to be able to hold an arbitrary number of Items, an array of Items isn't the best solution, since the size of the array has to be specified in advance. This means that we need to anticipate the largest number of items we think the location will ever hold and then declare the array to be at least that large. This will waste space for most locations since most of the array elements will remain unused.

To solve this problem, we have made use of a library class called ArrayList, which is essentially a linked list data structure, but which allows array notation (that is, the square brackets) to access its elements. It also has several built-in methods for adding, searching and deleting elements in the list.

As we will see when we get into the .NET libraries in later chapters, whenever we use a library class, we need to inform the compiler that we are using the namespace in which that class is contained. ArrayList is in the System.Collections namespace, which explains the using statement on line 1. The ArrayList itself is declared on line 6.

Apart from storing items, the other main feature of a Room is that it has one or more exits to other locations. There are various ways this can be implemented, but the method we have used here is to provide an enum for the six possible directions (line 8) and a parallel array of strings to contain the names of these directions (line 12). Each Room has an array called exits (line 7) which will be of size 6. If the current location has an exit in a given direction, we store the reference to the other `Room` that can be reached through that exit in the corresponding place in the array. If no exit exists in a given direction, the corresponding array element will be `null`.

We have provided two constructors: one without parameters (line 15) and one that allows `description` to be specified (line 22).

`SetExit()` (line 29) allows one of the exits for a `Room` to be set. The first parameter is one of the `Direction` enum values and the second parameter is the `Room` to which the exit leads. We use a `Direction` to specify the direction of the exit since it is clearer than using a bare integer, as we'll see later when we come to set up the floor plan of the rooms. Note that we do need to cast a `Direction` to an `int` to use it as an array index, however.

`HasExit()` (line 34) returns the current value of the `exits` array for the specified direction. If no exit exists in that direction, `HasExit()` will return `null`.

`FindExit()` (line 39) is used to locate an exit when the direction is specified as a `string` rather than a `Direction`, and is used in response to a 'move' command. It just compares the input parameter with the strings in the `directionNames` array and then calls `HasExit()` to see if an exit exists in that direction.

`AddItem()` (line 49) allows an `Item` to be added to the `ArrayList`, using the library method `Add()` from the `ArrayList` class. It is always a good idea to check the MSDN documentation to see what methods are available for a class, since in most cases, the method you want will already be there.

`RemoveItem()` (line 54) takes a `string` as a parameter, and uses this to search for an `Item` in `itemArray` whose `description` contains this `string`. This is done in `FindItem()` (line 64), which loops through all the `Items` in the array and calls `MatchesDescription()` for each one until it either finds a match or hits the end of the array. If a match is found, the `Item` is returned, otherwise `null` is returned.

The result of calling `FindItem()` is used back in `RemoveItem()`. On line 57 we test whether an `Item` matching `itemDesc` was found. If it was, we remove it from `itemList` using the library method `Remove()` (line 59). We return `removedItem` (line 61) which will either be the `Item` that was removed, or `null` if no item was found.

Following this, we have defined a few properties. The `ToString()` method (line 105) produces a `string` containing the `Room`'s `description`, a list of available exits and a list of its `Items`. The `string` listing the exits is constructed by `ExitsToString()` (line 92) which returns an `ArrayList` containing the string representations of the exit directions. The number of elements and contents of this `ArrayList` is used back in `ToString()` (lines 112 to 128) to produce an appropriate message stating what exits are available.

The `Player` class is very similar to `Room`:

```
1. using System.Collections;
2.
3. public class Player
4. {
```

```
5.    private string name;
6.    private ArrayList itemList;
7.    private Room currentLocation;
8.    private int maxCarryWeight, carryWeight;
9.
10.   public Player()
11.   {
12.     Name = "";
13.     MaxCarryWeight = 0;
14.     CarryWeight = 0;
15.     itemList = null;
16.   }
17.
18.   public Player(string name, int carry)
19.   {
20.     Name = name;
21.     MaxCarryWeight = carry;
22.     CarryWeight = 0;
23.     itemList = new ArrayList();
24.   }
25.
26.   public string Name
27.   {
28.     get
29.     { return name; }
30.     set
31.     { name = value; }
32.   }
33.
34.   public int MaxCarryWeight
35.   {
36.     get
37.     { return maxCarryWeight; }
38.     set
39.     { maxCarryWeight = value; }
40.   }
41.
42.   public int CarryWeight
43.   {
44.     get
45.     { return carryWeight; }
46.     set
47.     {
48.       if (carryWeight <= maxCarryWeight)
49.       {
50.         carryWeight = value;
```

```
51.         }
52.      }
53.    }
54.
55.    public ArrayList ItemArray
56.    {
57.      get
58.      { return itemList; }
59.      set
60.      { itemList = value; }
61.    }
62.
63.    public Room CurrentLocation
64.    {
65.      get
66.      { return currentLocation; }
67.      set
68.      { currentLocation = value; }
69.    }
70.
71.    public bool AddItem(Item newItem)
72.    {
73.      if (newItem.Weight <= MaxCarryWeight - CarryWeight)
74.      {
75.        itemList.Add(newItem);
76.        CarryWeight += newItem.Weight;
77.        return true;
78.      }
79.      return false;
80.    }
81.
82.    public Item RemoveItem(string itemDesc)
83.    {
84.      Item removedItem = FindItem(itemDesc);
85.      if (removedItem != null)
86.      {
87.        itemList.Remove(removedItem);
88.        CarryWeight -= removedItem.Weight;
89.      }
90.      return removedItem;
91.    }
92.
93.    public Item FindItem(string itemDesc)
94.    {
95.      foreach (Item item in itemList)
96.      {
```

```
97.          if (item.MatchesDescription(itemDesc))
98.          {
99.             return item;
100.         }
101.      }
102.      return null;
103.   }
104.
105.   public override string ToString()
106.   {
107.      string playerInfo = "Name: " + name;
108.      if (itemList.Count != 0)
109.      {
110.         playerInfo += "\nCarrying:\n";
111.         foreach (Item item in itemList)
112.         {
113.            playerInfo += item.ToString() + "\n";
114.         }
115.         playerInfo += "Total weight: " + CarryWeight + "\n";
116.      }
117.      else
118.         playerInfo += "\nNot carrying anything.";
119.      return playerInfo;
120.   }
121. }
```

Most of the new features in `Player` mirror those in `Room`. The `Player` now stores an `ArrayList` of `Item`s (line 6) representing what is carried in the backpack. A `Player` is given a weight limit in `maxCarryWeight` and the currently carried weight is stored in `carryWeight` (line 8). `AddItem()` and `RemoveItem()` do much the same things as their counterparts in `Room`, except that the total weight carried by the player is updated and the `Player` is not allowed to pick up an item if it will exceed their weight allowance (line 73). `FindItem()` and `ToString()` also do essentially the same things that their counterparts in `Room` do. Since a `Player` can move around, we have added a `Room` field (line 7) which stores the current location.

Finally, we consider the `Adventure` class, which has undergone the most changes and additions:

```
1. using System;
2.
3. public class Adventure
4. {
5.    private Player gamePlayer;
6.    private Room[] rooms;
7.    private const int numRooms = 3;
8.    public enum Locn
```

```
9.    {
10.      Laboratory = 0,
11.      Dungeon = 1,
12.      Kitchen = 2
13.    }
14.
15.    public Adventure()
16.    {
17.      rooms = new Room[numRooms];
18.
19.      rooms[(int)Locn.Laboratory] =
20.        new Room("magic laboratory.");
21.      Item roomItem = new Item("crystal ball", 10);
22.      rooms[(int)Locn.Laboratory].AddItem(roomItem);
23.      roomItem = new Item("magic wand", 2);
24.      rooms[(int)Locn.Laboratory].AddItem(roomItem);
25.      roomItem = new Item("homunculus", 23);
26.      rooms[(int)Locn.Laboratory].AddItem(roomItem);
27.      roomItem = new Item("dusty tome", 7);
28.      rooms[(int)Locn.Laboratory].AddItem(roomItem);
29.
30.      rooms[(int)Locn.Dungeon] = new Room("dungeon.");
31.      roomItem = new Item("knife", 10);
32.      rooms[(int)Locn.Dungeon].AddItem(roomItem);
33.
34.      rooms[(int)Locn.Kitchen] = new Room("kitchen.");
35.      roomItem = new Item("carrot", 1);
36.      rooms[(int)Locn.Kitchen].AddItem(roomItem);
37.      roomItem = new Item("chicken", 3);
38.      rooms[(int)Locn.Kitchen].AddItem(roomItem);
39.
40.      rooms[(int)Locn.Laboratory].SetExit(
41.        Room.Direction.East, rooms[(int)Locn.Kitchen]);
42.      rooms[(int)Locn.Laboratory].SetExit(
43.        Room.Direction.Down, rooms[(int)Locn.Dungeon]);
44.      rooms[(int)Locn.Kitchen].SetExit(
45.        Room.Direction.West, rooms[(int)Locn.Laboratory]);
46.      rooms[(int)Locn.Dungeon].SetExit(
47.        Room.Direction.Up, rooms[(int)Locn.Laboratory]);
48.
49.      gamePlayer = new Player("Wibble the Wizard", 100);
50.      gamePlayer.CurrentLocation = rooms[(int)Locn.Laboratory];
51.    }
52.
53.    public void PlayGame()
54.    {
```

```
55.     Console.WriteLine("Welcome to Adventure!");
56.     string command;
57.     do
58.     {
59.       Console.Write("\n\nYour command -> ");
60.       command = Console.ReadLine().ToLower();
61.
62.       if (command.Equals("quit"))
63.         Console.WriteLine("Thanks for playing.");
64.       else if (command.Equals("help"))
65.         PrintHelp();
66.       else if (command.Equals("status"))
67.         Console.WriteLine(gamePlayer.ToString());
68.       else if (command.Equals("look"))
69.         Console.WriteLine(
70.           gamePlayer.CurrentLocation.ToString());
71.       else if (command.IndexOf("move") == 0 ||
72.         command.IndexOf("take") == 0 ||
73.         command.IndexOf("drop") == 0)
74.       {
75.         string[] words = command.Split();
76.         if (words[(int)Locn.Laboratory].Equals("move"))
77.           DoMove(words);
78.         else if (words[(int)Locn.Laboratory].Equals("take"))
79.           DoTake(words);
80.         else if (words[(int)Locn.Laboratory].Equals("drop"))
81.           DoDrop(words);
82.         else
83.           Console.WriteLine(
84.             "Sorry, don't understand that - try ⤸
               again.");
85.       }
86.       else
87.         Console.WriteLine(
88.           "Sorry, don't understand that - try again.");
89.     } while (!command.Equals("quit"));
90.   }
91.
92.   private void DoMove(string[] words)
93.   {
94.     if (words.Length < 2)
95.     {
96.       Console.WriteLine("You must specify a direction.\n " +
97.         "Try one of north, east, south, west, up or down.");
98.       return;
99.     }
100.    Room destination =
```

```
101.          gamePlayer.CurrentLocation.FindExit(words[1]);
102.      if (destination == null)
103.      {
104.        Console.WriteLine(
105.          "Sorry, you can't move in that direction.");
106.        return;
107.      }
108.      gamePlayer.CurrentLocation = destination;
109.      Console.WriteLine("You move to the " +
110.        destination.Description);
111.    }
112.
113.    private void DoTake(string[] words)
114.    {
115.      int taken = 0;
116.      for (int i = 1; i < words.Length; i++)
117.      {
118.        Item takenItem =
119.          gamePlayer.CurrentLocation.RemoveItem(words[i]);
120.        if (takenItem != null)
121.        {
122.          if (!gamePlayer.AddItem(takenItem))
123.          {
124.            Console.WriteLine("You can't carry any more.");
125.            gamePlayer.CurrentLocation.AddItem(takenItem);
126.            break;
127.          }
128.          else
129.          {
130.            taken++;
131.          }
132.        }
133.      }
134.      Console.WriteLine("You have taken " + taken +
135.        (taken == 1 ? " item" : " items") + ".");
136.    }
137.
138.    private void DoDrop(string[] words)
139.    {
140.      int dropped = 0;
141.      for (int i = 1; i < words.Length; i++)
142.      {
143.        Item takenItem = gamePlayer.RemoveItem(words[i]);
144.        if (takenItem != null)
145.        {
146.          gamePlayer.CurrentLocation.AddItem(takenItem);
```

```
147.            dropped++;
148.          }
149.        }
150.      Console.WriteLine("You have dropped " + dropped +
151.        (dropped == 1 ? " item" : " items") + ".");
152.    }
153.
154.    private void PrintHelp()
155.    {
156.      Console.WriteLine("Valid commands:\n" +
157.        "=============================================\n" +
158.        "look - shows current location & contents;\n" +
159.        "status - shows player's name and inventory;\n" +
160.        "take <list> - take one or more items;\n" +
161.        "drop <list> - drop one or more items;\n" +
162.        "move <direction> - move in the given direction;\n" +
163.        "quit - quit the program.\n");
164.    }
165.
166.    public static void Main(string[] args)
167.    {
168.      Adventure adventure = new Adventure();
169.      adventure.PlayGame();
170.    }
171. }
```

Adventure now contains an array of Rooms (line 6). We use an array rather than an ArrayList since the locations in a game would usually be defined in the game's design and wouldn't change. To make the rooms easier to refer to, we define a Locn enum (line 8).

In the constructor (line 15), we create the array and populate each Room with a few Items. We then define the map of the adventure by assigning exits to each Room (lines 40 to 47) and then create the Player (line 49) and assign its current location. Note that by using the Locn enumeration, the array elements are much easier to understand – we always know which location each array element refers to.

This simple adventure contains only three rooms, with the game starting off in the laboratory. The kitchen can be reached by moving east from the laboratory and dungeon by moving down.

The user interaction is handled in PlayGame() and the methods that it calls. The main loop (lines 57 to 89) prints a command prompt (line 59) and then calls ReadLine() from the Console class (line 60) to read in the command typed by the user.

Commands can be of two main types: single-word commands such as quit or look, and commands such as move or take that require one or more words after them. We deal with all the single-word commands first (lines 62 to 70), since they just involve calling ready-made methods or printing simple messages.

The multi-word commands all take much the same form, so we will consider only `take` in detail. A typical `take` command would have the form:

```
take ball tome bat
```

Some of the objects in the list may be found in the player's current location and others may not. The `take` command should be able to sort out those that are found and add them to the player's backpack, and ignore the others. It must also check that the player does not exceed the maximum weight that they can carry.

We first check for all possible types of multi-word command on line 71 by using `IndexOf()` to see if the command begins with `move`, `take` or `drop`. If so, we use the `Split()` method (again from the `string` class) to split the input command into an array of separate words. (The `Split()` method is C#'s answer to Java's `StringTokenizer` – there is no exact equivalent of `StringTokenizer` in C#, but one of the `Split()` methods – it has several overloaded forms – usually is a good substitute.) We then call the corresponding method to process that command. The `take` command is handled on line 78, where we test that the first word is precisely 'take'.

`DoTake()` (line 113) aims to transfer as many items as can be recognized from the player's current location to the player's inventory list. The `taken` variable (line 115) is used to count the number of successful transfers.

The loop (line 116) begins at `words[1]` since `words[0]` is the command word `take`. For each word in the array, it calls `RemoveItem()` for the player's `CurrentLocation`. If this returns `null`, no match could be found so we go on to the next word.

If a match is found, we attempt to add this `Item` to the player's inventory (line 122). If this fails, the player cannot carry anything more, so we print a message and replace the `Item` back in the player's `CurrentLocation`. At the end of `DoTake()` we print a message saying how many `Items` were taken successfully.

One advantage to designing the `take` command this way is that it is able to cope with surprisingly complex input without complaints or errors. For example, the commands:

```
take ball
take crystal ball
take the crystal ball
take crystal
take crys
```

all have the same (and presumably desired) effect of taking the crystal ball, because the `DoTake()` method matches the first `Item` it can find with each word in turn and just ignores words that it can't match. The method can run into problems if two objects have similar descriptions. For example, if a room contained both a crystal ball and a basketball, the command 'take ball' would just take whichever of the two objects was first in the `itemArray` for that `Room`. In that case, we would need to provide some string that was unique to the item we want to take.

`DoMove()` and `DoDrop()` work in a similar way, so their code should be fairly easy to follow.

A typical session with the game may look like this:

```
Welcome to Adventure!


Your command -> look
magic laboratory.
Contains:
crystal ball: (10)
magic wand: (2)
homunculus: (23)
dusty tome: (7)



Your command -> take ball tome bat
You have taken 2 items.


Your command -> status
Name: Wibble the Wizard
Carrying:
crystal ball: (10)
dusty tome: (7)



Your command -> move dungeon
You move to the dungeon.


Your command -> look
dungeon.
Contains:
knife: (10)



Your command -> drop ball
You have dropped 1 item.


Your command -> look
dungeon.
```

```
Contains:
knife: (10)
crystal ball: (10)
```

```
Your command -> quit
Thanks for playing.
```

Although this version of the adventure game is playable, in the sense that the player can move from one room to another and can pick up and drop objects, we have not yet added anything to make the game particularly interesting. This will follow in later versions.

Another problem with the current version is that of checking for input errors from the user. This can be extremely difficult to do effectively, since it is often far from easy to predict all of the 'wrong' input that users can produce. In the interest of brevity, this program does not contain many such checks, so if you download and play the game yourself you will probably find that it is fairly easy to break it.

For example, typing just the command 'take' on its own produces the message 'You have taken 0 items.' which isn't terribly helpful. In games, as in any software, careful thought should be given to the usability aspects of a program.

■ Summary

In this chapter we have considered some of the more advanced features in C#, such as constructors, static fields and methods, const and readonly parameters, operator overloading, namespaces and indexers. Again, many of these features reflect similar features in Java, but some (such as operator overloading) are new and others are implemented in subtly different ways.

As you proceed in your study and use of C#, you will no doubt form your own programming style in which you will take a liking to some of these features and scarcely use others. However, it is a good idea to have an acquaintance with all of them so that you can recognize them in other people's code.

Exercises

5.1 Consider the class `Circle` which represents a circle:

```
public class Circle
{
    private float radius;
    private float centreX, centreY;

    public override string ToString()
    {
    return "Centre at (" + centreX + ", " +
      centreY + "); radius = " + radius;
    }
}
```

(a) Consider also a class `TestCircle` which contains a `Main()` method designed to test the `Circle` class. What is printed when this method is run?

```
public class TestCircle
{
    public static void Main(string[] args)
    {
        Circle circle = new Circle();
        Console.WriteLine(circle.ToString());
    }
}
```

(b) Write a constructor for `Circle` that provides a default value of 1 for `radius` and default values of 0 for both `centreX` and `centreY`. What is printed now when the `Main()` method in part (a) is run?

(c) Write another constructor for `Circle` that allows all three data fields to be specified when a `Circle` instance is created with the `new` operator. Modify the code in the `Main()` method in part (a) so that `circle` is created with a radius of 10.7 and a centre at the point (12.5, 24.3). Compile your answer to check it.

(d) Look up the `Random` class in the MSDN documentation to discover how to generate random numbers. Add some code to `Main()` to produce an array of 10 `Circle`s, each of which has a randomly chosen radius with a value between 1 and 100 (as a `float`) and a random centre point with `centreX` and `centreY` chosen from the range –100 to +100 (also as `float`s).

(e) Look up the `Point` class in the documentation and use it to replace `centreX` and `centreY` in the `Circle` class. Redo parts (a) to (c) of this exercise, rewriting the constructor in each case to initialize a `Point` as part of the initialization of a `Circle`.

5.2 (a) Write a method called `GetRadius()` in `TestCircle` (defined in the previous exercise) that accepts a single `Circle` parameter and returns the radius of the circle.

(b) Write an overloaded version of `GetRadius()` which takes an array of `Circles` as a parameter and returns the average radius of all circles in the array.

(c) Review the `params` keyword in Chapter 4 and write an overloaded version of `GetRadius()` which takes several `Circles` as parameters and converts them into a single array, then returns the average radius. Will the compiler allow the methods in (b) and (c) to be present in the same class at the same time?

5.3 A *vector* can be used to represent a point in two dimensions by grouping the x and y coordinates together into a single object, as in **r** = [12, 3], which represents a point at x = 12 and y = 3. Two vectors can be added together by just adding their respective components together. For example, if we have two vectors **r** = [12, 3] and **s** = [5, 9], we can create a new vector **t** = **r** + **s** = [17, 12].

(a) Write a class `Vector` which can be used to represent a vector, and provide it with a constructor which allows the values of x and y to be specified. Then write an overloaded + operator which returns another `Vector` which is the sum of its two operands.

(b) Vectors may also be multiplied together in several ways. The simplest vector multiplication is called a *dot product* and produces a single number (not a vector) as its result, and is calculated by multiplying together the respective components of the two vectors and adding up the result. For example, with **r** and **s** as defined above, the dot product can be calculated as p = **r·s** = 12*5 + 3*9 = 87. Write an overloaded * operator which calculates the dot product of two `Vectors` and returns the result as a `double`.

5.4 Write a simple class or struct called `PhoneRecord` which contains a `string` field for storing a friend's name and an `int` field for storing their phone number. Write another class called `PhoneBook` which stores an array of `PhoneRecords`. Write two indexers for `PhoneBook`. The first should use a `string` as an index and return the phone number corresponding to a friend's name, while the second should do the reverse by accepting a phone number and return the name of the corresponding friend.

Write a test program that reads in a number of names and numbers from the command line and then asks the user to type in a name or a number and return the corresponding data.

5.5 Can you see why the program in the previous exercise might not work very well for storing mobile (or long-distance) phone numbers? How might you modify the program to fix this problem?

5.6 Another problem with the indexers in the phone number program is how to handle erroneous input. Try to think of a sensible response when the user enters a name or number that isn't in the stored data.

5.7 Write a cast for the `PhoneRecord` class in the previous exercise that returns the friend's name as a `string`. Is this really the best way of extracting the friend's name from a `PhoneRecord`?

Inheritance 6

6.1 ■ The concept of inheritance

Inheritance is one of the foundations of object-oriented programming, and grew out of the observation that many objects in real life can be grouped together according to the properties they have in common. For example, think of the people you know personally. Although these people will all differ from each other in many ways, they will also share many features. Each of them has a name, a birthday, an age, a gender, and so on. However, if you are a student at a college or university, it is very likely that many of your friends are also students. A student is, of course, a person, and therefore has all the properties that we just mentioned, but in addition to these properties, a student will be taking certain courses, will have a student ID number, an expected graduation date, and so on. Other people we know could be doctors, engineers, barbers, and so on, and each of these groups of people will have a set of properties that describe some aspect of their professions in addition to the properties they have by virtue of being ordinary people.

If we want to represent these various types of people by classes in a computer language, perhaps for the purpose of including them in a database, we *could* create a separate class for each type of person and include *all* the properties for that type within the class. However, this would mean that we would need to duplicate all the common properties (name, birthday, age, etc) within each class. This leads to (at least) two problems for the software developer.

First, of course, it is a lot of extra typing. The second problem, however, is much more serious – if we duplicate all the common properties in all the classes we write, then if we wish to add another property (such as a person's address) as a common property for all types of people, we need to insert this data field in all the classes we have written. It is very easy to miss out one of the classes by accident. This situation leads to code that is difficult to maintain, which is a recipe for introducing bugs.

The principle of inheritance solves this problem by allowing us to define a *base class* which contains all the fields that are common to a number of classes, and then to define a number of *derived classes*, each of which *inherits* the base class. Each derived class inherits all the (non-private) data fields and methods of its base class. This allows us to write a *single* class which contains all data fields and methods that are to be common to a number of classes, and then to include all these fields in the derived classes without rewriting them in each case. We can also update the set of common properties by changing only the base class, since any changes made to the base class are automatically inherited by all the derived classes.

It is important to note that in proper object-oriented design, inheritance should only be used in this way – it should *not* be used to patch up a bad class design. Any derived class should represent an object that is a specialized type of the object represented by the base class. This relationship is often called an 'is-a-type-of' relationship: a derived class 'is a type of' the base class. When you are designing the classes in an object-oriented project, always ask yourself whether one class is-a-type-of another class – if it is, there is a good case for one class to inherit the other.

6.2 ■ Syntax for inheritance

Let us consider an implementation of the person and student classes mentioned above to get an idea of how inheritance is handled in C#. We'll begin with a Person class:

```csharp
public class Person
{
  private string name;
  private int age;

  public Person()
  {
    name = "";
    age = 0;
  }

  public Person(string name, int initAge)
  {
    this.name = name;
    age = initAge;
  }

  public string PrintDescription()
  {
    return "Name: " + name + "; Age = " + age;
  }
}
```

We have only included a name and an age for the person to keep things simple. The class contains a pair of constructors (we will see why we need the zero-parameter constructor later) and a `PrintDescription()` method which allows the data to be retrieved as a `string`.

Now let us make our first attempt at a `Student` class which inherits `Person`:

```
public class Student : Person
{
   private string studentID;

   public Student(string initName, int initAge,
      string initStudentID)
   {
      name = initName;
      age = initAge;
      studentID = initStudentID;
   }
}
```

The first line of this class shows the syntax for denoting inheritance – a single colon (`:`) followed by the name of the base class (`Person`).

C# vs Java

In Java, the colon would be replaced by the Java keyword `extends`.

We then declare the `studentID` field. In fact, `Student` has three data fields, since it inherits `name` and `age` from `Person`. The `Student` constructor allows all three of these data fields to be initialized, and the `PrintDescription()` method prints them out.

When we try to compile this new derived class, however, we get three compiler errors:

```
'Person.name' is inaccessible due to its protection level
'Person.age' is inaccessible due to its protection level
'Person.name' is inaccessible due to its protection level
```

The problem is that the `name` and `age` fields in the base class, being `private`, are not accessible to *any* class outside of `Person` itself, not even a class which inherits `Person`. When we try to refer to these fields in the constructor and the `PrintDescription()` method in `Student`, we are not allowed to due to the protection level.

6.3 ■ Accessing base class data from a derived class

Java or C++ programmers will probably know that the solution to this problem is to declare `name` and `age` to be `protected` rather than `private` in the base class (although `protected` means different things in Java and C++, in both languages it will allow a derived class access to base class fields). As we will see, C# offers this solution as well, but there is another way around the problem that is worth considering first.

If we wish to be a purist about the principle of encapsulation, we might observe that we should have provided properties for `name` and `age` in `Person` in order to control the setting and getting of these fields. If such properties were provided, there shouldn't be any need to redefine them in a derived class. In other words, we should just be able to inherit the properties from the base class. In fact, we can do just that.

Suppose we add a property to `Person` to control access to each of `name` and `age`:

```
public string Name
{
  get
  {
    return name;
  }
  set
  {
    name = value;
  }
}

public int Age
{
  get
  {
    return age;
  }
  set
  {
    age = value;
  }
}
```

These properties are both `public` and are therefore accessible from any class, including a derived class. With this addition to `Person`, we can now rewrite `Student` to use the properties rather than the original variables:

```
public class Student : Person
{
  private string studentID;
```

```
public Student(string name, int initAge,
   string initStudentID)
{
   Name = name;
   Age = initAge;
   studentID = initStudentID;
}
}
```

With this change, everything compiles without errors. This solution to the problem of accessing data fields in the base class does not require any relaxation of the `private` restriction on these fields, and might therefore be seen as more in keeping with the principles of good object-oriented design.

C# does provide the `protected` keyword as well, however, so those converts from Java and C++ that feel more comfortable using it may do so. A `protected` field may be accessed directly either by its own class or by any class derived from that class.

To do things this way, we merely need to change the declarations of name and age in Person to:

```
protected string name;
protected int age;
```

We can now use the original form of Student, which refers directly to name and age without going through any properties. (If properties for name and age *had* been provided for the `protected` fields, we could of course use the second version of Student as well.)

C# vs Java

In C#, if a data field or method is not given an explicit accessibility (e.g. with the `private` or `public` keyword) the accessibility defaults to `private`. In Java, the default is `protected`.

C# vs Java

In C#, the `protected` keyword allows access to the class itself and also to any other class derived from that class. In Java, `protected` allows access to any class in the same *package*, whether or not that class is related to the original class by inheritance. Java does not provide a method whereby the accessibility of a field can be restricted to classes derived from the current class.

6.4 ■ Inheriting methods

We've seen above that data fields can be inherited in a natural way, but what about methods? In the Person class we defined a method called PrintDescription(), which produced a string containing the information stored in the class. Suppose we test our Person and Student classes with the following code:

```
public static void Main(string[] argv)
{
    Person me = new Person("Glenn", 25);
    Console.WriteLine(me.PrintDescription());
    Student kevin = new Student("Kevin", 19, "00121212");
    Console.WriteLine(kevin.PrintDescription());
}
```

We find the following output:

```
Name: Glenn; Age = 25
Name: Kevin; Age = 19
```

Since we did not write a PrintDescription() method in Student, the version that we wrote in Person is being used to print out Kevin's details. Thus methods are inherited in much the same way as data fields.

However, we can spot a problem here. The information printed out for a Student contains only those data fields that were inherited from Person. If we use the PrintDescription() method from Person, this is all the information that *can* be printed, since a base class never has any knowledge of the extra data fields that might be added to a class that inherits it. Information transfer in inheritance works in only one direction: from base to derived.

It would be much neater if we could write a PrintDescription() method for Student as well, and have it print out the studentID in addition to name and age. So let us try just adding PrintDescription() to Student:

```
public string PrintDescription()
{
    return "Name: " + Name + "; Age = " + Age +
        "; ID: " + studentID;
}
```

We find that this will give the desired output:

```
Name: Glenn; Age = 25
Name: Kevin; Age = 19; ID: 00121212
```

However, the compiler issues a warning about the new PrintDescription() method:

```
The keyword new is required on 'Student.PrintDescription()'
because it hides inherited member 'Person.PrintDescription()'.
```

To fully understand what this warning means, we need to explore a couple of other topics: *name hiding* and *polymorphism*. First, we need to clarify how constructors are used when an inherited object is created.

6.5 ■ Constructors and inheritance

When an object is created from a derived class, the constructors of both the base and derived classes are called during the construction of that object. For example, if we declare a Student using a declaration such as:

```
Student kevin = new Student("Kevin", 19, "00121212");
```

the base class constructor (that from Person) is called *first*, then the derived class constructor (from Student). This is easily verified by placing WriteLine() calls in the various constructors (or by using the debugger to trace the code if you are using Visual Studio).

Since there was no explicit code in the Student constructor to call the base class constructor, the zero-parameter constructor from Person is called by default. This can give rise to a curious compiler error if we are unaware of what is going on.

If you glance back at the definition of the Person class earlier in this chapter, you will see that we defined *two* constructors for Person, even though we only ever used the two-parameter version in any object declarations. The reason for this is that if Person had only the two-parameter constructor, then the declaration of Student kevin above would produce the compiler error:

```
No overload for method 'Person' takes '0' arguments.
```

The offending line is flagged as the three-parameter Student constructor in the Student class above, which may be a bit puzzling until we realize that this constructor is attempting to call a zero-parameter Person constructor to initialize the base component of the object, and that no such constructor exists.

There are two solutions to this problem. First, we can make sure that every class we write always has a zero-parameter constructor explicitly defined, which is usually a good idea.

The other solution involves making an explicit call to a base class constructor from the derived class constructor. Java provides the super keyword for doing this: in C# the keyword is base.

Rather than use the Student constructor that is in the class definition above, we could say instead:

```
public Student(string initName, int initAge,
    string initStudentID) : base(initName, initAge)
{
    studentID = initStudentID;
}
```

After the parameter list, we have added a single colon and then the keyword `base` followed by a parameter list that passes the name and age values to the base class constructor. In this case, the effect is to call the two-parameter `Person` constructor, which initializes the name and age fields. After this, any code in the body of the `Student` constructor is run.

Using the `base` keyword can avoid a lot of duplication of code if a lot of work is involved in initializing the base class data. Also, since an explicit call is made to a base class constructor, no implicit call to the zero-parameter base class constructor is attempted, so no such constructor need be provided.

6.6 ■ Name hiding

Name hiding occurs when one entity (variable or method) has the same name (and, in the case of methods, the same parameter list) as an existing name. Although C# allows name hiding in many cases, it is almost always bad programming practice to use it, since the confusion between two objects with the same name can cause errors.

One way name hiding can occur is if a method contains a local variable with the same name as a class data field. For example:

```
class HidingDemo
{
   private int number;

   public void HidingMethod()
   {
      int number = 6;
      if (number > 0)
      {
         // Do something
      }
   }
}
```

Here we have a class data field called `number`, which has the same name as the local variable inside `HidingMethod()`. The local variable hides the class data field for the duration of `HidingMethod()`, so that the `number` referred to within the `if` statement is the local variable within the method, not the class data field.

Although we have declared the local variable `number` to have the same data type as the class field, this is not required – the local `number` variable could be any data type. The same rules of name hiding apply. In any case, no error or warning is issued by the compiler.

It should be obvious that this sort of coding is error-prone, since it is easy to get confused about which `number` is being used at any given point.

This type of name hiding occurs within a single class. A second type of name hiding occurs when one variable or method in a base class is hidden by another variable or method with the same name in a derived class. This is the sort of name hiding that occurred in our attempt earlier to add a `PrintDescription()` method to `Student`. This type of name hiding *does* generate a compiler warning, as we've seen above. To see why a warning might be sensible, we need to understand the idea of polymorphism.

6.7 ■ Polymorphism

To understand the motivation for polymorphism, let us return to the example above with the `Person` and `Student` classes. We've seen that even though there is a good reason for defining two separate classes to represent 'ordinary' people and students, there are some cases where it would be more convenient if we could treat instances of both classes equivalently. For example, if we just want to see a description of a given friend, we would expect to just call the `PrintDescription()` method, no matter whether our friend is a `Person` or a `Student`.

A better example of why it is sometimes more convenient to be able to treat related objects in a uniform way would be if instead of just two friends we had, say, 50 friends, some of whom are students and others are not. We might think that we need to sort our friends into two groups and create an array of `Person`s for one group and an array of `Student`s for the other. This sort of thing could get very inconvenient if we started to classify our acquaintances into more groups, such as doctors, lawyers, plumbers, and so on.

Since the main premise on which inheritance is based is the idea that all members of classes that share a common base class must have in common the properties defined in that base class, it would make sense if there were some way of treating objects from all derived classes in a uniform way when we are dealing with properties or methods that are defined in that base class. This is the main motivation for polymorphism.

Key point

Polymorphism allows a reference to a base class to refer to an instance of any class derived from the base class as well.

Stated simply, if we declare a reference to a base class, we are allowed to attach that reference either to a base object or an object created from any class that inherits the base class. For example, using `Person` and `Student`, we can declare a reference to a `Person`:

```
Person friend;
```

and then set `friend` to refer either to a `Person`:

```
friend = new Person("Glenn", 25);
```

or to a `Student`:

```
friend = new Student("Kevin", 19, " 00121212");
```

This sort of initialization might look distinctly suspect, since it seems that we are attempting to assign an object of one type to a reference that was declared for a different type. Under normal circumstances, this sort of thing is prohibited by the compiler.

However, the key point is that `Student` inherits `Person`, so a `Person` reference is allowed to refer to a `Student` object. In fact, we can return to the test code we wrote above to try out the new `PrintDescription()` method, and rewrite it using polymorphism:

```
Person me = new Person("Glenn", 25);
Console.WriteLine(me.PrintDescription());
Person kevin = new Student("Kevin", 19, "00121212");
Console.WriteLine(kevin.PrintDescription());
```

We find that this compiles, but if we still have the same `PrintDescription()` method in `Student`, we still get the same warning about it hiding the `PrintDescription()` method in `Person`.

If we now run this code, we get the output:

```
Name: Glenn; Age = 25
Name: Kevin; Age = 19
```

which doesn't look terribly promising, since we have lost Kevin's ID from the output, even though the new `PrintDescription()` method is still there in `Student`. What has gone wrong? Clearly, the base class `PrintDescription()` method from `Person` is being called for both objects, so our use of polymorphism appears to have broken the code. The answer to the problem lies in the method by which C# works out which method to call when an object has been created using polymorphism.

6.8 ■ Virtual methods

Java programmers may have been feeling quite confident up to this point, since everything we have described in the last section about polymorphism is also true in Java, except for the very last point. If we had used polymorphism in Java to create the `kevin` object from `Student` and then called `PrintDescription()`, we *would* have called the method in `Student` and not the one in `Person`. So what is C# doing differently?

Languages such as C# or Java that support polymorphism may use a technique called *dynamic binding* to decide which method to call whenever a statement refers to a method that exists in both the base and derived classes. In code such as:

```
Person kevin = new Student("Kevin", 19, "00121212");
Console.WriteLine(kevin.PrintDescription());
```

`kevin` is declared as a reference to a `Person`, but is initialized to a `Student`. When the call to `PrintDescription()` is made in the second line, that call could refer to either the method declared in `Person` or the one with the same signature (recall that a method's signature is its name plus its parameter list) in the derived class `Student`. How does the program decide which one to call?

The rule that is always followed in C# (but not in Java) is that the base class method will be called *unless* it is declared as `virtual`. If the base class method is `virtual`, the derived class method will be called instead.

What this means is that if we want `kevin.PrintDescription()` to call the method from `Student`, we need to go back to the `Person` class and declare its `PrintDescription()` method as `virtual`. That is, we rewrite `Person`'s `PrintDescription()` method as:

```
// In Person class
public virtual string PrintDescription()
{
    return "Name: " + name + "; Age = " + age;
}
```

If we try this and run the program again, however, we still find the output to be:

```
Name: Glenn; Age = 25
Name: Kevin; Age = 19
```

so obviously this hasn't solved the problem. We should notice that the compiler is still issuing a warning, but the message has changed:

```
'Student.PrintDescription()' hides inherited member
'Person.PrintDescription()'. To make the current member
override that implementation, add the override keyword.
Otherwise add the new keyword.
```

The final alteration we need to make is to tell the compiler that we want `PrintDescription()` in `Student` (the derived class) to `override` the corresponding method in `Person` (the base class). To do this, we need to add the `override` keyword to `PrintDescription()` in the *derived* class `Student`:

```
// In Student class
public override string PrintDescription()
{
    return "Name: " + Name + "; Age = " + Age +
        "; ID: " + studentID;
}
```

Now, finally, we get a compilation without any errors or warnings, and the output is correct:

```
Name: Glenn; Age = 25
Name: Kevin; Age = 19; ID: 00121212
```

What actually happens in this process is that the compiler builds a *virtual method table* for each class that it compiles. This table contains a list of all methods that have been declared as virtual in that class. If polymorphism is then used in the program, that is, if a reference to a base class (such as Person) has been declared and that reference has subsequently been assigned to an instance of a derived class (such as Student), the runtime environment will check the virtual method table for the base class each time a method call is made. If the method (such as PrintDescription()) is listed as virtual, a check is made to see if an overridden version of that method has been defined in the derived class and, if so, that method is called instead.

The process is called *dynamic binding* because the actual version of the method that is called is only determined when the program is run, not when it is compiled.

Key point

Only virtual methods can be overridden.

The difference between C# and Java (and the reason why Java always calls the 'right' method even though it doesn't have either a virtual or override keyword) is that Java simply assumes that *all* methods in *all* classes are virtual. So wouldn't it be easier if C# did the same thing?

Well, it probably would be, but the reason that C# programmers are given the choice of which methods to make virtual is that making all methods virtual can slow down a program considerably. Suppose you had a large base class with several hundred methods in it, but that only two or three of these methods are overridden in a derived class. In Java, a reference to the base class would need to carry around (and constantly refer to) a virtual method table with several hundred entries in it. In C# the table would contain only those methods that are overridden, resulting in a significant performance gain.

C# vs Java

In Java, all methods in all classes are implicitly virtual. In C#, only those methods declared as virtual appear in the virtual method table.

A final note to C++ programmers. Polymorphism in C++ works in a similar way to C#, in that base class methods must be declared virtual if they are to be overridden. C++ does not have an override keyword, however, so all that need be done in C++ is the insertion of virtual into base class methods.

6.9 ■ Polymorphism and method parameters

Polymorphism is also commonly used in passing parameters to methods. If a method's parameter is declared to be of a base class type, it is legal to pass a derived class object to that method as well as a base class object.

For example, if we defined a method in some class that took a `Person` parameter, we could pass a `Person` object or a `Student` object to that method:

```
// Method within a class
public void ExaminePerson(Person person)
{
   string description = person.PrintDescription();
   Console.WriteLine(description);
}
```

We can call this method with an ordinary `Person` object:

```
Person person = new Person("Glenn", 25);
ExaminePerson(person);
```

We can call it with an object that has been defined using polymorphism:

```
Person person = new Student("Kevin", 19, "00121212");
ExaminePerson(person);
```

Finally, we can call it with a `Student` object that has been defined without using polymorphism:

```
Student kevin = new Student("Kevin", 19, "00121212");
ExaminePerson(kevin);
```

In the last example, even though polymorphism wasn't used in the creation of `kevin`, it is used in passing `kevin` as a paremeter to `ExaminePerson()`, since passing a parameter to a method involves an assignment from the object passed to the object declared as the method's parameter.

In all these cases, the same rules of polymorphism apply as in the ordinary assignment expressions treated earlier.

6.10 ■ Versioning

We saw above that in order to define a method in a derived class that overrides a method in the base class, we need to do two things. First, we need to specify the base class method as `virtual` and second, we need to specify the derived class method as `override`. We have seen the justification for using `virtual`, since it makes a program run faster by cutting down the size of the virtual method table, but if we have specified in the base class which methods are allowed to be overridden, why do we need this extra `override` keyword in the derived class? Surely the fact that a method in the derived class has the same name as a virtual method in the base class is enough for the compiler to realize that an override is intended (as it is in C++).

To see why C# demands an `override` to be explicitly stated, we need to consider what could happen during a long period of software development. Suppose that we (or some external software developer) write a class such as `Person` at some point in time. Initially the `Person` class is fairly primitive, containing no more than the version we have given above. Then we write another class, such as `Friend`, that inherits `Person`. In `Friend`, we add a method called `FormattedName()`, which might format the friend's name in some fancy way using some character graphics, for example. Since `FormattedName()` doesn't exist in the base class `Person`, we would write it within `Friend` without using any extraneous qualifiers:

```
public string FormattedName()
{
    // code to produce a fancy name
}
```

Some time (possibly months or years) later, the author of `Person` decides to release a new version of that class with a few upgrades, including a method called `FormattedName()`. Quite possibly, this new `FormattedName()` method in `Person` does something different from the one we added to `Friend`, but the problem is that if we attempt to use our existing `Friend` class with the new version of `Person`, there will be a name clash between the two methods.

In this case, since the inheritance relationship between `Person` and `Friend` was designed long before the new version of `Person` was released, this name clash couldn't have been planned, so an override of `FormattedName()` wasn't in the original design. If we attempt to recompile our old version of `Friend` with the new version of `Person`, we get a compiler warning stating that `FormattedName()` in `Friend` is *hiding* (not overriding) `FormattedName()` in `Person`.

The difference between hiding and overriding will only be noticed if we try to use polymorphism. For example, consider the following code:

```
Person me = new Person("Glenn", 25);
Person simon = new Friend("Simon", 27);
Friend john = new Friend("John", 28);
Console.WriteLine(me.FormattedName());
Console.WriteLine(simon.FormattedName());
Console.WriteLine(john.FormattedName());
```

If `FormattedName()` in `Friend` hides `FormattedName()` in `Person`, then the first two calls to `FormattedName()` will call the version from `Person`, and only the last will call the version from `Friend`, even though `simon` is a `Friend` object. If `FormattedName()` in `Friend` had been declared as an `override`, then the 'right' version would be called for `simon`.

The compiler warning mentioned above arises because `FormattedName()` in `Friend` was just declared as an ordinary method, without an `override` qualifier. We should take note of this warning since it indicates that something is wrong with our class design.

To fix the problem, we have essentially three options. To decide which is the correct choice, we need to think carefully about what relationship should exist between the two methods. Does `FormattedName()` in `Friend` do essentially the same job as the same method in `Person`, but customized slightly for the `Friend` class? If so, then it would make sense to declare it as an `override` (assuming that `FormattedName()` in the base class was declared as `virtual` – if not, this first option is not available):

```
public override string FormattedName()
{
  // code
}
```

If the two methods do totally different things, the best option (if possible) is to rename one of them to avoid the name hiding. However, in the scenario outlined above, this is not likely to be an option. If we wrote our `Friend` class years ago and have used it extensively in other code, some of which has been published or used in other projects, then renaming `FormattedName()` in `Friend` is not possible. Similarly, if the new version of the `Person` class is in an official release of code from some other developer, then we cannot expect *them* to rewrite their code just because one of the methods has the same name as one of ours.

In that case, the only option open to us is to make `FormattedName()` in `Friend` hide, rather than override, its sibling in `Person`. Although this is the default action of the compiler, we can get rid of the warning message by inserting the `new` keyword in the derived class's method definition:

```
public new string FormattedName()
{
  // code
}
```

Doing this doesn't break any existing code since it doesn't change the name of either the derived class method or the base class method. It merely confirms to the compiler that we wish the derived class version of `FormattedName()` to hide the corresponding version in the base class.

Thus the 'extra' `override` and `new` keywords required by C# are actually there for a good reason – to prevent problems with different versions of software.

6.11   ■ Inheriting static methods

A static method is inherited in the same way as an instance method, but it is not possible to override a static method. The reason for this is quite sensible. When a base class reference that has been assigned a derived class object calls an instance method, the virtual method table for the reference variable is consulted to see what class the reference currently refers to. If the method being called is declared as `virtual` in the base class and an overridden version exists, then the overridden version gets called. The point is that the program needs an instance of the class to be able to tell which method to call: base or derived.

Key point

Static methods cannot be overridden.

A static method is not associated with any particular instance of the class in which it is defined, so it makes no sense to provide an overridden version of such a method. If we do want a new version of a static method in a derived class, we must use name hiding to create this new version. For example, suppose we had a base class static method such as this:

```
class baseClass
{
    // Data fields and other methods

    public static void staticMethod()
    {
        // Statements
    }
}
```

We could define a new version of `staticMethod()` in a derived class that hides the version in the base class by saying:

```
class derivedClass
{
    // Data fields and other methods

    public new static void staticMethod()
    {
        // Statements
    }
}
```

Note that we have added the new keyword to the method definition. If we don't do this, we get a compiler warning. Although it is not technically an error to omit new, it is good practice to include it since it confirms that the programmer understands that this new method is hiding an existing method in a base class.

6.12 ■ The Object **class**

We've seen so far that we can build up our own hierarchies of classes by using inheritance. However, Java programmers may remember that in Java, every class inherits the class Object whether or not this is explicitly stated in the class declaration. In C#, a fundamental Object class is also provided, and is inherited by all classes by default.

Key point

All C# classes implicitly inherit System.Object. The object keyword is a shorthand for System.Object.

The full name of the C# Object class is System.Object, since it resides in the System namespace. (In Java, the Object class is a member of the java.lang package.) However, since System.Object is commonly used in C# code, a shorthand name is provided for this class: object (with a lower-case 'o'). The C# version of Object provides most of the same methods as in the Java version. All these methods are declared as virtual in Object, and may therefore be overridden in any user-defined class. Two of the most commonly used methods are ToString() and Equals().

6.12.1 ☐ The ToString() **method**

The ToString() method returns a string which (unless overridden) contains the data type of the object calling it. For example, if we called ToString() on the me and kevin objects in the example earlier in this chapter, as in the code:

```
Person me = new Person("Glenn", 25);
Person kevin = new Student("Kevin", 19, "00121212");
Console.WriteLine(me.ToString());
Console.WriteLine(kevin.ToString());
```

we would get the output:

```
Person
Student
```

Although this information is occasionally useful, we usually want to display the data stored in an object rather than just its data type. It is therefore standard practice to override ToString() in most user-defined classes. In fact, the PrintDescription() methods that we defined for Person and Student earlier would usually be written as overrides of ToString():

```
// In Person
public override string ToString()
{
   return "Name: " + Name + "; Age = " + Age;
}
```

and:

```
// In Student
public override string ToString()
{
   return "Name: " + Name + "; Age = " + Age +
     "; ID: " + studentID;
}
```

Note that the declaration of the method is the same in both classes: the method is declared as an override and returns a string. There is no need to declare the version of this method that is in Person to be virtual since Person itself inherits Object and is therefore providing an override of Object's ToString(). In fact, we get a compiler warning if we omit the override keyword from Person's (or Student's) version of ToString(), since we would be hiding the ToString() method in Object rather than overriding it.

6.12.2 ☐ The Equals() and ReferenceEquals() methods

There are three methods in Object designed to compare two objects for equality. To use these methods properly, it is important to understand that there are two fundamentally different ways in which two objects can be 'equal'.

The most common interpretation of equality is that the data stored in the two objects is equal. For example, if we declared two Persons:

```
Person me = new Person("Glenn", 25);
Person otherMe = new Person("Glenn", 25);
```

we would probably regard me and otherMe to be 'equal' because the name and age fields in the two objects contain the same data.

However, there is another way in which two objects can be compared for equality: by comparing the memory addresses at which they are stored. Since me and otherMe are two distinct objects that just happen to contain the same data, they are stored in two different memory locations, and are therefore *not* equal in this second sense. If, instead of the above two object declarations, we had said:

```
Person me = new Person("Glenn", 25);
Person otherMe = me;
```

then me and otherMe would refer to the same object and they would then be equal in both senses of the word.

The three `Object` methods for testing equality are `Equals(object x)`, `Equals(object x, object y)` and `ReferenceEquals(object x, object y)`. The `Equals(object x)` method is a virtual instance method, and compares the object that calls it with the object x passed in as a parameter. The other two methods are `static` methods, so they don't require an `Object` instance to be called. They compare the two `object`s passed in as parameters. All three methods return a `bool`.

The default versions of all three of these methods in the `Object` class all do the same type of equality testing: they compare the memory addresses of the two objects being compared. However, all user-defined classes should provide overridden versions of the two `Equals()` methods, since they are supposed to compare objects by comparing the data they contain. The default versions in `Object` cannot do this, of course, because `Object` doesn't contain any data fields and it cannot predict what data fields will be in classes that are derived from `Object`.

As an example, we provide an overridden `Equals()` method for `Person`:

```
1. public override bool Equals(object x)
2. {
3.    if (x == null || GetType() != x.GetType())
4.       return false;
5.
6.    Person otherPerson = (Person)x;
7.    if (otherPerson.Age != Age)
8.       return false;
9.    if (!otherPerson.Name.Equals(Name))
10.      return false;
11.   return true;
12. }
13.
14. public override int GetHashCode()
15. {
16.    return Age.GetHashCode();
17. }
```

For technical reasons, we have also provided an override of `GetHashCode()`, which is another of the methods in `Object`. We have only included the override of `GetHashCode()` here since we get a compiler warning if we override `Equals()` without it. (If you have not encountered the concept of hashing, most introductory books on data structures should describe it.)

There are a couple of important points to note about the `Equals()` method. First, since the parameter x passed into `Equals()` is declared as an `object`, by using polymorphism, *any* object can be passed in as this parameter, since *all* classes in C# inherit `Object` either directly or indirectly. The first thing we need to do, then, is to make sure that the object passed into `Equals()` is a `Person`.

The initial `if` statement (line 3) first tests if `x` is `null`. If not, it then calls the `GetType()` method (another method from the `Object` class, and therefore available to all objects). This method returns a `Type` object, where `Type` is a predefined class in the `System` namespace which contains information on an object's data type. The only property of a `Type` that we are interested in here is that two objects will have the same `Type` if and only if they are objects created from the same class. We can therefore compare the `Type` of the object calling `Equals()` with the `Type` of the parameter `x` and if they are not equal, we know that `x` is not a `Person`.

If we get past this `if` statement, we know `x` is a `Person`, so we can see about comparing it with `this` (the object that called `Equals()`). In order to access the data fields within `x`, however, we need formally to cast it to a `Person` (line 6). Once we've done this, we can compare the data fields of the two objects to determine if they are in fact equal.

We can customize the `static Equals(object x, object y)` method in much the same way, except we need to determine the types of both `x` and `y`, and if they are both `Persons`, we then need to cast both of them to `Person` objects and then compare their data fields:

```
public new static bool Equals(object x, object y)
{
    // Check for null values and compare runtime types.
    Person testPerson = new Person();
    if (x == null || y == null ||
        testPerson.GetType() != x.GetType() ||
        testPerson.GetType() != y.GetType())
        return false;
    // Cast x & y to a Person type
    Person person1 = (Person)x;
    Person person2 = (Person)y;
    if (person1.Age != person2.Age)
        return false;
    if (!person1.Name.Equals(person2.Name))
        return false;
    return true;
}
```

Since this version of `Equals()` is a `static` method, we need to use `new` rather than `override` in its definition in a derived class as described above. Also, since an instance of `Person` is not required to call this method, we can't be sure that either of its parameters `x` or `y` is actually a `Person`. To ensure that both `x` and `y` are `Persons`, we create a `testPerson` object and use it to compare with the `Type` of `x` and `y`. Once we are certain that both `x` and `y` are `Persons`, we can proceed to compare their data fields as before.

There is no need to override `ReferenceEquals()` since it merely compares the memory addresses of the two objects without examining their contents, and therefore works the same for all objects. It will therefore return `true` only if both its parameters refer to the same location in memory.

The following code tests the overridden `Equals()` methods above, and also the `ReferenceEquals()` method:

```
Person me = new Person("Glenn", 25);
Person otherMe = new Person("Glenn", 25);
Person kevin = new Student("Kevin", 19, "00121212");
Console.WriteLine("me.Equals(me): " + me.Equals(me));
Console.WriteLine("me.Equals(otherMe): " +
  me.Equals(otherMe));
Console.WriteLine("me.Equals(kevin): " + me.Equals(kevin));
Console.WriteLine("ReferenceEquals(me, me): " +
  ReferenceEquals(me, me));
Console.WriteLine("ReferenceEquals(me, otherMe): " +
  ReferenceEquals(me, otherMe));
Console.WriteLine("Equals(me, me): " + Equals(me, me));
Console.WriteLine("Equals(me, otherMe): " +
  Equals(me, otherMe));
Console.WriteLine("Equals(me, kevin): " +
  Equals(me, kevin));
me = otherMe;
Console.WriteLine("Assigned otherMe to me");
Console.WriteLine("ReferenceEquals(me, otherMe): " +
  ReferenceEquals(me, otherMe));
```

The output from this code is:

```
me.Equals(me): True
me.Equals(otherMe): True
me.Equals(kevin): False
ReferenceEquals(me, me): True
ReferenceEquals(me, otherMe): False
Equals(me, me): True
Equals(me, otherMe): True
Equals(me, kevin): False
Assigned otherMe to me
ReferenceEquals(me, otherMe): True
```

Our overridden `Equals()` correctly determines that `me` and `otherMe` are equal, since although they are different objects (and therefore reside at different memory locations) they do contain the same data. The `ReferenceEquals()` method, however, finds that `me` and `otherMe` are not equal, since it is comparing the memory addresses rather than the contents of the objects.

The `static Equals()` method is also showing the correct results.

After the assignment `me = otherMe`, both references are pointing at the same object, so `ReferenceEquals()` now finds that they are equal.

6.13 ■ **Boxing and unboxing**

How does inheritance relate to value types such as the primitive data types and structs? Since these data types are not classes, it is not possible to derive any other data types from them. That is, we cannot say something like:

```
class myInt : int
{
}
```

There is one important exception to the no-inheritance rule for value types, however, and that is that all value types *do* still implicitly inherit object. This means that methods such as ToString() and Equals() can be used (and even overridden) with structs in the same way as with ordinary classes.

Since the primitive data types such as int and float are aliases for structs (see Chapter 4), they implicitly inherit object as well, which means that it is possible to call ToString() directly on an int:

```
int x = 42;
Console.WriteLine("x = " + x.ToString());
```

In fact, we can even call object's methods directly on a constant:

```
Console.WriteLine("x = " + 42.ToString());
```

Of course, there is no particular reason to do this, since we could just as well have written:

```
int x = 42;
Console.WriteLine("x = " + x);
```

or

```
Console.WriteLine("x = " + 42);
```

and obtained the same output. However, the fact that this sort of thing is possible reveals some important points about how C# handles value variables.

A value variable such as an int is actually stored as a simple four-byte quantity in the same way as in Java or C++. If a value variable is used in a context where it needs to behave like an object rather than just a primitive quantity, C# performs an operation known as *boxing*, which is essentially building a box around the primitive type to convert it into an object.

Java programmers may be familiar with Java's so-called *wrapper classes* such as Integer and Float. Since an int in Java is always a value variable, it is not possible to use it in expressions such as x.toString() as we did above in the C# example. In Java, we first need to wrap the value variable within an object and then call the desired methods:

```
// Wrapping an int within an object (Java code)
int x = 42;
Integer xInt = new Integer(x);
System.out.println("x = " + xInt.toString());
```

The boxing process in C# is essentially the same as explicitly creating a wrapper object in Java, except than in C#, no explicit intermediate class such as `Integer` is required. The conversion from value type to object happens invisibly.

C# also allows us to create a 'wrapped' `object` out of a value type, although again, no special class is needed to do this – we just use the `object` class directly. For example, we can define an `object` to represent an `int`:

```
int x = 96;
object xBox = x;
Console.WriteLine("Boxed x = " + xBox);
```

The output from this code is:

```
Boxed x = 96
```

This process resembles the definition of an intermediate class such as `IntBox`:

```
class IntBox
{
   int number;

   public IntBox(int init)
   {
     number = init;
   }
}
```

The line

```
object xBox = x;
```

amounts to saying:

```
IntBox xBox = new IntBox(x);
```

Notice that this operation actually *copies* the value of x into `number`, rather than making both xBox and x refer to the same object in memory. This means that if we modified the example above by changing x after boxing it, the value printed by the `WriteLine()` statement would not change. That is, if we said:

```
int x = 96;
object xBox = x;
x = 42;
Console.WriteLine("Boxed x = " + xBox);
```

the output would still be:

```
Boxed x = 96
```

A boxed object can be unboxed to reclaim the original value variable. Doing this always requires an explicit cast, since the compiler will have 'forgotten' what the original data type was. For example, if we want to unbox xBox back into an int, we could say:

```
int y = (int)xBox;
```

When unboxing objects, we need to be careful that the data type into which we do the unboxing is the correct type. Using an incorrect type will not generate any warnings or errors from the compiler, but will usually throw a runtime exception. For example, if we tried:

```
byte z = (byte)xBox;    // Runtime error
```

the code would compile, but the program would crash since the original data stored in xBox was an int.

The problem here is not that we might lose data when converting from an int to a byte, but rather that the data types in the object and value variable to which we are trying to unbox it do not match. The problem resides in the data type we have specified in the cast, not in the data type on the left side of the assignment. For example, even if we tried unboxing an int to a long, where no data loss can occur, as in:

```
long w = (long)xBox;    // Runtime error
```

we will still get a runtime error. It *is* acceptable to unbox xBox to an int and then assign the result to a long, since this just uses C#'s built-in implicit casting rules to convert one data type to a more general one:

```
long w = (int)xBox;    // No error
```

6.14 ■ Structs and inheritance

A C# struct, as we saw in Chapter 4, is a value data type. Although a struct implicitly inherits object in the same way that primitive data types do, no other inheritance is permitted with structs. We cannot derive a struct from another struct or from a class, so we cannot use polymorphism with a struct as a base class.

The fact that a struct implicitly inherits object does allow us to override any virtual method in object. The two most useful methods to override are probably ToString() and Equals() as we did for classes above. The syntax for overriding methods in a struct is the same as with a class.

A struct can be boxed and unboxed in the same way as a primitive value type (since primitive data types are just structs anyway), and the same cautions apply – be sure to unbox a boxed struct back into the same data type it came from originally.

As a simple example of a boxed struct consider the following code:

```
public struct BoxStruct
{
  public int a, b;

  public BoxStruct(int initA, int initB)
  {
    a = initA;
    b = initB;
  }

  public override string ToString()
  {
    return "a = " + a + "; b = " + b;
  }
}

public class BoxingDemo
{
  public static void Main(string[] args)
  {
    BoxStruct box = new BoxStruct(4, 5);
    object boxObj = box;
    Console.WriteLine(boxObj.ToString());
  }
}
```

The `BoxStruct` shows an example of an overridden `ToString()` method. A `BoxStruct` is declared in `Main()`, then converted to an `object`. The last line of `Main()` calls the `ToString()` by using the boxed object rather than the original `struct`. This produces the output:

```
a = 4; b = 5
```

because `ToString()` in `object` is a virtual method, so the overridden version is called.

However, if we attempted to refer to `boxObj.a` or `boxObj.b`, this would produce a compiler error even though these fields are public, since the compiler sees `boxObj` as an `object`, not a `BoxStruct`, and `object` does not have data fields named `a` or `b`. To access these data fields starting from `boxObj`, we need to unbox it back to a `BoxStruct`:

```
BoxStruct unboxed = (BoxStruct)boxObj;
Console.WriteLine("unboxed.a = " + unboxed.a);
```

Finally, note that the boxing operation when applied to a `struct` also produces a copy of the original `struct` and not just a new reference to the original `struct`. This means that any changes to the original `struct` after boxing it will not affect the boxed copy. Consider the code:

```
BoxStruct box = new BoxStruct(4, 5);
object boxObj = box;
box.a = 45;
box.b = 97;
Console.WriteLine("boxObj: " + boxObj.ToString());
Console.WriteLine("box: " + box.ToString());
```

The output is:

```
boxObj: a = 4; b = 5
box: a = 45; b = 97
```

Changing the values of a and b in box did not affect the the data fields in boxObj.

6.15 ■ The is operator

One problem with polymorphism is that it is sometimes not obvious what data type a reference variable refers to. For example, if we declare the variable

```
Person me;
```

then by the rules of polymorphism, me can refer to a Person or to any class, such as Student, that inherits Person, and we can change what me refers to dynamically as a program runs. We cannot, therefore, tell what type of object is referred to by me just by looking at its declaration.

It is sometimes important to know the type of object to which a reference refers. For example, suppose we add a method to Student that is not present in the Person base class, such as getID() to retrieve the studentID field:

```
public string getID()
{
   return studentID;
}
```

Since this method exists only in the derived class, we can call it only if we are sure that the object is a Student and not a Person. When we use polymorphism to create the Student, we can say something like this:

```
Person kevin = new Student("Kevin", 19, "00121212");
string kevinID = ((Student)kevin).getID();
```

Note that we need to be sure that kevin refers to a Student before we can be sure that the second line will run without errors.

The is operator provides an easy way of determining whether a given variable is compatible with a particular data type. To avoid any possibility of error in the previous example, we can say:

```
Person kevin = new Student("Kevin", 19, "00121212");
if (kevin is Student)
```

```
{
   string kevinID = ((Student)kevin).getID();
}
```

The is operator tests to see if its left operand is an instance of the data type given as its right operand, and returns a boolean value with the result. It will also return true if the data type of the object on the left is derived from the data type on the right, so that in the above example, the expression kevin is Person would also return true. The is operator is therefore equivalent to Java's instanceof operator.

In other words, is may be used to determine if the variable on the left is compatible with the data type on the right. The is operator will also work with value types. For example:

```
int x = 42;
Console.WriteLine("int is int: " + (x is int));
Console.WriteLine("int is byte: " + (x is byte));
Console.WriteLine("int is long: " + (x is long));
```

produces the output:

```
int is int: True
int is byte: False
int is long: False
```

This shows that is will not implement any implicit casts between value types. Even though an int can be implicitly converted to a long, the expression x is long will always return false if x is an int. Similarly, is reports false for a comparison of an int with a byte.

The is operator will apply boxing and unboxing if required to convert one type into another. For example:

```
int x = 42;
object xObj = x;
Console.WriteLine("boxed int is int: " + (xObj is int));
```

produces the output:

```
boxed int is int: True
```

The is operator detects that if the object xObj is unboxed, it will produce an int, and therefore returns true.

6.16 ■ The as operator

The keyword as can cast an object or value into a *reference* data type under certain conditions. These conditions are fairly restrictive, so as is not all that useful. We will not go into the details of the operator here, since the full set of rules under which as can be used are fairly complex. However, we will give a simple example to show how it might be used.

```
object [] asTest = new object[6];
asTest[0] = "a string";
asTest[1] = "number: " + 34;
asTest[2] = "hello";
asTest[3] = 123;
asTest[4] = 123.4;
asTest[5] = null;

for (int i=0; i < asTest.Length; i++)
{
   string s = asTest[i] as string;
   if (s != null)
      Console.WriteLine ("Element " + i + ": '" + s + "'" );
   else
      Console.WriteLine ("Element " + i +
         ":  is not a string" );
}
```

We declare an array of `object`s and initialize the elements of the array to various data types. Elements 0 through 2 are initialized to `string`s, elements 3 and 4 are initialized with numbers that are converted to `object`s via boxing, and element 5 is set to `null`.

Inside the `for` loop, we use `as` to attempt to convert each element of the array to a `string`. If such a conversion is possible, `as` will perform the operation just like an explicit cast. If the conversion is not possible, `as` returns `null`. We can therefore test the `string` `s` to see if it is `null`. If not, we have a valid `string` which can then be printed out. Otherwise, we print a message that that element is not a string.

The output from this code is:

```
Element 0: 'a string'
Element 1: 'number: 34'
Element 2: 'hello'
Element 3:  is not a string
Element 4:  is not a string
Element 5:  is not a string
```

The `as` operator can cope with conversions to and from `object` but the number of other applications is fairly limited, and most of its features can be duplicated by ordinary implicit or explicit casts and boxing.

6.17 ■ Sealed classes and methods

C# provides the `sealed` keyword which may be used in two main ways. First, an entire class can be declared as `sealed` in order to prevent that class from being inherited. This is equivalent to declaring a class in Java as `final`. For example, if we decided that the `Student` class that we have used for several examples in this chapter should not be inherited, we can declare it as `sealed`:

```
public sealed class Student : Person
{
  // data and methods
}
```

Why would we want to prevent a class from being inherited? The main reason is security. Many classes that are part of the System namespace are vital to the proper running of .NET. If a programmer could inherit these classes, they may be able to override some of the methods in them to break into secure areas of a computer system.

A classic example is the String class (both in C# and Java) which is used in many critical areas of the virtual machine that runs programs. String in C# is a sealed class to prevent programmers from inheriting it and overriding some of its methods. If it were possible, for example, to create a derived class MyString, we could use polymorphism to pass a MyString object to any method in any class that expected a String. If we had enough knowledge of a program and the data it accessed, some of these overrides could be written to access 'secure' data.

If we still wish to allow users to inherit a class we have written, but wish to prevent particular methods in that class from being overridden, we have the option of sealing only those methods rather than the entire class. Java also allows particular methods within a class to be declared as final even if the class as a whole is not final.

Only an override of a method that is declared as virtual in the base class can be sealed, as opposed to Java, where *any* method can be declared as final. The restriction of sealed to overridden methods in C# makes sense, since if we wish to prevent a method in the base class from being overridden, we simply do not declare it to be virtual in the first place. In Java, all methods are implicitly virtual, and therefore could be overridden if we did not declare them as final.

As an example, suppose we wished to allow the Student class to be inherited, but wished to prevent the ToString() method in Student from being overridden in any class derived from Student. We add the sealed keyword to the definition of ToString() in the Student class:

```
public sealed override string ToString()
{
  return "Name: " + Name + "; Age = " + Age +
    "; ID: " + studentID;
}
```

When applied to a method, sealed must always appear in conjunction with override.

Suppose we now define a new class called FirstYearStudent which inherits Student. Attempting to define an override of ToString() produces a compiler error, but it is still possible to add a new version of ToString() to FirstYearStudent, since this version hides, rather than overrides, ToString() in Student:

```
public class FirstYearStudent : Student
{
  public new string ToString()
  {
    // code goes here
  }
}
```

This will not cause security problems, since even if we use polymorphism to create a `FirstYearStudent` from a `Student` reference variable, calling `ToString()` will still call the version from `Student`, not `FirstYearStudent`. There is thus no way for a disreputable programmer to introduce an over-ridden `ToString()` method into existing code.

6.18 ■ Abstract classes

We have seen that the main idea behind inheritance is that common properties and methods can be extracted from a number of similar classes and stored in a common base class. In the case of `Person` and `Student`, both classes could represent real objects in the program. A `Person` is just someone who has no special properties (at least in the context of the program), and is someone about whom we wish to store only some basic information. A `Student` includes all the properties of a `Person`, but adds some more that are particular to being a student, such as an ID code.

In some cases, however, the properties stored in a base class may not be enough to specify a 'real' object. A somewhat overused, but still appropriate, example is that of geometric shapes. If we think of two-dimensional shapes in particular, they all have an area and a perimeter. However, specifying *just* the area and perimeter of a shape is not enough to say what kind of shape it is. It could be a rectangle, triangle, circle, and so on. It still makes sense to have a base class in this case, but it does *not* make sense to allow objects to be created from it.

C#, like Java, provides the *abstract class* for such a case. The rules for creating and using abstract classes are much the same in the two languages, but we shall review them here for completeness.

An abstract class cannot be used to create objects – that is, it is not possible to use the `new` operator with an abstract class. As such, the only possible role for an abstract class is as a base class in an inheritance relationship.

Methods within an abstract class may be normal methods, as found in an ordinary class, or they too may be abstract. If a method is declared abstract, it has no body – it consists of only a method declaration (the return type, name and parameter list, together with any other modifiers such as `public` or `override`) followed by a semi-colon. An abstract method *must* be over-ridden in any class that inherits the abstract class. Thus an abstract method is essentially the opposite of a sealed method – it forces the inheriting class to provide an implementation of it.

Abstract classes may themselves inherit other classes (either abstract or normal), and may override methods in these inherited classes.

Let us illustrate these ideas by defining TwoDimShape as an abstract base class for a number of two-dimensional shapes:

```
1.  public abstract class TwoDimShape
2.  {
3.      protected double area;
4.      protected double perimeter;
5.
6.      public abstract void CalcArea();
7.      public abstract void CalcPerimeter();
8.
9.      public override string ToString()
10.     {
11.         string info = "Area: " + area +
12.             "; Perimeter: " + perimeter + "\n";
13.         return info;
14.     }
15. }
```

An abstract class must include the abstract keyword in its definition (line 1). The class declares a couple of data fields (lines 3 and 4) to represent the area and perimeter of a general geometric shape.

Lines 6 and 7 define two abstract methods which will calculate the area and perimeter, respectively. Since these methods are declared abstract, they must be overridden in any class that inherits TwoDimShape.

The ToString() method shows that an abstract class can define non-abstract methods, and also that it can override methods from its base class. Abstract classes, like all classes in C#, also inherit the global object class, so they may override methods such as ToString(), just like any other class.

An abstract method, such as CalcArea() or CalcPerimeter(), is implicitly virtual, since it must be overridden in any derived class. Somewhat bizarrely, however, it is a syntax error to include the virtual keyword in an abstract method's declaration.

We can define a Rectangle class that inherits TwoDimShape:

```
1.  public class Rectangle : TwoDimShape
2.  {
3.      protected double length, width;
4.
5.      public Rectangle(double len, double wid)
6.      {
7.          length = len;
8.          width = wid;
9.          CalcArea();
10.         CalcPerimeter();
```

```
11.    }
12.
13.    public override void CalcArea()
14.    {
15.       area = length * width;
16.    }
17.
18.    public override void CalcPerimeter()
19.    {
20.       perimeter = 2 * (length + width);
21.    }
22.
23.    public override string ToString()
24.    {
25.       string info = "Length: " + length +
26.          "; Width: " + width + "\n";
27.       info += base.ToString();
28.       return info;
29.    }
30. }
```

This class inherits area and perimeter, and adds length and width (line 3). The constructor (lines 5 to 11) requires initial values for length and width and then calls CalcArea() and CalcPerimeter() to calculate area and perimeter. These methods are defined on lines 13 to 21, and are required in Rectangle since they were declared as abstract in the base class TwoDimShape. Not only must these methods be present, but they *must* be declared as override methods – we cannot attempt to hide the abstract methods in the base class.

Finally, we provide an override of ToString() (lines 23 to 29). On line 27, we use the ToString() method defined in TwoDimShape, illustrating that non-abstract methods defined within abstract classes are still accessible in the normal way.

To use Rectangle, we can create a third class which declares a Rectangle object and calls its ToString() method:

```
public class MainClass
{
   public static void Main(string[] args)
   {
      Rectangle shape = new Rectangle(3, 4);
      Console.WriteLine(shape.ToString());
   }
}
```

The output from this code is:

```
Length: 3; Width: 4
Area: 12; Perimeter: 14
```

One final note about abstract classes. Although we cannot create an object directly from an abstract class using the `new` operator, as in:

```
TwoDimShape shape = new TwoDimShape();    // Not allowed
```

we *can* declare a *reference* to an abstract class and then use polymorphism to assign this reference to an object from a derived class. In other words, we could have written the `Main()` method above as:

```
public class MainClass
{
   public static void Main(string[] args)
   {
      TwoDimShape shape = new Rectangle(3, 4);
      Console.WriteLine(shape.ToString());
   }
}
```

This means that all the advantages of using polymorphism that were discussed earlier in this chapter can be gained by using references to abstract classes as well as to ordinary base classes. In particular, we can define methods that take references to abstract classes as parameters.

6.19 ■ Interfaces

Interfaces are similar to, but more restrictive than abstract classes. Like an abstract class, an interface must be implemented (inherited) by a regular class in order to be used. However, unlike an abstract class, an interface may not contain any data fields or 'regular' methods. Any method declared in an interface is essentially abstract, in that we are not allowed to add any code body to it, although the `abstract` keyword is not attached to the method declaration.

Java programmers who have done any programming involving event handlers will be familiar with interfaces in Java. All events in Java are handled by means of implementing *listener* interfaces. Each listener defines one or more methods which must be implemented by the class that implements the interface. The `ActionListener` that is used to respond to `ActionEvents`, such as those generated by pressing a `JButton`, contains a single method called `actionPerformed()` which is called when the event is received. Code for handling the `ActionEvent` is placed within this method.

Although events are handled differently in C#, the interface concept is much the same in C# as in Java, so any experience in dealing with Java interfaces should serve the programmer well in C#.

Interfaces are treated somewhat differently than classes in object-oriented design. Whereas class inheritance should always be based on the 'is a type of' relationship between derived and base classes, an interface is usually used to define one or more methods that are used by a number of different classes. As such, an interface does not normally represent an 'object' within the design in the same way that a class does.

As an example, let us add an interface to the geometry example we used in the section on abstract classes. This interface will provide two methods which allow different types of information on the geometric shapes to be generated as strings.

```
public interface IShapeInfo
{
   string DimensionInfo();
   string ShapeInfo();
}
```

The `DimensionInfo()` method will generate as a string the dimensions of the particular shape – in the case of the `Rectangle`, it will display `length` and `width`. Similary, `ShapeInfo()` will display `area` and `perimeter`.

Note that we have given the interface a name beginning with an upper-case 'I'. Although an interface can be given any alphanumeric string (that does not begin with a number) just like a class, it is conventional to begin interface names with 'I' to distinguish them from classes.

We will demonstrate the use of `IShapeInfo` first by having the `Rectangle` class implement it directly:

```
public class Rectangle : TwoDimShape, IShapeInfo
{
   // Other fields and methods as in previous example

   public string DimensionInfo()
   {
      return "Length: " + length + "; Width: " + width + "\n";
   }

   public string ShapeInfo()
   {
      return base.ToString();
   }
}
```

The `Rectangle` class now inherits the abstract class `TwoDimShape` defined in the last section, and it also implements the `IShapeInfo` interface. Note that, unlike Java, C# makes no distinction between *inheriting* a class and *implementing* an interface – both the class and the interface are listed together within the same list. In Java, we would need to use `extends` to indicate class inheritance and `implements` to indicate interface implementation.

Like Java, however, once we state that we are implementing an interface, we must provide implementations for all methods declared in the interface. We have therefore added definitions for `DimensionInfo()` and `ShapeInfo()` to the `Rectangle` class, as shown. Although no access modifier was specified for these methods in the interface definition, whenever an interface method is implemented in a class, the method *must* be declared `public`. Note, however, that the methods in `Rectangle` are *not* declared as `override`, even though it may appear that we are overriding their declarations in `IShapeInfo`. In fact, implementing a method that is declared in an interface is not considered to be an override, and the use of `override` in the method definition is an error.

To illustrate how the interface can be used in practice, we will modify `MainClass` from our earlier example:

```
public class MainClass
{
   public static void PrintInfo(IShapeInfo shape)
   {
      Console.WriteLine(shape.DimensionInfo());
      Console.WriteLine(shape.ShapeInfo());
   }

   public static void Main(string[] args)
   {
      Rectangle shape = new Rectangle(3, 4);
      PrintInfo(shape);
   }
}
```

We have added a `PrintInfo()` method that takes an `IShapeInfo` parameter, illustrating that interfaces, like abstract classes, may be used to define reference variables even though they cannot be used to create objects on their own. This means that `PrintInfo()` can accept any object that is an instance of a class that implements the `IShapeInfo` interface. The output of this code is:

```
Length: 3; Width: 4

Area: 12; Perimeter: 14
```

Note that the `shape` parameter within `PrintInfo()` can refer only to those methods declared within `IShapeInfo`. In particular, attempting to call methods that are defined only in `Rectangle` or in `TwoDimShape` but not in `IShapeInfo` will *not* work. For example:

```
public static void PrintInfo(IShapeInfo shape)
{
   Console.WriteLine(shape.DimensionInfo());
   shape.CalcPerimeter();     // Error: can't call this
   Console.WriteLine(shape.ShapeInfo());
}
```

The call to `CalcPerimeter()` will generate a compiler error since this method is not declared in `IShapeInfo`, even though it is declared in `Rectangle`'s other base class, `TwoDimShape`. To access `CalcPerimeter()` from within `PrintInfo()` we would need to change the offending line to:

```
((TwoDimShape)shape).CalcPerimeter();
```

or

```
((Rectangle)shape).CalcPerimeter();
```

That is, we need to provide an explicit cast to either `TwoDimShape` or `Rectangle`.

As a second example of interface implementation, we can shift the implementation of `IShapeInfo` from `Rectangle` to its abstract base class `TwoDimShape`. We change the definition of `TwoDimShape` from its form in the last section to this new version:

```
public abstract class TwoDimShape : IShapeInfo
{
   protected double area;
   protected double perimeter;

   public abstract void CalcArea();
   public abstract void CalcPerimeter();
   public abstract string DimensionInfo();
   public abstract string ShapeInfo();

   public override string ToString()
   {
      string info = "Area: " + area +
         "; Perimeter: " + perimeter + "\n";
      return info;
   }
}
```

Since we don't have enough information in `TwoDimShape` to write a body for `DimensionInfo()` (since it depends on the dimensions defined for a particular shape), it is legal for an abstract class to 'implement' an interface method by declaring that method as an `abstract` method. In effect, we are passing the buck from the abstract class along to whatever normal class inherits the abstract class.

Making this change requires a couple of modifications to `Rectangle`. Instead of the version given earlier in this section, we now use the following:

```
public class Rectangle : TwoDimShape
{
   // Other fields and methods as in previous example
```

```
public override string DimensionInfo()
{
  return "Length: " + length + "; Width: " + width + "\n";
}

public override string ShapeInfo()
{
  return base.ToString();
}
}
```

We have dropped IShapeInfo from the list of inherited classes and interfaces in the first line. The other change is that we have now declared DimensionInfo() and ShapeInfo() as override, since these two methods are now overriding the declarations in the abstract base class, rather than the original versions in the interface.

In case you are feeling somewhat confused by these rules (when to use override, when methods should be declared public, and so on), you should feel reassured that the C# compiler is very helpful with its error messages if you do get something wrong, so it is usually very easy to correct the mistake.

The code given earlier in MainClass will work for this new version without any changes.

6.20 ■ Case study: the adventure game

Now that we have an understanding of inheritance, we are in a position to expand our adventure game case study considerably. In this section, we will introduce a number of derived classes to represent specialized objects that may appear in the game.

We will also take this opportunity to add a number of new commands to the game and in the process produce a game with enough interest to be playable. The amount of code that has been added at this stage is considerable, so it is best to begin with an overview of the structure of the game in this new version.

6.20.1 □ Using inheritance

The last version of the game (section 5.12) contained only four classes. The Item class allowed objects to be placed in rooms or in the player's backpack, the Room class allowed rooms to be created, the Player class represented the user's character in the game and the Adventure class started things off by creating all the objects and then kept things going by parsing the input commands.

'Real' adventure games (that is, those you can buy from computer software shops) have considerably more variety than this. In particular, these games usually contain several types of items, different types of rooms, and many varieties of creatures, some of which are friendly and others that will attack you.

These commercial games are the products of many people working over many months or years, so we obviously can't expect to approach the richness and variety of these games in a relatively simple case study in this book. However, we can get some inspiration from these commercial games and try to capture their spirit in our modest offering here.

We'll begin with a summary of the new features that are to be added to the game. First, we'll introduce a number of new item types that allow specialized items to be included. We've taken these types from the traditional 'sword and sorcery' type of adventure game.

The specialized types are:

- food: eating food boosts the player's energy;
- weapon: the player may wield a weapon to boost combat performance;
- armour: wearing armour protects the player from enemy attack;
- potion: quaffing a potion bestows extra abilities on the player for a limited time;
- ring: wearing a ring also bestows special abilities for as long as the ring is worn;
- wand: magic wands can be zapped at enemies.

Each of these item types represents a distinct concept in the game, and therefore each type is a good candidate for a separate class. However, it should be clear that all these item types have properties such as weight and a description in common, so they can all be viewed as specialized types of the Item class. It makes sense, therefore, to use Item as a base class for all these classes.

However, if we think about these items in a bit more depth, we might also recognize that potions, rings and wands are magical, while food, weapons and armour are not. (In many adventure games, of course, weapons and armour can have magical properties, but to keep things simple, we are not going to use magic weapons or armour here.) We might therefore create a class called MagicItem as a base class for the three magic item types. MagicItem would itself inherit Item, but since there are no direct instances of a MagicItem in the game, we can declare it as an abstract class.

The decision to make MagicItem abstract implies that all magic items will have classes of their own that derive from MagicItem. In the current design of the program, this is true, since we are considering only potions, rings and wands, but in a future expansion of the game, we might introduce unique types of magic item. By making MagicItem abstract, we are imposing the condition on all extensions of the game that any future types of magic item we add must have new classes created for them. This probably wouldn't be a major consideration, but it is worth noting that design decisions always have knock-on effects for future versions of the software.

The inheritance diagram in Figure 6.1 illustrates how these item classes relate to each other. We'll consider the details of these specialized classes below – for now, the main point is that they do fit together nicely using an inheritance relationship.

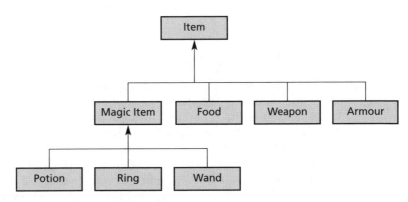

Figure 6.1 Inheritance diagram for the adventure game

Having weapons and armour isn't much use unless there are things to fight, so we need to introduce some opponents for the player's character. In line with most fantasy adventures, we will call these opponents *monsters*. The system of combat involves the player fighting a monster with both combatants trying to reduce the energy points of their opponent to zero. Clearly, players and monsters share a number of properties, so it is natural to ask if some sort of inheritance would be appropriate here as well.

In a richer version of an adventure game, there would be a number of different types of monsters, so we could build up an inheritance hierarchy for characters in the game similar to that for items. To keep the game manageable, however, we will consider all monsters to be of the same general type (that is, although monsters can have different names, they all have the same types of abilities). The player will have all the abilities of the monsters (though probably not to the same degree), but will also have some extra properties, such as the ability to wear armour, wield a weapon and use magic items.

It therefore makes sense to define a base class called Character which will be used on its own to create instances of monsters, and a derived class called Player which inherits Character and adds the special properties and abilities of the player.

We could also extend the game's class model by defining special types of locations and create an inheritance hierarchy here too, but hopefully by now you are getting the idea of how inheritance is being used, so we will simply define all the locations in the game to be of the same type. However, if you want to extend the game yourself by defining your own location classes, it is a good exercise in using inheritance.

The final list of classes is therefore:

- Adventure: class containing Main() and containing the initialization and command-handling code;
- Room: used for creating all locations in the game;
- Character: used for creating all types of monsters, and also as a base class for Player;
- Player: inherits Character and is used to create the main player character;
- Item: base class for all item types;
- Food: inherits Item, used for food objects;
- Weapon: inherits Item, used for non-magical weapons;
- Armour: inherits Item, used for non-magical armour;
- MagicItem: abstract class that inherits Item; base class for all magic item types;
- Potion: inherits MagicItem; represents potions that can be quaffed;
- Ring: inherits MagicItem; represents rings that can be worn;
- Wand: inherits MagicItem; represents wands that can be zapped in combat.

The contents of these classes are most easily shown on a diagram (Figure 6.2). Professional object-oriented designs are drawn using UML (Universal Modelling Language). Although we are not assuming a knowledge of UML on the part of the reader, we can use a simplified version of UML to display the class relationships, since the diagram is quite easy to understand.

In Figure 6.2, each class is represented as a box with two compartments. The top compartment shows the name of the class and the lower compartment shows the properties of the class that can be represented by primitive data types such as int or string. Thus the Player class contains three primitive properties called MaxCarry, CarryWeight and PotionTime (which will be explained below).

The lines connecting a pair of classes indicate that one class contains one or more instances of the other class as properties. The numbers at the ends of each line indicate how many instances of that class are involved. For example, the line joining Adventure with Player indicates that one instance of Adventure contains one Player (since there is a 1 at each end of the line). The line joining Adventure and Room shows that one Adventure contains '1 to n' Locations, that is, that it contains at least one and possibly many Locations. The line with the arrowhead connecting Player with Character indicates the inheritance relationship as described earlier.

The relations shown in the diagram can be summarized by saying that an instance of Adventure contains one Player and a number of Locations. The Player is associated with a single Room (that is, the player can only be in one place at a time) and may carry a number of Items (and by extension, other item types derived from Item). The '0..n' on the link between Player and Item indicates that a player may be carrying any number (including zero) of items.

Similarly, a Room is associated with one Player, and may also contain a number of Items.

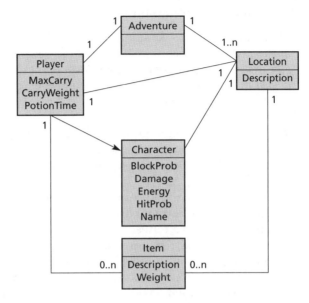

Figure 6.2 Relationships between classes in the adventure game

The specialized item types derived from Item have not been shown on the diagram to avoid clutter. However, we can summarize these relations as follows.

The specialized item types apply only to a Player, and a Player is allowed the following:

- A single Weapon may be wielded. Wielding another Weapon replaces the existing Weapon with the new one. The currently wielded Weapon becomes the WieldedWeapon field in Player.
- A single Armour may be worn. Wearing another Armour replaces the current one. The currently worn Armour becomes the WornArmour field in Player.
- A single Potion may be quaffed, with this Potion then becoming the QuaffedPotion for the Player. No further Potion may be quaffed until the QuaffedPotion wears off. The PotionTime field in Player keeps track of how many turns remain in the current QuaffedPotion.
- A single Ring may be worn (using the 'adorn' command), and becomes the WornRing field of Player. The 'unadorn' command removes the Ring.

There are no 'unwield' or 'unwear' commands for weapons or armour, since it is assumed that the player will always want to wield a weapon and wear armour. An 'unadorn' command is provided for rings, since it can be useful to remove the effects of all rings at times.

Other specialized types such as Food and Wand may be eaten or zapped, respectively, but otherwise have no special relation with a Player.

6.20.2 ☐ **Adding new commands**

In addition to the look, status, take, drop and move commands that were in the previous version, we'll now add in several more commands that will give the game a good set of actions. Most of these commands have been mentioned in passing while discussing the new classes above, but we'll summarize them here for reference:

- ■ wield <weapon>: requires a Weapon as a parameter, and either wields a weapon for the first time when the command is first used, or replaces the existing weapon with a new one. The old weapon is put into the player's backpack.
- ■ wear <armour>: requires an Armour as a parameter and, as with wield, either puts on armour the first time it is used, or replaces existing armour. In the latter case, the old armour is put into the backpack.
- ■ quaff <potion>: requires a Potion parameter. The player can only quaff a potion if no other potion is currently in effect. A potion has a duration parameter that specifies how many turns its effects last. Once an existing potion has worn off, a new one can be quaffed.
- ■ eat <food>: requires a Food parameter. Eating food increases the player's energy by an amount that depends on the food. The player can eat as much food as desired – there is no upper limit to the amount of energy a player can have.
- ■ adorn <ring>: requires a Ring parameter. The player can wear only one ring at a time. The previous ring must be removed with unadorn before a new ring can be put on. A ring can affect several of the player's properties – the details depend on the ring.
- ■ unadorn: no parameters. Removes a ring, if one is being worn. The effects of the ring cease once it is removed.
- ■ zap <wand>: requires a Wand parameter. The player need only have the wand in the backpack in order to zap it – it does not need to be wielded or held. The effect of a wand is usually to inflict damage on an opponent. A wand has a limited number of charges. Each time the wand is zapped, it loses one charge. When the number of charges reaches zero, the wand crumbles into dust. A wand may be zapped in a room without a monster, but this still uses up a charge.
- ■ attack: no parameters. If the player is in a room with a monster, the player attacks the monster. The results of an attack depend on the statistics of the player and monster (see the rules of combat below).

The commands are all handled, as before, in Adventure, although numerous method calls to the other classes are made. We will consider the details when we present the code below.

6.20.3 ☐ **Rules of combat**

Adventure games have many different rules for running combat sequences. Most of the later games use real-time combat, in which the player and the opponents attack each other at the same time. Many older (and some modern) games use a *turn-based* system in which each opponent in combat takes turns, similar to a game of chess. The turn-based system is considerably easier to program, so we'll use it for our case study.

The combat turns are based on commands given by the player. Passive commands such as 'look' or 'status' are not considered to use up any time and do not count as combat turns, so the monster does not get an extra chance to attack the player after a 'look'. Similarly, if the user enters an invalid command, either by typing in something that is not recognized or by attempting an illegal operation such as 'eat sword', this does not count as a combat turn.

A monster is given an attack on the player at the end of each turn in which the player remains in the same location as the monster, and where the player does something that counts as a time-consuming turn. This means that entering the room containing the monster gives the monster the first attack on the player. After this, if the player remains in the same room and gives commands like 'take', 'drop', 'wield' and so on, the monster will get an attack after each of these commands. The best option for the player, of course, is to 'attack' and try to defeat the monster.

If the player's energy is getting low (remember a free check can always be made by using 'status'), the best option is simply to move to a different location, since the monster will not get a free attack on the player if the player leaves the room.

When an attack is made by either side, we need to determine if the attacker hits the opponent and, if so, how much damage is done. Again, every adventure game seems to have its own rules for working this out, so we will use a fairly simple system.

The `Character` class contains properties related to combat as follows:

- `HitProb`: the probability that the attacker scores a 'hit' on the opponent. This is determined partly by the type of attacker (different monsters can have different `HitProb`s) and, for the player, partly by the weapon being wielded and by any magic items that may be in effect. For example, using a sword instead of your bare fists will increase your `HitProb` by an amount given in the `Weapon` object that represents the sword. Some potions and rings can change `HitProb` as well.
- `BlockProb`: the probability that the defender successfully blocks an attack. The blocking probability depends on such things as the armour being worn and also on the innate ability of the character to dodge or deflect an attack. Some magic items can also change `BlockProb`. For example, wearing a ring of invisibility increases your `BlockProb` since an invisible target is much harder to hit.

Both `HitProb` and `BlockProb` are expressed as percentages. They are combined to determine if an attack succeeds by using the formula:

```
ProbSuccess = HitProb(A) * (100 - BlockProb(D)) / 100
```

where `HitProb(A)` is the `HitProb` for the attacker and `BlockProb(D)` is `BlockProb` for the defender.

The logic behind this formula is that in order for an attack to succeed, the attacker must make a successful hit (given by `HitProb`) *and* the hit must get through the defender's defence. Since `BlockProb` is the probability that the defender is able to block the attack, `100 - BlockProb` is the probability that a hit is *not* blocked.

For example, if the attacker has a `HitProb` of 50 and the defender has a `BlockProb` of 70, then `ProbSuccess` is 50 * 30 / 100 = 15, meaning that for this particular attacker and defender, only 15 per cent of the attacks will be successful.

This technique may seem a little involved, but we need a way of taking into account both the weapon and combat skills of the attacker and defensive skills of the opponent.

The `Character` class also contains a `Damage` property, which is the maximum damage that can be inflicted in a successful attack. The actual amount of damage done is chosen randomly from one energy point up to `Damage` points.

We have now covered the basics of the design of the adventure game, so we can have a look at the code. This program is by far the largest we have considered so far in this book, so we will need to take it in stages.

6.20.4 ☐ `Item` classes

First, we'll consider the inheritance hierarchy for the various item types. The `Item` class remains virtually unchanged from the previous version in Chapter 5, but we reproduce it here for convenience.

```
1. public class Item
2. {
3.    protected string description;
4.    protected int weight;
5.
6.    public Item()
7.    {
8.       description = "";
9.       weight = 0;
10.   }
11.
12.   public Item(string description, int weight)
13.   {
14.      Description = description;
```

```
15.       Weight = weight;
16.    }
17.
18.    public string Description
19.    {
20.       get
21.       { return description; }
22.       set
23.       { description =  value; }
24.    }
25.
26.    public int Weight
27.    {
28.       get
29.       { return weight; }
30.       set
31.       { weight = value; }
32.    }
33.
34.    public override string ToString()
35.    {
36.       string itemInfo = description;
37.       itemInfo += ": (" + weight + ")";
38.       return itemInfo;
39.    }
40.
41.    public bool MatchesDescription(string itemDesc)
42.    {
43.       string thisLower = this.Description.ToLower();
44.       string otherLower = itemDesc.ToLower();
45.       if (thisLower.IndexOf(otherLower) != -1)
46.          return true;
47.       return false;
48.    }
49. }
```

The Item class represents the main style that is used for all the classes that inherit it. The data fields are now declared as protected instead of private, since this class will serve as a base class and we want these data fields to be inherited. A zero-parameter constructor is provided (line 6), which allows derived classes to define their own constructors that do not explicitly call the base class constructor using the base() keyword. If this constructor were not defined, we would need to include an explicit call to the other constructor on line 12 in all derived-class constructors.

In this and the other item-derived classes, we provide C# properties for all the data fields (lines 18 to 32). In most cases, these properties simply return the data field for the get operation and set the field to value for set. In a few cases, we will perform some checks on the value before assigning it to the data field. All basic properties in which the field value is simply returned or assigned without any other checks being made have essentially the same simple form, so in later classes we will omit these properties to save space. The complete code is, as usual, available from the book's web site.

Most classes in the adventure game also have an override version of ToString() (line 34). Since we are still dealing with a text-only program, these methods are used to construct the string that is to be printed whenever a description of the object is required.

The final method in Item is MatchesDescription() (line 41), which performs a case-insensitive search for the input string itemDesc within the Description property. This method is used in commands such as 'take' and 'drop', as we described in Chapter 5.

Referring back to the inheritance diagram for the item classes above, we see that there are three non-abstract classes that inherit Item directly: Armour, Food and Weapon. These three classes are all fairly similar in style to Item.

The Armour class is:

```
public class Armour : Item
{
   protected int blockProb;

   public Armour()
   {
      blockProb = 0;
   }

   public Armour(string description, int weight) :
      base(description, weight)
   {
      blockProb = 0;
   }

   public int BlockProb
   {
      get
      { return blockProb; }
      set
      { blockProb = value; }
   }
}
```

The first line indicates that Armour inherits Item and therefore inherits Item's Description and Weight properties (and their underlying data fields). Actually, it is worth pointing out that even if we had declared Item's two fields as private instead of protected, Armour could still effectively

inherit them provided that `Item` contained the two public properties
`Description` and `Weight` that provide a link to the private data fields. This
is not a particularly good design practice, however, since if we really do want
`Armour` to inherit `Item`'s data fields, we should specify that directly by making these fields `protected` in `Item` as we have done here.

   `Armour` adds a new field called `blockProb` which is the probability of that
armour blocking an opponent's attack. We are interpreting `blockProb` as the
difference to the player's overall blocking probability that wearing the
armour will make. That is, if the player has an innate blocking probability of,
say, 25 per cent and some armour has a `blockProb` of 30, then wearing the
armour will give the player an overall blocking probability of 55 per cent

   The accessibility of `blockProb` is set to `protected` which allows any
classes that inherit `Armour` to access it. Although we do not derive any classes from `Armour` in this version of the adventure game, it is easy to envision
a more advanced version with specialized armour types (such as shields,
suits of mail, helmets, gloves, boots and so on) which could be implemented as descendents of `Armour`.

   `Armour` provides two constructors, the second of which makes an explicit
call to `Item`'s two-parameter constructor using `base()`. Note that we have
opted to allow only the description and weight of the armour to be set through
the constructor. Setting `blockProb` requires using the `BlockProb` property.
This is not an essential feature of the class – we could certainly have added an
extra parameter to the `Armour` constructor to allow `blockProb` to be initialized there. However, it is sometimes better to require the programmer to set
field values explicitly using properties since this requires the actual name of
the property to appear in the code, rather than a string of bare numbers in a
constructor call. Many of the .NET library classes take this approach and provide only a zero-parameter constructor (although many others do provide several overloaded versions of the constructor). It is largely a matter of personal
programming style.

   The `Food` class is similar to `Armour`:

```
public class Food : Item
{
   protected int energy;

   public Food()
   {
      Energy = 0;
   }

   public Food(string description, int weight) :
      base(description, weight)
   {
      Energy = 0;
   }
```

```
public int Energy
{
   get
   { return energy; }
   set
   { energy = value; }
}
}
```

The `energy` represents the gain to a player's energy when the food is eaten using the 'eat' command. Otherwise, the structure of the class is the same as that of `Armour`.

The last direct descendant of `Item` is `Weapon`:

```
public class Weapon : Item
{
   protected int damage;
   protected int hitProb;

   public Weapon()
   {
      Damage = 0;
      HitProb = 0;
   }

   public Weapon(string description, int weight) :
      base(description, weight)
   {
      Damage = 0;
      HitProb = 0;
   }

   public int Damage
   {
      get
      { return damage; }
      set
      { damage = value; }
   }

   public int HitProb
   {
      get
      { return hitProb; }
      set
      { hitProb = value; }
   }
}
```

The damage field specifies the additional *maximum* damage that can be done with a successful hit using this weapon. The damage field from Weapon is added to the current damage value in the player's statistics to determine the overall maximum damage that can be inflicted from a single hit. In practice, if the player is wielding the weapon and makes a hit, the damage is determined by choosing a random number between 1 and the damage value in the *player* object, not the weapon object.

The hitProb field is the *difference* to the player's hit probability that is made by wielding this weapon. As with blockProb in Armour, the hitProb of a Weapon is added to that of the player when the weapon is wielded.

The fourth class that inherits Item directly is the abstract MagicItem class, which serves as the base class for magic item types such as potions, rings and wands. Its definition is:

```
public abstract class MagicItem : Item
{
   protected int hitProb, blockProb, energy, damage;

   public MagicItem()
   {
      HitProb = 0;
      BlockProb = 0;
      Energy = 0;
      Damage = 0;
   }

   public MagicItem(string description, int weight) :
      base(description, weight)
   {
      HitProb = 0;
      BlockProb = 0;
      Energy = 0;
      Damage = 0;
   }

   public int HitProb
   {
      get
      { return hitProb; }
      set
      { hitProb = value; }
   }

   public int BlockProb
   {
      get
      { return blockProb; }
```

```
      set
      { blockProb = value; }
   }

   public int Energy
   {
      get
      { return energy; }
      set
      { energy = value; }
   }

   public int Damage
   {
      get
      { return damage; }
      set
      { damage = value; }
   }
}
```

`MagicItem` declares four data fields: `hitProb`, `blockProb`, `energy` and `damage`. The method used for implementing a magic item of any type is to define its effect on each of these four parameters, even though the item itself might seem quite exotic. For example, a ring of invisibility will display a message such as 'You shimmer and disappear' when it is put on, but internally, its effect must be defined by giving values for each of these four parameters. In practice, its effect is implemented by giving a bonus to `blockProb`, since being invisible makes the player harder to hit. The other three parameters would be set to zero for this ring. Other magic item types have their effects defined in the same way.

The keyword `abstract` has been added to the declaration of this class, indicating that it does not represent any actual objects that will exist in the program. Rather, it serves as a base class that collects together a number of common properties from the classes that inherit it.

Making `MagicItem` abstract means that we cannot create any objects from it directly. However, we may still use polymorphism to declare a reference to a `MagicItem` and then set this reference to an object of any class that inherits `MagicItem`. We will see below that the `Potion`, `Ring` and `Wand` classes inherit `MagicItem` so it is legal to say, for example:

```
MagicItem magItem1 = new Potion();
```

The `Potion` class describes the effects of a potion:

```
public class Potion : MagicItem
{
   protected int duration;
   protected string quaffString;
```

```csharp
protected string wearOffString;

public Potion()
{
   Duration = 0;
   QuaffString = "";
   WearOffString = "";
}

public Potion(string description, int weight) :
   base(description, weight)
{
   Duration = 0;
   QuaffString = "";
   WearOffString = "";
}

public int Duration
{
   get
   { return duration; }
   set
   { duration = value; }
}

public string QuaffString
{
   get
   { return quaffString; }
   set
   { quaffString = value; }
}

public string WearOffString
{
   get
   { return wearOffString; }
   set
   { wearOffString = value; }
}
}
```

A potion is a magic drink which is contained in a small bottle or vial. To use it, the player issues the 'quaff' command which causes the potion to be drunk. The quaffString is printed on screen just after the quaff command is given, and will give some information on the effect of the potion. A potion will have an effect for a given number of turns, given by duration. When the potion wears off, the `wearOffString` is printed to let the player know that something has changed in their statistics (although it may not indicate that the change is due to the potion wearing off, but that's part of the mystery of playing the game).

The `Ring` class is similar:

```
public class Ring : MagicItem
{
    protected string adornString;
    protected string unadornString;

    public Ring()
    {
        AdornString = "";
        UnadornString = "";
    }

    public Ring(string description, int weight) :
        base(description, weight)
    {
        AdornString = "";
        UnadornString = "";
    }

    public string UnadornString
    {
        get
        { return unadornString; }
        set
        { unadornString = value; }
    }

    public string AdornString
    {
        get
        { return adornString; }
        set
        { adornString = value; }
    }
}
```

A `Ring` is put on using the 'adorn' command (to distinguish it from 'wear' which is used for armour). The `adornString` message is printed when the ring is put on, and `unadornString` when it is removed, using the 'unadorn' command. All the effects of a `Ring` are contained in the properties defined in the `MagicItem` class, so no new properties are needed.

Finally, the Wand class is:

```
public class Wand : MagicItem
{
   int charges;
   string zapString;

   public Wand()
   {
      Charges = 0;
      ZapString = "";
   }

   public Wand(string description, int weight) :
      base(description, weight)
   {
      Charges = 0;
      ZapString = "";
   }

   public int Charges
   {
      get
      { return charges; }
      set
      { charges = value; }
   }

   public string ZapString
   {
      get
      { return zapString; }
      set
      { zapString = value; }
   }
}
```

The wand can be zapped a limited number of times given by the charges field, after which it crumbles to dust and disappears from the player's inventory. Each time the wand is zapped, zapString is printed to the screen.

6.20.5 ☐ Character **classes**

The other use of inheritance in the adventure game is with the Character and Player classes. As described above, Character will serve as the class from which monsters are created, and also as a base class for Player. The Character class is formed from the earlier version of Player (that we used in Chapter 5) by separating out those features that are common to monsters and players.

```
1. using System.Collections;
2.
3. public class Character
4. {
5.    protected string name;
6.    protected ArrayList itemList;
7.    protected int hitProb;
8.    protected int blockProb;
9.    protected int energy;
10.   protected int damage;
11.
12.   public Character()
13.   {
14.     Name = "";
15.     itemList = null;
16.     InitializeFields();
17.   }
18.
19.   public Character(string name)
20.   {
21.     Name = name;
22.     itemList = new ArrayList();
23.     InitializeFields();
24.   }
25.
26.   private void InitializeFields()
27.   {
28.     Energy = 0;
29.     HitProb = 0;
30.     BlockProb = 0;
31.     Damage = 0;
32.   }
33.
34.   public string Name
35.   {
36.     get
37.     { return name; }
38.     set
39.     { name = value; }
40.   }
41.
42.   public int Energy
43.   {
44.     get
45.     { return energy; }
46.     set
```

```
47.      { energy = value; }
48.    }
49.
50.    public int HitProb
51.    {
52.      get
53.      { return hitProb; }
54.      set
55.      { hitProb = value; }
56.    }
57.
58.    public int Damage
59.    {
60.      get
61.      { return damage; }
62.      set
63.      { damage = value; }
64.    }
65.
66.    public int BlockProb
67.    {
68.      get
69.      { return blockProb; }
70.      set
71.      { blockProb = value; }
72.    }
73.
74.    public ArrayList ItemList
75.    {
76.      get
77.      { return itemList; }
78.      set
79.      { itemList = value; }
80.    }
81.
82.    public virtual bool AddItem(Item newItem)
83.    {
84.      ItemList.Add(newItem);
85.      return true;
86.    }
87.
88.    public virtual Item RemoveItem(string itemDesc)
89.    {
90.      Item removedItem = FindItem(itemDesc);
91.      if (removedItem != null)
92.      {
```

```
93.          ItemList.Remove(removedItem);
94.        }
95.        return removedItem;
96.      }
97.
98.      public Item FindItem(string itemDesc)
99.      {
100.        foreach (Item item in ItemList)
101.        {
102.          if (item.MatchesDescription(itemDesc))
103.          {
104.            return item;
105.          }
106.        }
107.        return null;
108.      }
109.
110.      public override string ToString()
111.      {
112.        string playerInfo = "Name: " + name;
113.        playerInfo += "\nEnergy: " + energy;
114.        playerInfo += "\nHit probability: " + HitProb;
115.        playerInfo += "\nDamage on hit: " + Damage;
116.        playerInfo += "\nBlocking probability: " + BlockProb;
117.        if (itemList.Count != 0)
118.        {
119.          playerInfo += "\nCarrying:\n";
120.          foreach (Item item in ItemList)
121.          {
122.            playerInfo += item.ToString() + "\n";
123.          }
124.        }
125.        else
126.          playerInfo += "\nNot carrying anything.";
127.        playerInfo += "\n";
128.        return playerInfo;
129.      }
130. }
```

A `Character` has a `name` and `itemList` as before (lines 5 and 6). We have added `hitProb` for the probability that the character can hit an opponent in combat, `blockProb` for the probability that a hit from an opponent can be blocked, `energy` for storing the total life energy and `damage` for the maximum damage that can be done if a successful hit is made. As mentioned earlier when we discussed the various item classes, each of these four fields can be altered by using weapons, food, armour or magic items.

Character defines public properties for all these parameters on lines 34 to 80. The methods for adding and removing items from the character's inventory (lines 82 to 108) are the same as those used in the Player class from Chapter 5, and have been moved into the Character class since they are common to all characters in the game. Notice, though, that we have declared a couple of these methods to be virtual, since we will find they need to be overridden in the Player class, since a player has a weight limit on the amount that can be carried, so we can't just keep adding items indefinitely without checking this limit. Finally, ToString() (line 110) prints out all the information for a Character.

The Player class inherits Character and adds a few more properties and methods that cater for the player's needs:

```
1. using System.Collections;
2.
3. public class Player : Character
4. {
5.     protected Room currentLocation;
6.     protected int maxCarryWeight, carryWeight;
7.     protected Ring wornRing;
8.     protected Potion quaffedPotion;
9.     protected int potionTime;
10.    protected Weapon wieldedWeapon;
11.    protected Armour wornArmour;
12.
13.    public Player()
14.    {
15.        MaxCarryWeight = 0;
16.        CarryWeight = 0;
17.        WornRing = null;
18.        QuaffedPotion = null;
19.        PotionTime = 0;
20.    }
21.
22.    public Player(string name) : base(name)
23.    {
24.        MaxCarryWeight = 0;
25.        CarryWeight = 0;
26.        WornRing = null;
27.        QuaffedPotion = null;
28.        PotionTime = 0;
29.    }
30.
31.    public int MaxCarryWeight
32.    {
33.        get
34.        { return maxCarryWeight; }
35.        set
```

```
36.        { maxCarryWeight = value; }
37.      }
38.
39.      public int CarryWeight
40.      {
41.        get
42.        { return carryWeight; }
43.        set
44.        {
45.          if (carryWeight <= maxCarryWeight)
46.          {
47.            carryWeight = value;
48.          }
49.        }
50.      }
51.
52.      public Ring WornRing
53.      {
54.        get
55.        { return wornRing; }
56.        set
57.        { wornRing = value; }
58.      }
59.
60.      public Potion QuaffedPotion
61.      {
62.        get
63.        { return quaffedPotion; }
64.        set
65.        { quaffedPotion = value; }
66.      }
67.
68.      public int PotionTime
69.      {
70.        get
71.        { return potionTime; }
72.        set
73.        {
74.          potionTime = value;
75.          if (potionTime <= 0)
76.          {
77.            potionTime = 0;
78.          }
79.        }
80.      }
81.
82.      public Weapon WieldedWeapon
```

```
83.     {
84.       get
85.       { return wieldedWeapon; }
86.       set
87.       { wieldedWeapon = value; }
88.     }
89.
90.     public Armour WornArmour
91.     {
92.       get
93.       { return wornArmour; }
94.       set
95.       { wornArmour = value; }
96.     }
97.
98.     public Room CurrentLocation
99.     {
100.      get
101.      { return currentLocation; }
102.      set
103.      { currentLocation = value; }
104.    }
105.
106.    public override bool AddItem(Item newItem)
107.    {
108.      if (newItem.Weight <= MaxCarryWeight - CarryWeight)
109.      {
110.        itemList.Add(newItem);
111.        CarryWeight += newItem.Weight;
112.        return true;
113.      }
114.      return false;
115.    }
116.
117.    public override Item RemoveItem(string itemDesc)
118.    {
119.      Item removedItem = FindItem(itemDesc);
120.      if (removedItem != null)
121.      {
122.        itemList.Remove(removedItem);
123.        CarryWeight -= removedItem.Weight;
124.      }
125.      return removedItem;
126.    }
127.
128.    public void SetEffects(Item usedItem)
129.    {
```

```
130.      if (usedItem is MagicItem)
131.      {
132.        MagicItem magicItem = (MagicItem)usedItem;
133.        blockProb += magicItem.BlockProb;
134.        damage += magicItem.Damage;
135.        energy += magicItem.Energy;
136.        hitProb += magicItem.HitProb;
137.      }
138.    }
139.
140.    public void RemoveEffects(Item usedItem)
141.    {
142.      if (usedItem is MagicItem)
143.      {
144.        MagicItem magicItem = (MagicItem)usedItem;
145.        blockProb -= magicItem.BlockProb;
146.        damage -= magicItem.Damage;
147.        energy -= magicItem.Energy;
148.        hitProb -= magicItem.HitProb;
149.      }
150.    }
151.
152.    public override string ToString()
153.    {
154.      string playerInfo = "Name: " + name;
155.      playerInfo += "\n------> Stats:";
156.      playerInfo += "\nEnergy: " + energy;
157.      playerInfo += "\nHit probability: " + HitProb;
158.      playerInfo += "\nDamage on hit: " + Damage;
159.      playerInfo += "\nBlocking probability: " + BlockProb;
160.      playerInfo += "\n<-------";
161.      if (itemList.Count != 0)
162.      {
163.        playerInfo += "\n******> Contents of pack:\n";
164.        foreach (Item item in itemList)
165.        {
166.          playerInfo += item.ToString() + "\n";
167.        }
168.        playerInfo += "Total weight: " + CarryWeight + "\n";
169.        playerInfo += "\n<******";
170.      }
171.      else
172.        playerInfo += "\nNot carrying anything.";
173.      if (WieldedWeapon == null)
174.      {
175.        playerInfo += "\nYou are not wielding a weapon.";
```

```
176.        }
177.        else
178.        {
179.          playerInfo +=
180.              "\nYou are wielding " + WieldedWeapon.⤶
                    Description;
181.        }
182.
183.        if (WornArmour == null)
184.        {
185.          playerInfo += "\nYou are not wearing any armour.";
186.        }
187.        else
188.        {
189.          playerInfo += "\nYou are wearing " +
190.              WornArmour.Description;
191.        }
192.
193.        playerInfo += "\n";
194.        if (WornRing != null)
195.          playerInfo += "\nWearing " + WornRing.Description;
196.        if (QuaffedPotion != null)
197.          playerInfo += "\nQuaffed " + QuaffedPotion.⤶
                  Description   +
198.            " with " + PotionTime +
199.            (PotionTime == 1 ? " turn" : " turns") + " ⤶
                  remaining.";
200.        return playerInfo;
201.    }
202. }
```

The fields added to `Player` show which room the player is in (line 5), the
maximum weight that can be carried and the current weight of the items in
the backpack (line 6), which ring is being worn (line 7 – `null` if no ring is
being worn), which potion is currently in effect, if any (line 8), which
weapon is currently being wielded (line 10) and which armour is currently
being worn (line 11). The properties defined on lines 31 to 104 allow external access to these fields. Note that some of these properties contain some
extra code to check the validity of the value that is being assigned to the
data field. For example, a check is made (lines 45 to 48) that
`maxCarryWeight` is not exceeded by `carryWeight`.

As mentioned when we discussed `Character`, `AddItem()` and `RemoveItem()`
need to be overridden in `Player` to take account of the weight limit on items
being carried. `Player`'s version of `AddItem()` is on line 106, and does a check
that the item being added to the player's inventory does not cause the total
weight to exceed `MaxCarryWeight`. If it does, nothing is added to `itemList`
and the method just returns `false` to indicate that the addition did not work.

RemoveItem() (line 117) must be overridden since when an item is removed from the inventory, its weight must be subtracted from CarryWeight.

The SetEffects() method (line 128) takes an Item as a parameter. The present version of SetEffects() only does anything if Item is in fact a MagicItem (line 130), but in principle could be extended to handle any type of Item. The method applies the various modifications caused by the MagicItem to the player's statistics. Similarly, RemoveEffects() (line 140) subtracts the effects of a MagicItem when it is removed or wears off.

Finally, ToString() prints out all the information on the player, including such information as what weapon is being wielded, what armour and ring are being worn, what potion has been quaffed and so on.

6.20.6 ☐ The Room class

Room has changed very little from its form in Chapter 5 and is included here for reference:

```csharp
using System.Collections;

public class Room
{
  private string description;
  private ArrayList itemList;
  private Room[] exits;
  public enum Direction
  {
    North, East, South, West, Up, Down
  }
  public string[] directionNames =
    { "north", "east", "south", "west", "up", "down" };
  private Character monster;

  public Room()
  {
    description = "";
    itemList = null;
    exits = null;
    monster = null;
  }

  public Room(string description)
  {
    Description = description;
    itemList = new ArrayList();
    exits = new Room[6];
    monster = null;
```

```
   }

public void SetExit(Direction dir, Room loc)
{
   exits[(int)dir] = loc;
}

public Room HasExit(Direction dir)
{
   return exits[(int)dir];
}

public Room FindExit(string dirString)
{
   for (int i = 0; i < directionNames.Length; i++)
   {
      if (dirString.Equals(directionNames[i]))
         return HasExit((Direction)i);
   }
   return null;
}

public void AddItem(Item newItem)
{
   itemList.Add(newItem);
}

public Item RemoveItem(string itemDesc)
{
   Item removedItem = FindItem(itemDesc);
   if (removedItem != null)
   {
      itemList.Remove(removedItem);
   }
   return removedItem;
}

public Item FindItem(string itemDesc)
{
   foreach (Item item in itemList)
   {
      if (item.MatchesDescription(itemDesc))
      {
         return item;
      }
   }
```

```csharp
        return null;
    }

    public string Description
    {
        get
        { return description; }
        set
        { description =   value; }
    }

    public ArrayList ItemList
    {
        get
        { return itemList; }
        set
        { itemList = value; }
    }

    public Character Monster
    {
        get
        { return monster; }
        set
        { monster = value; }
    }

    private ArrayList ExitsToString()
    {
        ArrayList exitStrings = new ArrayList();
        for (int i = 0; i < exits.Length; i++)
        {
            if (exits[i] != null)
            {
                exitStrings.Add(directionNames[i]);
            }
        }
        return exitStrings;
    }

    public override string ToString()
    {
        string locationInfo = "\n=========================";
        locationInfo += "\nYou are in the " + description + "\n";

        // Print exits
```

```
ArrayList exitStrings = ExitsToString();
if (exitStrings.Count == 0)
{
  locationInfo += "\nThere are no exits from this room.";
}
else if (exitStrings.Count == 1)
{
  locationInfo += "\nThere is one exit " + exitStrings[0];
}
else
{
  locationInfo += "\nThere are " + exitStrings.Count +
    " exits: ";
  foreach (string exit in exitStrings)
  {
    locationInfo += exit + " ";
  }
}

// Print contents
if (itemList.Count != 0)
{
  locationInfo += "\nContains:\n";
  foreach (Item item in itemList)
  {
    locationInfo += item.ToString() + "\n";
  }
}
else
  locationInfo += "\nThere are no items here.";

if (Monster != null)
{
  locationInfo += "\nThere is a " + Monster.Name +
    " here.";
}

    locationInfo += "\n=======================";
  return locationInfo;
  }
}
```

We are still using the same method for storing valid exits from each location, so the reader is directed to Chapter 5 for a description of the fields and methods in this class.

6.20.7 ☐ The `Adventure` class – initialization and command handling

Finally, we come to the `Adventure` class, which brings all the other classes together and manages the actual game play. This class has expanded considerably from its earlier version, so it is best if we break it up and consider the parts separately. We begin by looking at the data fields and initialization code:

```
1.  using System;
2.  using System.Collections;
3.
4.  public class Adventure
5.  {
6.      private Player gamePlayer;
7.      private Room[] rooms;
8.      private Random random = new Random();
9.      private const int numRooms = 3;
10.
11.     public enum Locn
12.     {
13.        Laboratory = 0,
14.        Dungeon = 1,
15.        Kitchen = 2
16.     }
17.
18.     public Adventure()
19.     {
20.        SetupRooms();
21.        AddItems();
22.        SetupMap();
23.        AddMonsters();
24.        SetupPlayer();
25.     }
26.
27.     private void SetupRooms()
28.     {
29.        rooms = new Room[numRooms];
30.
31.        rooms[(int)Locn.Laboratory] = new
32.           Room("magic laboratory.");
33.        rooms[(int)Locn.Dungeon] = new Room("dungeon.");
34.        rooms[(int)Locn.Kitchen] = new Room("kitchen.");
35.     }
36.
37.     private void AddItems()
38.     {
39.        Food food;
40.        Weapon weapon;
```

```
41.        Armour armour;
42.        Ring ring;
43.        Potion potion;
44.        Wand wand;
45.
46.        // Laboratory
47.        ring = new Ring("an invisibility ring", 1);
48.        ring.AdornString =  "You shimmer and then disappear";
49.        ring.UnadornString = "You become visible again";
50.        ring.BlockProb = 30;
51.        rooms[(int)Locn.Laboratory].AddItem(ring);
52.
53.        ring = new Ring("a power ring", 1);
54.        ring.AdornString = "You feel more powerful";
55.        ring.UnadornString = "The feeling of power fades";
56.        ring.HitProb = 25;
57.        rooms[(int)Locn.Laboratory].AddItem(ring);
58.
59.        potion = new Potion("an energy potion", 2);
60.        potion.Duration = 5;
61.        potion.QuaffString = "You feel healthier";
62.        potion.WearOffString = "The healthy feeling wears off";
63.        rooms[(int)Locn.Laboratory].AddItem(potion);
64.
65.        wand = new Wand("a fire wand", 3);
66.        wand.Charges = 7;
67.        wand.ZapString = "A bolt of fire bursts from the wand";
68.        wand.Damage = 6;
69.        rooms[(int)Locn.Laboratory].AddItem(wand);
70.
71.        // Kitchen
72.        food = new Food("a carrot", 1);
73.        food.Energy = 5;
74.        rooms[(int)Locn.Kitchen].AddItem(food);
75.        food = new Food("some chicken", 3);
76.        food.Energy = 8;
77.        rooms[(int)Locn.Kitchen].AddItem(food);
78.
79.        weapon = new Weapon("a knife", 10);
80.        weapon.Damage = 4;
81.        weapon.HitProb = 20;
82.        rooms[(int)Locn.Kitchen].AddItem(weapon);
83.    }
84.
85.    private void SetupMap()
86.    {
```

```
87.      rooms[(int)Locn.Laboratory].SetExit(Room.Direction.↩
         East,
88.        rooms[(int)Locn.Kitchen]);
89.      rooms[(int)Locn.Laboratory].SetExit(Room.Direction.↩
         Down,
90.        rooms[(int)Locn.Dungeon]);
91.      rooms[(int)Locn.Kitchen].SetExit(Room.Direction.West,
92.        rooms[(int)Locn.Laboratory]);
93.      rooms[(int)Locn.Dungeon].SetExit(Room.Direction.Up,
94.        rooms[(int)Locn.Laboratory]);
95.    }
96.
97.    private void AddMonsters()
98.    {
99.      Character monster = new Character("zombie");
100.     monster.BlockProb = 30;
101.     monster.Damage = 4;
102.     monster.Energy = 8;
103.     monster.HitProb = 60;
104.     Armour armour = new Armour("leather armour", 15);
105.     armour.BlockProb = 20;
106.     monster.ItemList.Add(armour);
107.     rooms[(int)Locn.Dungeon].Monster = monster;
108.   }
109.
110.   private void SetupPlayer()
111.   {
112.     gamePlayer = new Player("Wibble the Wizard");
113.     gamePlayer.Energy = 12;
114.     gamePlayer.HitProb = 60;
115.     gamePlayer.Damage = 2;
116.     gamePlayer.BlockProb = 20;
117.     gamePlayer.MaxCarryWeight = 100;
118.     gamePlayer.CurrentLocation = rooms[(int)Locn.↩
         Laboratory];
119.   }
120.
121.   // Other code to follow…
122. }
```

The game contains a `Player` (line 6) and an array of `Locations` (line 7). We also create a `Random` object (line 8) which is used to generate pseudo-random numbers. (We'll consider this class a bit more when it is used below.)

The constructor (line 18) calls several methods to set up the game. First, we call `SetupRooms()` (line 27) which just creates the bare `Room` objects. We are still using the same three locations we used in the previous version, but it should be obvious how to extend the game by adding more rooms.

Then we call `AddItems()` (line 37), which adds the items to the various locations at the start of the game. The code in `AddItems()` is fairly straightforward as it just creates a series of items of various types, assigns properties to them and then assigns each item to one of the `Locations` created in `SetupRooms()`.

Next, we call `SetupMap()` (line 85) which defines the exits from each location – these are the same as in the earlier version. Then `AddMonsters()` (line 97) is called to add creatures to the locations. In this case, we add only a single monster (a zombie) to the dungeon. The monster is declared as a `Character` (line 99), its properties are assigned and it is given something to carry (in this case, some leather armour). All items carried by a monster are dropped when the monster is killed and thus become available to the player as 'rewards' for killing the monster.

The final stage in the initialization is `SetupPlayer()` (line 110) which defines the initial statistics of the player.

After the initialization, the game itself begins when `PlayGame()` is called. Its code is:

```
1.  public void PlayGame()
2.  {
3.      string command;
4.      Console.WriteLine("Welcome to Adventure!");
5.      bool validTurn;
6.      do
7.      {
8.          validTurn = false;
9.          Console.Write("\n\nYour command -> ");
10.         command = Console.ReadLine().ToLower();
11.         string[] words = command.Split();
12.
13.         if (words[0].Equals("quit"))
14.             Console.WriteLine("Thanks for playing.");
15.         else if (words[0].Equals("help"))
16.             PrintHelp();
17.         else if (words[0].Equals("status"))
18.             Console.WriteLine(gamePlayer.ToString());
19.         else if (words[0].Equals("look"))
20.             Console.WriteLine(gamePlayer.
21.                 CurrentLocation.ToString());
22.         else if (words[0].Equals("move"))
23.             validTurn = DoMove(words);
24.         else if (words[0].Equals("take"))
25.             validTurn = DoTake(words);
26.         else if (words[0].Equals("drop"))
27.             validTurn = DoDrop(words);
28.         else if (words[0].Equals("eat"))
29.             validTurn = DoEat(words);
30.         else if (words[0].Equals("adorn"))
```

```
31.          validTurn = DoAdorn(words);
32.       else if (words[0].Equals("unadorn"))
33.          validTurn = DoUnadorn();
34.       else if (words[0].Equals("quaff"))
35.          validTurn = DoQuaff(words);
36.       else if (words[0].Equals("wield"))
37.          validTurn = DoWield(words);
38.       else if (words[0].Equals("wear"))
39.          validTurn = DoWear(words);
40.       else if (words[0].Equals("zap"))
41.          validTurn = DoZap(words);
42.       else if (words[0].Equals("attack"))
43.          validTurn = DoPlayerAttack();
44.       else
45.          Console.WriteLine(
46.            "Sorry, don't understand that - try again.");
47.
48.       if (validTurn)
49.       {
50.          if (gamePlayer.CurrentLocation.Monster != null)
51.          {
52.             DoMonsterAttack();
53.          }
54.          if (gamePlayer.PotionTime > 0)
55.          {
56.             gamePlayer.PotionTime--;
57.             if (gamePlayer.PotionTime == 0)
58.             {
59.                CancelPotion();
60.             }
61.          }
62.       }
63.    } while (gamePlayer.Energy > 0 && !command.Equals("quit"));
64. }
```

PlayGame()'s role is to accept commands from the user and deal with each command by calling the appropriate methods in this and other classes. It also must manage some bookkeeping to keep track of things like monster attacks and potion durations.

The validTurn variable (line 5) is used to determine if the user's most recent command resulted in a game action that caused some time to pass. This is used in deciding whether or not a monster should get an attack. As we mentioned earlier when describing the game design, a monster is only allowed an attack if the player does something (such as 'take' or 'drop') that requires some time.

The main game loop begins on line 6. The command is read in and split into a words array as in earlier versions (lines 9 to 11). We then enter a long if statement (lines 13 to 46) to determine which command was issued. We'll consider each command on its own below.

At the end of each command, `PlayGame()` determines if any extra actions need to occur (lines 48 to 62). First, if there is a monster in the same location as the player (line 50) `DoMonsterAttack()` is called to give the monster an attack on the player. We also check (line 54) if a potion is currently in effect and, if so, decrement its time. If this causes the potion to expire, `CancelPotion()` is called (line 59) to remove the effects of the potion.

We'll now have a look at the methods that implement the various commands. The 'quit', 'status' and 'look' commands just call methods in other classes that we have already examined. Of the other commands, the easiest is `PrintHelp()` which just prints out a description of the available commands:

```
private void PrintHelp()
{
   Console.WriteLine("Valid commands:\n" +
      "=========================================\n" +
      "look - shows current location & contents;\n" +
      "status - shows player's name and inventory;\n" +
      "take <list> - " +
         "take one or more items from current location;\n" +
      "drop <list> - drop one or more items from
      inventory;\n" +
      "move <direction> - move in the given direction;\n" +
      "wield <weapon> - " +
         "wield a weapon (weapon must be carried);\n" +
      "wear <armour> - " +
         "wear some armour (armour must be carried);\n" +
      "quaff <potion> - quaff a potion;\n" +
      "eat <food> - eat some food;\n" +
      "adorn <ring> - put on a ring;\n" +
      "unadorn - take off your ring;\n" +
      "zap <wand> - zap a wand (wand must be carried);\n" +
      "attack - attack a monster in the room;\n" +
      "\n" + ------------------------------/
      "quit - quit the program.\n");
}
```

The 'move' command is similar to its form in the previous version:

```
private bool DoMove(string[] words)
{
   if (words.Length < 2)
   {
      Console.WriteLine("You must specify a direction.\n " +
         "Try one of north, east, south, west, up or down.");
      return false;
   }
   Room destination =
      gamePlayer.CurrentLocation.FindExit(words[1]);
```

```
if (destination == null)
{
  Console.WriteLine(
    "Sorry, you can't move in that direction.");
  return false;
}
gamePlayer.CurrentLocation = destination;
Console.WriteLine("You move to the " +
  destination.Description);
if (destination.Monster != null)
{
  Console.WriteLine("\nThere is a " +
    destination.Monster.Name + " here.");
}
return true;
}
```

We have added a check at the end to see if there is a monster in the room and print a message if so. The player will be attacked by this monster at the end of the turn, but the code for this is in PlayGame() at the end of the main loop (see above).

The DoTake() and DoDrop() methods are also quite similar to earlier versions:

```
private bool DoTake(string[] words)
{
  int taken = 0;
  if (words.Length < 2)
  {
    Console.WriteLine("You must specify something
    to take.");return false;
  }
  for (int i = 1; i < words.Length; i++)
  {
    Item takenItem =
      gamePlayer.CurrentLocation.RemoveItem(words[i]);
    if (takenItem != null)
    {
      if (!gamePlayer.AddItem(takenItem))
      {
        Console.WriteLine("You can't carry any more.");
        gamePlayer.CurrentLocation.AddItem(takenItem);
        break;
      }
      else
      {
        taken++;
      }
```

```
      }
    }
    Console.WriteLine("You have taken " + taken +
      (taken == 1 ? " item" : " items") + ".");
    return taken > 0;
  }

  private bool DoDrop(string[] words)
  {
    int dropped = 0;
    if (words.Length < 2)
    {
      Console.WriteLine("You must specify something to drop.");
      return false;
    }
    for (int i = 1; i < words.Length; i++)
    {
      Item takenItem = gamePlayer.RemoveItem(words[i]);
      if (takenItem != null)
      {
        gamePlayer.CurrentLocation.AddItem(takenItem);
        dropped++;
      }
    }
    Console.WriteLine("You have dropped " + dropped +
      (dropped == 1 ? " item" : " items") + ".");
    return dropped > 0;
  }
```

`DoTake()` attempts to locate the items in the `Room`'s item list by calling
`RemoveItem()`. For each item, we test to see if the player can carry it without exceeding the weight limit. If not, the item is placed back in the `Room`'s
list. The method returns a `bool` which indicates whether anything was actually taken. This value is assigned to the `validTurn` flag, which in turn is
used to determine whether monsters get an attack and potion durations get
decremented back in `PlayGame()`'s main loop.

`DoDrop()` attempts to find each item in the player's inventory and, if
found, the item is transferred to the current location's item list. Again, a
`bool` is returned indicating whether any items were actually dropped.

The remaining commands are new to this version. `DoEat()` lets the player eat one or more items of food that are being carried:

```
  private bool DoEat(string[] words)
  {
    int eaten = 0;
    if (words.Length < 2)
    {
      Console.WriteLine("You must specify some food to eat.");
```

```
      return false;
    }
    for (int i = 1; i < words.Length; i++)
    {
      Item takenItem = gamePlayer.RemoveItem(words[i]);
      if (takenItem != null)
      {
        if (takenItem is Food)
        {
          gamePlayer.Energy += ((Food)takenItem).Energy;
          Console.WriteLine("You eat " + takenItem.
          Description); eaten++;
        }
        else
        {
          Console.WriteLine("You cannot eat " +
            takenItem.Description);
          gamePlayer.AddItem(takenItem);
        }
      }
    }
    Console.WriteLine("You have eaten " + eaten +
      (eaten == 1 ? " item" : " items") + ".");
    return eaten > 0;
}
```

DoEat() works in much the same way as DoDrop(). After removing each item to be eaten from the player's inventory, we test that the item is in fact a Food object. If so, the player's Energy is increased by the Energy value of the food. If the item was found in the player's backpack but is not a Food, a message saying that 'you cannot eat' the item is printed. DoEat() returns a bool indicating if anything was actually eaten.

The player can wear a ring by giving the 'adorn' command, which calls DoAdorn():

```
private bool DoAdorn(string[] words)
{
  if (gamePlayer.WornRing != null)
  {
    Console.WriteLine("You are already wearing a ring.");
    return false;
  }
  if (words.Length < 2)
  {
    Console.WriteLine("You must specify a ring to put on.");
    return false;
```

```
    }
    Item takenItem = gamePlayer.RemoveItem(words[1]);
    if (takenItem != null)
    {
      if (takenItem is Ring)
      {
        gamePlayer.WornRing = (Ring)takenItem;
        gamePlayer.SetEffects(takenItem);
        gamePlayer.CarryWeight += gamePlayer.WornRing.Weight;
        Console.WriteLine(((Ring)takenItem).AdornString);
        return true;
      }
      else
      {
        Console.WriteLine("You cannot put on " +
          takenItem.Description);
        gamePlayer.AddItem(takenItem);
        return false;
      }
    }
    return false;
  }
```

This method works in almost the same way as `DoEat()`. The main differences are that the method must first check if a ring is already being worn, since only one ring is allowed to be worn at a time. If no ring is being worn, the ring to be put on is located in the player's backpack. If the item is found, it is checked to see if it is a `Ring` object. If so, the player's `WornRing` is set to the ring and `SetEffects()` is called to apply whatever magic effects the ring bestows. We need to add the ring's weight back onto the player's `CarryWeight` property since `RemoveItem()` deducts the weight of the item removed. Finally, we write out the ring's `AdornString` to let the user know what effects the player experiences when the ring is put on.

The 'unadorn' command calls `DoUnadorn()`:

```
private bool DoUnadorn()
{
  if (gamePlayer.WornRing == null)
  {
    Console.WriteLine(
      "You are not wearing a ring at the moment.");
    return false;
  }
  gamePlayer.RemoveEffects(gamePlayer.WornRing);
  Console.WriteLine(gamePlayer.WornRing.UnadornString);
  gamePlayer.ItemList.Add(gamePlayer.WornRing);
  gamePlayer.WornRing = null;
  return true;
}
```

If a ring is being worn, RemoveEffects() is called to cancel its effects and then UnadornString is printed to describe how the player feels when the ring is removed. We add the ring back to the player's ItemList which restores it in the backpack, and WornRing is set to null to indicate that the player is no longer wearing a ring.

Quaffing a potion calls DoQuaff():

```
private bool DoQuaff(string[] words)
{
    if (gamePlayer.QuaffedPotion != null)
    {
        Console.WriteLine("You have already quaffed a
            potion.\n" +
            "You must wait until it wears off.");
        return false;
    }
    if (words.Length < 2)
    {
        Console.WriteLine("You must specify a potion to quaff.");
        return false;
    }
    Item takenItem = gamePlayer.RemoveItem(words[1]);
    if (takenItem != null)
    {
        if (takenItem is Potion)
        {
            Potion quaffed = (Potion)takenItem;
            gamePlayer.QuaffedPotion = quaffed;
            gamePlayer.PotionTime = quaffed.Duration;
            gamePlayer.SetEffects(takenItem);
            Console.WriteLine(quaffed.QuaffString);
            return true;
        }
        else
        {
            Console.WriteLine("You cannot quaff " +
                takenItem.Description);
            gamePlayer.AddItem(takenItem);
            return false;
        }
    }
    return false;
}
```

Since only one potion can be in effect at a time, we first check the player's QuaffedPotion to see if it is null. If no potion is currently in effect, the potion to be quaffed is removed from the player's inventory and checked to be sure it is a Potion object. If so, the player's QuaffedPotion is set to this potion, and the `PotionTime` is set to the potion's `Duration`. This sets the time remaining for the potion to remain in effect. As with a ring, `SetEffects()` is called to apply the potion's effects, and `QuaffString` is printed to display the potion's effects to the user.

There is no command to end the effects of a potion, but when `PotionTime` drops to zero, we call `CancelPotion()` from the end of the main loop in `PlayGame()`:

```
private void CancelPotion()
{
   if (gamePlayer.QuaffedPotion != null)
   {
     Console.WriteLine(gamePlayer.QuaffedPotion.WearOffString);
     gamePlayer.RemoveEffects(gamePlayer.QuaffedPotion);
     gamePlayer.QuaffedPotion = null;
     gamePlayer.PotionTime = 0;
   }
}
```

`CancelPotion()` carries out the bookkeeping tasks to remove the effects of the current potion.

Wielding a weapon calls `DoWield()`:

```
private bool DoWield(string[] words)
{
   if (words.Length < 2)
   {
     Console.WriteLine("You must specify a weapon to wield.");
     return false;
   }
   Item takenItem = gamePlayer.RemoveItem(words[1]);
   if (takenItem != null)
   {
     if (takenItem is Weapon)
     {
       if (gamePlayer.WieldedWeapon != null)
       {
         gamePlayer.HitProb -=
           gamePlayer.WieldedWeapon.HitProb;
         gamePlayer.Damage -= gamePlayer.WieldedWeapon.Damage;
         gamePlayer.ItemList.Add(gamePlayer.WieldedWeapon);
       }
       Weapon weapon = (Weapon)takenItem;
       gamePlayer.WieldedWeapon = weapon;
       gamePlayer.HitProb += gamePlayer.WieldedWeapon.HitProb;
       gamePlayer.Damage += gamePlayer.WieldedWeapon.Damage;
       gamePlayer.CarryWeight += weapon.Weight;
```

```
        Console.WriteLine("You are now wielding " +
            weapon.Description);
        return true;
    }
    else
    {
        Console.WriteLine("You cannot wield " +
            takenItem.Description);
        gamePlayer.AddItem(takenItem);
        return false;
    }
}
return false;
}
```

Although only one weapon can be wielded at a time, there is no 'unwield' command. It is assumed that if the player is already wielding a weapon when a new 'wield' command is given, the new weapon will simply replace the existing one. Therefore, there is no check at the start of `DoWield()` to see if the player is already wielding a weapon.

After the usual checks that the right type of item has been chosen, we then check if the player is currently wielding a weapon. If so, we stow it in the backpack and remove its effect on the player's `HitProb` and `Damage`. Then we wield the new weapon by applying its effects.

Wearing armour works in a similar fashion by calling `DoWear()`:

```
private bool DoWear(string[] words)
{
    if (words.Length < 2)
    {
        Console.WriteLine(
            "You must specify some armour to wear.");
        return false;
    }
    Item takenItem = gamePlayer.RemoveItem(words[1]);
    if (takenItem != null)
    {
        if (takenItem is Armour)
        {
            if (gamePlayer.WornArmour != null)
            {
                gamePlayer.BlockProb -=
                    gamePlayer.WornArmour.BlockProb;
                gamePlayer.ItemList.Add(gamePlayer.WornArmour);
            }
            Armour armour = (Armour)takenItem;
            gamePlayer.WornArmour = armour;
```

```
      gamePlayer.BlockProb += armour.BlockProb;
      gamePlayer.CarryWeight += armour.Weight;
      Console.WriteLine("You are now wearing " +
        armour.Description);
      return true;
    }
    else
    {
      Console.WriteLine("You cannot wear " +
        takenItem.Description);
      gamePlayer.AddItem(takenItem);
      return false;
    }
  }
  return false;
}
```

Armour, like weapons, cannot be removed without wearing another bit of armour in its place. The logic in this method is therefore essentially the same as in `DoWield()`.

Zapping a wand calls `DoZap()`:

```
private bool DoZap(string[] words)
{
  if (words.Length < 2)
  {
    Console.WriteLine("You must specify a wand to zap.");
    return false;
  }
  Item takenItem = gamePlayer.FindItem(words[1]);
  if (takenItem != null)
  {
    if (takenItem is Wand)
    {
      Wand wand = (Wand)takenItem;
      Console.WriteLine(wand.ZapString);
      if (gamePlayer.CurrentLocation.Monster != null)
      {
        Character monster =
          gamePlayer.CurrentLocation.Monster;
        int probSuccess = 100 - monster.BlockProb;
        if (random.Next(100) < probSuccess)
        {
          int damage = random.Next(wand.Damage) + 1;
          monster.Energy -= damage;
          Console.WriteLine("The wand does " + damage +
            (damage == 1 ? " point" : " points") +
```

```
                    " of damage to the " + monster.Name);
                if (monster.Energy <= 0)
                {
                    MonsterDead();
                }
            }
        }
        wand.Charges--;
        if (wand.Charges <= 0)
        {
            Console.WriteLine("The wand crumbles to dust.");
            gamePlayer.RemoveItem(wand.Description);
        }
        return true;
    }
    else
    {
        Console.WriteLine("You cannot zap " +
            takenItem.Description);
        return false;
    }
  }
  Console.WriteLine("No such item.");
  return false;
}
```

A wand need only be in the inventory to be zapped, so no checks are
required that the wand is held or worn. Since zapping the wand does not
remove it from the inventory, we use `FindItem()` rather than `RemoveItem()`
to locate it.

When the wand is zapped, `ZapString` is printed to describe the effects. A
wand can be zapped anywhere, but if a monster is present in the same room,
the damage caused by the wand is applied to the monster. A wand is
assumed to have a 100 per cent hit probability, so to work out the probability of a successful hit on the monster we need consider only the monster's
`BlockProb`, so we define `probSuccess` as `100 - monster.BlockProb`. We
then need to produce a random number to determine if the monster is in
fact damaged by the wand.

C#'s `Random` class allows the production of so-called *pseudo-random
numbers*. They are called 'pseudo' (false) since the random number
sequence is actually produced by a definite algorithm rather than by a truly
random process. The pattern of numbers produced by the algorithm does
satisfy numerous statistical tests for randomness, so the method is commonly used even though the numbers are not really random.

Recall that we initialized the `random` object in its declaration at the start
of the `Adventure` class. There are several methods for producing random
numbers from this object, but probably the most common is `Next()` which

generates the next number in the sequence. `Next()` has three overloaded versions which allow random numbers to be produced in various ranges. The form used here provides one parameter: `Next(100)`. This generates a random integer between 0 and 99.

We can use this value to determine whether zapping the wand causes a hit by comparing the random value with `probSuccess`. To see why this works, suppose `probSuccess` is 75, meaning that 75 per cent of the time the wand should hit the monster.

If the number produced by `Next(100)` is truly random in the range from 0 to 99, then it should produce a number less than 75 (that is, between 0 and 74), 75 per cent of the time. Therefore, the comparison `if (random.Next(100) < probSuccess)` should be true `probSuccess` per cent of the time, which is what we want.

If the hit is successful, we find how much damage the wand does by using `Next()` again. This time we want a value between 1 and the wand's `Damage` property. Since `Next()` with a single parameter always produces a number between 0 and its parameter value, we add 1 to the value returned. (There is a two-parameter version of `Next()` which allows a lower and upper limit to be specified, so we could have used that as well.)

After doing damage to the monster, we check to see if the monster is dead yet. If so, we call `MonsterDead()`:

```
private void MonsterDead()
{
   Character monster = gamePlayer.CurrentLocation.Monster;
   if (monster == null) return;
   Console.WriteLine("\nYou have killed the " + monster.Name);
   ArrayList items = monster.ItemList;
   if (items != null && items.Count > 0)
   {
      foreach (Item item in items)
      {
         gamePlayer.CurrentLocation.ItemList.Add(item);
      }
   }
   gamePlayer.CurrentLocation.Monster = null;
}
```

This method drops all the items carried by the monster, making them available in the Room's item list so the player can 'take' them if desired. The monster is also removed from the Room by setting the Room's Monster property to `null`.

Back in `DoZap()`, the final check we need to do is to see if all the wand's charges have been used up. If so, we print a message that the wand crumbles to dust and remove the wand from the player's inventory.

The last command is 'attack' which calls `DoPlayerAttack()`:

```csharp
private bool DoPlayerAttack()
{
  Character monster = gamePlayer.CurrentLocation.Monster;
  if (monster == null)
  {
    Console.WriteLine("There is nothing here to attack.");
    return false;
  }
  int probSuccess = gamePlayer.HitProb *
    (100 - monster.BlockProb) / 100;
  if (random.Next(100) < probSuccess)
  {
    int hitDamage = random.Next(gamePlayer.Damage) + 1;
    monster.Energy -= hitDamage;
    Console.WriteLine("\nYou hit the " + monster.Name +
      " and do " +
      hitDamage + (hitDamage == 1 ? " point" : " points") +
      " of damage.");
    if (monster.Energy <= 0)
    {
      MonsterDead();
    }
  }
  else
  {
    Console.WriteLine("\nYou miss the " + monster.Name + ".");
  }
  return true;
}
```

We first check that there is a monster in the room. If so, we work out the probability of a successful hit by the player on the monster by using the formula described earlier. The `Next()` method from `Random` is used again to determine if the player hits the monster, and if so, the amount of damage done is also determined randomly, this time using the current damage rating of the player.

At the end of each turn in which the player is in the same room as a monster, the monster gets its turn to attack, using `DoMonsterAttack()`:

```csharp
private bool DoMonsterAttack()
{
  Character monster = gamePlayer.CurrentLocation.Monster;
  if (monster == null)
    return false;
  int probSuccess = monster.HitProb *
```

```
      (100 - gamePlayer.BlockProb) / 100;
   if (random.Next(100) < probSuccess)
   {
      int hitDamage = random.Next(monster.Damage) + 1;
      gamePlayer.Energy -= hitDamage;
      Console.WriteLine("\nThe " + monster.Name +
         " hits you and does " +
         hitDamage + (hitDamage == 1 ? " point" : " points") +
         " of damage.");
      if (gamePlayer.Energy <= 0)
      {
         PlayerDead();
      }
   }
   else
   {
      Console.WriteLine("\nThe " + monster.Name +
         " attacks you but misses.");
   }
   return true;
}
```

`DoMonsterAttack()` works essentially like `DoPlayerAttack()` in reverse. After a successful hit, a check is made to see if the player has been killed and, if so, we call `PlayerDead()`:

```
private void PlayerDead()
{
   Console.WriteLine("\nUnfortunately, you are dead.");
   Console.WriteLine("\nWe hope you enjoyed the game.");
}
```

At present, `PlayerDead()` just prints out a farewell message. The game ends back in the main loop in `PlayGame()` if the player's `Energy` drops to 0. It would be fairly easy to add some code to offer the user a chance to play again. We would need to reset everything to its original configuration by redoing the initialization methods.

Finally, the `Main()` method just creates an `Adventure` object and calls `PlayGame()` to get the game going:

```
public static void Main(string[] args)
{
   Adventure adventure = new Adventure();
   adventure.PlayGame();
}
```

This has been a long example, but hopefully if you have persevered with it you have seen a substantial sample of how inheritance can be used in a more sizeable project. In projects of this size, it is important to give considerable thought to the structure of the program before jumping in and writing code. We laid out the class design and described the methods required at the start of this section, and only then got into the details of the code. If you don't take this bit of extra planning time, you will usually find that you need to keep chopping and changing the code as you write it, especially if you are fairly inexperienced at programming in C#. The resulting code will be the worse for it as well.

■ Summary

In this chapter we have introduced the concepts of inheritance and polymorphism, both of which are fundamental ideas in object-oriented programming. We have seen that C#'s implementation of these ideas provides somewhat more flexibility than that of Java. In particular, C# allows us to define which methods are virtual, which can result in considerably more efficient code.

We have also examined a number of other C# keywords and language features related to inheritance, such as boxing, the `is` operator, abstract classes and interfaces.

The extended case study in which the adventure game was expanded into a fully fledged textual game provides a substantial example of how inheritance can be used in a larger project.

Exercises

6.1 Write down a list of properties that could be associated with various forms of land transport, such as cars, buses, trucks, bicycles, motorcycles, tricycles and so on. Examine the list of properties to see which properties are common to all the forms of transport that you have considered. Group these properties into a base class, and then define a number of derived classes, one for each specific type of transport.

6.2 Broaden the scope of the previous exercise by considering other forms of transportation such as water and air transport. Consider a few specific types of transport within each of these overall categories, such as canoe, rowboat and oil tanker for water transport, and helicopter, 747 and hang glider for air transport. Create an inheritance structure for each of these other types of transport.

6.3 Examine your overall list of classes after completing the previous two exercises to see if there are any properties common to *all* types of transportation. Separate out these properties and define a new class which could be the base class of the three main classes (land, water and air transport) that you defined earlier. Note how inheritance can be a hierarchical structure with many layers. As the scope of the system that is to be modelled using inheritance grows, new levels or generality emerge, which allow new layers to be created in the inheritance tree.

6.4 Define a class `Tutor` which inherits the `Person` class used in the text. `Tutor` should represent a tutor or professor who teaches one or more courses at a college or university. A `Tutor` should have a few extra properties in addition to those inherited from `Person` such as an office location (as a `string`), a list of courses taught (use an array of `strings` to list the course titles) and any others you think would be relevant. Write out some skeleton C# code for this class, showing the inheritance relationship, the new data fields and a set of C# properties for getting and setting their values.

6.5 Modify the previous exercise by defining a `Course` class which contains details of an individual course taught at a college or university. The `Course` class should contain data fields such as the course code (e.g. Computing 101), the course title ('Introduction to Programming using C#', for example) and other information as required. Replace the array of `strings` in the `Tutor` class with an array of `Courses`.

6.6 A possible design for a program that represents students and tutors at a college would be to make `Student` and `Tutor` inherit `Course` so that each student and tutor is associated with the course they either take or teach. Why would this *not* be an appropriate use of inheritance?

6.7 Write an override of the `ToString()` method that returns a `string` containing the data in a `Tutor` object in some neatly formatted form.

6.8 Write overrides of the two `Equals()` methods that may be used in `Tutor`. The methods should return `true` if all the data in the corresponding fields of the two `Tutor` objects contain the same data.

6.9 Write a method in the `Person` class called `HasName()`. The method should contain a single `string` parameter, and should return a `bool` value indicating whether the `Person`'s name matches that passed in as a parameter. The match should be case-insensitive (see the documentation on the `String` class to find a way of doing this). Make sure this method is available to all classes derived from `Person`.

6.10 Write a program which defines an array of `Person` references. After initialization, the program should print a top-level menu which offers the user the choice of adding a new person's data to the array, or of searching for a person with a given name.

If the person elects to add a new person, the next menu should ask whether that person is to be an ordinary `Person`, a `Student` or a `Tutor`. When the user makes their selection, print the appropriate prompts to get the required information for that type of person, create a new object of the appropriate class and add it to the first available element in the array. Note that you can use polymorphism to add an object of any of the three classes to the array.

If the person elects to search for a person by name, use the `HasName()` method from the previous exercise to do the search. If the person is found, use the `is` operator to determine what type of object it is, and then call the correct `ToString()` method to print out the data for that person.

Exceptions

7

7.1 ■ Encountering exceptions

Java programmers will be no strangers to exceptions, even if they have never written code to generate or handle them. The most common cause of a Java program crash is some form of unhandled exception, and probably the most common of these is the NullPointerException. If you have run a Java program from a console window you will probably have seen the printout of the current *stack trace* (list of methods that were being called) when the program died. The first line of the error printout describes the particular exception that occurred.

If you have delved a bit deeper into Java's exception handling, you may have written some code that uses the try...catch block, which can be used to handle built-in exceptions in Java. If you have delved even more deeply, you may have written your own exception classes. We will see in this chapter that C#'s exception handling features are very similar to those of Java, so the transition between the two languages is quite painless.

First, let us consider a C# program that generates, or *throws*, an exception so we can see what happens if we make no effort to handle it when it occurs.

```
1. using System;
2.
3. public class ExceptionDemo1
4. {
5.    public static void Main(string[] args)
6.    {
7.       int x, y;
8.       Console.Write("Enter two ints: ");
9.       string intString = Console.ReadLine();
10.      string[] splitInts = intString.Split();
11.      x = int.Parse(splitInts[0]);
12.      y = int.Parse(splitInts[1]);
13.      Console.WriteLine(x + "/" + y + " = " + x / y);
14.   }
15. }
```

This simple program prompts the user to enter two integers on the same line. These ints are then stored in a string, which is then split into two separate strings within the array splitInts. The two elements of this array are converted to ints, and the final line prints out the quotient of these two numbers.

There is no explicit error handling in this code, but clearly there are several things that could go wrong with the user input. The user might type in no or only one integer, or possibly some text that is not a number at all.

They might type in two integers, but the second one could be zero, causing an attempt to divide by zero in the last line.

Suppose we make the latter mistake. Running the program may cause a 'Just-in-time debugging' dialog to appear if the code was compiled in Debug mode under Visual Studio, but if the offer to run the debugger is refused, the following output appears in the console window:

```
Enter two ints: 3 0

Unhandled Exception: System.DivideByZeroException:
Attempted to divide by zero.
    at ExceptionDemo1.Main(String[] args)
in c:\csharpbook\programs
\chap07\exceptiondemo1\exceptiondemo1.cs:line 13
```

Clearly the attempt to divide by zero has been detected and caused a System.DivideByZeroException to be thrown. Since there is no handler for this exception in the program code, .NET itself catches the exception and generates the error message. The process is very similar to that in Java – if there is no explicit code to catch an exception in Java, the Java virtual machine catches the exception and generates the stack trace error message.

If we try a couple of other errors, we can see a couple of other exceptions that are in the .NET repertoire. For example, we can try entering only a single integer, which results in the message:

```
Enter two ints: 3

Unhandled Exception: System.IndexOutOfRangeException:
Index was outside the bounds of the array.
    at ExceptionDemo1.Main(String[] args)
in c:\csharpbook\programs
\chap07\exceptiondemo1\exceptiondemo1.cs:line 12
```

The error is on line 12 and results from our attempt to access splitInts[1], since we only entered a single number.

We can also try entering some non-numerical text instead of ints, and we get:

```
Enter two ints: x y

Unhandled Exception: System.FormatException:
Input string was not in a correct format.
    at ExceptionDemo1.Main(String[] args)
in c:\csharpbook\programs
\chap07\exceptiondemo1\exceptiondemo1.cs:line 11
```

In this case, the error is on line 11 and results from our attempt to use int.Parse() to convert the string 'x' to an int.

We can see that the .NET system contains a number of built-in exceptions (in fact there are close to 100) that respond to different types of errors. In the current program, however, encountering any of these exceptions still causes the program to crash, so we need to see how to handle them more gracefully.

Key point

Runtime errors can generate one of .NET's built-in exceptions. If the exception is not caught, the program will crash.

7.2 ■ Handling exceptions

The techniques in C# for handling exceptions are essentially the same as in Java. We must enclose the code that can throw an exception within a `try` block and add one or more `catch` blocks after the `try`. The general format is as follows:

```
try
{
  // Code that can throw exceptions
}
catch (<Exception type 1>)
{
  // Code to handle exceptions of type 1
}
catch (<Exception type 2>)
{
  // Code to handle exceptions of type 2
}
// Other catch blocks may be added here
catch
{
  // Code to handle all exceptions not already caught
}
finally
{
  // Code that is run whether or not an exception is
  // caught.
}
```

Code that can throw one or more types of exception is placed within the `try` block at the start. Following the `try` block, we must add at least one `catch` block, although we can have as many more as we need. Each `catch` block can specify, much like a method parameter, a particular exception type that it will catch. The third `catch` block shown here has no parameter, and will catch *any* type of exception.

Catch blocks are checked in the order they are written and once one of them is activated (by having the thrown exception match the type in that catch's parameter), the exception is deemed to have been handled and all later catch blocks are ignored.

The finally block at the end is *always* run, whether or not any exception was thrown. This is useful in cases where there is some clean-up code (such as closing open files or database connections) that should be done in all cases, whether or not anything goes wrong with the program.

Before we delve more deeply into the rules that try...catch blocks must satisfy, let us see how this structure works with the program example above. We will add exception-handling code to the program to catch all three types of exception that we have seen above. When we do this, we must remember that the body of a try or a catch is a compound statement and, as such, defines its own local scope for variable declarations. We therefore have to be careful not to confine existing declarations (such as x and y above) to local scopes where they are not accessible to other areas of the code where they are needed.

```
1.  using System;
2.
3.  public class ExceptionDemo1
4.  {
5.    public static void Main(string[] args)
6.    {
7.      int x, y;
8.      bool correct = true;
9.      do
10.     {
11.       try
12.       {
13.         Console.Write("Enter two ints: ");
14.         string intString = Console.ReadLine();
15.         string[] splitInts = intString.Split();
16.         x = int.Parse(splitInts[0]);
17.         y = int.Parse(splitInts[1]);
18.         Console.WriteLine(x + "/" + y + " = " + x / y);
19.         correct = true;
20.       }
21.       catch (DivideByZeroException exception)
22.       {
23.         Console.WriteLine("Error: denominator is zero. " +
24.           "Please try again.");
25.         correct = false;
26.       }
27.       catch (IndexOutOfRangeException exception)
28.       {
```

```
29.             Console.WriteLine("Error: must enter 2 ints. " +
30.                 "Please try again.");
31.             correct = false;
32.         }
33.         catch (FormatException exception)
34.         {
35.             Console.WriteLine("Error: numbers not in correct " +
36.                 "int format. Please try again.");
37.             correct = false;
38.         }
39.         catch
40.         {
41.             Console.WriteLine("Error: incorrect input. " +
42.                 "Please try again.");
43.             correct = false;
44.         }
45.     } while (!correct);
46.   }
47. }
```

In order to make use of the catch blocks, we have added a do...while loop which continues asking for input until none of the three exceptions is thrown. The bool flag correct is set to false if any of the exceptions occurs, which causes the loop to continue.

In this example, the three types of exception can occur more or less independently of each other, so it doesn't really matter in which order we place the catch blocks. In each case, we simply print an error message and ask the user to try again. However, the final catch block which is designed to catch any exception that is not one of the three specified earlier, must come at the end, since if it were placed earlier, it would be activated by one of the three specific exceptions we are attempting to catch on their own. A typical session with this program might be as follows.

```
Enter two ints: 3 0
Error: denominator is zero. Please try again.
Enter two ints: 3
Error: must enter 2 ints. Please try again.
Enter two ints: x y
Error: numbers not in correct int format. Please try again.
Enter two ints: 111111111111111111111 3
Error: incorrect input. Please try again.
Enter two ints: 99 3
99/3 = 33
```

The first three attempts to input the data each generate one of the three specific exceptions for which we are checking, so the resulting error messages make sense and the user has some guidance on what to do to correct their mistake. However, the fourth attempt, where the user has typed in 11111111111111111111, does not generate one of the three specific exceptions, and therefore gets caught by the general `catch` block at the end. This produces the not terribly helpful message 'Error: incorrect input.' This, as the reader will no doubt be aware, is a common problem with a lot of software – the user does something wrong and the program complains but tells them nothing about how to fix it.

In almost all cases, this is the result of lazy programming and inadequate testing on the part of the software developer. In this case, for example, the actual exception that was thrown in the fourth attempt was an `OverflowException`, which results from the input number being too large for an `int`. A properly coded version of this example should have a specific `catch` block for this exception and a clear error message when it occurs.

7.3 ■ Exceptions and inheritance

C++ programmers may know that in C++, any data type may be thrown as an exception, so that a `catch` block may even use primitive data types such as `int` as their parameter. In C#, as in Java, a parameter passed to a `catch` block must be an instance of a specific base class, or of a class derived from it. In C#, the base class of all exception classes is `System.Exception`. Consulting the C# documentation will reveal that all the exceptions considered above are derived ultimately from this class.

This fact means that the rules of polymorphism come into effect whenever we pass an exception object to a `catch` block. That is, the class specified as the data type of the parameter in a `catch` will match an exception of that class or of any class derived from it.

Most of the pre-defined exceptions that arise in practice are in fact derived from `System.SystemException`, which is in turn derived from `System.Exception`. For example, `FormatException` and `IndexOutOfRange Exception` that we used above are both directly derived from `System. SystemException`. Some exceptions are even further down the inheritance hierarchy. `DivideByZeroException` is derived from `ArithmeticException` which is in turn derived from `System.SystemException`. `Arithmetic Exception` is also the base class for `OverflowException`.

We can use the inheritance relationships of exceptions to provide intermediate `catch` blocks that catch all exceptions of a particular type, without having to make reference to the blanket `catch` block without any parameters. For example, we could catch all `ArithmeticExceptions` in the previous example with code such as this:

```
try
{
    // Code
}
```

```
catch (ArithmeticException exception)
{
  Console.WriteLine(exception.Message +
    " Please try again.");
  correct = false;
}
catch (IndexOutOfRangeException exception)
{
}
catch (FormatException exception)
{
}
catch
{
}
```

In this case, the first `catch` block would catch both `DivideByZero Exceptions` and `OverflowExceptions`. The problem with doing this, of course, is that we won't know which precise type of exception was thrown, so the error message can't be as specific as we may like.

This problem can be solved in most cases by making use of the actual exception object that is passed to the `catch` block as a parameter. All of the .NET built-in exception classes have a `string` message field that contains a fairly clear description of what the problem is. In the example above, we have printed out this message as part of the error message so that the user knows more specifically what is wrong.

With this new way of handling `ArithmeticExceptions`, a typical session could look like this:

```
Enter two ints: 3 0
Attempted to divide by zero. Please try again.
Enter two ints: 11111111111111111 3
Value was either too large or too small for an int. Please
try again.
```

We can see that the message attached to the exception itself generated enough information to identify the problem with the input. Of course, even this might not be a clear enough message, depending on the audience for which the program is intended. If the expected users are not avid computer users, it is unlikely they would know what an 'int' is, so in that case, we would need to split up the `catch` block into two separate blocks and write error messages for each case.

Another possibility for fine-tuning exception handling is to make use of the `is` operator, discussed in Chapter 6. We could retain the single `catch` block for handling the `ArithmeticException` and its derived classes, but replace it with the following:

```
    catch (ArithmeticException exception)
    {
      if (exception is DivideByZeroException)
        Console.WriteLine("Dividing by zero." +
          " Please try again.");
      else if (exception is OverflowException)
        Console.WriteLine("The number is too big." +
          " Please try again.");
      else
        Console.WriteLine(exception.Message +
          " Please try again.");
      correct = false;
    }
```

We can use is to detect the actual class of which exception is an instance, and tailor our error messages accordingly.

7.4 ■ Throwing exceptions

The examples in the previous section relied on the underlying program to produce, or *throw* an exception which was then caught by a catch statement. Some exceptions in C# are thrown by built-in operators, while others are thrown by library methods.

For example, the division operator / will throw a DivideByZero Exception if its right operand is 0. The array index operator [] will throw an IndexOutOfBoundsException if its parameter is not an int that lies within the bounds of the array. The Parse() method of the int class will throw a FormatException if its parameter is not a string that represents an int. In all these cases, the code that throws the exception is hidden away in the definition of the operator or method, so we cannot see how it is done.

In fact, it is quite easy to throw our own exceptions using the throw keyword. For example, we can perform a test on the value y in the previous code to see if it is zero before we do the division and, if it is, throw our own DivideByZeroException before we attempt to do the division. The modified code looks like this:

```
    try
    {
      Console.Write("Enter two positive ints: ");
      string intString = Console.ReadLine();
      string[] splitInts = intString.Split();
      x = int.Parse(splitInts[0]);
      y = int.Parse(splitInts[1]);
      if (y == 0)
      {
        throw new DivideByZeroException();
```

```
  }
  Console.WriteLine(x + "/" + y + " = " + x / y);
  correct = true;
}
catch (DivideByZeroException exception)
{
  Console.WriteLine("Error: denominator is zero. " +
    "Please try again.");
  correct = false;
}
```

The `throw` keyword must be followed by an `Exception` object. When a `throw` is executed, it acts like a break within the `try` block. All code following the `throw` within the `try` block is skipped and control is passed to the `catch` statements that follow the `try` block. If a `catch` with a parameter that matches the type of exception produced by the `throw` is found, control passes into that `catch` block.

In this example, of course, we have no need to write an explicit `throw` since the division operator would do it for us, but we will see later that it is possible to define customized exception classes, and instances of these must be thrown in user-defined code.

7.5 ■ Data carried by exceptions

So far, we have used the various exception types only as labels to distinguish which type of error has occurred. Exceptions can also carry information on the error which can help us find the problem that produced it. Java veterans will no doubt be familiar with the stack trace that appears in the console window if we don't put a section of code in a `try...catch` block. C# will produce much the same sort of thing for an uncaught exception, but as with Java, C# also provides a way of printing the stack trace out explicitly, using the `StackTrace` property in the `Exception` class.

When we create a new exception to `throw`, we can also specify a `string` in the constructor which serves as an error message that can be printed out in a `catch` block. We can modify the example above to add a message and a stack trace to the output when a `DivideByZeroException` is thrown:

```
try
{
  Console.Write("Enter two positive ints: ");
  string intString = Console.ReadLine();
  string[] splitInts = intString.Split();
  x = int.Parse(splitInts[0]);
  y = int.Parse(splitInts[1]);
  if(y == 0)
  {
```

```
      throw new DivideByZeroException(
        "Error: your second number must not be 0.");
   }
   Console.WriteLine(x + "/" + y + " = " + x / y);
   correct = true;
}
catch (DivideByZeroException exception)
{
   Console.WriteLine(exception.Message);
   Console.WriteLine(exception.StackTrace);
   correct = false;
}
```

In declaring and throwing the `DivideByZeroException`, we have added the message 'Error: your second number must not be 0.' to the constructor. In the `catch` for this exception we print out this message, followed by the `StackTrace`. A typical session with this code would produce the output:

```
Enter two positive ints: 3 0
Error: your second number must not be 0.
   at ExceptionDemo.Main(String[] args) in c:\books\mybooks\
   csharpbook\programs\chap07\exceptiondemo\exceptiondemo.cs:
   line 31
```

In this case, the code that threw the exception was written directly in `Main()` so we only get a single method in the stack trace. In practice, we will usually be using methods in other classes which themselves may be derived from classes in the .NET libraries, so the stack trace will be considerably longer in those cases.

7.6 ■ User-defined exceptions

Although the .NET library comes with a good collection of exception classes, there are cases where it would be convenient to be able to write our own to cope with errors that are specific to a particular program. As in Java, writing customized exception classes is quite simple.

As with all the system exceptions, a custom exception must inherit the `System.Exception` class either directly or indirectly. Although it is perfectly legal to declare a new exception as a direct descendent of `System.Exception`, it is better practice to derive it from `System.ApplicationException`. This class is a direct descendent of `System.Exception` and actually adds no new fields or methods. Its only purpose is to provide a unique base class for all user-defined exceptions so that they may easily be distinguished from system-defined exceptions.

An exception need not have any functionality to be useful – simply having a distinct exception class that is tailored to a particular type of error allows us to test for that type of error and produce a customized error message to improve the user interface. As a simple example, we can modify the program above so that it will only accept positive integers. Since there is no system-defined exception class that tests for negative numbers, we can define our own exception class called `NegativeValueException`:

```
public class NegativeValueException : ApplicationException
{}
```

The class inherits all its functionality from `ApplicationException`, which in turn inherits everything from `Exception`. We can use this class to add a check that both numbers are positive:

```
try
{
   Console.Write("Enter two positive ints: ");
   string intString = Console.ReadLine();
   string[] splitInts = intString.Split();
   x = int.Parse(splitInts[0]);
   y = int.Parse(splitInts[1]);
   if(x < 0 || y < 0)
   {
      throw new NegativeValueException();
   }
      Console.WriteLine(x + "/" + y + " = " + x / y);
      correct = true;
}
catch (NegativeValueException exception)
{
   Console.WriteLine(
      "Error: both numbers must be positive.");
   correct = false;
}
// other catch blocks
```

In this case, there is no alternative to using a `throw` statement, since no system-defined operator or method knows anything about a `NegativeValueException` and therefore will not throw it.

A typical session using this exception would be:

```
Enter two positive ints: -20 2
Error: both numbers must be positive.
```

Since user-defined exceptions inherit all the functionality of the `Exception` class, we can assign messages to them as well. We can add a couple of constructors to our `NegativeValueException` to make it a bit more useful:

```
public class NegativeValueException : ApplicationException
{
   public NegativeValueException() :
```

```
    base()
  { }

  public NegativeValueException(string message) :
    base(message)
  { }
}
```

Again, there is no functionality here that is not present in the base class, but we can now create a `NegativeValueException` by passing a `string` to its constructor to set up an explicit error message. We can replace the `throw` statement above with:

```
if(x < 0 || y < 0)
{
  throw new NegativeValueException(
    "Error: both values must be positive.");
}
```

and the corresponding `catch` block with:

```
catch (NegativeValueException exception)
{
  Console.WriteLine(exception.Message);
  correct = false;
}
```

A typical session using this new code would be:

```
Enter two positive ints: -20 5
Error: both values must be positive.
```

7.7 ■ When to use exceptions

Exceptions are designed to handle errors that are largely outwith the program's control, in the sense that they arise from unpredictable sources such as user input, network errors, inaccessible or missing files and so on. In general it is not a good idea to use exceptions as a replacement for an `if...else` or `switch` statement.

For example, it would be possible to add another exception class to our previous example which deals with the case where the user's input is correct (that is, both numbers are positive). If we called this new exception class `CorrectInputException`, we could then add a check such as:

```
if (x > 0 && y > 0)
{
  throw new CorrectInputException();
}
```

and then add another `catch` block that produces the desired output from the program:

```
catch(CorrectInputException exception)
{
    Console.WriteLine(x + "/" + y + " = " + x / y);
    correct = true;
}
```

Although this would work in principle, it is bad programming practice because an exception is being produced when the program is actually working properly.

A `throw` is an unconditional break in the program flow and for it to work correctly, a `catch` must be provided in the code. If there is no `catch` for a thrown exception, the program will crash.

Key point

Exceptions should only be used to catch errors in a program.

The general rule for using exceptions is therefore that they should only appear in cases where an error from an external source might occur – all other conditions should be handled using 'ordinary' code (usually an `if` statement).

■ Summary

Exceptions are provided in C# to allow a way of catching runtime errors in a program and handling them smoothly without causing a program crash. Exceptions should be caught and appropriate action taken, such as producing a clear error message to let the user know what has gone wrong.

Exceptions in C# work in much the same way as they do in Java.

Exercises

7.1   Extend the example given in the chapter (where two numbers are read in and one divided by the other) so that the program runs in a loop. Each iteration of the loop should ask the user for two numbers, then print a menu offering the numbered options 1. Add, 2. Subtract, 3. Multiply, 4. Divide. Handle the exceptions described in the example in this chapter, but arrange the exception handling code so that entering invalid input gives the user a second chance to enter the data for the chosen operation, before going back to the beginning of the loop to request another pair of numbers for a new operation.

Add another user-defined exception to handle the case of a menu choice being outside the bounds 1 to 4.

7.2 The static method `Math.Sqrt()` (part of the `Math` class) returns the square root of a non-negative number. Write a test program that runs a loop that asks the user for a number and then prints out the square root of that number. The program should stop when the user enters zero.

What is printed out when the user enters a negative number? Look up this 'value' in the documentation to discover what it means if you haven't seen it before.

Use the `NegativeValueException` defined in the chapter to catch negative input and print an error message instead of the value that is produced by default.

7.3 Write a program which asks the user for an email address and checks that the address has a 'valid' form (that is, that it has the form xxxx@yyyy.zzz, so there should be some text, then an @ symbol, then some more text, then a dot, and finally some more text at the end). Investigate the `String` class to find methods for doing this, or alternatively, investigate the `Regex` class and build a *regular expression* to match a valid email address. Write an `EmailException` class and throw an instance of it if the entered string is not a valid email address.

Events and delegates 8

8.1 ■ Events

As a prelude to the next chapter where we begin our discussion of Windows programming using C# and .NET, we need to investigate how events are generated and handled in C#. Event handling should be familiar to any Java programmer who has produced graphical user interface (GUI) programs, since components such as buttons and menu items generate events which must be handled in order for them to do anything.

We will first review what events are and how they are handled in Java, then proceed to describe how they are generated and handled in C#.

Although events are encountered mainly in GUI programs, they can be used in any program, even console ones. An event is really just a signal that is sent to a running program indicating that something has occurred which may require the program to respond in some way. Events are generated from *user interaction*, as when the user presses or moves the mouse, presses a key on the keyboard, selects a menu item in the program, and so on. Other events not specifically associated with a user action can be generated by the operating system, such as various events that are sent when a program starts up or shuts down.

Although there are a large number (typically several hundred) of types of event, most programs only wish to respond to a handful of these, at least in the sense of producing a visible reaction. Typically, a method for handling a particular type of event is added to one of the classes in the program and arrangements must be made for that method to be called whenever the specific type of event occurs.

We have seen that events are generated outside the program by user interaction or the operating system, and that we can provide methods within the program that respond to these events. The problem is how to connect the two ends of the process. Let us see briefly how this is done in Java.

8.2 ■ Events in Java

In all versions of Java since 1.1, event handling is done using *listener* interfaces. To see how this works, suppose we have a graphical component such as a button (an instance of the JButton class in Java's Swing package, say) and we wish to add some code that is run whenever the button is pushed. Pressing a JButton generates an ActionEvent which, besides stating that an event has happened, contains other information about the event such as the object that generated it (the JButton) and so on.

In order for this ActionEvent to have any effect, it must be trapped by the program and caused to run some code. In Java, this is done by attaching an ActionListener to the JButton. An ActionListener (actually a class that implements the ActionListener interface) contains a method called actionPerformed(ActionEvent e) which is designed to receive an ActionEvent as its parameter. When the button is pressed, an ActionEvent is generated and sent to the JButton object, which then checks to see if it has an ActionListener attached to it. If it does, it calls the actionPerformed() method from that ActionListener. (In fact, we can attach several ActionListeners to a single JButton and the actionPerformed() methods of all these listeners will be called whenever an ActionEvent is received. Most buttons only have a single ActionListener, however.)

In Java, therefore, each component is sent a notification of any events that are associated with it, and it is up to the programmer to add listeners for those types of events that should produce a response. As each Java component typically can respond to several types of event, a given component can have several different types of listeners attached to it. Interacting with the component in different ways will generate different types of events, each of which will call methods from different listeners.

The connection between an event and the method it calls is therefore determined entirely by the listener interface. As in C#, implementing an interface in Java means that any methods declared by that interface must be implemented. Therefore, any class that implements a listener interface must provide the event handling method(s) required by that interface. In this way, Java provides a connection between a component and the method that is called when that component receives an event without having to pass the actual name of the method to the component – the method is part of the interface that has been implemented.

As we will see, event handling in C# uses a somewhat different technique. To understand how events are handled in C# we first need to understand delegates.

8.3 ■ Delegates

Ultimately, event handling must come down to connecting an event with the method that is supposed to run when the event is received. We've seen that Java uses listener interfaces to achieve this.

Some GUI systems written in C and C++ use *callback functions* to connect events with their handlers. In this system, a separate handler function (method) is written for each type of event, and the correct handler function is passed as a parameter to another function which uses the handler function to process the event. In this way we need to write only a single function to sort out the various events that impinge on a program. We merely pass this function the correct tool (in the form of another function passed in as a parameter) to handle a particular event correctly. If the idea of passing a method as a parameter to another method seems odd to you as a Java programmer, it is probably because Java does not support it.

C# does not support directly the passing of one method to another, at least not by simply putting a method's name as a parameter in another method's parameter list. However, C# does introduce a new type of class called a *delegate* which does essentially the same thing.

Although the main use of delegates in C# is as part of the event handling process, they can also be used on their own, and it is perhaps easier to understand how they work by examining a simple delegate without any events to confuse us. It may not become clear exactly how delegates are used until we reach the end of the example below, but be patient – all will be revealed.

When a delegate is declared, it must specify the exact type of method which it represents. This type includes not only the name and parameter list, but also the return type. Some books say that a delegate specifies the *signature* of a method, but as we saw in Chapter 5, our definition of the signature of a method includes its name and parameter list but excludes its return type, so it is not quite the same thing. To avoid confusion with the term signature as used in this book, we will just refer to the 'type' of a method when discussing delegates.

A delegate declaration looks a lot like a method declaration, without the method code following it. A typical declaration looks like this:

```
public delegate int ArithOperation(int num1, int num2);
```

This declaration declares a `delegate` class named `ArithOperation` which can represent methods that return an `int` and take two `int`s as parameters. It is important to note that this declaration specifies only the *type* of the method which can be represented by the delegate. In particular, the name `ArithOperation` is *not* the name of any particular method – it is the name of the *delegate class*.

This declaration is actually a class declaration in disguise. The keyword `delegate` tells the compiler that a class that inherits `System.Delegate` is being declared, and it will then take care of the details. It will name this class `ArithOperation` and store the details of the method's type as data fields in the class. All the other functionality of the new `ArithOperation` class is inherited from `System.Delegate`.

Since `ArithOperation` is a class, we can use it to declare objects, much like any other class. The only difference is that a delegate class has a specific type of constructor which must be used when making a declaration. This constructor takes a single parameter which must be the name of a method whose type matches that of the delegate.

For example, if we had a method `Plus()` defined as follows:

```
public int Plus(int num1, int num2)
{
   return num1 + num2;
}
```

then we could declare a delegate representing `Plus()` by writing:

```
ArithOperation arithOp = new ArithOperation(Plus);
```

If we had another method with a different type, as in:

```
public void OtherMethod(float x)
{
   // ......
}
```

then the declaration:

```
ArithOperation arithOp = new ArithOperation(OtherMethod);
```

would not compile, since the constructor parameter is a method with the wrong type.

Now all this may be fine, but it is probably still far from obvious how a delegate can be used for anything useful. Unfortunately, most examples that could be presented at this stage are not terribly realistic in that they could be done more easily without using delegates, but we will give a simple example so you can see how they work in practice. When we study event handling later, delegates will become truly useful.

As an example of delegates in action, the following program asks the user to enter two `int`s and then calculates four arithmetic operations using these two numbers. Each operation uses a separate method, and a delegate is used to pass each method in turn into another method that prints out the results.

```
 1. using System;
 2.
 3. class DelegateDemo
 4. {
 5.    public delegate int ArithOperation(int num1, int num2);
 6.
 7.    public int Arithmetic(ArithOperation operation,
 8.       int num1, int num2)
 9.    {
10.       return operation(num1, num2);
11.    }
12.
13.    public int Plus(int num1, int num2)
14.    {
15.       return num1 + num2;
16.    }
17.
18.    public int Minus(int num1, int num2)
19.    {
20.       return num1 - num2;
21.    }
```

```
22.
23.    public int Times(int num1, int num2)
24.    {
25.      return num1 * num2;
26.    }
27.
28.    public int Divide(int num1, int num2)
29.    {
30.      return num1 / num2;
31.    }
32.
33.    public void Calculator()
34.    {
35.      int num1, num2;
36.      ArithOperation[] arithOp =
37.      {
38.        new ArithOperation(Plus),
39.        new ArithOperation(Minus),
40.        new ArithOperation(Times),
41.        new ArithOperation(Divide)
42.      };
43.      string[] operatorSymbol = { "+", "-", "*", "/" };
44.
45.      do
46.      {
47.        Console.Write("Enter two ints (0 0 to end): ");
48.        string intString = Console.ReadLine();
49.        string[] splitInts = intString.Split();
50.        num1 = int.Parse(splitInts[0]);
51.        num2 = int.Parse(splitInts[1]);
52.        if(num1 == 0 && num2 == 0) break;
53.        for(int i = 0; i < arithOp.Length; i++)
54.        {
55.          Console.WriteLine(num1 + operatorSymbol[i] + num2 +
56.            " = " + Arithmetic(arithOp[i], num1, num2));
57.        }
58.      } while (num1 != 0 && num2 != 0);
59.    }
60.
61.    static void Main(string[] args)
62.    {
63.      DelegateDemo demo = new DelegateDemo();
64.      demo.Calculator();
65.    }
66. }
```

We've made use (line 5) of the same delegate that we declared earlier. Line 7 declares a method that takes an `ArithOperation` delegate and two `int`s as parameters. On line 10, this method uses the delegate to call the method that it represents and returns the result.

Lines 13 to 31 provide the four arithmetic methods, each of which has the correct type to be used with `ArithOperation`. The `Calculator()` method (line 33) is the control centre of the program and brings everything together. Lines 36 to 42 create an array of delegate objects, with each initialized to one of the four arithmetic operations. Line 43 declares a `string` array which is used in printing out the results.

The loop on line 45 includes much of the code from the example in the last chapter on exceptions (although the exception code has been omitted to keep things simple here). The user is prompted to enter two integers, which are extracted from the input string and converted to `int`s. The loop on line 53 calls `Arithmetic` and passes it each element of the `arithOp` array in turn. For example `arithOp[0]` is a delegate for the `Plus()` method, so we are essentially passing the `Plus()` method as a parameter into the `Arithmetic()` method. Back in `Arithmetic()` on line 10, the delegate `operation`, which is now a delegate representing `Plus()`, is called, which in turn calls `Plus()`, passing it `num1` and `num2`. The value returned from `Plus()` is also returned from the `operation` delegate. The other three methods `Minus()`, `Times()` and `Divide()` are all passed into `Arithmetic()` in a similar way.

A typical session with this program is:

```
Enter two ints (0 0 to end): 5 9
5+9 = 14
5-9 = -4
5*9 = 45
5/9 = 0
Enter two ints (0 0 to end): 123 -9034
123+-9034 = -8911
123--9034 = 9157
123*-9034 = -1111182
123/-9034 = 0
Enter two ints (0 0 to end): 0 0
Press any key to continue
```

Obviously, this program could have been written more simply without delegates by just calling the four methods directly. However, it does illustrate how a delegate can be used to pass one method as a parameter into another.

8.4 ■ Multicast delegates

C# delegates can be *multicast* delegates, which means that a delegate class can represent more than one method at a time. In the preceding example, we defined an array of four delegates and attached a single method to each one. We can rewrite this example to use only a single delegate which refers to all four arithmetic methods.

If we add more than one method to a delegate, there is an extra restriction on the method type: the method must be `void` – that is, it cannot return anything. The reason for this is fairly obvious, since if a delegate contains several methods that each return their own values, which value would the delegate itself return? To solve this problem, multicast delegates are restricted to `void` methods.

To convert our earlier example into one using a multicast delegate, we need to convert the four arithmetic operation methods to void methods, so we have put the output code inside these methods rather than in the `Calculator()` method. The result is as follows:

```
 1. using System;
 2.
 3. class MulticastDemo
 4. {
 5.    public delegate void ArithOperation(int num1, int num2);
 6.
 7.    public void Arithmetic(ArithOperation operation,
 8.       int num1, int num2)
 9.    {
10.       operation(num1, num2);
11.    }
12.
13.    public void Plus(int num1, int num2)
14.    {
15.       Console.WriteLine(num1 + " + " + num2 + " = " +
16.          (num1 + num2));
17.    }
18.
19.    public void Minus(int num1, int num2)
20.    {
21.       Console.WriteLine(num1 + " - " + num2 + " = " +
22.          (num1 - num2));
23.    }
24.
25.    public void Times(int num1, int num2)
26.    {
27.       Console.WriteLine(num1 + " * " + num2 + " = " +
28.          (num1 * num2));
```

```
29.     }
30.
31.     public void Divide(int num1, int num2)
32.     {
33.       Console.WriteLine(num1 + " / " + num2 + " = " +
34.         (num1 / num2));
35.     }
36.
37.     public void Calculator()
38.     {
39.       int num1, num2;
40.       ArithOperation arithOps = new ArithOperation(Plus);
41.       arithOps += new ArithOperation(Minus);
42.       arithOps += new ArithOperation(Times);
43.       arithOps += new ArithOperation(Divide);
44.
45.       do
46.       {
47.         Console.Write("Enter two ints (0 0 to end): ");
48.         string intString = Console.ReadLine();
49.         string[] splitInts = intString.Split();
50.         num1 = int.Parse(splitInts[0]);
51.         num2 = int.Parse(splitInts[1]);
52.         if(num1 == 0 && num2 == 0) break;
53.         Arithmetic(arithOps, num1, num2);
54.       } while (num1 != 0 && num2 != 0);
55.     }
56.
57.     static void Main(string[] args)
58.     {
59.       MulticastDemo demo = new MulticastDemo();
60.       demo.Calculator();
61.     }
62. }
```

The delegate declaration on line 5 is changed to specify a void return type. The Arithmetic() method on line 7 is also now void as are the four arithmetic operations that follow it.

In the Calculator() method on line 37, we declare a single delegate (line 40) and initialize it by adding the Plus() method to it. On lines 41 to 43, we add the other three methods to the *same* delegate. Note that the += operator is implicitly overloaded for delegates to allow them to add new methods.

Within the loop on line 45, the same code as before is used to request input from the user, but now we need make only a single call to the Arithmetic() method on line 53 in order to invoke all four arithmetic operations. Arithmetic() is passed the parameter arithOps which is the delegate containing all the arithmetic operation methods. When this delegate is run (line 10) it will call each of the methods that has been added to it, in the order in which they were added. The output from this program is therefore the same as in the previous example.

Although multicast delegates are not really necessary for this simple program, their application to event handling allows a single event to call multiple event handlers. In this way, C# is able to duplicate Java's event handling technique where a number of listeners for a particular event type can be added to a single component.

8.5 ■ Handling events

Now that we have seen how delegates work, we can return to how C# generates and handles events. In fact, a C# event is nothing more than a delegate with a particular method type. Each method that is added to the event delegate becomes an event handler that is called whenever that event occurs.

The only condition that an event delegate must satisfy is that its type is of the form:

```
public delegate void EventName(object source,
    EventArgs eventInfo);
```

The delegate must have a `void` return type (since it must allow multicasting so that more than one handler method can be attached to a given event). The event's name (shown as `EventName` here) can be anything you like. The parameter list must have the form shown – two parameters, where the first parameter represents the source of the event and the second parameter contains any extra information that is to accompany the event.

In a GUI program, for example, `source` could be a button component that is pressed to generate the event, and `eventInfo` could be `null` if no extra information about the button is needed. On the other hand, if the source of the event is a mouse click in a graphics window, `source` could be the window object containing the graphics and `eventInfo` could contain the pixel coordinates of the mouse cursor when the mouse was clicked.

Since `source`'s data type is given as `object`, the source of an event can be any data type, since all data types inherit `object`. The `EventArgs` class is defined in the `System` namespace and is an empty class. Its only purpose is to define a base class for the second parameter in an event delegate, so that any extra information accompanying an event must be contained within a class that inherits `EventArgs`.

The easiest way to understand how an event delegate is used to generate events is to look at a simple example. The following program presents yet another form of the arithmetic calculator given above. This time, the user is presented with a list of options at each point. First, the user must enter two integers, after which the menu will expand to allow these integers to be added or subtracted, or else the user can choose to enter another pair of integers, replacing the first two. A 'quit' option is also included at each stage.

After a pair of numbers is entered, the 'add' and 'subtract' options are handled by generating an event which is then handled by a separate method. Since we are dealing with a text-based program rather than a GUI program, the 'source' of the event is taken to be a `string` containing either `"Add"` or `"Subtract"`. In the next chapter, when we study simple Windows programs, we will rewrite this program in a GUI version where 'add' and 'subtract' become buttons that are pressed. In that case, the buttons will become the sources of the events.

We will present the code at this point and discuss it further afterwards.

```
1.  using System;
2.
3.  class EventDemo
4.  {
5.     public delegate void ArithDelegate(string source,
6.         EventArgs eventInfo);
7.     public event ArithDelegate ArithEvent;
8.     int num1, num2;
9.
10.    public void ReadInts()
11.    {
12.       Console.Write("Enter two integers: ");
13.       string intString = Console.ReadLine();
14.       string[] splitInts = intString.Split();
15.       num1 = int.Parse(splitInts[0]);
16.       num2 = int.Parse(splitInts[1]);
17.    }
18.
19.    public void EventHandler(string source, EventArgs eventInfo)
20.    {
21.       if(source.Equals("Add"))
22.       {
23.          Console.WriteLine(num1 + " + " + num2 + " = " +
24.             (num1 + num2));
25.       }
26.       else if(source.Equals("Subtract"))
27.       {
28.          Console.WriteLine(num1 + " - " + num2 + " = " +
29.             (num1 - num2));
30.       }
31.    }
32.
33.    public void Calculator()
34.    {
35.       ArithEvent += new ArithDelegate(EventHandler);
```

```
36.        int choice;
37.        bool firstIntsEntered = false;
38.        do
39.        {
40.          Console.WriteLine("\nSelect an option: ");
41.          Console.WriteLine("1. Enter new numbers");
42.          if(firstIntsEntered)
43.          {
44.             Console.WriteLine("2. Add");
45.             Console.WriteLine("3. Subtract");
46.          }
47.          Console.WriteLine("4. Quit\n");
48.          Console.Write("Enter your choice: ");
49.          string intString = Console.ReadLine();
50.          choice = int.Parse(intString);
51.          switch (choice)
52.          {
53.            case 1:
54.               ReadInts();
55.               firstIntsEntered = true;
56.               break;
57.            case 2:
58.               ArithEvent("Add", null);
59.               break;
60.            case 3:
61.               ArithEvent("Subtract", null);
62.               break;
63.          }
64.       } while (choice != 4);
65.     }
66.
67.     static void Main(string[] args)
68.     {
69.        EventDemo demo = new EventDemo();
70.        demo.Calculator();
71.     }
72. }
```

The event delegate is declared on line 5. The first parameter is given as a `string`, but since `string` inherits `object`, the principle of polymorphism allows the declaration to match the required form.

In this program, we will not make use of the `EventArgs` parameter at all, since all the information that we need about the event is contained in `source`. In fact, this is the only case where the second parameter of an event delegate should be given as the `EventArgs` base class. Since `EventArgs` is an empty class, it cannot store any information, so if the second parameter of the event delegate is `EventArgs`, this is a way of stating that this parameter will not be used. We will see an example below where this parameter is used, and in that case we need to create a new class that inherits `EventArgs` and add some data fields to this class in order to carry the information.

Line 7 creates an instance of `ArithDelegate` called `ArithEvent`. Note that the keyword `event` forms part of the declaration. In fact, this is not necessary – the program will work perfectly well even if `event` is omitted from line 7. The `event` keyword is an indication to the compiler that this declaration should be compatible with the data type required to represent an event. That is, if `event` is present, the compiler will check that `ArithDelegate`'s type conforms to that required for an event delegate, with the first parameter an `object` and the second an `EventArgs`. It is always a good idea to use this keyword as a safeguard against coding errors.

To see how this event delegate is used, we follow the program as it starts. In `Main()` (line 67), we call `Calculator()` to get things started. The first thing `Calculator()` does (line 35) is add the method `EventHandler()` (line 19) to the event delegate. This means that every time an `ArithEvent` occurs, `EventHandler()` should be called.

How do we make an `ArithEvent` occur? If we follow the code in `Calculator()`, the lines up to line 50 print out the menu and read the user's choice from the menu. When the program starts, the user is given only option 1 (enter two integers) and option 4 (quit). Once the user has entered two numbers, the menu expands to include option 2 (add) and 3 (subtract). Let us suppose the user has entered the numbers 24 and 4, and then selected option 2 to add them. In the `switch` statement (line 51), `choice` is 2, so line 58 will be run. This line is:

```
ArithEvent("Add", null);
```

Since `ArithEvent` is an instance of the delegate `ArithDelegate`, the two parameters must match those given in the delegate's type. The first parameter is the `string` `"Add"`, which is fine, and the second parameter is given as `null`, indicating that we are not passing in an `EventArgs` object. This is also fine provided we don't try to make use of the `EventsArgs` parameter anywhere within the event handler.

Since the `EventHandler()` method was added to the `ArithEvent` delegate (line 35), `ArithEvent` will call `EventHandler()` and pass its two parameters along to it. Thus within `EventHandler()` (line 19), `source` is `"Add"` and `eventInfo` is `null`. Therefore, the `if` condition on line 21 will be true, and the output will be

```
24 + 4 = 28
```

We can see from this example that events don't use any features of C# apart from those inherent in delegates. The `event` keyword is purely a bit of insurance to make sure that the delegate's type is of the required form, but in this example, the program would actually work equally well even if the delegate were of some other form. The requirement that all events are delegates with a particular type is needed when a programmer must write event handlers for system-defined events. By using a consistent type for all events, it is easier to write event handlers since they must always have the same parameter list.

When we study GUI programming in the next chapter, the only part of the event processing process we will need to worry about is writing the handler method (`EventHandler()` in this example). The declaration of the event delegate and the generation of the events will be done by .NET and is hidden from the application coder. Once we write the event handler we then just need to add it to the event delegate, as we did in this example on line 35.

8.6 ■ Threads

Most operating systems are *multi-tasking* systems, in that even though they are running on a single processor they can give the illusion of running several processes at the same time. It is only an illusion, since a single processor can only handle one process at a time. The operating system manages multi-tasking by allocating a small time slice to each process in turn, so that one process gets a bit of time, is then *swapped out* into memory and the next process is given its share of time and so on.

Within a single process, some programs provide the ability to run separate sub-processes in a similar way. Each sub-process is run in a separate *thread*. The various threads within a single process are managed by that process rather than directly by the operating system, so the programmer has the ability to control what happens in the thread.

Both Java and C# provide relatively simple methods for defining and managing threads within a program, although the two languages implement threads in somewhat different ways. We'll begin with a quick reminder of how Java manages threads and then proceed to describe C#'s facilities for threading. We have included the initial discussion of threads in this chapter on delegates, since as we will see, C# uses a delegate to provide the method that is to be run by a thread.

8.6.1 ☐ Threads in Java

Java contains a `Thread` class which can be used to create an instance of a thread in a program. When a `Thread` is created, it must be registered with an object that implements the `Runnable` interface. `Runnable` declares only a single method called `run()`, so writing a class that implements `Runnable` requires writing an implementation of `run()` within that class.

When a Java `Thread` has been created and registered, it can then be started in its own sub-process by calling the `start()` method. This method in turn consults the `Runnable` object with which the `Thread` was registered and calls the `run()` method from that object. The `run()` method contains whatever code is to be run in the new thread.

Earlier versions of Java provided methods for stopping, pausing and resuming a `Thread`, but these were removed in later versions of the language since they caused scheduling problems. As a result, stopping or pausing a thread in Java is a somewhat cumbersome procedure. We will see that the process is easier in C#.

8.6.2 ☐ Threads in C#

The main difference between threads in Java and C# is that in C#, rather than registering an *object* with a thread, a particular *method* within an object is registered when a thread is created. This is done by associating a new `Thread` with a `ThreadStart` delegate, with the delegate representing the method which should be run in the thread.

This will be easier to understand with a simple example, so consider the `SimpleThread` class below:

```
1. using System;
2. using System.Threading;
3.
4. public class SimpleThread
5. {
6.    Thread testThread;
7.
8.    public void RunThread()
9.    {
10.      for (int i = 0; i < 5; i++)
11.      {
12.         Console.WriteLine("Thread time: " + (i * 100)
            + " ms.");
13.         Thread.Sleep(100);
14.      }
15.    }
16.
17.    public static void Main(string[] args)
18.    {
19.      SimpleThread simpleThread = new SimpleThread();
20.      ThreadStart threadDelegate =
21.         new ThreadStart(simpleThread.RunThread);
22.      simpleThread.testThread = new Thread(threadDelegate);
23.      simpleThread.testThread.Start();
24.      for (int i = 0; i < 5; i++)
25.      {
26.         Console.WriteLine("Main time: " + (i * 100) + "
            ms.");
27.         Thread.Sleep(100);
28.      }
29.    }
30. }
```

In this program, the idea is to run the code in RunThread() (line 8) in a separate thread, while at the same time running the code in Main() itself. We therefore need to create a Thread and tell this thread that when it starts it should call RunThread().

This is done by first creating a ThreadStart delegate which represents RunThread() (line 20). ThreadStart is a predefined delegate class which can only represent a method with the following type:

```
void ThreadStartMethod();
```

That is, any method represented by ThreadStart must have no parameters and be void.

Having created the ThreadStart delegate, we can now create the Thread itself (line 22) and pass the delegate as the parameter to the Thread constructor. At this point, the Thread is fully defined and connected to the method that it must run, but it has not yet been started. This is done by calling Start() on the Thread object (line 23). Start() consults the delegate to find out what method should be run, and that method is started in its own thread.

This means that the program above splits into two separate threads starting at line 23. The code in RunThread() should run in parallel with and independently of any other code that follows line 23 in Main(). The code in RunThread() prints a message every 100 milliseconds, as does the code in the loop on line 24 in Main(). The time delay between successive messages was inserted so that the output can reveal that the two blocks of code are in fact running in parallel.

A typical output from the program is as follows:

```
Main time: 0 ms.
Thread time: 0 ms.
Main time: 100 ms.
Thread time: 100 ms.
Thread time: 200 ms.
Main time: 200 ms.
Thread time: 300 ms.
Main time: 300 ms.
Thread time: 400 ms.
Main time: 400 ms.
```

It can be seen that the output from the two blocks of code does indeed get mixed together, so that it is obvious that there are two threads running in parallel. A couple of things are worthy of note, however.

First, notice that the output from line 26 appears *before* that from RunThread(), even though the thread was started before the loop in Main() is run. The reason for this is that although Start() on line 23 does indeed start the thread running before the loop in Main() is entered, setting up a thread involves a fair bit of preliminary work before the code itself starts running in the thread. This setup work delays the output from the loop in RunThread() long enough for the loop in Main() to go through its first iteration.

Second, notice that the output from the two threads is not strictly synchronized, in that the 100 and 200 millisecond lines from RunThread() are printed together, while most of the other lines alternate with those from Main(). This is because the two threads are managed independently of each other, and the time allocated to each thread depends on other things such as the other processes running on the same machine and so on. In fact, running the same program several times usually produces slight differences in the relative ordering of the output from the two threads.

This illustrates an important point about threading: for unsynchronized threads such as these, it is not possible to predict the order in which the instructions in the two threads will be run relative to each other, or which thread will finish first.

You might also wonder what happens if the thread running Main() finishes before the thread running RunThread(). Does the program just quit and kill off the secondary thread before it is finished? In fact, the overall process that manages all the threads in a program will continue running until all the threads in that process have finished, so we don't need to worry about parts of the program not being given enough time to complete.

Another interesting feature of using a delegate to define the entry point for a thread is that, since the type of the method represented by the delegate has a void return type, the ThreadStart delegate can be used as a multicast delegate, as described earlier in this chapter. This feature is not often used, but we could, for example, add a second method called RunThread2() to the SimpleThread class, and then add this method to the ThreadStart delegate in Main(). That is, we could add the following method to the class:

```
public void RunThread2()
{
   for (int i = 0; i < 50; i++)
   {
      Console.WriteLine("Thread2 time: " + (i * 100) +
         " ms.");
      Thread.Sleep(100);
   }
}
```

and then add the following line after line 21 above:

```
threadDelegate += new ThreadStart(simpleThread.RunThread2);
```

The ThreadStart delegate now has two methods (RunThread and RunThread2) attached to it, so it will run both these methods when the thread starts. Note, however, that these two methods are being run by the *same* thread, so they will be run serially rather than in parallel.

8.6.3 ☐ **Uses of threads**

Like Java, a C# program has several threads running by default when it starts. One of these threads runs the code in Main() and another runs the garbage collector.

In text-only programs such as this, the main use of secondary threads is in running long calculations in the background while the main thread allows the user to interact with the program in other ways. This sort of design means that the user does not have to wait for a long calculation to finish if there are other things that can be done that require less time.

We will see in Chapter 10 that threads are also very useful in graphical programs when we wish to run an animation without locking up a program and disabling user input.

■ Summary

This chapter has introduced the idea of a delegate and illustrated how it can be used to represent other methods within a program. The main use of delegates in C# is as event handlers, since they allow us to attach methods to particular events generated from user interaction and other sources. We will see how this works in a GUI program in the next chapter.

We also introduced threads, since a thread uses a delegate to determine which method should be run when it is started.

Exercises

8.1 Write a class called Greetings which contains several methods that construct a string which provides a greeting for a particular occasion, such as a birthday, Christmas, wedding anniversary, etc. Each method should accept a single string as a parameter. For example, a method called Birthday() would accept a string that could contain a person's name and return a string that combined this name with a greeting to produce a message such as 'Happy Birthday, Philip!'.

Within the Greetings class, define a delegate that represents methods with the same type as those of the greetings methods. Then provide a method which asks the user for a name, then displays a menu listing the available greetings and asks the user to select a greeting. The program should then use the delegate to call the correct greeting method and print out the resulting message.

8.2 Modify the program in the previous exercise so that each greetings method prints the message directly rather than returning a string, and thus make each method void so that it can be used with a multicast delegate. Modify the menu system so that the user can specify more than one greeting for each name entered, then add the corresponding methods to the delegate so that a single delegate call prints all the desired methods.

GUI programming with Windows Forms $\qquad$ 9

9.1 ■ Using the .NET libraries

Although everything we have seen so far has relied on a console window for its output, C# and .NET are, of course, designed mainly for graphical user interface (GUI) programs, since the vast majority of software packages available today are of this form.

Besides moving from textual to GUI programs, there is another fundamental change in this chapter. Up to now, we have concentrated on describing the C# language – its keywords, data types and statements. We did make use of a few external classes for such things as reading and writing output to the console, dealing with exceptions and so on. However, most of the code used only elements of the C# language.

However, as we mentioned in Chapter 1, C# is part of the much larger .NET programming environment. One of the main ideas behind .NET is that classes can be written in any .NET-compliant language and linked in with classes written in any other .NET-compliant language. We can write one class in C#, another in Visual Basic .NET and yet another in Visual C++ .NET, then link them all together to produce a single executable program.

In order to make this sort of multi-language programming possible, the .NET class libraries have been written so that they are accessible to any .NET-compliant language. This means that classes such as `Console` and `Exception` that we have used in earlier chapters are also available to Visual Basic .NET and Visual C++ .NET programs in the same form as we have used them in C# programs. The only difference is that the appropriate syntax for each language must be used to call the class methods.

This concept of language-independent classes will probably be new to Java programmers, but in practice it shouldn't cause any problems. If we restrict ourselves to using only C# in writing a program, the fact that the class libraries are also available to other languages will not affect the coding at all.

9.2 ■ Writing GUI code in C# – the choice of environment

Depending on your Java background, you may be used to writing Java code in a simple text editor such as Notepad and then using a console window to run the `javac` Java compiler, followed by a `java` command to run the program, or you may have used some sort of *development environment* in which various tools are available to help you structure your code, find compilation errors, trace the code using a debugger and so on.

Most environments beyond a simple text editor will have some sort of *code generation* feature in which a skeleton class or method definitions will be produced for you. More advanced environments provide graphical editors that help you place components such as buttons and menus onto the background window or panel, and then generate the code that makes these components appear when the program is run.

Although these facilities can be helpful, they suffer from two major problems. First, most code generation systems produce much more code than is really needed to display the interface you've drawn in the editor. This excessive code not only slows down the compilation and running of the program, but makes the code harder to read and maintain.

Second, this automated code usually hinders the understanding of what the program is actually doing. Since this book's primary concern is to help you, the reader, *understand* how C# works, we want to keep the amount of extraneous code to a minimum. (There is, of course, another reason why some readers may not wish to use a development environment – cost. Most of the professional development packages are not cheap.)

For these reasons, we will take what may seem to some readers a more primitive approach to writing Windows code in C#. Although this may involve a bit more typing (but not all that much), the gain in understanding should more than offset the wear and tear on your fingers. Once you understand how C# works in a GUI programming situation, you are, of course, free to use all the graphical features of your favourite code-writing environment.

At the time of writing, the most common development environment for C# is Microsoft's Visual Studio .NET, 2003 edition. Since this system is so commonly used, we will describe how to write 'minimal' code using it, but the techniques we use should work equally well if your only environment is a simple text editor and console window.

If you have written any GUI code in Java, you will be familiar with Java's `import` statement, which imports external packages into your program and thus allows access to the classes within these packages. For example, if we want to use the `JFrame` class (which produces a top-level window) from within Java's Swing package, we would need the statement:

```
import javax.swing.JFrame;
```

at the start of any file that refers to `JFrame`s. Alternatively, if we want to use a number of classes from within the Swing package, we can import them all at once with the statement:

```
import javax.swing.*;
```

How do we link in the external libraries in C# that we need to write Windows programs? In previous chapters where we dealt with text-only programs, we used the statement

```
using System;
```

at the start of most of our files. This allowed us to write text to the console window with a statement such as

```
Console.WriteLine("Some text.");
```

Since `Console` is a class within the `System` namespace, we can see that `using` works in a similar way to `import`. In Java, an `import` statement will not compile unless the compiler can find the file containing the package to which the `import` refers. This is specified in Java's 'classpath', which can be given as part of the Java compiler command line as in

```
javac -classpath <list of directories>
```

In C#, in order to allow a `using System` statement to be accepted by the compiler, a *reference* to a thing called an *assembly* containing the `System` namespace must be made. If we are using a command line to compile the code, a reference can be made using the `/r` option in the compiler command. To refer to `System`, we can say:

```
csc /r:System.dll CodeFile.cs
```

Veteran Windows users will recognize the `System` assembly as a DLL (dynamic linked library), that is, a collection of classes that is linked into the program when it runs and is not stored in the .exe file produced by the compiler.

Depending on how the system paths are set up on your computer, you may need to give the full pathname to the assembly file, so the above line may need to look something like:

```
csc
  /r:C:\Windows\Microsoft.NET\Framework\v1.0.3705\System.dll
  CodeFile.cs
```

where the whole command would be typed on a single line in the console. The actual path may vary on your machine depending on where you installed Windows and what version of Visual Studio you have installed. The version number may be different from 1.0.3705.

In fact, you probably won't need to add a reference to `System.dll` from the command line since the basic `System` namespace is referenced by default anyway. However, to use other assemblies you may need to add explicit references in the compiler command. Multiple assemblies can be referenced by giving a comma-separated list of files:

```
csc /r:System.dll,System.Windows.Forms.dll CodeFile.cs
```

9.3 ■ Windows code in Visual Studio .NET

Even for code purists, writing C# Windows code entirely in a text editor can be a bit tedious, so we can use Visual Studio .NET to manage the code we write, but we will try to avoid its excesses by preventing it from generating its own code. This is not that difficult, but we do need to set up a project in a special way to get it to work.

To demonstrate, we will write a simple program which does nothing more than display an empty window on the screen. First, create a new project by selecting the File menu, then New → Project. In the New Project dialog, select 'Visual C# Projects' in the 'Project Types' list, and 'Empty Project' in the 'Templates' list. Give the project a name (we will use SimpleForm in what follows) and a location, and click OK.

An 'empty project', as its name implies, has no code files in it, so our first task is to add one. In the 'Solution Explorer' (if Solution Explorer isn't visible, select the View menu and choose 'Solution Explorer'), right-click on the name of the project, and select 'Add new item'. Choose 'Code file' from the 'Templates' list, give the new file a name such as SimpleForm.cs (with a .cs extension) and click OK.

Insert the following code into this code file (we'll explain what it does below):

```
using System;
using System.Windows.Forms;

class SimpleForm : Form
{
  public static void Main()
  {
    SimpleForm simpleForm = new SimpleForm();
    Application.Run(simpleForm);
  }
}
```

If you try to compile this code, you will get two errors. The first error says: 'SimpleForm.cs(2): The type or namespace name "Windows" does not exist in the class or namespace "System" (are you missing an assembly reference?)'. The error is on line 2, so is a problem with the using statement, and the clue to fixing it is that we are, in fact, missing an assembly reference as it suggests.

This program *could* be compiled from the command line using the command

```
csc /r:System.dll,System.Windows.Forms.dll SimpleForm.cs
```

In Visual Studio .NET, however, we need to add a *reference* to System.dll and System.Windows.Forms.dll in the Solution Explorer. To do this, expand the branch labelled with the project name (SimpleForm, if you've been following along) and you should see a node labelled 'References'. Right-click on this and select 'Add reference'. In the dialog that appears, select the .NET tab, and then scroll down until you get to System.dll. Select it, then press the 'Select' button on the right, then repeat the process to select System.Windows.Forms.dll, then press OK. Expanding the References node in Solution Explorer should now show System and System.Windows.Forms listed. The program should now compile and run without errors.

Running this program first displays a console window, and then a small, empty square window appears. The window has a normal title bar (except there is no text in it), with an icon in the upper-left corner that contains a system menu, and the usual three buttons in the upper-right corner allowing us to minimize, maximize and close the window.

9.4 ■ Console versus Windows programs

If we close this empty window by clicking the 'X' button in the upper-right corner, the console window shows 'Press any key to continue', as happens with a text-only application such as those we have shown in earlier chapters. This isn't normal behaviour for a 'true' Windows program, so what's going on?

In fact, if we use Visual Studio .NET to generate a 'true' Windows application (this can be done by selecting 'Windows application' from the 'Templates' list in the New Project dialog at the start), we get a ready-made program that will show the same empty window when it compiles and runs, except there is no console window in the background.

The key to the difference is that true Windows programs make no reference to a console – in fact, the very concept of a console is absent from such programs. When generating the executable file using the C# compiler, there is an option that can specify whether a console or Windows application is to be generated. When we chose an 'Empty Project' instead of a 'Windows Application', this option was set to 'console'. To change it to a proper Windows application, right-click on the project name (`SimpleForm`) in Solution Explorer and select 'Properties'. Select Common Properties → General from the list and find 'Output Type' in the 'Application' list, then select 'Windows Application' from the combo box and click OK. Now run the program again and you will see the empty window appear but without a console window in the background.

Since a true Windows program doesn't have a console to start it up, why don't we leave our program set to 'Windows Application'? For one very good reason: since a Windows Application has no access to a console, we cannot print any output using `Console.WriteLine()`. In your Java programming career, you probably made good use of Java's `System.out.println()` to print out the state of variables or control paths in your program as you were debugging it. The only way we can access equivalent functionality in C# is to leave the program output type set to 'Console'. Once we have finished debugging the program and want to release it to our clients, we would recompile it with the output type set to 'Windows' to get rid of the console.

But what if we have dozens of `Console.WriteLine()` statements scattered throughout the code? Do we have to go through and remove them all when we recompile the program as a Windows application? No, since a Windows program will simply ignore all calls to the console, so the output will not appear anywhere.

9.5 ■ The structure of a Windows program

Now let us consider what the code given in the simple example above actually does. We repeat the code for convenience:

```
using System;
using System.Windows.Forms;

class SimpleForm : Form
{
  public static void Main()
  {
    SimpleForm simpleForm = new SimpleForm();
    Application.Run(simpleForm);
  }
}
```

The class `SimpleForm` inherits `Form`, which is the main window class in the `System.Windows.Forms` namespace (so its full name is `System.Windows.Forms.Form`). A `Form` in C# acts much like a `JFrame` in Java Swing – it is a top-level container into which other components can be placed. By creating a custom class that inherits `Form`, we are creating the main window for our application, and we can add other components to produce the layout we wish.

In `Main()`, we create an instance of `SimpleForm` and then call `Application.Run()` on this instance. The `Application` class is also in the `System.Windows.Forms` namespace, and contains several methods (all static) and properties that manage the running of a Windows application. `Application.Run()` is the standard way of starting a Windows program, and its parameter should be the main window that is the basis of the GUI display. In other words, the `Form` that is passed to `Application.Run()` is the one that, when closed, shuts down the entire program.

9.6 ■ Editing a Windows Form

One final note about the `SimpleForm` program before we progress to something a bit more interesting. In Visual Studio .NET, a class that inherits `Form` is interpreted by the editor as one for which the Form Editor can be invoked. If you look in Solution Explorer at the node corresponding to the `SimpleForm` class file (with the label `SimpleForm.cs`), you will see the accompanying icon looks like a little dialog box. If you right-click on this node and select 'View Designer', the main editor window switches to a graphical display of the form and allows you to edit it by placing components such as buttons on the form.

This Form Editor can be useful for laying out components, but you should beware that every time you do anything using this editor, changes are made automatically to the code file. If you want to keep your code 'clean', you may want to avoid using the Form Editor.

To see the effects of using the Form Editor, try adding a single button to the form. Display the Toolbox (by using the View menu and selecting Toolbox), then open the list of Windows Forms components. Select the Button from this list and then click the mouse anywhere on the form. A button with the label 'button1' should appear.

Now look in the code file for `SimpleForm` to see what changes have been made to the code. We find the following lines have been added:

```
private System.Windows.Forms.Button button1;

private void InitializeComponent()
{
  this.button1 = new System.Windows.Forms.Button();
  this.SuspendLayout();
  //
  // button1
  //
  this.button1.Location = new System.Drawing.Point(112, 72);
  this.button1.Name = "button1";
  this.button1.TabIndex = 0;
  this.button1.Text = "button1";
  //
  // SimpleForm
  //
  this.AutoScaleBaseSize = new System.Drawing.Size(5, 13);
  this.ClientSize = new System.Drawing.Size(292, 273);
  this.Controls.AddRange(new System.Windows.Forms.Control[]
    {this.button1});
  this.Name = "SimpleForm";
  this.ResumeLayout(false);
}
```

As we will see later, we do not actually need all this code to display the button, so it is one example of how code-generating environments can quickly bloat your source code files. What's worse is that going back to the design editor and deleting the button doesn't delete all the code that was inserted.

Because we have been developing our program starting from an Empty Project, we will also find that this added code will not compile until we add another assembly reference for the `System.Drawing` namespace that is used at several points.

9.7 ■ Building a first GUI program from scratch

As a first example of a Windows Forms program built without the aid of any code-generation tools, let us write a program which displays the small form with a single button in it that we produced at the end of the previous section. The complete program is:

```
using System;
using System.Windows.Forms;
using System.Drawing;

class SimpleForm : Form
{
    Button button;

    public SimpleForm()
    {
        button = new Button();
        button.Text = "Press me!";
        button.Location = new Point(100, 100);
        button.Size = new Size(80, 25);
        this.Controls.Add(button);
    }

    public static void Main()
    {
        SimpleForm simpleForm = new SimpleForm();
        Application.Run(simpleForm);
    }
}
```

The code should be fairly obvious since the Windows Forms components are logically structured, and it is easy to understand their various properties by using the documentation for the classes. We add a Button as a data field in the class. We then add a constructor for the class and inside here, we create the Button, set its text to 'Press me!', its location to pixel coordinates (100, 100) and its size to a width of 80 pixels and a height of 25 pixels. The Point and Size classes are from the System.Drawing namespace, which is why we have a using System.Drawing statement on line 3.

The last line in the constructor accesses a property of a Form called Controls, which contains a list of the controls attached to the Form. The Add() method just adds the Button to the list of controls managed by this Form. Whenever a Form is displayed, it automatically displays all controls that it contains, so we don't need any special code to display the Button.

When this program is run, we see the result shown in Figure 9.1.

Figure 9.1 Interface displayed by the `SimpleForm` class

The button is displayed properly and can be pressed with the mouse, but of course nothing happens when it is pressed. To make something happen, we need to add an event handler to the program that responds to the event generated by a button press.

9.8 ■ Adding an event handler

From Chapter 8, we know that events in C# are really delegates, and that to handle an event we must write a method with a particular parameter list and add this method to the list of methods contacted by the delegate.

As we mentioned in Chapter 8, adding an event handler for a GUI component is much easier than the event example we presented in that chapter, since the process of *generating* the event is all done within the code for the component, so all we have to do is write a method that responds to the event, and add this method to the event delegate.

We will write a very simple event handler to begin with:

```
public void ButtonPressed(object source, EventArgs info)
{
   Console.WriteLine("Button pressed.");
}
```

Recall from Chapter 8 that all event handler methods must have the same type: they must all be `void` and must all take two parameters. The first parameter must be an `object` (or class derived from `object`) and the second must be an `EventArgs` (or class derived from it).

The `ButtonPressed()` method is added to the `SimpleForm` class above. To connect this method with the `Button`, we need to add it to the `Button`'s event delegate. A `Button`, like most components in Windows Forms, can generate a number of different types of events, so we need to specify the event to which we wish to respond. As usual, a complete list of the available events is found in the documentation for the `Button` class.

In our case, we want to respond to the button being pressed, and the correct event delegate is called `Click`. To connect the event delegate for the `Click` event to the `ButtonPressed()` event handler method, we add the following line as the last line in the `SimpleForm` constructor:

```
button.Click += new EventHandler(ButtonPressed);
```

Running the program now will produce the same display as before, but if we press the button, the text 'Button pressed.' appears in the console window. Note that this will only work if the program is being run as a console application – if you run it as a Windows application, pressing the button will have no effect.

Incidentally, the entire code for this program is 29 lines. Producing the equivalent program using Visual Studio's 'Windows Application' option in the New Project dialog requires 94 lines. Admittedly it is faster to write since most of the code is generated for you, but the resulting code is a lot harder to understand.

9.9 ■ Layouts: anchors and docks

If you have done any GUI programming in Java, you may well be wondering about the last example. We specified the button's location and size using precise pixel coordinates, while in Java all positioning and sizing of components is usually handled by Java's layout managers such as `FlowLayout`, `GridLayout` and so on. Are there C# equivalents of these layout managers?

The short answer is 'no, there aren't'. C# does provide some simple formatting tools with anchors and docks which we will discuss in a minute, but nothing approaching the versatility of Java's layout managers. Some Java programmers may think of this as a blessing, since layout managers in Java are notoriously difficult to master. However, once they are understood, they do provide elegant solutions to laying out containers, and they provide component systems that resize perfectly with their containers.

One of the main reasons that Java uses the layout manager system is that it is platform independent, and cannot rely on the same graphical layouts being available on all platforms. Using a relative positioning method provides much greater portability. Since .NET and C# are (for the moment) designed for Windows only, platform independence wasn't a consideration in their design. However, it does seem rather short-sighted to restrict .NET to a hard-coded pixel coordinate system rather than using the layout manager method.

The only facilities for defining layouts in C#, apart from hard-coding the bounds of a control, are *anchors* and *docks*. The Anchor property of a control allows the distance of each edge of the control from the corresponding edge of the client area to be fixed, meaning that the control retains its position relative to the enclosing container if the container is resized. A control may also be *docked* so that it nestles up against one of the edges of its container, as is common with toolbars and status bars.

An anchor is specified by setting a control's Anchor property to one or more of the options in the AnchorStyles enumeration. The choices are None, Top, Bottom, Left or Right. It is possible to combine several of these options by using the bitwise OR operator |. The default for a control is actually AnchorStyles.Left | AnchorStyles.Top, which means that a control retains its distance from the left and top edges of its container if the form is resized. This is easily demonstrated by resizing the window produced by SimpleForm above – the 'Press me' button remains the same distance from the top-left corner.

We can reset the Anchor so that the button remains the same distance from the bottom right by inserting the following line in the SimpleForm constructor:

```
button.Anchor = AnchorStyles.Bottom | AnchorStyles.Right;
```

Setting Anchor to AnchorStyles.None causes a control to retain its position relative to all four sides, which means that if the button starts off centred, it will remain centred as the form is resized.

So far, all the Anchor options just cause the control to adjust its position when the form is resized, leaving its size unchanged. Including opposite edges in an Anchor, however, will cause the control to stretch or shrink when the container is resized. For example, if we say:

```
button.Anchor = AnchorStyles.Left | AnchorStyles.Right;
```

then the left and right sides of the button are anchored to the corresponding edges of the container. Changing the width of the container causes the button's width to increase or decrease so that the sides of the button remain the same distance from sides of the form. This can cause the button to disappear completely if the container's width is reduced too much.

Although the Anchor property may seem easy to use and fairly powerful, it falls far short of Java's layout managers. The main problem is that there is no way of anchoring one control *to another control* rather than just to the edge of the container. This makes mimicking such things as Java's GridLayout and BorderLayout very difficult, which means that it is not easy to build sensible resizing behaviour into a C# GUI.

One way of adding sensible resizing behaviour into a Windows Forms program is to write a customized handler for the Layout event, which is generated whenever a form is resized. By recalculating the sizes and positions of the controls whenever the form is resized, we can ensure that the layout still looks correct for various sizes and shapes of the form. We include an example of this in the pizza-ordering program later in this chapter.

The `Dock` property allows a control to be docked along one of the edges of its container. Docking a control causes it to expand to fill the entire edge of the container, no matter what size it was given originally. Setting the `Dock` property requires choosing one of the options in the `DockStyle` enumeration, which have the same names as those in `AnchorStyles`. The main difference between anchoring and docking is that only one `DockStyle` may be selected at a time, since it doesn't make sense to try to dock a control along two edges at once.

To dock a button along the bottom edge, we can say:

```
Button.Dock = DockStyle.Bottom;
```

9.10 ■ Using the MSDN documentation

Glancing back at the `SimpleForm` program above, we can see that we set several properties of the `Button` by writing the statements:

```
button.Text = "Press me!";
button.Location = new Point(100, 100);
button.Size = new Size(80, 25);
```

The fields `Text`, `Location` and `Size` are all C# properties of the `Button` class (or of its base class), and allow many of the visible features of the `Button` to be specified.

This is the most common method by which features of GUI components are specified in Windows Forms. All components have a large number of properties that can be set, and the main 'secret' of efficient programming using .NET is to know how to discover what properties are available for the various components.

One of the most important skills to be learned when using large libraries such as those in .NET is how to use the documentation for the various classes in the library. The main source for .NET documentation is the MSDN (Microsoft Developer Network) library. If you have a full installation of Visual Studio .NET, you will have a version of the MSDN library that was current when the CDs were released. For an up-to-date version, you can use the on-line MSDN documentation available at http://msdn.microsoft.com/library/. If you have Internet access, the on-line version is recommended as it is always up to date.

It is worth taking a few minutes to understand how to use the MSDN library, since you will (or should) refer to it frequently as you develop C# code. First, we need to know how to find the page we want. Let us find the documentation for the `Button` class in the on-line MSDN library.

Unfortunately, the structure of the MSDN web site seems to change frequently (in fact, it changed several times during the writing of this book), so there is no guarantee that the instructions that follow will still apply when you are reading the book.

If we are searching for documentation on a C# class, the best place to start is to expand the .NET Development node in the tree on the left of the http://msdn.microsoft.com/library/ page. Then select, in turn, .NET Framework SDK, .NET Framework, Reference and finally Class Library. The main panel on the right should now display a list of all the namespaces in the .NET class library. You may want to bookmark this page in your web browser – that way, if the link changes again you should be redirected to the new location.

Starting from the Class Library page, select the namespace containing the class you want – in this case System.Windows.Forms for the Button class. This can be done either by expanding the Class Library node in the tree on the left, or by scrolling down the main panel until a link to System.Windows. Forms is found.

Within the System.Windows.Forms node, find 'Button class'. This will give an overview of the `Button` class. At the top of each overview page for a class is the inheritance hierarchy – we can see that `Button` actually has a hierarchy of five base classes extending back to `System.Object`.

Beneath the inheritance hierarchy is a grey box showing the declaration of the class in the various .NET languages. Remember that .NET is a language-independent library, so that all its classes are available in all languages that .NET supports. In the documentation, we see the `Button` class declared in Visual Basic, C#, C++ and JScript. From the C# declaration (or any of the others, if you are comfortable with the syntax in these other languages) we see that `Button` inherits `ButtonBase` as its immediate base class, and also implements the `IButtonControl` interface. (We can tell that `IButtonControl` is an interface and not a class, since .NET naming conventions specify that interface names begin with 'I'.)

Beneath the grey box are several sections giving general information on the class. Next, for most classes, some example code is given as to how they might be used. The usefulness of the example code varies, depending on what we want to do with the class. Keep in mind that most classes have a large number of properties and methods, so one or two examples can't cover all possible uses of the class.

At the bottom of the documentation page is a 'See also' section which often contains useful links to other related classes. For `Button`, there are links to `RadioButton` and `CheckBox` which are two other common controls that are related to the push button.

The most useful link from an overview page, however, is usually the 'members' page. Clicking on 'Button members' brings up a page giving a complete list of all properties, constructors, methods and events available in the `Button` class. In this list we will find the three properties used in the `SimpleForm` program earlier, along with many other properties.

Many of the properties and methods are inherited from one of `Button`'s base classes, and this is noted in the documentation. Also, many of the entries contain examples of how to use that property or method, or links to other pages containing examples.

It should be obvious from the number of entries on the 'Button members' page that no book can give a comprehensive coverage of everything that can be done, even with this single class, let alone with all the .NET library classes. This is why it is so important to master the skill of using the MSDN documentation to discover the capabilities of the various classes. In most cases, a property or method already exists to do whatever you want to do in a program, so it is well worth scanning the documentation to see what's available before embarking on writing your own code.

Although the MSDN library is the main source of information on the .NET libraries, there are many other sites on the Internet that contain articles, information and examples of .NET code, and the volume of information is growing rapidly as .NET and C# gain in popularity. Using one of the many Internet search facilities will usually bring up a list of sites containing information on almost any .NET class, so it is well worth trying a web search if you get stuck with a coding problem.

9.11 ■ A simple calculator in Windows Forms

As a slightly more involved example of a GUI program using Windows Forms which illustrates some of the properties of the controls, we will convert the text version of the arithmetic calculator program that we introduced in Chapter 8 into a full GUI program. The general layout of the program will provide two text boxes into which users can type the two numbers, and a button control for each of the arithmetic operations. The answer will be displayed in another text box, but editing in this last text box will not be allowed. The interface should look like Figure 9.2.

Figure 9.2 Interface for the simple calculator program

We'll present the complete code for this program, although it can be a bit tedious to read, since most of the code just sets the various properties of the controls. However, it is a good example for getting an idea of just how easy it is to set up most of the properties of controls. The code follows:

```
1.  using System;
2.  using System.Drawing;
3.  using System.Windows.Forms;
4.
5.    public class ArithmeticForm : Form
6.    {
7.      private Label enterIntsLabel;
8.      private TextBox num1TextBox;
9.      private TextBox num2TextBox;
10.     private Label answerLabel;
11.     private TextBox answerTextBox;
12.     private Button addButton;
13.     private Button subtractButton;
14.
15.     public ArithmeticForm()
16.     {
17.        InitializeComponents();
18.     }
19.
20.     private void InitializeComponents()
21.     {
22.        enterIntsLabel = new Label();
23.        num1TextBox = new TextBox();
24.        num2TextBox = new TextBox();
25.        addButton = new Button();
26.        subtractButton = new Button();
27.        answerLabel = new Label();
28.        answerTextBox = new TextBox();
29.
30.        Font labelFont = new Font("Arial", 10.5f,
              FontStyle.Bold);
31.        Font buttonFont = new Font("Arial", 10,
32.           FontStyle.Bold | FontStyle.Italic);
33.        Font textBoxFont = new Font("Arial", 10,
              FontStyle.Bold);
34.
35.        enterIntsLabel.Location = new Point(16, 30);
36.        enterIntsLabel.Size = new Size(160, 20);
37.        enterIntsLabel.Text = "Enter 2 integers:";
38.        enterIntsLabel.Font = labelFont;
39.
40.        num1TextBox.Location = new Point(16, 56);
41.        num1TextBox.Size = new Size(80, 20);
42.        num1TextBox.Font = textBoxFont;
43.        num1TextBox.TabIndex = 0;
44.
```

```
45.        num2TextBox.Location = new Point(128, 56);
46.        num2TextBox.Size = new Size(80, 20);
47.        num2TextBox.Font = textBoxFont;
48.        num2TextBox.TabIndex = 1;
49.
50.        addButton.Location = new Point(16, 112);
51.        addButton.Size = new Size(80, 25);
52.        addButton.Text = "&Add";
53.        addButton.Font = buttonFont;
54.        addButton.BackColor = Color.Honeydew;
55.        addButton.ForeColor = Color.DarkGreen;
56.        addButton.TabIndex = 2;
57.        addButton.Click += new EventHandler(addButton_Click);
58.
59.        subtractButton.Location = new Point(128, 112);
60.        subtractButton.Size = new Size(80, 25);
61.        subtractButton.Text = "&Subtract";
62.        subtractButton.Font = buttonFont;
63.        subtractButton.BackColor = Color.PeachPuff;
64.        subtractButton.ForeColor = Color.DarkRed;
65.        subtractButton.TabIndex = 3;
66.        subtractButton.Click +=
67.           new EventHandler(subtractButton_Click);
68.
69.        answerLabel.Location = new Point(16, 155);
70.        answerLabel.Size = new Size(65, 16);
71.        answerLabel.Text = "Answer:";
72.        answerLabel.Font = labelFont;
73.
74.        answerTextBox.Location = new Point(80, 152);
75.        answerTextBox.ReadOnly = true;
76.        answerTextBox.Size = new Size(120, 20);
77.        answerTextBox.Font = textBoxFont;
78.        answerTextBox.BackColor = Color.White;
79.        answerTextBox.TabStop = false;
80.
81.        ClientSize = new Size(225, 205);
82.        this.BackColor = Color.FromArgb(255, 200, 150);
83.        Controls.AddRange(
84.          new Control[] {
85.                           answerTextBox,
86.                           answerLabel,
87.                           subtractButton,
88.                           addButton,
89.                           num2TextBox,
90.                           num1TextBox,
```

```
91.                              enterIntsLabel
92.                         }
93.          );
94.       Text = "Arithmetic Demo";
95.       }
96.       private void addButton_Click(object sender, EventArgs e)
97.       {
98.          int num1 = int.Parse(num1TextBox.Text);
99.          int num2 = int.Parse(num2TextBox.Text);
100.         answerTextBox.Text = "" + (num1 + num2);
101.      }
102.
103.      private void subtractButton_Click(object sender,
104.         EventArgs e)
105.      {
106.         int num1 = int.Parse(num1TextBox.Text);
107.         int num2 = int.Parse(num2TextBox.Text);
108.         answerTextBox.Text = "" + (num1 - num2);
109.      }
110.
111.      public static void Main()
112.      {
113.         Application.Run(new ArithmeticForm());
114.      }
115.  }
```

Lines 7 through 13 declare the controls that appear on the form. We've seen the Button earlier, and we've added some Labels and TextBoxes. The constructor (line 15) calls InitializeComponents() to set up the controls and add the event handlers.

We create the controls by calling their default constructors on lines 22 to 28. Next, we create some Fonts which define text styles that will be used in the various controls. The Font class is similar to Java's Font class, in that it allows us to specify font names, sizes and styles (bold, italic, etc). The Font constructor comes in several overloaded versions, but here we have used a three-parameter form to specify the font name as 'Arial', the size and the style. The labelFont and textBoxFont are bold, while the buttonFont is bold and italic. Note that we use a bitwise OR operator | to combine the two FontStyle values (line 32).

Starting on line 35, we define the properties of the various controls. Most of this code should be fairly obvious, so we will just mention a few of the highlights.

As in the earlier example, we specify a Location and Size for all the controls. All three types of control that we are using in this example have a Text property, but since we want the TextBoxes to be empty when the program starts, we do not set Text for them.

The two TextBoxes for entering the two numbers and the two Buttons for doing the calculations have a TabIndex property assigned to them. Most Windows programs that contain controls allow the user to press the Tab key to move from one control to the next. The order in which the controls receive *focus* (that is, become the active control that can receive input from the keyboard) is specified by the `TabIndex` property. The first control in the tab series should have its `TabIndex` set to 0, with other controls set to 1, 2, 3, and so on in the desired order.

By default, controls that accept user input (such as `Buttons` and `TextBoxes`) are included in the tab sequence, while those that are passive controls (such as `Labels`) are not. In this example, the `answerTextBox` control is meant to be a passive control, since its purpose is to display the answer, and should not accept input. We exclude it from the tab sequence by setting its `TabStop` property to `false` (line 79). The user is also prohibited from interacting with `answerTextBox` by setting its `ReadOnly` property to `true` (line 75).

The `Buttons` have *mnemonic keys* defined for them. A mnemonic key allows the `Button` to be 'clicked' (that is, it sends a 'click' event for that `Button`) by using the keyboard rather than the mouse. To use a `Button`'s mnemonic, the Alt key is held down and one of the alphanumeric keys is pressed. The key that is to be used for a given `Button` should be one of the letters in the `Button`'s `Text`, and is specified by placing a `&` (ampersand) before that letter in the `Text` string (line 52 for the Add button and 61 for Subtract). The mnemonic letter is shown underlined when the `Button` is displayed, as can be seen from Figure 9.2

The `Buttons` also show how the `ForeColor` and `BackColor` can be set. For the Add button, this is done on lines 54 and 55. The .NET `Color` class comes with a large number of pre-defined colours (note that the American spelling of 'color' must be used when referring to the `Color` class), some with quite exotic names. For example, we set the `BackColor` of the Add button to 'Honeydew' which is a light yellowish green. For controls with text, the `ForeColor` defines the colour of the text. The Add button therefore has dark green text on a honeydew background, and the Subtract button has dark red text on a peach puff background. (These colours will, of course, not be visible in the book, but running the program will reveal them in all their glory.)

Colours may also be specified using standard RGB notation, as we have done on line 82 where we set the `BackColor` for the form itself. The `Color` class contains a static method `FromArgb()` which has a number of overloaded forms. The one we have used here takes three parameters, giving the red, green and blue components of the colour. Each of these three parameters can have a value between 0 and 255. Pure red, for example, is (255, 0, 0), yellow is (255, 255, 0) and so on. The colour we have given on line 82 is a shade of orange. We will consider colours in more detail when we study graphics in Chapter 10.

After all the components have been defined, we set up the properties of the form itself, beginning on line 81, where we set the size of the form's *client area*. The client area of a form is the area of the main display panel, excluding the title bar, menu (if there is one, which there isn't here), border frame, and so on. Since the positioning of the controls usually takes place entirely within the client area, this size is the best one to specify when deciding on the dimensions of the form.

In the earlier example, containing only a single `Button`, we used `Controls.Add()` to add the `Button` to the form. Here we demonstrate a method for adding a range of controls to the form in a single statement. The `AddRange()` method takes as its parameter an array of `Control`. On line 83, we call `AddRange()` and define an array as its parameter, filling the array with all the controls we just created. The order in which the controls are listed doesn't matter, since they have all had their positions defined earlier, so they should all appear in the correct locations.

On line 94, we set the `Text` for the form itself, which defines the text that appears in the title bar at the top of the frame.

Lines 97 through 109 define the event handlers for the two `Button`s, and these handlers are added to the event delegates for the 'click' event for the `Button`s on lines 57 and 66.

Finally, the whole program is started in `Main()` on line 111.

9.12 ■ Error handling and the `ErrorProvider` control

The GUI version of the simple calculator in the last section lacks one important feature: the ability to detect input errors in the two text boxes. As we saw in Chapter 7, the standard way of handling errors is by means of exceptions. We can use exceptions to detect errors in GUI programs as well, but .NET provides a convenient control for reporting to users that they have made errors in input. In this section, we'll introduce the `ErrorProvider` control to report invalid input into the two text boxes in the simple calculator.

An `ErrorProvider` can display a flashing red icon containing an exclamation mark next to the control into which the user has made incorrect input. When the mouse pointer hovers over the icon, a tooltip message explaining the problem can be displayed (see Figure 9.3).

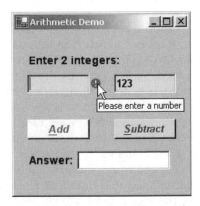

Figure 9.3 An `ErrorProvider` displays an icon with an exclamation mark and a popup message if incorrect or no input is provided

We will also coordinate the contents of the two text boxes with the state of the two buttons. The buttons will be disabled (unable to be pushed) until both text boxes contain valid integers.

Since most of the code is the same as in the original `ArithmeticForm` class, we'll refer back to the code in the previous section and indicate where the new code is inserted.

First, we'll need to use some classes from a new namespace, so we insert the following statement after line 3:

```
using System.ComponentModel;
```

We need to add the `ErrorProvider` as a class field. After line 13, we insert the declaration:

```
private ErrorProvider errorProvider;
```

The single `ErrorProvider` can be used to report errors in any number of controls, as we will see below. To initialize it, we insert a call to its constructor after line 28:

```
errorProvider = new ErrorProvider();
```

All the controls are created and initialized in the same way as before, but we do need a way of testing the contents of the text boxes to see if they contain valid integers. As we mentioned earlier, each control in .NET is capable of generating a variety of event types. We've seen only the `Click` event in the `Button` class so far, but over the course of the book, we will see many other examples of events and their handlers.

In this case, we are interested in checking the contents of a `TextBox` for validity as an `int`. The process of a control acquiring focus, having data entered into it, and then losing focus actually generates several events, any or all of which can be handled in our code. Let us consider the process for a `TextBox`.

First, when the `TextBox` is *entered* (by having the mouse clicked over it, for example) an `Enter` event is generated. The process of entering a control also gives it *focus*, but a separate `GotFocus` event is also generated after `Enter`, although for controls, handling `Enter` is usually all that is necessary.

After the `TextBox` receives focus, the user can interact with it by typing characters on the keyboard. The default response of a `TextBox` to keyboard events is, of course, to echo the keys as characters in the box. However, each keystroke also generates several events which can be handled in the code.

When focus passes from the `TextBox` to another control on the form, a `Leave` event is generated. After leaving a control, a `Validating` event is generated. The handler for `Validating` should contain some code that tests the user's input to see if it is valid for the intended purpose. For example, a text box that is meant to contain an email address could be tested to ensure that the string contains '@' and at least one '.'.

A `Validating` event delegate contains a `bool Cancel` property, which should be set to `true` if the input is not valid. If this is done, the remaining events in the focus series are skipped. If `Cancel` is `false`, the next event generated is `Validated`, indicating that the `Validating` event succeeded.

The handler for this event could be used to remove any error messages displayed with previous, invalid input, for example. Finally, there is a `LostFocus` event to finish the sequence.

We can use `Validating` and `Validated` events to perform the tests on the data entered into the `TextBox`es. By consulting the documentation for these two events, we find that `Validating` is a delegate for a `CancelEvent Handler` (a descendant of `EventHandler`) while `Validated` is a delegate for the standard `EventHandler`. We therefore add the following methods to provide the event handlers for these two events:

```csharp
private void OnValidating(object sender, CancelEventArgs e)
{
  if(sender is TextBox)
  {
    if (!ValidateNumber((TextBox)sender))
    {
      e.Cancel = true;
    }
  }
}

private void OnValidated(object sender, EventArgs e)
{
  if(sender is TextBox)
  {
    errorProvider.SetError((TextBox)sender, "");
  }
}

private bool ValidateNumber(TextBox textBox)
{
  string numText = textBox.Text;
  if(numText.Equals(""))
  {
    errorProvider.SetError(textBox, "Please enter a number");
    return false;
  }
  try
  {
    int.Parse(numText);
  }
  catch (Exception ex)
  {
    errorProvider.SetError(textBox,
      "Number must be an integer");
    return false;
  }
  return true;
}
```

Before we explain this code, we will finish off the modifications to the program by adding event handlers for Validating and Validated to the two TextBoxes. After line 43, we insert the two lines:

```
num1TextBox.Validating +=
    new CancelEventHandler(OnValidating);
num1TextBox.Validated +=
    new EventHandler(OnValidated);
```

These lines add the handlers to the first TextBox. We add a similar pair of lines after line 48 to provide handlers for the other TextBox:

```
num2TextBox.Validating +=
    new CancelEventHandler(OnValidating);
num2TextBox.Validated +=
    new EventHandler(OnValidated);
```

Now let us consider what the event handling code does. Referring to OnValidating() above, we test that sender is a TextBox, and if so, call ValidateNumber() to test the text that the user has entered in the box.

ValidateNumber() extracts the text from the TextBox and first tests to see if the user has entered anything in the box at all. If not, the errorProvider has its error message set to 'Please enter a number', and the control to which it refers is set to textBox which is the object that generated the Validating event. Note that the single errorProvider can serve multiple controls, since the control to which it is to refer is passed to errorProvider as the first parameter.

If the user *has* typed something in the box, the next bit of code in ValidateNumber() checks that this text is a valid integer. This time, we use a try block to catch any exceptions thrown by the int.Parse() method. We don't need to save the int returned by this method, since all we are doing is checking that numText contains a string that can be parsed to a valid int. If an exception is thrown, the errorProvider has its message set to 'Number must be an integer'.

If either of these tests is failed, the errorProvider will flash the error icon next to the control that was passed to it in its parameter list. If the contents of the text box pass both tests, ValidateNumber() returns true.

Back in OnValidating(), we see that if the value returned from ValidateNumber() is false, the Cancel property of the CancelEventArgs parameter is set to true. This has two effects in the program.

First, it prevents the Validated event from being generated. Second, it retains the focus in the TextBox which generated the original Validating event, thus forcing the user to enter correct data before proceeding. Attempting to press either button when invalid data has been entered in a text box will cause the text box with the current focus to validate its contents and, if the validation fails, the user will be forced to go back and correct the data in that text box.

There is still a flaw in this program in that if the user enters a *correct* integer in the first text box and then presses a button *without* shifting the focus to the second text box, the second text box doesn't get a chance to validate itself and an unhandled exception gets thrown. This can be solved by inserting a check at the start of the two `Button` event handlers. We insert the following code after line 97 and again after line 105:

```
if (num1TextBox.Text.Equals("") ||
   num2TextBox.Text.Equals(""))
   return;
```

At the time of writing, there is a nasty bug in the use of the `Validating` event. The problem is that once a control that has validation checking attached to it gets the focus, the user cannot do anything else in the program until valid data is entered in the control. It is not even possible to shut down the program by pressing the 'X' in the title bar. Hopefully this will be sorted out in future versions of .NET.

9.13 ■ Checkboxes and radio buttons

We've now seen the essentials of setting up a Windows Form and adding controls to it. Although .NET, like most GUI environments, has a large number of controls that can be placed on forms, they all work in much the same way. The control has its position and location defined, is added to the form, and has one or more event handlers attached to it.

Although the various controls all work in similar ways, many controls have their own peculiarities, so it is worth considering the more commonly used ones in some detail. We'll begin in this section with checkboxes and radio buttons.

A checkbox is a control allowing the user to select or unselect a little square by clicking on the control. It is used to indicate a yes/no choice for an option that is independent of any other option.

Radio buttons usually occur in groups of two or more, since they allow the user to select one option out of several mutually exclusive choices. The name 'radio button' comes from the panel of buttons typically found on car radios, allowing one station to be selected quickly. Pushing any of the radio's buttons selects that station and deselects all the others.

As a simple demonstration program using the `CheckBox` and `RadioButton` controls, we'll write an application that allows the user to order a pizza by specifying the type of crust (deep pan or thin and crispy) and choose several toppings. The interface looks like Figure 9.4.

We use radio buttons to offer the choice of crust, since a pizza can only have one type of crust at a time. Checkboxes are used to select the toppings, since we can have several toppings on each pizza. A selected item has its text displayed in bold. Note that each of the two groups of buttons is enclosed in a border with a title. This uses the `GroupBox` control.

Figure 9.4 Interface for the pizza ordering program

The button at the bottom displays a small message box summarizing the order (Figure 9.5).

Figure 9.5 Message box displaying a summary of the order

The complete code for the program follows:

```
1.  using System;
2.  using System.Drawing;
3.  using System.Windows.Forms;
4.
5.  public class PizzaForm : Form
6.  {
7.      private GroupBox crustBox, toppingBox;
8.      private RadioButton deepPanRadio, thinCrispyRadio;
9.      private CheckBox[] toppings;
10.     private const int NumberOfToppings = 4;
11.     private Button orderButton;
12.     private Font checkedFont =
13.        new Font("Arial", 8, FontStyle.Bold);
14.     private Font uncheckedFont =
15.        new Font("Arial", 8, FontStyle.Regular);
16.
```

```
17.    public PizzaForm()
18.    {
19.      InitializeComponents();
20.    }
21.
22.    private void InitializeComponents()
23.    {
24.      crustBox = new GroupBox();
25.      crustBox.Bounds = new Rectangle(20, 20, 130, 75);
26.      crustBox.Text = "Select crust:";
27.
28.      deepPanRadio = new RadioButton();
29.      deepPanRadio.Bounds = new Rectangle(10, 15, 100, 20);
30.      deepPanRadio.Text = "Deep pan";
31.      deepPanRadio.CheckedChanged += new EventHandler
          (OnClick);
32.
33.      thinCrispyRadio = new RadioButton();
34.      thinCrispyRadio.Bounds = new Rectangle(10, 45, 110,
          20);
35.      thinCrispyRadio.Text = "Thin and crispy";
36.      thinCrispyRadio.Checked = true;
37.      thinCrispyRadio.Font = checkedFont;
38.      thinCrispyRadio.CheckedChanged +=
39.        new EventHandler(OnClick);
40.      crustBox.Controls.AddRange(new Control[]
41.        { deepPanRadio, thinCrispyRadio }
42.      );
43.
44.      toppingBox = new GroupBox();
45.      toppingBox.Size = new Size(200, 80);
46.      toppingBox.Text = "Select toppings:";
47.
48.      toppings = new CheckBox[NumberOfToppings];
49.      for (int i = 0; i < NumberOfToppings; i++)
50.      {
51.        toppings[i] = new CheckBox();
52.        toppings[i].Click += new EventHandler(OnClick);
53.        toppingBox.Controls.Add(toppings[i]);
54.      }
55.
56.      toppings[0].Bounds = new Rectangle(10, 15, 90, 20);
57.      toppings[0].Text = "Olives";
58.
59.      toppings[1].Bounds = new Rectangle(10, 45, 90, 20);
60.      toppings[1].Text = "Anchovies";
61.
```

```
62.     toppings[2].Bounds = new Rectangle(100, 15, 90, 20);
63.     toppings[2].Text = "Pepperoni";
64.
65.     toppings[3].Bounds = new Rectangle(100, 45, 90, 20);
66.     toppings[3].Text = "Mushrooms";
67.
68.     orderButton = new Button();
69.     orderButton.Size = new Size(90, 30);
70.     orderButton.Text = "&Place order";
71.     orderButton.Click += new EventHandler(OnClick);
72.
73.     ClientSize = new Size(225, 250);
74.     this.BackColor = Color.FromArgb(255, 200, 150);
75.     this.Controls.AddRange(
76.       new Control[] { crustBox, toppingBox, orderButton }
77.     );
78.
79.     Text = "Greasy Pizzas R Us";
80.     this.Layout += new LayoutEventHandler(OnLayoutForm);
81.
82.     Rectangle screenSize = Screen.GetWorkingArea(this);
83.     this.Location =
84.       new Point(screenSize.Width/2 - this.Size.Width/2,
85.       screenSize.Height/2 - this.Size.Height/2);
86.   }
87.
88.   private void OnLayoutForm(object sender,
         LayoutEventArgs args)
89.   {
90.     if (sender == this)
91.     {
92.       crustBox.Location = new Point(
93.         this.ClientSize.Width/2 - crustBox.Size.
           Width/2, 20);
94.       toppingBox.Location = new Point(
95.         this.ClientSize.Width/2 - toppingBox.Size.Width/2,
96.         crustBox.Location.Y + crustBox.Size.Height + 20);
97.       orderButton.Location = new Point(
98.         this.ClientSize.Width/2 - orderButton.Size.
           Width/2,
99.         toppingBox.Location.Y + toppingBox.Size.
           Height + 20);
100.    }
101.  }
102.
103.  private void OnClick(object sender, EventArgs args)
104.  {
```

```
105.    if (sender is CheckBox)
106.    {
107.       CheckBox checkBox = (CheckBox)sender;
108.       if (checkBox.Checked)
109.          checkBox.Font = checkedFont;
110.       else
111.          checkBox.Font = uncheckedFont;
112.    }
113.    else if (sender is RadioButton)
114.    {
115.       RadioButton radioButton = (RadioButton)sender;
116.       if (radioButton.Checked)
117.          radioButton.Font = checkedFont;
118.       else
119.          radioButton.Font = uncheckedFont;
120.    }
121.    else if (sender == orderButton)
122.    {
123.       string orderDescription = "You have ordered a\n";
124.       if (deepPanRadio.Checked)
125.       {
126.          orderDescription += "deep pan pizza with\n";
127.       }
128.       else if (thinCrispyRadio.Checked)
129.       {
130.          orderDescription += "thin and crispy pizza
               with\n";
131.       }
132.       for (int i = 0; i < NumberOfToppings; i++)
133.       {
134.          if (toppings[i].Checked)
135.          {
136.             orderDescription += toppings[i].Text + " ";
137.          }
138.       }
139.       MessageBox.Show(orderDescription, "Your order");
140.    }
141.  }
142.
143.  public static void Main()
144.  {
145.     Application.Run(new PizzaForm());
146.  }
147. }
```

The controls are set up in InitializeComponents() (line 22), so we'll examine what happens here. We first set up the box where the type of crust is selected. Since the idea behind a group of radio buttons is that only one out of the group can be selected at any one time, we need a way of assigning a radio button to a particular group. This is done by creating a *container* control and putting the radio buttons inside it. There are two containers in common use: the GroupBox (used here) and the Panel. The GroupBox allows a border with a title to be drawn around a set of controls, while the Panel can be invisible if all we want is a way of grouping controls together without changing their appearance.

These container controls act like mini-forms, in that controls can be added to them in the same way as to a top-level Form. The locations of the controls that are added to containers are relative to the upper-left corner of the container, and not to the overall Form.

Let us see how this works in the case of the GroupBox that holds the radio buttons for selecting the type of crust. The properties of the GroupBox are set on lines 24 to 26. We have used the Bounds property to set the location and size of the box in a single command – this is equivalent to separate statements setting Location and Size properties as we did in the calculator example. A Rectangle constructor takes four parameters: the first two are the coordinates of the upper-left corner and the next two are the width and height.

Next we create the two RadioButtons (lines 28 to 38). When we set the Bounds (lines 29 and 34) we must remember that the location coordinates are relative to the GroupBox into which we are placing the buttons. We add the two RadioButtons to the GroupBox on line 40.

We have added event handlers to the RadioButtons on lines 31 and 38. These handlers respond to the CheckedChanged event which occurs when the state of the button changes from checked to unchecked or vice versa. If all we were interested in was the state of the radio buttons when the main 'Place order' button is pushed, we wouldn't need to add event handlers to the radio buttons or the checkboxes, since we can just read their states when the button is pushed. However, to demonstrate that RadioButtons and CheckBoxes can generate events themselves, we've added event handlers that change the font of the buttons' text when they are selected. The event handler is the OnClick() method (line 103), which we will consider below.

We have set up the RadioButton group so that thinCrispyRadio is checked when the program starts (line 36). Since we are using a special bold font for checked buttons, we set the font on line 37.

The GroupBox that holds the CheckBoxes that allow the pizza toppings to be selected is set up on lines 44 to 46. Note that we specify only a size and not a location for toppingBox. The reason for this is that locations of the GroupBoxes are set dynamically whenever the main Form is displayed or resized, in order to keep them centred horizontally in the main frame. We'll see how this is done a little later.

Lines 48 to 54 create the array of CheckBoxes and assign event handlers to them so that their font can be changed when they are clicked. Incidentally, the reason we didn't use the Click event for the RadioButtons is that when one RadioButton is clicked, the others also change state at the same time, but only the button that was clicked actually generates a Click event. As a result, we would need a more circuitous route to update the fonts of all the radio buttons if we only listened for Click events from them. By listening instead for a CheckChanged event, we receive events from all RadioButtons whenever any one of them is clicked.

Lines 56 to 66 set up the CheckBoxes, again relative to the toppingBox that contains them. Lines 68 to 71 set up the 'Place order' button, including its event handler. Lines 73 to 77 set up the properties of the main form and add the two GroupBoxes and the Button to it.

Line 80 adds a handler for the Layout event, which is sent whenever anything happens to the main form that requires a recalculation of the layout of its components. This happens when the form is displayed when the program starts, and whenever the main frame is resized. The handler for this event is OnLayoutForm() (line 88). Here we position the two GroupBoxes and the Button so that they are always centred horizontally in the frame. This is done by using the ClientSize property of the Form to obtain the width of the client area. The crustBox is positioned 20 pixels below the title bar, and the other components are placed relative to the components above them, with a gap of 20 pixels between each pair of components.

The main form is also centred relative to the overall monitor screen on lines 82 to 85. The Screen class is a member of Windows.Forms that contains a number of properties and methods that allow information on the display device to be retrieved. The GetWorkingArea() method returns a Rectangle that contains the width and height of the visible area on the monitor (effectively it returns the current display resolution).

In fact, if we just want to display the form centred on the screen, there is a shorthand way of doing this. We could just insert the following line in the constructor:

```
StartPosition = FormStartPosition.CenterScreen;
```

FormStartPosition contains several properties that can be used to define the starting position of a form. However, the longer method used in the code above is useful to know if you want to customize the form's location.

Finally, we consider the event handler for the various buttons and checkboxes. The OnClick() method (line 103) handles events from all the RadioButtons, CheckBoxes and the Button. If the event is received from a CheckBox we set the font according to whether the box is checked or not (lines 105 to 112). If the sender is a RadioButton we do the same thing (lines 113 to 120). Notice that we can use the same OnClick method to respond to Click events from CheckBoxes and CheckChanged events from RadioButtons, since they both use the same type of delegate (that is, a delegate that expects a method that takes an ordinary EventArgs parameter).

If the sender is orderButton, we construct a message stating what the user has ordered by scanning the states of the RadioButtons and the CheckBoxes. We then use a popup MessageBox to display the order. The MessageBox class contains a number of methods for creating pre-configured message and information dialogs (similar to Java Swing's JOptionPane), and is very useful for quick display of a program's state.

9.14 ■ **Menus**

.NET provides two main types of menus, according to where they appear: standard menus which are attached to the menu bar which appears just below the title bar in a top-level frame, and context menus which may be attached to any control and which popup in response to a right mouse click.

Both types of menu are quite easy to add to a GUI program, so we present another example program illustrating both of them. Along the way we will also introduce a few other features that are useful in Windows programming.

The sample program displays a digital clock which updates its time every second. The interface is customizable in that the main window can be resized, and the text within the window will also resize to fit the new window size as best it can. The background and text colours may also be set using a standard Windows `ColorDialog`. Finally, a couple of radio buttons at the bottom allow either the local time or 'coordinated universal time' (what used to be called Greenwich Mean Time or GMT).

The main frame contains a menu which allows the colours to be set, and also allows the program to be shut down without using the 'X' button in the title bar. The radio buttons are each provided with a context menu which allows some information on what they do to be displayed. The main interface of the program is shown in Figure 9.6

Figure 9.6 Interface for the digital clock program

The code for the program follows:

```
1. using System;
2. using System.Drawing;
3. using System.Windows.Forms;
4.
5. public class ClockForm : Form
6. {
7.   private enum TimeType { Local, UTC };
8.
9.   private Panel timePanel;
10.  private RadioButton utcRadio, localRadio;
11.  private Label timeLabel;
```

```
12.    private MenuItem formMenu, colorMenu,
13.      backgroundMenu, foregroundMenu, exitMenu;
14.    private MenuItem utcHelpMenu, localHelpMenu;
15.    private Timer secondsTimer;
16.    private TimeType timeType;
17.
18.    public ClockForm()
19.    {
20.      InitializeComponents();
21.    }
22.
23.    private void InitializeComponents()
24.    {
25.      backgroundMenu = new MenuItem("&Background",
26.        new EventHandler(OnClick), Shortcut.CtrlB);
27.      foregroundMenu = new MenuItem("&Foreground",
28.        new EventHandler(OnClick), Shortcut.CtrlF);
29.      colorMenu = new MenuItem("&Colour",
30.        new MenuItem[] {backgroundMenu, foregroundMenu});
31.      MenuItem separator = new MenuItem("-");
32.      exitMenu = new MenuItem("E&xit",
33.        new EventHandler(OnClick));
34.      formMenu = new MenuItem("&Form",
35.        new MenuItem[] {colorMenu, separator, exitMenu});
36.      Menu = new MainMenu(new MenuItem[] { formMenu } );
37.
38.      ClientSize = new Size(200, 100);
39.      timeLabel = new Label();
40.      DateTime now = DateTime.Now;
41.      timeLabel.Text = now.ToString("T");
42.      Controls.Add(timeLabel);
43.
44.      timePanel = new Panel();
45.      Controls.Add(timePanel);
46.      utcRadio = new RadioButton();
47.      utcRadio.Text = "UTC";
48.      utcRadio.Click += new EventHandler(OnClick);
49.      utcHelpMenu = new MenuItem("What's this?",
50.        new EventHandler(OnClick));
51.      utcRadio.ContextMenu = new ContextMenu(
52.        new MenuItem[] { utcHelpMenu }
53.      );
54.
55.      localRadio = new RadioButton();
56.      localRadio.Text = "Local";
57.      localRadio.Click += new EventHandler(OnClick);
```

```
58.      localRadio.Checked = true;
59.      timeType = TimeType.Local;
60.      localHelpMenu = new MenuItem("What's this?",
61.        new EventHandler(OnClick));
62.      localRadio.ContextMenu = new ContextMenu(
63.        new MenuItem[] { localHelpMenu }
64.      );
65.
66.      timePanel.Controls.AddRange(new Control[]
67.        { localRadio, utcRadio }
68.      );
69.
70.      secondsTimer = new Timer();
71.      secondsTimer.Interval = 1000;
72.      secondsTimer.Enabled = true;
73.      secondsTimer.Tick += new EventHandler(OnTick);
74.
75.      Text = "ColourClock";
76.      Layout += new LayoutEventHandler(OnLayoutForm);
77.      Rectangle screenSize = Screen.GetWorkingArea(this);
78.      Location = new Point(screenSize.Width/2 - Size.
         Width/2,
79.        screenSize.Height/2 - Size.Height/2);
80.    }
81.
82.    private void OnLayoutForm(object sender,
83.      LayoutEventArgs args)
84.    {
85.      if (sender == this)
86.      {
87.        Rectangle clientRect = ClientRectangle;
88.        timeLabel.Bounds =
89.          new Rectangle(clientRect.X, clientRect.Y,
90.          clientRect.Width, clientRect.Height - 20);
91.        timeLabel.TextAlign = ContentAlignment.MiddleCenter;
92.        timeLabel.Font =
93.          new Font("Arial", ClientSize.Height/4);
94.
95.        timePanel.Bounds = new Rectangle(clientRect.X,
96.          clientRect.Height - 20, clientRect.Width, 20);
97.        localRadio.Bounds = new Rectangle(
98.          timePanel.Width/8, 0, timePanel.Width/2, 20);
99.        utcRadio.Bounds = new Rectangle(
100.         5*timePanel.Width/8, 0, timePanel.Width/2, 20);
101.      }
102.    }
103.
```

```
104.    private void OnClick(object sender, EventArgs args)
105.    {
106.      if (sender == backgroundMenu || sender ==
          foregroundMenu)
107.      {
108.        ColorDialog colorDialog = new ColorDialog();
109.        if (colorDialog.ShowDialog() == DialogResult.OK)
110.        {
111.          if (sender == backgroundMenu)
112.            timeLabel.BackColor = colorDialog.Color;
113.          else if (sender == foregroundMenu)
114.            timeLabel.ForeColor = colorDialog.Color;
115.        }
116.      }
117.      else if (sender == utcRadio)
118.      {
119.        timeType = TimeType.UTC;
120.        OnTick(null, null);
121.      }
122.      else if (sender == localRadio)
123.      {
124.        timeType = TimeType.Local;
125.        OnTick(null, null);
126.      }
127.      else if (sender == utcHelpMenu)
128.      {
129.        MessageBox.Show("Coordinated Universal Time (GMT)",
130.          "UTC");
131.      }
132.      else if (sender == localHelpMenu)
133.      {
134.        MessageBox.Show("Your local time", "Local");
135.      }
136.      else if (sender == exitMenu)
137.      {
138.        Application.Exit();
139.      }
140.    }
141.
142.    private void OnTick(object sender, EventArgs args)
143.    {
144.      DateTime now = new DateTime();
145.      if (timeType == TimeType.Local)
146.        now = DateTime.Now;
147.      else if (timeType == TimeType.UTC)
148.        now = DateTime.UtcNow;
149.      timeLabel.Text = now.ToString("T");
```

```
150.      }
151.
152.    public static void Main()
153.    {
154.        Application.Run(new ClockForm());
155.    }
156. }
```

The client area of the main frame consists of a `Label` that displays the time, and takes up most of the space, and a `Panel` at the bottom that contains the two radio buttons. Recall from the previous section that in order for a set of `RadioButtons` to form a mutually exclusive group, they must be enclosed in either a `GroupBox` or `Panel`.

Let us consider the structure of the menu first. When expanded, the menu looks like Figure 9.7.

Figure 9.7 Menus in the digital clock program

The main menu contains two items, 'Colour' and 'Exit', separated by a horizontal dividing line. The 'Colour' menu contains two submenu items for setting the background and foreground colours.

In .NET, the menu bar itself is represented by the `Menu` property of a `Form`. This property is assigned to a `MainMenu` object, which contains an array of `MenuItems`. Each `MenuItem` defines one of the menu headers that appears in the menu bar. In this program, we have only one such header for the 'Form' menu, so the `MainMenu` contains an array of only a single `MenuItem`.

Submenus, such as the 'Colour' menu here, are formed by attaching another array of `MenuItems` to the top-level `MenuItem`. In the code, we create the `MenuItems` for setting the colours on lines 25 to 30. Note that the `MenuItem` constructor has a number of overloads, depending on what sort of `MenuItem` is being defined – that is, whether the `MenuItem` is one that generates an event on which the program should act, or whether it is a header for other `MenuItems`. The `backgroundMenu` and `foregroundMenu` objects are ones that generate `Click` events, so we construct them by giving them a name, an event handler, and in this case, a shortcut key. Shortcut keys are defined by choosing constants from the `Shortcut` class. In this case we attach Ctrl+B to the 'Background' menu and Ctrl+F to the 'Foreground' menu.

The `colorMenu` (line 29) is created with a name and an array of `MenuItem`s which define the items that are attached to it as a submenu. No event handler is attached to this item since it is not itself a selection in the menu – it is only a header for other selections.

Line 31 adds the horizontal line between 'Colour' and 'Exit'. This is done by creating a `MenuItem` with a single dash as its parameter.

The `formMenu` is the top-level menu (the one whose header appears in the menu bar), and is built (line 34) by adding an array consisting of `colorMenu`, the `separator`, and `exitMenu`. Finally, the menu bar itself is assigned on line 36.

Event handlers for `MenuItem`s work the same way as those for `Button`s, so we use the single `OnClick` method (line 104) to handle all `Click` events in this program. We'll consider the various things it does when we come to them.

After creating the menus, we set up the `Label` that displays the time (line 39). To get the current system time, we use `DateTime.Now`, which returns a `DateTime` that contains the date and time, accurate to roughly 10 ms. To convert this to a displayable string, we use the `ToString()` method, but make use of one of its features that we have not yet encountered. Looking up the documentation for `ToString()` we find that it takes a `string` parameter which tells it how to format its output. If `ToString()` is printing a `DateTime` we can format the output in several ways. The 'T' parameter used on line 41 displays a 'short time', which is the hour, minute and nearest second (without any fractional part).

Starting on line 44, we create the `Panel` and add the radio buttons to it. This is done in much the same way as in the previous section. Selecting one of the radio buttons sets a parameter that specifies which time we wish to display (local or UTC). The extra bit here is the addition of a `ContextMenu` to the radio buttons. A `ContextMenu` is just like an ordinary menu except that it can appear anywhere on a form. Rather than being attached to a menu bar, a `ContextMenu` is attached to a specific control via that control's `ContextMenu` property. We create a `MenuItem` on line 49 and attach it to `utcRadio`'s `ContextMenu` property on line 51. This means that right-clicking on `utcRadio` with the mouse will display the menu at the position of the mouse pointer. If the 'What's this?' menu item is selected, a `Click` event is generated in the usual way. A `ContextMenu` is also attached to `localRadio` on lines 60 to 64 (see Figure 9.8).

Figure 9.8 Context menu in the digital clock program

The next new feature is the use of a `Timer` on line 70. We want the `Label`'s display to update once per second to show the new time. A `Timer` control generates an event at a fixed interval, which is specified in milliseconds (line 71). We start the `Timer` by setting its `Enabled` property to `true` (or by calling its `Start()` method). At each interval, the `Timer` generates a `Tick` event, so in order to update the display we add an event handler on line 73. This calls `OnTick()` (line 142) which refreshes the `Label`'s display, according to which type of time we wish to see, as specified by clicking one of the radio buttons as described earlier.

As with the pizza selection example, we leave the specification of the bounds of the `Label` and `Panel` to the `OnLayoutForm()` method (line 82), which allows these controls to be resized with the frame. As well as resizing the controls, we also scale the font used to display the time (line 92), although this is not perfect since it still requires the `Label` to be wide enough for the time to be displayed on one line. The positions of the radio buttons within the panel are also scaled with the frame.

Selecting one of the 'Colour' menu items brings up a `ColorDialog` which allows the user to select a colour, which is then assigned to either the foreground or background of the `Label` (lines 108 to 115).

9.15 ■ Dialogs, status bars and toolbars

Most GUI applications of any size contain one or more *dialog boxes*, which are separate windows that are displayed to allow the user to enter data or interact with the program in other ways. Status bars and toolbars are also fairly standard features in GUI programs, and we shall see that .NET provides support for both these features.

We will describe some of the properties of these three features first, and then present a substantial example that includes all of them along with a few other features that are useful in building GUI programs. This example is a version of the Windows Notepad program, which allows text files to be viewed, edited and saved to disk.

9.15.1 □ Dialogs

Unlike Java, which provides a separate `JDialog` class for implementing dialogs, .NET treats popup dialogs in exactly the same way as the `Form` that is used to display the main window of a program. Since the process of creating a dialog by adding controls to it is identical to that for creating the main window, we need not dwell on the process of actually building a dialog. The main skills to be mastered in using dialogs involve the interaction between the dialog and its owner – that is, the class that contains the code that displays the dialog in the first place.

Dialogs come in two varieties: *modal* and *non-modal*. A modal dialog, once displayed, must be dismissed (usually by clicking an 'OK' or a 'Cancel' button) before any other part of the interface can be accessed. The name 'modal' implies that the *mode* of interaction with the program has been changed from the main window to the dialog, and the dialog therefore locks the focus of the program upon itself until it is dismissed. Most dialogs in common applications are modal since, in most cases, it would be dangerous to allow the user to alter things in the main display and in the controls within the dialog at the same time.

Non-modal dialogs, as you might expect, allow the user to interact with the underlying window while they are still displayed. Since a non-modal dialog allows the user to switch back and forth between the main application and the dialog box, it should be used with care. A common example of a non-modal dialog is the find and replace dialog in word processors and code editors.

The standard procedure for building a dialog is to create a new class that inherits Form, create and add the various controls to the dialog to build its interface, and then provide a means by which the dialog can interact with its parent window, if required. The method of interaction is different for modal and non-modal dialogs, so we'll consider each separately.

For a modal dialog, typically the user enters data into various controls such as text boxes, list boxes and so on and, when they are satisfied with their entries, press 'OK' to transfer the information to the main window or, if they decide to quit without making any changes, press 'Cancel' to close the dialog and leave everything as it was.

Therefore, in addition to any controls for data entry, virtually all modal dialogs will have an 'OK' and a 'Cancel' button. .NET recognizes that these features are very common and provides special properties in a Form that allow them to be added without requiring separate event handlers to be written for them. These properties are called AcceptButton and CancelButton, and should be set to Buttons that have been created as controls displayed on the dialog. Clicking either of these buttons causes the dialog to close and return a value specified in the DialogResult enumeration. This value can be used in the parent class to determine which button the user pressed to close the dialog, and thus what action should be taken. For example, if the returned value is DialogResult.OK, the user wishes the data entered in the dialog to be applied to the program, so the calling method should provide code to do this. A returned value of DialogResult.Cancel indicates that the user wishes all entries in the dialog to be discarded. We will see examples of these two buttons in the Notepad example below.

A non-modal dialog is a bit more complicated, since it is possible for information entered into the dialog to be applied to the underlying window while the dialog is still visible. This means that we cannot just wait for the user to press an 'OK' or 'Cancel' button before taking any action. The dialog needs some way of communicating with its parent window on a continuing basis.

There are two ways this communication can be provided, but only one of them is recommended. The first (and faulty) method is to provide a public method in the main window which can be called by code from within the dialog class. This isn't a very good way of doing things, however, since it ties the dialog to the specific class that calls it. For example, suppose a non-modal dialog that allowed the user to search for a string within some text displayed on the main window required the main window class to contain a method called `FindText()` which did the actual searching. This `FindText()` method would be called whenever the user pressed a 'Find' button on the dialog. Doing things this way would require *all* classes that wanted to display this dialog to provide a method called `FindText()`, which could cause problems if that name has already been used for a different, unrelated method.

A much better way is to put the onus on the dialog to provide the machinery for the communication with its parent. This can be done quite easily by defining a customized event that is generated by the dialog whenever the user pressed the 'Find' button. The parent class can then add a handler for this event (and it can also call this event handler anything it likes). We have already seen in Chapter 8 how to define our own events, so this won't be too difficult. Basically, we add an event handler for the `Click` event of the 'Find' button in the dialog. This event handler in turn generates an instance of the customized event we have defined within the dialog.

Back in the main window class, we add a handler for this customized event. Thus, whenever the user clicks 'Find', the `Click` event from that button generates a custom event which is picked up by the handler in the main window, and that handler does whatever is required in the main class. Again, we will see an example of this in the program below.

Many modal dialogs now require some interaction with their parent window before they are closed. The most common example of this is the 'Apply' button which is now found on many dialogs in Windows programs, and which allows the user to apply the options specified in the dialog without having to close the dialog first. The same technique as that used to handle buttons in non-modal dialogs can be applied to such buttons in modal dialogs as well.

9.15.2 ☐ Status bars

A *status bar* is a control that typically extends across the bottom of a `Form` and is used to display information about the state of the program, or sometimes helpful messages explaining how controls work. A word processor's status bar, for example, typically contains the page, line and column numbers of the current location of the cursor and various other information.

.NET provides a dedicated `StatusBar` class with a lot of helpful properties that make using status bars quite easy. A `StatusBar` may be added to a `Form` simply by setting its parent to be that `Form`. By default, a `StatusBar` is docked to the bottom of the `Form` (docking was covered in section 9.9).

Rather than display information directly in the status bar, it is more usual to define one or more `StatusBarPanels` which are inserted inside the `StatusBar`. Each `StatusBarPanel` can contain text or an icon.

The Notepad example in section 9.16 shows several `StatusBar` features.

9.15.3 ☐ **Toolbars**

A *toolbar* is a strip of icons each of which acts as a button which, when pressed, generates an event that causes some change to the program. Common actions contained in toolbars are saving and loading files, copying, pasting, printing and so on. Often, toolbars provide shortcuts for menu items, and as a result many toolbar buttons will duplicate events generated by menus.

Although there is a `ToolBar` class in .NET, .NET's treatment of toolbars is actually quite clumsy and awkward to use, especially when it comes to associating events with individual toolbar buttons. There are two main hurdles to overcome in using a `ToolBar`. First, we need to create the toolbar and associate it with the images used for its buttons. Second, we need to connect these buttons with the events that they should generate when pushed.

Let us consider the connection between a toolbar and its button images first. The images can be provided either as separate bitmaps, each in its own file, or as a single strip image containing all the individual button icons pasted together. Since it is more common to find the images in separate files, we'll consider that case here. If you have Visual Studio .NET installed, you will find many of the more common toolbar images in a sub-directory of Visual Studio .NET. A typical path is Program Files\Microsoft Visual Studio .NET\Common7\Graphics\bitmaps. You can also use Visual Studio's (or many other programs') bitmap editor to create your own bitmaps.

Once we have the images prepared, we need to connect them to a `ToolBar`. The first step is loading the images into a C# program. Although this can be done directly from the bitmap file, it is a cleaner solution to embed the images directly into the .exe file that contains the application itself. If you are using Visual Studio .NET to develop your code, this can be done by starting in Solution Explorer (use the View menu to display Solution Explorer if it's not visible), right-clicking on the project and selecting Add → 'Add existing item'. In the dialog that appears, select 'Image files' in the 'Files of type' box and then find the bitmap files you want to add to the project. The bitmap files should now appear within your list of project files in Solution Explorer.

To embed each bitmap file in the .exe file, select the bitmap file in Solution Explorer and display its properties window. Set the 'Build Action' property to 'Embedded Resource' and you're done.

If you want to embed the bitmap files by using a command-line option for the compiler, use the `/res` (or `/resource`) option. For example, to embed a bitmap file called `Open.bmp`, use the command line:

```
csc /res:Open.bmp,DialogDemo.Open.bmp DialogDemo.cs
```

Here we have specified the filename (`Open.bmp`) and after it, the name by which it will be referred to within the code (`DialogDemo.Open.bmp`). The `DialogDemo` class is the class that will load the bitmap image into the program, so the name of the resource inside the code prepends the class name onto the file's name. The `DialogDemo.cs` file is, of course, the C# source code file. If we wish to embed several bitmap files, we need a separate /res entry for each file.

With these preparations made, we can see a typical `ToolBar` creation sequence in C# code:

```
Bitmap[] iconImage = new Bitmap[numberToolBarButtons];
iconImage[0] = new Bitmap(GetType(), "DialogDemo.Open.bmp");
// Add other images here
ImageList imageList = new ImageList();
for (int i = 0; i < numberToolBarButtons; i++)
   imageList.Images.Add(iconImage[i]);
toolBar = new ToolBar();
toolBar.Parent = this;
toolBar.ImageList = imageList;
ToolBarButton[] toolBarButton =
   new ToolBarButton[numberToolBarButtons];
for (int i = 0; i < numberToolBarButtons; i++)
   toolBarButton[i] = new ToolBarButton();
toolBarButton[0].ImageIndex = 0;
// Set the image indexes of remaining buttons
```

We create an array of `Bitmap`s (here `numberToolBarButtons` is a `const` defined earlier in the class that specifies the number of toolbar buttons). The `Bitmap` constructor we use here is designed for loading images that have been embedded in the .exe file – there are other versions of the constructor that allow us to load bitmaps directly from disk files.

This constructor's first parameter must specify the data type of the class that is loading the image, so we call `GetType()` to get this. The second parameter is the name by which the resource is referenced. This is the same name as that specified in the command-line entry above. If you used Visual Studio .NET to embed the resource, then make sure the correct class name is prepended to the file name.

After loading the button images, we create an `ImageList` and add each bitmap to it. Then we create the `ToolBar` itself, set its parent to the `Form` in which it is to appear, and then attach the `ImageList` to it.

Finally, we need to create an array of `ToolBarButton`s, and then set the `ImageIndex` of each button so that it corresponds to the correct entry in the `ImageList`.

If all this seems like a lot more work than Java's much simpler way of handling toolbars, we are not done yet. We must still attach event handlers to the toolbar. We might think that the easiest way of doing this is to attach an event handler to each `ToolBarButton`, but in fact, this is not possible, since a `ToolBarButton` does not, in fact, generate any events (or at least any that are useful). Only the toolbar itself can generate any events, and there is only a single event (`ButtonClick`) which is generated no matter which button on the toolbar is clicked. We must sort out, within the event handler, which button was actually pushed and then call the correct action.

The event handler is a special type, so a typical event handler definition is:

```
toolBar.ButtonClick +=
  new ToolBarButtonClickEventHandler(OnToolBarButton);
```

The handler method must sort out which button was actually pushed and act accordingly. The information on which button was pushed is contained within the `ToolBarButtonClickEventArgs` parameter passed to the event handler. This parameter has a `Button` property that contains the actual `ToolBarButton` reference for the button that was pushed.

However, typically a toolbar button duplicates a menu item, so it would be nice if we could associate a `ToolBarButton` with a `MenuItem`. We can do this by defining the `Tag` property for each `ToolBarButton`. A `Tag` can be anything (it is defined as an `object`), so we can simply attach the actual `MenuItem` as the `Tag`. Thus the final bit of code we need to initialize a `ToolBar` is a set of `Tag`s:

```
toolBarButton[0].Tag = openMenu;
```

Here, we have attached `openMenu` (which is a `MenuItem`) as the `Tag` for the first `ToolBarButton`.

Finally, we can look at the event handler for the `ButtonClick` event:

```
private void OnToolBarButton(object sender,
  ToolBarButtonClickEventArgs args)
{
  if (args.Button.Tag == openMenu)
    OnOpen(null, null);
  else if (args.Button.Tag == saveMenu)
    OnSave(null, null);
  else if (args.Button.Tag == fontMenu)
    OnFont(null, null);
  else if (args.Button.Tag == findMenu)
    OnFind(null, null);
}
```

We examine the `Tag` to see to which menu command the pushed toolbar button corresponds, and then call the event handler for that menu command to process the toolbar's event. The two `null` parameters passed to the event handlers assume that these handlers do not need the source or the `EventArgs` parameters to carry out their commands – if they did, we would need to take more care in passing the correct values to these handlers.

As you can see, this is an excessively cumbersome and clumsy way of handling toolbars, but once we have written the code for one toolbar, we can always use it as a template for producing others. If you are using Visual Studio .NET, there is a toolbar editor that can be used to accomplish most of the preceding tasks, although the code within the event handler must, of course, still be written by hand.

9.16 ■ Example: a Notepad clone

We will now present a complete program that implements some of the features of the standard Notepad program that has come with Windows since ancient times. The program consists of three classes: one for the main window, one for a modal dialog that allows the text in the title bar of the main window to be set (not particlarly useful, but it illustrates a simple modal dialog), and a more useful non-modal dialog which allows the user to search for a given string in the text that is displayed on the main window.

The main window contains a menu, toolbar, main display area and a status bar, as shown in Figure 9.9.

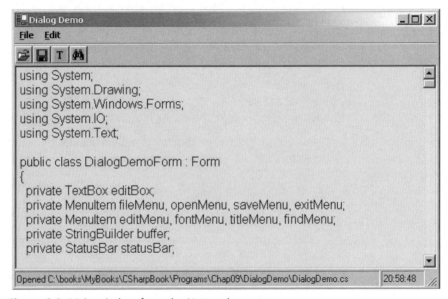

Figure 9.9 Main window from the Notepad program

The status bar displays various messages, including help text for the menu items, the name of saved and opened files, and so on. It also displays the current time on the right, which is updated each second. This time panel also displays a tooltip (not shown) that shows the current date.

The toolbar contains buttons for opening and saving files, a button which displays a font selection dialog, and another button which opens the text search dialog.

The title section dialog is modal, and contains only a `Label` and `TextBox` in addition to the standard buttons (Figure 9.10).

The non-modal 'Find text' dialog allows the user to find the first occurrence of the entered string (Figure 9.11).

Figure 9.10 Modal dialog for setting the title

Figure 9.11 Non-modal dialog for text searching

Extending its functionality to allow more general searches would not be diffi-cult, but we've omitted this to keep an already long example from getting longer.

In order that the reader can see how everything fits together, we will pres-ent the complete code for the three classes. First, we present the main Form:

```
1.  using System;
2.  using System.Drawing;
3.  using System.Windows.Forms;
4.  using System.IO;
5.  using System.Text;
6.
7.  public class DialogDemoForm : Form
8.  {
9.     private TextBox editBox;
10.    private MenuItem fileMenu, openMenu, saveMenu, exitMenu;
11.    private MenuItem editMenu, fontMenu, titleMenu, findMenu;
12.    private StringBuilder buffer;
13.    private StatusBar statusBar;
14.    private StatusBarPanel statusInfoPanel, timePanel;
15.    private ToolBar toolBar;
16.    private const int numberToolBarButtons = 4;
17.
18.    public DialogDemoForm()
19.    {
20.       InitializeComponents();
21.    }
22.
23.    private void InitializeComponents()
24.    {
25.       openMenu = new MenuItem("&Open", new
          EventHandler (OnOpen),
26.          Shortcut.Ctrl0);
```

```
27.     saveMenu = new MenuItem("&Save", new
        EventHandler(OnSave),
28.       Shortcut.CtrlS);
29.     MenuItem separator = new MenuItem("-");
30.     exitMenu = new MenuItem("E&xit", new
        EventHandler(OnClick));
31.     fileMenu = new MenuItem("&File", new MenuItem[]
32.       {openMenu, saveMenu, separator, exitMenu});
33.     openMenu.Select += new EventHandler(OnMenuSelect);
34.     saveMenu.Select += new EventHandler(OnMenuSelect);
35.     exitMenu.Select += new EventHandler(OnMenuSelect);
36.
37.     fontMenu = new MenuItem("Fo&nt", new
        EventHandler(OnFont),
38.       Shortcut.CtrlN);
39.     titleMenu =
40.       new MenuItem("&Title", new EventHandler(OnTitle),
41.       Shortcut.CtrlT);
42.     findMenu = new MenuItem("&Find", new
        EventHandler(OnFind),
43.       Shortcut.CtrlF);
44.     editMenu = new MenuItem("&Edit", new MenuItem[]
45.       {fontMenu, titleMenu, findMenu});
46.     fontMenu.Select += new EventHandler(OnMenuSelect);
47.     titleMenu.Select += new EventHandler(OnMenuSelect);
48.     findMenu.Select += new EventHandler(OnMenuSelect);
49.
50.     Menu = new MainMenu(new MenuItem[] { fileMenu,
        editMenu } );
51.
52.     editBox = new TextBox();
53.     editBox.Multiline = true;
54.     editBox.ScrollBars = ScrollBars.Vertical;
55.     editBox.HideSelection = false;
56.     editBox.TextAlign = HorizontalAlignment.Left;
57.     editBox.Font = new Font("Arial", 12);
58.     Controls.Add(editBox);
59.
60.     statusBar = new StatusBar();
61.     statusBar.Parent = this;
62.     statusBar.ShowPanels = true;
63.     statusInfoPanel = new StatusBarPanel();
64.     statusInfoPanel.AutoSize = StatusBarPanelAutoSize.
        Spring;
65.     timePanel = new StatusBarPanel();
66.     timePanel.Text = DateTime.Now.ToLongTimeString();
67.     timePanel.AutoSize = StatusBarPanelAutoSize.Contents;
```

```
68.    timePanel.ToolTipText = DateTime.Now.
       ToShortDateString();
69.    Timer panelTimer = new Timer();
70.    panelTimer.Tick += new EventHandler(OnTimer);
71.    panelTimer.Interval = 1000;
72.    panelTimer.Start();
73.    statusBar.Panels.AddRange(
74.       new StatusBarPanel[] { statusInfoPanel,
          timePanel } );
75.
76.    Bitmap[] iconImage = new Bitmap[numberToolBarButtons];
77.    iconImage[0] = new Bitmap(GetType(), "DialogDemo.
       Open.bmp");
78.    iconImage[1] = new Bitmap(GetType(), "DialogDemo.
       Save.bmp");
79.    iconImage[2] = new Bitmap(GetType(), "DialogDemo.
       Font.bmp");
80.    iconImage[3] = new Bitmap(GetType(), "DialogDemo.
       Find.bmp");
81.    ImageList imageList = new ImageList();
82.    for (int i = 0; i < numberToolBarButtons; i++)
83.       imageList.Images.Add(iconImage[i]);
84.    toolBar = new ToolBar();
85.    toolBar.Parent = this;
86.    toolBar.ImageList = imageList;
87.    ToolBarButton[] toolBarButton =
88.       new ToolBarButton[numberToolBarButtons];
89.    for (int i = 0; i < numberToolBarButtons; i++)
90.       toolBarButton[i] = new ToolBarButton();
91.    toolBarButton[0].ImageIndex = 0;
92.    toolBarButton[0].Tag = openMenu;
93.    toolBarButton[0].ToolTipText = "Open file";
94.    toolBarButton[1].ImageIndex = 1;
95.    toolBarButton[1].Tag = saveMenu;
96.    toolBarButton[1].ToolTipText = "Save file";
97.    toolBarButton[2].ImageIndex = 2;
98.    toolBarButton[2].Tag = fontMenu;
99.    toolBarButton[2].ToolTipText = "Change font";
100.   toolBarButton[3].ImageIndex = 3;
101.   toolBarButton[3].Tag = findMenu;
102.   toolBarButton[3].ToolTipText = "Search for text";
103.   toolBar.Buttons.AddRange(toolBarButton);
104.   toolBar.ButtonClick +=
105.      new ToolBarButtonClickEventHandler
          (OnToolBarButton);
106.
107.   ClientSize = new Size(500, 300);
108.
```

```
109.      Text = "Dialog Demo";
110.      Layout += new LayoutEventHandler(OnLayoutForm);
111.      StartPosition = FormStartPosition.CenterScreen;
112.      MenuComplete += new EventHandler(OnMenuComplete);
113.    }
114.
115.    private void OnLayoutForm(object sender, LayoutEvent
        Args args)
116.    {
117.      if (sender == this)
118.      {
119.        Rectangle clientRect = ClientRectangle;
120.        editBox.Bounds = new Rectangle(clientRect.X,
121.          clientRect.Y + toolBar.Height + 3,
122.          clientRect.Width, clientRect.Height -
123.          toolBar.Height - statusBar.Height - 3);
124.      }
125.    }
126.
127.    private void OnTimer(object sender, EventArgs args)
128.    {
129.      timePanel.Text = DateTime.Now.ToLongTimeString();
130.      timePanel.ToolTipText = DateTime.Now.ToString("D");
131.    }
132.
133.    private void OnToolBarButton(object sender,
134.      ToolBarButtonClickEventArgs args)
135.    {
136.      if (args.Button.Tag == openMenu)
137.        OnOpen(null, null);
138.      else if (args.Button.Tag == saveMenu)
139.        OnSave(null, null);
140.      else if (args.Button.Tag == fontMenu)
141.        OnFont(null, null);
142.      else if (args.Button.Tag == findMenu)
143.        OnFind(null, null);
144.    }
145.
146.    private void OnOpen(object sender, EventArgs args)
147.    {
148.      OpenFileDialog openDialog = new OpenFileDialog();
149.      openDialog.Filter =
150.        "Text files (*.txt)|*.txt|All files (*.*)|*.*";
151.      openDialog.FilterIndex = 2;
152.      if (openDialog.ShowDialog() == DialogResult.OK)
153.      {
154.        StreamReader streamReader =
155.          new StreamReader(openDialog.FileName);
```

```
156.          string line;
157.          buffer = new StringBuilder();
158.          while ((line = streamReader.ReadLine()) != null)
159.          {
160.            buffer.Append(line + "\r\n");
161.          }
162.          streamReader.Close();
163.          editBox.Text = buffer.ToString();
164.          statusInfoPanel.Text = "Opened " + openDialog.↩
              FileName;
165.        }
166.    }
167.
168.    private void OnSave(object sender, EventArgs args)
169.    {
170.      SaveFileDialog saveDialog = new SaveFileDialog();
171.      saveDialog.Filter =
172.        "Text files (*.txt)|*.txt|All files (*.*)|*.*";
173.      saveDialog.FilterIndex = 2;
174.      if (saveDialog.ShowDialog() == DialogResult.OK)
175.      {
176.        StreamWriter streamWriter =
177.          new StreamWriter(saveDialog.FileName);
178.        streamWriter.Write(editBox.Text);
179.        streamWriter.Close();
180.        statusInfoPanel.Text = "Saved " + saveDialog.↩
            FileName;
181.      }
182.    }
183.
184.    private void OnFont(object sender, EventArgs args)
185.    {
186.      FontDialog fontDialog = new FontDialog();
187.      fontDialog.Font = editBox.Font;
188.      if (fontDialog.ShowDialog() == DialogResult.OK)
189.      {
190.        editBox.Font = fontDialog.Font;
191.      }
192.    }
193.
194.    private void OnTitle(object sender, EventArgs args)
195.    {
196.      TitleDialog titleDialog = new TitleDialog();
197.      titleDialog.StartPosition = FormStartPosition.↩
            CenterScreen;
198.      if (titleDialog.ShowDialog() == DialogResult.OK)
199.      {
```

```
200.          Text = titleDialog.TitleText;
201.      }
202.  }
203.
204.  private void OnFind(object sender, EventArgs args)
205.  {
206.      FindDialog findDialog = new FindDialog();
207.      findDialog.Owner = this;
208.      findDialog.StartPosition = FormStartPosition.
          CenterScreen;
209.      findDialog.Find += new EventHandler(FindText);
210.      findDialog.Show();
211.  }
212.
213.  private void FindText(object sender, EventArgs args)
214.  {
215.      FindDialog findDialog = (FindDialog)sender;
216.      string findText = findDialog.FindText;
217.      if (findText.Length > 0)
218.      {
219.          int findLocation = editBox.Text.IndexOf(findText);
220.          if (findLocation > -1)
221.          {
222.              editBox.SelectionStart = findLocation;
223.              editBox.SelectionLength = findText.Length;
224.              editBox.ScrollToCaret();
225.          }
226.          else
227.          {
228.              statusInfoPanel.Text = "Text not found.";
229.          }
230.      }
231.  }
232.
233.  private void OnMenuSelect(object sender, EventArgs
      args)
234.  {
235.      if (sender == openMenu)
236.          statusInfoPanel.Text = "Opens a file from disk.";
237.      else if (sender == saveMenu)
238.          statusInfoPanel.Text = "Saves a file to disk.";
239.      else if (sender == exitMenu)
240.          statusInfoPanel.Text = "Quits the program.";
241.      else if (sender == fontMenu)
242.          statusInfoPanel.Text = "Sets the font in
              the text box.";
243.      else if (sender == titleMenu)
```

```
244.          statusInfoPanel.Text = "Sets the text in the ⤵
              title bar.";
245.        else if (sender == findMenu)
246.          statusInfoPanel.Text = "Search for text ⤵
              in main display.";
247.      }
248.
249.      private void OnMenuComplete(object sender, ⤵
         EventArgs args)
250.      {
251.        statusInfoPanel.Text = "";
252.      }
253.
254.      private void OnClick(object sender, EventArgs args)
255.      {
256.        if (sender == exitMenu)
257.        {
258.          Application.Exit();
259.        }
260.      }
261.
262.      public static void Main()
263.      {
264.        Application.Run(new DialogDemoForm());
265.      }
266. }
```

The components of the main window are created in `Initialize Components()` (line 23). The menu is created in the usual way, although we have added handlers for the `Select` event (lines 33 to 35 and 46 to 48). This event is generated when a menu item is selected by moving the mouse over it or by using the keyboard. The handler method `OnMenuSelect` (line 233) provides some help text in the status bar for each menu item. (We will explain `statusInfoPanel` below when we consider the status bar.)

The main display area for the text file is a `TextBox` (lines 52 to 55). The `TextBox` is a multiline box with a vertical scrollbar. Note that, unlike Java, the scrollbar is an integral part of the control rather than a separate control (like the `JScrollPane` in Java) into which the control must be placed.

The `HideSelection` property (line 55) specifies whether any selected text in the `TextBox` should be deselected when the control loses focus. We must set this to `false` since otherwise any text found when using the Find dialog below will not be highlighted in the main display.

The status bar is created on lines 60 to 74. Rather than using `Controls.Add()` to add the status bar to the main form, we set its `Parent` to be the enclosing frame (line 61). We use two `StatusBarPanels` to display the information in the status bar, so we turn on `ShowPanels` (line 62). The first panel (`statusInfoPanel`) is to be used to display the information messages such as help for menu items and which files have been opened or saved. We set its `AutoSize` to `StatusBarPanelAutoSize.Spring` which causes it to stretch (like a spring) to fill in all space not taken up by other panels in the status bar. It is this panel which is used in the OnMenuSelect() method (line 233) for displaying menu help.

The other panel (timePanel) is used for displaying the current time, updated each second. Its AutoSize is set to Contents, meaning that the panel is sized to fit the string that is displayed within it. The time is initialized on line 68, and a Timer is created to update this time (lines 69 to 72) in the same way as in the Clock example presented earlier. The Timer's event handler (line 127) updates the status bar display (line 129) and also sets this panel's tooltip to display the current date (line 130).

The code for creating the toolbar is on lines 76 to 105 and has been discussed above in the introduction on toolbars. The code here provides a complete example of a toolbar displaying four buttons. The event handler for the toolbar buttons is on line 133 and illustrates the correspondence between the toolbar buttons and the menu items they duplicate.

A few properties of the overall form are set up on lines 109 to 112. We have added a handler for the MenuComplete event, which is generated whenever a menu loses focus. The handler (line 249) clears the text in the status bar.

The layout of the form is defined in OnLayoutForm() (line 115). Note that we don't need to layout the toolbar or status bar, since they are managed by the parent form. We do, however, need to allow for the sizes of the toolbar and status bar when positioning the TextBox, which is meant to fit between them with a three-pixel gap at the top and bottom.

The event handler for the 'Open' menu item and toolbar button (line 146) illustrates the use of the built-in OpenFileDialog which displays the standard Windows file selection dialog. (The code within OnOpen() really should be enclosed in a try-catch block to handle file I/O exceptions, but we have omitted this to save space.)

A filename filter is defined on line 149 – this allows the file selector to display only files with certain extensions. We have provided two file types in the filter. Each type is specified as two strings separated by a vertical bar. The first string is the description that appears in the file selector dialog, and the second string is the pattern to match when selecting files from the current directory. Thus, the first file type on line 150 is specified as 'Text files (*.txt)|*.txt' which means that 'Text files (*.txt)' will appear in the 'Files of type' combo list in the dialog, and the directory will be searched to display all files that match the '*.txt' pattern specified in the second part of the description.

We can specify which filter is used when the dialog first appears by specifying the FilterIndex (line 151). Perversely, the FilterIndex value for the first filter in the list is 1, not 0, so the FilterIndex must be about the only indexed list in the language that does not start from zero by default. The code on line 151 therefore initializes the dialog to display 'All files' when it first appears.

The remaining code in OnOpen() illustrates the reading of text from a text file. The easiest way of doing this is to use a StreamReader (line 154) which can be created by using the FileName obtained from the file selector dialog. The StreamReader contains a number of methods that make reading text easy to do, such as the ReadLine() method (line 158) which reads a single line of text from the file.

We could use a `string` together with its `+=` operator to append each line to a string and build up a copy of the file in the program. However, this technique is not very efficient since each time some text is 'appended' to a `string` a new `string` must be created which causes a lot of processing overhead. A better way is to use a `StringBuilder` (line 157), whose `Append()` method does not require the creation of a new object with each line added to the `StringBuilder`. (A `StringBuilder` is similar to Java's `StringBuffer`.)

When all the text in the file has been read, we close the `StreamReader` (line 162) and then display the text in the `TextBox` (line 163) and display a message in the status bar.

The handler for the 'Save' menu item (line 168) works much like the `OnOpen()` method in reverse. We use a `StreamWriter` to write text to a disk file. This time, we can simply copy the entire contents of the `TextBox` and use the `Write()` method (line 178) to write the whole lot at once, rather than having to split up the text into separate lines.

The handler for the 'Font' menu item (line 184) displays the Windows font selection dialog and just sets the `TextBox`'s `Font` to the selection of the user.

The handler for the 'Title' menu item (line 194) retrieves the text entered by the user in the `TitleDialog` (considered below) and sets the main form's `Text` to this value. Note that we use `ShowDialog()` (line 198) to display the dialog in the same way as in the built-in dialogs for saving and loading files. `ShowDialog()` displays a *modal* dialog, and prevents access to the underlying window until the dialog is dismissed.

Finally, the 'Find' menu command is handled by `OnFind()` (line 204). The code that defines the Find dialog as a non-modal dialog occurs here rather than in the `FindDialog` class which we consider later. By setting the dialog's `Owner` as the main form (line 207) we ensure that the dialog always appears on top of the parent, and that if the main window is minimized, the dialog also disappears.

The key line that makes the dialog non-modal is line 210, where we use `Show()` rather than `ShowDialog()` to display the dialog. `Show()` displays a `Form` but allows access to the underlying, parent form at the same time.

We will consider the communication between the main form and the `FindDialog` below, but we will examine here how the search of the text is done once the search string has been retrieved from `FindDialog`.

As we will see below, when the user clicks the 'Find' button in `FindDialog`, the `FindText()` method in the main class (line 213) is called to handle the event. We can then retrieve the search string from `FindDialog` (lines 215 and 216). We first check that the user has actually entered a search string by checking that the string's length is greater than zero (line 217). If so, we use the `IndexOf()` method in the `string` class to search for the text (line 219). `IndexOf()` returns -1 if it cannot find the string, so we check this condition (line 220). If the string was found, we can set the `SelectionStart` and `SelectionLength` properties of the `TextBox` to highlight the string in the main display. To ensure that the selection is visible, we call `ScrollToCaret()` (line 224), which scrolls the text until the current selection is visible. If the string is not found, we display a message in the status bar (line 228).

As mentioned above, this simple searching procedure will only find the first occurrence of the search string. There are several overloads of `IndexOf()` that could be used to provide a better search by allowing searches for other occurrences. Other methods in `string` could be used to provide a case-insensitive search, or we could make use of the `Regex` class to search for *regular expressions*, which allow pattern matching.

We now consider the code for the modal dialog that allows the user to set the text in the title bar:

```
1. using System;
2. using System.Drawing;
3. using System.Windows.Forms;
4.
5. public class TitleDialog : Form
6. {
7.    TextBox titleBox;
8.
9.    public TitleDialog()
10.   {
11.      Text = "Select title";
12.      FormBorderStyle = FormBorderStyle.FixedDialog;
13.      ControlBox = false;
14.      MinimizeBox = false;
15.      MaximizeBox = false;
16.
17.      Label label = new Label();
18.      label.Text = "Enter title bar caption:";
19.      label.Bounds = new Rectangle(8, 5, 150, 20);
20.      titleBox = new TextBox();
21.      titleBox.Bounds = new Rectangle(8, 25, 150, 20);
22.
23.      this.Controls.AddRange(
24.         new Control[] { label, titleBox }
25.      );
26.
27.      Button button = new Button();
28.      button.Parent = this;
29.      button.Text = "OK";
30.      button.Bounds =
31.         new Rectangle(8, titleBox.Bottom + 5, 60, 20);
32.      button.DialogResult = DialogResult.OK;
33.      AcceptButton = button;
34.
35.      button = new Button();
36.      button.Parent = this;
37.      button.Text = "Cancel";
38.      button.Bounds =
39.         new Rectangle(98, titleBox.Bottom + 5, 60, 20);
```

```
40.        button.DialogResult = DialogResult.Cancel;
41.        CancelButton = button;
42.
43.        ClientSize = new Size(180, 80);
44.      }
45.
46.      public string TitleText
47.      {
48.        get
49.        {
50.          return titleBox.Text;
51.        }
52.      }
53. }
```

The dialog has a few settings made in the constructor (lines 11 to 15) which are fairly standard for a dialog. The FixedDialog border style provides a non-resizable, heavy border, and turning off ControlBox, MinimizeBox and MaximizeBox eliminates all the controls from the title bar. Several other properties may be worth defining here as well, such as setting ShowInTaskbar to false if you don't want a separate icon for the dialog to appear in the Windows task bar. Explore the documentation for Form to see what else is available.

Then we create and add the label and TextBox (lines 17 to 25). The OK and Cancel buttons are then created (lines 27 to 41). By setting the dialog's AcceptButton property to the OK button (line 33) we associate the OK button with the Enter key on the keyboard, so that pressing this key will close the dialog and return DialogResult.OK to the main form. Similarly, by setting the CancelButton property to the Cancel button, hitting the Esc key will close the dialog and return DialogResult.Cancel. Notice that we don't define event handlers for either of these buttons – setting the DialogResult property for a button (lines 32 and 40) provides the intended behaviour.

Once again, a reminder that there is nothing in the TitleText class that specifies whether the dialog is modal or non-modal – that is done by choosing whether to use ShowDialog() or Show() to display it as we mentioned earlier.

Finally, we consider the code for the non-modal, text search dialog:

```
1. using System;
2. using System.Drawing;
3. using System.Windows.Forms;
4.
5. public class FindDialog : Form
6. {
7.    TextBox findBox;
8.    public event EventHandler Find;
9.
10.   public FindDialog()
11.   {
12.     Text = "Find text";
```

```
13.      FormBorderStyle = FormBorderStyle.FixedDialog;
14.      ControlBox = false;
15.      MinimizeBox = false;
16.      MaximizeBox = false;
17.
18.      Label label = new Label();
19.      label.Text = "Enter search text:";
20.      label.Bounds = new Rectangle(8, 5, 150, 20);
21.      findBox = new TextBox();
22.      findBox.Bounds = new Rectangle(8, 25, 150, 20);
23.
24.      this.Controls.AddRange(
25.        new Control[] { label, findBox }
26.          );
27.
28.      Button button = new Button();
29.      button.Parent = this;
30.      button.Text = "Find";
31.      button.Bounds =
32.        new Rectangle(8, findBox.Bottom + 5, 60, 20);
33.      AcceptButton = button;
34.      button.Click += new EventHandler(OnFind);
35.
36.      button = new Button();
37.      button.Parent = this;
38.      button.Text = "Close";
39.      button.Bounds =
40.        new Rectangle(98, findBox.Bottom + 5, 60, 20);
41.      CancelButton = button;
42.      button.Click += new EventHandler(OnClose);
43.
44.      ClientSize = new Size(180, 80);
45.    }
46.
47.  private void OnClose(object sender, EventArgs args)
48.  {
49.    Close();
50.  }
51.
52.  private void OnFind(object sender, EventArgs args)
53.  {
54.    if (Find != null)
55.    {
56.      Find(this, args);
57.    }
58.  }
59.
```

```
60.    public string FindText
61.    {
62.      get
63.      {
64.        return findBox.Text;
65.      }
66.    }
67. }
```

The design of this dialog is similar to `TitleDialog`. The only real difference in the constructor is that we have not defined a `DialogResult` for either of the buttons, since the dialog is intended to be non-modal, so the dialog won't be called using `ShowDialog()`. The `DialogResult` serves as the return value from `ShowDialog()` and thus won't be needed here.

Since there is no default event handler provided for these buttons, we must add our own (lines 34 and 42). We also specify the 'Find' button as the `AcceptButton` so that the user can enter some search text and then hit 'Enter' to do the search back in the main form. Similarly, the 'Close' button is specified as the `CancelButton` (line 41).

The key point in this dialog is the way the 'Find' button communicates its event back to the parent form. This is done by creating a custom event delegate called `Find` (line 8). The parent form then adds its own event handler to this delegate when the `FindDialog` object is created (see line 209 in the main `DialogDemo` class, where `DialogDemo`'s `FindText` method is added to the `Find` delegate).

Back in `FindDialog`, the `Click` event for the 'Find' button has `OnFind()` (line 52) defined as its handler. This method checks if `Find` is `null` (as it would be if no methods had been added to it in the parent form). If not, it then calls the delegate (line 56) to run any event handlers that have been added to it.

The sequence of events that occurs when the 'Find' button is pressed is then: first `OnFind()` within `FindDialog` is called, then the `Find` delegate runs `FindText()` back in `DialogDemo`.

9.17 ■ Other controls

.NET contains many other GUI controls that can be used in programs written with Windows Forms, but we do not have the space to go into all of them in this book. We will meet some of the other controls in examples in the remaining chapters in this book, however, to give you a flavour for how they can enhance the interface of a program.

There are several controls that allow lists of items to be displayed. These include the `ComboBox` (a list that contracts to a single entry with a small button on one side that allows the user to expand the list and select an item from it), the `ListBox`, which is similar to a `ComboBox` except that the list is displayed in a rectangular frame with scrollbars, if needed, the `TreeView`, which displays a tree-like view of hierarchical data such as folders and files on a disk and so on. We will see an example of the `ListBox` in the GUI version of the adventure game case study at the end of Chapter 10.

As mentioned earlier, most controls work in much the same way at their lowest level. The control is created, given a size and position within a container, and added to the container. If the control is to be used for more than just the display of information, one or more event handlers needs to be attached to respond to user interaction.

Despite the common base shared by controls, each individual control has its own peculiarities, so it is a good idea to get an example of a specific control before trying to use it within your own programs. The first place to look should be the MSDN documentation, as most of the entries there for GUI controls contain at least one sample program illustrating how it can be used. Although MSDN provides a good introduction to the use of controls, often you will want to do something a bit more involved and will find that the documentation doesn't have quite the examples you need. In that case, a search of the web is the best way to continue.

■ Summary

This chapter has introduced GUI programming using Windows Forms. This is a large topic so only some of the most commonly used controls are described here, but the guidelines given in this chapter should be applicable to most of the other controls.

The basic procedure for adding a control to a form is to create the control, define its size and position within its container, add it to the container, and, if necessary, attach the appropriate event handlers to allow the user to interact with the control.

Documentation and examples of other controls may be found in the MSDN library, in more detailed books on GUI programming using .NET and C#, and on the web.

Exercises

9.1 Write a simple GUI program that consists of only a blank form. Refer to the documentation for the `Form` class and see how many properties you can set in the C# code that will affect the way the form appears when the program runs. Try such things as changing the background colour, changing its size and so on.

9.2 Again by referring to the documentation for `Form`, investigate the events that can be generated by a `Form` and add some event handlers to the blank form from the previous exercise. Some events you could try handling are `Click` (when the mouse is clicked over the form), `DoubleClick`, `BackColorChanged` and so on. The simplest response to an event is just to print a message in the console window, but you could try a few other simple responses such as displaying a `MessageBox` or changing the colour of the form.

9.3 Either by adding controls to your blank form program from the previous exercise, or by starting from scratch, write a Windows Forms program that displays a single `TextBox` and a `Button`. When the user types some text into the `TextBox` and then presses the `Button`, display a `MessageBox` that contains the text from the `TextBox`. As always, if you are unsure how to proceed, use the simple event-handling example from the text and examine the MSDN documentation to see what properties of the `TextBox` and `Button` might help you.

9.4 Suppose you wanted to restrict the text that was typed into the `TextBox` in the previous exercise so that only numbers are allowed. Add an `ErrorProvider` to the program in the previous exercise so that a flashing icon is displayed if the user attempts to push the `Button` with either no text or non-numerical text in the `TextBox`. Use a helpful error message in the tooltip message that appears when the mouse hovers over the icon.

9.5 Write a Windows Forms application which displays a simple multiple choice test. The test should contain at least three questions, each of which should have three possible answers. For example, you might ask 'What is the largest planet in our solar system?' and provide the answers A. Earth, B. Saturn, C. Jupiter. Use a `Label` to display the question and radio buttons to display the possible answers to each question.

At the bottom of the client area, provide a `Button` which can be pressed when the user has selected all the answers. The event handler for the `Button` should check the user's answers and display a `MessageBox` stating the score (and possibly the correct answers).

9.6 Add a dialog box to the quiz program in the previous exercise. The dialog should replace the `MessageBox` that is displayed when the user presses the button to check the answers, and should request the player's name in addition to displaying their score. The program should store a list of player's names and associated scores. (The list can be stored as an array, so that only the last 10 scores are stored, for example.)

Add a menu to the program which contains a menu item that displays a `MessageBox` showing a list of all the players who have done the quiz and their scores. (This assumes that the list is fairly short so it will fit comfortably on screen.)

9.7 Replace the `MessageBox` in the preceding exercise with a dialog that contains a `ListBox` that displays the players and scores.

A `ListBox` displays a list of items within a scrollable panel. The `ListBox` control can be created and added to a container in the same way as any other control, so add a `ListBox` (along with a `Label` to state what is displayed in the `ListBox`) to the dialog's `Form`, making its size large enough to view three or four scores at once.

To add items to a `ListBox`, you need to deal with the `Items` property of the `ListBox`. Starting with the MSDN documentation for the `ListBox` (make sure you read the documentation for the `Windows.Forms` version of the `ListBox`, as there is another version that is used in designing web pages), find the description of the `Items` property. You will discover that `Items` is a `ListBox.ObjectCollection` object, so look at the members of this class to discover the `Add()` method for adding an item to the `Items` of a `ListBox`. You should find some sample code illustrating how to add items to the `ListBox`, so use this as a model to construct the list of players and scores in your dialog.

9.8   Add another menu item that allows the user to save the scores list in a text file on disk. Use the 'Save' option in the Notepad example in the text as a model. This command should display a `SaveFileDialog` as in the text, and save the scores in a file with a `.scr` extension.

9.9   Add a toolbar to the quiz program from the preceding exercises. The toolbar should contain two buttons: one that duplicates the menu command for displaying the `MessageBox` or dialog (depending on whether you implemented the dialog) that shows the scores, and the other which duplicates the menu command for saving the scores to disk.

Graphics 10

10.1 ■ Graphics: Java versus .NET

Java graphics programmers will find much that is familiar in .NET's graphics capabilities, but there are a few key differences as well. To set the scene, we'll briefly review some of the main points in Java graphics programming.

Depending on the version of Java you are using, the main class used for producing graphics is either Graphics or Graphics2D. The Graphics class has been around since the earliest versions of Java and provides only fairly limited capabilities, such as the drawing of lines, text and basic shapes. With Java 1.2 (sometimes known, confusingly, as Java 2), the Java 2D packages introduced the Graphics2D class, which inherits Graphics and provides a much larger library of drawing methods. The Java 2D package also redefined the methods by which graphics are produced, introducing the Shape interface for representing an arbitrary curve and the Stroke and Paint interfaces for line styles, fill colours and patterns.

In order to produce any graphics in a Java component, its *graphics context*, represented by either a Graphics or Graphics2D object, must be obtained. All Java components contain a paint() method which is called to draw and update the control's graphics throughout its lifetime. The graphics context provides the interface between the code and the various device drivers that drive the display devices such as monitors and printers. The paint() method is called automatically by the Java Virtual Machine whenever the component needs to be redrawn, and in general is never called directly by the programmer. The JVM will obtain the graphics context and send it to the paint() method automatically, so the programmer need not worry about where to find a Graphics object. If the programmer wishes to force a redraw at some point, a call to repaint() can be made, which in turn calls paint() after obtaining the graphics context behind the scenes.

One of the key features of the Java graphics context is that Graphics and Graphics2D contain a number of *states* into which they can be set. These states are then used in all drawing operations until they are changed in the code. The states include such things as the *stroke* (essentially a type of pen) that is used to draw lines and the *paint* that is used to fill shapes. A stroke and paint can be set in Graphics2D and these drawing attributes are used to draw all shapes until they are replaced. In a sense, the graphics context may be thought of as the artist that does all the drawing and painting, and the graphics state is similar to putting a particular pen and brush in the artist's hands which are then used to draw everything until the artist is given a different pen or brush. In other words, the qualities of the line and fill patterns are properties of the *artist* and not of the shapes being drawn.

The .NET graphics model is known as GDI+ (for Graphics Device Interface), and is similar to the Java model in many ways, in that a graphics context is required to do any drawing, and all graphics are drawn in an `OnPaint()` method which is called by the underlying program manager in response to a message requesting a control to be drawn or redrawn. Much of the functionality in Java 2D is also available in .NET's graphics libraries.

Probably the biggest difference between Java 2D and .NET's GDI+ is that GDI+ is an (almost) *stateless* graphics model. This means that the qualities of a line or shape are associated directly with the shape rather than with the graphics context. We say that GDI+ is 'almost' stateless, since there are a few properties that can be set within the graphics context, but most of the more common properties must be attached to each line or shape.

In one sense, this probably seems more logical from an object-oriented standpoint, since most of us would think of things like a line's colour and thickness as being properties of the line rather than of the artist doing the drawing. However, it does seem to make a less efficient graphical coding system, since we must remember to pass a pen and a brush to every shape that we want to draw, rather than just setting these things up once in the graphics context and using them to draw a number of shapes.

The stateless graphics context is a rather curious choice for the .NET engineers to make since the older Microsoft Foundation Classes (MFC) system that will (hopefully) ultimately be replaced by .NET uses the graphics context (or, as it is called in MFC, the *device context*) to store the drawing objects such as pens and brushes. At any rate, it is something of which Java graphics programmers should beware, since it is easy to forget to provide the drawing tools for every object we wish to draw.

In this chapter we will give an overview of the main types of graphics that can be coded in .NET and C#. The general field of computer graphics is usually divided into two main areas: *vector graphics* and *raster graphics*.

Vector graphics are drawn using mathematical formulas to determine which pixels to light up, and as such, the built-in methods for producing this type of graphics are restricted to those that produce fairly simple shapes such as lines, rectangles and ellipses. Because they involve a fair bit of calculation, vector graphics can be expensive (in processor time) to produce, but their main advantage is that, because they use equations to define a shape, they are easily scaled to produce an accurate representation of the image at any size.

Raster graphics are constructed by displaying an array of predefined pixel values, usually stored as an image file such as a bitmap or JPEG. Raster graphics are thus used to display images such as icons, photographs and so on. Because a raster image is defined using a fixed array of pixel values, it often does not scale very well, since some form of interpolation between pixel values (in the case of a larger image) or omission of some information (in the case of a smaller image) is needed.

Although it is often not treated as a separate type of graphics, the production of text has become specialized enough that it is worth considering on its own. Text can be produced using vector graphics if mathematical formulas defining the outlines of the letters are specified, or as raster graphics if a letter's shape is just defined by a bitmap.

We will begin with some examples of how to produce some basic, static shapes such as lines, rectangles and more general two-dimensional shapes. We will illustrate how these shapes can be varied by changing their colours, fill patterns and so on.

We will then move on to consider how .NET handles simple raster graphics by seeing how image files can be displayed within controls on a form.

An important feature of any reasonable graphics library is the ability to *transform* an existing image by actions such as *translation* (moving the object to a new location without changing its shape or orientation), *rotation*, *scaling* (making the object larger or smaller without changing its relative proportions) and *shearing* (stretching the object along a given direction). .NET provides built-in methods for these basic transforms which duplicate those provided in Java 2D's `AffineTransform` class.

Finally in this chapter, we will consider some simple animations by combining repeated graphical drawing with a timer to provide the connection between successive frames.

10.2 ■ Vector graphics

10.2.1 □ Colo(u)rs

In order to do any drawing, we need to know something about how colours are represented in .NET. First, of course, is the usual transatlantic difference in spelling. Since Microsoft is an American company, we have to use the American spelling of `Color` whenever we want to refer to the `Color` class.

Java programmers will probably be familiar with Java's `Color` class, which has several predefined colours such as `Color.Red`, `Color.Green` and so on. In .NET, there are 140 predefined named colours, making something of an artist's paradise. Old favourites such as `Red` are there, but we now have more exotic names such as `Honeydew` (a pale green), `Thistle` (well, I do live in Scotland), `PapayaWhip` and `PeachPuff`. Have a look at the documentation for the `Color` class for a complete list.

If you can't find just the right shade amongst the 140 predefined colours, it is easy enough to create your own colour by specifying the precise values of red, green and blue using one of the static `FromArgb()` methods in the `Color` class. Each of these methods returns a `Color` object constructed from the values passed in as parameters.

The RGB colour model creates all colours that can be represented on a standard display device by specifying each of red, green and blue with a value between 0 and 255. When all three colours are 255, we get white, and when all are 0 we get black. All other shades can be produced by other mixtures.

The 'A' in `FromArgb()` corresponds to the so-called *alpha* value of a colour, which denotes its transparency, and is also represented by a value between 0 and 255. An alpha of 255 is the default value and gives a totally opaque colour. An alpha of 0 is totally transparent (and therefore invisible). Intermediate values of alpha allow some of the background image to 'show through' the colour. The effect is achieved by combining the background colours with the foreground colours to produce the transparency.

For example, since yellow is a combination of red and green, we can produce a half-transparent yellow with the call:

```
Color transYellow = Color.FromArgb(128, 255, 255, 0);
```

where the parameters are alpha, red, green and blue, in that order.

10.2.2 ☐ Drawing shapes – the Pen class

The easiest way to illustrate how .NET handles some simple vector graphics is to give a sort of 'Hello line' example:

```
1. using System;
2. using System.Drawing;
3. using System.Windows.Forms;
4.
5. public class DrawLine : Form
6. {
7.    public DrawLine()
8.    {
9.       ClientSize = new Size(100, 100);
10.   }
11.
12.   protected override void OnPaint(PaintEventArgs args)
13.   {
14.      Graphics g = args.Graphics;
15.      Pen pen = new Pen(Color.Red);
16.      g.DrawLine(pen, 10, 20, 80, 90);
17.   }
18.
19.   public static void Main()
20.   {
21.      Application.Run(new DrawLine());
22.   }
23. }
```

Simple vector graphics requires the System.Drawing namespace (line 2). This program produces a form with a client area of 100 by 100 pixels, but no controls – we are drawing directly on the form's client area.

The OnPaint() method (line 12) shows the basics of producing a drawing. Notice that this method is declared as protected override. This is essential, since OnPaint() is actually an event handler that is declared in the Control class (which is a base class of all forms and controls). If the OnPaint() method in the derived class is not declared as an override, it hides the method in the base class, which means that it will not be interpreted as the event handler for the Paint event, which is sent whenever a redraw of the form is required. As a result, no graphics will appear.

The PaintEventArgs parameter contains the Graphics object which is required for all drawing operations so, unlike the paint() method in Java, we must extract Graphics first (line 14) before we can apply it to drawing operations.

Since all drawing operations must have a pen provided for them, we cannot just call a drawing method without creating a pen first (line 15). The Pen class contains several properties which define the properties of the line, such as its colour, width, dash pattern and so on, although we've only specified the colour here.

The line itself is drawn by the DrawLine() method from the Graphics class (line 16). The parameters passed to DrawLine() consist of the pen followed by the x and y coordinates of the start point, then the x and y coordinates of the end point.

Coordinates for all drawing operations are specified using pixel coordinates, where the x (horizontal) coordinate is measured from the left border increasing to the right, and the y (vertical) coordinate is measured from the top border increasing downwards. Note that this coordinate system is different from that commonly used to plot graphs and charts in mathematics, in that the y axis in computer graphics is inverted. The reason for this is historical, since in raster display devices such as a monitor, the electron beam scans the screen in horizontal rows from top to bottom.

The (not very impressive) result of this program is as shown in Figure 10.1.

Figure 10.1 Output of the DrawLine program

The Graphics class contains a number of methods that allow basic vector shapes to be drawn. All these methods require a Pen as their first parameter, followed by values that are appropriate to the type of shape being drawn. For DrawLine() we just specify two sets of coordinates for the start and end points of the line.

Some of the other methods include DrawRectangle(), DrawPolygon() and DrawEllipse() which are all fairly obvious and easy to use. The DrawString() method is used to draw text, which we will consider later in this chapter.

Some drawing methods have a related version that allows arrays of shapes to be displayed. For example, the DrawLines() method takes as its parameters a Pen and an array of Points. The Point class consists simply of X and Y properties which contain the pixel coordinates. For example, the following code draws three connected line segments using a solid black line 3 pixels wide:

```
Pen pen = new Pen(Color.Black, 3);
Point[] points =
{
   new Point( 10,   10),
   new Point( 10,  100),
   new Point(200,   50),
   new Point(250,  300)
};
g.DrawLines(pen, points);
```

The first segment connects the first two points (10, 10) and (10, 100). The next segment connects the second and third points (10, 100) and (200, 50) and so on.

There is also a DrawRectangles() method for drawing an array of rectangles.

Using these basic drawing methods is quite easy, so the best way to get used to them is just to experiment by drawing a few shapes with different pen types and drawing shapes. Use the documentation to see what variations are available.

10.2.3 ☐ Filling shapes – the Brush classes

Any of the shapes in the Graphics library that contain an *interior* can also be filled. Although it may seem obvious what an 'interior' of a shape is, we will see that it actually does require a precise definition.

Simple shapes such as rectangles and ellipses have obvious interiors, and a filled rectangle, for example, can be drawn using FillRectangle(). Just as drawing a shape requires a Pen, so filling a shape requires a Brush. A Brush specifies the colour or other pattern that is used to fill an enclosed area. The simplest fill pattern is just a solid colour, but a Brush can also contain simple geometric patterns such as hatching, colour gradients and even full images.

It is important to note that filling and drawing are two separate operations – a rectangle produced with FillRectangle() will contain only the interior of the rectangle displayed using a particular Brush. There will not be any outline of the edges of the rectangle. If we want both a filled interior and a drawn outline, we need to call FillRectangle() and then DrawRectangle(). It is a good idea to call these two methods in that order, since calling them the other way round can sometimes overwrite part of the border with the fill pattern.

The Brush class itself is actually abstract, and thus cannot be used to create a brush directly. We must use one of the brush classes that inherits Brush and provides a concrete implementation.

There are five such classes from which to choose. Two of these are in the System.Drawing namespace and the other three are in System.Drawing. Drawing2D.

The first two classes are SolidBrush, used to fill shapes with a solid colour, and TextureBrush, used to fill shapes with raster images. Let's consider a simple SolidBrush fill first. The following code draws a rectangle filled with light blue and bordered by a solid blue-violet line:

```
Pen pen = new Pen(Color.BlueViolet, 2);
Brush brush = new SolidBrush(Color.LightBlue);
g.FillRectangle(brush, 10, 10, 200, 150);
g.DrawRectangle(pen, 10, 10, 200, 150);
```

The SolidBrush constructor comes in only one form, which requires a Color parameter that specifies the solid fill colour. The result of this code is as shown in Figure 10.2.

Figure 10.2 A filled rectangle created using SolidBrush

The TextureBrush is almost as simple to use – all we need to do is load an image into the TextureBrush and then use it to fill a shape. As a sample image, we will use a JPEG file containing a digital photo of the author's wallpaper (Figure 10.3).

Figure 10.3 The original JPEG image used as a texture

The following code loads this JPEG file into an `Image` and then creates a `TextureBrush` using this `Image` as its paint:

```
Image wallpaper = Image.FromFile("wallpaper.jpg");
brush = new TextureBrush(wallpaper);
g.FillEllipse(brush, 10, 10, 200, 150);
g.DrawEllipse(pen, 10, 10, 200, 150);
```

The `FromFile()` method takes the filename as its parameter. We've just used the bare filename since the 'wallpaper.jpg' file is in the same directory as the executable file – if it is somewhere else, we can insert the full pathname. We then use the texture to fill an ellipse (just for variety), with the result as shown in Figure 10.4.

Figure 10.4 A filled ellipse created using `TextureBrush`

The `HatchBrush` provides a number of predefined hatching patterns. The constructor allows us to specify the hatching style, which must be selected from the `HatchStyle` enumeration. The colour used for the hatching pattern must also be specified. The background colour may also be specified in the constructor as a third parameter, but if this is omitted, the background colour defaults to black.

Although there is a large selection of hatching patterns available, you might not find quite the one you want. If you need to make up your own hatching pattern, save it as an image file and use `TextureBrush` instead.

A simple example of a `HatchBrush` is as follows:

```
using System.Drawing.Drawing2D;

brush = new HatchBrush(HatchStyle.DiagonalCross,
    Color.BlueViolet, Color.White);
g.FillEllipse(brush, 10, 10, 200, 150);
g.DrawEllipse(pen, 10, 10, 200, 150);
```

The extra `using` statement is needed to access this and the next two brush classes, since they are in the separate `Drawing2D` namespace. This produces the image in Figure 10.5.

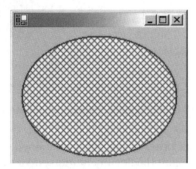

Figure 10.5 A hatched ellipse created using `HatchBrush`

The `LinearGradientBrush` allows a fill pattern that gradually fades from one colour into another. It comes in several varieties, but we'll just examine one here to give you an idea of its capabilities.

The two-point `LinearGradientBrush` requires that we specify two points on the drawing surface. We then specify two solid colours. The gradient fill begins with the first colour at the first point and then gradually fades the fill into the other colour at the second point. The banding pattern is repeated over the entire fill area, although the precise banding pattern can be varied by setting the `WrapMode`.

Here's a little example of a gradient fill using blue and yellow as the anchor colours:

```
Brush brush = new LinearGradientBrush(new Point(10, 10),
   new Point(50, 50), Color.Blue, Color.Yellow);
((LinearGradientBrush)brush).WrapMode =
   WrapMode.TileFlipXY;
g.FillEllipse(brush, 10, 10, 200, 150);
g.DrawEllipse(pen, 10, 10, 200, 150);
```

To set `WrapMode`, we need to cast `brush` to `LinearGradientBrush`, since `WrapMode` isn't a property in the abstract `Brush` class. The default `WrapMode` is `Tile`, which draws a band from the first colour to the second, then starts over again with another band from first colour to second. The `TileFlipXY` mode flips the colour scheme at each repetition, so that the first band is drawn from blue to yellow, then the second from yellow to blue and so on. This usually produces a more pleasing result. The result looks as shown in Figure 10.6.

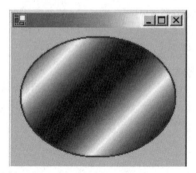

Figure 10.6 A repeating gradient fill created using LinearGradientBrush

Various other effects can be obtained with the different types of linear gradients – explore the documentation and try a few examples to see what's available.

The final, and fanciest, brush is the PathGradientBrush, which is essentially a generalization of the LinearGradientBrush, in that it allows colour gradients to be defined within curves of arbitrary shape, and with more than two colours.

A path gradient is defined by specifying a boundary shape as a polygon defined by an array of Points, and an additional point called the centre point. An array of Colors can then be associated with the array of Points, and an additional Color associated with the centre point.

For example, we can define a triangular brush as shown in Figure 10.7.

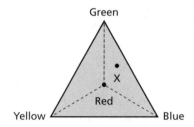

Figure 10.7 Definition of a triangular path gradient brush

The border is defined by an array of three Points, each of which has an associated Color as shown. The centre point has the Color red associated with it. The path gradient works out the colour of a point such as X within the boundary of the triangle by considering the three colours at the corners of the smallest internal triangle that contains the centre point and encloses X, which in this case consists of the red, green and blue points. The actual colour assigned to X is worked out by weighting the three colours according to X's distance from each of the three points: the closer to a point the more that point's colour contributes to the overall colour assigned to X.

The code for producing a triangular brush like this one is as follows:

```
Point[] fillPoint =
  { new Point(110, 10),
    new Point(210, 160),
    new Point(10, 160) };
PathGradientBrush pathBrush =
  new PathGradientBrush(fillPoint);
pathBrush.CenterColor = Color.Red;
Color[] surround =
  { Color.Green, Color.Blue, Color.Yellow };
pathBrush.SurroundColors = surround;
g.FillRectangle(pathBrush, 10, 10, 200, 150);
Pen pen = new Pen(Color.BlueViolet, 2);
g.DrawRectangle(pen, 10, 10, 200, 150);
```

We define the array of `Points` to create the triangle, then create a `PathGradientBrush` and provide the array to its constructor to define the triangular brush. The `CenterColor` is set to red (it is black by default). We then define an array of `Colors` to be associated with the original `fillPoint` array – each `Color` is associated with each `Point` in turn automatically when we assign the `Color` array as `pathBrush`'s `SurroundColors`.

We then call `FillRectangle()` to apply the brush. The result looks like Figure 10.8 (although admittedly it loses much of its impact if it can't be viewed in colour).

Figure 10.8 Result of filling a rectangle with the triangular brush defined in Figure 10.7

Note that even though we applied the brush to the entire rectangle, only the triangle gets painted – the portion of the rectangle that is not painted by the triangle is not painted, and in fact the brush allows any other graphics previously drawn in this area to show through.

We didn't specify the location of `CenterPoint` explicitly in this example since by default it is located at the point found by averaging all the boundary points. We can define `CenterPoint` to be anywhere we like, however –

even outside the boundary. The result can be a bit unexpected at times. For example, if we modify the example above by adding the line:

```
pathBrush.CenterPoint = new Point(0, 0);
```

we set the centre point to be the upper-left corner of the rectangle. The resulting image is as Figure 10.9.

Figure 10.9 Result of moving the centre point of the brush outside its boundary

Since the brush was applied to the entire rectangle, the algorithm above for determining the colour of each point is applied, which causes the triangular section in the upper left to be coloured in since the centre point is now outside the central triangular region.

We do have to be a bit careful when specifying the boundary, and make sure that the array of Points actually defines a two-dimensional area, rather than just a line segment. For example, if we had tried the array (by mistake, of course!):

```
Point[] fillPoint =
  { new Point(110, 10),
    new Point(210, 10),
    new Point(10, 10) };
```

then all three points have the same *y* coordinate, so the 'boundary' is just a horizontal line segment. Attempting to run the program with this border causes an 'out of memory' error, presumably because the underlying algorithm uses recursion to attempt to fill the rectangle using the path provided. Since the path does not define a two-dimensional region, it is impossible to fill the rectangle. (Probably the underlying code should be tightened up a bit to detect this situation and throw a more sensible exception.)

A PathGradientBrush will also accept a GraphicsPath as its boundary instead of an array of Points. A GraphicsPath is a general class that allows pretty well any shape to be defined – we will consider it in more detail later in this chapter.

Finally, `PathGradientBrush`es can be tiled in various ways to produce an overall texture for an area. Tiling is always done using the `Rectangle` property of the brush – that is, even though we may have defined a triangular outline as in the above example, the shape that is tiled is the rectangle that encloses the triangle.

By default, the `WrapMode` of the brush is set to `WrapMode.Clamp`, which means that only one instance of the shape is drawn. There are several other `WrapMode`s which produce various tiling effects. The simplest is `WrapMode.Tile` which just copies the base figure horizontally and vertically to fill the shape.

For example, we can reduce the size of the triangular brush used in the previous example and turn on tiling:

```
Point[] fillPoint =
   { new Point(10, 10),
     new Point(110, 10),
     new Point(10, 85) };
PathGradientBrush pathBrush =
   new PathGradientBrush(fillPoint);
pathBrush.CenterColor = Color.Red;
Color[] surround =
   { Color.Green, Color.Blue, Color.Yellow };
pathBrush.SurroundColors = surround;
pathBrush.WrapMode = WrapMode.Tile;
g.FillRectangle(pathBrush, 10, 10, 200, 150);
Pen pen = new Pen(Color.BlueViolet, 2);
g.DrawRectangle(pen, 10, 10, 200, 150);
```

The result looks like that shown in Figure 10.10.

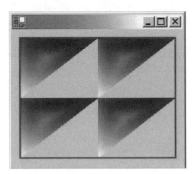

Figure 10.10 A tiled path gradient brush

It is also possible to flip the brush horizontally and/or vertically at each repetition by using the other wrapping modes: `TileFlipX`, `TileFlipY` and `TileFlipXY`. For example, `TileFlipXY` produces the result shown in Figure 10.11.

Figure 10.11 A tiled path gradient brush with the brush flipped after each repetition

It is possible to set the enclosing `Rectangle` of the brush to a custom value, which can produce some interesting effects. Finally, by combining two or more brushes, where one brush neatly fills in the gaps left by the other one, we can produce an almost endless variety of effects, even tiling patterns that appear non-rectangular. Just experiment to see what you can create.

10.2.4 ☐ Brushes as pens

If you've glanced through the list of constructors for a `Pen`, you may have noticed that some of them accept a `Brush` as a parameter. In fact, a `Pen` can use a `Brush` as its 'ink' when drawing curves. Any brush can be used in a `Pen`, so we'll just give a simple example in which we'll draw the border in the last path gradient example using the wallpaper `TextureBrush` from earlier. We replace the `Pen` used to draw the border with the following:

```
Image wallpaper = Image.FromFile("wallpaper.jpg");
Brush imageBrush = new TextureBrush(wallpaper);
Pen pen = new Pen(imageBrush, 10);
g.DrawRectangle(pen, 10, 10, 200, 150);
```

This draws a 10-pixel wide frame using the wallpaper pen around the tiled triangles. The result is as shown in Figure 10.12.

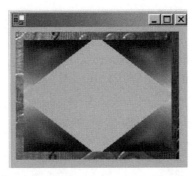

Figure 10.12 A texture brush used as a pen to draw a border

10.3 ■ The GraphicsPath

If you have explored the Shape interface and its implementations in Java 2D, you will know that it supports a wide variety of shapes which can be constructed from primitive vector graphics such as lines, rectangles and ellipses. A Shape can be constructed in other ways in Java, for example, by obtaining the outline of some text. A Java Shape can also be transformed using the AffineTransform class to produce translated, rotated, scaled or sheared versions of the original shape.

The .NET equivalent of Shape is the GraphicsPath, and it (and other associated classes) allows much the same sort of operations as its Java counterpart. A complete exploration of GraphicsPath would take up too much of this book, but we'll give an overview of some of its more useful features.

In its simplest form, a GraphicsPath can be treated almost as an off-screen Graphics object, since it contains many methods analogous to those of Graphics for defining shapes.

For example, here is a version of the first vector graphics example presented earlier in this chapter in which a GraphicsPath is used to draw a line segment:

```
using System.Drawing;
using System.Drawing.Drawing2D;
using System.Windows.Forms;

public class DrawLine : Form
{
  public DrawLine()
  {
    ClientSize = new Size(300, 300);
    StartPosition = FormStartPosition.CenterScreen;
  }

  protected override void OnPaint(PaintEventArgs args)
  {
```

```
        Graphics g = args.Graphics;
        GraphicsPath path = new GraphicsPath();
        Pen pen = new Pen(Color.Red);
        path.AddLine(10, 20, 80, 90);
        g.DrawPath(pen, path);
    }

    public static void Main()
    {
        Application.Run(new DrawLine());
    }
}
```

GraphicsPath is part of the System.Drawing.Drawing2D namespace, so remember to add a using statement to include this.

In OnPaint() we create a new GraphicsPath and add a line segment to it. Note that unlike the corresponding AddLine() method in Graphics, we do *not* specify the Pen that is used to draw the shape when adding it to the GraphicsPath. A GraphicsPath defines only the *shape* of the figure and not its actual appearance on screen. This must still be done when we use Graphics itself to draw the path using the DrawPath() method, which takes a Pen and a GraphicsPath as its parameters.

This program illustrates the division of labour that occurs when using a GraphicsPath. The geometric path itself is defined within GraphicsPath, and is then drawn to the screen, or *rendered*, as a separate operation. Only Graphics can do rendering, since Graphics contains the code that interfaces with the device drivers for the display devices such as monitors and printers. GraphicsPath is a purely internal class that can do the mathematics required to calculate and transform shapes, but it can't display them.

Clearly, there isn't much point in using GraphicsPath if all we want to do is duplicate the capabilities of Graphics itself. To understand the power of a GraphicsPath, we first need to understand exactly what a path is.

A GraphicsPath is really just a generalization of the simpler vector curves we've already met. When we use one of the built-in Graphics classes such as DrawLine() to draw a vector shape, what actually happens inside the method? Since all the shapes are drawn on a digital display such as a monitor, we need to convert the abstract mathematical shape into a collection of pixels that are to be lit up. Although there are some specialized algorithms that determine which pixels to illuminate for some common curved shapes such as circles, most shapes are displayed by breaking them down into a series of line segments, and then applying an underlying algorithm to draw each line segment. We can therefore define any shape as a collection of line segments, and this is essentially all that a GraphicsPath is.

The line segments within a GraphicsPath are collected together into one or more *subpaths*. Within each subpath, the line segments are all connected together to form a continuous curve, and the line segments within one subpath are disconnected (not joined) to the line segments in any other subpath.

A simple example of a path containing two subpaths is a rectangle and a circle placed side by side. The rectangle contains four line segments that are connected to form the rectangular shape; the circle contains enough line segments to approximate a circular shape within the constraints imposed by the digital display.

A subpath may consist of either a *closed* or *open* curve. A closed curve is one where the end of each line segment joins up with the beginning of the next one, and the last line segment joins up to the first one so that there are no 'loose ends' on any of the line segments. An open curve, as you might expect, is a curve that does have loose ends. A rectangle and circle are both closed curves.

10.4 ■ Filling shapes

As we've seen above, a GraphicsPath only defines the shape but must leave the rendering to Graphics. However, it is important to realize when building a GraphicsPath that it can be rendered in two fundamental ways: by being *drawn* or by being *filled*. The drawing operation applies a Pen to trace the outline of the shape as defined by the series of line segments. A filling operation can only be applied to a closed shape, and consists of filling the interior using a Brush, in much the same way as we did with our earlier examples using Graphics. If a filling operation is applied to an open curve, Graphics will close the curve first, by adding an extra line segment to connect the last line segment in the path to the first one.

Filling a simple closed shape such as a rectangle is a fairly obvious operation, but how is a more complex shape such as a polygon with overlapping edges filled? Graphics offers two *filling modes* in its FillPolygon() and FillPath() methods, so a quick explanation of what they are is in order.

The easiest fill mode to understand is Alternate. To see how this works, consider Figure 10.13.

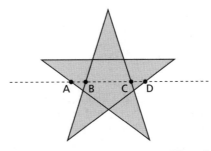

Figure 10.13 Diagram used to define the Alternate fill mode

The five-pointed star is defined by five points and drawn by drawing the five line segments that connect these points. If we use FillPolygon() to fill this star and set the FillMode to Alternate, the algorithm that is applied works by using a horizontal scan line (shown as dashed in the figure) to fill each row of pixels in the figure. For a particular row such as the one shown in the figure, we start at the left end of the scan line, and assume that this is outside the figure and therefore is not part of the filled region. Moving to the right along the scan line, we reach the first point (A) where the scan line intersects one of the line segments that defines the figure. As soon as we cross one of the line segments, we alternate the fill state from 'off' to 'on'. The portion of the scan line between points A and B is therefore drawn in. When we reach point B, we alternate the fill state back to 'off', so the section from B to C is not filled. Similarly, the section from C to D is filled, and then when we leave the figure at point D, filling is off again, so the remainder of the scan line (out to the right margin of the window) is not drawn.

The algorithm has to have some special cases defined to deal with things like horizontal edges and vertices in the figure to be filled, but these are all worked out to give sensible results (see an introductory textbook on computer graphics for details).

We can see the results of applying the alternating fill algorithm to a five-pointed star by writing a little program that draws it. We replace the OnPaint() method in the previous example with the following:

```
protected override void OnPaint(PaintEventArgs args)
{
    Graphics g = args.Graphics;
    Point[] points =
        {
            new Point(5, 88), new Point(195, 88),
            new Point(41, 200), new Point(100, 19),
            new Point(159, 200)
        };
    GraphicsPath path = new GraphicsPath(FillMode.Alternate);
    Brush brush = new SolidBrush(Color.Red);
    path.AddLines(points);
    g.FillPath(brush, path);
}
```

The points of the star are defined as an array of Points (the coordinates are worked out using a little geometry – a good exercise for the reader). We create a GraphicsPath and set its FillMode to Alternate in the constructor. We can add an array of Points to a GraphicsPath using AddLines(), and then use FillPath() to fill the result. Note that the points array actually defines an *open* curve, since the last point is not equal to the first one. FillPath() will therefore provide this extra line segment before applying the filling algorithm. The result is as shown in Figure 10.14.

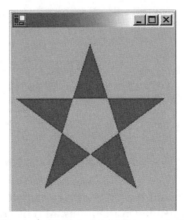

Figure 10.14 Result of filling a five-point star in `Alternate` mode

The `Winding` filling mode is a little trickier to understand, and we don't want to get bogged down with a complicated definition that accounts for all the special cases. Basically, we need to calculate an integer called the *winding number* for each point in the figure. The winding number is a measure of how many times the figure 'winds around' the given point. If the winding number is zero, the point is assumed to lie outside the figure and is not filled, otherwise the point is inside and therefore filled.

To calculate the winding number in most cases, we can use the following method. Referring back to the figure used to demonstrate the horizontal scan line above, suppose we want to determine if a point in the middle region of the star (between points B and C) is to be filled. We can draw a line (called a *ray*) from that point to infinity (or at least beyond the bounds of the figure) and observe the points where this line crosses the line segments that make up the figure. For our example, we can use the line extending to the right, so it will intersect the figure at points C and D (although we could equally well have used the line going to the left through points B and A, or any other line, not necessarily a horizontal one).

Next, we need to assign a *direction* to each line segment that makes up the figure. We can do this by starting at the first point (the upper-left point of the star, as defined in the example C# code above) and then trace out the figure in the order given by the list of points. This results in the situation shown in Figure 10.15.

To calculate the winding number of point P, we observe which direction each line segment in the figure crosses the ray heading away from point P. If the direction is left to right (as viewed by a traveller moving along the ray away from P) we add 1 to the winding number; if the direction is right to left, we subtract 1. In the example shown here, we can see that both line segments crossed by the ray are left to right relative to the ray, so the winding number of P is 2.

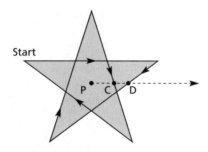

Figure 10.15 Diagram used to define the winding number

You should try a few other examples to convince yourself that any point that lies inside (in the informal sense of lying within the bounds of the line segments) the star has a non-zero winding number, and any point outside the star has a zero winding number. Therefore, if we use the winding number rule, all points inside the star will be filled. It is worth experimenting with other polygons, either on paper or in C# code, to see what sort of effects you can generate using the two fill modes.

We can see this by running the above code after changing the parameter passed to the GraphicsPath constructor to FillMode.Winding. The result is as shown in Figure 10.16.

Figure 10.16 Result of filling a five-point star in Winding mode

In general, the winding fill mode will usually result in complex polygons (ones where some of the edges intersect each other) that are completely filled, while the alternating fill mode will give more of a patchwork effect. There are some pathological cases where a winding fill mode will leave some gaps in the interior and if we really do want a solid fill in these cases, we'll need to patch up the figure with some extra graphics, but these are fairly uncommon.

10.5 ■ Transformations and the `Matrix` class

As we've mentioned several times, .NET provides ways by which shapes can be *transformed* in various ways. Readers who have used Java's `Affine Transform` class will be familiar with the basics of affine transformations, but we will provide a summary of the ideas here.

A general *transformation* of a two-dimensional shape can distort the shape in any fashion we like – we can move, rotate, stretch, or even break the shape up if we want to.

An *affine transformation* is a particular type of transformation that must satisfy certain conditions, and can be defined precisely using mathematical terminology, but for our purposes a less rigorous definition will be more useful. Basically, an affine transformation must preserve all parallel lines in a shape. That is, if two lines are parallel before an affine transformation, they must also be parallel afterwards. Note that is *not* the same as saying that the angle between any pair of lines must remain unchanged during the transformation. All we are stating is that lines that are parallel must remain so.

Both Java and .NET provide four basic types of affine transformation in two-dimensional graphics: translation, rotation, scaling and shearing.

Translation simply moves the shape from one location to another without changing its shape, orientation or size. Rotation again does not change the curve's shape or size, but merely rotates the figure relative to some fixed centre point. Scaling changes the figure's size without moving or rotating it, and without distorting the figure in any way. Shearing distorts the figure along a direction parallel to a fixed line, such as the x or y axis.

We will present some simple examples of all four of these transformations to give a better idea of what they involve. To do this, we must introduce the `Matrix` class which is used to specify the transformations, and is roughly equivalent to Java's `AffineTransform` class.

First, a brief word about why the affine transformation class is called `Matrix`. As you can discover by consulting an introductory textbook on computer graphics, it is possible to represent any affine transformation in terms of a mathematical object called a *matrix*. Since we are not expecting readers to have a mathematical background, we do not want to get into the details here, but if you happen to know a bit of elementary matrix theory, the idea is to represent each point in the figure to be transformed as a *vector* with three components. Two of these components represent the x and y coordinates of the point and the third component, introduced to make the equations easier to deal with, is always 1. An affine transformation such as a rotation can then be calculated by defining a 3-by-3 matrix containing numbers which depend on the angle of rotation. Multiplying the vector representing the point by this matrix produces another 3-component vector which contains the transformed coordinates of the point. If we multiply all the points that define a shape by the same matrix, the net effect is to transform the entire shape. For simple shapes, this requires relatively few calculations, since we only need to transform the end points of each line segment in the shape, and then just connect up the new end points to produce the transformed figure. This simplified procedure only works for affine transformations, since more general transformations could turn a straight line into an arbitrary curve. For these more general transformations, we would therefore need to apply a mathematical formula to *all* points that made up the original shape, which drastically increases the amount of computation required.

If we develop the theory of affine transformations, we would find that all such transformations (in two dimensions, anyway) can be represented by 3-by-3 matrices. The .NET Matrix class uses these matrices to implement transformations, hence its name.

One feature of the matrix representation of a transformation does have to be understood, even if we are not delving into the details of the numbers within a given matrix. We can combine two or more separate transformations by multiplying together the individual matrices for each transformation. For example, if we want to translate an object from one point to another and then rotate it after it arrives at its new position, we can create one matrix called T for the translation and another matrix called R for the rotation. Due to the peculiarities of matrix arithmetic, however, the *order* in which the multiplication is done *does* matter, and is in fact opposite to what you are probably used to. The order in which a series of transformations is applied to a shape is read from *right* to *left* in a matrix product. Thus the composite transformation consisting of a translation first followed by a rotation would be given by the matrix product $R * T$. Even if you don't understand how to multiply matrices on paper, you need to understand this point since the methods in the Matrix class offer a choice as to the order in which two matrices are multiplied together.

We have seen above that the distinction between GraphicsPath and Graphics classes is that GraphicsPath can only be used to define a shape, while Graphics must be used to render the shape onto an output device such as a monitor or printer. However, if we consult the documentation, we will discover that Graphics has a Transform *property* while GraphicsPath has a Transform() *method*. Both of these Transforms use a Matrix to specify their value, so why the difference in the implementation?

If you cast your mind back to the section where we introduced Graphics, we said then that Graphics is an 'almost stateless' graphics system, by which we meant that the Pen or Brush required to draw each figure had to be specified with each drawing or filling command. The 'almost' means that there are *some* properties or states that *can* be set in Graphics, and the transformation is one of these states.

We can therefore set the Transform property of Graphics to a particular Matrix, and then use the various drawing and filling methods of Graphics to render some shapes. The Transform will be applied to all these shapes until it is changed.

In contrast, in `GraphicsPath`, transformations are implemented by means of a *method* rather than a property. This means that we are not setting a state in `GraphicsPath` that is applied to future points that are added to the path; rather, we are applying a transformation to whatever path exists in the `GraphicsPath` at the time the `Transform()` method is called.

The differences between the two transformations methods will become easier to see once we have considered a few examples.

10.5.1 □ Translation

The simplest type of transformation is the translation, which involves just moving the shape parallel to itself (that is, without rotation or deformation of any kind).

Although a `Matrix` can be defined by giving the individual numerical elements within the transformation matrix, the most common way of defining a `Matrix` is using one of the convenience methods from the `Matrix` class. For translation, there is a `Translate()` method which takes the x and y values by which the object should be translated.

The following version of `OnPaint()` can be used in place of the `OnPaint()` method in the sample programs earlier in this chapter. It tiles the client area of the main `Form` with small ellipses.

```
protected override void OnPaint(PaintEventArgs args)
{
    Graphics g = args.Graphics;
    Pen pen = new Pen(Color.Black);
    for (int x = 0; x < ClientRectangle.Width; x += 40)
    {
        for (int y = 0; y < ClientRectangle.Height; y += 20)
        {
            Matrix trans = new Matrix();
            trans.Translate(x, y);
            g.Transform = trans;
            g.DrawEllipse(pen, 0, 0, 40, 20);
        }
    }
}
```

The method uses a nested `for` loop to tile the background, and a new translation is defined for each iteration through the loop. This example applies the transform as a property of `Graphics` before `DrawEllipse()` is called each time. The output of the program looks like Figure 10.17.

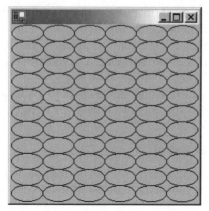

Figure 10.17 Pattern created by repeatedly translating an ellipse

We could produce the same result using a GraphicsPath and its Transform() method as follows:

```
protected override void OnPaint(PaintEventArgs args)
{
    Graphics g = args.Graphics;
    Pen pen = new Pen(Color.Black);
    for (int x = 0; x < ClientRectangle.Width; x += 40)
    {
        for (int y = 0; y < ClientRectangle.Height; y += 20)
        {
            GraphicsPath path = new GraphicsPath();
            path.AddEllipse(0, 0, 40, 20);
            Matrix trans = new Matrix();
            trans.Translate(x, y);
            path.Transform(trans);
            g.DrawPath(pen, path);
        }
    }
}
```

Here, we create a new GraphicsPath and translate it (rather than setting the Transform property in Graphics) at each iteration in the loop. This is, of course, much less efficient than the previous method, since now we are creating a new object for each ellipse, while in the previous example we just used Graphics to draw the ellipse at a translated location.

You might wonder if these two examples are as efficient as they could be in any case. In particular, is it really necessary to create a new Matrix with each iteration of the loop? That is, could we just omit the line:

```
Matrix trans = new Matrix();
```

from the inner `for` loop, since surely we are just setting the `Matrix`'s translation by using the `Translate()` method and we could do that with an existing `Matrix` without having to create a new one.

If we try this, however, it doesn't work, and the reason is that `Translate()` (along with the other convenience methods in the `Matrix` class for defining the other types of transformation) doesn't just set the `Matrix` to be a single translation. Rather, it *multiplies* the existing `Matrix` by another matrix that implements the required translation. That is, the `Translate()` method actually applies the translation after any other transformations that may already be in the `Matrix`. So instead of applying the desired translation each time, it is compounding it with all the translations that have happened in previous loop iterations.

We can avoid this and still avoid creating a new `Matrix` each time if we use the `Reset()` method to restore the `Matrix` to an *identity* transformation (that is, a transformation that doesn't change the shape at all). So we could rewrite our first example in a slightly more efficient form as:

```
protected override void OnPaint(PaintEventArgs args)
{
  Graphics g = args.Graphics;
  Pen pen = new Pen(Color.Black);
  Matrix trans = new Matrix();
  for (int x = 0; x < ClientRectangle.Width; x += 40)
  {
    for (int y = 0; y < ClientRectangle.Height; y += 20)
    {
      trans.Reset();
      trans.Translate(x, y);
      g.Transform = trans;
      g.DrawEllipse(pen, 0, 0, 40, 20);
    }
  }
}
```

We could do a similar thing with the second example using `GraphicsPath`, but there is one crucial difference. The `Transform()` method from `GraphicsPath` actually changes the coordinates of the path stored within the `GraphicsPath` and it does not save the original values of these points, so we can't 'undo' a transformation applied to a `GraphicsPath` unless we save the transformation values and then reverse the transformation. There is a `Reset()` method in `GraphicsPath`, but this erases all the points stored, rather than restoring them to some earlier state.

To save the previous transformation and then reverse it before applying the new transformation, we can alter the `GraphicsPath` example above to:

```
protected override void OnPaint(PaintEventArgs args)
{
  Graphics g = args.Graphics;
```

```
Pen pen = new Pen(Color.Black);
Matrix trans = new Matrix();
Matrix oldMatrix = new Matrix();
GraphicsPath path = new GraphicsPath();
path.AddEllipse(0, 0, 40, 20);
for (int x = 0; x < ClientRectangle.Width; x += 40)
{
   for (int y = 0; y < ClientRectangle.Height; y += 20)
   {
     path.Transform(oldMatrix);
     trans.Reset();
     trans.Translate(x, y);
     oldMatrix = trans.Clone();
     oldMatrix.Invert();
     path.Transform(trans);
     g.DrawPath(pen, path);
   }
 }
}
```

Within each iteration, we begin by reversing the transformation of path that we applied on the previous iteration (on the first iteration, oldMatrix is the identity transformation and so does not change path). We then reset the Matrix and create the new translation, as before. Next, we take a clone of the Matrix, and then apply Invert() to this clone. The inverse of a Matrix provides a transformation that undoes the original transformation. We can then apply the transformation to path and draw it.

It is debatable how much more efficient this method is, however, since the Clone() still requires creating a new Matrix, and transformations and matrix inversions all require a fair bit of calculation.

10.5.2 ☐ Rotations

From now on, we will use only the Transform() method on a GraphicsPath for illustrating transformations, since apart from the differences between the Graphics Transform property and the Transform() method in GraphicsPath outlined above, the actual use of the various transformations in building up a Matrix is the same in both cases.

The Rotate() method in Matrix may look incomplete on first inspection, since the only parameter it accepts is the angle of rotation. There is no way of specifying the point about which the rotation is to occur – the Rotate() method always rotates about the origin.

The trick here is to translate the shape first so that the desired rotation point is at the origin, then do the rotation, then translate it back to its original position. Thus we need to do a compound transform consisting of three separate operations.

The following code uses the five-pointed star from earlier examples, and rotates it by 45 degrees about its centre:

```
1.  protected override void OnPaint(PaintEventArgs args)
2.  {
3.      Graphics g = args.Graphics;
4.      Point[] points =
5.          {
6.              new Point(5, 88), new Point(195, 88),
7.              new Point(41, 200), new Point(100, 19),
8.              new Point(159, 200)
9.          };
10.     GraphicsPath path = new GraphicsPath(FillMode.Winding);
11.     Brush brush = new SolidBrush(Color.Red);
12.     path.AddLines(points);
13.
14.     Point centre = new Point();
15.     for (int i = 0; i < points.Length; i++)
16.     {
17.         centre.X += points[i].X;
18.         centre.Y += points[i].Y;
19.     }
20.     centre.X /= points.Length;
21.     centre.Y /= points.Length;
22.
23.     Matrix transform = new Matrix();
24.     transform.Translate(-centre.X, -centre.Y);
25.     transform.Rotate(45f, MatrixOrder.Append);
26.     transform.Translate(centre.X, centre.Y,
27.         MatrixOrder.Append);
28.     path.Transform(transform);
29.     g.FillPath(brush, path);
30. }
```

After setting up the star in the same way as before, we must calculate its centre point by averaging the locations of the five points (lines 14 to 21). We then create the compound transformation on lines 23 to 27. We first translate the star so that its centre is at the origin (line 24), then apply the rotation (line 25), and then translate it back to its original position (lines 26 and 27).

Note a couple of things about this code. First, somewhat unusually for methods taking angles as parameters, the `Rotate()` expects its angle in degrees rather than the more usual (and less useful) radians. Second, in order to ensure the transformations are done in the right order, we add a `MatrixOrder.Append` parameter to each of the transformations. The default for these methods is `MatrixOrder.Prepend`, which causes each operation to occur *before* the last one added. This seemingly perverse behaviour is due to the matrix multiplication rules described above.

The output of this program is as shown in Figure 10.18.

Figure 10.18 A star rotated about its centre

10.5.3 ☐ Scaling

Scaling works by multiplying all the x coordinates of a path by a horizontal scaling factor and all the y coordinates by a vertical scaling factor. As with rotation, this method of scaling effectively scales all distances relative to the origin, so if we simply apply a Scale() method to a figure that is not at the origin and expect it to appear in the same place but larger or smaller, we will find instead that the figure has also moved from its original location.

The solution to this problem is the same as for rotation: if we want to scale an object *in place*, we must first translate it so that its centre is at the origin, then apply Scale(), and then translate it back to its original location.

We can illustrate this by adding in a call to Scale() in the rotation example above. If we insert the line:

```
transform.Scale(0.5f, 0.75f, MatrixOrder.Append);
```

after line 25 (that is, if we do the scaling when the star's centre is at the origin), we will multiply the star by a factor of 0.5 horizontally and 0.75 vertically. The result is as shown in Figure 10.19.

10.5.4 ☐ Shearing

Shearing is most easily thought of in terms of a pack of playing cards. Begin by placing the pack of cards on the table in front of you, squared up so that the cards form a vertical pile. Now push the pack over in such a way that the bottom card remains where it was, and each card above the bottom card gets pushed over slightly more than the one below it. The result is that the pack of cards now has a sloping profile rather than the vertical profile with which it began.

Figure 10.19 The star from Figure 10.18 with an additional scaling transformation

Mathematically, we can express a shear using a simple equation for the x and y coordinates of each point in the figure:

```
x(after) = x(before) + shearX * y(before)
y(after) = y(before) + shearY * x(before)
```

where `x(after)` is the x coordinate of the point after the shear operation, `x(before)` is the x coordinate before the shear, and `shearX` and `shearY` are constants called the horizontal and vertical shear constants respectively.

The first equation means simply that each point's x coordinate gets shifted over by an amount that is proportional to the y coordinate of that point. In other words, the further along the y axis a point lies, the more its x coordinate gets shifted, resulting in the effect we saw with the pack of cards.

The `Shear()` method requires us to specify values for `shearX` and `shearY`. From the above equations, using `shearX = shearY = 0` results in no changes at all, so to produce a mild shear we should use values fairly close to 0.

It is easiest to see the effects of a shear if we isolate it from other transformations, but as usual, if we apply a shear to an object that is not centred at the origin, the effect will probably not be what we imagine. We'll therefore illustrate a shear by replacing line 25 (the rotation line) in the previous example illustrating rotation with the following line:

```
transform.Shear(0.3f, 0f, MatrixOrder.Append);
```

This shears the star horizontally but not vertically. The result is as shown in Figure 10.20.

When viewing this figure, it is important to remember that the star has not been rotated, only sheared. We can see that those parts of the star with larger y coordinates (towards the bottom of the figure) have been sheared more than those at the top.

Figure 10.20 A star sheared horizontally

10.6 ■ Fonts and drawing strings

.NET provides a great many features that allow text to be drawn and formatted, but we do not have the space to cover them all in detail. In this section, we will cover the basics of creating a string from a particular font and drawing it on the screen. Like other graphics such as lines and ellipses, a string may also be added to a `GraphicsPath`, which allows some quite impressive text effects to be created.

The simplest way to add text to a graphical display is to call `DrawString()` from `Graphics`. This method comes in six overloaded forms, but even the simplest of these requires a fair bit of information. First, of course, we need to supply the string itself, but we also need to provide a `Font`, a `Brush` and the `Point` at which the string should be displayed. We have seen all of these classes before, with the exception of `Font`, so we'll take a quick look at fonts here.

The `Font` class comes with 13 (yes, 13) constructors to choose from. The simplest of these requests a 'family name' and a 'size' for the font. The family name of a font is the usual name you have probably seen when selecting fonts in a word processor, such as 'Times New Roman', 'Arial' or 'Courier New'. The size is specified, by default, in units called *points*. A point is a historical unit dating from the days of typesetting, and is officially 1/72 inch. How big a 12-point font actually appears on your monitor, of course, depends on the current screen resolution, but typically the font that appears in dialog boxes and ordinary text in documents in a word processor is somewhere in the 8 to 10 point range, so you can use that as a guide to the smallest size of text that is easily readable in most situations. The best thing is to experiment and see what gives the desired effect.

Armed with this information, we can produce some text with the following code:

```
protected override void OnPaint(PaintEventArgs args)

{
   Graphics g = args.Graphics;
   string someText = "Some text";
   Font font = new Font("Arial", 20);
   Brush brush = new SolidBrush(Color.Red);
   Point point = new Point(10, 20);
   g.DrawString(someText, font, brush, point);
}
```

This will draw 'Some text' in 20-point (largish) Arial font using a solid red brush, with the upper-left corner of the text located at the point (10, 20).

Since text is drawn using Graphics, all the enhancements that we have illustrated in our earlier examples with vector graphics can be applied to text as well. We can use various types of Brush to produce text with colour gradients or bitmap patterns, we can apply a Matrix to produce text that is transformed in various ways, and so on.

The one thing we *can't* do if we stick to using just Graphics to display text is produce text that is drawn with one Brush for a fill pattern and a Pen for the outline. However, since GraphicsPath allows text to be added to a general path, we can solve that problem by using GraphicsPath to store the text before drawing it.

The following OnPaint() method illustrates how this might be done by producing the string 'Some text' drawn with a honeydew brush and then outlined with a black pen. The text is also rotated about its centre to illustrate how the centre of a line of text may be found.

```
1.  protected override void OnPaint(PaintEventArgs args)
2.  {
3.     Graphics g = args.Graphics;
4.     string someText = "Some text";
5.     int leftText = 10, topText = 100;
6.
7.     FontFamily fontFamily = new FontFamily("Arial");
8.     Font font = new Font(fontFamily, 40, FontStyle.Bold);
9.     GraphicsPath path = new GraphicsPath(FillMode.Winding);
10.    path.AddString(someText, fontFamily,
11.       (int)FontStyle.Bold, 40,
12.       new Point (leftText, topText),
13.       StringFormat.GenericDefault);
14.
15.    SizeF textSize = g.MeasureString(someText, font);
16.    Point centre = new Point();
17.    centre.X = (int)(leftText + textSize.Width) / 2;
18.    centre.Y = (int)(topText + textSize.Height) / 2;
19.
```

```
20.    Matrix transform = new Matrix();
21.    transform.Translate(-centre.X, -centre.Y);
22.    transform.Rotate(45f, MatrixOrder.Append);
23.    transform.Translate(centre.X, centre.Y,
       MatrixOrder.Append);
24.    path.Transform(transform);
25.
26.    Brush brush = new SolidBrush(Color.Honeydew);
27.    g.FillPath(brush, path);
28.    Pen pen = new Pen(Color.Black, 2);
29.    g.DrawPath(pen, path);
30.    g.DrawString(someText, font, brush, new Point(10, 200));
31. }
```

Let us consider the code in sections. First, we create the text and specify its position (lines 4 and 5). Next, we define the Font that is to be used to display the text. However, when adding a string to a GraphicsPath, we cannot just specify the Font in which the string is to be drawn. Rather, we must define a FontFamily and derive the Font from it. A FontFamily is a class that defines the main properties of a particular font design, from which specific instances of the font can be created. For example, here (line 7) we create the 'Arial' FontFamily, which defines all fonts that are based on the Arial specifications.

We can derive a particular Font from a FontFamily by using another of Font's 13 constructors (line 8), where we specify the FontFamily, the size of the font (40 points here) and the style of the font (bold, italic and so on). The choices for style are contained in the FontStyle enumeration.

Then we create the GraphicsPath (line 9), and then (line 10) we add a string to the path. The AddString() method from GraphicsPath allows a string to be added, but only if we specify the font information in terms of the FontFamily, and not the actual Font itself, even though we need to repeat all the information required in the Font constructor back on line 8. The parameters in AddString() are, first, the string to be added to the path and then the FontFamily object.

Next, we provide the font style, but AddString() will not accept one of the FontStyle enumeration values directly – instead it must be cast to an int. After that comes the font size, then the location of the text, and finally a StringFormat parameter. StringFormat is used mainly in formatting text that is to be displayed on multiple lines, as in a word processor, and we will not consider it further here. If you only need basic text display, just use StringFormat.GenericDefault as we have here.

If all we want is to display the text within a GraphicsPath, we don't actually need the Font object we created on line 8. However, in many cases we need some specific information about the font to position the text correctly in relation to other objects in the scene or, as here, to calculate the centre of the string so that we may rotate the text relative to the centre point.

To this end, we use MeasureString() from Graphics to find the dimensions (in pixels, not points) of a string displayed using a particular font. This is shown on line 15, where the result is returned as a `SizeF`, which stores the width and height of the text in `float` values. We use this information together with the starting point of the text on lines 17 and 18 to calculate the mid-point of the displayed string.

Once we have this information, we use a `Matrix` to rotate the string through 45 degrees as we did with the star in the earlier example (lines 20 to 24).

Finally, we illustrate how to draw text using a `Brush` for the interior and a `Pen` for the outline (lines 26 to 29). On line 30 we just draw another string using `DrawString()` from `Graphics` for comparison. The result is as shown in Figure 10.21.

Figure 10.21 Text outline drawn with a `Pen` for the outline and a `Brush` for the interior

We close this section on text with a cautionary word on fonts. Most Windows installations include a large number of fonts that are installed by default. Many users will add other fonts found on cover disks of computer magazines, on the web or even ones they have designed themselves. While some of these fonts may look attractive, if you are writing a program that is intended for widespread use in locations with which you have no direct connection it is a bit risky to assume that everyone will have all the exotic fonts you have used in writing the program.

Therefore, although it will probably crimp your artistic style, it is best to stick to those fonts that are almost certainly on everyone's computer, such as Arial, Times New Roman, Courier and so on. If your program requests a font that is not installed, it is usually not a complete disaster, since Windows will attempt to substitute an existing font. This means that text will usually appear in some form on a graphics display – it just might not look quite as you intended.

10.7 ■ Raster graphics

As we mentioned at the beginning of this chapter, general images such as digital or scanned photographs are displayed using *raster graphics*, in which the information required to display the image is stored simply as an array of colour values rather than as a set of mathematical formulas for drawing and filling the curves.

Veterans of Java's image-handling features will know that it is fairly easy to load an image from a disk file and manipulate it in various ways within the program. Java is somewhat limited in the image formats that it can support (at least without obtaining some third-party packages to supplement the basic Java Development Kit), but it does support the display of the popular GIF and JPEG formats.

More battle-hardened veterans who have used the Microsoft Foundation Classes (MFC) for writing Visual C++ programs will have unpleasant memories of image handling, since MFC provided no built-in support for any image types apart from the Windows bitmap (BMP) format.

.NET's image handling features will be good news for both groups, since in general, loading, editing and saving images is easy in C#. As usual, there are a great many features available, so in this section we will tour the highlights and direct you to the documentation to see what else is available.

10.7.1 □ Displaying an image from a disk file

We've already seen how to use an image file as a `Brush` earlier in this chapter, so it should come as no surprise that it is quite simple to display an unadulterated image in the client area of a `Form`. The following code does just that:

```
using System;
using System.Drawing;
using System.Windows.Forms;
using System.Drawing.Imaging;

public class ImageShow : Form
{
  public ImageShow()
  {
  }

  protected override void OnPaint(PaintEventArgs args)
  {
    Graphics g = args.Graphics;
    Image dundee = Image.FromFile("Dundee.jpg");
    Size dundeeSize = dundee.Size;
    ClientSize = dundeeSize;
```

```
      g.DrawImage(dundee, new Rectangle(0, 0,
        dundeeSize.Width, dundeeSize.Height));
      dundee.Save("Dundee.gif", ImageFormat.Gif);
    }

    public static void Main()
    {
      Application.Run(new ImageShow());
    }
  }
```

As usual, the code for displaying the image is in the OnPaint() method, since Graphics is in charge of drawing raster images as well as vector shapes.

The image (a JPEG file in this case) is loaded from disk using the FromFile() method in the Image class. Image is actually an abstract class and cannot be used on its own to instantiate objects, but it contains a number of static methods that allow images to be created in various ways.

In order to fit the main frame to the image, we obtain its size and use it to set the ClientSize. The DrawImage() method in Graphics allows the image to be drawn in various ways (the method actually has 30 overloads!). Here, we specify the Rectangle which is to be occupied by the image. The dimensions of the rectangle are taken from the size of the image, but this is not necessary. If we specify different dimensions, the image is scaled to fit the rectangle.

The last line in OnPaint() shows how to save an Image to a disk file, possibly in a different image format. Here we save the original JPEG image as a GIF. The second parameter to Save() specifies the image format, and uses the specification of the format given in an ImageFormat object. ImageFormat is a class in System.Drawing.Imaging, so remember to add a using statement for that namespace.

10.7.2 ☐ Drawing on an image

An Image has its own Graphics object which can be used to add customized graphics to a raster image. For example, the following OnPaint() method adds a caption to the picture of Dundee in the upper-left corner:

```
protected override void OnPaint(PaintEventArgs args)
{
  Graphics g = args.Graphics;
  Image dundee = Image.FromFile("Dundee.jpg");
  Size dundeeSize = dundee.Size;
  ClientSize = dundeeSize;
  Graphics dundeeG = Graphics.FromImage(dundee);
  dundeeG.DrawString("View of Dundee from the Law",
    new Font("Arial", 14), new SolidBrush(Color.Black),
    0, 0);
```

```
    g.DrawImage(dundee, new Rectangle(0, 0,
      dundeeSize.Width, dundeeSize.Height));
    dundee.Save("DundeeLabel.jpg", ImageFormat.Jpeg);
}
```

We use the static `FromImage()` method from `Graphics` to obtain a graphics context called `dundeeG` for the `Image` containing the photo of Dundee. We can then use `dundeeG` to draw on the photo in exactly the same way as we use `g` to draw on the client area of the main `Form`. Here we use `DrawString()` to add the caption 'View of Dundee from the Law'. (The Law is a large hill in the centre of Dundee – 'law' is actually Gaelic for 'hill'.) The last line saves the titled image to a new JPEG file.

It is important to remember that in order for any drawing done on an `Image` to be visible, it must be done *before* the image is drawn to a visible component. The `Image` itself is really an offscreen buffer and does not appear until it is drawn using `DrawImage()` to display it on a component that is part of the visible interface. Therefore, if we had placed the `g.DrawImage(...)` line before the `dundeeG.DrawString(...)` line in the above code, the caption would not appear on screen, although it *would* still appear in the saved file, since the file stores the contents of the `Image`, and is not just a copy of what appears on the screen.

The output of the program is as shown in Figure 10.22 (the image here is a smaller size than that which would appear on screen, so the text in the upper-left corner may be hard to read). It is a photograph I took of Dundee, Scotland (where I work) on an admittedly rare sunny day in August 2002.

Figure 10.22 A JPEG image of Dundee with a caption added at the upper left

The view looks south over the River Tay, and shows the locally famous Tay Railway Bridge (more than 3 km or 2 miles long) in the centre of the picture.

Clearly, all the techniques illustrated earlier in this chapter can be applied to producing graphics overlaid on raster images, so the possibilities are literally limitless. In addition to adding vector graphics to a raster image, it is also possible to combine several raster images, since the Graphics object of one image can be used to draw another image on top of it, using DrawImage().

Although the methods given above for transforming vector shapes will also work on raster images, some of the versions of DrawImage() provide easier ways of implementing transforms such as rotations and shearing. Have a look through the documentation to see the possibilities.

10.8 ■ Mouse events

Adding handlers for mouse events is fairly straightforward. Handlers are provided for all the usual mouse events such as pressing and releasing a button, moving the mouse, and entering, leaving and hovering over a form. The general procedure for adding a handler for a mouse event is the same for all events, so we'll give a few examples here and then summarize by listing the handlers that are available.

As a first example, we will write a little program that detects the 'mouse down' event when a mouse is clicked over a blank form. Depending on which button is pressed, a red, green or blue square is drawn at the location of the mouse pointer. The code is as follows.

```
1. using System;
2. using System.Drawing;
3. using System.Windows.Forms;
4.
5. public class MouseDemo1 : Form
6. {
7.    const int squareSide = 10;
8.
9.    public MouseDemo1()
10.    {
11.       ClientSize = new Size(300, 300);
12.       BackColor = Color.WhiteSmoke;
13.       StartPosition = FormStartPosition.CenterScreen;
14.    }
15.
16.    protected override void OnMouseDown(MouseEventArgs args)
17.    {
18.       Graphics g = CreateGraphics();
19.       Pen pen = new Pen(Color.Black);
```

```
20.        if (args.Button == MouseButtons.Left)
21.           pen = new Pen(Color.Red);
22.        else if (args.Button == MouseButtons.Middle)
23.           pen = new Pen(Color.Green);
24.        else if (args.Button == MouseButtons.Right)
25.           pen = new Pen(Color.Blue);
26.        g.DrawRectangle(pen,
27.           args.X - squareSide/2,
28.           args.Y - squareSide/2,
29.           squareSide, squareSide);
30.     }
31.
32.     public static void Main()
33.     {
34.        Application.Run(new MouseDemo1());
35.     }
36. }
```

Notice that this program has no override of OnPaint()– all the graphics are drawn in OnMouseDown() (line 16), which is the override of the mouse down handler in the Form class. This handler is called whenever any of the mouse buttons is pressed down (there is a separate OnMouseUp() handler that is called when a button is released). A Graphics object for drawing is created (line 18) and a default pen is created (line 19).

The MouseEventsArgs parameter that is passed to OnMouseDown() (and to all other mouse event handlers) contains all the information about which button was pressed, what the coordinates of the mouse cursor are and so on. We illustrate here how to detect which button was pressed by using the Button property. This value has a value that is defined as a MouseButtons property. On a standard PC mouse, Left and Right refer to the left and right buttons. Middle refers to the middle button if there is one, and also to the mouse wheel if it is used as a button.

Running this program displays a blank form, and clicking one of the mouse buttons over the client area draws a little square of the correct colour at each point. Everything appears to work well, but if you cover up the window and then redisplay it, all the squares disappear.

The reason for this is that when a window is displayed or restored after being hidden or minimized, any graphics that are to appear must be defined in OnPaint(). Since this program has no OnPaint() override, no graphics appear.

The solution is to save the squares in an internal data structure as they are entered with the mouse, and then put graphics commands in OnPaint() that display the squares. There are various ways this can be done, but one solution is as follows.

```
1.  using System;
2.  using System.Drawing;
3.  using System.Drawing.Drawing2D;
4.  using System.Windows.Forms;
5.  using System.Collections;
6.
7.  public class MouseDemo2 : Form
8.  {
9.    const int squareSide = 10;
10.   private ArrayList squareList = new ArrayList();
11.
12.   public MouseDemo2()
13.   {
14.     ClientSize = new Size(300, 300);
15.     BackColor = Color.WhiteSmoke;
16.     StartPosition = FormStartPosition.CenterScreen;
17.   }
18.
19.   protected override void OnMouseDown(MouseEventArgs args)
20.   {
21.     Pen pen = new Pen(Color.Black);
22.     if (args.Button == MouseButtons.Left)
23.       pen = new Pen(Color.Red);
24.     else if (args.Button == MouseButtons.Middle)
25.       pen = new Pen(Color.Green);
26.     else if (args.Button == MouseButtons.Right)
27.       pen = new Pen(Color.Blue);
28.     squareList.Add(new SquareSymbol(pen, args.X, args.Y));
29.     Invalidate();
30.   }
31.
32.   protected override void OnPaint(PaintEventArgs args)
33.   {
34.     Graphics g = args.Graphics;
35.     foreach (SquareSymbol square in squareList)
36.     {
37.       g.DrawRectangle(square.pen,
38.         square.x - squareSide/2,
39.         square.y - squareSide/2,
40.         squareSide, squareSide);
41.     }
42.   }
43.
44.   public static void Main()
45.   {
46.     Application.Run(new MouseDemo2());
```

```
47.    }
48. }
49.
50. public struct SquareSymbol
51. {
52.    public int x, y;
53.    public Pen pen;
54.
55.    public SquareSymbol(Pen p, int xx, int yy)
56.    {
57.       x = xx;
58.       y = yy;
59.       pen = p;
60.    }
61. }
```

We have added a little utility class called `SquareSymbol` (line 50) which stores the coordinates of the centre of each square that is to be drawn, along with a `Pen` that defines the drawing colour.

The `OnMouseDown()` handler (line 19) is similar to the previous version, except that it now uses an `ArrayList` to store a `SquareSymbol` (line 28) each time the mouse is clicked. A call to `Invalidate()` (line 29) then calls `OnPaint()` (line 32) to actually draw the squares. This version of the program behaves in the same way as the previous one when the mouse is clicked over the form's client area, but now the squares are saved and redrawn whenever the window is hidden and redisplayed.

This example illustrates an important point about graphics – all graphics are recreated whenever a window must be redisplayed, and this must be done by drawing the graphics in `OnPaint()`.

10.8.1 ☐ Mouse events example: checkers game

As a final example of mouse event handling, we will present a simple checkers (draughts) game. The program allows two humans to play checkers by dragging checkermen over a checkerboard. It does not check that moves are legal, nor does it actually provide a computer-based opponent.

Figure 10.23 shows the display of the program, and illustrates a black piece being dragged by the mouse over a red piece.

The program draws the board as a grid of grey and pink squares and then draws the current setup of the pieces on top. A piece can be moved by clicking on the square containing it with the left mouse button and then dragging (moving the mouse while holding down the left button) the mouse to the square to which the piece is to move. The piece will follow the mouse as it is dragged, and when the mouse button is released over the destination square, the piece is drawn centred in that square.

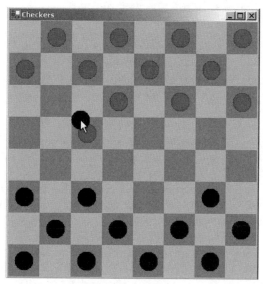

Figure 10.23 A checkers board showing a piece being dragged by the mouse

The only check the program makes during a move is that the destination square is not already occupied by another piece. If it is, the piece being moved just snaps back to its starting square. A piece can be removed from the board by right-clicking on it.

The code for the game is as follows. We will describe the details following the code listing.

```
1.  using System;
2.  using System.Drawing;
3.  using System.Drawing.Drawing2D;
4.  using System.Windows.Forms;
5.  using System.Collections;
6.
7.  public class Checkers : Form
8.  {
9.      readonly int squareSide = 50;
10.     readonly int pieceDiameter = 30;
11.     readonly Color blackSquare = Color.DarkGray;
12.     readonly Color redSquare = Color.Pink;
13.     readonly Color blackPiece = Color.Black;
14.     readonly Color redPiece = Color.Red;
15.     private ArrayList pieces = new ArrayList();
16.     private Piece selected = null;
17.     private int selectedX, selectedY;
18.     private Rectangle oldSquare;
19.
```

```
20.    public Checkers()
21.    {
22.      ClientSize = new Size(8*squareSide, 8*squareSide);
23.      Text = "Checkers";
24.      StartPosition = FormStartPosition.CenterScreen;
25.      CreatePieces();
26.    }
27.
28.    protected override void OnMouseDown(MouseEventArgs args)
29.    {
30.      selected = GetSelectedPiece(args.X, args.Y);
31.      if (selected == null) return;
32.      if (args.Button == MouseButtons.Left)
33.      {
34.        selectedX = selected.x;
35.        selectedY = selected.y;
36.        oldSquare = new Rectangle(selected.x, selected.y,
37.          squareSide, squareSide);
38.      }
39.      else if (args.Button == MouseButtons.Right)
40.      {
41.        pieces.Remove(selected);
42.        selected = null;
43.        Invalidate();
44.      }
45.    }
46.
47.    protected override void OnMouseMove(MouseEventArgs args)
48.    {
49.      if (selected == null) return;
50.      selected.x = args.X - squareSide/2;
51.      selected.y = args.Y - squareSide/2;
52.      Rectangle newSquare = new Rectangle
         (selected.x, selected.y,
53.        squareSide, squareSide);
54.      Rectangle clipRect = Rectangle.Union
         (oldSquare, newSquare);
55.      Invalidate(clipRect);
56.      oldSquare = newSquare;
57.    }
58.
59.    protected override void OnMouseUp(MouseEventArgs args)
60.    {
61.      if (selected == null) return;
62.      Square square = SquareOccupied(args.X, args.Y);
63.      if (square.piece != null)
```

```
64.      {
65.         selected.x = selectedX;
66.         selected.y = selectedY;
67.      }
68.      else
69.      {
70.         selected.x = square.x;
71.         selected.y = square.y;
72.      }
73.      selected = null;
74.      Invalidate();
75.   }
76.
77.   private Square SquareOccupied(int mouseX, int mouseY)
78.   {
79.      for (int x = 0; x < 8; x++)
80.      {
81.         for (int y = 0; y < 8; y++)
82.         {
83.            Rectangle square = new Rectangle(x*squareSide,
84.               y*squareSide, squareSide, squareSide);
85.            if (square.Contains(mouseX, mouseY))
86.            {
87.               foreach (Piece piece in pieces)
88.               {
89.                  if (piece != selected &&
90.                                          square.Contains
                                            (piece.x,
                                            piece.y))
91.                     return new Square(x * squareSide,
92.                        y * squareSide, piece);
93.               }
94.               return new Square(x * squareSide,
95.                  y * squareSide, null);
96.            }
97.         }
98.      }
99.      // Should never get here
100.     return null;
101.  }
102.
103.  private Piece GetSelectedPiece(int x, int y)
104.  {
105.     foreach(Piece piece in pieces)
106.     {
107.        Rectangle square = new Rectangle(piece.x, piece.y,
```

```
108.              squareSide, squareSide);
109.         if (square.Contains(x, y))
110.         {
111.             return piece;
112.         }
113.       }
114.     return null;
115.   }
116.
117.   private void CreatePieces()
118.   {
119.     // Red pieces at top of board
120.     Brush redBrush = new SolidBrush(redPiece);
121.     Brush blackBrush = new SolidBrush(blackPiece);
122.     for (int x = 0; x < 8; x++)
123.     {
124.       for (int y = 0; y < 3; y++)
125.       {
126.         if ((x + y) % 2 == 1)
127.         {
128.             pieces.Add(new Piece(redBrush, squareSide*x,
129.               squareSide*y));
130.         }
131.       }
132.       for (int y = 5; y < 8; y++)
133.       {
134.         if ((x + y) % 2 == 1)
135.         {
136.             pieces.Add(new Piece(blackBrush, squareSide*x,
137.               squareSide*y));
138.         }
139.       }
140.     }
141.   }
142.
143.   private void DrawBoard(Graphics g)
144.   {
145.     for (int x = 0; x < 8; x++)
146.     {
147.       for (int y = 0; y < 8; y++)
148.       {
149.         Color brushColor = (x + y) % 2 == 0 ?
150.           redSquare : blackSquare;
151.         Brush brush = new SolidBrush(brushColor);
152.         g.FillRectangle(brush, x*squareSide,
               y*squareSide,
```

```
153.                  squareSide, squareSide);
154.            }
155.        }
156.    }
157.
158.    private void DrawPieces(Graphics g)
159.    {
160.        int pieceOffset = (squareSide - pieceDiameter) / 2;
161.        foreach (Piece piece in pieces)
162.        {
163.            g.FillEllipse(piece.brush,
164.                piece.x + pieceOffset,
165.                piece.y + pieceOffset,
166.                pieceDiameter, pieceDiameter);
167.        }
168.    }
169.
170.    protected override void OnPaint(PaintEventArgs args)
171.    {
172.        Graphics g = args.Graphics;
173.        DrawBoard(g);
174.        DrawPieces(g);
175.    }
176.
177.    public static void Main()
178.    {
179.        Application.Run(new Checkers());
180.    }
181. }
182.
183. public class Piece
184. {
185.    public int x, y;
186.    public Brush brush;
187.
188.    public Piece(Brush b, int xx, int yy)
189.    {
190.        x = xx;
191.        y = yy;
192.        brush = b;
193.    }
194. }
195.
196. public class Square
197. {
198.    public int x, y;
```

```
199.    public Piece piece;
200.
201.    public Square(int xx, int yy, Piece p)
202.    {
203.        x = xx;
204.        y = yy;
205.        piece = p;
206.    }
207. }
```

The program defines a couple of utility classes for storing components in the game. Piece (line 183) stores the coordinates of the piece on the board and the Brush that is used to draw it, while Square (line 196) stores the coordinates of a square on the board and the piece (if any) that is on that square.

The constructor (line 20) initializes the form and then calls CreatePieces() to define the initial setup of the pieces on the board. CreatePieces() (line 117) creates a number of Piece objects and stores them in the pieces ArrayList. Note that CreatePieces() does not actually draw any graphics, since this is done by an automatic call to OnPaint() when the window is first displayed.

OnPaint() (line 170) calls DrawBoard() (line 143) to draw the squares on the board and then DrawPieces() (line 158) to draw the pieces on top of the squares. Each piece is drawn as a circle that is sized to fit inside the square with space between it at the square's edges. The sizes of the squares and pieces are defined by a couple of readonly parameters on lines 9 and 10.

The pieces are stored in an ArrayList called pieces, so we just need to loop through this list using a foreach loop (line 161) and extract the coordinates of each piece to draw it onto the board.

At this point, the initial setup of the board is complete, and the program will wait for user interaction. This is done by the user clicking on a square containing a piece. (In a proper checkers game, black must move first by dragging one of the black pieces diagonally forward by one square, but the program does not check this. Any piece can be moved to any empty square.)

The sequence of mouse events required to move a piece is therefore a mouse down, followed by a number of mouse move events and ending with a mouse up. Let us look at the handlers for each of these events.

OnMouseDown() (line 28) calls GetSelectedPiece() to try to select the piece that is in the square selected by the user. GetSelectedPiece() loops through all the pieces in the pieces list trying to find a piece in the selected square. This is most easily done by using the Contains() method in the Rectangle class to see if a particular point lies within a rectangle. On line 107 we create a Rectangle representing the chosen square and then test it to see if it contains the point clicked by the mouse (line 109). If no piece is in the square selected by the user, null is returned (line 114). OnMouseDown() therefore has no effect on the graphics – it simply selects the piece to be moved, if any.

OnMouseDown() also handles removal of a piece from the board (line 39) when the right button is clicked. In this case, all we need to do is call the Remove() method from ArrayList to remove selected and then redraw the board.

If the mouse is now dragged, OnMouseMove() (line 47) is called. We first check that a piece has actually been selected (line 49), since if the user clicked on an empty square, dragging the mouse should have no effect.

For a selected piece, the idea is to have the image of the piece follow the mouse pointer smoothly as it is dragged across the board. We therefore set the selected piece's coordinates to those of the mouse pointer (offset by half a square's width so that the piece is centred on the mouse pointer – lines 50 and 51). We could simply call Invalidate() to redraw the board at this point, but in most cases this will cause the entire board to flicker noticeably as the piece is dragged.

The flickering is caused by a rapid succession of calls to OnPaint() each time a mouse move event is generated, which is typically every few milliseconds. For all but the most powerful graphics cards, it is difficult to redraw a large area such as the entire window entirely smoothly, so some flickering is unavoidable.

We can reduce (although not usually eliminate entirely) the flickering by clipping the region that is redrawn. When a single piece is moved, the only area on the board that requires redrawing is the union of the square surrounding the old position of the piece with the square surrounding the new position. We define a Rectangle called oldSquare (line 18) for storing the previous position of the piece and then calculate the new position on line 52. Using the Union() method from Rectangle (line 54) produces a larger rectangle that contains both squares, and we can use that to define a clipping region for the call to Invalidate() (line 55).

When the piece reaches its destination square, we can release the mouse button to drop the piece in place. This calls OnMouseUp() (line 59), which in turn calls SquareOccupied() (line 77) to locate the square over which the mouse button was released. SquareOccupied() locates this square and then checks to see if there is a piece on that square already (loop on line 87). SquareOccupied() returns a Square object which either contains the piece on that square (line 91) or null if the square is empty (line 94).

Back in OnMouseUp() we send the piece being moved back to its starting point if the destination square is occupied (line 63), or else move it to the new square if it is empty (line 68). In this case, we can redraw the entire board (line 74) since only a single mouse up event is generated by releasing the mouse button, so continuous flickering won't be a problem.

10.8.2 ☐ Other mouse events

The other mouse events work in much the same way as those illustrated above. In addition to mouse down and mouse up, there is also a mouse click event, which is generated immediately before mouse up, and can be handled with an OnClick() method. There is also an OnDoubleClick() handler for double-clicks of the mouse.

Rotating (as opposed to clicking) the mouse wheel can be handled with `OnMouseWheel()`. The `MouseEventArgs` parameter has a `Delta` property which contains the number of notches or *detents* the wheel has been moved. `Delta` actually returns a value of 120 for each detent moved on the wheel, so you will need to divide the `Delta` value by 120 to get the actual number of notches moved. Forward detents (away from the user) are assigned positive values and backward detents (toward the user) negative ones. Thus rolling the wheel 3 notches towards you will generate a `Delta` of –360.

There are three other mouse events that do not return precise information about the mouse's location, but only general information about the mouse leaving, entering or hovering over a control or form. `OnMouseLeave()` and `OnMouseEnter()` are generated whenever the mouse pointer leaves or enters the form or control's boundary. They are passed an ordinary `EventArgs` parameter rather than a `MouseEventArgs`. `OnMouseHover()` is called whenever the mouse hovers over a control. The most common response to a hover is the display of a tooltip.

Finally, it should be mentioned that event handlers can be added to a form or control in the usual way, rather than by an explicit override of the base class handlers. For example, we could add an event handler for the mouse down event to a form by adding the following line to a constructor:

```
this.MouseDown += new EventHandler(MouseDownHandler);
```

We could then write the `MouseDownHandler()` method as usual:

```
public void MouseDownHandler(MouseEventArgs args)
{
    // handler code
}
```

10.9 ■ Keyboard events

The main keyboard event handlers respond to key down and key up events. The corresponding handlers, `OnKeyDown()` and `OnKeyUp()` can be added to a form or control in the same way as a mouse handler. Keyboard event handlers are passed `KeyEventArgs` as a parameter, which contains information such as which key was pressed, which modifier keys (shift, control and alt) were pressed at the same time and so on.

We will present a simple modification of the `MouseDemo2` program above in which pressing the R, G or B key draws a red, green or blue square at a random position on the client area. Holding down the shift key will fill the square in red, holding down control will fill it in green, and holding down shift and control together will fill the square in yellow. The complete program follows:

```
1. using System;
2. using System.Drawing;
3. using System.Windows.Forms;
4. using System.Collections;
5.
6. public class KeyboardDemo : Form
7. {
8.    const int squareSide = 10;
9.    private ArrayList squareList = new ArrayList();
10.   private Random random = new Random();
11.
12.   public KeyboardDemo()
13.   {
14.     ClientSize = new Size(300, 300);
15.     BackColor = Color.WhiteSmoke;
16.     StartPosition = FormStartPosition.CenterScreen;
17.   }
18.
19.   protected override void OnKeyDown(KeyEventArgs args)
20.   {
21.     Pen pen = new Pen(Color.Black);
22.     if (args.KeyCode == Keys.R)
23.       pen = new Pen(Color.Red);
24.     else if (args.KeyCode == Keys.G)
25.       pen = new Pen(Color.Green);
26.     else if (args.KeyCode == Keys.B)
27.       pen = new Pen(Color.Blue);
28.     else
29.       return;
30.
31.     Brush brush = new SolidBrush(Color.White);
32.     if (args.Modifiers == Keys.Shift)
33.       brush = new SolidBrush(Color.Red);
34.     else if (args.Modifiers == Keys.Control)
35.       brush = new SolidBrush(Color.Green);
36.     else if (args.Modifiers == (Keys.Control | Keys.Shift))
37.       brush = new SolidBrush(Color.Yellow);
38.
39.     squareList.Add(new SquareSymbol(pen, brush,
40.       random.Next(ClientSize.Width),
41.       random.Next(ClientSize.Height)));
42.     Invalidate();
43.   }
44.
45.   protected override void OnPaint(PaintEventArgs args)
46.   {
```

```
47.        Graphics g = args.Graphics;
48.        foreach (SquareSymbol square in squareList)
49.        {
50.          g.FillRectangle(square.brush,
51.              square.x - squareSide/2,
52.              square.y - squareSide/2,
53.              squareSide, squareSide);
54.          g.DrawRectangle(square.pen,
55.              square.x - squareSide/2,
56.              square.y - squareSide/2,
57.              squareSide, squareSide);
58.        }
59.    }
60.
61.    public static void Main()
62.    {
63.        Application.Run(new KeyboardDemo());
64.    }
65. }
66.
67. public struct SquareSymbol
68. {
69.    public int x, y;
70.    public Pen pen;
71.    public Brush brush;
72.
73.    public SquareSymbol(Pen p, Brush b, int xx, int yy)
74.    {
75.        x = xx;
76.        y = yy;
77.        pen = p;
78.        brush = b;
79.    }
80. }
```

We have modified the `SquareSymbol` utility class (line 67) so that it holds a `Brush` as well as a `Pen`, allowing the square to be filled and outlined in different colours.

When a key is pressed, `OnKeyDown()` (line 19) is called. The identity of the pressed key can be extracted from the `KeyEventsArgs` parameter, as on line 22. The easiest way to do this is to examine the `KeyCode` property and compare it with a list of properties in the `Keys` enumeration, which contains an entry for each key on the keyboard (and a few that probably aren't on your keyboard as well). Letter keys have an obvious entry, which is just the letter that was pressed, such as `Keys.R` on line 22. Other keys usually have a fairly obvious name, such as `F1` to `F24` for the function keys (although it is unlikely your keyboard goes beyond F12), `Left`, `Right`, `Up` and `Down` for the arrow keys and so on. Number keys have a `D` before the number, so that `Keys.D1` is the 1 key and so on. Explore the documentation for the `Keys` enumeration to see a complete list.

It should be pointed out that only one `KeyCode` is ever returned for a given key on the keyboard, even if some of the modifier keys such as Shift or Control are pressed at the same time. For example, pressing the 'T' key always returns a `KeyCode` of `Keys.T`, even if the Shift key is also pressed. Information about the modifier keys is contained in `KeyData`, which combines the `KeyCode` with the modifier keys that have been pressed, and in the `Modifiers` property, which we've used on lines 32 to 37 to extract information about the extra keys. Generally, if you want a control that reproduces characters from the keyboard in the same way as a text editor, you should use one of the ready-made text controls such as those discussed in Chapter 9.

The `KeyValue` property returns the numerical value (that is, the ASCII or Unicode value) of the key that was pressed. For example, pressing 'A' generates a `KeyValue` of 65.

The `Modifiers` property may be compared to the `Keys` entries for the modifier keys to see which ones were pressed. We can check for single modifier keys, as on line 32 where we check for the Shift key and on line 34 for Control, or for combinations of keys, such as Shift and Control together on line 36. To combine modifiers, use a bitwise OR operator to combine the relevant `Keys` values.

Note that modifier keys such as Shift or Control do produce key events even if they are held down on their own. This fact is used by some programs to build things like volume controls into the shift keys, since just holding them down generates events that can be handled and translated into commands within the program. It is also important to remember that holding down a key causes it to repeat, and each repeat generates a separate key down event for that key. In the program above, for example, if you hold down the R key, a succession of red squares will be drawn.

Once we've set the pen and brush for the square, we generate a random position for it using a `Random` object called `random` on lines 39 to 41, and add it to the list.

The `OnPaint()` method (line 45) draws the filled interior and then the outline of each square in the usual way.

10.10 ■ Animation – threads revisited

All the graphics we have seen so far are either static, in the sense that a single image is drawn on the screen, or dynamic only when the user interacts with the scene, as when using the mouse to drag a checker piece across the board.

In many cases, adding animation to a graphical scene can greatly enhance the display. The concept behind computer animation is the same as that used in creating animated cartoons: an animated image is produced by drawing a number of still images and showing them at a rate that gives the illusion of continuous movement.

We have already seen a simple example of animation in the digital clock program presented in Chapter 9. There, the `Timer` class was used to generate an event every second to update the clock. We could also use `Timer` to produce the animation example in this section, but we will present the example using 'proper' threads in order to illustrate how they can be used.

We have seen in Chapter 8 that a program can be paused for a given number of milliseconds by calling `Thread.Sleep()`, so this is a natural way to produce animation. We can prepare a number of images or *frames* that are to be displayed at regular intervals and use `Thread.Sleep()` to pause slightly in between each pair of frames.

As cinema fans will know, the usual rate at which films are shown is around 24 frames per second, so the delay between successive frames is about 42 milliseconds. A longer delay tends to produce a jerky image. If you plan on producing animation, it would be worth experimenting with various delay times to see what gives the best results.

Although the theory of animation is simple enough – just produce a number of images and display them with a time delay – there are a few problems that can arise in practice. One problem we have already met in the checkers example above: rapid repainting of a large graphical area usually causes flickering of the image, unless a very powerful graphics card and associated hardware are being used. We have already seen how clipping can be used to reduce this problem to some extent, but if you want to produce animation where the entire image changes from one frame to the next, clipping is not possible, and some flickering will usually have to be endured.

The other problem is rather different, and fortunately easier to solve. When an animation is running, it is usually done by using a loop in the C# code to iterate over the frames to be displayed. In a GUI program, an animated image often occupies only part of the display, with various controls such as buttons and menus occupying other areas. A common interface provides buttons to allow the animation to be paused and resumed, or to allow the display to be altered. This is done in the usual way, by attaching event handlers to the controls which change parameters in the code that are in turn used to determine how the display should look.

The problem is that as long as the animation runs, it locks out all other processing in the same program, meaning that all controls essentially become disabled (although they do still seem to respond to user input, in that buttons can still be pressed and so on) until the animation finishes. If the animation is infinite, we obviously have a problem.

The solution, as you may already have guessed, is to run the animation in a separate thread, thus freeing up the main thread in the program so that it can respond to events. This is a common technique whenever some time-consuming sub-process is to be run without locking out the user interaction to the main GUI.

A simple example will illustrate the problem and how it can be solved. The `Animation` program produces an interface with some buttons in a panel on the left, and a main display area on the right that runs an animation. The animation consists of a sequence of lines or ellipses drawn at random locations and using random colours. Pressing the 'Start' button starts the animation going, after which the 'Start' caption is to be changed to 'Pause', so that pressing this button again should pause the animation. When paused, the button's caption is changed to 'Resume', and pressing it yet again lets the animation continue from where it left off. The 'Clear' button clears the display without stopping the animation if it is running, and 'Quit' exits the program.

The two radio buttons allow the user to select whether to draw lines or ellipses, and should make the change as soon as one of them is selected, even if the animation is running at the time.

If we write this program without defining a separate thread in which the animation can be run, we find that after starting the animation, the controls have no further effect and the only way to stop the program is by typing Control-C in the console window (if it was started from a console) or by using more drastic measures such as using Windows Task Manager if it is running on its own.

The solution is clearly to create a separate thread which is used to do all the drawing, and retain the original thread for handling the various events from the controls. The code for the `Animation` class is as follows:

```
 1. using System;
 2. using System.Threading;
 3. using System.Drawing;
 4. using System.Drawing.Drawing2D;
 5. using System.Windows.Forms;
 6.
 7. public class Animation : Form
 8. {
 9.    private Panel controlPanel, drawingPanel;
10.    private Button pauseButton, clearButton, quitButton;
11.    private RadioButton linesRadio, ellipsesRadio;
12.    private Thread drawThread;
13.    private ShapeType shapeType;
14.    private Color backColor = Color.WhiteSmoke;
15.
16.    public enum ShapeType
17.    { Lines, Ellipses }
18.
19.    public Animation()
20.    {
21.      ClientSize = new Size(500, 400);
22.      SetupControlPanel();
23.      drawingPanel = new Panel();
```

```
24.      drawingPanel.Bounds = new Rectangle ⮌
         (controlPanel.Width, 0,
25.        ClientSize.Width - controlPanel.Width, ⮌
           ClientSize.Height);
26.      drawingPanel.BackColor = backColor;
27.      Controls.Add(drawingPanel);
28.      StartPosition = FormStartPosition.CenterScreen;
29.
30.      ThreadStart drawStart = new ThreadStart(DrawShapes);
31.      drawThread = new Thread(drawStart);
32.    }
33.
34.    private void SetupControlPanel()
35.    {
36.      controlPanel = new Panel();
37.      controlPanel.Bounds = new Rectangle(0, 0,
38.        ClientSize.Width/5, ClientSize.Height);
39.      controlPanel.BackColor = Color.Beige;
40.      this.Controls.Add(controlPanel);
41.
42.      // Radio buttons
43.      GroupBox radioGroup = new GroupBox();
44.      radioGroup.Text = "Select shape";
45.      linesRadio = new RadioButton();
46.      linesRadio.Text = "Lines";
47.      linesRadio.Bounds = new Rectangle(8, 15, 70, 25);
48.      linesRadio.Checked = true;
49.      shapeType = ShapeType.Lines;
50.      linesRadio.Click += new EventHandler(radio_Click);
51.      radioGroup.Controls.Add(linesRadio);
52.
53.      ellipsesRadio = new RadioButton();
54.      ellipsesRadio.Text = "Ellipses";
55.      ellipsesRadio.Bounds = new Rectangle(8,
56.        linesRadio.Bounds.Y + linesRadio.Height + 5, 70, 25);
57.      ellipsesRadio.Click += new EventHandler(radio_Click);
58.      radioGroup.Controls.Add(ellipsesRadio);
59.      radioGroup.Bounds = new Rectangle(5, 5, 90, 75);
60.      controlPanel.Controls.Add(radioGroup);
61.
62.      // Buttons
63.      pauseButton = new Button();
64.      pauseButton.Text = "Start";
65.      pauseButton.Bounds = new Rectangle(8, ⮌
         radioGroup.Bounds.Y +
66.        radioGroup.Height +  5, 85, 25);
```

```
67.      pauseButton.Click += new EventHandler ⤸
         (pauseButton_Click);
68.      controlPanel.Controls.Add(pauseButton);
69.
70.      clearButton = new Button();
71.      clearButton.Text = "Clear";
72.      clearButton.Bounds = new Rectangle(8, ⤸
         pauseButton.Bounds.Y +
73.         pauseButton.Height +  5, 85, 25);
74.      clearButton.Click += new EventHandler ⤸
         (clearButton_Click);
75.      controlPanel.Controls.Add(clearButton);
76.
77.      quitButton = new Button();
78.      quitButton.Text = "Quit";
79.      quitButton.Bounds = new Rectangle(8, ⤸
         clearButton.Bounds.Y +
80.         clearButton.Height +  5, 85, 25);
81.      quitButton.Click += new EventHandler ⤸
         (quitButton_Click);
82.      controlPanel.Controls.Add(quitButton);
83.    }
84.
85.    private void radio_Click(object sender, EventArgs args)
86.    {
87.      if (sender == linesRadio)
88.        shapeType = ShapeType.Lines;
89.      else if (sender == ellipsesRadio)
90.        shapeType = ShapeType.Ellipses;
91.    }
92.
93.    private void clearButton_Click(object sender, ⤸
       EventArgs args)
94.    {
95.      Graphics g = drawingPanel.CreateGraphics();
96.      Brush brush = new SolidBrush(backColor);
97.      g.FillRectangle(brush, 0, 0,
98.         drawingPanel.Width, drawingPanel.Height);
99.    }
100.
101.   private void quitButton_Click(object sender, ⤸
       EventArgs args)
102.   {
103.     drawThread.Abort();
104.     Application.Exit();
105.   }
```

```
106.
107.    private void pauseButton_Click(object sender, ⤸
        EventArgs args)
108.    {
109.      if (sender == pauseButton)
110.      {
111.        if ((drawThread.ThreadState & ThreadState. ⤸
           Suspended) != 0)
112.        {
113.          drawThread.Resume();
114.          pauseButton.Text = "Pause";
115.        }
116.        else if ((drawThread.ThreadState &
117.            (ThreadState.Running | ThreadState.WaitSleepJoin))
118.            != 0)
119.        {
120.          drawThread.Suspend();
121.          pauseButton.Text = "Resume";
122.        }
123.        else if (drawThread.ThreadState == ThreadState. ⤸
           Unstarted)
124.        {
125.          drawThread.Start();
126.          pauseButton.Text = "Pause";
127.        }
128.      }
129.    }
130.
131.    private void DrawShapes()
132.    {
133.      Graphics g = drawingPanel.CreateGraphics();
134.      Random random = new Random();
135.      int x1, y1, x2, y2;
136.      Pen pen = new Pen(Color.Black);
137.      while (true)
138.      {
139.        pen = new Pen(Color.FromArgb(
140.          random.Next(255), random.Next(255), ⤸
          random.Next (255)));
141.        x1 = random.Next(drawingPanel.Width);
142.        y1 = random.Next(drawingPanel.Height);
143.        x2 = random.Next(drawingPanel.Width);
144.        y2 = random.Next(drawingPanel.Height);
145.        switch (shapeType)
146.        {
147.          case ShapeType.Lines:
```

```
148.              g.DrawLine(pen, x1, y1, x2, y2);
149.              break;
150.          case ShapeType.Ellipses:
151.              g.DrawEllipse(pen, x1, y1, x2, y2);
152.              break;
153.          }
154.          Thread.Sleep(100);
155.       }
156.    }
157.
158.    public static void Main()
159.    {
160.       Application.Run(new Animation());
161.    }
162. }
```

The constructor (line 19) calls `SetupControlPanel()` to create the panel and the controls, then (lines 23 to 27) creates the panel which will display the animation. On lines 30 and 31 we define the `Thread` (see Chapter 8 for a discussion of how threads are created) and register `DrawShapes()` as the method that should be run when the thread is started.

`SetupControlPanel()` (line 34) sets up the radio buttons and ordinary buttons in the usual way, and adds event handlers to all the controls.

When the program is run, the user should first press the 'Start' button, which calls the event handler `pauseButton_Click()` (line 107). The behaviour of the handler depends on the state of the thread. The possible states of a `Thread` are defined in the `ThreadState` enumeration, which we use in the event handler to determine what action should be taken when the button is pressed.

The first time the button is pressed, the thread has not yet been run at all, so its state is `Unstarted` (line 123). In this case, we call `Start()` for the thread (line 125) and change the button's caption to 'Pause' (line 126). We will return to the other two possibilities within this event handler after we consider the code for producing the animation.

When we created the thread on line 31, we registered `DrawShapes()` (line 131) as the method that should be run when the thread starts. `DrawShapes()` obtains the `Graphics` object for `drawingPanel` (line 133) rather than for the entire form, so we can use coordinates that are local to `drawingPanel`.

The main loop (line 137) is an infinite loop which will draw a new shape every 100 milliseconds until the user presses the button to interrupt the animation. Some random values for the colour and location of the shape are selected (lines 139 to 144) and then a `switch` (line 145) draws the shape depending on the value of `shapeType`, which is set in the event handler for the radio buttons (line 85). At the end of each iteration, `Thread.Sleep()` is called (line 154) to introduce a delay of 100 milliseconds between shapes.

Returning to `pauseButton_Click()`, we can now see what happens when the user wishes to pause the animation. When a thread is running, its state is set to `Running`, but from the code in `DrawShapes()`, we see that most of the time the thread will probably be asleep due to the `Thread.Sleep()` on line 154. A sleeping thread is in a *blocked* state, which is represented by `WaitSleepJoin` in its `ThreadState` property. We can therefore check to see if the thread is in either of the states `Running` or `WaitSleepJoin` (line 116) and, if so, call `Suspend()` to suspend its operation.

Note that we use a bitwise AND `&` operator to compare the `ThreadState` property with values from the `ThreadState` enumeration. Using an equality test `==` would not always work, since it is possible for a thread to be in more than one state at a time. For example, if the thread is in `WaitSleepJoin` when it is suspended, it will then be in both `WaitSleepJoin` since it has been blocked by the `Thread.Sleep()` call, and it will also be in a `Suspended` state.

The final operation is the resumption of a suspended thread, so the test on line 111 deals with that. We call `Resume()` to start the thread from where it left off.

It is worth noting that although the drawing and the event handling are being run in separate threads, they both have access to the same data fields within the program. This allows a radio button click to have an immediate effect on a running thread by changing the type of shape that is drawn. If the animation is running and drawing lines, for example, clicking on the 'Ellipses' radio button calls the event handler on line 85, which sets `shapeType` to `ShapeType.Ellipses`. This new value is then used on the next iteration of the `while` loop in `DrawShapes()` where the `switch` statement will now draw ellipses on line 151.

The 'Clear' button calls the handler on line 93, which just clears all the previous graphics from the panel. This handler will work whether or not the thread is currently running.

The 'Quit' button calls the handler on line 101, which first kills the thread by calling `Abort()` and then exits the program. Failing to stop a running thread before shutting down a program can cause an exception to be thrown.

10.11 ■ Case study: the adventure game graphical interface

Now that we have covered the elements of GUI and graphics in .NET, we can extend our adventure game case study (last considered in Chapter 6) so that it has a graphical interface. Readers who have played commercial games will be aware that the graphical interfaces in many games are reaching levels of sophistication undreamed of only a few years ago. Not surprisingly, we won't be able to approach this standard in graphics in the example presented here, but hopefully the version of the adventure game presented in this chapter will give you an idea of how a GUI can be attached to our previous text-only program.

The only change to the actual content of the game that we will make in this chapter is to add a few more rooms so that the player has a bit more area to explore. The types of items and the commands available will not be changed from the earlier version.

10.11.1 ☐ **The interface to the game**

Before we get into details, Figure 10.24 shows what the game looks like when it is first loaded.

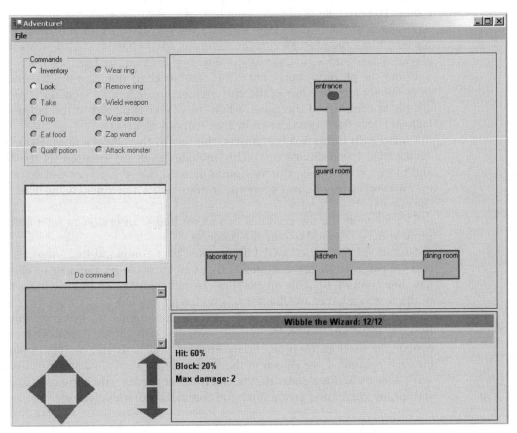

Figure 10.24 Graphical interface for the adventure game

The available commands are displayed using a set of radio buttons in the upper-left corner. Beneath these command buttons is a ListBox which will list the options (usually available items in the player's backpack or in a room) that some commands such as 'take' or 'drop' require. Under the ListBox is a button labelled 'Do command' which is pressed when the user has selected the command and the required options. Only those commands that are possible at the current turn are enabled.

Under the button is a grey message area where information is printed. This information consists of such things as the messages that appear when a ring is worn or a potion is quaffed, descriptions of combat and so on.

Under the information box is a set of buttons that allow the player to move between rooms. These are actually non-rectangular Buttons (we will see how to create these below). Only those buttons that correspond to available exits from the current room will be enabled.

The large area on the upper right is used to draw a map of the current level. Each room is drawn as a rectangle, and passages between rooms are also indicated. The current location of the player is shown as a red blob in one of the rooms. The brief name of each room is displayed within each rectangle.

The area at the bottom right displays the player's current statistics. The top bar shows the player's current energy as a bar chart, and also prints the player's name and actual number of energy points on the bar.

Under the player's energy bar is another bar chart that displays the energy points for any monster in the current location. When no monster is present (as at the start of the game, when the player is placed in the entrance hallway), this bar is just shown in grey without any text.

Underneath these two bar graphs, the rest of the player's information is displayed using ordinary text. This includes such information as the hit and block probabilities, the maximum damage that the player can do, and information on any items (weapons, armour, potions or rings) being used by the player.

The menu at the top contains two menu items: an option to start a new game and a command to exit the program.

One useful feature of a GUI as opposed to a command-line interface is that we can restrict the commands that can be made by the user to eliminate incorrect input. This means that error-checking code that we included in the text version from Chapter 6 is no longer needed.

Writing a GUI that allows only correct commands is, however, fairly tricky in itself, since we have to make sure that only those controls that can actually be used at the moment are enabled, that only the correct options for each command are shown in the list box and so on. However, this extra work does make for a game that is much easier to play, since the user won't waste time correcting errors or trying commands that don't work.

10.11.2 ☐ Class design

The class design is essentially the same as it was in Chapter 6, since we are not changing the underlying operation of the game. An extra class has been added for the non-rectangular buttons used for movement.

The main change is that the Adventure class is no longer the starting point for the program. We have added an AdventureForm class that manages the GUI aspects, so we have moved Main() to this class. AdventureForm now contains an instance of Adventure, since Adventure still stores all the actual data on what rooms (and their contents) are in the game and other information on the player. The `Adventure` class has not changed much apart from adding the code to set up the extra rooms in this expanded version.

We have also made a few minor changes in the `Room` class to make the map easier to draw. The other classes for the various item types, monsters and the player have not changed at all.

10.11.3 ☐ **The GUI code**

Since virtually all the new code is in `AdventureForm`, we'll analyze this class in some detail. One of the unfortunate aspects of writing GUI code, even without using the code-generation features of an environment such as Visual Studio .NET, is that rather a lot of code is needed to get the components up and running. It can help to organize this code into methods so we can separate out the various sections of the GUI.

10.11.4 ☐ `AdventureForm` – **initialization**

We will examine `AdventureForm` in stages, which will allow us to discuss the main features of each part of the GUI. First, we look at the data fields and constructor:

```
 1. using System;
 2. using System.Drawing;
 3. using System.Windows.Forms;
 4. using System.Collections;
 5.
 6. public class AdventureForm : Form
 7. {
 8.    public Adventure adventure;
 9.
10.    MenuItem fileMenu;
11.    MenuItem newGameMenu, exitMenu;
12.
13.    const int leftMargin = 20;
14.
15.    GroupBox commandBox;
16.    RadioButton inventoryRadio,
17.       takeRadio, dropRadio,
18.       eatRadio, lookRadio,
19.       quaffRadio, adornRadio,
20.       unadornRadio, wieldRadio,
21.       wearRadio, attackRadio,
22.       zapRadio, lastCommand;
23.    RadioButton[] radioArray;
24.    public TextBox messageBox;
25.    ListBox commandOptionsListBox;
```

```
26.    Label instructionLabel;
27.    Button goButton;
28.
29.    int mapLevel, minXMap, maxXMap, minYMap, maxYMap;
30.
31.    ArrowButton[] moveButton;
32.    const int arrowWidth = 50, arrowHeight = 30;
33.
34.    private enum Command
35.    {
36.       Inventory, Look, Take, Drop, Eat,
37.       Quaff, Adorn, Unadorn, Wield, Wear,
38.       Attack, Zap
39.    }
40.    Command selectedCommand;
41.
42.    public AdventureForm()
43.    {
44.       adventure = new Adventure();
45.       this.Layout += new LayoutEventHandler(OnLayoutForm);
46.       this.Closing +=
47.          new System.ComponentModel.CancelEventHandler(OnQuit);
48.       this.Text = "Adventure!";
49.       InitializeComponents();
50.    }
51.
52.    private void InitializeComponents()
53.    {
54.       ClientSize = new Size(800, 600);
55.       StartPosition = FormStartPosition.CenterScreen;
56.       SetupMenus();
57.       SetupCommandRadioButtons();
58.       SetupMoveButtons();
59.       BackColor = Color.FromArgb(255, 220, 170);
60.       Controls.AddRange(
61.          new Control[] { commandBox }
62.          );
63.    }
```

Line 8 declares the adventure object, which is now subservient to AdventureForm. All the details of the rooms, monsters, player and various items are still created in Adventure, but the display of these features will be handled in AdventureForm.

The menu items are declared on lines 10 and 11. The const leftMargin (line 13) is used to specify the size of the margin between the edge of the form and the controls on the left side of the client area. It is always a good idea to use consts for quantities like this since it provides an easy-to-understand name within the program, and also allows the margin to be changed easily by just changing this one quantity instead of hunting through the program to find all the places where we specify a margin size.

Lines 15 to 27 declare the various controls (apart from the arrow buttons, which we'll get to later) that appear on the left side of the form. Line 29 declares a few parameters that are used in drawing the map in the upper right. Finally, the arrow buttons are declared on line 31 and a couple of parameters relating to them on line 32.

The enum on line 34 is used to provide human-readable names for the commands, and is used in processing each command. Finally, the constructor (line 42) creates adventure, adds a handler to the main form to allow the graphics to be redrawn if the window is resized and then calls Initialize Components() (line 52) to set up the various controls.

InitializeComponents() also adds a handler for the form's Closing event (line 46). This event is generated when the 'Close' button (the little 'X' in the upper-right corner) is pressed. In order to avoid the program closing unintentionally, we provide a confirmation dialog in the OnQuit() handler method:

```
private void OnQuit(object sender,
   System.ComponentModel.CancelEventArgs args)
{
   string message = "Do you really want to quit?";
   string caption = "Quit game";
   MessageBoxButtons buttons = MessageBoxButtons.YesNo;
   DialogResult result;

   result = MessageBox.Show(this, message, caption, buttons,
      MessageBoxIcon.Question);

   if(result == DialogResult.Yes)
   {
      Application.Exit();
   }
   else
   {
      args.Cancel = true;
   }
}
```

OnQuit() displays a MessageBox asking the user to confirm they really want the program to quit. If not, then we set args.Cancel to true to prevent the closing action from continuing, which causes the form to remain visible and the program to continue running.

InitializeComponents() delegates most of the initialization work to other methods, since there is quite a bit to do. We'll consider each of these methods separately, beginning with SetupMenus():

```
   private void SetupMenus()
   {
     exitMenu = new MenuItem("E&xit",
       new EventHandler(OnMenu));
     newGameMenu = new MenuItem("&New game",
       new EventHandler(OnMenu));
     fileMenu = new MenuItem("&File",
       new MenuItem[] {newGameMenu, exitMenu});
     Menu = new MainMenu(new MenuItem[] { fileMenu } );
   }
```

Both menu items are handled by `OnMenu()`:

```
1. private void OnMenu(object sender, EventArgs args)
2. {
3.   if (sender == exitMenu)
4.   {
5.     string message = "Do you really want to quit?";
6.     string caption = "Quit game";
7.     MessageBoxButtons buttons = MessageBoxButtons.YesNo;
8.     DialogResult result;
9.
10.    result = MessageBox.Show(this, message, caption,⟲
         buttons,
11.       MessageBoxIcon.Question);
12.
13.    if(result == DialogResult.Yes)
14.    {
15.      Application.Exit();
16.    }
17.   }
18.   else if (sender == newGameMenu)
19.   {
20.     string message =
21.       "Do you really want to start a new game?\n" +
22.       "This will erase the current game.";
23.     string caption = "New game";
24.     MessageBoxButtons buttons = MessageBoxButtons.YesNo;
25.     DialogResult result;
26.
27.     result = MessageBox.Show(this, message, caption,⟲
          buttons,
28.        MessageBoxIcon.Question);
29.
30.     if(result == DialogResult.Yes)
31.     {
32.       adventure = new Adventure();
```

```
33.          EnableMoveButtons();
34.          EnableCommands();
35.          Invalidate();
36.      }
37.  }
38. }
```

Both the menu items give commands that will erase the current game, so they both provide a message box asking for confirmation. The 'Exit' command just calls `Application.Exit()` to stop the program.

Starting a game can be achieved just by creating a new `Adventure` object (line 32) since all the startup code is in that class. We then need to refresh the controls and graphics on the GUI, which we do on lines 33 and 34. We'll consider these methods in more detail below.

The next method in `InitializeComponents()` is `SetupCommandRadio Buttons()`, which contains a lot of repetitive code for creating the radio buttons and their associated controls for displaying and requesting information:

```
1. private void SetupCommandRadioButtons()
2. {
3.   commandBox = new GroupBox();
4.   commandBox.Bounds = new Rectangle(leftMargin,
      20, 230, 175);
5.   commandBox.Text = "Commands";
6.
7.   int buttonX = 10, buttonY = 15;
8.   int buttonWidth = 100, buttonHeight = 20;
9.   int buttonSpacing = 5;
10.  inventoryRadio = new RadioButton();
11.  inventoryRadio.Bounds = new Rectangle(buttonX, buttonY,
12.     buttonWidth, buttonHeight);
13.  inventoryRadio.Text = "Inventory";
14.  inventoryRadio.Click += new EventHandler(OnCommand);
15.
16.  lookRadio = new RadioButton();
17.  buttonY += buttonHeight + buttonSpacing;
18.  lookRadio.Bounds = new Rectangle(buttonX,
19.     buttonY, buttonWidth, buttonHeight);
20.  lookRadio.Text = "Look";
21.  lookRadio.Click += new EventHandler(OnCommand);
22.
23.  takeRadio = new RadioButton();
24.  buttonY += buttonHeight + buttonSpacing;
25.  takeRadio.Bounds = new Rectangle(buttonX,
26.     buttonY, buttonWidth, buttonHeight);
27.  takeRadio.Text = "Take";
28.  takeRadio.Click += new EventHandler(OnCommand);
```

```
29.
30.    dropRadio = new RadioButton();
31.    buttonY += buttonHeight + buttonSpacing;
32.    dropRadio.Bounds = new Rectangle(buttonX,
33.       buttonY, buttonWidth, buttonHeight);
34.    dropRadio.Text = "Drop";
35.    dropRadio.Click += new EventHandler(OnCommand);
36.
37.    eatRadio = new RadioButton();
38.    buttonY += buttonHeight + buttonSpacing;
39.    eatRadio.Bounds = new Rectangle(buttonX,
40.       buttonY, buttonWidth, buttonHeight);
41.    eatRadio.Text = "Eat food";
42.    eatRadio.Click += new EventHandler(OnCommand);
43.
44.    quaffRadio = new RadioButton();
45.    buttonY += buttonHeight + buttonSpacing;
46.    quaffRadio.Bounds = new Rectangle(buttonX,
47.       buttonY, buttonWidth, buttonHeight);
48.    quaffRadio.Text = "Quaff potion";
49.    quaffRadio.Click += new EventHandler(OnCommand);
50.
51.    buttonX = inventoryRadio.Bounds.X +
52.       inventoryRadio.Bounds.Width + 5;
53.    buttonY = inventoryRadio.Bounds.Y;
54.    adornRadio = new RadioButton();
55.    adornRadio.Bounds = new Rectangle(buttonX,
56.       buttonY, buttonWidth, buttonHeight);
57.    adornRadio.Text = "Wear ring";
58.    adornRadio.Click += new EventHandler(OnCommand);
59.
60.    unadornRadio = new RadioButton();
61.    buttonY += buttonHeight + buttonSpacing;
62.    unadornRadio.Bounds = new Rectangle(buttonX,
63.       buttonY, buttonWidth, buttonHeight);
64.    unadornRadio.Text = "Remove ring";
65.    unadornRadio.Click += new EventHandler(OnCommand);
66.
67.    wieldRadio = new RadioButton();
68.    buttonY += buttonHeight + buttonSpacing;
69.    wieldRadio.Bounds = new Rectangle(buttonX,
70.       buttonY, buttonWidth, buttonHeight);
71.    wieldRadio.Text = "Wield weapon";
72.    wieldRadio.Click += new EventHandler(OnCommand);
73.
```

```
74.     wearRadio = new RadioButton();
75.     buttonY += buttonHeight + buttonSpacing;
76.     wearRadio.Bounds = new Rectangle(buttonX,
77.        buttonY, buttonWidth, buttonHeight);
78.     wearRadio.Text = "Wear armour";
79.     wearRadio.Click += new EventHandler(OnCommand);
80.
81.     zapRadio = new RadioButton();
82.     buttonY += buttonHeight + buttonSpacing;
83.     zapRadio.Bounds = new Rectangle(buttonX,
84.        buttonY, buttonWidth, buttonHeight);
85.     zapRadio.Text = "Zap wand";
86.     zapRadio.Click += new EventHandler(OnCommand);
87.
88.     attackRadio = new RadioButton();
89.     buttonY += buttonHeight + buttonSpacing;
90.     attackRadio.Bounds = new Rectangle(buttonX,
91.        buttonY, buttonWidth, buttonHeight);
92.     attackRadio.Text = "Attack monster";
93.     attackRadio.Click += new EventHandler(OnCommand);
94.
95.     radioArray = new RadioButton[] {
96.        inventoryRadio, lookRadio,
97.        takeRadio, dropRadio,
98.        eatRadio,
99.        quaffRadio, adornRadio,
100.       unadornRadio, wieldRadio,
101.       wearRadio, attackRadio,
102.       zapRadio
103.    };
104.    EnableCommands();
105.
106.    commandBox.Controls.AddRange(radioArray);
107.
108.    instructionLabel = new Label();
109.    instructionLabel.Bounds = new Rectangle(leftMargin,
110.       commandBox.Location.Y + commandBox.Height ⤶
          + 5, 230, 18);
111.    instructionLabel.Text = "";
112.    Controls.Add(instructionLabel);
113.
114.    commandOptionsListBox = new ListBox();
115.    commandOptionsListBox.Bounds = ⤶
       new Rectangle(leftMargin,
116.       instructionLabel.Location.Y + ⤶
          instructionLabel.Height + 5,
```

```
117.          230, 125);
118.      commandOptionsListBox.SelectedValueChanged +=
119.        new EventHandler(OnSelect);
120.    Controls.Add(commandOptionsListBox);
121.
122.    goButton = new Button();
123.    int goButtonWidth = 100;
124.    int goButtonHeight = 25;
125.    goButton.Bounds = new Rectangle(
126.      commandOptionsListBox.Location.X +
127.      commandOptionsListBox.Width/2 - goButtonWidth/2,
128.      commandOptionsListBox.Location.Y +
129.      commandOptionsListBox.Height + 5,
130.      goButtonWidth, goButtonHeight);
131.    goButton.Text = "Do command";
132.    goButton.Enabled = false;
133.    goButton.Click += new EventHandler(OnGo);
134.    Controls.Add(goButton);
135.
136.    messageBox = new TextBox();
137.    messageBox.Multiline = true;
138.    messageBox.ReadOnly = true;
139.    messageBox.ScrollBars = ScrollBars.Vertical;
140.    messageBox.Bounds = new Rectangle(leftMargin,
141.      goButton.Location.Y + goButton.Height + 5, 230, 100);
142.    Controls.Add(messageBox);
143. }
```

Most of this method should be fairly obvious, since it just sets up the various radio buttons in a similar way to the example earlier in Chapter 9. We have added event handlers for the Click event for each radio button, which means that they act in a similar way to a regular Button. We've used radio buttons instead, since it allows the user to see which command they just selected, which is needed in some cases since some commands (such as 'take' and 'drop') require the user to select some items from a list. All the radio buttons are given the same event handler: OnClick().

One of the key points in any GUI is that controls should only be enabled when they can be used. Many of the radio button commands are only available in certain cases. For example, 'take' should only be available when there are items in the current room that can be taken, 'drop' when the player's backpack has something in it and so on.

On line 95, we group the radio buttons together into an array and then call EnableCommands(), which checks all the conditions for the various buttons to be enabled or disabled and sets them accordingly:

```
public void EnableCommands()
{
  takeRadio.Enabled =
    adventure.GamePlayer.CurrentLocation.ItemList.Count > 0;
  dropRadio.Enabled = adventure.GamePlayer.ItemList.Count > 0;
  eatRadio.Enabled =
    CountItemsOfType(Type.GetType("Food")) > 0;
  quaffRadio.Enabled =
    CountItemsOfType(Type.GetType("Potion")) > 0 &&
    adventure.GamePlayer.QuaffedPotion == null;
  adornRadio.Enabled =
    CountItemsOfType(Type.GetType("Ring")) > 0 &&
    adventure.GamePlayer.WornRing == null;
  unadornRadio.Enabled =
    adventure.GamePlayer.WornRing != null;
  wieldRadio.Enabled =
    CountItemsOfType(Type.GetType("Weapon")) > 0;
  wearRadio.Enabled =
    CountItemsOfType(Type.GetType("Armour")) > 0;
  zapRadio.Enabled =
    CountItemsOfType(Type.GetType("Wand")) > 0;
  attackRadio.Enabled =
    adventure.GamePlayer.CurrentLocation.Monster != null;
  foreach (RadioButton radio in radioArray)
  {
    if (!radio.Enabled && radio.Checked)
    {
      radio.Checked = false;
      lastCommand = null;
      commandOptionsListBox.Items.Clear();
      break;
    }
  }
}
```

Many of these commands need to know whether the player is carrying items of a specific type, such as rings or potions. Since we have used a separate derived class for each item type (see the version of the game in Chapter 6 where we introduced inheritance), we can count the number of items in the player's inventory that are of specific class types. This is done using the CountItemsOfType() method, which takes as its parameter a System.Type object. Each data type in C# has an associated System.Type object which can be obtained using the static method GetType() from the System.Type class. GetType() takes a string parameter which gives the name of the class (or other data type) for which the System.Type object is required.

For example, when we are counting the number of `Food` items being carried, we make the call:

```
eatRadio.Enabled =
  CountItemsOfType(Type.GetType("Food")) > 0;
```

`CountItemsOfType()` is fairly simple:

```
private int CountItemsOfType(Type itemType)
{
  ArrayList items = adventure.GamePlayer.ItemList;
  int numItems = 0;
  foreach (Item item in items)
  {
    if (item.GetType() == itemType)
    {
      ++numItems;
    }
  }
  return numItems;
}
```

We use a second version of `GetType()`, which can be called for any object, to obtain the `System.Type` of each item in the player's item list and compare this type with the `itemType` parameter, keeping a count of the number of such items in the player's item list.

Returning to `EnableCommands()`, some commands require an extra check to make sure that the rules of the game are being followed. For example, it is only possible to quaff one potion at a time, so we enable the 'Quaff potion' button only if (a) the player is carrying some potions and (b) no other potion is currently in effect. A similar check must be carried out when attempting to wear a ring. The `attackRadio` button is only enabled if there is a monster at the current location.

After enabling and disabling the various buttons, we need to check that the currently selected button is not now disabled. This can happen, for example, if the player selects 'Eat food' and is currently carrying only one item of food. If the player eats that one item, then they no longer have any food in their backpack, so the 'Eat food' button will be disabled, but still be selected. In this case, the final `foreach` loop locates the checked button and clears it if it is disabled. This results in none of the radio buttons being checked, so we clear the `lastCommand` record to show that the previous command is not valid any more. We also clear the list of options displayed in the list box.

Returning to `SetupCommandRadioButtons()`, after creating the radio buttons, we need to create the other controls that provide and request information. The `instructionLabel` is a one-line label (lines 108 to 112) that appears just below the command buttons, and gives information related to the selected command. For example, if 'Look' is done on an empty room, `instructionLabel` says 'The room is empty.'.

Next (line 114), we add the `ListBox` which contains the items that may be selected for various commands, such as `Food` for 'Eat' and so on. We add (line 118) a handler for the `SelectedValueChanged` event, since we need a way of telling if the user has made any selections from this list in order to provide a valid command. For example, if the user selects 'Take' but then does not select anything to take, the 'take' command is not valid and should not be issued. Only when a command is valid does the 'Do command' button become enabled. The `OnSelect()` handler merely enables this button:

```
private void OnSelect(object sender, EventArgs args)
{
  if (sender == commandOptionsListBox)
  {
    goButton.Enabled = true;
  }
}
```

The 'Do command' button (called `goButton`) itself is added on line 122, with an event handler called `OnGo()`. Finally, a `TextBox` called `messageBox` for displaying general messages about the play of the game, such as reports of the progress of combat or the effects of potions, rings or wands, is added (line 136).

We will return to consider the processing of commands after we have completed looking at the setup of the controls and graphics.

10.11.5 ☐ Non-rectangular buttons

Back in `InitializeComponents()`, the last setup operation is the creation of the arrow buttons for moving between rooms. This setup is done in `SetupMoveButtons()`:

```
private void SetupMoveButtons()
{
  moveButton = new ArrowButton[6];
  for (int i = 0; i < 6; i++)
  {
    moveButton[i] =
      new ArrowButton((Room.Direction)i);
    moveButton[i].Click +=
      new EventHandler(OnArrowButton);
  }
  moveButton[(int)Room.Direction.North].Bounds =
    new Rectangle(leftMargin + arrowHeight + 3,
      messageBox.Location.Y + messageBox.Height + 5,
      arrowWidth, arrowHeight);
  moveButton[(int)Room.Direction.East].Bounds =
```

```
      new Rectangle(leftMargin + arrowHeight + arrowWidth + 3,
        messageBox.Location.Y + messageBox.Height +
        arrowHeight + 5, arrowHeight, arrowWidth);
    moveButton[(int)Room.Direction.South].Bounds =
      new Rectangle(leftMargin + arrowHeight + 3,
        messageBox.Location.Y + messageBox.Height +
        arrowHeight + arrowWidth + 5, arrowWidth, arrowHeight);
    moveButton[(int)Room.Direction.West].Bounds =
      new Rectangle(leftMargin + 3,
        messageBox.Location.Y + messageBox.Height +
        arrowHeight + 5, arrowHeight, arrowWidth);
    moveButton[(int)Room.Direction.Up].Bounds =
      new Rectangle(leftMargin + messageBox.Width - arrowWidth,
        messageBox.Location.Y + messageBox.Height + 5,
        arrowWidth, arrowWidth);
    moveButton[(int)Room.Direction.Down].Bounds =
      new Rectangle(leftMargin + messageBox.Width - arrowWidth,
        messageBox.Location.Y + messageBox.Height +
        arrowWidth + 8, arrowWidth, arrowWidth);
    for (int i = 0; i < 6; i++)
    {
      moveButton[i].SetRegion();
    }
    Controls.AddRange(moveButton);
    EnableMoveButtons();
}
```

The buttons for moving between rooms, visible in the lower left of the main window in Figure 10.24, are *non-rectangular* buttons, something we have not yet met. C# makes it quite easy to create user-defined buttons such as these, so we'll have a look at how it's done.

A user-defined button requires its own class, which inherits Button. Most of the functionality of a button is therefore just inherited, and we need only add those methods that customize its appearance and behaviour. We have created the ArrowButton class which provides the necessary methods.

In SetupMoveButtons(), we create an array of six ArrowButtons in the initial for loop and attach a handler for Click to each button. We then set the bounds for each of these buttons by using measurements that are relative to messageBox which is the TextBox immediately above them. After this, we use another for loop to define the shape of each button using SetRegion(), and then we call EnableMoveButtons() to determine which buttons should be enabled and disabled.

To understand how all this works, we need to look at the code for ArrowButton:

1. using System;
2. using System.Drawing;

```
 3. using System.Drawing.Drawing2D;
 4. using System.Windows.Forms;
 5.
 6. public class ArrowButton : Button
 7. {
 8.    Room.Direction direction;
 9.    Color NormalColor = Color.Red,
10.       PressedColor = Color.Yellow,
11.       DisabledColor = Color.Gray;
12.
13.    public ArrowButton(Room.Direction dir)
14.    {
15.       direction = dir;
16.       BackColor = NormalColor;
17.    }
18.
19.    public new bool Enabled
20.    {
21.       set
22.       {
23.          base.Enabled = value;
24.          if (Enabled)
25.             BackColor = NormalColor;
26.          else
27.             BackColor = DisabledColor;
28.       }
29.       get
30.       {
31.          return base.Enabled;
32.       }
33.    }
34.
35.    public Room.Direction Direction
36.    {
37.       get
38.       { return direction; }
39.    }
40.
41.    public void SetRegion()
42.    {
43.       GraphicsPath outline = new GraphicsPath();
44.       switch (direction)
45.       {
46.          case Room.Direction.North:
47.             outline.AddPolygon(
48.                new Point[]
```

```
49.              {
50.                new Point(Width/2, 0),
51.                new Point(Width, Height),
52.                new Point(0, Height)
53.              });
54.            break;
55.          case Room.Direction.East:
56.            outline.AddPolygon(
57.              new Point[]
58.              {
59.                new Point(0, 0),
60.                new Point(Width, Height/2),
61.                new Point(0, Height)
62.              });
63.            break;
64.          case Room.Direction.South:
65.            outline.AddPolygon(
66.              new Point[]
67.              {
68.                new Point(0, 0),
69.                new Point(Width, 0),
70.                new Point(Width/2, Height)
71.              });
72.            break;
73.          case Room.Direction.West:
74.            outline.AddPolygon(
75.              new Point[]
76.              {
77.                new Point(Width, 0),
78.                new Point(Width, Height),
79.                new Point(0, Height/2)
80.              });
81.            break;
82.          case Room.Direction.Up:
83.            outline.AddPolygon(
84.              new Point[]
85.              {
86.                new Point(0, Height/3),
87.                new Point(Width/2, 0),
88.                new Point(Width, Height/3),
89.                new Point(2*Width/3, Height/3),
90.                new Point(2*Width/3, Height),
91.                new Point(Width/3, Height),
92.                new Point(Width/3, Height/3)
93.              });
94.            break;
```

```
95.            case Room.Direction.Down:
96.              outline.AddPolygon(
97.                new Point[]
98.                {
99.                  new Point(Width/3, 0),
100.                 new Point(2*Width/3, 0),
101.                 new Point(2*Width/3, 2*Height/3),
102.                 new Point(Width, 2*Height/3),
103.                 new Point(Width/2, Height),
104.                 new Point(0, 2*Height/3),
105.                 new Point(Width/3, 2*Height/3)
106.               });
107.             break;
108.        }
109.        Region = new Region(outline);
110.    }
111.
112.    protected override void OnPaint(PaintEventArgs e)
113.    {
114.        Graphics g = e.Graphics;
115.        g.FillRectangle(new SolidBrush(BackColor), 0, 0,
116.            ClientSize.Width, ClientSize.Height);
117.    }
118.
119.    protected override void OnMouseDown(MouseEventArgs e)
120.    {
121.        BackColor = PressedColor;
122.        base.OnMouseDown(e);
123.    }
124.
125.    protected override void OnMouseUp(MouseEventArgs e)
126.    {
127.        BackColor = NormalColor;
128.        base.OnMouseUp(e);
129.    }
130. }
```

Each button has a distinctive shape depending on which direction it represents. The four compass directions (north, east, south and west) are represented by triangles while up and down are drawn as arrows, as can be seen on the screenshot of the game (Figure 10.24).

When we create our own buttons, we are responsible for drawing anything that appears on them, and also for changing the button's appearance when it is clicked with the mouse. To do this, we need to override the OnPaint() event handler to draw the graphics on the button, and also the OnMouseDown() and OnMouseUp() event handlers to change the graphics when the button is pressed. Further customization is also possible – for example, we could override OnMouseEnter() and OnMouseLeave() to have the button change its shape when the mouse passes over it.

In `ArrowButton`, an enabled button in a resting state is coloured a solid red. When the button is pressed, its colour changes to yellow while the mouse button is held down, then back to red when the mouse button is released. The `Colors` are defined on line 9, and the overridden event handlers are on lines 119 to 129. Note that we call the base class event handlers as well – this is essential if we want to add another event handler to the button when it is used in `AdventureForm`. We added a handler for `Click` back in `SetupMoveButtons()` in `AdventureForm`, and this would not work unless the base class handlers for the mouse events were called in `ArrowButton`.

A button may also be enabled or disabled by setting its `Enabled` property. We usually wish to change the button's appearance when it is disabled, so we do this by defining our own `Enabled` property (line 19). Since `Enabled` in the base `Button` class is not declared as `virtual`, we cannot override it in `ArrowButton`. We therefore declare it as `new` on line 19 which hides the property from the base class.

The `OnPaint()` method (line 112) is quite simple here in that all it does is paint the button with a solid colour. Since graphics may be drawn on a button just like any other component, the graphics here can be as elaborate as you like.

All we have done so far is describe how to draw our own graphics on a button, but we have not yet said how to make the button non-rectangular. In fact, this requires nothing more than defining the desired shape as a `GraphicsPath` and then setting the button's `Region` property using this shape. This is done for the six different button shapes in `SetRegion()` (line 41 – recall that `SetRegion()` was called from `SetupMoveButtons()`). The `outline` variable is a `GraphicsPath` that contains the outline shape of the button, and it is defined according to the `direction` of the button that we defined earlier. At the end of the method (line 109) we assign the `Region` by passing `outline` to the `Region` constructor (`Region` is a class in `System.Drawing` and can be used for other things than defining button shapes).

Once we have finished the `ArrowButton` class, we can use it just like an ordinary `Button` back in `AdventureForm`. Recall that we registered `OnArrowButton()` as the event handler for clicking on one of the arrow buttons. Its code follows:

```
public void OnArrowButton(object sender, EventArgs args)
{
  ArrowButton arrow = (ArrowButton)sender;
  string dirString =
    Room.directionNames[(int)arrow.Direction];
  adventure.DoMove(dirString);
  messageBox.Text = "You move to the " +
    adventure.GamePlayer.CurrentLocation.Description +
    DoValidTurn();
  EnableMoveButtons();
```

```
    Invalidate();
    UpdateCommand();
    if (adventure.GamePlayer.Energy <= 0)
        EndGame();
}
```

This method extracts the direction moved from the button and then calls the old `DoMove()` method from `Adventure` that we used back in Chapter 6. A message is displayed in `messageBox` stating the room into which we moved. The last few lines call several methods to update the display after the move. We shall consider these methods later.

This completes the definition of the control panel on the left side of the main form. We now consider the map and stats area on the right.

10.11.6 ☐ Drawing the map

Adventure game maps range from the very simple to the fiendishly complex, with some of them employing algorithms from graph theory to plot out routes between points. For our purposes, we will use a fairly simple system, but one that is flexible enough to allow a good variety of floor layouts for each level in the game.

In our previous version of the game, we defined the map by specifying the exits from each room, stating the direction of the exit and the other room to which it leads. Although we could probably work out an algorithm for drawing a map from this information alone, it is much easier to pin down the location of each room by specifying some coordinates for it.

To this end, we modify the `Room` class slightly by adding three data fields: `x`, `y` and `level`. Each room is assigned to one particular level, with the starting level as level 0. In this version of the game, level 0 contains five rooms (entrance, guard room, kitchen, laboratory and dining room). The laboratory contains an exit down to the dungeon, which is therefore on level –1. There are three rooms on level –1: the dungeon, a jail and a storeroom.

Within each level, each room has `x` (measured from left to right) and `y` (measured from the top downwards) coordinates. A new constructor is provided in `Room` to allow a room to be declared with its three coordinates. The `SetupRooms()` method in the old `Adventure` class thus becomes in the new version:

```
private void SetupRooms()
{
    rooms = new Room[NumRooms];

    rooms[(int)Locn.Laboratory] =
        new Room(0, 2, 0, "laboratory");
    rooms[(int)Locn.Kitchen] = new Room(1, 2, 0, "kitchen");
    rooms[(int)Locn.Entrance] = new Room(1, 0, 0, "entrance");
    rooms[(int)Locn.GuardRoom] =
```

```
      new Room(1, 1, 0, "guard room");
  rooms[(int)Locn.DiningRoom] =
      new Room(2, 2, 0, "dining room");
  rooms[(int)Locn.Jail] = new Room(0, 0, -1, "jail");
  rooms[(int)Locn.Dungeon] = new Room(1, 0, -1, "dungeon");
  rooms[(int)Locn.Storeroom] =
      new Room(2, 0, -1, "storeroom");
}
```

Here, the first three parameters in each constructor call are x, y and level. Thus the laboratory is at (x, y) = (0, 2) and on level 0 and so on.

Once this information is stored, how do we use it to draw the map of a given level? This is done in DrawMap() in AdventureForm:

```
1.  private void DrawMap(Graphics g)
2.  {
3.      Pen pen = new Pen(Color.Green);
4.      Rectangle clientRect = ClientRectangle;
5.      int mapLeft = commandBox.Bounds.X + commandBox.⤹
          Width + 5;
6.      int mapTop = commandBox.Bounds.Y;
7.      int mapWidth = ClientRectangle.Width -
8.          (commandBox.Bounds.X + commandBox.Width + 20);
9.      int mapHeight = 2*ClientRectangle.Height/3;
10.     g.DrawRectangle(pen,
11.        mapLeft, mapTop, mapWidth, mapHeight);
12.
13.     mapLevel = adventure.GamePlayer.CurrentLocation.Level;
14.     MapLimits();
15.
16.     int xRoomSize = mapWidth / (maxXMap - minXMap + 1);
17.     int yRoomSize = mapHeight / (maxYMap - minYMap + 1);
18.     for (int i = 0; i < Adventure.NumRooms; i++)
19.     {
20.        if (adventure[i].Level == mapLevel)
21.        {
22.           DrawRoom(g, mapLeft,
23.              mapTop, xRoomSize, yRoomSize, adventure[i]);
24.        }
25.     }
26. }
```

DrawMap() is called from AdventureForm's OnPaint() method, so we can obtain the Graphics object from OnPaint() and pass it along to DrawMap().

The first section of DrawMap() (lines 3 to 11) just draws a frame around the area to be used for the map. The frame is scaled to the current size of the client area, so resizing the overall window causes the map to change size.

We obtain the player's current level on line 13 and then call MapLimits() to determine the layout of the rooms on that level. The code is:

```
private void MapLimits()
{
    minXMap = 10000;
    maxXMap = -10000;
    minYMap = 10000;
    maxYMap = -10000;
    for (int i = 0; i < Adventure.NumRooms; i++)
    {
        if (adventure[i].Level == mapLevel)
        {
            if (minXMap > adventure[i].X)
                minXMap = adventure[i].X;
            if (maxXMap < adventure[i].X)
                maxXMap = adventure[i].X;
            if (minYMap > adventure[i].Y)
                minYMap = adventure[i].Y;
            if (maxYMap < adventure[i].Y)
                maxYMap = adventure[i].Y;
        }
    }
}
```

This method just loops through all the Rooms in the game and records the limits of x and y for all rooms on the current level. We therefore know the extent of the rooms in the horizontal and vertical, and how many squares in each direction we must allocate. For example, on level 0, x ranges between 0 and 2, as does y, so we must allow for a 3 × 3 grid to be able to draw all the rooms. On the lower level, x ranges from 0 to 2 but all y values are 0, so a single row of 3 cells is all we need.

The information calculated by MapLimits() is used back in DrawMap() to work out the size of the rectangle that is allocated to each room (lines 16 and 17). We then loop through all Rooms in the game and call DrawRoom() for all rooms that are on the current level (lines 18 to 25).

The DrawRoom() method does all the actual drawing:

```
1. private void DrawRoom(Graphics g, int mapLeft, int mapTop,
2.     int xRoomSize, int yRoomSize, Room room)
3. {
4.     int roomX = mapLeft + (room.X - minXMap) * xRoomSize;
5.     int roomY = mapTop + (room.Y - minYMap) * yRoomSize;
6.
7.     Pen pen = new Pen(Color.BlueViolet, 2);
8.     Brush brush = new SolidBrush(Color.LightBlue);
```

```
 9.
10.   g.FillRectangle(brush, roomX + xRoomSize/3,
11.     roomY + yRoomSize/3, xRoomSize/3, yRoomSize/3);
12.   g.DrawRectangle(pen, roomX + xRoomSize/3,
13.     roomY + yRoomSize/3, xRoomSize/3, yRoomSize/3);
14.
15.   if (room.Exit(Room.Direction.East) != null)
16.   {
17.     g.FillRectangle(brush, roomX + 2*xRoomSize/3 - 2,
18.       roomY + 4*yRoomSize/9,
19.       xRoomSize/3 + 2, yRoomSize/9);
20.   }
21.   if (room.Exit(Room.Direction.West) != null)
22.   {
23.     g.FillRectangle(brush, roomX - 2,
24.       roomY + 4*yRoomSize/9,
25.       xRoomSize/3 + 4, yRoomSize/9);
26.   }
27.   if (room.Exit(Room.Direction.North) != null)
28.   {
29.     g.FillRectangle(brush, roomX + 4*xRoomSize/9,
30.       roomY - 2,
31.       xRoomSize/9, yRoomSize/3 + 4);
32.   }
33.   if (room.Exit(Room.Direction.South) != null)
34.   {
35.     g.FillRectangle(brush, roomX + 4*xRoomSize/9,
36.       roomY + 2*yRoomSize/3 - 2,
37.       xRoomSize/9, yRoomSize/3 + 4);
38.   }
39.
40.   Font font = new Font("Arial", 8);
41.   brush = new SolidBrush(Color.Black);
42.   Point point = new Point(roomX + xRoomSize/3,
43.     roomY + yRoomSize/3);
44.   g.DrawString(room.Description, font, brush, point);
45.
46.   if (adventure.GamePlayer.CurrentLocation == room)
47.   {
48.     brush = new SolidBrush(Color.Red);
49.     g.FillEllipse(brush, roomX + 4*xRoomSize/9,
50.       roomY + 4*yRoomSize/9, xRoomSize/9,
51.       yRoomSize/9);
52.   }
53. }
```

The location of the rectangle for the given room is calculated (lines 4 and 5) from the map's position and the x and y coordinates of the room itself. After defining a pen and brush (lines 7 and 8), we draw the room (lines 10 to 13). The room does not fill all the space allocated to it since we need some space to draw the passages between rooms. Here, we have chosen to make the room's rectangle fill the middle third of the overall cell.

The exits from each room are drawn by filling a rectangle that has a width that is one-third of that of the room's outline (and therefore one-ninth of the overall cell size). The possible exits are drawn on lines 15 to 38 (up and down exits are not drawn – these are visible from the arrow buttons in the control panel).

We could put a number of embellishments within a room, such as symbols to indicate what the room contains, a graphic for the monster and so on. To keep things fairly short, we've just written the room's name at the top of the rectangle (lines 40 to 44) and drawn a red ellipse in the room containing the player (lines 46 to 52). You may wish to add some extra graphics to display more information.

10.11.7 ☐ Displaying the player's statistics

The final bit of the display is the stats area at the bottom right. The display shows the current energy of the player (and that of the monster, if there is one in the room) as a bar chart. The bar shows the player's maximum energy and current energy as shown in Figure 10.25.

Figure 10.25 Customized bar charts for displaying statistics of player and opponent

Below this we show the other stats of the player as ordinary text. This display is produced by DrawStats():

```
1. private void DrawStats(Graphics g)
2. {
3.    Pen pen = new Pen(Color.Blue);
4.    Rectangle clientRect = ClientRectangle;
5.    int statsLeft = commandBox.Bounds.X + commandBox.
       Width + 5;
6.    int statsTop =
7.       commandBox.Bounds.Y + 2*ClientRectangle.Height/3 + 5;
8.    int statsWidth = ClientRectangle.Width -
9.       (commandBox.Bounds.X + commandBox.Width + 20);
10.   int statsHeight = ClientRectangle.Height/3 - 30;
11.   g.DrawRectangle(pen,
```

```
12.         statsLeft, statsTop, statsWidth, statsHeight);
13.
14.     int energyX = statsLeft + 5;
15.     int energyY = statsTop + 5;
16.     int energyWidth = statsWidth - 10;
17.     int energyHeight = 20;
18.     Player player = adventure.GamePlayer;
19.     int currentEnergy = player.Energy < 0 ? 0 : player.Energy;
20.     int currentEnergyWidth =
21.         energyWidth * currentEnergy / player.MaxEnergy;
22.     string energyString = player.Name + ": " + player.Energy +
23.         "/" + player.MaxEnergy;
24.     DrawBarGraph(g, energyX, energyY, energyWidth, ⮌
            energyHeight,
25.         currentEnergyWidth, energyString, Color.LightGray,
26.         Color.Salmon);
27.
28.     Character monster = player.CurrentLocation.Monster;
29.     energyY += energyHeight + 5;
30.     if (monster != null)
31.     {
32.         currentEnergy = monster.Energy < 0 ? 0 : monster.Energy;
33.         currentEnergyWidth = energyWidth * currentEnergy /
34.             monster.MaxEnergy;
35.         energyString = monster.Name + ": " + monster.Energy +
36.             "/" + monster.MaxEnergy;
37.         DrawBarGraph(g, energyX, energyY,
38.             energyWidth, energyHeight,
39.             currentEnergyWidth, energyString, Color.LightGray,
40.             Color.SkyBlue);
41.     }
42.     else
43.     {
44.         DrawBarGraph(g, energyX, energyY,
45.             energyWidth, energyHeight,
46.             0, "", Color.LightGray, Color.LightGray);
47.     }
48.
49.     Font font = new Font("Arial", 10, FontStyle.Bold);
50.     Brush brush = new SolidBrush(Color.Black);
51.     energyY += energyHeight + 5;
52.     g.DrawString("Hit: " + player.HitProb + "%", font, brush,
53.         energyX, energyY);
54.     energyY += energyHeight;
55.     g.DrawString("Block: " + player.BlockProb + "%",
56.         font, brush,
```

```
57.        energyX, energyY);
58.     energyY += energyHeight;
59.     g.DrawString("Max damage: " + player.Damage, font, brush,
60.        energyX, energyY);
61.     if (player.WornArmour != null)
62.     {
63.        energyY += energyHeight;
64.        g.DrawString("Wearing " + player.WornArmour.⤶
           Description,
65.           font, brush, energyX, energyY);
66.     }
67.     if (player.WieldedWeapon != null)
68.     {
69.        energyY += energyHeight;
70.        g.DrawString("Wielding " +
71.           player.WieldedWeapon.Description, font, brush,
72.           energyX, energyY);
73.     }
74.     energyX += statsWidth/2;
75.     energyY = statsTop + 15 + energyHeight;
76.     if (player.QuaffedPotion != null)
77.     {
78.        energyY += energyHeight;
79.        g.DrawString("Quaffed " +
80.           player.QuaffedPotion.Description +
81.           " (" + player.PotionTime + " turns left)", font,⤶
           brush,
82.           energyX, energyY);
83.     }
84.     if (player.WornRing != null)
85.     {
86.        energyY += energyHeight;
87.        g.DrawString("Wearing " +
88.           player.WornRing.Description, font, brush,
89.           energyX, energyY);
90.     }
91. }
```

Most of this method (from line 49 onwards) just writes out the statistics as text. The method begins by drawing a frame around the statistics area (lines 3 to 12). The bar charts for the player and monster are created by retrieving the player's MaxEnergy (the player's energy when at full health) and current Energy and working out the size of the 'active' portion of the bar compared to the overall length of the bar. We then call DrawBarGraph() to draw the bar itself.

This bar graph looks very similar to the 'progress bar' that is often seen to indicate the progress of an operation such as a program installation. There is, in fact, a `ProgressBar` class in Windows Forms, but it is quite primitive and is not really suitable for what we want here.

We have therefore implemented `DrawBarGraph()` by using ordinary graphics commands:

```
private void DrawBarGraph(Graphics g, int x, int y,
    int width, int height,
    int activeWidth, string text,
    Color back, Color front)
{
    Brush brush = new SolidBrush(back);
    g.FillRectangle(brush, x, y, width, height);
    brush = new SolidBrush(front);
    g.FillRectangle(brush, x, y, activeWidth, height);
    Font font = new Font("Arial", 10, FontStyle.Bold);
    SizeF textSize = g.MeasureString(text, font);
    Point stringLoc = new Point();
    stringLoc.X = (int)(x + width/2 - textSize.Width/2);
    stringLoc.Y = (int)(y + 2);
    brush = new SolidBrush(Color.Black);
    g.DrawString(text, font, brush, stringLoc);
}
```

This method has a large number of parameters which allow the bar to be customized in several ways. The `x` and `y` parameters specify the upper-left corner of the bar, and `width` and `height` its overall size. Note that `width` is the maximum width of the bar, allocated to `MaxEnergy`. The `activeWidth` is the width allocated to the current energy of the player or monster. The `text` is printed on top of the bar after both background and active portions have been filled in. Finally, `back` and `front` are the colours used for the background and foreground respectively. We use the `MeasureString()` method from `Graphics` to find the size of the text and use this information to centre it horizontally on the bar.

This completes the setup of the interface.

10.11.8 ☐ Event handlers

The other main section of the GUI programming provides the event handlers for the various controls. Most of these handlers simply call methods in the classes that we wrote for the text version in Chapter 6.

As we mentioned earlier, most commands in the game require two stages. First, the user must select the command itself ('take', 'look' and so on). For some commands such as 'look' and 'inventory', clicking the corresponding radio button then produces the required information and no other action is needed. Most commands, however, do require extra information from the user. For example, 'take' requires a list of items in the current room that the player wishes to pick up. For these commands, the list of available options is printed in the ListBox and the user must select at least one of these in order to complete the command. Commands that require this additional information can only be completed when the 'Do command' button is enabled by the program, and this only happens when the user has selected something from the list.

We saw in the code above that an event handler for the Click event was attached to all the command radio buttons. The OnCommand() method handles directly those commands that require no further information from the user, and populates the list box with the available options for all other commands:

```
1. public void OnCommand(object sender, EventArgs args)
2. {
3.    int items;
4.    lastCommand = (RadioButton)sender;
5.    if (sender == inventoryRadio)
6.    {
7.        commandOptionsListBox.SelectionMode =
        SelectionMode.None;
8.        ShowInventory();
9.        commandOptionsListBox.Enabled = false;
10.        selectedCommand = Command.Inventory;
11.    }
12.    else if (sender == lookRadio)
13.    {
14.        ShowLocationContents(
15.            adventure.GamePlayer.CurrentLocation);
16.        commandOptionsListBox.Enabled = false;
17.        selectedCommand = Command.Look;
18.    }
19.    else if (sender == takeRadio)
20.    {
21.        commandOptionsListBox.SelectionMode =
22.            SelectionMode.MultiExtended;
23.        commandOptionsListBox.Enabled = true;
24.        items = ShowLocationContents(
25.            adventure.GamePlayer.CurrentLocation);
26.        if (items > 0)
27.            instructionLabel.Text = "Select item(s) to take:";
28.        selectedCommand = Command.Take;
29.    }
30.    else if (sender == dropRadio)
31.    {
32.        commandOptionsListBox.SelectionMode =
33.            SelectionMode.MultiExtended;
```

```
34.        commandOptionsListBox.Enabled = true;
35.        items = ShowInventory();
36.        if (items > 0)
37.          instructionLabel.Text = "Select item(s) to drop:";
38.        selectedCommand = Command.Drop;
39.      }
40.    else if (sender == eatRadio)
41.    {
42.        commandOptionsListBox.SelectionMode =
43.          SelectionMode.MultiExtended;
44.        commandOptionsListBox.Enabled = true;
45.        items = ShowItemsOfType(Type.GetType("Food"));
46.        if (items > 0)
47.          instructionLabel.Text = "Select item(s) to eat:";
48.        else
49.          instructionLabel.Text = "You have nothing to eat.";
50.        selectedCommand = Command.Eat;
51.    }
52.    else if (sender == quaffRadio)
53.    {
54.        commandOptionsListBox.SelectionMode =
           SelectionMode.One;
55.        commandOptionsListBox.Enabled = true;
56.        int numItems = ShowItemsOfType(Type.GetType("Potion"));
57.        if (numItems > 0)
58.          instructionLabel.Text = "Select potion to quaff:";
59.        else
60.          instructionLabel.Text = "You have no potions.";
61.        selectedCommand = Command.Quaff;
62.    }
63.    else if (sender == adornRadio)
64.    {
65.        commandOptionsListBox.SelectionMode =
           SelectionMode.One;
66.        commandOptionsListBox.Enabled = true;
67.        int numItems = ShowItemsOfType(Type.GetType("Ring"));
68.        if (numItems > 0)
69.          instructionLabel.Text = "Select ring to wear:";
70.        else
71.          instructionLabel.Text = "You have no rings.";
72.        selectedCommand = Command.Adorn;
73.    }
74.    else if (sender == unadornRadio)
75.    {
76.        if (adventure.GamePlayer.WornRing == null)
77.        {
```

```
78.        instructionLabel.Text = "You are not wearing
           a ring.";
79.      }
80.    else
81.    {
82.      commandOptionsListBox.Items.Clear();
83.      adventure.DoUnadorn();
84.      instructionLabel.Text = "You remove the ring.";
85.    }
86.    selectedCommand = Command.Unadorn;
87.  }
88.  else if (sender == wieldRadio)
89.  {
90.    commandOptionsListBox.SelectionMode =
         SelectionMode.One;
91.    commandOptionsListBox.Enabled = true;
92.    int numItems = ShowItemsOfType(Type.GetType("Weapon"));
93.    if (numItems > 0)
94.      instructionLabel.Text = "Select weapon to wield:";
95.    else
96.      instructionLabel.Text = "You have no weapons.";
97.    selectedCommand = Command.Wield;
98.  }
99.  else if (sender == wearRadio)
100. {
101.   commandOptionsListBox.SelectionMode =
         SelectionMode.One;
102.   commandOptionsListBox.Enabled = true;
103.   int numItems = ShowItemsOfType(Type.GetType("Armour"));
104.   if (numItems > 0)
105.     instructionLabel.Text = "Select armour to wear:";
106.   else
107.     instructionLabel.Text = "You have no armour.";
108.   selectedCommand = Command.Wear;
109. }
110. else if (sender == zapRadio)
111. {
112.   commandOptionsListBox.SelectionMode =
         SelectionMode.One;
113.   commandOptionsListBox.Enabled = true;
114.   int numItems = ShowItemsOfType(Type.GetType("Wand"));
115.   if (numItems > 0)
116.     instructionLabel.Text = "Select wand to zap:";
117.   else
118.     instructionLabel.Text = "You have no wands.";
119.   selectedCommand = Command.Zap;
```

```
120.    }
121.    else if (sender == attackRadio)
122.    {
123.       commandOptionsListBox.Items.Clear();
124.       selectedCommand = Command.Attack;
125.       string message = adventure.DoPlayerAttack();
126.       message += DoValidTurn();
127.       messageBox.Text = message;
128.    }
129.    goButton.Enabled = false;
130.    Invalidate();
131.    EnableCommands();
132.    if (adventure.GamePlayer.Energy <= 0)
133.       EndGame();
134. }
```

The selected command is saved as `lastCommand` (line 4) so that it can be repeated, if appropriate, as the player moves between rooms using the arrow buttons. This means that the player can select the 'look' command and then see the contents of each room as the player walks through the various rooms on the map.

The remainder of the method from line 5 onwards provides handler code for all the radio buttons. In most cases, this code should be fairly obvious so we won't go into detail for all of them.

Most of the commands use `commandOptionsListBox` either to display some read-only information (as in the 'look' and 'inventory' commands) or to display a list of options from which the user can choose. For the latter group, some commands allow only a single selection (as in 'quaff' or 'wield', for example) while others allow multiple selections (as in 'eat' or take'). The state of the list box must thus be set properly before the user is allowed to make any selections.

The code for the 'inventory' command (line 5) displays the contents of the player's backpack in `commandOptionsListBox` as read-only (non-selectable) information. We therefore set the `SelectionMode` of the list box to `None` (line 7). Doing this prohibits the user from making any selections, but the text in the box still appears as normal black font, which could mislead the user into thinking that a selection was still possible. We therefore disable the list box (line 9) which changes the text to grey. (Actually, disabling the control also prevents the user from making any selections, so we don't really need line 7, but we've included it to show how a list box can prevent selections from being made.)

As an example of a command where multiple selections are allowed, we can have a look at 'take' (line 19). Here the `SelectionMode` is set to `MultiExtended`, which not only allows multiple items to be selected, but also allows the Shift, Ctrl and arrow keys to be used. The Shift key is used to select a range of items by selecting the first item with the mouse as usual, then scrolling to the end of the range, holding down the Shift key and selecting the last item with the mouse. All items between these two will also be selected.

To select two items without including the range between them, select the first with the mouse and then hold down Ctrl and select the second.

The list box is loaded with the items currently in the room by calling `ShowLocationContents()` (line 24):

```
private int ShowLocationContents(Room location)
{
  commandOptionsListBox.Items.Clear();
  commandOptionsListBox.Items.AddRange(
    location.ItemList.ToArray());
  int items = location.ItemList.Count;
  if (items > 0)
  {
    instructionLabel.Text = "The " + location.Description +
      " contains:";
  }
  else
  {
    instructionLabel.Text = "The " + location.Description +
      " is empty";
  }
  return items;
}
```

The list box is cleared of existing entries and then filled with the contents of `location`. Note that we can convert an `ArrayList` to an array by calling `ToArray()` and that this array can be used to populate a `ListBox` directly, without using a loop.

We then display an appropriate message in `instructionLabel`, which appears directly above the list box. In the case of the 'take' command, the message is changed to 'Select item(s) to take' if there are some items in the room (line 26).

An example of a command where only a single selection is allowed is 'quaff' (line 52). The `SelectionMode` is set to `One` (line 54). We only want to list the potions being carried by the player, so we use `ShowItemsOfType()` to select and display items of a specific type. This method is a slight variant of `CountItemsOfType()` that we saw earlier:

```
private int ShowItemsOfType(Type itemType)
{
  commandOptionsListBox.Items.Clear();
  ArrayList items = adventure.GamePlayer.ItemList;
  int numItems = 0;
  foreach (Item item in items)
  {
    if (item.GetType() == itemType)
    {
```

```
        commandOptionsListBox.Items.Add(item);
        ++numItems;
    }
  }
  return numItems;
}
```

The list box is cleared and the player's inventory is searched for items whose object type matches `itemType`. Any such items are added to the list box.

Each control handler also sets a `selectedCommand` parameter, which is used in the second stage of command handling after the user has selected some items from the list box. When 'Do command' is pressed, we need to know which command is to be processed.

The only command that is significantly different from all the others is 'attack'. The handler for 'attack' (line 121) clears the list box and then calls `DoPlayerAttack()` from the original `Adventure` class, which we considered in Chapter 6. The 'attack' command is special in that it is the only command that does not require any additional information from the user, yet still uses up game time. This is why `DoValidTurn()` is called (line 126) to give the monster a chance to attack and to do some other bookkeeping. The results of a round of combat are then displayed in the `messageBox` below the 'Do command' button.

Before we consider the handler for 'Do command', it is worth looking at the last few lines in `OnCommand()`. Line 129 disables the 'Do command' button after any radio button is selected. This makes sense since, if the selected command merely produces information without requiring any further input, there is nothing more that needs to be done, so 'Do command' should not be enabled. On the other hand, if the user *does* need to input some more data by selecting something from the list box, then 'Do command' should not be enabled until that information is provided.

On line 130, `Invalidate()` is called to refresh the graphics. Some commands change the state of the player so we need to refresh the information in the display.

Line 131 calls `EnableCommands()` which we looked at earlier. This method enables or disables each radio button depending on the current state of the player, and must be called after each command since the player's state could change.

Finally (line 132) we check to see if the player has been killed as a result of the last command and, if so, call `EndGame()` to display a message and offer a new game.

After `OnCommand()`, the 'Do command' button may be enabled. If so, it must be pressed to complete the command. Its handler is `OnGo()`:

```
private void OnGo(object sender, EventArgs args)
{
    if (sender == goButton)
```

```
    {
      switch (selectedCommand)
      {
        case Command.Take:
            DoTake();
            break;
        case Command.Drop:
            DoDrop();
            break;
        case Command.Eat:
            DoEat();
            break;
        case Command.Quaff:
            DoQuaff();
            break;
        case Command.Adorn:
            DoAdorn();
            break;
        case Command.Wield:
            DoWield();
            break;
        case Command.Wear:
            DoWear();
            break;
        case Command.Zap:
            DoZap();
            break;
      }
      goButton.Enabled = false;
      EnableCommands();
      Invalidate();
    }
  }
}
```

This method just delegates the handler to the method for that specific
command. We will list the code for all these methods here, although most of
them are quite similar to each other, so we'll only consider a few of them in
any detail:

```
1. private void DoTake()
2. {
3.    ListBox.SelectedObjectCollection selectedItems =
4.       commandOptionsListBox.SelectedItems;
5.    foreach (Item item in selectedItems)
6.    {
7.       if (adventure.GamePlayer.AddItem(item))
8.       {
```

```
 9.          adventure.GamePlayer.CurrentLocation.RemoveItem(
10.            item.Description);
11.        }
12.      }
13.    int items =
14.      ShowLocationContents(
15.        adventure.GamePlayer.CurrentLocation);
16.    if (items > 0)
17.      instructionLabel.Text = "Select item(s) to take:";
18.    messageBox.Text = DoValidTurn();
19. }
20.
21. private void DoDrop()
22. {
23.    ListBox.SelectedObjectCollection selectedItems =
24.      commandOptionsListBox.SelectedItems;
25.    foreach (Item item in selectedItems)
26.    {
27.      adventure.GamePlayer.RemoveItem(item.Description);
28.      adventure.GamePlayer.CurrentLocation.AddItem(item);
29.    }
30.    int items = ShowInventory();
31.    if (items > 0)
32.      instructionLabel.Text = "Select item(s) to drop:";
33.    messageBox.Text = DoValidTurn();
34. }
35.
36. private void DoEat()
37. {
38.    ListBox.SelectedObjectCollection selectedItems =
39.      commandOptionsListBox.SelectedItems;
40.    string itemsEaten = "";
41.    int itemCount = 0;
42.    foreach (Item item in selectedItems)
43.    {
44.      adventure.GamePlayer.RemoveItem(item.Description);
45.      adventure.GamePlayer.Energy += ((Food)item).Energy;
46.      if (adventure.GamePlayer.Energy >
47.          adventure.GamePlayer.MaxEnergy)
48.        adventure.GamePlayer.MaxEnergy =
49.          adventure.GamePlayer.Energy;
50.      itemsEaten += item.Description;
51.      itemCount++;
52.      if (itemCount < selectedItems.Count - 1)
53.      {
54.        itemsEaten += ", ";
```

```
55.       }
56.       else if (itemCount == selectedItems.Count - 1)
57.       {
58.         itemsEaten += " and ";
59.       }
60.     }
61.     int items = ShowItemsOfType(Type.GetType("Food"));
62.     if (items > 0)
63.       instructionLabel.Text = "Select item(s) to eat:";
64.     else
65.       instructionLabel.Text =
66.         "You have nothing to eat in your pack.";
67.     messageBox.Text = "You eat " + itemsEaten + ⮠
        DoValidTurn();
68. }
69.
70. private void DoQuaff()
71. {
72.     Potion potion = (Potion)commandOptionsListBox.⮠
        SelectedItem;
73.     string potionDesc =
74.       commandOptionsListBox.SelectedItem.ToString();
75.     adventure.DoQuaff(potionDesc);
76.     int items = ShowItemsOfType(Type.GetType("Potion"));
77.     if (items > 0)
78.       instructionLabel.Text = "Select potion to quaff:";
79.     else
80.       instructionLabel.Text =
81.         "You have no potions in your pack.";
82.     messageBox.Text = potion.QuaffString + DoValidTurn();
83. }
84.
85. private void DoAdorn()
86. {
87.     Ring ring = (Ring)commandOptionsListBox.SelectedItem;
88.     string ringDesc =
89.       commandOptionsListBox.SelectedItem.ToString();
90.     adventure.DoAdorn(ringDesc);
91.     ShowItemsOfType(Type.GetType("Ring"));
92.     instructionLabel.Text = "";
93.     messageBox.Text = ring.AdornString + DoValidTurn();
94. }
95.
96. private void DoWield()
97. {
98.     string weapon =
```

```
 99.        commandOptionsListBox.SelectedItem.ToString();
100.     adventure.DoWield(weapon);
101.     int items = ShowItemsOfType(Type.GetType("Weapon"));
102.     if (items > 0)
103.        instructionLabel.Text = "Select weapon to wield:";
104.     else
105.        instructionLabel.Text =
106.           "You have no weapons in your pack.";
107.     messageBox.Text = "You are now wielding " + weapon +
108.        DoValidTurn();
109. }
110.
111. private void DoWear()
112. {
113.     string armour =
114.        commandOptionsListBox.SelectedItem.ToString();
115.     adventure.DoWear(armour);
116.     int items = ShowItemsOfType(Type.GetType("Armour"));
117.     if (items > 0)
118.        instructionLabel.Text = "Select armour to wear:";
119.     else
120.        instructionLabel.Text =
121.           "You have no armour in your pack.";
122.     messageBox.Text = "You are now wearing " + armour +
123.        DoValidTurn();
124. }
125.
126. private void DoZap()
127. {
128.     string message = "";
129.     Wand wand = (Wand)commandOptionsListBox.SelectedItem;
130.     string wandDesc =
131.        commandOptionsListBox.SelectedItem.ToString();
132.     message += adventure.DoZap(wandDesc);
133.     int items = ShowItemsOfType(Type.GetType("Wand"));
134.     if (items > 0)
135.        instructionLabel.Text = "Select wand to zap:";
136.     else
137.        instructionLabel.Text = "You have no wands
            in your pack.";
138.     messageBox.Text = message + DoValidTurn();
139. }
```

Most commands follow the model exemplified by `DoTake()` (line 1). We extract the selected items from the list box and store them in a `Selected ObjectCollection`. A `foreach` loop can iterate over the items in this collection and process each item in turn. For 'take' we attempt to add an item to the player's inventory (which can fail if the item exceeds the weight limit for the player – see code in Chapter 6).

After completing the command, we update the display (lines 13 to 17) and call `DoValidTurn()` to allow monsters to attack and update potion times if required.

Most of the other commands work in a similar fashion – the selected item(s) are processed by calling the appropriate method from the `Adventure` class or some other class from the text version of the program. After this, `DoValidTurn()` is called to update the situation in the game.

The 'eat' command (line 36) is a bit different in that if eating some food increases the player's `Energy` beyond `MaxEnergy`, `MaxEnergy` is increased to this new value. This means that eating food can permanently increase the player's maximum energy. (We're treating all food in the game as health food.)

Commands such as 'quaff' (line 70) that require exactly one selected item can obtain this item directly by using the `SelectedItem` property of the list box (line 72).

There are a few other utility methods that we have not discussed but these do not do anything complex or mysterious and can be examined in the complete code available on the book's web site.

■ Summary

In this chapter, we have introduced some of .NET's facilities for producing graphics. Like Java, C# requires a *graphics context* to provide the interface between the code and the output devices on which the images are displayed. Simple graphics can be produced using the `Pen` and `Brush` for drawing and filling. More effects can be produced by using the various transformations, and by defining more complex shapes using a `GraphicsPath`.

We also had a look at drawing text using `Fonts`, handling mouse events, and producing animation by using a separate thread to run the graphics, thus avoiding locking up the main program.

Finally, a full GUI version of the adventure game case study was produced illustrating how the concepts of the last two chapters can be brought together into a larger program.

Exercises

10.1 Write a program that displays a plain form with a background painted with a hatched brush. Use the `ClientArea` property of the form to determine the size of the rectangle to fill.

10.2 Write a program that fills the form with a series of concentric rectangles, each one smaller than the last, and with all rectangles centred in the form's client area. Each rectangle should have a random solid colour as a fill pattern and a black border.

10.3 Write a simple plotting program that will draw an x–y graph from a set of data. To keep things simple, assume that the x and y values both range between 0 and 100. Generate some data by creating an array of 100 `ints` and fill the array with values of your choice (or use `Random` to produce some random values). Use this array for the y values and assume that the x values consist of the integers from 1 to 100.

For the first version of the program, use the left and bottom edges of the client area as the y and x axes respectively and just write some code that calculates the correct location of each point to be plotted, then join up all the points with straight line segments.

Various enhancements to the plotting program in the previous exercise are possible, so try implementing a few of them. For example, draw a rectangular frame within the client area that leaves a margin between the frame and the edges of the form. Draw the graph so that all the points fit inside this frame, and then draw a label using text on the x and y axes. The label on the y axis should be rotated by 90 degrees so that the text reads upwards.

10.5 Enhance the graph program by using a gradient brush to provide a transition between two pastel shades in the background.

10.6 Investigate some of the properties of a `Pen` that allow the style of line to be customized. In particular, examine `DashStyle`, which allows dotted and dashed lines to be drawn, `LineJoin`, which allows corners (places where two lines meet) to be customized, `StartCap`, `EndCap` and `DashCap`, which allow the shapes of the ends of lines to be customized and so on. Many of these properties show up best if the lines are fairly thick.

10.7 Write a simple 'whiteboard' application which displays a blank form with a white background and allows the user to draw on it using the mouse. To do this, you will need to use 'mouse move' events in pairs and draw a line segment for each mouse move event after the first. In this first version, don't worry about saving the lines (meaning that the graphics will be lost if the window is hidden and then redisplayed).

10.8 Enhance the program in the previous exercise so that the lines making up a drawing are saved in a data structure and drawn in `OnPaint()`, thus allowing the drawing to survive minimizing and restoring the window.

10.9   Further enhance the whiteboard program by adding a menu with a command allowing the drawing to be saved as a JPEG file on disk. Use a `SaveFileDialog` to allow the user to choose a file name.

10.10 Add another option to the drawing program to allow an image file to be read in from a disk file, and then edited by using the mouse to draw lines on top of the image. The resulting image could then be saved to disk as a new file.

10.11 Write a program which displays a blank form with a small square displayed in the middle. Add a mouse event handler so that when the mouse is clicked inside the square, the square moves a short distance in a random direction (up, down, left or right). The motion should be animated, so that the square appears to drift over the distance, rather than just jump to its new location. If the square hits an edge of the form, it should bounce back in the opposite direction. (Hint: examine the `Rectangle.Contains()` method to see how to detect when the mouse is clicked within the square.)

10.12 Alter the checkers game by changing the way the piece is moved. Rather than dragging the piece with the mouse, click the mouse on the piece that is to be moved, then click on the destination square. If the destination is valid, the piece should slide from the source to the destination using animation in a separate thread. Once you have the animation working, try to add in code so that if the mouse is clicked anywhere on the board before the animation is complete, the move is aborted and the piece snaps back to its starting square.

Databases

11

11.1 ■ The basics

For better or worse, databases are now a part of everyday life in computing. They form the core of accounting systems, many web sites, and many home PC users' CD collections. Because databases are so common and relatively easy to use, it is good news that C# and .NET provide solid support for interacting with most common databases.

Since this book is not a textbook on databases, we won't give a comprehensive survey of database theory, but since we don't assume any prior knowledge of databases on the part of the reader, we will provide an outline of what databases are and how to communicate with them.

A database is, not surprisingly, a program that stores data in a structured way. The most important function of a database is its ability to allow *queries* to be made of its data. For example, if you have stored information on your book collection in a database, you might want to get a list of all books written by a particular author, or on a particular subject, or you might even want a list of all books that are longer than 300 pages.

In order to achieve this, we need to design the structure of the database carefully so that the retrieval operation is both possible and relatively easy. To get an idea of what's involved, let's start with a list of several books (not all of which actually exist), for each of which we will list the author(s), title and number of pages:

Author(s)	Title	No. of pages
Wibble, Zaphod	Wibble's Guide to the Classics	345
Asimov, Isaac	The Complete Stories, Vol. 1	429
Asimov, I.	The Complete Stories, Vol. 2	464
Dium, T. & Moron, Oxy	Honest Politicians	24
Wibble, Z. Q.	Wibble's Guide to Heavy Metal	297

It may seem that the simplest way of storing these books in a database would be to just store the information on each book as a single string in a text file, such as:

```
Author:"Wibble, Zaphod";Title:"Wibble's Guide to the
Classics";Pages:345
Author:"Asimov, Isaac";Title:"The Complete Stories, Vol. 1";
Pages:429
Author:"Asimov, I.";Title:"The Complete Stories, Vol. 2";
Pages:464
```

```
Author:"Dium,T & Moron, Oxy";Title:"Honest Politicians";
Pages:24
Author:"Wibble, Z.Q.";Title:"Wibble's Guide to Heavy Metal";
Pages:297
```

With the data stored in this way, we could, for example, search for all books by Asimov by looking at each line in the file, finding the word 'Author', and then searching between the double quotes following 'Author' for the name 'Asimov'.

Although this method would work in principle, it is inefficient in practice, since it requires a sequential search through a lot of text, much of which is not relevant to the query we are making.

Rather than a 'flat file' format such as this, a database makes use of *tables* for defining key features of the data that is being stored. Designing the table structure of a database is similar to designing the class structure of an object-oriented program. We need to identify those features of the data that are most useful in classifying it, and which will best facilitate any queries we might wish to do.

As with object-oriented design, there is often not a single 'correct' design for a database, but there are designs that certainly make more sense than others. For our book data, we need to think about the objects that are being described and ask how they relate to each other. The central object type in a book database is, of course, the book itself. We therefore create one table called 'Books' for storing information on individual books.

Like a class, a table has individual data fields that describe properties of the objects that are stored in the table. Each book can have one or more authors, a title, and a number of pages. (Books can, of course, have many other properties such as publisher, ISBN, price, publication date, and so on, but to keep things simple, we will just consider author, title and number of pages here.) We could, therefore, just define an authors field, a title field and a number of pages field in our book table.

But does this really organize the data in the most efficient way? We've seen that one book can have more than one author, so do we just list all the authors in the table's 'Author' field? Or do we allow a single book to have more than one 'Author' field?

What about the authors themselves? Here, we have stored only the author's name, but we might want the database to store other information about each author, such as their birth and death dates, their nationality, and so on. Also, one author can be associated with more than one book. If we did specify extra information about each author, does this mean we would need to repeat the information with each book the author wrote (or co-wrote)? Doing this not only wastes space, but also opens the database up to potential errors, since we might make a mistake in copying the information from one book to the next.

Another problem is evident from the data listed above: sometimes the same author is written differently, as in 'Asimov, Isaac' and 'Asimov, I.'. If these both refer to the same person, we don't want them listed as two separate entries in the table.

Clearly using just a single table to store the book data is not very efficient. A better design is to create a separate table for authors, and then somehow link the 'Authors' table to the 'Books' table to indicate which authors wrote which books. A common method of doing this is to add a numerical *key* to each author and book and use these keys to link the tables. We can then use this key as a reference in another table. As an example, we rewrite the data above as two tables, one for authors and one for books. We'll deal with the links between the tables later.

Authors

AuthorKey	Name
1	Wibble, Zaphod Q
2	Asimov, Isaac
3	Dium, T
4	Moron, Oxy

Books

BookKey	Title	Number of pages
1	Wibble's Guide to the Classics	345
2	The Complete Stories, Vol. 1	429
3	The Complete Stories, Vol. 2	464
4	Honest Politicians	24
5	Wibble's Guide to Heavy Metal	297

If each book had only a single author, we could add another column to the Books table to provide a link to that book's author. For example, we could list the *first* author of each book this way for our data above:

Books

BookKey	Title	Number of pages	Author
1	Wibble's Guide to the Classics	345	1
2	The Complete Stories, Vol. 1	429	2
3	The Complete Stories, Vol. 2	464	2
4	Honest Politicians	24	3
5	Wibble's Guide to Heavy Metal	297	1

This form of linking works well if there is a 'one-to-many' relationship between two tables, that is, if at most one record in one table can be connected to many records in another table. It is certainly a better solution than entering all the author's details alongside every book written by that author, since we can change or add information about a given author by changing only the record corresponding to that author in the Authors table.

A common problem in database design occurs when two tables have a 'many-to-many' relationship. This is actually the case with our book example, since each author can write more than one book, and each book can have more than one author. The solution of adding a single Author field in the Books table will not work in a many-to-many relationship, since each data field can only store a single value.

To solve this problem, we revert back to the original form of the Books table (the form without the extra column for Authors). To link together these two tables connected by a many-to-many relationship and store the information about which authors wrote which books, we provide a *link table* which contains only two columns – the key from the 'Authors' table and the corresponding key from the 'Books' table which corresponds to the book written by that author:

AuthorBook links

AuthorKey	BookKey
1	1
1	5
2	2
2	3
3	4
4	4

This table shows that author 1 (Wibble, Zaphod Q) wrote book 1 (Wibble's Guide to the Classics) and also book 5 (Wibble's Guide to Heavy Metal), author 2 wrote books 2 and 3, and that authors 3 and 4 both worked on book 4. The combination of all three of these tables contains all the information specified in the original data, but in a form that makes it much easier to search, expand and maintain.

For example, we need enter the information for a given author only once, since we can use the author's key number to refer to that author in the books table rather than duplicating the author's name for each book. Also, if we want to add more information on each author such as their birth and death dates, we can simply add a couple of extra columns to the Authors table, without having to modify either of the Books or Authors–Books tables.

This sort of table structure relies on each entry in each table having a unique identifier, which in the Books and Authors tables is the 'BookKey' or 'AuthorKey' field. A data field in a table that is guaranteed to be unique for each entry in the table and is used as a reference in other tables is called a *primary key*. Although the primary key in the Authors and Books tables is a single number in our example here, this is not necessary. Any field containing any type of data that is unique for each entry in the table can be used as a primary key. In fact, even combinations of more than one field can be used as a primary key, provided that each combination is unique for each table entry.

For example, in the Authors–Books link table, neither column on its own can be used as a primary key since both columns contain duplicate entries. However, the combination of the two columns always gives a unique combination of the two key values and so both columns together can be used as a primary key.

The allowed relationships between pairs of tables can be enforced by defining *relationships* between tables. For example, we can enforce a one-to-many or many-to-many relationship between two tables by setting up these relationships in the database. These rules have no effect on data input unless we violate them, in which case the database engine will generate an error message stating that we have tried to enter invalid data. This process is known as enforcing relational integrity.

Although there is much more that can be said about building a database, this brief introduction contains most of what you will need to know to write C# code to add and delete records from an existing database, and to write queries to extract information from it.

11.2 ■ SQL

We now have some idea how information is stored in a database, but so far we have seen neither how we actually add this information, nor how we can extract information once it has been added.

If you have used a database such as Microsoft Access which has a (moderately) user-friendly front end which allows you to add data by filling out a form and run queries by answering a few questions about what you are looking for, you have been shielded from what is going on underneath during the process of accessing the database. Since our goal in this chapter is to drive a database (and not just those with user-friendly front ends) from within a C# program, we need to delve a bit more deeply.

Most interaction with databases is done by using Structured Query Language, or SQL for short. Although for some complex operations SQL statements can get quite involved, happily most simple database operations such as inserting, updating and querying a database require only very simple SQL statements.

It is actually possible to create a database's tables, define relationships, add and delete records, update data within individual records, and perform queries of almost unlimited complexity using SQL. A complete treatment of SQL is a topic for a book on its own, but the point is that the *interaction* between a database and an external program written in C# takes place by sending the database SQL statements from within the C# program. If the SQL statement is a query, the database will send back a response containing a set of records that satisfy the query, and the C# program can then use or display these results as it sees fit.

We will cover a few of the simpler SQL statements that can be used for adding, updating and deleting records, and for querying a database. In section 11.3, we will see how to connect to an existing database from within C# and then use these SQL statements to interact with the database.

11.2.1 □ Data types

Before we can add any records to a table, we must decide what data types are to be used to represent each data field in the table. It must be remembered when building a database table that the data types allowed depend on the database program that is used to manage the database itself and *not* on the language (such as C#) that will be used to interact with the database. Unfortuately, although many data types are common across database programs, there is not universal agreement on all the types that are available. We'll therefore restrict ourselves to the more common ones that are (or should be) universal.

The data types fall into three main categories: numerical data, text or character data, and binary data. The numerical data types are used to store data that is purely numerical, without any textual or binary components. Text data fields can store strings of ASCII or Unicode characters. Binary data fields can essentially store any type of data, but are more commonly used to store images and other types of multimedia. Databases also provide a special data type for storing dates and times. In our brief introduction to SQL we will consider only numerical and textual data fields.

For the three tables above, we could define the data types as follows:

Authors – data types

AuthorKey	int
Name	char

Books – data types

BookKey	int
Title	char
Number of Pages	int

AuthorBook – data types

AuthorKey	int
BookKey	int

We have indicated the primary keys in each table in bold.

11.2.2 ☐ **Inserting a new record**

Once we have the tables defined, we can add new records to a table by using SQL's INSERT statement. For example, if we wish to add a new record to the Authors table for 'Asimov, Isaac', we could use the statement:

```
INSERT INTO Authors VALUES(1, 'Asimov, Isaac')
```

This statement assumes that there is no record in the Authors table with an AuthorKey value of 1. If there were, and we had defined AuthorKey as a primary key in the Authors table, the database would complain that we were attempting to add a record with a key that already existed in the table.

If we are using a single numerical field as the primary key, a simple way of guaranteeing a unique value is to retrieve the maximum existing key value and then add 1 to it. This can be done using SQL's SELECT MAX statement:

```
SELECT MAX(AuthorKey) FROM Authors
```

In practice, primary keys can be more complex data types or comprise more than one data field, so a different algorithm may be needed in other cases. The important thing is to have *some* way of ensuring that the primary key is unique.

A second point to notice about the INSERT statement above is that the numeric field is *not* enclosed in quotes, while the text field *is* enclosed in quotes. This is always required in an SQL statement: all text fields must always be enclosed in single quotes. If the text string that we wish to insert itself contains a quote character, this must be doubled up before enclosing the entire string in quotes. For example, if we wanted to store the author Sean O'Reilly we would need an INSERT statement like this:

```
INSERT INTO Authors VALUES(5, 'O''Reilly, Sean')
```

The parameters in the VALUES part of the statement must be listed in the same order as the data fields in the table are defined. If we wish to leave one of the data fields blank, we must pass the string NULL (not in quotes) as the parameter for that field. A NULL field in SQL is a special value which indicates that no actual data has been stored in that location.

Although it is traditional to write SQL keywords such as INSERT, INTO and so on in uppercase, most implementations of SQL are not case-sensitive. It is still better to use uppercase however, to make the keywords stand out.

After we've inserted the four authors above into the Authors table, we can insert records for the five books in our list. Doing this requires inserting a record first in the Books table, and then one or more entries in the AuthorBook link table to connect that book with its author(s). For example, to insert the first book, we would use the two statements:

```
INSERT INTO Books VALUES(1,
  'Wibble''s Guide to the Classics', 345)
INSERT INTO AuthorBook VALUES(1, 1)
```

To insert book number 4 which has two authors, we write:

```
INSERT INTO Books VALUES(4, 'Honest Politicians', 24)
INSERT INTO AuthorBook VALUES(3, 4)
INSERT INTO AuthorBook VALUES(4, 4)
```

11.2.3 ☐ Queries

Once we have some data in the database, we can run some queries on it. The main SQL command for querying is SELECT, which can be used in a number of ways.

The simplest SELECT command retrieves all data from a single table:

```
SELECT * FROM Authors
```

This returns all data fields from all records in the Authors table, so the result of the query is a *record set* consisting of the data in the table:

1	Wibble, Zaphod Q
2	Asimov, Isaac
3	Dium, T
4	Moron, Oxy

The * after SELECT is a wild card character which indicates that all data fields should be returned.

More usually, we wish to retrieve only some of the data fields, or else impose a *filter* on the query so that only records satisfying certain criteria are returned. A few examples will illustrate some common cases.

First, if we want a list of the authors without their associated keys, we can specify that we want only the Name field from the Authors table returned:

```
SELECT Name FROM Authors
```

This returns the record set:

Wibble, Zaphod Q
Asimov, Isaac
Dium, T
Moron, Oxy

We can specify some search criteria using a WHERE clause in the SELECT statement. For example, if we want a list of books with more than 300 pages, we can write:

```
SELECT * FROM Books WHERE NumberOfPages > 300
```

This returns the record set:

1	Wibble's Guide to the Classics	345
2	The Complete Stories, Vol. 1	429
3	The Complete Stories, Vol. 2	464

We can search for a substring in a text field using the LIKE clause:

```
SELECT * FROM Books WHERE Title LIKE '%Guide%'
```

This returns:

1	Wibble's Guide to the Classics	345
5	Wibble's Guide to Heavy Metal	297

In this SELECT statement, records where the Title field contains the substring 'Guide' are returned. Note that the per cent character % is used as a wild card to match any string, so the search text '%Guide%' matches any string with 'Guide' anywhere within it. If we had searched for '%Guide', we would match a string that ended with 'Guide' (and would get an empty record set, since no book has a title ending with 'Guide').

We can combine criteria using the AND keyword, so if we wanted all books whose title contained 'Guide' and that had more than 300 pages, we would say:

```
SELECT * FROM Books WHERE Title LIKE '%Guide%'
AND NumberOfPages > 300
```

This produces the single record:

1	Wibble's Guide to the Classics	345

SQL also contains an OR keyword for combining clauses in a WHERE statement.

If we want a selected list of fields to be returned, we can separate them with commas, so we could get a list of book titles and page numbers without the keys for books with more than 300 pages by saying:

```
SELECT Title,NumberOfPages FROM Books WHERE
NumberOfPages > 300
```

which returns the set:

Wibble's Guide to the Classics	345
The Complete Stories, Vol. 1	429
The Complete Stories, Vol. 2	464

Other more esoteric things can be done with SELECT, but these examples should demonstrate most of the common cases.

11.2.4 ☐ Joins

The examples of SELECT statements in the last section omitted one very common query – that involving linked tables. For example, if we wanted a list of all books by a certain author, we need to combine data from the Authors and Books tables to do the search. Since the only link is through the AuthorBook link table, how do we do this?

Let us approach this step by step. We know that the link between a book and its authors is contained in the AuthorBook table, where each record contains an author key and a book key. Let us start by generating a record set which expands the record set in AuthorBook so that each AuthorKey is listed next to the *title* of the book corresponding to that author rather than just the book key value.

The original AuthorBook table looks like this:

AuthorKey	BookKey
1	1
1	5
2	2
2	3
3	4
4	4

so what we want is a record set that looks like this:

1	Wibble's Guide to the Classics
1	Wibble's Guide to Heavy Metal
2	The Complete Stories, Vol. 1
2	The Complete Stories, Vol. 2
3	Honest Politicians
4	Honest Politicians

We can achieve this by using an INNER JOIN to join the AuthorBook table to the Books table. An INNER JOIN forms part of a SELECT statement, as follows:

```
SELECT AuthorBook.AuthorKey, Books.Title
FROM Books INNER JOIN AuthorBook ON
Books.BookKey = AuthorBook.BookKey
```

To understand what is happening here, we need to consider the FROM clause first. The second line states that an INNER JOIN should be done between the Books and AuthorBook tables. An INNER JOIN combines two tables into one table, ON some condition being true. The condition in this case is that the BookKey field in the Books table must match the BookKey field in the AuthorBook table. The inner join therefore examines each record in the Books table and compares it in turn with each record in the AuthorBook table. If a record in AuthorBook has a BookKey value that matches the BookKey value in the record from the Books table, these two records are combined into a single record and added to the joined table. The result of this INNER JOIN gives the combined table shown here:

Books Table			AuthorBook Table	
BookKey	**Title**	**NumberOfPages**	**AuthorKey**	**BookKey**
1	Wibble's Guide to the Classics	345	1	1
5	Wibble's Guide to Heavy Metal	297	1	5
2	The Complete Stories, Vol. 1	429	2	2
3	The Complete Stories, Vol. 2	464	2	3
4	Honest Politicians	24	3	4
4	Honest Politicians	24	4	4

The three columns on the left come from the Books table, and the two on the right from AuthorBook. Now that we have the combined table, we can apply the SELECT part of the statement above to it. This SELECT clause says to select AuthorBook.AuthorKey (column 4) and Books.Title (column 2) from this joined table. Doing this results in the record set shown above.

We now have a table that links a book with its author(s), but we haven't yet retrieved the actual name of the author. To do this, we need to bring the Authors table into the picture. We could get the author's name instead of just the AuthorKey by joining AuthorBook with Authors *before* doing the join with Books. That is, we can try a statement like this:

```
SELECT Authors.Name, Books.Title
FROM Books INNER JOIN
(Authors INNER JOIN AuthorBook ON
Authors.AuthorKey = AuthorBook.AuthorKey)
ON Books.BookKey = AuthorBook.BookKey
```

The third and fourth lines (within the parentheses) join Authors and AuthorBook to produce the table:

Authors		AuthorBook	
AuthorKey	**Name**	**AuthorKey**	**BookKey**
1	Wibble, Zaphod Q	1	1
1	Wibble, Zaphod Q	1	5
2	Asimov, Isaac	2	2
2	Asimov, Isaac	2	3
3	Dium, T	3	4
4	Moron, Oxy	4	4

Taking the INNER JOIN of this table with Books produces a combined table as follows:

Books			Authors		AuthorBook	
1	Wibble's Guide to the Classics	345	1	Wibble, Zaphod Q	1	1
5	Wibble's Guide to Heavy Metal	297	1	Wibble, Zaphod Q	1	5
2	The Complete Stories, Vol. 1	429	2	Asimov, Isaac	2	2
3	The Complete Stories, Vol. 2	464	2	Asimov, Isaac	2	3
4	Honest Politicians	24	3	Dium, T	3	4
4	Honest Politicians	24	4	Moron, Oxy	4	4

Finally, if we select Authors.Name and Books.Title from this table, we get the desired record set:

Wibble, Zaphod Q	Wibble's Guide to the Classics
Wibble, Zaphod Q	Wibble's Guide to Heavy Metal
Asimov, Isaac	The Complete Stories, Vol. 1
Asimov, Isaac	The Complete Stories, Vol. 2
Dium, T	Honest Politicians
Moron, Oxy	Honest Politicians

This may seem like a lot of work just to get a simple author–title list, but in fact the amount of calculation that is required to do the inner joins is much less than if we had simply stored the data in a flat file format as we did at the beginning of this chapter. It also ensures that there is as little duplication of data as possible, since there is only one record for each author, and one record for each book.

One handy SQL clause that is often used with queries is ORDER BY which allows a result set to be sorted by one or more of its data fields. For example, if we wanted to sort the list above by author, we would add the clause

```
ORDER BY Authors.Name
```

to the end of the statement above. This results in the output:

Asimov, Isaac	The Complete Stories, Vol. 1
Asimov, Isaac	The Complete Stories, Vol. 2
Dium, T	Honest Politicians
Moron, Oxy	Honest Politicians
Wibble, Zaphod Q	Wibble's Guide to the Classics
Wibble, Zaphod Q	Wibble's Guide to Heavy Metal

We can sort the output first by author and then by title by adding a list of fields to the ORDER BY clause:

```
ORDER BY Authors.Name, Books.Title
```

This produces:

Asimov, Isaac	The Complete Stories, Vol. 1
Asimov, Isaac	The Complete Stories, Vol. 2
Dium, T	Honest Politicians
Moron, Oxy	Honest Politicians
Wibble, Zaphod Q	Wibble's Guide to Heavy Metal
Wibble, Zaphod Q	Wibble's Guide to the Classics

where the last two rows are reversed from the earlier output.

Getting a list of books by a particular author is now just a matter of appending a WHERE clause to the end of this statement:

```
SELECT Authors.Name, Books.Title
FROM Books INNER JOIN
(Authors INNER JOIN AuthorBook ON
Authors.AuthorKey = AuthorBook.AuthorKey)
ON Books.BookKey = AuthorBook.BookKey
WHERE Authors.Name LIKE 'Asimov%'
```

This statement retrieves all books whose author's name begins with 'Asimov':

Asimov, Isaac	The Complete Stories, Vol. 1
Asimov, Isaac	The Complete Stories, Vol. 2

11.2.5 ☐ **Updates**

SQL provides the UPDATE statement to allow existing records in a database to be edited. UPDATE is combined with a SET clause that provides a list of fields to update, together with the new values for each field. UPDATE can be combined with a WHERE clause to filter the records that are updated.

For example, if we wanted to change the title and number of pages of the book with BookKey = 1, we could say:

```
UPDATE Books SET NumberOfPages = 357, Title = 'New Title'
WHERE BookKey = 1
```

If an UPDATE statement does not contain a WHERE clause, it will apply the updates to *all* records in the table (so be careful!).

11.2.6 ☐ **Deleting records**

The last SQL command we will consider in this brief tour is DELETE, which can be used to delete one or more records from a table. DELETE is used together with a FROM clause to specify the table from which records should be removed, and usually with a WHERE clause to provide a filter on which records should be deleted.

For example, we can delete a specific author from the Authors table by saying:

```
DELETE FROM Authors WHERE Name LIKE 'Wibble%'
```

Deletion must be used with care, since it is not reversible. Also, in databases with link tables, such as AuthorBook in our example above, we must remember to delete all references to the deleted record in any link tables *before* deleting the record itself. As with the UPDATE statement, if no WHERE clause is present, *all* records from the named table will be deleted (so be *very* careful!).

For example, if we wanted to delete Wibble from the Authors table we have to note that Wibble occurs twice in the AuthorBook table, since he is the author of two of the books in the Books table. We could delete these two records from AuthorBook, and then delete Wibble's record from Authors, but if we do that, two books in the Books table will have no authors, since there are no entries in AuthorBook for those books once Wibble has been removed. It is possible that this is what we intended since some books don't have any specific authors listed, but it is more likely that this is an error, and that we need to update AuthorBook with another record to provide an author for these two books. Deletion is not always a straightforward process in a linked database!

In databases that support *referential integrity* the database itself will generate an error message if you attempt to delete a record that is linked to another table. However, not all databases support referential integrity, so you must take care to update all tables if a record is to be deleted.

11.3 ■ Driving databases from C#

Now that we've covered the basics of databases and SQL, we can have a look at how to manage databases from within a C# program. If you have done any database programming in Java using the `java.sql` package, you should find the procedures quite similar in C#. We won't go into any comparisons between C# and Java at this stage, however, since no prior knowledge of database programming is assumed of readers.

The .NET namespaces that allow interaction with databases are known collectively as ADO .NET. The acronym ADO stood originally (in pre-.NET days) for ActiveX Data Objects. Since ActiveX technology has been effectively replaced by .NET, the acronym is something of a misnomer when we are talking about ADO .NET, but the name has stuck in any case.

Before we can do any actual database programming using SQL, we first need to connect to the database from within a C# program. Unfortunately, the procedure for doing this varies with the database. Since C# and .NET are Microsoft products, it is natural that the best support for database connections within .NET is provided for Microsoft databases such as Access and SQL Server. However, it is possible to connect to most databases using the .NET database classes.

.NET provides two main namespaces containing classes for dealing with databases: `System.Data.OleDb` and `System.Data.SqlClient`. The first namespace is designed to work with any database that supports the ODBC (Open DataBase Connectivity) API (application programming interface). OleDB is Microsoft's implementation of ODBC, and has been available in one form or another for many years – long before .NET came on the scene. The `System.Data.OleDb` namespace is a class library that implements OleDB for the .NET programming environment. It supports not only Microsoft databases such as Access and SQL Server, but other popular databases such as MySQL, which is an open source database available free of charge to non-commercial users.

The `System.Data.SqlClient` namespace is designed specifically for Microsoft's SQL Server, and can produce significantly faster code when used with that database. To a large extent, the two namespaces provide parallel versions of the same methods, although SqlClient provides some extra features not available in OleDb.

To keep things as general as possible, we will use OleDb for most of our database code, but if your own personal database is SQL Server it would pay you to use SqlClient code instead. Where there is a difference between the two methods of writing database code in C#, we will present both techniques.

11.4 ■ ODBC drivers

The first, and often the trickiest, step in writing database code in C# (or any language) is finding the right statements to connect to the database of your choice. First of all, of course, you must install the database software and get it running. This is not something we can cover in this book, since each database has its own installation methods and setup parameters, all of which should be detailed in the documentation that comes with the database.

Most databases also come with some sort of interface that allows tables to be constructed, data entered and edited, and SQL queries to be run. Some databases such as MySQL provide minimal GUI support and must be driven from a command line (unless a third-party GUI front end is obtained), while others like Access provide a complete GUI front end which includes wizards for building and querying databases and even generating formatted reports from the data.

Since our goal here is to write C# programs that handle the interface between the user and the database, the provisions of the database for direct input from the user need not concern us – we will be providing all the code for managing the database from within C#. However, before we can do that, we need a way for a C# program to communicate with the database program itself.

Since OleDb uses the ODBC system, any database with which we wish to communicate must have an *ODBC driver* installed. This driver runs separately from any C# program that communicates with it, and must be installed separately. Commercial databases will probably have a driver supplied with them, or have one available on a web site. Unfortunately, locating and installing these drivers can be a difficult job, and is not something we can address in this book, since there are many different varieties of database around. We will present examples for Microsoft's Access and SQL Server, and for MySQL in this book, but if you have a different database running on your own machine, it should be possible to adapt these examples to work in that case. The best route to follow is to do a web search using the name of your database (such as MySQL, for example) and 'ODBC driver' as keywords. For most popular databases you should find web sites that offer downloads of the ODBC drivers and instructions on how to install them. We will provide an example using MySQL below.

11.5 ■ Connecting to a database from C#

Assuming we have the ODBC driver for the database installed, we can now turn our attention to connecting to this database from within C#. To keep the example concrete, let us assume that we have installed both Access and SQL Server. In both of these, we have defined a new database called BookTest, and we have inserted into this database the data contained in the Books, Authors and AuthorBook tables that we used in the section on SQL. For now, we'll assume that we have done all this by using the features in the database package itself (rather than from a C# program) so that we have a ready made database to play with from within our C# program.

The first job is to connect to the database. We will present a complete program that connects to the database and uses a simple SQL statement to retrieve the list of authors from the Authors table:

```
1.  using System;
2.  using System.Data.OleDb;
3.
4.  public class MySQLDemo
5.  {
6.    public static void Main(string[] args)
7.    {
8.      string source;
9.
10.     // Access
11.     //source = "Provider=Microsoft.Jet.OLEDB.4.0;" +
12.     //   @"Data Source=C:\Books\MyBooks\CSharpBook\
                BookTest.mdb";
13.
14.     // SQL Server
15.     source = "Provider=SQLOLEDB;server=(local);" +
16.       "uid=<MyUsername>;" +
17.       "password=<MyPassword>;database=BookTest";
18.
19.     OleDbConnection oleConn = new OleDbConnection(source);
20.
21.     try
22.     {
23.       oleConn.Open();
24.       string sql = "SELECT * FROM Authors";
25.       OleDbCommand command = new OleDbCommand(sql, oleConn);
26.       OleDbDataReader reader = command.ExecuteReader();
27.       while (reader.Read())
28.       {
29.         Console.WriteLine(reader[0] + " " + reader[1] );
30.       }
31.     }
32.     catch (Exception ex)
33.     {
34.       Console.WriteLine(ex.ToString());
35.     }
36.     finally
37.     {
38.       oleConn.Close();
39.     }
40.   }
41. }
```

We need to reference the `System.Data.OleDb` namespace (line 2) to access the OleDb library.

A connection to a database is made by creating an `OleDbConnection` object. The parameter that is passed to its constructor is a `string` containing the information required to locate the database driver and connect to it. We've shown typical connection strings for connecting to Access and SQL Server. Obviously only one of these strings should be active at any one time, so we've commented out the Access string on lines 11 and 12, and made the SQL Server string on lines 15 to 17 active. If you want to try this code with an Access database on your own computer, uncomment the Access string and comment out the SQL Server string. Since the Access database is found by stating the full path name to the `.mdb` file, you will probably have to change this to match the location of the database file on your computer.

A compulsory component in the connection string is a *provider*. A provider is essentially a service external to the C# program which allows `OleDbConnection` to connect to the database engine we are using. Unfortunately, these providers have rather cryptic names, so if you wish to use a database other than Access or SQL Server, you will need to find out what provider is required.

For Access, the provider is 'Microsoft.Jet.OLEDB.4.0' as shown on line 11, and for SQL Server it is 'SQLOLEDB' (line 15).

Although it is possible to use Access over a network, its most common use is probably as a stand-alone database on a single computer, so we will consider that case here. If you wish to connect to an Access database stored on your local machine, the only other parameter that is required in the connection string is the 'Data Source', which should be specified as the full path name of the database file (all Access database files have a `.mdb` extension). Be careful to spell 'Data Source' as two words separated by only a *single* space. If you omit the space or insert more than one, you will get the obscure error message 'Could not find installable ISAM'.

Be careful also not to leave any blanks anywhere else in the connection string. For example, it is an error to put blanks around the = in any of the parameter specifications.

The connection string for SQL Server can be a bit more complicated. If you want to use SQL Server on the same machine as the C# program, you can specify 'server=(local)' as shown on line 15. It is also possible to connect to a remotely running SQL Server by inserting the IP address in place of '(local)'.

The `uid` and `password` fields will, of course, depend on whatever you have chosen for your username and password when setting up the database program. The values given on lines 16 and 17 are of course not my real username and password, and you will need to alter these in your own code.

Finally, we must specify the name of the database we wish to access through the driver – in this case we are connecting to `BookTest`.

When the string is complete, we create a new `OleDbConnection` object (line 19). To get things going, we need to call `Open()` to actually make the connection (line 23). Note that we have enclosed all the code that actually communicates (or tries to) with the database within a `try` block. This is highly recommended since it can sometimes take several tries to get the connection string right, especially if you are trying to get a new database type to work. You might spell your username or password incorrectly, or get the database name wrong or make any of a number of other errors, so it is important to catch any exceptions that are thrown so you can see what's gone wrong.

If the connection is successful, we can start talking to the database using SQL statements. We will delve more deeply into how this is done later in this chapter, but this simple example should give an idea of how easy database manipulation from within C# really is.

We define an SQL statement as a `string` (line 24), and then create an `OleDbCommand` object containing the statement and the connection object (line 25). If the command is a query, as it is here, we can create an `OleDb Reader` to receive the results of the query by calling the command's `Execute Reader()` method (line 26). The reader retrieves each record in the result set as an array of data fields, with one element for each field in that record. For example, since we are reading all columns from the Authors table, each reader result will be an array of two elements, one for the AuthorKey and the other for the Name. We can iterate through a reader in a loop (line 27) and use ordinary array notation to access each element (line 29).

The output from this program (assuming all the database connections work properly) is:

```
1 Wibble, Zaphod Q
2 Asimov, Isaac
3 Dium, T
4 Moron, Oxy
```

which we can see matches the contents of the Authors table given in the section on SQL above.

11.6 ■ Accessing other databases from C# – MySQL example

As we mentioned above, connecting from C# to a Microsoft database is fairly easy, since all the support is built into either the database or .NET. If we wish to connect to another database, however, things can get a bit more problematic.

Although we can't give complete instructions for all known databases, we will provide an example of how to get MySQL working with C#. This section assumes that you have installed MySQL and have either mastered the command-line interface that comes with it, or else have installed one of the GUI front ends to MySQL that allows easier access to its functions.

The process consists of several steps:

1. Download and install an ODBC driver for MySQL.

2. Download and install the ODBC .NET Data Provider from Microsoft.

3. Create a sample database in MySQL using either its command line or a GUI front end.

4. Create a Data Source Name (DSN) for this database.

5. Write some C# code to connect to the MySQL database.

First, we must locate and download an ODBC driver for MySQL. At the time of writing, this can be found on MySQL's web site at http://www. mysql.com by following the Connector/ODBC link. This is a fairly painless procedure which just involves running a setup file.

Next, we will need the ODBC .NET Data Provider. This proved somewhat more difficult to find on Microsoft's web site, but at the time of writing was available from http://msdn.microsoft.com/library/default.asp?url=/downloads/list/netdevframework.asp (the entire URL must of course be on a single line). Scroll down the page to find the ODBC .NET Data Provider. Again, this is just a matter of running the downloaded file to install it. (Note that like many pages on Microsoft's web site, this page tends to move around, as it did during the course of writing this book, but hopefully if you visit the location above you will be redirected to the current site if it has moved again.)

Next, create the BookTest database under MySQL, either by entering commands at a command line or by using a GUI front end. Instructions for doing this should be included either with MySQL itself or with the front end you are using. You will need to create the three database tables (Authors, Books and AuthorBook) and enter the data above into each table.

Now, grant permission for access to this database with the MySQL server. The easiest way to do this is by the command line. Open a console window and change directory to the 'bin' directory under your MySQL installation. For example, if you installed MySQL on the C drive in the directory mysql, this directory will be C:\mysql\bin. From this directory, issue the command:

```
mysql -u root -p
```

This logs you into the MySQL server as the 'root' (administrator) user. The -p will prompt for a password – enter whatever password you defined when you installed MySQL. Once logged in, issue the command:

```
grant all on BookTest.* to csharp@127.0.0.1 identified by
'password'
```

Again, the whole command should be on one line. This creates a new user called 'csharp' (you can, of course, specify whatever username you like here) with the password 'password' (again, choose your own password). The 'csharp' user has been granted full access privileges to the BookTest database. (The '@127.0.0.1' bit after the 'csharp' username means that the user csharp is running on the local machine, as 127.0.0.1 is the IP address of a local computer.)

The next step is to register a Data Source Name (DSN) with Windows for this new database. To do this under Windows XP (other versions should be similar), open Windows Explorer, then the Control Panel, then Administrative Tools, then Data Sources (ODBC). Select the User DSN tab and then click 'Add'. If you successfully added the MySQL ODBC driver earlier, you should see MySQL in the list of drivers. Select this and then click 'Finish' to bring up the MySQL driver dialog.

Although there are a lot of boxes here, we only need to fill in a few of them. First, think of a DSN by which you can identify the database – something like `mysql_csharp` would do for this example. Enter this in the Windows DSN Name box.

In MySQL host, enter 127.0.0.1 if you only plan on using MySQL locally on a stand-alone PC. If you want to connect to a remote server, enter its IP address or Internet name. Under MySQL database name, enter BookTest if you are using the BookTest database. Finally, fill in the username and password you used in the 'grant' command above.

That completes the preparatory work, so we can now write some C# code. We will write a version of the example program in the last section that accesses the MySQL database. Apart from the connection string, the code is essentially identical to that we saw earlier, except that different classes are used to provide the database access.

```csharp
1.  using System;
2.  using System.Data;
3.  using Microsoft.Data.Odbc;
4.
5.  public class MySQLDemo
6.  {
7.    public static void Main(string[] args)
8.    {
9.      string source;
10.     source = "DSN=mysql_csharp";
11.     OdbcConnection odbcConn = new OdbcConnection(source);
12.     try
13.     {
14.       odbcConn.Open();
15.       string sql = "SELECT * FROM Authors";
16.       OdbcCommand command = new OdbcCommand(sql, odbcConn);
17.       OdbcDataReader reader = command.ExecuteReader();
18.       while (reader.Read())
19.       {
20.         Console.WriteLine(reader[0] + " " + reader[1] );
21.       }
```

```
22.       }
23.       catch (Exception ex)
24.       {
25.          Console.WriteLine(ex.ToString());
26.       }
27.       finally
28.       {
29.          odbcConn.Close();
30.       }
31.    }
32. }
```

In order to access MySQL databases from within C#, we need to use the add-on `Microsoft.Data.Odbc` namespace that we downloaded in step 2 above. This namespace is contained in the file `Microsoft.Data.Odbc.dll`, which was installed at that time. To use the classes in this namespace, add the `using` statement shown on line 3. You will also need to add this namespace to the list of references in your project (or onto the compiler's command line).

This namespace contains a set of classes that parallel those in the OleDb set that we used earlier. To get the class names in this new set, just replace 'OleDb' in the previous namespace with 'Odbc' in the new one. Thus, we have an `OdbcConnection` class for connecting to a database, and so on.

Apart from this, the only difference is in the connection string on line 10. Note that we no longer specify a provider; rather we have a DSN clause that uses the DSN we defined in the Data Source (ODBC) dialog above. Apart from that, we just add the `uid` and `pwd` clauses (although you may find you don't need them). After that, the connection and interaction with the database is identical to the earlier example.

11.7 ■ SQL Server and the `SqlClient` namespace

Finally, we mention the `System.Data.SqlClient` namespace which contains another parallel set of classes specifically designed for efficient access to SQL Server. We can generate an equivalent program to our first example above by replacing 'OleDb' in class names with 'Sql':

```
using System;
using System.Data.SqlClient;

public class SQLOptimum
{
  public static void Main(string[] args)
  {
    string source;
    source = "server=(local);" +
```

```
    "uid=<Username>;password=<Password>;database=BookTest";
SqlConnection sqlConn = new SqlConnection(source);
try
{
  sqlConn.Open();
  string sql = "SELECT * FROM Authors";
  SqlCommand command = new SqlCommand(sql, sqlConn);
  SqlDataReader reader = command.ExecuteReader();
  while (reader.Read())
  {
    Console.WriteLine(reader[0] + " " + reader[1] );
  }
}
catch (Exception ex)
{
  Console.WriteLine(ex.ToString());
}
finally
{
  sqlConn.Close();
}
}
}
```

The only differences here are that we add a `using` statement for the `SqlClient` namespace, and that a 'provider' is no longer required in the connection string. Apart from that, the `SqlClient` classes mirror the functionality of the `OleDb` ones, although in some classes there are extra methods.

It is unlikely that any difference in speed will be noticed unless we are dealing with large databases or making a large number of SQL requests. However, if your code is to be used exclusively with SQL Server, it makes sense to use the `SqlClient` namespace in order to optimize performance.

11.8 ■ Running SQL commands

We'll now examine .NET's capabilities for communicating with databases by sending them SQL commands. For most of this discussion we will use the `OleDb` namespace, but you should keep in mind that the code will also work if you use `SqlClient` or `Odbc` as well, depending on which database you wish to connect to. The only real difference apart from the class names is in the connection string, which we have covered in the preceding sections.

For now, we will use only text programs to test the various methods in `OleDb`, but we will integrate these methods into GUI programs later in this chapter. Since it can be difficult to provide a good interface to a database using only a command-line interface, the programs in this section will be quite simple.

The main class used to send SQL commands to a database is `OleDbCommand` (or its equivalents `SqlCommand` and `OdbcCommand`). Within this class, there are three methods that are used for sending various types of commands: `ExecuteScalar()`, `ExecuteReader()` and `ExecuteNonQuery()`. The first two are used to submit a query and the last, as its name implies, is used for all non-query commands such as INSERT, DELETE and UPDATE.

11.8.1 ☐ Querying

We'll begin by taking a closer look at how queries can be sent to a database and the result sets retrieved in C#. For these examples, we will assume that the BookTest database has been constructed and that it contains the data used earlier in this chapter in our discussion of SQL.

The two methods used for querying are `ExecuteScalar()`, which is used to submit a query whose result consists of a single value, such as a count of the number of records satisfying a particular set of conditions, and `ExecuteReader()` which is used to submit a more general query using the SELECT command, which can return a result set consisting of one or more records from the database.

For our first example, we will show a complete program that illustrates `ExecuteScalar()`. Subsequent programs will show only the code that actually creates and submits the SQL command, since all other parts of the program are identical to our first example.

We can query the database to find the number of records in the Authors table as follows:

```
using System;
using System.Data.OleDb;

public class QueryDemo
{
  public static void Main(string[] args)
  {
    string source;
    source = "Provider=Microsoft.Jet.OLEDB.4.0;" +
      @"Data Source=C:\Books\MyBooks\CSharpBook\BookTest.mdb";
    OleDbConnection oleConn = new OleDbConnection(source);
    try
    {
      oleConn.Open();
      string sql = "SELECT COUNT(*) FROM Authors";
      OleDbCommand command = new OleDbCommand(sql, oleConn);
      int count = (int)command.ExecuteScalar();
      Console.WriteLine("Number of authors: " + count);
    }
    catch (Exception ex)
```

```
    {
      Console.WriteLine(ex.ToString());
    }
    finally
    {
      oleConn.Close();
    }
  }
}
```

We are using the Access database containing BookTest that we used earlier, although this program would also work with the SQL Server version if we replaced the connection string with that for SQL Server given above.

The query is constructed in the `try` block, where we use the SQL function COUNT() to request the number of records in the Authors table. An `OleDbCommand` is created using this command string, and then `Execute Scalar()` is called to send the command to the database. `ExecuteScalar()` returns an `object`, since the result of the query need not always be the same data type. This means that we must cast the result into whatever data type we are expecting from the query. In this case, since a count should be an `int`, we cast the returned value to `int`, and then print it to the console. The output from this program is:

```
Number of authors: 4
```

A count can be qualified in the same way as a SELECT statement by adding a WHERE clause. For example, we can count how many authors' names begin with the string 'Asimov'

```
try
{
  oleConn.Open();
  string sql = "SELECT COUNT(*) FROM Authors " +
    "WHERE Name LIKE 'Asimov%'";
  OleDbCommand command = new OleDbCommand(sql, oleConn);
  int count = (int)command.ExecuteScalar();
  Console.WriteLine("Number of authors: " + count);
}
```

This produces the output:

```
Number of authors: 1
```

Incidentally, when specifying longer SQL commands in C# code, it is common to split them over several lines, as we have done here. If you do this, remember to leave a blank at the end of each line to separate each word in the SQL command from the next. Failure to do this can result in error messages that can be a bit confusing. For example, if we specified our `sql` string in the previous example as:

```
string sql = "SELECT COUNT(*) FROM Authors" +
    "WHERE Name LIKE 'Asimov%'";
```

that is, we omitted the blank at the end of the first line after Authors, we get
the error:

```
System.Data.OleDb.OleDbException: Syntax error in FROM clause.
```

since the actual string that was sent to the database was: 'SELECT
COUNT(*) FROM AuthorsWHERE Name LIKE "Asimov%"'.

To perform more general queries that return result sets containing entire
records from the database, we use `ExecuteReader()`. We have already seen a
brief example of this method above, but let us consider it here in more detail.

To begin, we'll consider a slight variant on the original example. The following code constructs an `OleDbDataReader` that reads all the records in
the Authors table:

```
OleDbDataReader reader = null;
try
{
   string sql = "SELECT * FROM Authors";
   OleDbCommand command = new OleDbCommand(sql, oleConn);
   reader = command.ExecuteReader();
   while (reader.Read())
   {
     for (int i = 0; i < reader.FieldCount; i++)
       Console.Write(reader[i] + " ");
     Console.WriteLine();
   }
   reader.Close();
}
catch (Exception ex)
{
   Console.WriteLine(ex.ToString());
}
finally
{
   if (reader != null)
     reader.Close();
   oleConn.Close();
}
```

We've given a broader view of this program since it is important to ensure
that a reader is closed after use. We declare the `OleDbDataReader` before the
`try` block to give it a wider scope, and initialize it to `null`. Within the `try`
block, we construct the query and the command as usual. We then call
`ExecuteReader()` to run the query and retrieve the result set.

The result set is essentially a linked list of records from the database, and when the reader is created, its marker is positioned before the first record in the result set. The `Read()` method must be called to advance the marker to the first record. We use `reader.Read()` as the parameter inside the `while` loop, since `Read()` returns a `bool` value which is false if there are no more records available.

Inside the `while` loop, we want to print out all the fields (columns) for a given record on a single line. A reader has a `FieldCount` property which contains the number of fields in the current record, so we use that as the termination condition for the `for` loop which writes out each column of the record. The output is:

```
1 Wibble, Zaphod Q
2 Asimov, Isaac
3 Dium, T
4 Moron, Oxy
```

Note that the reader can be treated like an array when accessing the data fields of the current record. The array bracket notation `[]` can be used to specify a given column in the record.

The parameter inside the array brackets is an `int` in this example, but it can also be the name of the column in the table. For example, if we wanted to print out the AuthorKey column from the current record, we can refer to it as `reader["AuthorKey"]`. If we use an `int` as the array parameter, we need to know the order in which the columns are stored within each record, which will be determined by the original SQL statement. In this case, since we specified 'SELECT * FROM Authors', each record in the result set contains all the columns from the Authors table arranged in the same order as they were defined when the table was built.

After processing all the records, we call `Close()` to close the reader. This is an important step, since a reader effectively locks an `OleDbConnection` until it is closed. We could not do anything else with the database connection after using the reader if we forgot to close it.

The list of records within a reader is a 'one way' list, in that we can only step through it in one direction. There is no 'previous record' method in the `OleDbDataReader` class, so once we've stepped through the result set we would need to call `ExecuteReader()` again to refresh the list if we wanted to step through it again. We'll see a much more flexible way of reading the results of a query when we examine the `DataSet` class later in this chapter.

Since each column in a database table can contain data in various formats and data types, the value returned by a reference to the reader array is an `object`, and if it is to be assigned to a particular data type, it must be cast. For example, if we wanted to store the AuthorKey value in an `int` variable, we could say:

```
int authorKey = (int)reader["AuthorKey"];
```

However, the `OleDbDataReader` class contains a number of 'Get' methods that do this conversion for you, removing the need for a cast. For example, we could replace the `while` loop in the above example with:

```
while (reader.Read())
{
  Console.WriteLine(reader.GetInt32(0) +
    ": " + reader.GetString(1));
}
```

which produces the output:

```
1: Wibble, Zaphod Q
2: Asimov, Isaac
3: Dium, T
4: Moron, Oxy
```

In this case, however, the parameter of each 'Get' method must be the column index as an integer, and not the column name.

11.8.2 ☐ Non-queries

For all SQL commands that do not request information from the database (basically, any SQL command that doesn't involve SELECT), the `ExecuteNonQuery()` method should be used. This method returns an `int` which indicates the number of records in the database that were affected by the command.

As a simple example, we can insert a new author in the Authors table:

```
try
{
  oleConn.Open();
  string sql =
    "INSERT INTO Authors VALUES (5, 'Tolkien, J R R')";
  OleDbCommand command = new OleDbCommand(sql, oleConn);
  int rowsAffected = (int)command.ExecuteNonQuery();
  Console.WriteLine("Number of rows affected: "
    + rowsAffected);

  sql = "SELECT * FROM Authors";
  command = new OleDbCommand(sql, oleConn);
  reader = command.ExecuteReader();
  while (reader.Read())
  {
    Console.WriteLine(reader.GetInt32(0) +
      ": " + reader.GetString(1));
  }
  reader.Close();
}
```

We use `ExecuteNonQuery()` to send the INSERT command and then `ExecuteReader()` to read the Authors table and print out the new contents. The output is:

```
Number of rows affected: 1
1: Wibble, Zaphod Q
2: Asimov, Isaac
3: Dium, T
4: Moron, Oxy
5: Tolkien, J R R
```

Incidentally, if you try to run this program twice, you'll get an error on the second run, because AuthorKey is defined as a primary key for the Authors table, so attempting to insert the value 5 twice would violate the rule that primary keys have to be unique.

This problem illustrates that adding or modifying records in a database usually requires more care than simply querying existing data. We need to ensure that primary keys are unique, that relationships aren't violated and so on. These problems more properly belong in a textbook on databases, but we will illustrate some techniques when we consider some GUI applications later in this chapter.

11.8.3 ☐ Prepared statements

In addition to the three methods in `OleDbCommand` described above, there is a fourth method which is often useful when the actual parameter values that are to be passed to a command are not known at compile time. This is the `Prepare()` method.

The `Prepare()` method accepts an SQL command with one or more placeholders in it. Each placeholder is filled in with a parameter whose value can be changed during the course of the program. As an example, we will show a program which inserts a number of authors in the Authors table by reading in the author's name at a command prompt and then passing this name as a parameter to a prepared SQL statement. This program also illustrates one method by which we can ensure that the primary key is unique for each new record.

```
1. try
2. {
3.     oleConn.Open();
4.     string sql = "SELECT MAX(AuthorKey) FROM Authors";
5.     OleDbCommand maxCommand = new OleDbCommand(sql,
           oleConn);
6.     int authorKey = (int)maxCommand.ExecuteScalar();
7.
8.     OleDbCommand command = new OleDbCommand(null, oleConn);
9.     command.CommandText = "INSERT INTO Authors VALUES
           (?, ?)";
```

```
10.    command.Parameters.Add("authorKey", OleDbType.Integer);
11.    command.Parameters.Add("authorName", OleDbType.Char, 80);
12.    command.Prepare();
13.    do
14.    {
15.      Console.Write("Author's name: ");
16.      string authorName = Console.ReadLine();
17.      if (authorName.Equals("quit"))
18.        break;
19.      authorKey++;
20.      command.Parameters["authorKey"].Value = authorKey;
21.      command.Parameters["authorName"].Value = authorName;
22.      command.ExecuteNonQuery();
23.    } while (true);
24.
25.    sql = "SELECT * FROM Authors";
26.    command = new OleDbCommand(sql, oleConn);
27.    reader = command.ExecuteReader();
28.    while (reader.Read())
29.    {
30.      Console.WriteLine(reader.GetInt32(0) +
31.        ": " + reader.GetString(1));
32.    }
33.    reader.Close();
34. }
```

We can ensure that the primary key (AuthorKey) is unique by using SQL's
MAX function to retrieve the maximum AuthorKey currently in the database
(line 4). We store this in the int authorKey (line 6) and then increment this
value to provide an AuthorKey for each new author we add to the table.

To create a prepared statement, we begin by defining an OleDbCommand
with a null command string (line 8). We then assign its command text on
line 9, but notice that there are two ? symbols in the statement. These act
as placeholders for the actual values that will be inserted later.

In order to fill in these placeholders with real values later, we need to
define a parameter for each placeholder. This parameter must be an
instance of OleDbParameter. The Parameters property of the command
provides access to the OleDbParameterCollection, which is a list of
parameters that are attached to the command. The collection's Add()
method allows parameters to be added to this list, but we must ensure that
they are added in the same order that they occur in the CommandText.

We add the two parameters on lines 10 and 11. The first argument
("authorKey" on line 10, for example) to Add() specifies a name for the
parameter by which it can be referred to later.

The Add() method has a number of overloaded forms which allow parameters to be defined in various ways. However, for a prepared SQL statement,
we *must* use a version of Add() that allows the data type of the parameter

to be specified. This means that we must use one of the overloads of `Add()` that accepts an `OleDbType` parameter. `OleDbType` contains an `enum` list of the standard data types that are used in databases, so we should choose the `OleDbType` that matches the datatype for the parameter we are defining. In our case, the first parameter is for AuthorKey, which is an `int`, so we use the data type `OleDbType.Integer`. The second parameter, for the Name column, is a string, but if we look in the `OleDbType` documentation we will not find a 'String' type listed. However, we can use `Char` instead, as this maps to the String class.

The `Char` type represents a data type of variable size, and for such types we must also specify the maximum size allowed for a parameter of this type. This is given by the third parameter to `Add()` – here we specify a maximum of 80 characters.

When we have added the parameters to the collection, we call the `Prepare()` method on line 12. This essentially 'compiles' the `CommandText` so that parameter values can be passed to it, be incorporated into the SQL statement and then sent on to the database.

We see how this statement is used inside the loop on line 13. A prompt requests a name for the author to be added to the table. If the user enters 'quit' the loop is terminated.

On line 19, we increment `authorKey` to provide a unique AuthorKey primary key value. Then we set the values of the two parameters in the command. We use the parameter name that was specified in the call to `Add()` earlier, and access the parameter's `Value` property to assign a value to it.

When both parameters have had values assigned to them, we call `ExecuteNonQuery()` to run the INSERT SQL command.

The loop allows as many authors as required to be added, after which we use a SELECT statement to print out the new state of the Authors table (line 25).

A typical session with this program would look like this:

```
Author's name: Bradbury, Ray
Author's name: Herbert, Frank
Author's name: Jones, J V
Author's name: Goodkind, Terry
Author's name: quit
1: Wibble, Zaphod Q
2: Asimov, Isaac
3: Dium, T
4: Moron, Oxy
5: Tolkien, J R R
6: Bradbury, Ray
7: Herbert, Frank
8: Jones, J V
9: Goodkind, Terry
```

11.9 ■ DataSets

As we've seen, the data reader classes are easy to use for retrieving a result set from an SQL query, but restrictive in that they only allow us to traverse the list of records once by successively calling the Read() method. We cannot back up in the list and if we wish to run through the list more than once, we need to re-query the database to refresh the list.

.NET provides a much more powerful and flexible class for dealing with results sets, and indeed with data sets of any form: the DataSet class. A DataSet is essentially a database in its own right, in that it allows tables to be created within it, with each table containing its own set of columns and rows. A DataSet even allows relationships to be defined between tables, and constraints (such as primary keys) to be defined on one or more columns within each table.

We'll delve a bit more deeply into a DataSet's capabilities later, but we'll begin by illustrating its most common use: as a receptacle for the result set from a query to a 'real' database. The easiest way to illustrate the DataSet is with a brief example. Since it's been a while since we presented a complete program, and since there are a couple of changes required for using the DataSet outside the try block, we will present the complete program here. As with our earlier examples, the code assumes that the BookTest database is being used, and that all the data described earlier has been entered into the tables in that database.

We can load the entire contents of the Authors table into a DataSet and then print out the results to the console using the following code:

```
1. using System;
2. using System.Data;
3. using System.Data.OleDb;
4.
5. public class DataSetDemo
6. {
7.   public static void Main(string[] args)
8.   {
9.     string source;
10.     source = "Provider=Microsoft.Jet.OLEDB.4.0;" +
11.       @"Data Source=C:\Books\MyBooks\CSharpBook\
         BookTest.mdb";
12.
13.     OleDbConnection oleConn = new OleDbConnection(source);
14.     try
15.     {
16.       oleConn.Open();
17.       string sql = "SELECT * FROM Authors";
18.       OleDbDataAdapter command =
19.         new OleDbDataAdapter(sql, oleConn);
```

```
20.        DataSet dataSet = new DataSet();
21.        command.Fill(dataSet, "AuthorInfo");
22.        foreach (DataRow row in dataSet.Tables[0].Rows)
23.        {
24.           Console.WriteLine(row[0] + " - " + row[1]);
25.        }
26.        Console.WriteLine("\nEntries in reverse order:");
27.        for (int i = dataSet.Tables["AuthorInfo"]
           .Rows.Count - 1;
28.           i >= 0; i--)
29.        {
30.           DataRow row = dataSet.Tables["AuthorInfo"].Rows[i];
31.           Console.WriteLine(row["AuthorKey"] + ": "
32.              + row["Name"]);
33.        }
34.     }
35.     catch (Exception ex)
36.     {
37.        Console.WriteLine(ex.ToString());
38.     }
39.     finally
40.     {
41.        oleConn.Close();
42.     }
43.   }
44. }
```

Since `DataSet` is in the `System.Data` namespace, we need to add a new `using` statement (line 2). Also, since some of the base classes referenced from `DataSet` rely on XML, we need to add a reference to `System.XML` in the references list (either in Visual Studio's project, or in the command line for the compiler).

As with the examples in the last section, we are using the Access database to illustrate, but the example will work with SQL Server as well if the connection string on lines 10 and 11 is changed.

After opening the database (line 16) and defining the SQL statement (line 17), we must create (line 18) an `OleDbDataAdapter` to provide the interface between the database and the `DataSet`. Note that this line replaces the creation of the `OleDbCommand` that we used in our earlier examples, since the data adapter will handle the transmission of the SQL command to the database and the retrieval of the result set.

Next, we create the `DataSet` (line 20). Although the contents of the `DataSet` can be defined by hand (by writing code to define the tables and their columns), the easiest way to use a `DataSet` to retrieve a result set from a query is to use the `Fill()` method from `OleDbDataAdapter` (line 21). `Fill()` takes two parameters: the first is the `DataSet` to fill, and the second is the name of the table that should be created to hold the records returned from the query. Although this name is usually the same as the table from which the query is made, it need not be, and in this example we have deliberately given the table a different name ('AuthorInfo') from the table in the database.

The `Fill()` method loads the results of the query into the `DataSet`'s AuthorInfo table, in the process creating enough columns in the table to store the data fields in the result set. The names of these columns will be taken from their names in the database, so in this case, the `DataSet` will have two columns named 'AuthorKey' and 'Name'. We will see later that if we wish to change these names it is easy enough to do so. In most cases, to avoid confusion we will want to keep the same names, but sometimes the column names in the database are fairly cryptic and if we want to use the `DataSet` to display the data to the user, it is handy to be able to provide more user-friendly column titles.

Once we have filled the `DataSet` with the result set from the database, the `DataSet` becomes a totally independent repository of that data. We could, for example, close the connection to the database after the `Fill()` method is called and then deal with the `DataSet` off-line. This also means that any changes made to the `DataSet` have no effect on the data in the original database, although it is possible to write back any changes to the database if we wish to.

As we mentioned above, a `DataSet` has its own set of tables, each of which has its own set of columns. The `DataSet` class has a number of properties that allow easy access to these internal components. We'll explore the details in the next section, but the code in the current example shows a couple of methods.

We list the contents of the `DataSet` in two ways to show the flexibility of the interface. On line 22, we use a `foreach` loop to iterate through the set of `Rows` in the AuthorInfo table. Each `DataSet` has a `Tables` property which is an array of the tables that have been added to the `DataSet`. Each element with `Tables` is a `DataTable` object, and can be referenced by its index number as we do on line 22, or by the name of the table, as we do on line 27. Although a `DataSet` can hold any number of `DataTables`, the `Fill()` method is only capable of filling one table at a time. We could produce a complete replica of the BookTest database within a `DataSet` by adding another couple of tables named Books and AuthorBook to the `DataSet` and then calling `Fill()` for these two tables.

A `DataTable` has a `Rows` property, which is an array of the records in the table, each of which is a `DataRow` object. A `DataRow` is an array of `objects`, each element of which is one data field from the record. Each element within `Rows` can be referenced by its index number as on line 24, or by the name of the column it belongs to, as on lines 31 and 32.

The loop on line 22 iterates through the `DataRows` in ascending order, and just to illustrate that the data in a `DataSet` can be accessed in any order, we list the data in reverse order in the loop on line 27. The output from the program is (assuming that the example at the end of the last section that adds several new authors to the database has been run):

```
1 - Wibble, Zaphod Q
2 - Asimov, Isaac
3 - Dium, T
4 - Moron, Oxy
5 - Tolkien, J R R
6 - Bradbury, Ray
7 - Herbert, Frank
8 - Jones, J V
9 - Goodkind, Terry

Entries in reverse order:
9: Goodkind, Terry
8: Jones, J V
7: Herbert, Frank
6: Bradbury, Ray
5: Tolkien, J R R
4: Moron, Oxy
3: Dium, T
2: Asimov, Isaac
1: Wibble, Zaphod Q
```

To change the column names, we can insert the following code *after* the `Fill()` statement on line 21:

```
dataSet.Tables[0].Columns[0].ColumnName = "Primary Key";
dataSet.Tables[0].Columns[1].ColumnName = "Author's name";
```

It is important to change the column names after filling the `DataSet`, since the `Fill()` method tries to match the existing column names to the column names in the database table. If we change the `DataSet`'s column names before filling it, the two columns will be ignored and two new columns will be added to the table with the names from the database's Authors table.

It is possible to build a 'hand made' `DataSet` by specifying the tables it should contain and defining the contents of each of these tables in code, but for our purposes in this book we will not need this level of control over a `DataSet`. However, there are several examples in the MSDN documentation and on the web if you wish to do it yourself. It is worth pointing out that although a `DataSet` is most often used to store a result set from a database query, it can also store data obtained from any source. We can read data in from a text file or even specify the data within the C# code and build an 'internal' database inside the program using a `DataSet`.

11.10 ■ **Databases and Windows Forms: `DataGrids`**

We've seen that a `DataSet` is a powerful class for representing data retrieved from a database, but it really comes into its own when used together with a `DataGrid` in a Windows program.

The `DataGrid` is a Windows Form control which displays data in a tabular form similar to that in a spreadsheet. We will illustrate the use of a `DataGrid` by loading the Authors table from BookTest into one and then using it as an interface for adding, deleting and modifying records in the original database.

The main interface to the DataGridDemo program is as shown in Figure 11.1. The `DataGrid` occupies the main display and contains two columns showing the data from the Authors table. Each cell in this grid is editable. At the bottom there is a button which when pressed transmits any changes in the data back to the original Access database.

The `DataGrid` actually displays data from a `DataSet`, and does not itself have a direct link to the original database except through this `DataSet`. Thus any changes made to the `DataGrid` affect only the data stored in the `DataSet`, which we must remember is only a copy of the data from the database. Pressing the 'Update' button causes the data from the `DataSet` to be sent back to the original database using SQL commands.

(Incidentally, you may come across some books that use terms such as 'persisting the data' when talking about saving data back to the database. I do not wish to contribute to the breakdown in English grammar that seems to be emerging from the computing community – 'persist' is an intransitive verb (look it up!), so it is correct to say that something can persist, but it is not correct to say that something can be persisted. And let's not even mention 'leveraging'…)

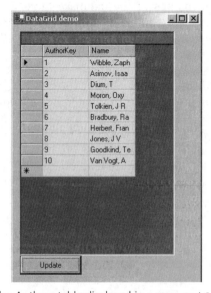

Figure 11.1 Data in the Authors table displayed in a `DataGrid`

The initial interface of the program shows the entries from the Authors table that are there following our sample code from earlier in this chapter. The DataGrid uses a default width for all columns, which as you can see from the figure gives too much space to AuthorKey and not enough to Name, but this can be corrected in the code, which we will do later. For now we want to concentrate on the interaction between the DataGrid, DataSet and the original database. (The columns can be resized by dragging their boundaries with the mouse anyway.)

This interface is used much like that in an ordinary database table – the individual text cells are all editable, so the user can make changes to existing database records just by clicking in the cell and typing. New records can be added at the bottom by clicking in the line with a * at the left.

The code for this program is as follows:

```
1. using System;
2. using System.Data;
3. using System.Data.OleDb;
4. using System.Drawing;
5. using System.Windows.Forms;
6.
7. class DataGridDemo : Form
8. {
9.     DataGrid dataGrid;
10.    Button updateButton;
11.    DataSet dataSet;
12.    OleDbDataAdapter adapter;
13.    OleDbCommandBuilder builder;
14.    OleDbConnection oleConn;
15.
16.    public DataGridDemo()
17.    {
18.      InitializeComponents();
19.    }
20.
21.    public void InitializeComponents()
22.    {
23.      ClientSize = new Size(300, 400);
24.      Text = "DataGrid demo";
25.
26.      dataGrid = new DataGrid();
27.      dataGrid.Bounds = new Rectangle(10, 10, 250, 350);
28.
29.      updateButton = new Button();
30.      updateButton.Bounds = new Rectangle(10, 360, 100, 30);
31.      updateButton.Text = "Update";
32.      updateButton.Click += new EventHandler(OnUpdate);
```

```
33.      Controls.Add(updateButton);
34.
35.      InitializeDatabase();
36.      Controls.Add(dataGrid);
37.
38.      Rectangle screenSize = Screen.GetWorkingArea(this);
39.      Location =
40.        new Point(screenSize.Width/2 - Size.Width/2,
41.        screenSize.Height/2 - Size.Height/2);
42.    }
43.
44.    private void InitializeDatabase()
45.    {
46.      string source = "Provider=Microsoft.Jet.OLEDB.4.0;" +
47.        @"Data Source=C:\Books\MyBooks\CSharpBook\
         BookTest.mdb";
48.      oleConn = new OleDbConnection(source);
49.
50.      string sql;
51.      try
52.      {
53.        oleConn.Open();
54.        sql = "SELECT MAX(AuthorKey) FROM Authors";
55.        OleDbCommand command = new OleDbCommand(sql, oleConn);
56.        int maxKey = (int)command.ExecuteScalar();
57.        sql = "SELECT * FROM Authors";
58.        adapter = new OleDbDataAdapter(sql, oleConn);
59.        builder = new OleDbCommandBuilder(adapter);
60.        dataSet = new DataSet();
61.        adapter.Fill(dataSet, "Authors");
62.        dataSet.Tables["Authors"].PrimaryKey =
63.          new DataColumn[]
64.          {dataSet.Tables["Authors"].Columns["AuthorKey"]};
65.        dataSet.Tables["Authors"].Columns["AuthorKey"].
66.          AutoIncrement = true;
67.        dataSet.Tables["Authors"].Columns["AuthorKey"].
68.          AutoIncrementSeed = maxKey + 1;
69.
70.        dataGrid.SetDataBinding(dataSet, "Authors");
71.      }
72.      catch (Exception ex)
73.      {
74.        Console.WriteLine(ex.ToString());
75.      }
76.      finally
77.      {
```

```
78.        oleConn.Close();
79.    }
80.  }
81.
82.    private void OnUpdate( object sender, EventArgs e )
83.    {
84.      if(dataSet.HasChanges())
85.      {
86.        adapter.Update(dataSet, "Authors");
87.        dataSet.AcceptChanges();
88.      }
89.    }
90.
91.    public static void Main(string[] args)
92.    {
93.        Application.Run(new DataGridDemo());
94.    }
95. }
```

Most of the code in `InitializeComponents()` should be fairly obvious as it sets up the controls on the form in the same way as we did in Chapter 9. A `DataGrid` is just like any other control in this respect – we create it and give it its bounds on lines 26 and 27.

The `InitializeDatabase()` method (line 44) contains a few new features. We use the same Access database that we have used for earlier examples. After opening the database connection (line 53), we find the maximum AuthorKey using the SQL MAX() function (lines 54 to 56). This value will be used later for assigning AuthorKeys to new entries.

Since we will be loading the data into a `DataSet`, we create an `OleDbDataAdapter` on line 58. The next line introduces a `OleDbCommandBuilder`, which is a very handy class, but its use requires a little explanation.

One feature of the adapter classes that we have not yet mentioned is that they have four properties which can contain SQL statements for querying, inserting, updating and deleting records from the database to which the adapter is connected. The four corresponding properties in the `OleDbData Adapter` class (and the other adapter classes as well) are `SelectCommand`, `InsertCommand`, `UpdateCommand`, and `DeleteCommand`. When we pass the SQL string to the `OleDbDataAdapter` constructor on line 58, we are in fact initializing the `SelectCommand` property, but the other three commands are not initialized by default.

The remaining three commands are used by the adapter whenever we wish to write changes *back* to the database. If all we want to do is just view the current contents of the database, then there is no need to provide any values for these three commands, which is the default behaviour. However, in this example, we wish to use the `DataGrid` to allow the user to make changes to the database, so we will need these commands.

The main difference between a `SelectCommand` and the other three commands is that when we wish to change something in the database, we won't know in advance which records will be affected by the changes. For example, if we wish to insert a new author into the Authors table, we don't know what that author's name will be when the program is compiled, so obviously we can't program the name into the code.

We have seen earlier that it is possible to define prepared statements in which we can leave some placeholders that can be filled in later, and this is, in fact, the approach taken with these three command properties of an adapter. However, defining an appropriate command statement isn't quite as simple as just providing an SQL statement with a few placeholders in it – we actually need to do a fair number of other chores to set everything up properly. Although it is possible to do this ourselves, it is much easier to use a command builder class such as `OleDbCommandBuilder` to do it for us.

A command builder deduces the forms of the other three command statements by examining the form of `SelectCommand`. If we want to see what commands it generates, this can be done by retrieving the `CommandText` property for each command. We can insert the following code after line 59, for example:

```
Console.WriteLine(builder.GetInsertCommand().CommandText
    + "\n");
Console.WriteLine(builder.GetUpdateCommand().CommandText
    + "\n");
Console.WriteLine(builder.GetDeleteCommand().CommandText);
```

This produces the output:

```
INSERT INTO Authors( AuthorKey , Name ) VALUES ( ? , ? )

UPDATE Authors SET AuthorKey = ? , Name = ? WHERE
( (AuthorKey = ?) AND ((? IS NULL AND Name IS NULL) OR
(Name = ?)) )

DELETE FROM  Authors WHERE ( (AuthorKey = ?) AND ((? IS
NULL AND Name IS NULL) OR (Name = ?)) )
```

The structure of these statements is deduced from the original `SelectCommand` that we provided in the program (line 57):

```
SELECT * FROM Authors
```

The * wildcard has been expanded by connecting to the database, and thus the command builder knows that Authors has two columns named AuthorKey and Name. From this it constructs the commands for inserting, updating and deleting a record from the Authors table.

The `InsertCommand` has two placeholders that are filled in by the two values entered into the `DataGrid` by the user (as we will see below).

The other two commands refer to existing records in the table, and so need a way of identifying which record is to be changed. The `UpdateCommand`, for example, sets AuthorKey and Name to two new values, but to identify the correct record to alter, the *previous* values of these two fields are used (a `DataSet` actually stores both the old and new values for any changed records to allow this comparison to take place). The WHERE clause therefore first matches the *old* values of AuthorKey and Name to locate the correct record. The section of this clause that checks the condition

```
((? IS NULL AND Name IS NULL) OR (Name = ?))
```

allows for the case where Name is NULL (that is, there is no entry in the Name field), *or* where Name has a given value. The same check is not done for AuthorKey, since AuthorKey is identified in the database as a primary key, and keys cannot be NULL. The same conditions are checked for the `DeleteCommand`.

The handy thing about a command builder is that it not only constructs these commands automatically, but also takes care of all the other chores that are required to set them up. As we will see a bit later, all that is required to transfer changes from a `DataSet` back to the original database is that the `Update()` method is called from the adapter – the command builder provides all the relevant SQL statements to do the updating.

After creating the adapter and builder, we create and fill the `DataSet` (lines 60 and 61). Lines 62 to 68 illustrate how to set some of the properties of a `DataSet` to make data entry a bit easier. A `DataSet` is able to mimic most of the features of a 'real' database, including the definition of primary keys, relationships and so on. On line 62, for example, we define a primary key for the Authors table within the `DataSet` so that it matches the primary key in the database. The `PrimaryKey` property may be set for a `DataTable`, and must be an *array* of `DataColumns`, since in general, a primary key can be one or more columns in a table. In this case, the primary key is only one column, so we just create it by defining an array dynamically. For a table such as AuthorBook, where two columns jointly define the primary key, we would create an array containing both columns.

Setting the `PrimaryKey` property for a table has the same effect in a `DataSet` as in a database – the `DataSet` will require that all primary keys are unique. If this condition is violated during data entry into a `DataGrid` a message box pops up informing the user of the error and offering a chance to fix it.

Line 65 declares the AuthorKey column to be an AutoIncrement column. This means that each time we create a new record in the `DataGrid`, the value of AuthorKey is set automatically to one more than the last value. The `AutoIncrementSeed` property (line 67) specifies the value at which AuthorKey should begin. We use the maxKey value we determined earlier (line 56) to start the autoincrementing off at a value one greater than the largest existing AuthorKey.

We can set other properties of the `DataSet` if we require – just refer to the MSDN documentation to see what is available. Once the `DataSet` is set up, we can *bind* it to the `DataGrid` by calling `SetDataBinding()` (line 70). A `DataGrid` can only display one table at a time (recall that a `DataSet` can store multiple tables) so the second parameter of `SetDataBinding()` is the name of the table we wish to display.

This completes the initial setup of the interface. The user can now insert new authors and change or delete existing ones as often as required. The code to handle all these changes is internal to the `DataGrid` and need not concern us here. What is important to remember is that the `DataGrid` communicates all these changes to the `DataSet` to which it is bound, and the `DataSet` will keep track of the states of all the rows. In particular, it tags each row with a label such as 'Added', 'Deleted', and so on.

When the user is happy with the changes that have been made in the `DataGrid`, the 'Update' button is pressed, which calls the `OnUpdate()` event handler (line 82). We first test the `dataSet` to see if any changes have been made (line 84) and, if so, call `Update()` to transmit these changes to the database. This is done by the adapter, which in turn uses the various commands that were created for it by the command builder earlier. The adapter tests each row in the `DataSet` to see if it has changed, and if so, it examines the tag for that row to see what type of change has occurred. If a row is new (that is, it wasn't in the original database), it will be marked as 'Added' so the `InsertCommand` will be run to insert a new record into the database. Similarly, if a row was deleted, it will be tagged as 'Deleted' and the `DeleteCommand` is run to remove it from the database.

After all the changes have been saved to the database, we call `Accept Changes()` (line 87) on the `DataSet`. This clears all the tags on the `DataSet`'s rows, so that the `DataSet` will be reset to the 'unchanged' state. Further modifications in the `DataGrid` will then start from that point, and only further changes will be updated the next time the 'Update' button is pressed.

If the `DataSet` contains a large number of records, the time taken to do an update can be reduced by using the `GetChanges()` method to obtain a second `DataSet` that contains only rows from the original `DataSet` that have changed since the last update. In this case, we could write instead of lines 86 and 87:

```
DataSet changeSet = dataSet.GetChanges();
adapter.Update(changeSet, "Authors");
dataSet.Merge(changeSet);
dataSet.AcceptChanges();
```

To complete the program, a test for any unsaved changes should be made when the program is shut down, and the user given the chance to save these changes.

The `DataSet`–`DataGrid` combination is an elegant system for interacting with a database in a GUI environment, and can do much more than we have space to cover here. If you want to explore further, have a look at the MSDN documentation for the various classes involved, or consult a specialized book on databases in .NET.

11.11 ■ More with `DataGrid`s and `DataSet`s

We've seen in the last section a few of the basic things that we can do using a `DataGrid` to display a `DataSet`. There is a great deal more that can be done using `DataSet`s and `DataGrid`s, so we will present another example in this section that illustrates a few of these features.

First, let's consider a problem with the simple example in the previous section. We saw how to display a `DataGrid` that allowed the user to add new records to the Authors table in the main database. We did not, however, consider adding a new book to the Books table. If we recall the structure of the BookTest database from earlier in this chapter, we will notice that adding a book to the database requires making an entry in the Books table, but also adding a new record to the AuthorBook link table for each author of the book.

In principle, this is easy enough to do, but from a GUI perspective, we need a way to present a list of authors to the user from which a selection can be made, and then we need to link this selection to the new record in the Books table to produce the entries in the AuthorBook table.

In this example program, we do this by using a `CheckedListBox` to provide a list of authors, and a `DataGrid` in which the user can type the title and number of pages of the new book. Along the way we will get some experience with a few more Windows Forms controls. The interface is as shown in Figure 11.2.

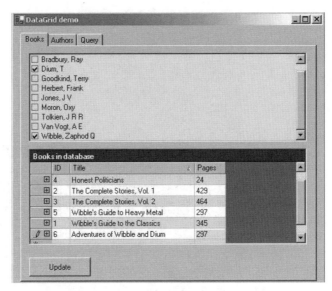

Figure 11.2 Form for adding a book to the database

The main interface uses a `TabControl` with three tabs. The first is the one shown in the figure which allows the user to add a new book to the database. The second tab allows the Authors table to be edited (Figure 11.3).

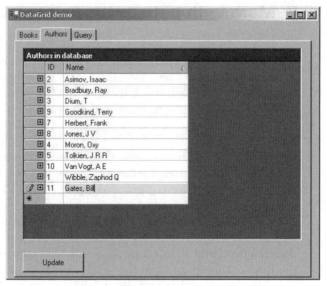

Figure 11.3 Form for editing authors in the database

The final tab allows the user to query the database and get a list of all books by a given author (Figure 11.4).

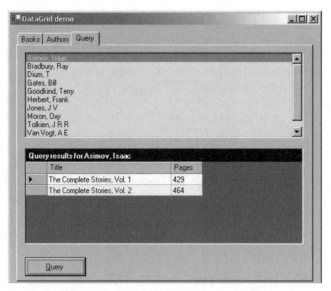

Figure 11.4 Form for obtaining a list of books by a given author

We have also formatted the DataGrids by giving them titles, defining some widths for the columns, changed the column headers, and provided contrasting colours for alternating rows in the table.

The complete code for this program is a fair bit longer than the sample programs we have used so far, so we will break the code up into sections and deal with each in turn.

We begin with the using statements and class declarations:

```
1. using System;
2. using System.Data;
3. using System.Data.OleDb;
4. using System.Drawing;
5. using System.Windows.Forms;
6.
7. class BookDB : Form
8. {
9.    DataGrid authorGrid, bookGrid, queryGrid;
10.   TabControl tabControl;
11.   TabPage bookPage, authorPage, queryPage;
12.   CheckedListBox authorList;
13.   ListBox authorQueryList;
14.   Button updateAuthorsButton, updateBooksButton, queryButton;
15.   DataSet dataSet;
16.   OleDbDataAdapter authors, books, AuthorBook;
17.   OleDbCommandBuilder authorBuilder, bookBuilder,
18.      AuthorBookBuilder;
19.   OleDbConnection oleConn;
20.
21.   public BookDB()
22.   {
23.      InitializeComponents();
24.   }
25.
26.   #region Initializations
27.   public void InitializeComponents()
28.   {
29.      ClientSize = new Size(500, 400);
30.      Text = "DataGrid demo";
31.
32.      tabControl = new TabControl();
33.      tabControl.Bounds = new Rectangle(10, 10, 480, 390);
34.      Controls.Add(tabControl);
35.      InitializeBookPage();
36.      InitializeAuthorPage();
37.      InitializeQueryPage();
38.      InitializeDatabase();
39.      SetupGridStyles();
40.
```

```
41.       Rectangle screenSize = Screen.GetWorkingArea(this);
42.       Location = new Point(screenSize.Width/2 - Size.Width/2,
43.          screenSize.Height/2 - Size.Height/2);
44.    }
```

This section of code just sets up the various Windows Forms controls that are needed in the GUI on lines 9 to 14, and then the database objects on lines 15 to 19. The constructor (line 21) calls `InitializeComponents()` (line 27) which in turn calls a number of other methods to set up the tab pages and database connections.

The three methods that set up the tab pages are as follows:

```
1. private void InitializeAuthorPage()
2. {
3.    authorPage = new TabPage("Authors");
4.    tabControl.TabPages.Add(authorPage);
5.    updateAuthorsButton = new Button();
6.    updateAuthorsButton.Text = "Update";
7.    updateAuthorsButton.Bounds =
8.       new Rectangle(10, 330, 100, 30);
9.    updateAuthorsButton.Click += new EventHandler(OnUpdate);
10.   authorPage.Controls.Add(updateAuthorsButton);
11.
12.   authorGrid = new DataGrid();
13.   authorGrid.Bounds = new Rectangle(10, 10, 450, 300);
14.   authorGrid.CaptionText = "Authors in database";
15.   authorGrid.CaptionBackColor = Color.DarkGreen;
16.   authorPage.Controls.Add(authorGrid);
17. }
18.
19. private void InitializeBookPage()
20. {
21.   bookPage = new TabPage("Books");
22.   tabControl.TabPages.Add(bookPage);
23.
24.   updateBooksButton = new Button();
25.   updateBooksButton.Text = "Update";
26.   updateBooksButton.Bounds = new Rectangle(10,
         330, 100, 30);
27.   updateBooksButton.Click += new EventHandler(OnBooksUpdate);
28.   bookPage.Controls.Add(updateBooksButton);
29.
30.   authorList = new CheckedListBox();
31.   authorList.Bounds = new Rectangle(10, 10, 450, 140);
32.   authorList.CheckOnClick = true;
33.   bookPage.Controls.Add(authorList);
34.
```

```
35.     bookGrid = new DataGrid();
36.     bookGrid.Bounds = new Rectangle(10, 160, 450, 150);
37.     bookGrid.CaptionText = "Books in database";
38.     bookGrid.CaptionBackColor = Color.DarkRed;
39.     bookPage.Controls.Add(bookGrid);
40. }
41.
42. private void InitializeQueryPage()
43. {
44.     queryPage = new TabPage("Query");
45.     tabControl.TabPages.Add(queryPage);
46.     queryButton = new Button();
47.     queryButton.Text = "&Query";
48.     queryButton.Bounds = new Rectangle(10, 330, 100, 30);
49.     queryButton.Click += new EventHandler(OnQuery);
50.     queryPage.Controls.Add(queryButton);
51.
52.     authorQueryList = new ListBox();
53.     authorQueryList.Bounds = new Rectangle(10, 10, 450, 140);
54.     queryPage.Controls.Add(authorQueryList);
55.
56.     queryGrid = new DataGrid();
57.     queryGrid.Bounds = new Rectangle(10, 160, 450, 150);
58.     queryGrid.CaptionBackColor = Color.DarkBlue;
59.     queryGrid.ReadOnly = true;
60.     queryPage.Controls.Add(queryGrid);
61. }
```

The Authors tab page defines the `Button` and `DataGrid`, attaches an event handler to the `Button` (line 9) and sets a couple of display properties for the `DataGrid` (lines 14 and 15).

The Books tab page is set up in a similar way (line 19). The `Button`, `CheckedListBox` and `DataGrid` are initialized and added to the page.

Finally, the Query page is set up on line 42. The author list here is displayed using an ordinary `ListBox`, and the results of the query are displayed using another `DataGrid`.

These three methods all just set up the appearance of the program. The actual database connections are done in `InitializeDatabase()`:

```
1. private void InitializeDatabase()
2. {
3.     string source = "Provider=Microsoft.Jet.OLEDB.4.0;" +
4.         @"Data Source=C:\Books\MyBooks\CSharpBook\
            BookTest.mdb";
5.     oleConn = new OleDbConnection(source);
6.
7.     string sql;
```

```
8.    try
9.    {
10.     oleConn.Open();
11.     sql = "SELECT MAX(AuthorKey) FROM Authors";
12.     OleDbCommand command = new OleDbCommand(sql, oleConn);
13.     int maxAuthorKey = (int)command.ExecuteScalar();
14.     sql = "SELECT * FROM Authors";
15.     authors = new OleDbDataAdapter(sql, oleConn);
16.     authorBuilder = new OleDbCommandBuilder(authors);
17.     dataSet = new DataSet();
18.     authors.Fill(dataSet, "Authors");
19.
20.     dataSet.Tables["Authors"].PrimaryKey =
21.       new DataColumn[]
22.       {dataSet.Tables["Authors"].Columns["AuthorKey"]};
23.     dataSet.Tables["Authors"].Columns["AuthorKey"].
24.       AutoIncrement = true;
25.     dataSet.Tables["Authors"].Columns["AuthorKey"].
26.       AutoIncrementSeed = maxAuthorKey + 1;
27.
28.     sql = "SELECT MAX(BookKey) FROM Books";
29.     command = new OleDbCommand(sql, oleConn);
30.     int maxBookKey = (int)command.ExecuteScalar();
31.     sql = "SELECT * FROM Books";
32.     books = new OleDbDataAdapter(sql, oleConn);
33.     bookBuilder = new OleDbCommandBuilder(books);
34.     books.Fill(dataSet, "Books");
35.      dataSet.Tables["Books"].PrimaryKey =
36.       new DataColumn[]
37.       {dataSet.Tables["Books"].Columns["BookKey"]};
38.     dataSet.Tables["Books"].Columns["BookKey"].
        AutoIncrement =
39.       true;
40.     dataSet.Tables["Books"].Columns["BookKey"].
41.       AutoIncrementSeed = maxBookKey + 1;
42.
43.     sql = "SELECT * FROM AuthorBook";
44.     AuthorBook = new OleDbDataAdapter(sql, oleConn);
45.     AuthorBookBuilder = new OleDbCommandBuilder(AuthorBook);
46.     AuthorBook.Fill(dataSet, "AuthorBook");
47.     dataSet.Tables["AuthorBook"].PrimaryKey =
48.       new DataColumn[]
49.       {
50.         dataSet.Tables["AuthorBook"].Columns["AuthorKey"],
51.         dataSet.Tables["AuthorBook"].Columns["BookKey"]
52.       };
```

```
53.
54.     dataSet.Relations.Add("AuthorLink",
55.        dataSet.Tables["Authors"].Columns["AuthorKey"],
56.        dataSet.Tables["AuthorBook"].Columns["AuthorKey"]);
57.     dataSet.Relations.Add("BookLink",
58.        dataSet.Tables["Books"].Columns["BookKey"],
59.        dataSet.Tables["AuthorBook"].Columns["BookKey"]);
60.     dataSet.EnforceConstraints = true;
61.
62.     DataViewManager dataViewManager =
63.        new DataViewManager(dataSet);
64.     dataViewManager.DataViewSettings["Authors"]
        .Sort = "Name";
65.     dataViewManager.DataViewSettings["Books"].Sort = "Title";
66.     authorGrid.SetDataBinding(dataViewManager, "Authors");
67.     bookGrid.SetDataBinding(dataViewManager, "Books");
68.
69.     dataSet.Tables["Authors"].DefaultView.Sort = "Name";
70.     authorList.DataSource =
71.        dataSet.Tables["Authors"].DefaultView;
72.     authorList.DisplayMember = "Name";
73.     authorList.ValueMember = "AuthorKey";
74.     authorQueryList.DataSource =
75.        dataSet.Tables["Authors"].DefaultView;
76.     authorQueryList.DisplayMember = "Name";
77.     authorQueryList.ValueMember = "AuthorKey";
78.  }
79.  catch (Exception ex)
80.  {
81.     Console.WriteLine(ex.ToString());
82.  }
83.  finally
84.  {
85.     oleConn.Close();
86.  }
87. }
```

This method provides links between the database and all the DataGrids and lists that display information from the database. We use the same technique as earlier to determine a primary key value for adding a new author – we use an SQL MAX command to determine the largest AuthorKey currently in the database (line 11) and then create a local parameter maxAuthorKey which can be used to generate a new key value.

On lines 14 to 18, we create a DataSet and fill it with the contents of the Authors table. We'll connect this DataSet to the DataGrid (authorGrid) later. First, we set up a few properties of this DataSet on lines 20 to 26, by defining a primary key for it and turning on AutoIncrement for this key value in the Authors table. The Books DataGrid is set up in a similar way on lines 28 to 41.

On lines 43 to 52, we set up the AuthorBook table within the DataSet, which seems unnecessary since we don't actually display its contents anywhere in the program. However, if we load this table into the DataSet it is then possible to duplicate the structure of the original database within the DataSet, which allows us to define relationships between the tables in the DataSet that mirror those in the database.

We do this on lines 54 to 60 by adding a couple of relationships to the Relations property of the DataSet. Each relationship consists of a name (as a string) followed by the column that is to be the parent of the relationship, and then the column that is the child in the relationship. For example, on line 54 we create a relation between the AuthorKey column in the Authors table and the AuthorKey column in the AuthorBook table. We'll see what these relations can be used for a bit later. On line 60, we set EnforceConstraints to 'true' to force the DataSet to enforce these relationships in any changes that are applied to the DataSet by the user.

Although we could bind a DataGrid directly to a DataSet as we did in the simpler example in the last section, we can provide more control over what data is displayed in a DataGrid by first attaching a DataView to the DataSet. A DataView contains a number of properties that allow the data in a DataSet to be *filtered* (in much the same way as with a WHERE clause in SQL) and sorted.

Each table in a DataSet has a DefaultView property which is a DataView object that can be assigned properties to specify filters or sorting procedures for that table. For example, on line 69 we specify that the records in the Authors table should be sorted according to the data in the Name column. It is possible to sort on two or more columns by giving a list of columns in the Sort property. We can also specify ascending or descending sorts by using the keywords ASC and DESC. For example, we could specify that the Books table be sorted primarily in ascending order by title and then secondarily in descending order by number of pages by saying:

```
dataSet.Tables["Books"].DefaultView.Sort =
    "Title ASC, NumberOfPages DESC";
```

Filters can be applied using the RowFilter property in a DataView. Most of the simple SQL expressions that work in a WHERE clause will work here as well. For example, we could specify that only books with more than 200 pages should be included by saying:

```
dataSet.Tables["Books"].DefaultView.RowFilter =
    "NumberOfPages > 200";
```

Filtering is also possible on the *state* of a row rather than its contents by using the RowStateFilter property. The state is determined by whether the row has just been added, modified or deleted. The set of possible states is

defined as an enum in the DataViewRowState class and further documentation can be found there. We can for example, list only those rows that have
just been added by saying:

```
dataSet.Tables["Books"].DefaultView.RowStateFilter =
   DataViewRowState.Added;
```

We can unify the DataViews for a DataSet under a common roof by cre-
ating a DataViewManager for that DataSet, as we do on line 62. A
DataViewManager allows properties to be set up for each table in the
DataSet that it manages by using the DataViewSettings property. For
example, on lines 64 and 65 we define the sorting order for the Authors and
Books tables within the DataSet.

Curiously, a DataViewManager only works if the data is subsequently displayed in a DataGrid, and not if the data is displayed in other controls such
as a ListBox. It is for this reason that we have defined both a
DataViewManager *and* set the DefaultView property for the Authors table
in the code here. Setting only the DataViewManager would not sort the data
that appears in the ListBox or CheckedListBox.

Once we have set up the properties of the data that we wish to display, we
need to connect the DataView or DataViewManager with the GUI control
that will display the data. For a DataGrid, we use SetDataBinding() as in
our earlier example (lines 66 and 67). Note that we bind authorGrid and
bookGrid to the DataViewManager rather than directly to the DataSet. This
allows the sorting and filtering properties defined within the manager to be
displayed in the DataGrids.

Since DataViewManagers don't work with controls other than DataGrid,
we must bind the CheckedListBox and ListBox to the DefaultView within the Authors table. For example, on lines 70 to 73, we set the DataSource
for the authorList (which is the CheckedListBox that displays the authors
on the Books tab) to the DefaultView in the Authors table. We specify
which column the list should display by setting the DisplayMember property (line 72). We can, however, tell the list to store a different column as the
value of a given item by setting its ValueMember, which we do on line 73. If
we then retrieve the value of a selected item later, we will get back the
AuthorKey (which is not displayed on screen) rather than the Name, which
is displayed. The ListBox used for listing the authors on the Query tab is
set up in a similar way (lines 74 to 77).

Before we consider the event handlers, we will show how to set up the
properties of the columns and rows displayed within a DataGrid. This is
done in the SetupGridStyles() method:

```
1. private void SetupGridStyles()
2. {
3.    DataGridTableStyle style = new DataGridTableStyle();
4.    style.MappingName = "Books";
5.    style.BackColor = Color.White;
6.    style.AlternatingBackColor = Color.PeachPuff;
```

```
7.     DataGridTextBoxColumn[] bookColumns =
8.        new DataGridTextBoxColumn[3];
9.     bookColumns[0] = new DataGridTextBoxColumn();
10.    bookColumns[0].HeaderText = "ID";
11.    bookColumns[0].MappingName = "BookKey";
12.    bookColumns[0].Width = 30;
13.    bookColumns[1] = new DataGridTextBoxColumn();
14.    bookColumns[1].HeaderText = "Title";
15.    bookColumns[1].MappingName = "Title";
16.    bookColumns[1].Width = 200;
17.    bookColumns[2] = new DataGridTextBoxColumn();
18.    bookColumns[2].HeaderText = "Pages";
19.    bookColumns[2].MappingName = "NumberOfPages";
20.    bookColumns[2].Width = 50;
21.    style.GridColumnStyles.AddRange(bookColumns);
22.    bookGrid.TableStyles.Add(style);
23.
24.    style = new DataGridTableStyle();
25.    style.MappingName = "Authors";
26.    style.BackColor = Color.White;
27.    style.AlternatingBackColor = Color.Honeydew;
28.    DataGridTextBoxColumn[] authorColumns =
29.       new DataGridTextBoxColumn[2];
30.    authorColumns[0] = new DataGridTextBoxColumn();
31.    authorColumns[0].HeaderText = "ID";
32.    authorColumns[0].MappingName = "AuthorKey";
33.    authorColumns[0].Width = 30;
34.    authorColumns[1] = new DataGridTextBoxColumn();
35.    authorColumns[1].HeaderText = "Name";
36.    authorColumns[1].MappingName = "Name";
37.    authorColumns[1].Width = 200;
38.    style.GridColumnStyles.AddRange(authorColumns);
39.    authorGrid.TableStyles.Add(style);
40.
41.    style = new DataGridTableStyle();
42.    style.MappingName = "Query";
43.    style.BackColor = Color.White;
44.    style.AlternatingBackColor = Color.AliceBlue;
45.    DataGridTextBoxColumn[] queryColumns =
46.       new DataGridTextBoxColumn[2];
47.    queryColumns[0] = new DataGridTextBoxColumn();
48.    queryColumns[0].HeaderText = "Title";
49.    queryColumns[0].MappingName = "Title";
50.    queryColumns[0].Width = 200;
51.    queryColumns[1] = new DataGridTextBoxColumn();
52.    queryColumns[1].HeaderText = "Pages";
53.    queryColumns[1].MappingName = "NumberOfPages";
```

```
54.    queryColumns[1].Width = 50;
55.    style.GridColumnStyles.AddRange(queryColumns);
56.    queryGrid.TableStyles.Add(style);
57. }
```

The properties of the rows and columns displayed within a DataGrid are controlled by the DataGridTableStyle class. There are a large number of properties in this class so you should explore the documentation to see what's available. We only illustrate a few of the possibilities here.

First, we create a style for the bookGrid used to display the Books table on the Books tab. Each style must be linked to the table that it describes by specifying the MappingName (line 4). We then specify the two colours used as backgrounds on alternating rows (lines 5 and 6). To specify column properties, we create an array of DataGridTextBoxColumns (line 7). The size of this array must match the number of columns to be displayed – we can't just create a DataGridTextBoxColumn for one column that we want to customize and hope that some default style will be applied to the other columns. If we do that, only one column will be shown in the grid.

Each DataGridTextBoxColumn allows various properties to be specified for a given column. Again, we need to provide a MappingName (line 11) to link the column to the column in the DataSet that is supposed to display. We can change the text that is displayed at the top of the column by specifying HeaderText (line 10), and we can change the width by specifying a Width (line 12). Many other properties can be customized as well – see the documentation.

When we have finished customizing the columns, we add the array of DataGridTextBoxColumns to the GridColumnStyles property of the DataGridTableStyle (line 21) and then add the style itself to bookGrid (line 22). The rest of this method customized the other two DataGrids that appear in the program.

Finally, we consider the event handlers for the three Buttons, which provide the interaction between the program and the underlying database:

```
1.    #region Event handlers
2.    private void OnBooksUpdate(object sender, EventArgs e)
3.    {
4.      foreach (DataRow row in dataSet.Tables["Books"].Rows)
5.      {
6.        if (row.RowState == DataRowState.Added)
7.        {
8.          CheckedListBox.CheckedItemCollection checkedItems =
9.            authorList.CheckedItems;
10.         foreach (object item in checkedItems)
11.         {
12.           DataRowView viewItem = (DataRowView)item;
13.           dataSet.Tables["AuthorBook"].Rows.Add(new Object[]
14.             { viewItem["AuthorKey"], row["BookKey"] }
15.           );
```

```
16.          }
17.         }
18.        }
19.      OnUpdate(null, null);
20.    }
21.
22.    private void OnUpdate(object sender, EventArgs e)
23.    {
24.      if(dataSet.HasChanges())
25.      {
26.        AuthorBook.Update(dataSet, "AuthorBook");
27.        books.Update(dataSet, "Books");
28.        authors.Update(dataSet, "Authors");
29.        dataSet.AcceptChanges();
30.      }
31.    }
32.
33.    private void OnQuery(object sender, EventArgs e)
34.    {
35.      int selectedAuthor = (int)authorQueryList.SelectedValue;
36.      string sql = "SELECT  Books.Title,
         Books.NumberOfPages " +
37.        "FROM Books INNER JOIN " +
38.        "(Authors  INNER JOIN AuthorBook ON
         Authors.AuthorKey " +
39.        "= AuthorBook.AuthorKey) ON Books.BookKey = " +
40.        "AuthorBook.BookKey " +
41.        "WHERE Authors.AuthorKey = " + selectedAuthor;
42.      OleDbDataAdapter queryAdapter =
43.        new OleDbDataAdapter(sql, oleConn);
44.      DataSet querySet = new DataSet();
45.      queryAdapter.Fill(querySet, "Query");
46.      queryGrid.SetDataBinding(querySet, "Query");
47.      DataRowView selectedItem =
48.        (DataRowView)authorQueryList.SelectedItem;
49.      queryGrid.CaptionText = "Query results for " +
50.        selectedItem["Name"];
51.    }
52.    #endregion
53.
54.    public static void Main(string[] args)
55.    {
56.      Application.Run(new BookDB());
57.    }
58. }
```

Let us consider first the Books tab. The user can make a number of changes (additions, modifications to existing rows, and deletions) to the `DataGrid` storing the list of books before pressing the 'Update' button. As we described earlier, we can transfer the changes from the `DataSet` to the underlying database by calling the `Update()` method from the data adapter that filled the `DataSet` in the first place.

However, in this example, we have an extra complication: the three tables in the database are linked to each other, and making a change in one table can affect the other tables as well. When we add a new record to the Books table, for example, we must also add an entry to AuthorBook for each author of that book. Deleting a book requires deleting any entries referring to that book in AuthorBook as well.

The `OnBooksUpdate()` method (line 2) handles updates to the Books table and any related effects on the AuthorBook table. First, consider new books that have been added. When a user adds a new book, they will first select one or more authors for that book by checking items in the `CheckedListBox`, then clicking on the bottom row of the `bookGrid` (the row marked with a * in the left column) and typing in the title and number of pages of the new book. The `DataGrid` will automatically add a new record to the Books table in the `DataSet` to which it is bound, but it knows nothing about the need to create a new entry in the AuthorLink table, so we need to do that in the code.

This is done in the loop starting on line 4. We examine each row in the Books table and test its state to see if it is 'Added' (line 6). If so, we need to retrieve the authors that have been checked in the `CheckedListBox` and add an entry to `AuthorBook` for each author. We retrieve the list of checked authors on line 8, as a `CheckedItemCollection`. We then loop through each item in this collection (line 10). An item in a `CheckedItemCollection` is stored as a `DataRowView`, which allows us to read individual columns by using array notation and giving the column name as the array index. We can therefore extract the AuthorKey value from this item and use this value along with the BookKey value from the current row in the Books table to add a new row to the AuthorBook table in the `DataSet` (lines 12 to 15). Note that this only adds the row to the AuthorBook table in the `DataSet` – we have not yet done anything that affects the original database, since we haven't made any calls to `Update()`.

After adding the rows to the AuthorBook table, we call `OnUpdate()` (which is also the event handler for the 'Update' button on the Authors tab, as we'll see in a minute), and it updates all three of the tables, and then calls `AcceptChanges()` to reset the `DataSet` to an 'unchanged' state, in preparation for any more changes that the user may wish to make.

You may have noticed that something appears to be missing here. We have added code to update AuthorBook if we add a new book, but there is no code for deleting records from AuthorBook if we have deleted a book from the Books grid. Surely we should have to write a similar piece of code that checks for rows in the 'Deleted' state and then searches the AuthorBook table for rows that reference the deleted book, and mark each of these rows for deletion.

In fact, we don't need to do this since we have defined a relationship between the BookKey column in the Books table and the BookKey column in AuthorBook. By telling the `DataSet` to `EnforceConstraints` as we did above, it will do this search for us and delete all associated records from AuthorBook. This illustrates the reason we created the relationships in the first place – it saves us from writing a fair bit of code later on.

However, if you're even more observant, you may have noticed that there is a problem with the user interface here. The way the `OnBooksUpdate()` method is written, it attaches the list of authors *as it is when the Update button is pressed* to all 'Added' rows in the Books table. The most likely way a user would use this program, however, is to select an author, enter a book title, select another author, enter another book title and so on, and only after entering a number of books in this way to finally press Update to record all the changes in the database. Unfortunately for our user, what would get recorded is a list of books, but all these books would have the same author – the last author that was entered.

A similar problem occurs on the Authors tab. At present, we can add a number of new authors and then press 'Update' and each author is added correctly to the database. However, if we wish to delete an author, all entries in the AuthorBook table with a reference to that author will also be deleted, which could leave some books without any authors attached to them. A better response from the program would be to flag an error and prevent the user from deleting an author unless all books written by that author have been deleted first.

These problems point to what seems to be a rather serious limitation on the `DataGrid` control (at least at the time of writing – future versions of .NET may have addressed this). Let's consider the case of deleting an author for which there are still books written by that author in the database. The user would do this by selecting the row for that author in the `DataGrid` and then pressing the 'Delete' key on the keyboard. At present, the response of the program to this action is to delete the author from the display, although of course nothing is changed in the database until the 'Update' button is pressed.

Ideally, what should happen is that when the user presses the 'Delete' key, an error message should appear (say, a `MessageBox`) stating that since there are still books written by that author in the database, the author cannot be deleted. To make this happen requires an event to be generated from within the `DataGrid`. There is no such event in `DataGrid`, but there are four events within `DataTable` (which represents each table within a `DataSet`). These events are: `RowChanged`, `RowChanging`, `RowDeleted` and `RowDeleting`, which certainly look promising.

We should be able to add an event handler to the Authors table for the `RowDeleting` event (which occurs when a row is about to be deleted, as opposed to `RowDeleted`, which occurs after deletion is completed), do the check in the handler to see if any books by this author exist and, if so, generate an error message and prevent the deletion from occurring. This seems to be possible, except that the only way of preventing the deletion process is to throw an exception inside the RowDeleting event handler. Since the whole process which led to the RowDeleting event occurring was started inside a DataGrid, however, we have no access to the code which generates the event and nowhere to put a try/catch block to catch the exception. The net result is that the program crashes whenever the user tries to delete an author who has books in the database.

A number of other bugs have been reported in the use of a DataGrid in interfacing with a database in more complex situations. Hopefully future versions of .NET will address these problems, but for now, some careful thought is needed in using the system.

11.12 ■ Case study: the adventure game

Readers who have been following the adventure game case study so far will have noticed that setting up the game can be quite tedious, as we need to write separate blocks of code to add each item, room, monster and so on to the overall layout. As well, if we want to add more rooms or items, we need to add code to the program and recompile it. Clearly a more flexible method would be better.

One way of easing the process of creating the initial game is to store the required information in a database and then construct the map and its contents by reading in this data in the C# code. We'll illustrate how this could be done here.

11.12.1 □ Building a database for the adventure game

The first step is, of course, the construction of the database. As with our other examples in this chapter, we will use Access since it is the easiest system to use for small databases, but the same techniques could be used with other databases such as SQL Server or MySQL by adapting the code as described in this chapter.

The structure of the database can be based on the classes used to represent the various objects in the game. The tables and relationships we will use are shown in the diagram taken from Access (Figure 11.5).

The Room table represents all rooms in the game. The Description field is text that contains the name of the room, and also serves as the primary key for the Room table (we are therefore demanding that all rooms have unique names). The X, Y and Level fields specify the coordinates of the room. The six direction fields are all text fields that store the Description of the room that can be reached by moving in that direction, or NULL (the database NULL) if no exit exists in that direction. The Monster field stores the name of the monster, if any, in the room or NULL if there is no monster.

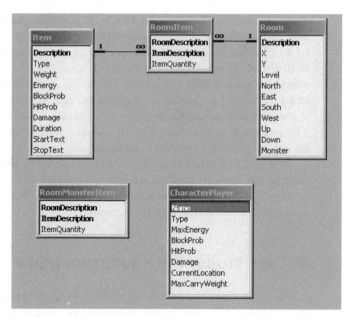

Figure 11.5 Tables and relationships in the database used in the adventure game

The Item table is used to define all types of item that are available in the game. The Item table's primary key is again the Description field, requiring each item to have a unique description. This table includes definitions of item types that are derived from `Item` in the code. The class name of a particular item is stored in the Type field, so a potion would have 'Potion' as its type.

Some of the fields in the Item table are generic fields that serve a purpose that is specific to the item type. The Duration field stores `duration` for a Potion or `charges` for a wand, and is empty for all other item types. StartText stores the string that is printed when some items are first used, such as `QuaffString` for a Potion, `AdornString` for a Ring and `ZapString` for a Wand. Similarly, StopText stores `WearOffString` for a Potion and `UnadornString` for a Ring.

Since a given room can store an arbitrary number of items, we provide a link table called RoomItem that links rooms to the items they store. We've added an extra field called ItemQuantity to this table to allow a room to store more than one instance of a given item.

The CharacterPlayer table contains definitions for the Player and all monsters. It is similar in concept to the Item table in that it contains a Type field to distinguish the Player object from monsters which are represented by the `Character` class. Notice that we only need to store those data fields that are initialized at the start of the game, so fields such as `QuaffedPotion`, `WornArmour` and so on are not included, since the player is assumed to be carrying no items at the start of the game. For the same reason, there is no link table connecting CharacterPlayer with Item. If we wish to modify this to allow a player to start off with some items, it is easy enough to add this link table.

Monsters in rooms, however, *can* carry objects which are dropped when the monster is killed. We can't provide this in the database by a link table between CharacterPlayer and Item, since CharacterPlayer contains the generic description of a particular type of monster, such as a zombie, and we can have more than one zombie in the game (that is, several rooms could have a monster of the same generic type).

Since only one monster is allowed per room, we have therefore provided a link table called RoomMonsterItem which provides a list of items carried by the monster in that room. This table contains only the descriptions of the room and item (along with the quantity of items) since the monster carrying these items is specified in the Room table under the entry for that particular room.

Once the database has been constructed, we can use Access's table interface (or build an Access form) to enter the data, or we could write a C# program to provide a customized interface for doing this if we wished. For the small size of the game we are considering here, this isn't worth the effort, since the data entry features provided by Access are adequate.

For example, the CharacterPlayer table after entering the player and a few monsters is shown in Figure 11.6.

Name	Type	MaxEnergy	BlockProb	HitProb	Damage	CurrentLocation	MaxCarryWeight
demon	Character	10	10	30	6		0
dragon	Character	25	40	70	8		0
giant spider	Character	14	20	30	6		0
snake	Character	7	45	25	5		0
Wibble the Wiz	Player	12	20	60	2	entrance	100
zombie	Character	8	30	60	4		0
		0	0	0	0		0

Figure 11.6 CharacterPlayer table in the adventure game database

11.12.2 ☐ Writing the C# code

Once we have enough data in the database to create a functioning game, we can write the C# code to build the game from the database. All the changes are in the `Adventure` class, since this is the only class that is used to initialize the game. The relevant portion of this class in its new version is as follows:

```
1. using System;
2. using System.Collections;
3. using System.Data;
4. using System.Data.OleDb;
5.
6. public class Adventure
7. {
8.     private Player gamePlayer;
9.     private Room[] rooms;
10.    private Random random = new Random();
```

```
11.    public int numRooms;
12.
13.    OleDbDataAdapter command;
14.    DataSet dataSet;
15.
16.    public Adventure()
17.    {
18.       SetupGameFromDB();
19.    }
20.
21.    private void SetupGameFromDB()
22.    {
23.       string source;
24.
25.       // Access database
26.       source = "Provider=Microsoft.Jet.OLEDB.4.0;" +
27.          @"Data Source=C:\Books\MyBooks\CSharpBook\
           Adventure.mdb";
28.       OleDbConnection oleConn = new OleDbConnection(source);
29.       dataSet = new DataSet();
30.       try
31.       {
32.          oleConn.Open();
33.          string sql = "SELECT * FROM Item";
34.          command = new OleDbDataAdapter(sql, oleConn);
35.          command.Fill(dataSet, "Item");
36.          dataSet.Tables["Item"].PrimaryKey =
37.             new DataColumn[]
38.                {dataSet.Tables["Item"].Columns["Description"]};
39.
40.          sql = "SELECT * FROM Room";
41.          command = new OleDbDataAdapter(sql, oleConn);
42.          command.Fill(dataSet, "Room");
43.          dataSet.Tables["Room"].PrimaryKey =
44.             new DataColumn[]
45.                {dataSet.Tables["Room"].Columns["Description"]};
46.
47.          sql = "SELECT * FROM CharacterPlayer";
48.          command = new OleDbDataAdapter(sql, oleConn);
49.          command.Fill(dataSet, "CharacterPlayer");
50.          dataSet.Tables["CharacterPlayer"].PrimaryKey =
51.             new DataColumn[]
52.                {dataSet.Tables["CharacterPlayer"].Columns
                    ["Name"]};
53.
54.          sql = "SELECT * FROM RoomItem";
55.          command = new OleDbDataAdapter(sql, oleConn);
```

```
56.          command.Fill(dataSet, "RoomItem");
57.
58.          sql = "SELECT * FROM RoomMonsterItem";
59.          command = new OleDbDataAdapter(sql, oleConn);
60.          command.Fill(dataSet, "RoomMonsterItem");
61.
62.          SetupRoomsDB();
63.          SetupPlayerDB();
64.        }
65.      catch (Exception ex)
66.      {
67.          Console.WriteLine(ex.ToString());
68.      }
69.      finally
70.      {
71.          oleConn.Close();
72.      }
73.    }
74.
75.    private void SetupRoomsDB()
76.    {
77.      // Create rooms
78.      numRooms = dataSet.Tables["Room"].Rows.Count;
79.      rooms = new Room[NumRooms];
80.      for (int i = 0; i < NumRooms; i++)
81.      {
82.        DataRow roomRow = dataSet.Tables["Room"].Rows[i];
83.        rooms[i] = new Room((int)roomRow["X"],
               (int)roomRow["Y"],
84.            (int)roomRow["Level"],
85.            (string)roomRow["Description"]);
86.      }
87.
88.      // Add exits
89.      for (int i = 0; i < NumRooms; i++)
90.      {
91.        DataRow roomRow = dataSet.Tables["Room"].Rows[i];
92.        Room currentRoom =
93.          FindRoom((string)roomRow["Description"]);
94.        int northColIndex =
95.          dataSet.Tables["Room"].Columns.IndexOf("North");
96.        for (int dir = northColIndex;
97.          dir < northColIndex + 6; dir++)
98.        {
99.          if (roomRow[dir].GetType() ==
100.            Type.GetType("System.String"))
101.          {
```

```
102.          string exitTo = (string)roomRow[dir];
103.          Room otherRoom = FindRoom(exitTo);
104.          currentRoom.SetExit((Room.Direction)
105.            (dir - northColIndex), otherRoom);
106.        }
107.      }
108.
109.      // Add monster, if any
110.      if (roomRow["Monster"].GetType() ==
111.        Type.GetType("System.String"))
112.      {
113.        string monsterName = (string)roomRow["Monster"];
114.        DataRow monsterRow =
115.          dataSet.Tables["CharacterPlayer"].Rows.
116.          Find(monsterName);
117.        Character monster = new Character();
118.        monster.Name = (string)monsterRow["Name"];
119.        monster.MaxEnergy = (int)monsterRow["MaxEnergy"];
120.        monster.Energy = monster.MaxEnergy;
121.        monster.BlockProb = (int)monsterRow["BlockProb"];
122.        monster.HitProb = (int)monsterRow["HitProb"];
123.        monster.Damage = (int)monsterRow["Damage"];
124.        currentRoom.Monster = monster;
125.      }
126.    }
127.
128.    // Add items to rooms
129.    for (int i = 0;
130.      i < dataSet.Tables["RoomItem"].Rows.Count; i++)
131.    {
132.      DataRow row = dataSet.Tables["RoomItem"].Rows[i];
133.      Room room = FindRoom((string)row["RoomDescription"]);
134.      DataRow itemRow = dataSet.Tables["Item"].Rows.
135.        Find((string)row["ItemDescription"]);
136.      int itemQuantity = (int)row["ItemQuantity"];
137.      for (int q = 0; q < itemQuantity; q++)
138.      {
139.      Item addItem = GetItem(itemRow);
140.        room.AddItem(addItem);
141.      }
142.    }
143.
144.    // Add items to monsters
145.    for (int i = 0;
146.      i < dataSet.Tables["RoomMonsterItem"]
        .Rows.Count; i++)
147.    {
```

```
148.        DataRow row = dataSet.Tables
           ["RoomMonsterItem"]. Rows[i];
149.        Room room = FindRoom((string)row["RoomDescription"]);
150.        DataRow itemRow = dataSet.Tables["Item"].Rows.
151.           Find((string)row["ItemDescription"]);
152.        int itemQuantity = (int)row["ItemQuantity"];
153.        for (int q = 0; q < itemQuantity; q++)
154.        {
155.        Item monsterItem = GetItem(itemRow);
156.           room.Monster.AddItem(monsterItem);
157.        }
158.     }
159.  }
160.
161.  private Item GetItem(DataRow itemRow)
162.  {
163.    Item addItem = null;
164.    String itemType = (string)itemRow["Type"];
165.    if (itemType.Equals("Item"))
166.    {
167.      addItem = new Item();
168.    }
169.    else if (itemType.Equals("Food"))
170.    {
171.      addItem = new Food();
172.      ((Food)addItem).Energy = (int)itemRow["Energy"];
173.    }
174.    else if (itemType.Equals("Weapon"))
175.    {
176.      addItem = new Weapon();
177.      ((Weapon)addItem).Damage = (int)itemRow["Damage"];
178.      ((Weapon)addItem).HitProb = (int)itemRow["HitProb"];
179.    }
180.    else if (itemType.Equals("Armour"))
181.    {
182.      addItem = new Armour();
183.      ((Armour)addItem).BlockProb = (int)itemRow
           ["BlockProb"];
184.    }
185.    else // MagicItem
186.    {
187.      if (itemType.Equals("Potion"))
188.      {
189.        addItem = new Potion();
190.        ((Potion)addItem).Duration = (int)itemRow
             ["Duration"];
191.        ((Potion)addItem).QuaffString =
```

```
192.                (string)itemRow["StartText"];
193.            ((Potion)addItem).WearOffString =
194.                (string)itemRow["StopText"];
195.          }
196.        else if (itemType.Equals("Ring"))
197.        {
198.            addItem = new Ring();
199.            ((Ring)addItem).AdornString =
200.                (string)itemRow["StartText"];
201.            ((Ring)addItem).UnadornString =
202.                (string)itemRow["StopText"];
203.        }
204.        else if (itemType.Equals("Wand"))
205.        {
206.            addItem = new Wand();
207.            ((Wand)addItem).Charges = (int)itemRow["Duration"];
208.            ((Wand)addItem).ZapString =
209.                (string)itemRow["StartText"];
210.        }
211.        ((MagicItem)addItem).BlockProb =
212.            (int)itemRow["BlockProb"];
213.        ((MagicItem)addItem).HitProb = (int)itemRow
               ["HitProb"];
214.        ((MagicItem)addItem).Damage = (int)itemRow["Damage"];
215.        ((MagicItem)addItem).Energy = (int)itemRow["Energy"];
216.      }
217.      addItem.Description = (string)itemRow["Description"];
218.      addItem.Weight = (int)itemRow["Weight"];
219.      return addItem;
220.   }
221.
222.   private void SetupPlayerDB()
223.   {
224.      DataRow playerRow = dataSet.Tables
          ["CharacterPlayer"].Rows.
225.        Find("Wibble the Wizard");
226.      gamePlayer = new Player((string)playerRow["Name"]);
227.      gamePlayer.MaxEnergy = (int)playerRow["MaxEnergy"];
228.      gamePlayer.Energy = gamePlayer.MaxEnergy;
229.      gamePlayer.HitProb = (int)playerRow["HitProb"];
230.      gamePlayer.Damage = (int)playerRow["Damage"];
231.      gamePlayer.BlockProb = (int)playerRow["BlockProb"];
232.      gamePlayer.MaxCarryWeight =
233.        (int)playerRow["MaxCarryWeight"];
234.      gamePlayer.CurrentLocation =
235.        FindRoom((string)playerRow["CurrentLocation"]);
236.   }
```

```
237.
238.    private Room FindRoom(string description)
239.    {
240.      foreach (Room room in rooms)
241.      {
242.        if (room.Description.Equals(description))
243.          return room;
244.      }
245.      return null;
246.    }
247.
248.    // Remainder of class as before
249. }
```

The plan is to read the entire database into a DataSet, since this makes finding the required bits of data much easier. We load the entire database since everything in the database is needed to create the game.

The data fields in Adventure have not changed much, but a couple of alterations are worth pointing out. We have made numRooms a variable (line 11) with its own property (not shown) since we do not know in advance how many rooms are to be in the game. For the same reason, we have removed the Locn enumeration that was used in earlier versions, since we also don't know in advance the names of the rooms we will be loading.

The database objects are declared on lines 13 and 14, and then the constructor calls the single method SetupGameFromDB() to get things going.

After connecting to the database (lines 26 to 28 – alter these lines if you want to use a different database or locate the database file in a different place), we load the entire database into the DataSet (lines 29 to 60). We then call SetupRoomsDB() and SetupPlayerDB() to set up the rooms, monsters and player.

SetupRoomsDB() (line 75) begins by creating the rooms array. We obtain the number of rooms from the DataSet Room table (line 78) and use this value to allocate the array (line 79). Since we need to create a separate Room object for each row in the Room table, we can just loop through these rows and extract the information needed to call the Room constructor (lines 80 to 86). Note that we can access the various columns within a DataRow by using the column name as an indexer, but we do need to cast the value to the required data type, since all column values in a DataRow are stored as objects.

After creating all the Rooms, we add the exits to each room (lines 89 to 107). To do this, we iterate through the Room table in the DataSet again. For each DataRow, we use FindRoom() to find the Room object corresponding to this row. FindRoom() (line 238) just loops through the rooms array searching for a Room with a description that matches its parameter.

Once we have the Room object, we set about adding any exits it may have. We are assuming that the Room table stores the exit data in consecutive columns in the order North, East, South, West, Up, Down, since this is the same order in which the exit data is stored in the Room class's Direction enumeration. We locate the column in the Room table storing the North exit by using `IndexOf()` (line 94). We can then loop over the six columns starting at this location (lines 96 to 107) to locate and attach the exits for that room.

To determine which entries in the Room table correspond to exits, we test the data type of each column (row 99). Columns with no exit string will have a `System.DBNull` stored there, while those with a string will have a `System.String` object.

Adding an exit to a `Room` requires locating the other `Room` to which the exit leads, so we do that by using `FindRoom()` again (line 103) and then `SetExit()` (line 104) to connect this room to the current room.

If the `Room` has a monster, we add it on lines 110 to 125. The monster's name is extracted from the `Room`'s data row (line 113) and the `DataRow` in the CharacterPlayer table corresponding to that name is found (line 114). The `Rows` property of a data table from a `DataSet` contains a `Find()` method that allows a search to be done on the `DataRows` in the collection. `Find()` will *only* search columns that are part of the table's primary key however, so we need to make sure we define the primary key for the table in the `DataSet`. Remember that even though we have defined a primary key in the original Access database, this information is not read in when we load the data in the internal `DataSet`. This is why we set the primary keys when we read in the data back on lines 33 to 60.

After the `DataRow` for the monster is located, it is just a matter of using the information in that row to define the properties of the monster (lines 117 to 123). Finally, we attach the monster to the current room (line 124).

Adding items to rooms works in a similar way (lines 129 to 142). We loop over all the rows in the RoomItem link table. For each row, we get the Room description (line 133) and then extract the `DataRow` for the corresponding item from the Item table, again using `Find()` (line 134). The `Item` object (or its derived class object) is created by the method `GetItem()`, which we will consider below. Finally, the ItemQuantity column is used to attach the correct number of this item to the room.

The process of adding items to monsters is very similar (lines 145 to 158).

`GetItem()` (line 161) builds an `Item` object (or an object from a class that inherits `Item`) from the data in a `DataRow` from the Item table. The trick here is to build an item of the correct data type, so we first obtain the data type from the Type column (line 164). The rest of the method then creates an item of the correct type and adds in the data fields that are appropriate for that type of item.

The player is set up by `SetupPlayerDB()` (line 222). This involves nothing more than locating the row containing the player's name (line 224) and then using the rest of the row to initialize all the player's parameters.

Although the amount of code is not trivial, it has the advantage of being fixed. Additions and alterations to the game can be made just by editing the database, so the C# program need not be modified unless we want to add something that requires a new class, such as a new type of item.

The one disadvantage to using the database approach for data storage is that it does require that the user have the database software installed on their system. In the next chapter we will have a look at another method which avoids this problem: XML.

■ Summary

This chapter has explored the facilities provided by .NET and C# for interfacing with databases. We began with a survey of the essentials of database design and the use of SQL for editing and querying databases.

Our survey of .NET's capabilities began with some simple classes that allow reading and displaying the data in a database in a one-way fashion. Then we explored the `DataSet` which is a powerful class capable of duplicating a database within C# code, and allowing most database operations to be performed on it.

The `DataGrid` control allows a reasonably versatile interface, both for displaying the results of queries and allowing editing of the original database. Due to some limitations in event handling, however, some aspects of the `DataGrid` require caution when they are used.

We concluded with another instalment in our continuing case study of the adventure game, in which the details of the initial setup of the game are stored in a database and read in to start the game off.

Exercises

11.1 Using a database of your choice (Access, SQL Server, or MySQL preferably, so you can connect to it using the code in this chapter), design a database for storing some data on a CD collection. Typical tables might be a Disk table for storing the data specific to a single CD, an Artists table (or a Composers table if your collection is classical) for storing details of the band(s) or composer(s) featured on the CD, and an ArtistDisk link table. In the CD table, provide a column for the CD's title and another for the number of tracks. Also provide a CDKey column which stores a number that is unique for each CD and can serve as the primary key.

The Artists table should contain a column for the artist's or composer's name and an ArtistKey to be used as a primary key. The ArtistDisk table contains only ArtistKey and DiskKey, which together form a primary key.

Using the Book database in the text as a model, enter some data into the CD database using the facilities provided by the database software. Data on five or so CDs, provided they feature different artists, should be enough for what follows.

11.2 Write a C# program that connects to the database you have just written. Be sure to follow through the steps in the text for the particular type of database you are using. Write an SQL statement and use the appropriate `DataReader` class to print to the console a complete list of the titles in the Disk table.

11.3 Modify the SQL statement in the previous question to print out only those CDs that have more than a certain number of tracks (choose the threshold value to be one that will return only some of the CDs in your database).

11.4 Write an SQL statement using an INNER JOIN that will return a record set where each record contains a CD title and the corresponding artist for that CD. Use the `DataReader` to run the query and print out the results.

11.5 Using the model in the text, write a Windows Form program containing a single `DataGrid`. Define a `DataSet` and load just the Artist table into the `DataSet`, then display the results in the `DataGrid`. The `DataGrid` should display both columns in the Artist table (ArtistKey and Name).

11.6 Add a `TextBox` and a `Button` to the form in the previous exercise. The user should be able to type a string in the box and then press the button to do a search of the Artist table for all names containing that string. For example, if the Artist table contained entries for Beethoven, Schubert and Schumann, typing in 'Schu' should return Schubert and Schumann, but not Beethoven. (Hint: recall the LIKE clause in SQL.)

11.7 Write another program (or add a `TabControl` to the program from the previous exercise and add the interface on a second tab) which displays a list of all CDs in the database. The display should contain a `DataGrid` with three columns: CD title, Artist and Number of Tracks (that is, none of the key values should be displayed).

11.8 Add a `TextBox` and `Button` to the interface in the previous exercise which allows the user to search for all CDs by artists whose name contains the string entered in the text box. Using the same example as in the previous search exercise, all CDs featuring works by Schubert or Schumann should be listed.

11.9 Returning to the program that displayed all artists in a `DataGrid`, use the model in the text to add code to this program allowing users to add extra artists to the Artist table in the original database. Use a `CommandBuilder` to provide the link between the `DataSet` and database, and add an Update button to allow the user to update the database after adding a new artist.

11.10 Link together the appropriate programs from the last few exercises, along with the examples in the text, to produce a complete interface to the CD database, allowing the user to add new entries in the Disk table, together with correct updates to the ArtistDisk link table.

11.11 Create a database that could be used to store the name and score of each player that plays the quiz game from Exercise 9.5 in Chapter 9. Read the names and scores from the database and display them in response to the menu item in Exercise 9.6 or 9.7.

XML 12

12.1 ■ Introduction

XML (Extensible Markup Language) has become a widely used technology over the past few years, especially with regard to the Internet. However, you could easily be forgiven for wondering (as I did) upon first encountering XML what all the fuss is about.

We will therefore begin this chapter with a survey of what XML is and how it can be used both for transmission of data over the Internet and for storing data locally within your own programs. As with databases, however, we must remember that this book is primarily a book on C#, so we can't go into serious depth on XML.

So what exactly *is* XML? Basically it is yet another way of storing and transmitting information. If you are familiar with HTML, the language used in writing most web pages, you will have seen an example of an XML representation of data. (Well, you *may* have seen a proper example of XML, since most web browsers will accept HTML that is not, strictly speaking, correctly formatted. Proper XML requires that all syntax rules be adhered to exactly.)

If you've never looked at HTML in any depth, don't worry – we won't be assuming any knowledge of HTML here. However, you might like to have a look at some HTML by loading up a web page (try to pick a web page with a fairly plain layout, consisting mainly of text). Most web browsers allow you to see the source code used to produce the page by selecting the View menu and then selecting Source. A text window containing the HTML source code should pop up.

Here's a simple example, condensed from my own web page:

```
<HTML>
<HEAD>
<TITLE>growe's real home page</TITLE>
</HEAD>
<BODY>
<H1 align=center>Welcome to growe's real home page</H1>
<CENTER>
   <P>The time now is 3/3/2003 3:50:09 PM in Dundee, UK</P>
</CENTER>
<!- Other code follows ->
</BODY>
</HTML>
```

The main thing to notice about this example is that it consists of a number of *tags* (words enclosed in angle brackets, such as <HEAD>). These tags define portions of the document and are interpreted by the web browser as instructions to display text or images in certain ways.

Each tag has a corresponding end tag, which consists of the same word as in the opening tag but preceded by a slash, such as `</HEAD>`. Tags in XML always come in pairs, with the first tag opening a region of the document and the end tag closing it. (Most browsers will accept HTML where not all opening tags have a corresponding end tag – this is what was meant earlier when it was stated that not all HTML is properly formed.)

With HTML, the meaning of each tag is defined by an HTML parser that is built into the program (usually a web browser such as Internet Explorer or Netscape) that is used to display the file. For example, text enclosed in the `<TITLE> … </TITLE>` tags is displayed in the title bar of the browser's window, text enclosed in `<H1> … </H1>` tags is displayed in a large font and so on.

In XML, the idea behind HTML is extended (hence the 'extensible' part of XML) to allow programmers to define their own tags, and to attach their own meanings to these tags. At first glance, this sounds like a powerful technology, since it should allow us to devise a markup language for pretty well anything: music, mathematics, share prices, whatever we like. At a second glance, however, we are brought back to earth with the question: how do we provide meaning for the tags we define? Since we can define *any* tags to represent *any* kind of data, surely the syntax of XML can't foresee every use to which it might be put, so a fair amount of work must be involved in defining meanings for these new tags that we invent.

Therein lies the 'catch' to XML. Devising a set of tags to store information is relatively easy for simple sets of data, but providing some environment in which these new tags actually have any meaning is the hard part. Fortunately, a lot of tools have been provided to ease the task, which is what makes XML so popular and powerful.

12.2 ■ Simple XML

To illustrate how we might design our own set of tags to define an XML document, we'll go back to the book example we used in Chapter 11 on databases. The information on each book we stored in the database consisted of its title, authors and number of pages. To store this information in XML, we'll define a `<BOOK>` tag to store the information on a single book, and then `<AUTHOR>` and `<TITLE>` tags to store each author and the title of the book. We also define a `<BOOKLIST>` tag to enclose a list of books.

An XML file containing a list of two books might look like this:

```
<?xml version="1.0" encoding="utf-8" ?>
<!-- Comment: A list of two books -->
<BOOKLIST>
  <BOOK NumPages="345">
    <AUTHOR>Zaphod Wibble</AUTHOR>
    <TITLE>Wibble's Guide to the Classics</TITLE>
  </BOOK>
```

```
<BOOK NumPages="429">
  <AUTHOR>Isaac Asimov</AUTHOR>
  <TITLE>The Complete Stories, Vol. 1</TITLE>
</BOOK>
</BOOKLIST>
```

Apart from the first line, which provides some standard information on the XML version being used, everything else in this example was simply invented on the spot. All the names of the tags were taken from what they are supposed to represent – they are not keywords in XML. So what makes this file XML as opposed to just a random text file?

The main thing that is required of an XML file is that it adhere to a certain structure which, at the ground level, is very simple. It is easiest to think of this structure as a *tree*, since we can most easily display the relationships between the various components that way.

Each portion of an XML file that is enclosed by a start and an end tag is called an *element*. At the top level, a single element must enclose all the other elements. In our example, the `<BOOKLIST>` element contains the entire file.

Within this top-level element may be placed any number of other elements, which may be nested to any depth. In this example, `<BOOKLIST>` contains two `<BOOK>` elements, each of which in turn contains an `<AUTHOR>` and a `<TITLE>`. Since a book could have more than one author, we could put more than one `<AUTHOR>` element within each `<BOOK>` element.

Besides containing other elements, a given element can also contain some ordinary text. In this example, `<AUTHOR>` and `<TITLE>` both contain text (the name of the author and the book's title, respectively), but the `<BOOK>` element does not contain any text.

An element can also have one or more *attributes* associated with it. An attribute has the form *name= value*, where *name* is the name of the attribute and *value* is a string that contains the value of the attribute. The value must always be enclosed in double quotes. The attributes are always enclosed within the opening tag of the element. In the example here, the `<BOOK>` element has a single attribute called `NumPages`, which contains the number of pages in the book.

Sometimes we can just define an element that contains no other elements or any text. For example, we might just include a `<BOOK>` element that contains a `NumPages` attribute but no authors or title (for example, the book could be a blank diary). In this case, XML allows the opening and closing tags of an element to be combined, so we could write the complete element as follows:

```
<BOOK NumPages="200" />
```

This line is equivalent to

```
<BOOK NumPages="200"></BOOK>
```

We could, of course, have defined a <NUMPAGES> element to store the number of pages and not used any attributes at all in this XML file. Generally, an attribute is appropriate for information that only occurs once for a given element, and usually can be described using a fairly short string. In many cases, it is just a matter of taste whether an attribute or element is used to store data.

XML files can contain comment lines, an example of which is shown in the file above. A comment is started with the string <!-- and ended with -->.

XML allows a few other types of statements to be included, but elements and attributes are sufficient to store most data, so we'll leave our description of XML at this point. However, in general, the term *node* is used to describe any individual part of an XML file, so start and end tags, attributes, text and even comments are all nodes.

To illustrate the tree structure of a typical XML file, we'll show the above book file as a tree diagram (Figure12.1).

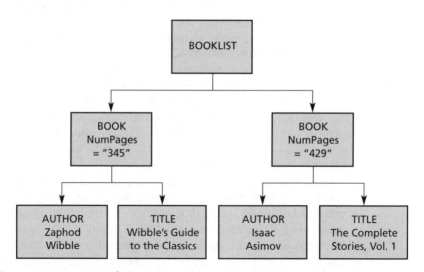

Figure 12.1 Structure of elements used to represent books as XML

The BOOKLIST node serves as the *root* of the tree (tree diagrams are usually drawn upside-down, with the root at the top). Every XML file must have an element that encompasses the entire file, which serves as the root of the tree structure. All other elements within the file are 'owned' by this root node.

Within the root node, we can add as many nodes of various types as we wish, provided that each node is well-formed, by obeying the syntax rules for that type of node. For example, if a node is an element, the element must have an opening and a closing tag. Within BOOKLIST we have two BOOK nodes, each of which contains an AUTHOR and a TITLE.

In the diagram, we've included the `NumPages` attribute and the text within the same box as the element that contains them. To be more precise, we could have shown attributes and text as separate children of their parent element, but that tends to make the tree diagram too cluttered.

As mentioned above, there is no restriction on the names given to the various elements; the only thing that really matters is that every element must come as a pair of tags, and the hierarchical, or tree, structure of the file must be preserved. This last rule means that we can't begin an element with an opening tag on one layer in the tree and end it on another level.

For example, the following file is not correctly formed XML since the `<AUTHOR>` element begins within the `<BOOK>` node but ends outside it:

```
<?xml version="1.0" encoding="utf-8" ?>
<BOOKLIST>
  <BOOK NumPages="345">
    <AUTHOR>Zaphod Wibble
    <TITLE>Wibble's Guide to the Classics</TITLE>
  </BOOK>
  </AUTHOR>
</BOOKLIST>
```

Another way of looking at this rule is that each end tag must match the *last* unmatched starting tag that occurs before it. In this example, then, the `</BOOK>` tag would try to match with the `<AUTHOR>` tag, since the `<TITLE>` element that comes between them is correctly matched.

Some browsers, such as later versions of Internet Explorer, will show a neatly formatted listing of an XML file if that file is loaded into the browser. In the absence of any other XML processing software, Internet Explorer can be used to parse XML files and test them for correctness. If an error is encountered, a reasonably clear error message is usually produced, showing the line where the error occurs.

As it stands, an XML file such as this book list isn't of much use since we haven't written any code that uses the data stored in the file. In the next section, we'll consider some of the ways an XML file such as this might be used.

12.3 ■ Using XML

As we've seen, an XML file on its own is not of much use, since it just contains some information in a form that is not terribly easy to read for humans. What can we do to make use of the information?

The main power of XML is that it is a universally accepted format for storing and transmitting data. It is extremely rare for the computing community to agree on a universal format for any sort of data storage or transmission, so the fact that XML has achieved such status is truly cause for celebration. Because we can rely on the XML standard, we can safely write software that reads in data in XML from a foreign source. Similarly, we can export data to clients using XML, confident that the client will be able to make sense of the result.

There are various ways we can use an XML data file. The simplest way is probably just to read it through from start to finish and extract the information we need as we progress through the file. Java programmers with some XML experience may have used the SAX (SAX is actually a second-order acronym: Simple API for XML) parser in earlier versions of Java which does just that. It provides a quick, one-way passage through an XML file, allowing a program to strip out relevant information as it finds it.

While this method is fine for some purposes, in many cases we need to move around inside the tree structure of the XML file to extract the information we want. In this case, we need a parser that recognizes the Document Object Model or DOM. Using the DOM to parse XML builds up a tree structure of the entire file within memory and allows the program to move backwards and forwards within this representation. Although DOM provides more flexibility in examining an XML file, it also requires considerably more memory, since the entire tree must be held in memory at once, unlike SAX, which just reads a line, gives us the chance to use it, and then throws it away to make room for the next line. Java also provides support for DOM in the JDOM package.

As we'll see in this chapter, .NET and C# provide comprehensive support for both ways of parsing XML.

Both these parsing techniques, however, pay no attention to the actual content of the XML – they just read the nodes and provide the information for the programmer to do with as they see fit. In many cases, we would like to extract information of a given type and discard the rest. For example, given a book file like the example above, we might want to extract a list of all the authors in the file. True, we could use a SAX-like parser and step through the entire file looking for AUTHOR tags, but this requires writing our own code to compare each tag's name with the string 'AUTHOR'. Many other types of search can be considerably more complex to program.

Because a search facility is so commonly needed in processing XML files, a separate language called XPath was developed to provide a powerful search facility. Although we don't have the space in this book to look at XPath in detail, we will see some simple examples of how it can be used in C# to search XML files.

Finally, another common task is that of *transforming* an XML file into another format. The most common example of such a transform is the conversion of the data stored in an XML file into HTML so it can be displayed on a web page. Yet another language called XSLT (Extensible Stylesheet Language for Transformations) has been developed to make such transformations easier to achieve. A common application of such a transformation is the production of HTML in response to a request to a web server. In this case the result of the XSLT transformation, instead of being written to a file on disk, is sent directly back to the client over the web to produce a dynamic web page.

You might find one aspect of all this a bit worrying. We've seen that XML imposes very few restrictions on the format of the file. We need only be sure that we have used a proper tree structure in building the file; there are no restrictions on the names of the tags, their arrangement relative to each other, or on the number or names of any attributes we attach to each tag.

If we are designing an XML file format for a particular purpose such as storing a list of data on books, it would seem safer if we could in some way *define* some additional restrictions on the file format in order to avoid errors such as assigning two titles to a book, omitting the author or numerous other errors we might make when entering the information into the file.

We can in fact define a *schema* for an XML file format which allows us to impose restrictions of this sort. Various types of schema exist, but a popular standard is the Document Type Definition or DTD. We'll see later how to write a simple DTD for the book list file, but again, if you want full details on this format or any of the other schemas sometimes used, you should consult a book on XML.

Once we have a schema, we can use it to *validate* the XML that is read into one of the parsers. The validation process will catch any errors that not only violate the basic syntax of XML itself, such as improperly matched tags within an element, but also any that violate the rules defined in the schema.

Hopefully you have now been convinced that XML does have a variety of useful applications, albeit with a not insignificant amount of effort on the part of the programmer.

To wrap up this section, we should mention that the various standards relating to XML are maintained and documented by the World Wide Web Consortium, known as W3C for short. Their web site (http://www.w3c.org) is a rich site for anyone wanting the final word on XML and its associated packages.

12.4 ■ Reading XML: `XMLTextReader`

We'll begin our examination of how C# and .NET can be used to process XML with the simplest case – that of one-directional reading and writing of XML. As mentioned above, this process is realized in Java through the use of SAX, and readers who have used SAX will find C#'s facilities for reading XML to be very similar.

As an XML example, we will use the book list given above. Probably the simplest thing we can do with this XML file is to read it in and print out the tags and the text content of all the nodes that have a textual component. The C# code for this is as follows.

```csharp
using System;
using System.Xml;

public class SimpleXML
{
    public static void Main(string[] args)
    {
        string fileName = "BookList.xml";
```

```
XmlTextReader reader = new XmlTextReader(fileName);
while(reader.Read())
{
  if (reader.NodeType == XmlNodeType.Text)
  {
    Console.WriteLine(reader.Value);
  }
  else if (reader.NodeType == XmlNodeType.Element)
  {
    Console.WriteLine(reader.Name);
  }
  else if (reader.NodeType == XmlNodeType.EndElement)
  {
    Console.WriteLine("/" + reader.Name);
  }
}
    }
}
```

The XML support in .NET is contained within the System.Xml name-space, so we need to include a using statement for it, and also include it in the list of resources used by the program.

This program relies on the BookList.xml file being in the same direct-ory as the executable program – if it isn't, you will need to modify the path to the file in the program.

The .NET analogue of the SAX parser is XmlTextReader, which takes an input stream as its source of data – here we just use the disk file.

The XmlTextReader steps through the XML source code using the Read() method. Each call to Read() reads one *node* (as defined above) from the XML, which is not necessarily one line from the file. Recall that each tag counts as a node, as does the text between a start and end tag. Each node that is read is assigned a particular type, which is one of the XmlNodeType enumeration.

The program here checks if the current node is of type Text, in which case it prints the Value of the node (which is just the text), or if the node is either the start or end tag. An XML start tag begins an Element and an end tag is an EndElement. Many other types of node can be detected by the XmlTextReader – see the documentation for details.

When we run this program using the BookList.xml file above, we get the following output:

```
BOOKLIST
BOOK
AUTHOR
Zaphod Wibble
/AUTHOR
TITLE
```

```
Wibble's Guide to the Classics
/TITLE
/BOOK
BOOK
AUTHOR
Isaac Asimov
/AUTHOR
TITLE
The Complete Stories, Vol. 1
/TITLE
/BOOK
/BOOKLIST
```

We can see that we can keep track of exactly where the parser is at each point by tracking the `Element` and `EndElement` names, although there is no way we can deduce the overall structure of the XML file from the `XmlTextReader` since it just plods through the file one node at a time and never builds the tree structure on which the file is based.

This sort of parser can be useful for extracting information from an XML file. For example, to get a list of authors, we could replace the `Main()` method above with:

```
public static void Main(string[] args)
{
   string fileName = "BookList.xml";
   XmlTextReader reader = new XmlTextReader(fileName);
   while(reader.Read())
   {
      if (reader.MoveToContent() == XmlNodeType.Element &&
         reader.Name.Equals("AUTHOR"))
      {
         Console.WriteLine(reader.ReadElementString());
      }
   }
}
```

The `MoveToContent()` method reads nodes until it finds a 'content' node, which includes `Element`, `EndElement`, `Text` and a few others. This method is a way of skipping over comments, whitespace and other nodes that are usually not of interest to the program. If the next content node encountered is an `Element`, and the `Element`'s name is 'AUTHOR', we then call `ReadElementString()` which reads the text component of an `Element`. The output of this program thus extracts the text from AUTHOR elements only, and produces:

```
Zaphod Wibble
Isaac Asimov
```

Note that the `XmlTextReader` acts like a bookmark in the XML file that it is reading. Methods such as `Read()` and `MoveToContent()` don't actually return parts of the file – rather they move the reader to a particular location in the file and then allow the programmer to use other methods or properties such as `Name` or `ReadElementString()` to retrieve information about the current node.

It is also important to realize that `XmlTextReader` does not allow us to back up at any point, so if we need information from a node we have to get it on the first (and only) pass through the file. If this turns out to be a problem, we need to use a different method of processing the XML file.

Because XML is a standard for storing and transmitting data, it is often used to communicate data between two applications that may have different uses for the same data set. For example, one application might need to load the book data into an internal data structure in C# so that more complex operations on the data, operations that are not easy or even possible with XML methods, can be done. In this case, we would like to build the C# data structure as we read through the XML file.

To see how this works, let us write a C# program that defines a `Book` class and then builds a list of `Books` by reading the data from `BookList.xml` using `XmlTextReader`.

First, we define a `Book` class for storing the information associated with each book:

```csharp
public class Book
{
  private string author;
  private string title;
  private int numPages;

  public string Author
  {
    set
    {
      author = value;
    }
    get
    {
      return author;
    }
  }

  public string Title
  {
    set
    {
      title = value;
```

```
      }
      get
      {
        return title;
      }
    }

    public int NumPages
    {
      set
      {
        numPages = value;
      }
      get
      {
        return numPages;
      }
    }

    public override string ToString()
    {
      string description = Title + " by " + Author;
      if (NumPages > 0)
      {
        description +=   "; " + NumPages + " pages.";
      }
      return description;
    }
}
```

This class simply declares fields for the author, title and number of pages, then provides a property for each field, and adds a `ToString()` override to allow a book's fields to be printed out. This method does not check for various error conditions such as a missing author or title, but it does allow for the case where `NumPages` has not been initialized and is therefore still zero.

The other class reads in the data for each book from an XML file and builds a list of `Books`:

```
1. using System;
2. using System.Xml;
3. using System.Collections;
4.
5. public class BuildBookList
6. {
7.   private ArrayList bookList;
8.
9.   public BuildBookList()
```

```
10.    {
11.       bookList = new ArrayList();
12.       ReadBookList();
13.    }
14.
15.    private void ReadBookList()
16.    {
17.       Book book = null;
18.       string text = null;
19.       string fileName = "BookList.xml";
20.       XmlTextReader reader = new XmlTextReader(fileName);
21.       while(reader.Read())
22.       {
23.         if (reader.NodeType == XmlNodeType.Text)
24.         {
25.            text = reader.Value;
26.         }
27.         else if (reader.NodeType == XmlNodeType.Element)
28.         {
29.            if (reader.Name.Equals("BOOK"))
30.            {
31.              book = new Book();
32.              bookList.Add(book);
33.              try
34.              {
35.                book.NumPages =
36.                    int.Parse(reader.GetAttribute("NumPages"));
37.              }
38.              catch  {}
39.            }
40.         }
41.         else if (reader.NodeType == XmlNodeType.EndElement)
42.         {
43.            if (reader.Name.Equals("AUTHOR"))
44.            {
45.              book.Author = text;
46.            }
47.            if (reader.Name.Equals("TITLE"))
48.            {
49.              book.Title = text;
50.            }
51.         }
52.       }
53.    }
54.
55.    private void WriteBookList()
```

```
56.    {
57.      foreach (object obj in bookList)
58.      {
59.        Book book = (Book)obj;
60.        Console.WriteLine(book.ToString());
61.      }
62.    }
63.
64.    public static void Main(string[] args)
65.    {
66.      BuildBookList buildBookList = new BuildBookList();
67.      buildBookList.WriteBookList();
68.    }
69. }
```

We use an `ArrayList` to store the list of `Books` (line 7). An `ArrayList` is C#'s version of a variable-length array or linked list, implemented in Java by a `Vector` or `LinkedList`. It is part of the `System.Collections` namespace which contains a number of useful utility classes for creating collections of objects.

The constructor (line 9) creates an empty `bookList` and calls `Read BookList()` to read the XML file and add the books to the list.

`ReadBookList()` is similar to the first version of the XML parser that we used earlier. It reads from `BookList.xml` (again assumed to be in the same directory as the executable version of the program) and uses `XmlText Reader` to step through the nodes in the file. When we encounter the start tag of a `BOOK` element (line 29), we create a new `Book` and add it to `bookList`. We then extract the `NumPages` attribute from the same node (lines 33 to 38). We've enclosed this code in a `try` block since we're allowing for the possibility that the `NumPages` attribute is not present for a given book. Calling `GetAttribute()` for a non-existent attribute name throws an exception, but since this isn't really an error, we just use a `catch` to skip over this case without taking any action (line 38).

At this point, the new `Book` will have only its `NumPage` field assigned a value (if the attribute exists), so we still need to read the author and title. These are contained in separate elements rather than attributes, however, and the information is contained as a text node within the corresponding element.

We could extract the information in various ways, but probably the easiest is to save a text node as a `string` whenever it is encountered (lines 23 to 26). Then, when we find the end tag of either an `AUTHOR` or `TITLE` element, assign the text that was just extracted to the correct field in the `Book` (lines 41 to 50). This code assumes that `AUTHOR` and `TITLE` elements will always have some text within them, which of course may not be true. There are two ways we could deal with this situation. One is to insert some more error-handling code in the class shown here, but the other is a more elegant and generally better solution: write a DTD for the book XML file and use validation in the parser to ensure that all `AUTHOR` and `TITLE` elements do contain text. We'll come back to this later when we consider DTDs.

We've added an extra book to the `BookList.xml` file to test what happens if we leave off the `NumPages` attribute:

```
<?xml version="1.0" encoding="utf-8" ?>
<BOOKLIST>
  <BOOK NumPages="345">
    <AUTHOR>Zaphod Wibble</AUTHOR>
    <TITLE>Wibble's Guide to the Classics</TITLE>
  </BOOK>
  <BOOK NumPages="429">
    <AUTHOR>Isaac Asimov</AUTHOR>
    <TITLE>The Complete Stories, Vol. 1</TITLE>
  </BOOK>
  <BOOK>
    <AUTHOR>Charles Dickens</AUTHOR>
    <TITLE>A Tale of Two Cities</TITLE>
  </BOOK>
</BOOKLIST>
```

When we run the program on this file, we get the output:

```
Wibble's Guide to the Classics by Zaphod Wibble; 345 pages.
The Complete Stories, Vol. 1 by Isaac Asimov; 429 pages.
A Tale of Two Cities by Charles Dickens
```

12.5 ■ Document Type Definitions – validating XML files

As mentioned above, a *well-formed* XML file is one that adheres to the basic tree structure required by the XML specifications. A well-formed file, however, may not conform to the structure that the programmer intended, in that it may contain tags that are not recognized by the parsing program or may have elements in the wrong place. It is therefore possible for a well-formed XML file to be *invalid*, in that it does not provide its data in a form recognizable by the parsing program.

In the book list example above, we could have a BOOK element that contained two or more TITLE elements, or we might have tried to enter an author's name as an attribute rather than as an AUTHOR element, or we could have made any of many other possible errors.

A basic XML parser will be able to detect if an XML file is not well-formed, but it has no way of testing whether the file is *valid*. We could attempt to test for validity by writing checks in the C# program that parses the XML, but in all but the simplest cases, this is an extremely tedious and error-prone method. It is much better to provide a *schema* that defines the conditions an XML file must satisfy for it to be valid, and then use a *validating parser* to parse the XML.

There are several schemas which may be used to define a valid XML structure for a given project. Probably the most common of these is the *Document Type Definition* or DTD, and it is the only one we will consider in this book. Another schema gaining in popularity is *XML Schema* – if you want to learn more about this technique, consult a book on XML.

Using a DTD to validate an XML document requires three actions from the programmer. First, we must write the DTD file that defines the constraints an XML document must satisfy to be valid. Second, we need to insert a line in any XML file that is to use this DTD that connects the XML document with the DTD. Finally, we need to write the parser in such a way that it uses the DTD to validate the XML document.

12.5.1 ☐ Writing DTDs

Although a DTD can get quite involved for more complex documents, it is fairly simple to compose a DTD for most basic XML documents. We will give an introduction to the more commonly used features of DTDs and refer you to a more detailed book on XML if you want to delve more deeply into the subject.

There are four fundamental keywords used in declaring the main parts of a DTD: ELEMENT, ATTLIST, ENTITY and NOTATION. We will only consider the first two, as they are all that are needed to specify most XML document structures.

We will present the DTD for the book list XML document and use it as a starting point for describing some of the features of these keywords. The DTD is stored in a file called `BookList.dtd` and looks like this:

```
<!ELEMENT BOOKLIST (BOOK*)>

<!ELEMENT BOOK (AUTHOR+, TITLE)>
<!ATTLIST BOOK NumPages CDATA #IMPLIED>

<!ELEMENT AUTHOR (#PCDATA)>

<!ELEMENT TITLE (#PCDATA)>
```

The ELEMENT keyword is used to specify the structure of an element. We can specify what other elements the element being declared can contain, whether it can contain a text node and so on. The structure of the ELEMENT declaration is:

```
<!ELEMENT element-name (content-model)>
```

or

```
<!ELEMENT element-name category>
```

The parts in italics are those which must be filled in to define the element. All the ELEMENTs in the book list DTD are of the first type (the content model type), but we'll also consider the category type briefly later.

An ELEMENT defined using the content model must provide a list of other nodes that may be contained within it. A DTD must always begin with the root element of the XML file, in this case BOOKLIST. The BOOKLIST element has its content model shown as (BOOK*) which means that it may contain any number (zero or more) BOOK elements and nothing else.

The asterisk (*) is a *regular expression* symbol which indicates zero or more of the element it follows. The other commonly used regular expression symbols are the plus sign (+) indicating 'one or more' and the question mark (?) indicating 'zero or one'.

This declaration of BOOKLIST means that an XML document may contain an empty list, as in:

```
<BOOKLIST>
</BOOKLIST>
```

or just:

```
<BOOKLIST/>
```

If we wanted to require that a BOOKLIST element contain at least one BOOK, we could change the first line to:

```
<!ELEMENT BOOKLIST (BOOK+)>
```

The declaration of the BOOK element is:

```
<!ELEMENT BOOK (AUTHOR+, TITLE)>
```

which specifies that a BOOK must contain at least one AUTHOR (but could contain more) and exactly one TITLE (since TITLE has no regular expression symbol following it). Further, the AUTHORs must precede the TITLE – in other words, the ordering of the elements in the content model is significant.

The next line declares the attribute of the BOOK element:

```
<!ATTLIST BOOK NumPages CDATA #IMPLIED>
```

This line uses the ATTLIST keyword. The general structure of an ATTLIST is:

```
<!ATTLIST element-name
    attribute1-name attribute-type default-type-or-value
    attribute2-name attribute-type default-type-or-value
    attribute3-name attribute-type default-type-or-value
    ...
>
```

After the keyword ATTLIST must come the name of the element to which these attributes are to be assigned. In our example, we are defining attributes for the BOOK element.

Following this, we may list as many attributes as we wish. Each attribute must have a name (such as NumPages) a type and a default type, which we shall consider below.

The attribute's type can be one of ten choices, only two of which we will consider here. The most common attribute type is CDATA, or character data, which means that any string is acceptable as a value for the attribute. The NumPages attribute is declared as CDATA. There is no way of restricting the type of string any further – for example, we cannot require that the string represents a number. This sort of processing would have to be written into the C# parsing program.

The other commonly used type is an *enumerated list*, which requires us to list all the acceptable choices for the attribute's value. We could, for example, add an attribute to AUTHOR allowing us to specify a title for each author:

```
<!ATTLIST AUTHOR Title (Mr | Ms | Dr | Prof) #IMPLIED>
```

In this case, if an AUTHOR element has a Title attribute, the value must be one of those listed. The choices are separated by the vertical bar | and are *not* enclosed in quotes.

The final entry in an attribute's declaration is its *default type* or *default value*. The possible values here are #REQUIRED, meaning that the attribute *must* appear every time the element is used, #IMPLIED, meaning that the attribute is optional (as is the case with NumPages) or #FIXED (with a default value provided afterwards), meaning that the attribute is optional but if it does appear, it *must* have the value given in the DTD. The most common default types are #REQUIRED and #IMPLIED.

It is also possible to supply just a default value for the attribute. If this is done, it means that the attribute itself is optional, and if it is does not appear in an element in the XML document, then the parser should provide the default value automatically. This behaviour is only guaranteed if the parser is a validating parser however, since a non-validating parser may not even read the DTD file.

For example, we could change the NumPages attribute so that it has a default value of 100 pages by saying:

```
<!ATTLIST BOOK NumPages CDATA "100" >
```

Note that default values must be enclosed in quotes.

Using this declaration would then provide a value of 100 pages for any BOOK element that did not have a NumPages attribute, such as the Charles Dickens book in the example earlier in this chapter.

There are a number of other features that are available in DTD authoring, but those described here should suffice for our needs.

12.5.2 ☐ DOCTYPE statements

The next stage in adding validation is the connection of the XML document with the DTD. Fortunately this is very easy, requiring only an extra line in the XML document. Again, there are variations in the way this can be done, but we'll just give the most common situation here for simplicity.

The connection between XML document and DTD is done by inserting a DOCTYPE statement into the XML document, usually immediately following the XML version definition line at the top. A typical DOCTYPE statement could be inserted into our `BookList.xml` file as follows:

```
<?xml version="1.0" encoding="utf-8" ?>
<!DOCTYPE BOOKLIST SYSTEM "BookList.dtd">
<BOOKLIST>
  <BOOK NumPages="345">
    <AUTHOR>Zaphod Wibble</AUTHOR>
    <TITLE>Wibble's Guide to the Classics</TITLE>
  </BOOK>
  <BOOK NumPages="429">
    <AUTHOR>Isaac Asimov</AUTHOR>
    <TITLE>The Complete Stories, Vol. 1</TITLE>
  </BOOK>
  <BOOK>
    <AUTHOR>Charles Dickens</AUTHOR>
    <TITLE>A Tale of Two Cities</TITLE>
  </BOOK>
</BOOKLIST>
```

The DOCTYPE statement shows the root node of the XML document (BOOKLIST), followed by the keyword SYSTEM and then the DTD filename in quotes. This will work provided that the DTD file is in the same directory as the XML file.

For use over the web, it is also possible to give a URL for the location of the DTD file, such as the (fictitious) web address:

```
<!DOCTYPE BOOKLIST SYSTEM "http://my.web.site/BookList.dtd">
```

12.5.3 ☐ Using a validating parser

The final stage in the validation process is also quite easy, since .NET provides a validating parser as part of its `System.Xml` namespace. To illustrate how this is used, we will provide a rewritten version of the `BuildBookList` class we used earlier to build an internal list of the books by parsing the `BookList.xml` file. The new class is called `ValidateBookList`:

```
1. using System;
2. using System.Xml;
3. using System.Xml.Schema;
4. using System.Collections;
5.
6. public class ValidateBookList
7. {
8.   private ArrayList bookList;
9.
```

```
10.    public ValidateBookList()
11.    {
12.      bookList = new ArrayList();
13.      ReadBookList();
14.    }
15.
16.    private void ReadBookList()
17.    {
18.      Book book = null;
19.      string text = null;
20.      string fileName = "BookList.xml";
21.      XmlTextReader textReader = new XmlTextReader(fileName);
22.      XmlValidatingReader reader =
23.        new XmlValidatingReader(textReader);
24.      reader.ValidationType = ValidationType.Auto;
25.      try
26.      {
27.        while(reader.Read())
28.        {
29.          if (reader.NodeType == XmlNodeType.Text)
30.          {
31.            text = reader.Value;
32.          }
33.          else if (reader.NodeType == XmlNodeType.Element)
34.          {
35.            if (reader.Name.Equals("BOOK"))
36.            {
37.              book = new Book();
38.              bookList.Add(book);
39.              try
40.              {
41.                book.NumPages =
42.                  int.Parse(reader.GetAttribute("NumPages"));
43.              }
44.              catch  {}
45.            }
46.          }
47.          else if (reader.NodeType == XmlNodeType.EndElement)
48.          {
49.            if (reader.Name.Equals("AUTHOR"))
50.            {
51.              book.Author = text;
52.            }
53.            if (reader.Name.Equals("TITLE"))
54.            {
55.              book.Title = text;
```

```
56.                    }
57.                 }
58.              }
59.           }
60.        catch (XmlSchemaException ex)
61.        {
62.           Console.WriteLine("Error reading " + fileName);
63.           Console.WriteLine(ex.Message);
64.        }
65.     }
66.
67.     public void WriteBookList()
68.     {
69.        foreach (object obj in bookList)
70.        {
71.          Book book = (Book)obj;
72.          Console.WriteLine(book.ToString());
73.        }
74.     }
75.
76.     public static void Main(string[] args)
77.     {
78.        ValidateBookList buildBookList = new ValidateBookList();
79.        buildBookList.WriteBookList();
80.     }
81. }
```

This class is very similar to BuildBookList, but as there are a few important differences at various places, we have included the whole class again.

We define the XmlTextReader as before on line 21, but instead of using it directly to parse the XML document, we create an XmlValidatingReader on line 22. Note that an XmlValidatingReader requires an XmlTextReader to provide the link with the XML file, since it takes this as the parameter to the constructor.

The ValidationType property (line 24) allows us to specify which type of validation the parser will do. The ValidationType.Auto value that is assigned here is actually the default value, and means that the parser will attempt to discover from the XML document what type of validation is required. It can do this by reading the DOCTYPE statement in the XML file. Other values for this property allow for several other standard types of XML validation which we will not cover in this book.

After this initialization is done, we can use the XmlValidatingReader in exactly the same way as we used the XmlTextReader before. All the methods for reading and examining XML documents are present in both classes and work in almost exactly the same way.

The 'almost' in the last sentence means that the validating reader will throw an XmlSchemaException if it finds part of the XML document that does not satisfy the DTD. This allows us to catch this exception and provide some sort of error handling when a bad XML file is encountered.

We have done this in the example program here by enclosing the reading statements within a try block (lines 25 to 59). The catch block (lines 60 to 64) prints out an error message that includes the file that was being read and the message from the exception. Note that XmlSchemaException is part of the System.Xml.Schema namespace, so a using statement is required (line 3) to access it.

We'll give a couple of examples to show what happens when we attempt to parse a well-formed but invalid XML file with this new version of the parser.

First, we violate the DTD by giving the first book two TITLEs:

```
<?xml version="1.0" encoding="utf-8" ?>
<!DOCTYPE BOOKLIST SYSTEM "BookList.dtd">
<BOOKLIST>
  <BOOK NumPages="345">
    <AUTHOR>Zaphod Wibble</AUTHOR>
    <TITLE>Wibble's Guide to the Classics</TITLE>
    <TITLE>Indispensible for Beethoven Buffs</TITLE>
  </BOOK>
  <BOOK NumPages="429">
    <AUTHOR>Isaac Asimov</AUTHOR>
    <TITLE>The Complete Stories, Vol. 1</TITLE>
  </BOOK>
  <BOOK>
    <AUTHOR>Charles Dickens</AUTHOR>
    <TITLE>A Tale of Two Cities</TITLE>
  </BOOK>
</BOOKLIST>
```

The output from attempting to parse this file is (formatted a bit to improve readability):

```
Error reading BookList.xml
Element 'BOOK' has invalid child element 'TITLE'.
An error occurred at file:///C
:/books/MyBooks/CSharpBook/Programs/Chap12/ValidateBookList/
BookList.xml(7, 6).
Wibble's Guide to the Classics by Zaphod Wibble; 345 pages.
```

The error message could be a bit cryptic since it states that BOOK has an invalid child element called TITLE, rather than stating that only one TITLE child is allowed, but at least it will direct us to the right general area when tracking down the error.

This example also illustrates again that the XmlReader classes read the file sequentially rather than attempting to construct the entire XML tree within the program. After the error message, we see that the book list actually does contain one entry which was created when the first TITLE element was read for the first BOOK. The validation error was only detected when the second TITLE element was found. This caused the exception to be thrown, which prevented any further processing of the XML document since the entire parsing loop is inside the `try` block.

As a second example, we try removing both the AUTHOR and TITLE elements from the second book:

```
<?xml version="1.0" encoding="utf-8" ?>
<!DOCTYPE BOOKLIST SYSTEM "BookList.dtd">
<BOOKLIST>
  <BOOK NumPages="345">
    <AUTHOR>Zaphod Wibble</AUTHOR>
    <TITLE>Wibble's Guide to the Classics</TITLE>
  </BOOK>
  <BOOK NumPages="429">
  </BOOK>
  <BOOK>
    <AUTHOR>Charles Dickens</AUTHOR>
    <TITLE>A Tale of Two Cities</TITLE>
  </BOOK>
</BOOKLIST>
```

This file produces the output:

```
Error reading BookList.xml
Element 'BOOK' has incomplete content. Expected 'AUTHOR'.
An error occurred at
file:///C:/books/MyBooks/CSharpBook/Programs/
Chap12/VerifyBookList/BookList.xml(9, 5).
Wibble's Guide to the Classics by Zaphod Wibble; 345 pages.
 by ; 429 pages.
```

This is a fairly clear error message and should enable us to track down the cause quite easily.

12.6 ■ The Document Object Model

As mentioned earlier, there are two main techniques for parsing XML documents. `XmlTextReader` provides a one-way trip through a document and is suited to extracting information from XML for use elsewhere. It takes no account of the tree structure of the document.

The second method makes use of the *Document Object Model* or DOM, which loads an entire XML document into the program and preserves its structure, allowing the program to navigate within the tree. The main DOM class is `XmlDocument`, which stores an entire XML document as a data structure within a C# program.

Once a document has been loaded, there are a number of methods in the XmlDocument class that can be used to navigate around the tree and extract information. The following program illustrates how to load an XmlDocument and use some of these methods to extract the author, title and number of pages for each of the books in the XML file used earlier.

```
1.  using System;
2.  using System.Xml;
3.  using System.Xml.Schema;
4.
5.  public class DomReader
6.  {
7.      private XmlDocument xmlDocument;
8.
9.      public DomReader()
10.     {
11.         xmlDocument = new XmlDocument();
12.         ReadBookList();
13.         PrintBookList();
14.     }
15.
16.     private void ReadBookList()
17.     {
18.         string fileName = @"BookList.xml";
19.         XmlTextReader textReader = new XmlTextReader(fileName);
20.         XmlValidatingReader reader =
21.             new XmlValidatingReader(textReader);
22.         reader.ValidationType = ValidationType.Auto;
23.         try
24.         {
25.             xmlDocument.Load(reader);
26.         }
27.         catch (XmlSchemaException ex)
28.         {
29.             Console.WriteLine("Error reading " + fileName);
30.             Console.WriteLine(ex.Message);
31.         }
32.     }
33.
34.     private void PrintBookList()
35.     {
36.         XmlNode currNode = xmlDocument.DocumentElement;
37.         if (currNode.HasChildNodes)
38.         {
39.             XmlNode book = currNode.FirstChild;
40.             while (book != null)
```

```
41.        {
42.            string bookDescription = "";
43.            XmlNode bookChild = book.FirstChild;
44.            while (bookChild != null)
45.            {
46.                if (bookChild.NodeType == XmlNodeType.Element)
47.                {
48.                    if (bookChild.Name.Equals("AUTHOR"))
49.                    {
50.                        bookDescription += "Author: " +
51.                            bookChild.InnerText + "; ";
52.                    }
53.                    else if (bookChild.Name.Equals("TITLE"))
54.                    {
55.                        bookDescription += "Title: " +
56.                            bookChild.InnerText + "; ";
57.                    }
58.                }
59.                bookChild = bookChild.NextSibling;
60.            }
61.            XmlAttributeCollection attributes = book.Attributes;
62.            if (attributes.Count > 0)
63.            {
64.                bookDescription += attributes["NumPages"].Value +
65.                    " pages";
66.            }
67.            Console.WriteLine(bookDescription + "\n");
68.            book = book.NextSibling;
69.        }
70.    }
71.  }
72.
73.  public static void Main(string[] args)
74.  {
75.      DomReader buildBookList = new DomReader();
76.  }
77. }
```

We declare the XmlDocument as a class member (line 7) since in most applications it will be used in various methods within the class. The constructor (line 9) initializes the XmlDocument and then uses it to load in an XML document from a file (in ReadBookList()) and print out the book list.

ReadBookList() (line 16) shows how to use validation in conjunction with XmlDocument. We create an XmlTextReader (line 19) connected to the disk file, then attach an XmlValidatingReader to the text reader (line 20), and finally use XmlDocument's Load() method (line 25) to load the document through the validating reader. The validation occurs in the same way as before, with an `XmlSchemaException` being thrown if some part of the XML document doesn't match the DTD, so we enclose the call to `Load()` within a `try` block.

Note that the call to `Load()` is all we need to do to read in the XML document, since `Load()` not only parses the XML file, but also builds the document tree within the `XmlDocument` object, rather than just reading through the file one line at a time.

Once we have loaded the document, we can navigate through it by using several other classes designed for the purpose. In `PrintBookList()`, we locate all BOOK nodes and then extract the author, title and number of pages for each book. Rather than doing this by iterating through the nodes of the XML document as we did before, we need to move about within the document tree. To do this, we need to start at the root of the tree (the BOOKLIST element), so we obtain this by using the `DocumentElement` property of `XmlDocument` (line 36).

Any node in a document tree is represented as an `XmlNode`, as with `currNode` on line 36. Since 'node' is a generic term for any component of an XML document, an `XmlNode` can store a variety of types of component, but it is relatively easy to extract the information we need from a given node, as we'll see below.

To extract the information on the books stored in the XML file, we need to traverse the tree starting from the root node. We begin this process on line 37 by testing if the root (BOOKLIST) has any children using the `HasChildNodes` property. (Recall that the DTD did allow BOOKLIST to be empty, so we do need to check for this.)

If the root node does have some children, we know from the DTD and the fact that this program uses validation when loading the document that all these children must be BOOK elements, so we don't need to check this here. We can therefore just load the first BOOK into an `XmlNode` using the `FirstChild` property of `rootNode` (line 39). This child is stored in an `XmlNode` called `book`, and this object is reused within the `while` loop (line 40) to examine all the BOOK elements in the document.

We will build up a description of each book in the string `bookDescription` (line 42). Since we know from the DTD that a BOOK element must have at least one AUTHOR and a TITLE, we know that all BOOK elements must have children, so we do not need to test for this before examining the children of the `book` node. We therefore begin by extracting the first child of `book` on line 43.

We'll build up the description by scanning through the children of each `book` node within the loop on line 44. As mentioned earlier, an `XmlNode` is a generic class designed to hold all types of node from an XML document, so we need to check that each node is of the desired type before we try to use it. We can do this by looking at its `NodeType` property (line 46) which returns an `XmlNodeType` value. We are looking for elements within the BOOK element, so we test that the current child of BOOK is of type `XmlNodeType.Element`. If it is, then we need to determine the name of the element (AUTHOR or TITLE).

We can get this from the Name property (line 48). (Note that Name returns different information depending on the type of the node – see the documentation for XmlNode for details.) If we have found an AUTHOR element, we can extract the author's name by using the InnerText property of the node (line 50). We use the same process to obtain the book's title (line 53).

After processing one of the children of a BOOK node, we can move along to the next child by using the NextSibling property (line 59). NextSibling returns an XmlNode if there is another sibling, or null if not.

We have not yet extracted the number of pages for the book, so we do this on line 61 by using the Attributes property of the book node. This returns a collection (essentially an array) of all attributes for that node (if the node is of a type that can have attributes, of course). Each element in this collection is an XmlAttribute. As line 64 shows, we can index the attributes in the collection using their names. Here we access the NumPages attribute's value and append it to bookDescription.

Once we have gathered all the information for the current book, we print it to the console (line 67) and then proceed to the next sibling of the root node (line 68).

The output of this program for the BookList.xml file we have been using throughout this chapter is:

```
Author: Zaphod Wibble; Title: Wibble's Guide to the
Classics; 345 pages

Author: Isaac Asimov; Title: The Complete Stories, Vol. 1;
429 pages

Author: Charles Dickens; Title: A Tale of Two Cities;
```

12.7 ■ Searching an XML tree with XPath

The example in the previous section shows how an XML document can be loaded into an XmlDocument and how the resulting tree can be navigated to extract information. The example works well if we need to process all the data stored in the document, but in some cases we need to extract a small subset of the total data collection by specifying some condition that the data should satisfy.

There is a standard language called XPath that is used to search XML documents for nodes satisfying certain conditions. The full specification for XPath is given on the W3C web site (www.w3c.org). Here we shall describe the basics of XPath in order that we may understand how it is used in C# and .NET.

At its simplest level, an XPath specifies a path starting at the root of the document and extending to some depth into the document tree. The slash symbol / is used to separate layers in the tree.

For example, the XPath expression:

```
/BOOKLIST/BOOK/AUTHOR
```

would search the document for all AUTHOR elements that were children of a BOOK element that is in turn a child of a BOOKLIST element.

Before we get too deeply into XPath syntax, we should show how XPath can be used in C# so you can try out the various path statements and see how they work.

.NET provides a set of classes for dealing with XPath searches, but before we examine these it is probably easier to use some of the search methods available in XmlDocument, since these also use XPath expressions.

As a simple example, we can replace the PrintBookList() method in the DomReader class in the last section with the following:

```
private void PrintBookList()
{
   string search = "/BOOKLIST/BOOK/AUTHOR";
   XmlNodeList authorList = xmlDocument.SelectNodes(search);
   foreach(XmlNode node in authorList)
   {
     Console.WriteLine(node.InnerText);
   }
}
```

We specify the XPath search statement as a string, and then use SelectNodes() to search the document tree for all nodes that satisfy this condition. (There is a SelectSingleNode() method if we only want the first occurrence of a node that matches the search condition.) The result is returned as an XmlNodeList, which is a list of XmlNodes. We can then loop through the list and print out the InnerText, which is the text component of the AUTHOR element. The result is:

```
Zaphod Wibble
Isaac Asimov
Charles Dickens
```

XPath allows more specific searches to be done by providing ways of specifying the actual value or values of the data at various places along the path. For example, if we wanted a list of all books by Isaac Asimov we can use the search string:

```
/BOOKLIST/BOOK[AUTHOR = 'Isaac Asimov']
```

That is, we apply conditions to a node by adding the condition in square brackets after the node name. The condition BOOK[AUTHOR = 'Isaac Asimov'] states that in order to be selected, the BOOK element must have a child element with the name AUTHOR, and that the value (text) of that element must be 'Isaac Asimov'. Note that a single = sign is used to specify the value in the condition. That is, a single = sign in XPath is an equality operator and not an assignment operator in this context.

The value of an attribute can be specified by giving the attribute name prefixed by an @ sign. For example, we can search for all books containing 429 pages by using the search string:

```
/BOOKLIST/BOOK[@NumPages = '429']
```

More complex searches can be done by using one of the XPath functions that are provided as part of the XPath specification. A complete list of standard XPath functions is available at the W3C web site.

As a simple example, if we are uncertain as to whether Isaac Asimov's name is given as 'Isaac Asimov', 'Asimov, Isaac', 'I. Asimov' or 'Asimov, I.', we can use the `contains()` function to test if the AUTHOR text field contains the string 'Asimov':

```
/BOOKLIST/BOOK[contains(AUTHOR, 'Asimov')]
```

The `contains()` function takes two parameters, the first of which is the string to be searched and the second of which is the search string. If we give an element name as the first parameter, the text component of that element is used as the string to be searched. This XPath expression will therefore find all BOOK elements that have an AUTHOR child that contains the string 'Asimov'.

As we mentioned earlier, .NET provides an XPath namespace which allows quick navigation within a document using XPath commands. The XPath classes provide read-only access to XML documents (we will see below that `XmlDocument` allows editing and writing of documents as well), and is primarily used as a front end for transforming XML into other document types using XSLT, as we will see later in this chapter.

At this point, however, we can give a simple example of how some of the XPath classes are used. The following code duplicates an earlier example by reading in the `BookList.xml` file, searching for all AUTHOR elements and writing out their text values.

```
1.  using System;
2.  using System.Xml;
3.  using System.Xml.Schema;
4.  using System.Xml.XPath;
5.
6.  public class DomReader
7.  {
8.      private XPathDocument xPathDocument;
9.      private XPathNavigator xPathNavigator;
10.
11.     public DomReader()
12.     {
13.         ReadBookList();
14.         PrintBookList();
15.     }
16.
```

```
17.    private void ReadBookList()
18.    {
19.      string fileName = "BookList.xml";
20.      XmlTextReader textReader = new XmlTextReader(fileName);
21.      XmlValidatingReader reader =
22.        new XmlValidatingReader(textReader);
23.      reader.ValidationType = ValidationType.Auto;
24.      try
25.      {
26.        xPathDocument = new XPathDocument(reader);
27.        xPathNavigator = xPathDocument.CreateNavigator();
28.      }
29.      catch (XmlSchemaException ex)
30.      {
31.        Console.WriteLine("Error reading " + fileName);
32.        Console.WriteLine(ex.Message);
33.      }
34.    }
35.
36.    private void PrintBookList()
37.    {
38.      string search = "/BOOKLIST/BOOK/AUTHOR";
39.      XPathNodeIterator nodes = xPathNavigator.Select(search);
40.      while (nodes.MoveNext())
41.      {
42.        Console.WriteLine(nodes.Current.Value);
43.      }
44.    }
45.
46.    public static void Main(string[] args)
47.    {
48.      DomReader buildBookList = new DomReader();
49.    }
50. }
```

Classes in the XPath namespace require a using System.Xml.XPath statement (line 4).

Using XPath classes requires two main steps. First, we load the document into an XPathDocument, and then we create an XPathNavigator to allow navigation within the document.

The creation of the XPathDocument is similar to the creation of an XmlDocument. If we require validation of the document, we create an XmlTextReader, then attach an XmlValidatingReader, and then create an XPathDocument, passing the XmlValidatingReader as a parameter to the constructor (lines 20 to 26).

An `XPathNavigator` can be created for any data store that implements the `IXPathNavigable` interface, although in practice it is used mainly for navigating through `XPathDocument`s. The `XPathNavigator` is the real power behind the XPath classes, as it provides all the methods for moving around and searching an XML document using XPath commands. We see how to create an `XPathNavigator` from an `XPathDocument` on line 27.

Once we have the `XPathNavigator`, we can start moving around the document in a variety of ways. The class contains 14 different methods for moving to a specified node in the tree, and also contains methods that allow searching of the tree using XPath commands. In our simple example here, we have used the `Select()` method (line 39) to select all AUTHOR elements.

Rather than return the results of the search as an array, the `Select()` method returns an `XPathNodeIterator`, which allows us to step through the list using the `MoveNext()` method. At each point in the iteration, we can access the current node using the `Current` property.

One thing should be noted about the object returned by `Current`: it is actually an `XPathNavigator` that is returned and not, say, an `XmlNode`. An `XPathNavigator` stores a marker to its current position in the tree as well as allowing movement within the tree. However, the `XPathNavigator` that is returned by the `Current` property should only be used to obtain properties of the current node, and should not be used to move away from that node to other parts of the tree. Attempting to move around in the tree can invalidate the state of the navigator which can cause the iteration to behave incorrectly.

In the example above, we have only used `Current` to access the `Value` property of the current node, which is the text belonging to the AUTHOR element.

12.8 ■ Editing and writing XML

.NET provides two main facilities for writing XML files from within a C# program. The first uses the `XmlTextWriter` class and is basically a mirror of `XmlTextReader` in that it allows XML to be written in a linear fashion with no recognition of the structure of the document. The second method writes an `XmlDocument` to a stream (such as a disk file), and translates all the internal structure of the document directly into XML code with a single method call.

The first method is probably used less than the second, since if we are building an XML document within C# code, we usually need to use `XmlDocument` in order to retain the structure of the document as it is built. However, it is worth having a look at a simple example of `XmlTextWriter` to illustrate how it is used.

12.8.1 ☐ **XmlTextWriter**

The following code writes a booklist XML file from scratch and inserts a single BOOK element in it:

```
string simpleFile = "Simple.xml";
XmlTextWriter simpleWriter =
    new XmlTextWriter(simpleFile, System.Text.Encoding.UTF8);
simpleWriter.Formatting = Formatting.Indented;
simpleWriter.WriteStartDocument();
simpleWriter.WriteDocType("BOOKLIST", null,
    "BookList.dtd", null);
simpleWriter.WriteStartElement("BOOKLIST");
simpleWriter.WriteStartElement("BOOK");
simpleWriter.WriteAttributeString("NumPages", "145");
simpleWriter.WriteElementString("AUTHOR", "Jules Verne");
simpleWriter.WriteElementString("TITLE",
    "Around the World in 80 Days");
simpleWriter.WriteEndElement();
simpleWriter.WriteEndElement();
simpleWriter.WriteEndDocument();
simpleWriter.Flush();
simpleWriter.Close();
```

As can be seen, the code consists of a number of fairly obvious method calls to produce the XML in a linear fashion. We begin by creating the XmlTextWriter, passing the name of the file to create, and an *encoding* option. UTF-8 encoding is fairly standard for most documents so the option given should work for most situations. It is also acceptable just to use a null here.

XmlTextWriter allows the XML to be formatted in various ways – probably the most useful formatting option is Indented, which produces nicely indented XML statements which make it easier for humans to read.

After this, we call WriteStartDocument(), which writes out the XML header line (containing the version number and encoding option, if any). After this, if we need validation to occur when the XML file is used, we can insert a call to WriteDocType(), which produces a DOCTYPE statement. This method contains four parameters which allow for all the various types of DOCTYPE that are available in the current XML standard. To produce the simple DOCTYPE we have used earlier in the section on validation, insert the name of the root element (BOOKLIST here) as the first parameter and the name of the DTD file as the third parameter, leaving the second and fourth parameters as null.

After the preliminaries, we can write out the XML code proper. Elements that contain more than just a text node can be written in stages, by beginning with a call to WriteStartElement(), in which we provide the element's name. Then we can insert the elements that are contained by the top-level element, as we have done here by inserting BOOK element and then the AUTHOR and TITLE elements contained within the BOOK.

An attribute can be attached to an element by using `WriteAttribute String()`, which takes two parameters: the name of the attribute and its value

Elements such as AUTHOR and TITLE, which contain text only, can be written with a single call to `WriteElementString()`, providing the element name and the text as the two parameters.

To complete a compound element after all its internals have been written, we just call `WriteEndElement()` without any parameters. Note that `XmlText Writer` is intelligent enough to keep track of the last element that was opened and will provide the correct closing tag each time this method is called.

We clean up with calls to `WriteEndDocument()`, `Flush()` and `Close()`. The output from this code looks like this:

```
<?xml version="1.0" encoding="utf-8"?>
<!DOCTYPE BOOKLIST SYSTEM "BookList.dtd">
<BOOKLIST>
  <BOOK NumPages="145">
    <AUTHOR>Jules Verne</AUTHOR>
    <TITLE>Around the World in 80 Days</TITLE>
  </BOOK>
</BOOKLIST>
```

12.8.2 □ Writing XML using `XmlDocument`

While this simple use of `XmlTextWriter` may be useful if you are reading in some data from an external source and translating it directly into XML, so that the structure of the data is known in advance and is not editable, a far more common situation is an interactive program in which the user may view existing data and edit it by changing existing entries, adding new entries or deleting existing entries. For this sort of flexibility, we need to maintain the structure of the XML document within the C# program, so we need to use `XmlDocument` to represent the XML internally.

`XmlDocument` and its associated classes provide a wide variety of methods for manipulating XML documents, so we will just illustrate some of the basics by presenting a GUI program in which the user can view the books in an existing XML file, and edit these contents by changing the data for existing books and adding or deleting books from the file.

The interface to the program is as shown in Figure 12.2.

The program reads the `BookList.xml` file upon startup and displays the titles of the books it finds in that file in a `ListBox` in the lower panel. If the user selects a title with the mouse, the details for that book are displayed in the text boxes at the top. The user can then edit these text boxes and press 'Change' to save the changes to the XML file.

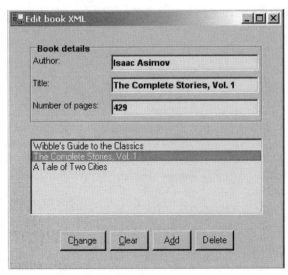

Figure 12.2 Interface to 'Edit book XML' program

Pressing 'Clear' clears all the data in the text boxes and deselects the list. If the user then types in data for a new book and presses 'Add', the new book is added to the XML file and the title list is updated to show the new entry. Finally, selecting a title in the list and pressing 'Delete' deletes the book from the XML file and updates the display.

The complete code for this example is fairly long, but much of the code deals with the initialization of the GUI, and we will not present this here since it uses no new techniques beyond those that were covered in Chapter 9. The complete program is available from the book's web site.

The remainder of the class is as follows:

```
1. using System;
2. using System.Drawing;
3. using System.Windows.Forms;
4. using System.Xml;
5. using System.Xml.Schema;
6.
7. public class EditXMLForm : Form
8. {
9.     private ListBox titleList;
10.    private GroupBox detailsBox;
11.    private TextBox authorBox, titleBox, numPagesBox;
12.    private Button applyButton, clearButton, addButton,
13.       deleteButton;
14.    private Font titleFont = new Font("Arial", 8,
       FontStyle.Bold);
15.    private Font labelFont =
```

```
16.      new Font("Arial", 8, FontStyle.Regular);
17.  private XmlDocument xmlDocument;
18.  private XmlNode selectedNode;
19.  private string fileName = "BookList.xml";
20.
21.  public EditXMLForm()
22.  {
23.     InitializeComponents();
24.     ReadBookXML();
25.     PopulateTitleList();
26.  }
27.
28.  private void ReadBookXML()
29.  {
30.     xmlDocument = new XmlDocument();
31.     XmlTextReader textReader = new XmlTextReader(fileName);
32.     XmlValidatingReader reader =
33.        new XmlValidatingReader(textReader);
34.     reader.ValidationType = ValidationType.Auto;
35.     try
36.     {
37.        xmlDocument.Load(reader);
38.        textReader.Close();
39.     }
40.     catch (XmlSchemaException ex)
41.     {
42.        Console.WriteLine("Error reading " + fileName);
43.        Console.WriteLine(ex.Message);
44.     }
45.  }
46.
47.  private void PopulateTitleList()
48.  {
49.     XmlNodeList titleNodeList =
50.        xmlDocument.GetElementsByTagName("TITLE");
51.     titleList.Items.Clear();
52.     foreach (XmlNode titleNode in titleNodeList)
53.     {
54.        titleList.Items.Add(titleNode.InnerText);
55.     }
56.  }
57.
58.  private void InitializeComponents()
59.  {
60.     // Code to set up GUI - see web site for details
61.  }
```

```
62.
63.    private void ClearDisplay()
64.    {
65.      authorBox.Text = "";
66.      titleBox.Text = "";
67.      numPagesBox.Text = "";
68.      titleList.ClearSelected();
69.      selectedNode = null;
70.    }
71.
72.    private void AddNewBook()
73.    {
74.      XmlElement newBook = xmlDocument.CreateElement("BOOK");
75.      XmlElement authorElement =
76.        xmlDocument.CreateElement("AUTHOR");
77.      authorElement.InnerText = authorBox.Text;
78.      newBook.AppendChild(authorElement);
79.      XmlElement titleElement =
80.        xmlDocument.CreateElement("TITLE");
81.      titleElement.InnerText = titleBox.Text;
82.      newBook.AppendChild(titleElement);
83.
84.      if (numPagesBox.Text.Length > 0)
85.      {
86.        newBook.SetAttribute("NumPages", numPagesBox.Text);
87.      }
88.      xmlDocument.DocumentElement.AppendChild(newBook);
89.      WriteBookXML();
90.    }
91.
92.    private void WriteBookXML()
93.    {
94.      XmlTextWriter textWriter =
95.        new XmlTextWriter(fileName, System.⤶
        Text.Encoding.UTF8);
96.      textWriter.Formatting = Formatting.Indented;
97.      xmlDocument.WriteContentTo(textWriter);
98.      textWriter.Close();
99.    }
100.
101.   private void OnLayoutForm(object sender, ⤶
       LayoutEventArgs args)
102.   {
103.     if (sender == this)
104.     {
105.       detailsBox.Location = new Point(
```

```
106.             this.ClientSize.Width/2 - detailsBox.
                 Size.Width/2, 20);
107.           titleList.Location = new Point(
108.             this.ClientSize.Width/2 - titleList.Size.Width/2,
109.             detailsBox.Location.Y + detailsBox.
                 Size.Height + 20);
110.           applyButton.Location = new Point(
111.             this.ClientSize.Width/2 - (applyButton.Size.Width +
112.             addButton.Size.Width + clearButton.Size.Width
113.             + deleteButton.Size.Width + 15)/2,
114.             titleList.Location.Y + titleList.Size.Height + 20);
115.           clearButton.Location = new Point(
116.             applyButton.Location.X + applyButton.
                 Size.Width + 5,
117.             titleList.Location.Y + titleList.Size.Height + 20);
118.           addButton.Location = new Point(
119.             applyButton.Location.X + applyButton.Size.Width +
120.             clearButton.Size.Width + 10,
121.             titleList.Location.Y + titleList.Size.Height + 20);
122.           deleteButton.Location = new Point(
123.             applyButton.Location.X + applyButton.Size.Width +
124.             clearButton.Size.Width + addButton.Size.Width + 15,
125.             titleList.Location.Y + titleList.Size.Height + 20);
126.         }
127.     }
128.
129.     private void OnSelectTitle(object sender,
         EventArgs args)
130.     {
131.       if (titleList.SelectedItem == null) return;
132.       string selectedTitle = titleList.
           SelectedItem.ToString();
133.       selectedNode = xmlDocument.SelectSingleNode(
134.         "/BOOKLIST/BOOK[TITLE = \"" + selectedTitle + "\"]");
135.       if (selectedNode != null)
136.       {
137.         XmlNode childNode =
138.           selectedNode.SelectSingleNode("TITLE");
139.         titleBox.Text = childNode.InnerText;
140.         childNode = selectedNode.SelectSingleNode("AUTHOR");
141.         authorBox.Text = childNode.InnerText;
142.         XmlAttributeCollection attributes =
143.           selectedNode.Attributes;
144.         if (attributes.Count > 0)
145.         {
146.           numPagesBox.Text = attributes["NumPages"].Value;
```

```
147.        }
148.      else
149.      {
150.        numPagesBox.Text = "";
151.      }
152.    }
153.  }
154.
155.  private void OnApply(object sender, EventArgs args)
156.  {
157.    if (sender == applyButton)
158.    {
159.      if (selectedNode != null)
160.      {
161.        XmlElement selectedElement = (XmlElement)
             selectedNode;
162.        XmlNode childNode =
163.          selectedElement.SelectSingleNode("TITLE");
164.        childNode.InnerText = titleBox.Text;
165.        childNode = selectedElement.SelectSingleNode
             ("AUTHOR");
166.        childNode.InnerText = authorBox.Text;
167.        if (numPagesBox.Text.Length > 0)
168.        {
169.          selectedElement.SetAttribute("NumPages",
170.            numPagesBox.Text);
171.        }
172.        else
173.        {
174.          selectedElement.RemoveAttribute("NumPages");
175.        }
176.        WriteBookXML();
177.        PopulateTitleList();
178.      }
179.    }
180.  }
181.
182.  private void OnClear(object sender, EventArgs args)
183.  {
184.    ClearDisplay();
185.  }
186.
187.  private void OnAdd(object sender, EventArgs args)
188.  {
189.    AddNewBook();
190.    PopulateTitleList();
```

```
191.    }
192.
193.    private void OnDelete(object sender, EventArgs args)
194.    {
195.      if (selectedNode != null)
196.      {
197.        XmlNode parent = selectedNode.ParentNode;
198.        parent.RemoveChild(selectedNode);
199.        WriteBookXML();
200.        ClearDisplay();
201.        PopulateTitleList();
202.      }
203.    }
204.
205.    public static void Main()
206.    {
207.      Application.Run(new EditXMLForm());
208.    }
209. }
```

The code in `InitializeComponents()` creates and places the various GUI controls, and adds event handlers to the `Button`s and `ListBox`. When the form is first displayed, `OnLayoutForm()` is called to position the controls on the client area. We'll consider the event handlers after considering the remaining setup code.

The initial XML file is read in using `ReadBookXML()` (line 28). This process is the same as that which we described earlier when introducing `XmlDocument`: the XML document is read in, using validation, and stored internally in `xmlDocument`.

After this, we fill `titleList` (the `ListBox` control that displays the book titles) in `PopulateTitleList()`. We use `GetElementsByTagName()` to retrieve a list of all TITLE elements in the XML document (lines 49–50). We then add the `InnerText` of each of these elements to `titleList` (lines 52 to 55) to create the initial display that is visible when the program loads.

After this, everything happens in one of the event handlers in response to a user action. First, suppose the user selects a book in the list by clicking on it with the mouse. This triggers a `SelectedItemChanged` event in the `ListBox`, to which we have attached the `OnSelectTitle()` method as an event handler (line 129).

Line 131 checks that an item has actually been selected, since when we clear the `ListBox` (by pressing the 'Clear' button; see below), this method is also called.

The main purpose of `OnSelectTitle()` is to display the details of the selected book in the text boxes at the top of the window. We therefore must find the element in `xmlDocument` corresponding to the title that was chosen by the user. We first extract the title that was selected (line 132). We can then use this title to search `xmlDocument` for the BOOK element that contains it as the text in its child TITLE element. We do this by using an XPath search string (lines 133 and 134). For example, if the user selected 'A Tale of Two Cities', the XPath string is:

```
/BOOKLIST/BOOK[TITLE = "A Tale of Two Cities"]
```

This statement states that the BOOK node (not the TITLE node) should be retrieved, which is what we want since we need to extract the other data relating to that book in order to display it in the text boxes.

At this point, we should make a comment about the use of quotes for delimiting strings in XPath search statements. Earlier, we used single quotes (apostrophes) to delimit the strings in attributes and XPath search strings, while here we have used the double quote (line 134). In fact, both attributes and XPath search strings may use either type of quote. We have used the double quote here since some book titles contain apostrophes (as in "Wibble's Guide to the Classics"), and if we use the double quote to delimit the string, single quotes are considered part of the string rather than delimiters.

This raises the fairly obvious question as to what to do if the string we are searching for itself contains both single and double quotes. Bizarrely, it seems that it is not possible to search for strings of this type. None of the standard procedures for escaping symbols by preceding them with the backslash character, or of doubling up apostrophes (as is done in SQL statements, for example), or of using the long form of special symbols such as `&quot;` for " or `&apos;` for ' seems to work, and the documentation offers no help.

Once we have found the BOOK element corresponding to the selected title, it is stored in `selectedNode`, and may then be used to extract the author and number of pages, which we do inside the `if` statement on lines 137 to 151.

This code illustrates that we may use XPath to search for a node starting at an internal element rather than at the root of the document. Line 137 searches for the TITLE element *relative* to `selectedNode`, so it will return the TITLE of the selected book. Line 139 then copies this text into `titleBox`, which is the `TextBox` displaying the book's title. Lines 140 and 141 do likewise for the AUTHOR element.

To extract the number of pages, we need to retrieve the `NumPages` attribute from the BOOK element. Since the DTD allows this node to be optional, we cannot be sure it will be there for every BOOK. We therefore first retrieve the list of attributes for `selectedNode` (line 142) and then check if this list has any elements in it (line 144). If so, we retrieve the value for `NumPages` and display it. If not, we clear `numPagesBox`, since otherwise selecting a book without a `NumPages` attribute after selecting one that did have one would leave the earlier `NumPages` value displayed.

Now let us assume that the user makes some changes to the selected book and wishes to save these changes in the XML file. After editing the text in the various `TextBoxes`, the 'Change' button is pressed, which calls `OnApply()` (line 155).

We wish to edit the various child nodes of the current BOOK element in response to the changes typed in by the user. In order to edit an element, we need to use the `XmlElement` class, which is derived from `XmlNode`. We therefore cast `selectedNode` to an `XmlElement` called `selectedElement` (line 161) to allow us to use the `XmlElement` methods for editing.

To update the title of the book, we search the element for its TITLE node (line 162) and then copy the text in `titleBox` into the `InnerText` property of the TITLE node (line 164). We repeat the process to update the AUTHOR (lines 165 to 166).

To update the number of pages, we examine what is in the `numPagesBox` text box. If the user has entered a value, we use `SetAttribute()` to set the value for the `NumPages` attribute (line 169). Note that `NumPages` is an attribute of a BOOK element, so we call `SetAttribute()` from `selectedElement`.

If the user has not entered anything in `numPagesBox`, we remove the `NumPages` attribute from `selectedElement` (line 174).

This completes the updating of the internal XML element within `xml Document`, but to complete the process we need to save the document to disk. For this, we call `WriteBookXML()` on line 176.

The code for `WriteBookXML()` begins on line 92. Writing an `XmlDocument` to disk is very simple – we first create an `XmlTextWriter` as we did in writing out the straightforward XML above (lines 94 to 96) and then just call `WriteContentTo()` from `xmlDocument` (line 97). This method handles the creation of all the elements internally so we don't need to worry about starting and ending elements and so forth.

After calling `WriteBookXML()` on line 176, we update the title list by calling `PopulateTitleList()` again (line 177). This will refresh the display by updating the title displayed in the list.

The other three buttons are all fairly simple. The 'Clear' button is connected to the `OnClear()` event handler (line 182) which just calls `Clear Display()`, the code for which is on line 63. We just clear all the text boxes and the title list box, and set `selectedNode` to `null`.

Adding a new book by pressing the 'Add' button calls `OnAdd()` on line 187, which in turn calls `AddNewBook()` to add the new book to the XML document and write it to disk, and then calls `PopulateTitleList()` to add the new title to the display.

`AddNewBook()` (line 72) illustrates how a brand new element can be added to an existing XML document. We create the element on line 74 by calling `CreateElement()` from `XmlDocument`. The parameter passed to this method is the name of the new element. We are adding a new BOOK so we create this here, and then add its child nodes to it later.

We then create another new element for the AUTHOR element that is to be a child of the new BOOK (line 75). The `InnerText` of the AUTHOR is copied from `authorBox`, and then `AppendChild()` is used to attach the AUTHOR to the new BOOK (line 78).

Note that the order in which new nodes are created and added is important if we want the new element to be consistent with the DTD, which specifies that any AUTHOR nodes must precede the TITLE node in a BOOK element.

Remember that XML writers do not validate documents when they write them, so it's up to you to make sure you create the XML documents correctly!

We repeat the process to add the TITLE (lines 79 to 82). Then we must deal with the NumPages attribute. First, we check (line 84) if the user has entered a value for the number of pages. If so, we use SetAttribute() as before (line 86) to set a NumPages attribute for the new BOOK. If there is no entry in numPagesBox we don't need to do anything, since a new element will not have any attributes unless we assign them using SetAttribute().

After we have finished creating the new BOOK, we must not forget to connect it to the existing document, and to do so in the right place. In this simple example, all BOOK elements are attached directly to the root of the document, so we can use the DocumentElement property of xmlDocument (line 88) to retrieve this root node and attach the new BOOK to it. In a more general situation, we may need to search for the correct node in the document first (using an XPath statement, for example) before attaching the new node.

After attaching the new node, we save the new document with Write BookXML() as before (line 89).

Finally, if the user selects a title and then presses 'Delete', we must delete the corresponding BOOK from the document. This is done with the OnDelete() event handler (line 193).

Deleting a node from an XML tree requires that we obtain the node's parent, so first we do this by using the ParentNode property (line 197). Once we have the parent, we can then call RemoveChild() to delete the selected book (line 198). After this, we call WriteBookXML() to save the document, then clear all the text boxes and selections with ClearDisplay() and finally update the title list with PopulateTitleList().

After using this program to add 'Around the World in 80 Days' by Jules Verne (with 534 pages), the XML file looks like this:

```
<?xml version="1.0" encoding="utf-8"?>
<!DOCTYPE BOOKLIST SYSTEM "BookList.dtd"[]>
<BOOKLIST>
  <BOOK NumPages="345">
    <AUTHOR>Zaphod Wibble</AUTHOR>
    <TITLE>Wibble's Guide to the Classics</TITLE>
  </BOOK>
  <BOOK NumPages="429">
    <AUTHOR>Isaac Asimov</AUTHOR>
    <TITLE>The Complete Stories, Vol. 1</TITLE>
  </BOOK>
  <BOOK NumPages="145">
    <AUTHOR>Charles Dickens</AUTHOR>
    <TITLE>A Tale of Two Cities</TITLE>
  </BOOK>
  <BOOK NumPages="534">
    <AUTHOR>Jules Verne</AUTHOR>
```

```
    <TITLE>Around the World in 80 Days</TITLE>
  </BOOK>
</BOOKLIST>
```

This example has shown a few of the simpler techniques for editing and writing XML documents. You should explore the documentation for `XmlDocument` and its associated classes such as `XmlElement` to learn more about what's available.

12.9 ■ Transforming XML – XSLT

We've seen in this chapter that XML can be handled within C# in a number of ways, many of which involve extracting the information within certain types of elements and using it for whatever purpose is required.

In fact, the process of *transforming* XML into other forms is so common that yet another language has been invented for doing just that. XSLT (Extensible Stylesheet Language for Transformations) allows *templates* for each type of element in an XML document to be defined. Each template converts the information contained in the original XML element into another representation.

XSLT is commonly used to convert XML into standard HTML for display on a web page, or to convert the information in one XML document into a different form based, perhaps, on a different DTD. The latter application is commonly used when sending information from one business or organization to another that uses a different format for representing similar information.

In principle, we could write C# code to do everything that XSLT does by just applying the .NET XML libraries that we have studied in this chapter, but XSLT makes most of these transformations much easier to accomplish. As with XPath and XML itself, XSLT has a large set of commands and statements which may be used, so we will examine only the basics here to give the reader a feel for how it can be used in a C# and .NET context. There are many books on XSLT which will explore the subject in greater depth.

As we mentioned earlier, XSLT allows a *template* to be defined for each type of element in an XML document. A template provides instructions on what information should be extracted from an element of the given type, and how it should be represented in the transformed document. The general form of an XSLT template is as follows:

```
<xsl:template match=XPath expression>
  XSLT instructions
</xsl:template>
```

Here, text that is in *italics* is just a description of the code that must be inserted at that point.

The XPath expression in the first line selects the nodes from the XML document to which the template should be applied. The XSLT instructions in the middle line define the transformations that will be applied to the nodes that are retrieved by the search pattern.

Note that an XSLT template definition looks a lot like an ordinary XML element in that it consists of a tag name (`xsl:template`) and has an opening and closing tag with content in the middle. All XSLT elements, however, have names that begin with the `xsl:` prefix. (In XML, a tag may be defined as belonging to a *namespace* in order to avoid clashes in names between XML documents. The namespace name precedes the regular name and is delimited with a colon. For more details on XML namespaces, consult a book on XML.)

An ordinary XML parser will not notice anything special about XSLT elements, so we need an XSLT parser to handle these statements. Parsers exist as stand-alone programs or as parts of other programs such as web browsers, but we shall be concerned only with the XSLT processors within .NET.

Typically, XSLT templates for transforming a particular type of XML document are stored in a separate file with a `.xsl` extension. A link between the XML document and the XSLT file is then made, either by inserting a line in the XML file, or by linking the two files in the code that processes them.

This will all make a lot more sense if we see a simple example. As usual, we will use our `BookList.xml` file as the XML document, and write a simple XSLT file that converts the information in the XML file to HTML so that it can be viewed as ordinary text in a web browser.

The XSLT file is as follows:

```
1.  <?xml version="1.0" encoding="UTF-8" ?>
2.  <xsl:stylesheet version="1.0"
3.    xmlns:xsl="http://www.w3.org/1999/XSL/Transform">
4.    <xsl:template match="/">
5.       <HTML>
6.         <HEAD>
7.           <TITLE>Book information</TITLE>
8.         </HEAD>
9.         <BODY>
10.          <xsl:apply-templates/>
11.        </BODY>
12.      </HTML>
13.    </xsl:template>
14.
15.    <xsl:template match="BOOK">
16.       <hr/>
17.       <b><xsl:value-of select="AUTHOR"/></b>
18.       <br/>
19.       <i><xsl:value-of select="TITLE"/></i>
20.       <xsl:if test="@NumPages">
21.          <br/>
22.          <xsl:value-of select="@NumPages"/> pages.
23.       </xsl:if>
24.    </xsl:template>
25.
26.  </xsl:stylesheet>
```

Lines 1 to 3 are standard introductory code for an XSLT file, and we won't delve into their meaning here since that would carry us too deeply into the innards of XSLT. Provided you insert these lines (and the last line, which closes the `xsl:stylesheet` tag) into all your XSLT files you should avoid problems at the top level.

After this introductory material, everything else in an XSLT file involves the definition of templates. The main template is defined on lines 4 through 13. The XPath pattern that is matched on line 4 is given as `"/"`, which matches the root node of an XML document. This should be the entry point of any XSLT file. We can select which nodes underneath the root we wish to transform within this top-level template.

One important point about XSLT files is that any text that is not part of an `xsl` tag is interpreted as text that is to be output. Thus all the text on lines 5 to 9 is just output directly to the HTML file we are building on disk. Although this text consists of valid XML, it is not interpreted as XSLT commands by the XSLT parser.

If you are not familiar with HTML, don't worry too much about what the HTML statements on lines 5 to 9 and elsewhere in this XSLT file are doing. The important thing at this point is to recognize that the XSLT file will send directly to the output stream any text that is not part of an `xsl` element. We will consider the HTML file that is produced as a result of the transformation below.

Line 10 contains the command `xsl:apply-templates`. This instructs the XSLT parser to search the remainder of the XSLT file to see if there are any template definitions that match other nodes that might be found in the XML document. We'll consider these below.

The remainder of the first template prints out a couple of closing tags for the HTML file (lines 11 and 12) and then closes the `xsl:template` tag (line 13).

The `xsl:apply-templates` command on line 10 is a bit like a method call, in that it redirects the parser to one of the other templates that may be defined elsewhere in the XSLT file. In our case, we have only one other template definition, beginning on line 15.

This template matches all BOOK elements in the XML document. Each time a BOOK is found, we first print out an `<hr>` tag (which draws a horizontal line across the web page). Then on line 17 we encounter a new type of XSLT command: `xsl:value-of`.

To understand what this command is doing, we first need to understand the idea of the *context node*. As XSLT processes an XML document, it keeps a marker to the node in the overall document that is being processed. This node is known as the context node, and many XSLT commands are given relative to the context node, while other commands will change the context node.

The `xsl:template` command will change the context node to whatever node is found when applying the `match`. Other XSLT commands are then issued relative to this context node.

The `match="BOOK"` will match each BOOK node in turn, so when the first BOOK is matched, the `xsl:value-of` command acts on that BOOK node. The `select` attribute of the `xsl:value-of` command is an XPath search string which is run starting at the context node. If the search results in a match, then xsl:value-of extracts the inner text from that element. The result of line 17 is therefore to extract the author's name from the AUTHOR element that is the child element of the current BOOK. This name will be output surrounded by <b> and </b> tags which makes it appear in boldface type on the web page. Similarly, line 19 locates the book's title and displays it in italics.

Those familiar with HTML might be wondering why we have specified the horizontal rule and break tags as <hr/> and <br/> respectively, rather than the more familiar <hr> and <br>. The reason is that an XSLT file is a proper XML document and thus must adhere to XML syntax rules, which require all elements to be closed. If we had given line 16 as just <hr>, for example, the parser would throw an exception and the transformation would fail. As we will see, the output to the HTML file writes an ordinary <hr> tag anyway, so the final product looks like normal HTML.

The final portion of the BOOK template deals with the optional NumPages attribute. Since we don't know in advance if a BOOK element will contain this attribute, we cannot automatically print out the number of pages.

XSLT has a conditional statement just like most other languages, so we can use xsl:if to check if the NumPages attribute exists first. The format of the xsl:if is:

```
<xsl:if test=boolean expression>
   do this if true
</xsl:if>
```

For the purposes of testing the existence of an attribute or element, we can just set the test to the name of the attribute or element. If the node exists, test will be true and if not, it will be false.

In this case, we check to see if the current BOOK element has a NumPages attribute and, if so, we use xsl:value-of to retrieve its value and print it out, followed by the word 'pages.'.

Now that we've seen a relatively simple XSLT file, we need to see how to connect it with the original BookList.xml document using C# code. This is, in fact, quite simple, as the example below shows:

```
1.  using System;
2.  using System.Xml;
3.  using System.Xml.Schema;
4.  using System.Xml.XPath;
5.  using System.Xml.Xsl;
6.  using System.IO;
7.
8.  public class XSLTDemo
9.  {
10.     private XPathDocument xPathDocument;
11.     private XPathNavigator xPathNavigator;
```

```
12.    private XslTransform xslTransform;
13.
14.    private void TransformBookList()
15.    {
16.       string fileName = "BookList.xml";
17.       XmlTextReader textReader = new XmlTextReader(fileName);
18.       XmlValidatingReader reader =
19.          new XmlValidatingReader(textReader);
20.       reader.ValidationType = ValidationType.Auto;
21.       xslTransform = new XslTransform();
22.       FileStream htmlFile = new FileStream("Books.html",
23.          FileMode.Create);
24.
25.       try
26.       {
27.          xPathDocument = new XPathDocument(reader);
28.          xslTransform.Load("BookWeb.xslt");
29.          xPathNavigator = xPathDocument.CreateNavigator();
30.          xslTransform.Transform(xPathNavigator, null,
              htmlFile);
31.       }
32.       catch (XmlSchemaException ex)
33.       {
34.          Console.WriteLine("Error reading " + fileName);
35.          Console.WriteLine(ex.Message);
36.       }
37.       catch (Exception ex)
38.       {
39.          Console.WriteLine("Error processing " + fileName);
40.          Console.WriteLine(ex.Message);
41.       }
42.    }
43.
44.    public static void Main(string[] args)
45.    {
46.       XSLTDemo buildBookList = new XSLTDemo();
47.       buildBookList.TransformBookList();
48.    }
49. }
```

A typical application uses an XPathDocument to hold the XML document, so we need to include a using System.Xml.XPath (line 4). To use the XSLT classes, we need to add a using System.Xml.Xsl (line 5). Finally, since we are writing the results directly to disk, we need to use a FileStream, which requires the System.IO namespace (line 6).

All the action takes place in `TransformBookList()` (line 14). We assume that both the XML document file `BookList.xml` and the XSLT file `BookWeb.xslt` are in the same directory as the executable file for the program – if not, you will need to adjust the file paths in the code.

We first set up the reader objects (lines 16 to 20). As before, we are using validation when we read in the XML document, so we first create an `XmlTextReader`, then an `XmlValidatingReader`. If you are not using validation (that is, you don't have a DTD), just skip the creation of the validating reader on lines 18 to 20 and use `textReader` directly.

The final bit of setup creates the output file as a `FileStream` (line 22). A more realistic application would probably use XSLT to transform some XML and send the resulting HTML directly over the web to a waiting client. We will consider this sort of thing in the next chapter, but for now we will just store the result on disk and then open a web browser to view the result afterwards.

Within the `try` block on line 25 we do the actual processing. We use `XPathDocument` to load the XML file (line 27) since the XSLT parser is designed to work most efficiently with an `XPathDocument` to process the various XPath searches that XSLT contains. Note that we do not actually need to write any `XPathDocument` method calls ourselves – this is all handled internally by the XSLT parser.

The `XslTransform` object loads in the XSLT command file (line 28), and an `XPathNavigator` is created (line 29). Finally, the XML document, XSLT command file and HTML output file are connected when we call `Transform()` on line 30. (The middle parameter in `Transform()` allows some optional parameters to be passed to the transformation, but we don't need those here.)

All the hard work is done in writing the XML and XSLT files. Once we have those, it is just a matter of writing a few lines in C# to use the XSLT to transform the XML. Since a lot of things *can* go wrong (mainly syntax errors in the XML or XSLT files) however, it is always a good idea to print out any exception messages, as we've done on lines 32 to 41.

The HTML file produced by this transformation is as follows:

```
<HTML>
  <HEAD>
    <META http-equiv="Content-Type" content="text/html;
      charset=utf-8">
    <TITLE>Book information</TITLE>
  </HEAD>
  <BODY>
    <hr>
    <b>Zaphod Wibble</b>
    <br>
    <i>Wibble's Guide to the Classics</i>
    <br>
    345 pages.
    <hr>
```

```
      <b>Isaac Asimov</b>
      <br>
      <i>The Complete Stories, Vol. 1</i>
      <br>
      429 pages.
      <hr>
      <b>Charles Dickens</b>
      <br>
      <i>A Tale of Two Cities</i>
   </BODY>
</HTML>
```

If you are familiar with HTML, this should look quite familiar. As a quick reminder, the HEAD section of an HTML document defines a few properties that don't appear in the main client area of the browser. In this case, the META element is actually inserted automatically by the `Transform()` method – this was not coded in the XSLT file. The TITLE element specifies the text that appears in the title bar of the browser window.

The BODY section defines the content that appears in the client area of the browser. The `<hr>` tag draws a horizontal line across the entire client area, `<b></b>` specifies that the enclosed text is in boldface, `<i></i>` draws text in italics and `<br>` causes a line break.

When loaded into a web browser, this file looks as shown in Figure 12.3.

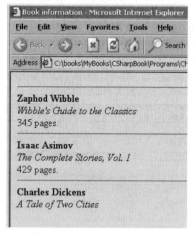

Figure 12.3 Result of translating XML into HTML using XSLT

Although this example has shown how to convert XML into ordinary HTML, it should be obvious that XSLT has great flexibility in its uses, as it can be used to transform XML into any format we like. To explore its capabilities further, you should consult a book on XML or have a look at the W3C web site http://www.w3c.org which contains the specifications and a reference page for XSLT and its commands.

12.10 ■ XML documentation in C# code

Java programmers should be familiar with the comprehensive documentation that comes with the Java Development Kit (JDK) and most other packages of Java classes. Many Java programmers will also be aware that this documentation is produced by a tool called `javadoc`, which scans Java source files looking for special types of comments that have been inserted by the programmer. `javadoc` will process these comments to create a set of HTML files giving comprehensive documentation for the classes and their data fields and methods.

A similar facility exists for authors of C# code, except that in line with .NET's philosophy of using XML for most forms of data handling, the 'special comments' that should be inserted into C# source code are written using XML. Also, rather than providing a separate application to produce the documentation, the C# compiler includes a `/doc` option which allows the documentation to be produced as part of the compilation process, so it is refreshed each time we compile the project.

A documentation comment may be inserted before a class declaration, a data field declaration and a method definition. All such comments must be on separate lines and must begin with a triple slash `///` rather than the double slash used for ordinary comments.

C# provides 15 XML tag names that may be used to provide documentation. We'll begin with a simple example of how to insert documentation.

We will use the example earlier in this chapter where we illustrated editing and writing XML. Below is a portion of the `EditXMLForm` class showing the documentation comments added. The code is omitted from the methods and not all the methods from the class are included, since the comments all follow the same pattern.

```
1. using System;
2. using System.Drawing;
3. using System.Windows.Forms;
4. using System.Xml;
5. using System.Xml.Schema;
6.
7. /// <summary>
8. /// Demonstrates editing and writing of XML
9. /// using <c>XmlDocument</c>
10. /// </summary>
11. public class EditXMLForm : Form
12. {
13.    /// <summary>
14.    /// Displays the list of titles from all BOOK elements
15.    /// </summary>
16.    private ListBox titleList;
17.    /// <summary>
```

```
18.    /// Groups the text boxes
19.    /// </summary>
20.    private GroupBox detailsBox;
21.    /// <summary>
22.    /// Allows the user to view and edit data for one book
23.    /// </summary>
24.    private TextBox authorBox, titleBox, numPagesBox;
25.
26.    /// <summary>
27.    /// Reads the initial XML document from <c>fileName</c>
28.    /// </summary>
29.    private void ReadBookXML()
30.    {
31.    }
32.
33.    /// <summary>
34.    /// Enters titles of books into <c>titleList</c>
35.    /// </summary>
36.    private void PopulateTitleList()
37.    {
38.    }
39.
40.    /// <summary>
41.    /// Sets up controls
42.    /// </summary>
43.    private void InitializeComponents()
44.    {
45.    }
46.
47.    /// <summary>
48.    /// Lays out the controls each time form is displayed
49.    /// </summary>
50.    /// <param name="sender">Assumed to be the main
       form</param>
51.    /// <param name="args">Not used</param>
52.    private void OnLayoutForm(object sender,
       LayoutEventArgs args)
53.    {
54.    }
55. }
```

The various XML tags can be used to provide documentation that will appear in certain places if an HTML page is produced from the XML (as we will see below). We begin by providing a general description of the EditXMLForm class using the <summary> tag (lines 7 to 10). The <c> tag is used on line 9 to mark up text that should be formatted as computer code.

Within a class, we can provide documentation for each variable declaration and method definition. In each case, all the XML that pertains to a particular field or method within the class must appear immediately before that field or method is defined. For example, we've provided a description of `titleList` with the comments on lines 13 to 15, and of `detailsBox` on lines 17 to 19. If we add a comment before a declaration that contains several objects, the same comment is applied to each object in the declaration. Thus the comment on lines 21 to 23 is applied to all three of the objects declared on line 24.

We have shown a few examples of adding documentation to methods on lines 26 to 54. For `void` methods that have no parameters, a simple `<summary>` is probably all that is needed in most cases. For methods having parameters, such as `OnLayoutForm()` on line 52, we provide a `<summary>` and then add a `<param>` element for each parameter in the method. The `<param>` takes the name of the parameter as an attribute, and the description of the parameter as its inner text.

All the methods in `EditXMLForm` are `void`, but if a method has a return value, we can add a `<return>` element to the documentation to explain what value is returned by the method.

If we are using a command-line compiler rather than Visual Studio .NET, we can produce an XML file from these comments by adding a `/doc` option to the compiler's command line. For this class, we could say:

```
csc /doc:EditXMLForm.xml EditXMLForm.cs
```

This will compile the C# source code as usual, but will also produce a file called `EditXMLForm.xml` containing a complete XML description of the documentation as obtained from the special comments in the source code. The compiler will also perform several checks on the XML comments to be sure they are correctly formatted. Warnings will even be issued if you have forgotten to add documentation to some of the public methods in the class.

It is up to you to decide what to do with the XML file that is produced (if you are feeling ambitious, you may want to try writing your own XSLT transformation to produce your own documentation style), but if you are using Visual Studio .NET, there is a facility which converts the XML into a set of HTML files that allow web-based documentation to be produced. Although we don't want to rely too much on Visual Studio .NET in this book, it is worth describing the procedure since there doesn't appear to be any other easy way of producing this type of documentation.

First, to get Visual Studio .NET to produce the XML file (without any extra HTML documentation), open Solution Explorer (using the View menu if it's not visible), select the project for which you want the XML file produced, then use the View menu to open the Property Pages for this project.

In the panel on the left, open Configuration Properties, then select Build. In the Outputs section, select XML Documentation File and enter the name of the file to which you want the XML documentation written. This file's location is relative to the home directory of the project. This file name is the same as the one that is specified with the `/doc` option in the command-line version above.

If you set an XML Documentation File, XML documentation will be produced automatically every time you compile the project.

To produce the HTML documentation, select the Tools menu and then choose Build Comment Web Pages, select the project(s) for which you want the documentation and the location on disk where it should be written and then click OK. You will get a separate folder called `CodeCommentReport` containing a number of files which together produce the web documentation. The main page that should be opened in a browser is called `Solution_name`.htm, where 'name' will be the name of the solution for which documentation was produced. The documentation for `EditXMLForm` is as shown in Figure 12.4.

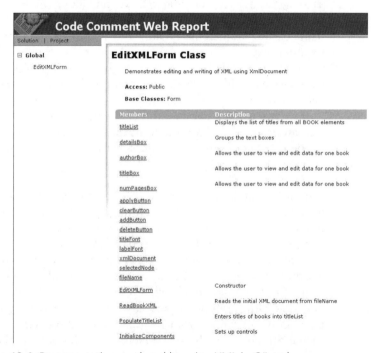

Figure 12.4 Documentation produced by using XML in C# code

Each data field and method name in the list is a link to a separate page where more details are provided on that item, depending on how much information was written into the comment in the source code. In any case, the name, data type (including complete namespace name) and accessibility (private, public, etc) of all data fields are given.

For complete information on the 15 XML tags that are available for formatting comments and a tutorial on the production of XML documentation, see the MSDN documentation (either on the web at msdn.microsoft.com or the documentation that comes with Visual Studio .NET). The tutorial can be found by searching for 'XML Documentation Tutorial'.

12.11 ■ Case study: saving and loading the adventure game

One common use of XML is as a format in which the state of a program may be saved to disk. We can demonstrate this by adding saving and loading features to the adventure game case study that we have been developing throughout the book.

The previous version of the game was presented in Chapter 11 where we added a database to store the data required to set the game up initially. The strategy we will use in adding saving and loading of a game in progress is that we only need to save that information that can change after the game starts. For example, the number of rooms in the game is determined by the data in the database, as are the connections between these rooms, so we need not save any of this information.

12.11.1 □ DTD for the Adventure XML file

Things that can change during the course of a game are the location and existence of items, the state of the monsters in the rooms, and the state of the player. The best way to plan out the structure of the XML file that will store this information is to write a DTD for it. The following DTD is stored in `Adventure.dtd`:

```
<!ELEMENT ADVENTURE (ROOM*, PLAYER)>

<!ELEMENT ROOM (ITEM*, MONSTER?)>
<!ATTLIST ROOM Description CDATA #REQUIRED>

<!ELEMENT PLAYER (ITEM*)>
<!ATTLIST PLAYER CurrentLocation CDATA #REQUIRED>
<!ATTLIST PLAYER Energy CDATA #REQUIRED>
<!ATTLIST PLAYER MaxEnergy CDATA #REQUIRED>
<!ATTLIST PLAYER BlockProb CDATA #REQUIRED>
<!ATTLIST PLAYER HitProb CDATA #REQUIRED>
<!ATTLIST PLAYER Damage CDATA #REQUIRED>
<!ATTLIST PLAYER CarryWeight CDATA #REQUIRED>
<!ATTLIST PLAYER QuaffedPotion CDATA #IMPLIED>
<!ATTLIST PLAYER PotionTime CDATA #IMPLIED>
<!ATTLIST PLAYER WieldedWeapon CDATA #IMPLIED>
<!ATTLIST PLAYER WornArmour CDATA #IMPLIED>
<!ATTLIST PLAYER WornRing CDATA #IMPLIED>

<!ELEMENT ITEM EMPTY>
<!ATTLIST ITEM Description CDATA #REQUIRED>
<!ATTLIST ITEM Charges CDATA #IMPLIED>

<!ELEMENT MONSTER EMPTY>
<!ATTLIST MONSTER Energy CDATA #REQUIRED>
```

The root node (document element) in the XML hierarchy is called ADVENTURE, and may contain zero or more ROOM elements and exactly one PLAYER. The only information we need to store about each room is its description and its contents (items and monster, if any). The ROOM element therefore accepts zero or more ITEMs and zero or one MONSTER. The room's description is stored as a required attribute.

The player has a large number of attributes to save, some of which are required and others optional. Technically, we could work out a lot of these values from the items being carried by the player, but it is easier just to save them as raw data. The PLAYER element may also contain zero or more ITEMs.

An ITEM consists only of a description, since we will look up the other data for an item in the database. The wand is the only item type that has a value that varies during play, so we add the extra attribute to store the number of charges left on a wand.

In a more complex game, items may have several properties that can vary as the game is played. Weapons and armour could wear out, food could decay and so on. In this case it may be better to create a separate element in the XML file for each item type, since each type will have its own set of attributes.

Finally, the only data we need to store for a monster is its current energy level. We do not need to save even the monster's name since all monsters are fixed to a particular room, and according to the DTD, the only place a MONSTER element can be found is as a child of ROOM. Since the monster's stats are created when the game is initialized and the only thing that can change is the monster's energy level, that's all we need to store. If a monster in a particular room has been killed by the time the game is saved, then the room's `Monster` property is `null` and no MONSTER element would be saved for that room.

12.11.2 ☐ C# code for saving the game as XML

Since the XML that is being written to disk is a fixed snapshot of the game, we could use `XmlTextWriter` to write out the XML statements one by one. However, it is more intuitive to build the document as a tree within the code before writing it out, so we'll use `XmlDocument` to construct the document first and then write it to disk using `WriteContentTo()` as we did in the example earlier in this chapter.

We have added a couple of items to the File menu allowing saving and loading – the code for this is not included here since it is a straightforward change to the menu.

Selecting 'Save game' on the menu calls `SaveGame()`:

```csharp
private void SaveGame()
{
    SaveFileDialog saveDialog = new SaveFileDialog();
    saveDialog.Filter = "Adventure games (*.adv)|*.adv";
    saveDialog.InitialDirectory = ".";
```

```
if (saveDialog.ShowDialog() == DialogResult.OK)
{
  BuildXML();
  XmlTextWriter textWriter =
    new XmlTextWriter(saveDialog.FileName,
      System.Text.Encoding.UTF8);
  textWriter.Formatting = Formatting.Indented;
  textWriter.WriteStartDocument();
  gameXML.WriteContentTo(textWriter);
  textWriter.Close();
}
}
```

This method displays a file selector and filters the displayed files so that only .adv files are shown. The actual XML document gameXML is built up in BuildXML() which we consider below. After this, we create a XmlTextWriter to write the header line using WriteStartDocument() and then write gameXML to the selected file using WriteContentTo().

BuildXML() looks like this:

```
1.  private void BuildXML()
2.  {
3.    gameXML = new XmlDocument();
4.    XmlDocumentType docType =
5.      gameXML.CreateDocumentType("ADVENTURE", null,
6.      "Adventure.dtd", null);
7.    gameXML.AppendChild(docType);
8.    XmlElement adventureElement =
9.      gameXML.CreateElement("ADVENTURE");
10.   gameXML.AppendChild(adventureElement);
11.   for (int i = 0; i < adventure.NumRooms; i++)
12.   {
13.     Room room = adventure[i];
14.     XmlElement roomElement = gameXML.CreateElement("ROOM");
15.     roomElement.SetAttribute("Description", room.
        Description);
16.     for (int j = 0; j < room.ItemList.Count; j++)
17.     {
18.       Item item = (Item)room.ItemList[j];
19.       XmlElement itemElement = gameXML.CreateElement
          ("ITEM");
20.       itemElement.SetAttribute("Description",
21.         item.Description);
22.       if (item.GetType() == Type.GetType("Wand"))
23.       {
24.         itemElement.SetAttribute("Charges",
25.           ((Wand)item).Charges.ToString());
```

```
26.         }
27.         roomElement.AppendChild(itemElement);
28.      }
29.      if (room.Monster != null)
30.      {
31.         XmlElement monsterElement =
32.            gameXML.CreateElement("MONSTER");
33.         monsterElement.SetAttribute("Energy",
34.            room.Monster.Energy.ToString());
35.         roomElement.AppendChild(monsterElement);
36.      }
37.      adventureElement.AppendChild(roomElement);
38.   }
39.
40.   XmlElement playerElement = gameXML.CreateElement("PLAYER");
41.   Player player = adventure.GamePlayer;
42.   playerElement.SetAttribute("CurrentLocation",
43.      player.CurrentLocation.Description);
44.   playerElement.SetAttribute("Energy",
45.      player.Energy.ToString());
46.   playerElement.SetAttribute("MaxEnergy",
47.      player.MaxEnergy.ToString());
48.   playerElement.SetAttribute("BlockProb",
49.      player.BlockProb.ToString());
50.   playerElement.SetAttribute("HitProb",
51.      player.HitProb.ToString());
52.   playerElement.SetAttribute("Damage",
53.      player.Damage.ToString());
54.   playerElement.SetAttribute("CarryWeight",
55.      player.CarryWeight.ToString());
56.   if (player.QuaffedPotion != null)
57.   {
58.      playerElement.SetAttribute("QuaffedPotion",
59.         player.QuaffedPotion.Description);
60.      playerElement.SetAttribute("PotionTime",
61.         player.PotionTime.ToString());
62.   }
63.   if (player.WieldedWeapon != null)
64.   {
65.      playerElement.SetAttribute("WieldedWeapon",
66.         player.WieldedWeapon.Description);
67.   }
68.   if (player.WornArmour != null)
69.   {
70.      playerElement.SetAttribute("WornArmour",
71.         player.WornArmour.Description);
```

```
72.    }
73.    if (player.WornRing != null)
74.    {
75.      playerElement.SetAttribute("WornRing",
76.        player.WornRing.Description);
77.    }
78.    for (int i = 0; i < player.ItemList.Count; i++)
79.    {
80.      Item item = (Item)player.ItemList[i];
81.      XmlElement itemElement = gameXML.CreateElement("ITEM");
82.      itemElement.SetAttribute("Description",
         item.Description);
83.      if (item.GetType() == Type.GetType("Wand"))
84.      {
85.        itemElement.SetAttribute("Charges",
86.          ((Wand)item).Charges.ToString());
87.      }
88.      playerElement.AppendChild(itemElement);
89.    }
90.    gameXML.DocumentElement.AppendChild(playerElement);
91. }
```

This method is a fairly straightforward construction of the document. On line 4 we create the DOCTYPE line which connects the XML file with the DTD file (which is assumed to be in the same directory).

The loop starting on line 11 saves the information on the rooms in the game. The inner loop (line 16) retrieves the information on the items stored in each room and attaches a node for each item to the corresponding room node.

If the room contains a monster, the code starting on line 29 inserts a MONSTER element as a child of the room. Finally, each room element is attached to the root element (line 37).

The player information is stored on lines 40 to 90 and again just consists in extracting the required information from the objects in the Adventure class and creating elements to insert into the XML document. The optional attributes (lines 56 to 77) are only inserted if the corresponding properties in the Player object are not null.

An example of a file created by this code is as follows:

```
<?xml version="1.0" encoding="utf-8"?>
<!DOCTYPE ADVENTURE SYSTEM "Adventure.dtd">
<ADVENTURE>
  <ROOM Description="laboratory" />
  <ROOM Description="kitchen" />
  <ROOM Description="entrance" />
  <ROOM Description="guard room" />
  <ROOM Description="dining room">
    <ITEM Description="roast beef" />
```

```
        <MONSTER Energy="10" />
    </ROOM>
    <ROOM Description="jail" />
    <ROOM Description="dungeon">
        <MONSTER Energy="2" />
    </ROOM>
    <ROOM Description="storeroom">
        <ITEM Description="an ice wand" Charges="2" />
        <MONSTER Energy="8" />
    </ROOM>
    <ROOM Description="king's bedroom">
        <ITEM Description="a shield potion" />
        <MONSTER Energy="7" />
    </ROOM>
    <ROOM Description="queen's bedroom">
        <ITEM Description="a jewelled dagger" />
    </ROOM>
    <ROOM Description="queen's closet">
        <MONSTER Energy="14" />
    </ROOM>
    <ROOM Description="turret">
    <ITEM Description="a banana split" />
        <MONSTER Energy="25" />
    </ROOM>
    <PLAYER CurrentLocation="dungeon" Energy="22" MaxEnergy="27"
        BlockProb="20" HitProb="80" Damage="6" CarryWeight="39"
        QuaffedPotion="an energy potion" PotionTime="2"
        WieldedWeapon="a knife">
        <ITEM Description="a carrot" />
        <ITEM Description="some chicken" />
        <ITEM Description="an invisibility ring" />
        <ITEM Description="a power ring" />
        <ITEM Description="an energy potion" />
        <ITEM Description="a fire wand" Charges="4" />
    </PLAYER>
</ADVENTURE>
```

12.11.3 ☐ C# code for loading a saved game

The strategy for loading a saved game is first to start a new game and then use the information read in from the XML file to update the information to the state that was saved. This was the rationale behind saving only that information that can change during the course of a game.

Selecting the 'Load game' menu item calls `LoadGame()`:

```
private void LoadGame()
{
  OpenFileDialog openDialog = new OpenFileDialog();
  openDialog.Filter = "Adventure games (*.adv)|*.adv";
  openDialog.InitialDirectory = ".";
  if (openDialog.ShowDialog() == DialogResult.OK)
  {
    gameXML = new XmlDocument();
    XmlTextReader textReader = new
      XmlTextReader(openDialog.FileName);
    XmlValidatingReader reader =
      new XmlValidatingReader(textReader);
    reader.ValidationType = ValidationType.Auto;
    try
    {
      gameXML.Load(reader);
      textReader.Close();
      RestoreGame();
    }
    catch (XmlSchemaException ex)
    {
      MessageBox.Show(ex.Message, "Error reading " +
        openDialog.FileName,
        MessageBoxButtons.OK, MessageBoxIcon.Error);
    }
  }
}
```

LoadGame() allows the user to select the file using a file selector dialog as usual. We then supply the standard code for creating a validating parser and then attempt to read the XML file. The Load() call is inside a try block since we have no guarantee that the XML in the file is valid. (Hopefully if the file was produced by the Adventure program it will be valid, but since XML is just text, it could easily be edited by the user, so could contain errors.)

If the XML is loaded successfully, it is stored in gameXML as an XML document. We then call RestoreGame() to transfer the information back into the Adventure object:

```
1. private void RestoreGame()
2. {
3.   adventure = new Adventure();
4.   XmlElement adventureElement = gameXML.DocumentElement;
5.   XmlNodeList roomList = adventureElement.SelectNodes
       ("ROOM");
6.   foreach (XmlNode roomNode in roomList)
7.   {
8.     Room room =
```

```
 9.           adventure.FindRoom(roomNode.Attributes[0].Value);
10.       room.ItemList.Clear();
11.       XmlNodeList itemList = roomNode.SelectNodes("ITEM");
12.       foreach (XmlNode itemNode in itemList)
13.       {
14.         Item item = adventure.GetItem(
15.           itemNode.Attributes["Description"].Value);
16.         room.AddItem(item);
17.         if (item.GetType() == Type.GetType("Wand") &&
18.           itemNode.Attributes["Charges"] != null)
19.         {
20.           ((Wand)item).Charges =
21.             int.Parse(itemNode.Attributes["Charges"].Value);
22.         }
23.       }
24.       XmlNode monsterNode =
25.         roomNode.SelectSingleNode("MONSTER");
26.       if (monsterNode != null)
27.       {
28.         room.Monster.Energy =
29.           int.Parse(monsterNode.Attributes["Energy"].Value);
30.       }
31.       else
32.       {
33.         room.Monster = null;
34.       }
35.     }
36.
37.     XmlNode playerNode =
38.       gameXML.DocumentElement.SelectSingleNode("PLAYER");
39.     Player player = adventure.GamePlayer;
40.     player.CurrentLocation = adventure.FindRoom(
41.       playerNode.Attributes["CurrentLocation"].Value);
42.     player.Energy =
43.       int.Parse(playerNode.Attributes["Energy"].Value);
44.     player.MaxEnergy =
45.       int.Parse(playerNode.Attributes["MaxEnergy"].Value);
46.     player.BlockProb =
47.       int.Parse(playerNode.Attributes["BlockProb"].Value);
48.     player.HitProb =
49.       int.Parse(playerNode.Attributes["HitProb"].Value);
50.     player.Damage =
51.       int.Parse(playerNode.Attributes["Damage"].Value);
52.     player.CarryWeight =
53.       int.Parse(playerNode.Attributes["CarryWeight"].Value);
```

```
54.    if (playerNode.Attributes["QuaffedPotion"] != null)
55.    {
56.      Potion potion = (Potion)adventure.GetItem(
57.        playerNode.Attributes["QuaffedPotion"].Value);
58.      player.QuaffedPotion = potion;
59.    }
60.    if (playerNode.Attributes["PotionTime"] != null)
61.    {
62.      player.PotionTime =
63.        int.Parse(playerNode.Attributes["PotionTime"].Value);
64.    }
65.    if (playerNode.Attributes["WieldedWeapon"] != null)
66.    {
67.      Weapon weapon = (Weapon)adventure.GetItem(
68.        playerNode.Attributes["WieldedWeapon"].Value);
69.      player.WieldedWeapon = weapon;
70.    }
71.    if (playerNode.Attributes["WornArmour"] != null)
72.    {
73.      Armour armour = (Armour)adventure.GetItem(
74.        playerNode.Attributes["WornArmour"].Value);
75.      player.WornArmour = armour;
76.    }
77.    if (playerNode.Attributes["WornRing"] != null)
78.    {
79.      Ring ring = (Ring)adventure.GetItem(
80.        playerNode.Attributes["WornRing"].Value);
81.      player.WornRing = ring;
82.    }
83.    player.ItemList.Clear();
84.    XmlNodeList playerItemList = playerNode.SelectNodes
       ("ITEM");
85.    foreach (XmlNode itemNode in playerItemList)
86.    {
87.      Item item = adventure.GetItem(
88.        itemNode.Attributes["Description"].Value);
89.      player.AddItem(item);
90.      if (item.GetType() == Type.GetType("Wand") &&
91.        itemNode.Attributes["Charges"] != null)
92.      {
93.        ((Wand)item).Charges =
94.          int.Parse(itemNode.Attributes["Charges"].Value);
95.      }
96.    }
97.    messageBox.Text = "";
98.    EnableMoveButtons();
```

```
99.    EnableCommands();
100.   Invalidate();
101. }
```

The process of restoring the data is a bit more involved than saving it, since we need to extract the correct information from the XML document and build it back into the various data structures in the Adventure object.

We begin by creating a new Adventure object (line 3) to restore the game to the starting conditions. Then we start the DocumentElement (the root node of the document – line 4) and extract an XmlNodeList containing all the ROOM nodes that are children of the root node (line 5). For each of these ROOM nodes, we need to update the item list and state of the monster in the corresponding Room object in the Adventure class. Remember that we stored the description of the room as the only ROOM attribute in the XML file, so we can use this value and the FindRoom() method (considered in Chapter 11) in Adventure to locate a Room object from its description string (line 8). We now have the actual Room object corresponding to the ROOM node in the XML document, so we can start updating the information in it.

We begin the updating process by clearing the item list in the room (line 10). This is necessary since some rooms have items placed in them when a new Adventure is created, and these items could have been picked up and removed by the player.

For a given room, we select all the children of that room that are ITEM nodes (line 11) and then loop through each item in the list to build the item and add it to the room.

The process for doing this is much the same as that used for adding items to rooms when a new game is created. We call the GetItem() method in Adventure (line 14) to build an item from its description. The version of GetItem() that was used in Chapter 11 took a DataRow as a parameter – here we have just added an overloaded version of GetItem() that looks up the correct DataRow in the DataSet Item table and then calls the original version of GetItem() to build the item.

When the item has been built, it is added to the room (line 16). Since wands are a special case in that the number of charges on the wand could have changed since the wand was created, we check this case on lines 17 to 22.

Note that when we attempt to use a Value stored in an attribute, the Value is always stored as a string in the XmlNode's attribute. If we want to use it as a numerical value (as with the charges on a wand), we must convert it in the appropriate way. Here, we use the int.Parse() method to convert the string to an int. Other numerical data types all have their own Parse() methods.

Next, we see if the room contains a monster (line 24) by searching for any children of the current room node with a MONSTER tag. If one is found, it means that the room had a monster in it when the game was saved, so we just set the monster's current energy to the saved value (line 28). Note that we do not have to create the monster since this was done when the new

`Adventure` object was created on line 3 and, since monsters never leave the room in which they were created, all the constant stats for the monster will already have been initialized. This simple system obviously would not work in a more complex game in which more than one monster was allowed in a room, or where monsters could move between rooms.

If there is no MONSTER node for the current room, we must set the room's `Monster` property to `null` (line 33) since this could mean that the room was created with a monster in it, but that it was killed before the game was saved.

The rest of the method restores the player's properties using much the same techniques as those used for restoring the rooms.

The end of the method (lines 97 to 100) updates the display to enable the move buttons and controls and refresh the map and statistics areas to show the state of the game as it was when it was saved.

We could, of course, have devised our own method of saving and loading games, but using XML has the advantage that it is a recognized format and .NET provides a number of powerful tools for manipulation of the results.

Another advantage is that, besides reading in the XML file to restore a game, we can also transform it using XSLT to produce a display (on a web page, for example) of the current state of a game in a different format if desired.

■ Summary

This chapter has introduced XML and described a few of its uses for storing and transmitting data. We then saw how C# can be used to read and process the information in an XML file, using either a serial parsing process or by storing the entire XML file in a tree structure within the program.

We then explored the DTD which can be used to validate the structure of an XML document, and then considered the use of XPath for searching an XML document for specific types of data. Methods of generating and editing XML were considered.

An introduction to XSLT showed some of the methods in C# for transforming XML into other forms, most notably HTML for display on web pages.

C# uses XML to produce documentation on the classes, fields and methods in source code, and an introduction to the production of this documentation was given.

Finally, we extended the adventure game case study by using XML to save and load a game in progress.

Exercises

12.1 Suppose you are in charge of a bookshop and wish to store customer records in an XML document. The data which should be stored consists of some data on each customer: the customer's name (compulsory), address (compulsory), phone numbers (optional, and more than one phone number is allowed – e.g. home, business, mobile, etc).

The name and each phone number should just be single strings, but the address should consist of a street name and number, town or city, country and post code or zip code.

Invent appropriate XML elements and attributes to store this information, using your judgement as to whether a data field is to be a separate element or an attribute within an existing element. Don't worry about validation at this stage.

Write out a sample XML document containing at least three customer records using a text editor.

12.2 Use an `XmlTextReader` to type out (to the console) just the names of the customers in your customer list from Exercise 12.1.

12.3 Write a complete Windows Forms application that displays the data in the customer XML list in the following way. First, create an `Address` class and a `Customer` class. Use an `XmlTextReader` to read all the information in the XML document and create a list or array of `Customer`s, each of which contains an `Address` data field, a `string` field for the customer's name and a list or array of `string`s for storing the phone numbers.

Display the information using an appropriate control, such as a `DataGrid` or `ListBox`. The data should be read-only, so you do not need to include any facilities for editing or writing any XML.

12.4 Read the documentation on the `DataSet` class that was used for storing an internal copy of a database in Chapter 11. Find out how to build a `DataSet` from data stored in data structures within the program, such as the array of `Customer`s that you created in Exercise 12.3. Note that this will require creating `DataTable`s which may be used to build the `DataSet`. In effect, what you are doing is creating an in-code database for storing the data contained in the original XML document.

12.5 Write a DTD for the Customer XML file, using the requirements in Exercise12.1. Modify the reader program from Exercise12.2 so that it validates the XML as it parses it. If your original XML document that you prepared in Exercise12.1 is valid, introduce some intentional errors into it to see what messages you get from the validating parser.

12.6 Investigate the XML Schema method of validating XML documents. A couple of good starting points are the XML Schema primer on the W3C web site (http://www.w3c.org/TR/xmlschema-0/) and the articles on XML Schema in the MSDN documentation. Numerous books on XML will also contain tutorials on XML Schema.

Use XML Schema to provide an alternative validation procedure for the Customer XML document.

12.7   Use an `XmlDocument` to read in the Customer XML document you created in Exercise12.1, and print out a list of customers' names in a console application.

12.8   Use an `XmlDocument` in conjunction with an XPath search statement to list all customers with an address in a particular city (modify your XML file so that not all customers have addresses in the city for which you are searching, just to test your program).

12.9   Write a Windows Forms application similar to the 'Edit book' program in the text that provides a GUI showing a list of customers' names in a `ListBox`. Selecting a customer should display their details in a number of `TextBox`es and allow the user to edit the details or delete the customer from the list. It should also be possible to add a new customer to the list. The changes should be saved to disk as a modified XML file.

12.10   Using XSLT and `XslTransform`, write an XSLT template that transforms the Customer XML document into plain text, with each customer's details formatted neatly so that it is easily readable by a human. Write the result to   the console.

12.11   If you know some basic HTML, write another XSLT template that converts the Customer XML file to a neatly formatted web page. Depending on your depth of HTML knowledge, you may wish to experiment with defining different fonts for different parts of each customer's details, make use of background and foreground colours and so on.

12.12   Add XML documentation to some or all of the programs you have written as exercises from this book. Generate a documentation web page for each program you document in this way.

Web pages and the Internet **13**

13.1 ■ Generating web pages

.NET provides comprehensive support for the creation of interactive web pages, and C# plays a central role behind the scenes in processing a user's interaction with web pages. The main technology used by .NET for managing web pages is ASP .NET (ASP stands for Active Server Pages). If you have done any programming with earlier versions of ASP, you will find that ASP .NET provides a lot more power and flexibility than its earlier incarnations.

ASP .NET is roughly analogous to Java Server Pages (JSP) in the Java world, but we are not assuming the reader to have progressed this far in their study of Java, so we will not compare the two systems here.

It is possible to write web pages using ASP .NET on its own, but this is a topic for a separate book. Since this book is primarily about C#, we don't want to dwell too much on the intricacies of ASP .NET itself. Rather we will concentrate on showing how C# may be used to drive a web page where the controls and layout of the page are determined by a skeleton ASP .NET file. We will find that if we use C# to provide most of the processing of a web page, we do not need to know that much about ASP .NET beyond the syntax for defining a few web controls that we wish to appear on the web page.

First, we will provide a brief overview of how a web server works, and how ASP .NET fits into this picture. We should note at this stage that in order to get any of the examples in this chapter to work on your own computer, you will need Microsoft's IIS web server, version 5 or later, to be installed. You do not need an active Internet connection, since all the web pages can be tested by using the 'localhost' address.

The Internet is basically a collection of *clients* requesting resources from *servers*. When we click on a link in a web browser such as Internet Explorer, the browser reads the address of the computer to which the link should lead. This address is usually in some textual form such as 'http://alife.mic.dundee.ac.uk/default.asp' (which is the URL, or *Uniform Resource Locator*, of my home page). If we have a connection to the Internet, the Internet service provider (ISP) will have access to a *domain name server* (DNS) which translates textual Internet addresses into a numerical IP (for Internet Protocol) address with four components, such as 134.36.34.124 (which happens to be the IP address of my office computer's web site). Routers around the world will relay the client's request through various networks until the request reaches its destination, which is the *web server* that plays host to the web site.

When the request reaches the web server, that part of the URL that describes the actual file or service that is requested (the file 'default.asp' in this case) will be read and, if the file can be found, it will be processed by the server and the result sent back to the client, which will then display it in the web browser.

We mentioned that the server needs to process the outgoing file before it is sent off to the client. If the file is straightforward HTML containing only text or images, little or no processing is usually required and the file is just sent off directly. However, if the file contains ASP .NET code, that code must be run by the server to produce the actual text that is sent to the client. It is this code that is the subject of this chapter.

13.2 ■ ASP .NET and C#

Before we present any code, a word is needed about how ASP .NET projects can be developed. Visual Studio .NET provides a comprehensive environment in which web applications can be created, so if you have it installed, you may wish to use it to follow along with the examples in this chapter. To create a new project in this way, select File → New → Project, then select 'Visual C# Projects' as the project type, and 'ASP .NET Web Application' as the template. Enter a name in the 'Location' box and then click OK. This should appear in the 'New Project' dialog as http://localhost followed by the project name. The actual files that are created should appear in the directory used by your web server to store its web pages. This directory is usually C:\Inetpub\wwwroot, but will depend on your configuration of IIS, since it is possible to change the directory where it stores its web sites.

Visual Studio .NET will then create a number of files (most of which you don't actually need for simple web pages). It will allow you to test your web site by running the project in the same way you would when developing an ordinary C# application, except that it will use Internet Explorer to display the web pages.

In this book, however, we would like to provide examples that can be developed without using Visual Studio .NET, so we will not use its development environment here. Besides allowing users who do not have Visual Studio .NET installed to run the examples, this also has the advantage of producing much less code.

Let us now turn to a simple example to see how ASP .NET and C# can work together to generate a web page and provide event handlers for controls on that page. We will present the example as two files: one containing ASP .NET code and the other containing C# code. ASP .NET code files should have the extension `.aspx`, since these files are the ones that are used as part of the URL when a browser is sending its request to the server. Using a consistent file extension allows the server to identify the incoming request as one that requires ASP .NET support.

We will write a simple ASP .NET page that displays a button and a label. When the button is pressed, the label should display the current date and time. We store the ASP .NET code in a file called TestASP.aspx:

```
1. <%@ Page Language="c#" AutoEventWireup="false"
2.   Src="TestASP.aspx.cs" Inherits="TestASP"%>
3. <!DOCTYPE HTML PUBLIC "-//W3C//DTD HTML 4.0
   Transitional//EN">
4. <HTML>
5.   <HEAD>
6.     <title>TestASP with C# Code-Behind Test</title>
7.   </HEAD>
8.   <body>
9.     <form id="Form1" method="post" runat="server">
10.       <asp:Button id="Button1" runat="server"
11.         Text="Press"></asp:Button>
12.       <hr>
13.       <asp:Label id="Label1" runat="server">Label
          </asp:Label>
14.     </form>
15.   </body>
16. </HTML>
```

If you're not overly familiar with HTML, don't worry too much since we won't be using a lot of complex HTML in this chapter, and you should be able to work out what most of the examples are doing once you understand a few of the basics. If you have read the start of Chapter 12 on XML this should also be helpful since the structure of an HTML file is much the same as XML.

ASP .NET files should always begin with a line similar to the one shown on lines 1 and 2. The `<%@ Page … %>` directive is ASP code (ASP commands are contained within the `<% … %>` delimiters), and is about the only ASP code we will see in this book. The components of this directive are as follows.

First, we specify the language (C#) that will be used to provide the background processing for events generated when the user interacts with the web page. Any language supported by .NET may be used here, but at present probably the two most popular choices would be `Language="vb"` (for Visual Basic .NET) and `Language="c#"`.

The `AutoEventWireup="false"` directive means that we will be providing our own event handlers for loading the page.

The last two directives provide the link between this ASP .NET file and the background C# code. This ASP .NET file was produced *without* using Visual Studio .NET's wizards, so the form of the file is slightly different from what you will get if you create an 'ASP .NET Web Application' using the wizard. On line 2, we specify the file `TestASP.aspx.cs` as the source (`Src`) file for the C# code that is the 'code behind' the ASP .NET page. In Visual Studio .NET, the word `Src` would be replaced by `Codebehind`. In fact, `Codebehind` means nothing to a web server and will be ignored if found in an ASP .NET file on its own. The `Src` keyword is recognized by the ASP .NET parser, however, and tells ASP .NET where to find the C# file that contains the support code. (Incidentally, if you are using Visual Studio .NET's wizard to produce the application, it can be a bit tricky trying to get the editor to display the C# source code corresponding to an ASP .NET file – this can be done most easily by right-clicking on the ASP .NET file's entry in Solution Explorer (use View → Solution Explorer if it's not visible) and then selecting 'View Code'.)

The last directive on line 2 says that this page 'inherits' something called TestASP. In fact what is happening here is that the ASP .NET page inherits the C# class named TestASP that is to be defined in the file TestASP.aspx.cs. We'll now examine this C# file to see how this works. (We'll come back to what the rest of the code in the ASP .NET file does later.)

The C# code file contains the following class definition:

```
using System;
using System.Web.UI;
using System.Web.UI.WebControls;

public class TestASP : Page
{
   protected Button Button1;
   protected Label Label1;

   protected override void OnInit(EventArgs args)
   {
      Button1.Click += new EventHandler(OnButton1Click);
   }

   protected void OnButton1Click(object sender, EventArgs
      args)
   {
      Label1.Text = "Time: " + System.DateTime.Now;
   }
}
```

The TestASP class inherits Page, which is found in the System.Web.UI namespace, and is the base class for a web page (in a similar way that Form is the base class for a window in a Windows Forms application).

We define two controls: a Button and a Label. We will see later in this chapter that controls that appear on web pages are *not* the same as the controls that are used on Windows Forms. This Button and Label are from the System.Web.UI.WebControls namespace, and are different classes entirely from Button and Label in System.Windows.Forms, although they are used in much the same way.

TestASP provides an override of the OnInit() method, which is called when the page is initialized. In this case we add an event handler to the button. The event handler is OnButton1Click() and simply sets the label's text to display the current time.

If these two files are placed together within a directory called TestASP that is in the web server's web site area, then the result can be tested by

opening a web browser and typing the URL `http://localhost/TestASP/`
`TestASP.aspx` into the address box. The initial display should look something like that shown in Figure 13.1.

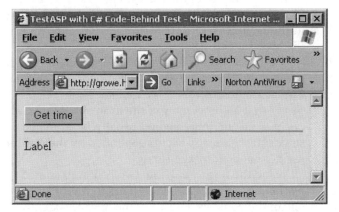

Figure 13.1 A simple ASP .NET page containing a button and a label

Pressing the button should change the display to show the current time
(Figure 13.2).

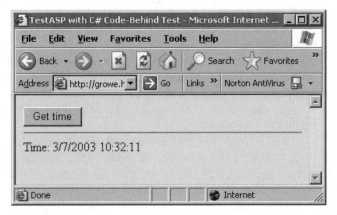

Figure 13.2 Pressing the button causes the current date and time to be displayed

13.2.1 ☐ **How it works**

The process may look a bit magical, since if we look at the C# class, there
seems to be a fair bit missing. In particular, there is no constructor and no code
that actually initializes the controls, so we might expect a 'null reference' error
when we try to run the program, but in fact everything seems to work.

The key is in the `Inherits="TestASP"` directive that appeared back on
line 2 of the ASP .NET file. This tells the ASP .NET processor that the page
that is defined in the ASP file should inherit the C# class `TestASP`. To see
how this works, we need to examine the ASP code a bit more closely.

Line 3 in `TestASP.aspx` above is a standard line that states that the document type (DOCTYPE) is HTML, and sets the DTD for the version of HTML that is being used (see the discussion of DTDs in Chapter 12).

The remainder of the file uses XML syntax to define the HTML file. HTML files have a HEAD section which contains information that is not displayed in the main area of the browser. In this case we set the title that appears in the browser's title bar.

The main section of the document is delimited by `<body>` tags, and contains an HTML `form`. (Note that this is not the same as a Windows `Form`!) The attributes of this `form` include `runat="server"`, which tells the web server that all processing of the form should take place at the server, not the client. This attribute should usually be attached to all ASP .NET controls, since otherwise, any events generated by them will remain on the client and not get handled by the server.

Inside the form we define two ASP web controls, which can be identified by the `asp:` namespace identifiers in their tags. The type of control must be one of the controls defined in the `System.Web.UI.WebControls` namespace we mentioned above when discussing the C# code. In order to provide a link with the C# class, we must ensure that the `id` of each control matches the object name that is defined for that control in the C# class. For example, we have called the `Button Button1` so the C# `Button` object must also be called `Button1`. The link between the C# base class and the ASP code is provided by the inheritance relation defined on line 2.

When this ASP .NET page is requested from the server, the server will first compile the 'code-behind' C# file `TestASP.aspx.cs` (which it finds by using the `Src` link on line 2 of the ASP code) and use the `TestASP` class found in that file as the base class for a 'class' that is implicitly defined within the ASP file. Any web controls declared in the base C# class must appear in the ASP page, although the ASP page can add extra controls that are not defined in the C# base class.

The reason that we do not need to instantiate the web controls in the C# class is that the controls themselves are created implicitly when the ASP page is created by the server for onward transmission to the client.

The key point in all of this is that by using a C# class as the code behind an ASP .NET page, we can use C# rather than a less powerful scripting language to produce all the code that is run whenever the user interacts with a web page.

So what actually gets sent to the client from the server after the ASP has been processed? This is easily discovered by using 'View Source' on the browser after the page has loaded. The initial display (when the label just shows the text 'Label') is produced by the HTML code:

```
<!DOCTYPE HTML PUBLIC
  "-//W3C//DTD HTML 4.0 Transitional//EN">
<HTML>
  <HEAD>
    <title>TestASP with C# Code-Behind Test</title>
```

```
    </HEAD>
    <body>
      <form name="Form1" method="post" action="TestASP.aspx"
        id="Form1">
        <input type="hidden" name="__VIEWSTATE"
          value="dDwtNjI3MTU0NjQyOzs+rSHg/p0cW4yG
          pT9Sc7NOeiEVsGc=" />
        <input type="submit" name="Button1" value="Get time"
          id="Button1" />
        <hr>
        <span id="Label1">Label</span>
      </form>
    </body>
</HTML>
```

The structure of this file looks similar to the HTML section of the original ASP file, except that the 'Get time' button is now shown as an input element and the label is a span element, both of which are standard HTML constructs.

The most curious addition, however, is a new input element with a name of __VIEWSTATE and a value that looks like some sort of secret code. This element is the key to how ASP .NET stores the *state* of a web page between submissions of the form.

ASP .NET pages are known as *stateless* pages because no information is stored on the server between client requests. We will see later, however, that the page does 'remember' user settings (such as text typed into text boxes, selections made from combo boxes and so on) from one request to the next. The way this is done is by encoding the content of a page into a hidden input element called __VIEWSTATE. When the page is resubmitted to the server, the information on the state of the page is also sent back in this element's coded value. The server can extract the current state of the various controls from this value and use this information to set each control properly before the response is sent back to the client.

For this reason, we can expect the content of __VIEWSTATE's value to change after each form submission, which is easily checked by examining the source code each time we press the 'Get time' button. After pressing it once, for example, the code sent to the browser becomes:

```
<!DOCTYPE HTML PUBLIC "-//W3C//DTD HTML 4.0 Transitional//EN">
<HTML>
  <HEAD>
    <title>TestASP with C# Code-Behind Test</title>
  </HEAD>
  <body>
    <form name="Form1" method="post" action="TestASP.aspx"
      id="Form1">
      <input type="hidden" name="__VIEWSTATE"
        value="dDwtNjI3MTU0NjQyO3Q8O2w8aTwxPjs+O2w8dD
        w7bDxpPDM+Oz47bDx0PHA8cDxsPFRleHQ7PjtsPFRpbWWU
```

```
6IDMvNy8yMDAzIDExOjI3OjQ5Oz4+Oz47Oz47Pj47Pj47
PkmX9PaCjIBB/H02VTrv7tuo07t5" />
<input type="submit" name="Button1" value="Get time"
   id="Button1" />
<hr>
<span id="Label1">Time: 3/7/2003 10:32:11</span>
  </form>
 </body>
</HTML>
```

Besides the different (and longer) value of __VIEWSTATE, we also notice that the label's text is shown as the current date and time, since the server constructs this string at its end and sends it back to the client.

13.3 ■ Web controls

The simple example in the previous section illustrates most of what we need to know about using C# as the power behind an ASP .NET web page. ASP .NET, of course, has a great deal of functionality that does not require the use of C#, but that is a topic for a different book and we will not delve into that here.

For web pages that contain basic GUI controls such as text boxes, buttons, list boxes and so on, there is little more that needs to be said, since the .NET Web Control library essentially mirrors the Windows Forms library. This means that most of what can be done with Windows Forms in a stand-alone application can also be done with ASP .NET, and in much the same way.

13.4 ■ Web controls and databases

Most substantial web installations now rely on databases to store and manage the information that is supplied to visitors to their sites. On-line shops maintain databases of their stock and customer orders, libraries keep records of the book collections and borrowers' records in databases, government organizations store everything from weather data to census information in databases and so on.

We have seen in earlier chapters how databases may be linked to Windows applications written in C#, and it should come as no surprise that all of these techniques can be used in programs in which C# provides the code behind an ASP .NET web page.

The methods for accessing the database in such cases are identical to those we have considered in Chapter 11, so we can proceed to use them directly here. As with Windows Forms, .NET's web control library provides a DataGrid in which results of a database query can be displayed. The display methods in the web version of DataGrid are a bit different from those used in Windows Forms, however, so it is worth running through a couple of examples to see how they are used.

13.5 ■ Case study: an on-line scores list for the adventure game

As a simple example of displaying the results of a database query using a `DataGrid` on a web page, we will provide a 'top scores' page for the adventure game that we have been using as a case study throughout the book.

The last version of the adventure (in Chapter 12, where we added game saving and loading using XML) did not have any way of providing a score for the player, so we first need to add that. We'll use a simple scoring method whereby the player gets 1 point for each energy point removed from a monster during combat. For example, if the player fights the zombie in the dungeon and removes 5 energy points and then goes into the dining room and fights the demon, removing 6 energy points from it, the player gets a total of 11 points (even if neither monster was killed). The code for calculating the score is straightforward and won't be shown here – the Chapter 13 version of the adventure game code contains the details and is available on the book's web site. The important thing is that the scores are saved to a database, so we can retrieve the data and display it on a web page.

To save the scores, we add a new table to the `Adventure.mdb` Access database. The table is called Scores and contains three columns: Name, Date and Score. Name is the player's game name (such as 'Wibble the Wizard' – we have also added an option for changing the player's name during game play if desired), Date is the date and time when the score was added to the database and Score is the numerical score. The Adventure application will automatically save the score whenever the player gets killed, starts a new game or quits the program. Again, the code for doing all this is straightforward, involving constructing an SQL INSERT statement and calling `Execute NonQuery()` to insert the data into the database.

What we would like to do here is to build a separate application (that is, not part of the Adventure project) that builds a web page displaying the scores in the database, listed in descending order. We'll do this in two stages. First, we'll just use an unadorned `DataGrid` to display the data, since this illustrates the basic technique, although it produces an ugly (but readable) web page.

Second, we will show some of the ways in which the display can be beautified by using *templates* for formatting the output data.

13.5.1 □ **The DataGrid web control**

The result of the first attempt at producing a scores list looks like that shown in Figure 13.3.

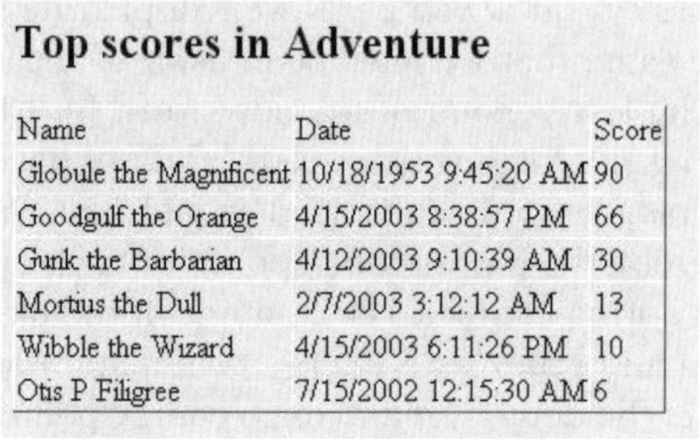

Top scores in Adventure

Name	Date	Score
Globule the Magnificent	10/18/1953 9:45:20 AM	90
Goodgulf the Orange	4/15/2003 8:38:57 PM	66
Gunk the Barbarian	4/12/2003 9:10:39 AM	30
Mortius the Dull	2/7/2003 3:12:12 AM	13
Wibble the Wizard	4/15/2003 6:11:26 PM	10
Otis P Filigree	7/15/2002 12:15:30 AM	6

Figure 13.3 Displaying data in a DataGrid web control

As you can see, the data is displayed clearly enough, although the format wouldn't win any beauty contests. The code for producing this consists of the usual .aspx file with a C# class providing the power behind the scenes. The .aspx file contains the following code:

```
<%@ Page Language="c#" AutoEventWireup="false"
   Src="TopAdventure.aspx.cs" Inherits="TopAdventure"%>
<!DOCTYPE HTML PUBLIC "-//W3C//DTD HTML 4.0 Transitional//EN">
<HTML>
  <HEAD>
    <title>Scores in Adventure</title>
  </HEAD>
  <body>
  <h2>Top scores in Adventure</h2>
    <form id="Form1" method="post" runat="server">
    <asp:DataGrid Runat="server" ID="adventureScores" />
    </form>
  </body>
</HTML>
```

Apart from the page's title, the entire output is produced by the DataGrid control called adventureScores. As the header line states, the ASP .NET file inherits a C# class called TopAdventure, which is contained in the C# code file:

```
using System;
using System.Web.UI;
using System.Web.UI.WebControls;
using System.Data;
using System.Data.OleDb;
```

```csharp
public class TopAdventure : Page
{
  protected DataGrid adventureScores;
  protected DataSet dataSet;
  protected OleDbDataAdapter command;

  protected override void OnInit(EventArgs args)
  {
    string source = "Provider=Microsoft.Jet.OLEDB.4.0;" +
        @"Data Source=C:\Books\MyBooks\CSharpBook\Programs\
        Chap13\Adventure\Adventure.mdb";
    OleDbConnection oleConn = new OleDbConnection(source);
    dataSet = new DataSet();
    try
    {
      oleConn.Open();
      string sql = "SELECT * FROM Scores ORDER BY Score
        DESC";
      command = new OleDbDataAdapter(sql, oleConn);
      command.Fill(dataSet, "Scores");
      adventureScores.DataSource = dataSet.Tables["Scores"];
      adventureScores.DataBind();
    }
    catch (Exception ex)
    {
      Console.WriteLine(ex.ToString());
    }
    finally
    {
      oleConn.Close();
    }
  }
}
```

The code should look familiar if you have read Chapter 11 on databases, since most of the steps involved in retrieving the information are identical to methods we introduced there. We open the database, construct an SQL command to retrieve the data from the Scores table (the 'ORDER BY Score DESC' clause sorts the data into descending order using the Score as the sort field), and then fill a DataSet with the result of the query.

The next two lines are new, however. The easiest way to load the data into a DataGrid is to set its DataSource to a table from the DataSet. Just setting the DataSource property only provides the link between the DataGrid and DataSet, however – in order to actually get the DataGrid to display the data, we must call DataBind().

This example shows how little code is actually needed to link a database to a web page, but the display leaves a lot to be desired. We'll now examine a few methods that can improve this situation.

13.5.2 ☐ Customizing a `DataGrid`

The `DataGrid` can be customized in a large number of ways to produce a prettier display. We will give an example here that uses the same data as in the previous section, but the reader is encouraged to browse the documentation to see what else is available.

To get an idea of what we are aiming for in the code, Figure 13.4 shows the new display as seen in a web browser.

Adventure game top scores

Name	Score	Date obtained
Globule the Magnificent	90	18 Oct 1953 (9:45 AM)
Goodgulf the Orange	66	15 Apr 2003 (8:38 PM)
Gunk the Barbarian	30	12 Apr 2003 (9:10 AM)
Mortius the Dull	13	07 Feb 2003 (3:12 AM)
Wibble the Wizard	10	15 Apr 2003 (6:11 PM)
Otis P Filigree	6	15 Jul 2002 (12:15 AM)

Figure 13.4 Displaying data in a customized `DataGrid` web control

To achieve these effects, we have customized the `DataGrid` by changing the code both in the `.aspx` file and in the background C# class. Many of the custom properties can be set in either location, but we have tried to emphasize the C# code here.

We'll begin by having a look at the new `.aspx` file:

```
1. <%@ Page Language="c#" AutoEventWireup="false"
2. Src="TopAdventure.aspx.cs" Inherits="TopAdventure"%>
3. <!DOCTYPE HTML PUBLIC "-//W3C//DTD HTML 4.0 ⤸
   Transitional//EN">
4. <HTML>
5.   <HEAD>
6.     <title>Scores in Adventure</title>
7.   </HEAD>
8.   <body>
9.     <form id="Form1" method="post" runat="server">
10.       <center>
11.       <asp:Label Runat="server" ID="headerLabel"/>
12.       </center>
13.       <asp:DataGrid
14.         AutoGenerateColumns="false"
15.         Runat="server" ID="adventureScores">
```

```
16.            <Columns>
17.
18.              <asp:BoundColumn
19.                  HeaderText="Name"
20.                  DataField="Name"
21.                />
22.
23.              <asp:BoundColumn
24.                  HeaderText="Score"
25.                  DataField="Score"
26.                />
27.
28.              <asp:BoundColumn
29.                  HeaderText="Date obtained"
30.                  DataField="Date"
31.                  DataFormatString="{0:dd MMM yyyy (h:mm tt)}"
32.                />
33.
34.            </Columns>
35.
36.          </asp:DataGrid>
37.        </form>
38.      </body>
39.  </HTML>
```

A `Label` has been added (line 11) to display the title on the page – its text is defined in the C# code as we'll see later.

The `DataGrid` itself is defined on lines 13 to 36. Glancing back at the picture above, it can be seen that we have customized each column in the grid by aligning the text differently in each case. The Name column uses left-aligned text, the Score column is right-aligned, and the Date column is centred. The default `DataGrid` applies the same alignment to all cells in the table, so we need to build up the `DataGrid` by hand if we want access to the individual columns within it.

This is indicated by line 14, where we set `AutoGenerateColumns` to `false`. By default, this property is true, which means that the `DataGrid` generates its columns by reading them from the data source to which it is bound. This restricts the display so that it can only show all the columns in the data source, and the order in which the columns are displayed must be the same as their order in the data source.

The `DataGrid`'s columns are defined within a `<Columns>` section (lines 16 to 34). There are several types of columns that can be inserted into a `DataGrid` – the complete list is shown in the documentation for `DataGrid`. The `BoundColumn` that we use here binds that column to a field in a data source, which for our purposes will be a column from the Scores table in the database. Other column types allow each entry in the `DataGrid` to appear as a button or as a hyperlink to a URL. It is also possible to make the cells in a column editable.

Each column type has a number of attributes that can be defined in the
.aspx file or in the C# code. Here, we have specified the HeaderText (the text
that appears at the top of the column) and the DataField (which is the name
of the column in the data source to which the DataGrid column is to be
bound). For the last column (displaying the date), we have added a
DataFormatString which uses standard string formatting code to indicate
how the date should be displayed. Complete information on formatting dates
and times can be found in the documentation for DateTimeFormatInfo.

We could set up all the other properties of the various controls in the
.aspx file, but it is more flexible to use the C# class that drives the web
page. Its code is as follows:

```
1. using System;
2. using System.Web.UI;
3. using System.Web.UI.WebControls;
4. using System.Data;
5. using System.Data.OleDb;
6. using System.Drawing;
7.
8. public class TopAdventure : Page
9. {
10.    protected DataGrid adventureScores;
11.    protected DataSet dataSet;
12.    protected OleDbDataAdapter command;
13.    protected Label headerLabel;
14.
15.    protected override void OnInit(EventArgs args)
16.    {
17.        headerLabel.Text = "Adventure game top scores";
18.        headerLabel.Height = 40;
19.        headerLabel.ForeColor = Color.Red;
20.        headerLabel.Font.Name = "Arial";
21.        headerLabel.Font.Size = 20;
22.        headerLabel.Font.Bold = true;
23.
24.        string source = "Provider=Microsoft.Jet.OLEDB.4.0;" +
25.            @"Data Source=C:\Books\MyBooks\CSharpBook
               \Programs\Chap13"
26.            + @"Adventure\Adventure.mdb";
27.        OleDbConnection oleConn = new OleDbConnection(source);
28.        dataSet = new DataSet();
29.        try
30.        {
31.            oleConn.Open();
32.            string sql = "SELECT * FROM Scores ORDER BY
                   Score DESC";
33.            command = new OleDbDataAdapter(sql, oleConn);
34.            command.Fill(dataSet, "Scores");
```

```
35.
36.            adventureScores.DataSource = dataSet.Tables["Scores"];
37.            adventureScores.DataBind();
38.
39.            adventureScores.HorizontalAlign =
               HorizontalAlign.Center;
40.            adventureScores.BackColor = Color.Black;
41.            adventureScores.BorderColor = Color.Black;
42.            adventureScores.BorderWidth = 5;
43.            adventureScores.CellPadding = 5;
44.            adventureScores.CellSpacing = 2;
45.            adventureScores.Font.Name = "Arial";
46.
47.            TableItemStyle adventureStyle = adventureScores.
               ItemStyle;
48.            adventureStyle = adventureScores.ItemStyle;
49.            adventureStyle.BackColor = Color.LightYellow;
50.            adventureStyle = adventureScores.AlternatingItemStyle;
51.            adventureStyle.BackColor = Color.MistyRose;
52.
53.            TableItemStyle headerStyle = adventureScores.
               HeaderStyle;
54.            headerStyle.HorizontalAlign = HorizontalAlign.Center;
55.            headerStyle.BackColor = Color.Red;
56.            headerStyle.ForeColor = Color.White;
57.            headerStyle.Font.Bold = true;
58.            headerStyle.Font.Name = "Arial";
59.
60.            DataGridColumnCollection cols = adventureScores.
               Columns;
61.            TableItemStyle itemStyle = cols[0].ItemStyle;
62.            itemStyle.HorizontalAlign = HorizontalAlign.Left;
63.            itemStyle = cols[1].ItemStyle;
64.            itemStyle.HorizontalAlign = HorizontalAlign.Right;
65.            itemStyle = cols[2].ItemStyle;
66.            itemStyle.HorizontalAlign = HorizontalAlign.Center;
67.        }
68.        catch (Exception ex)
69.        {
70.           Console.WriteLine(ex.ToString());
71.        }
72.        finally
73.        {
74.           oleConn.Close();
75.        }
76.    }
77. }
```

The text and properties of the page's title are defined on lines 17 to 22. Some properties of web controls are multi-layered, in the sense that we need to access an intermediate property to get at the specific property we want. One such property is the `Font`, which is actually represented by a `FontInfo` object (and not the `Font` object used in Windows Forms). Lines 20 to 22 illustrate accessing and defining several properties of the font for the page title. We could also have said:

```
FontInfo headerFont = headerLabel.Font;
headerFont.Name = "Arial";
headerFont.Size = 20;
headerFont.Bold = true;
```

The `Font` itself is read-only, so we can't prepare a `FontInfo` object in advance and then assign it to a web control's `Font` property.

Starting on line 24, we load the data into a `DataSet` as usual, and then (lines 36 and 37) bind the `DataGrid` to the `DataSet`'s Scores table. Calling `DataBind()` here causes the columns defined in the `.aspx` file to bind to the corresponding columns in the `DataSet` – we don't need to write a separate `DataBind()` call for each column.

If we stopped at this point, we would get a view similar to that shown in the last section, except that the columns would be in a different order (since we deliberately switched the Score and Date columns from their order in the `DataSet` just to show how it can be done). To provide the formatting of the table, we need to apply the formatting styles to the various bits of the `DataGrid` control.

First (lines 39 to 45) we define some properties that apply to the `DataGrid` as a whole. `HorizontalAlign` defines the alignment of the `DataGrid` relative to the web page, *not* the alignment of the text within each cell. On line 39, we set the control so that it should appear centred horizontally on the page.

The other properties should be fairly obvious, but it should be remembered that this example only uses a few of the many properties available. Have a look at the list of properties in the `DataGrid` documentation to see what's possible, and try things out for yourself.

Lines 47 to 51 illustrate the use of *styles* within a `DataGrid`. There are seven style properties that can be defined for various parts of the grid, each of which is represented by a `TableItemStyle`. In this example, we have defined an `ItemStyle` and an `AlternatingItemStyle`. The `ItemStyle` defines the parameters used to display the ordinary (that is, in the main body of the grid, excluding the header and footer, if any) cells in the grid. A `TableItemStyle` contains a number of properties that can be set to define the appearance of a given cell in the table. Here, we've just set the `BackColor` to `LightYellow`, but many more properties could be defined.

The `AlternatingItemStyle` defines properties for every second row in the table. This produces a banding effect which makes the rows in a large table easier to read, as can be seen in the picture above. Lines 53 to 58 define the properties for the header row in a similar way.

The styles considered so far all apply to *rows* within the table. It is also possible to define styles for individual columns. On lines 60 to 66, we set the horizontal alignment of the text in each column. To access individual columns, we need to use the `Columns` property of the `DataGrid`, which is a `DataGridColumnCollection` (line 60). Each column within this collection can be accessed using array notation, but in this case the array index *must* be an integer – it is not possible to use notation such as `cols["Name"]` to access the Name column. It is therefore important to remember the order in which the columns were defined. We can always refer back to the `.aspx` file to do this.

Each column has its own style properties, so we can access these and modify them to customize the appearance of the overall grid.

13.6 ■ Graphics on web pages

One of Java's main selling points originally was its provision of *applets*, which are Java programs that could be embedded within a web page. A Java applet allows much of the functionality of a stand-alone Java application, except that it is not allowed to access the hard disk of the client machine (for fairly obvious security reasons). In particular, a Java applet allows vector graphics and raster images to be displayed in exactly the same way as in a stand-alone application.

.NET does not have an equivalent to the Java applet, and as a result, the production of vector graphics is not as straightforward in an ASP .NET web page as it is in a stand-alone C# application (see Chapter 10 on graphics). However, by means of a little trick, it is actually fairly easy to embed graphics within an ASP .NET page.

The ASP .NET web controls library contains a control called `Image` which allows a static raster image (such as that loaded from a JPEG file) to be displayed as a control within an ASP .NET container. Note that the `Image` web control is quite different from the `Image` control in Windows Forms, since it does not allow the creation of a `Graphics` object and therefore does not allow any vector graphics to be drawn directly onto it.

The trick is to create an `Image` web control and direct it to load a JPEG disk file that has been created using a Windows Forms `Image` which, as we saw in Chapter 10, *does* allow drawing. We can create a `Graphics` object for the Windows Forms `Image`, create the graphics we need and save this image back to disk on the server as a JPEG file. Finally, we can make the web controls image, which is the one that is visible on the web page, load its data from the JPEG file created from the Windows Forms `Image`.

We present a simple example that shows how this can be done. First, the `.aspx` file, which contains only the outline of a `Table`:

```
<%@ Page Language="c#" AutoEventWireup="false"
  Src="GraphicsDemo.aspx.cs" Inherits="GraphicsDemo" %>
<!DOCTYPE HTML PUBLIC "-//W3C//DTD HTML 4.0 Transitional//EN">
```

```
<HTML>
  <HEAD>
    <title>ASP .NET Graphics Demo</title>
  </HEAD>
  <body>
    <h1>ASP .NET Graphics Demo</h1>
    The table contains an image generated using GDI+.
    <form runat="server" ID="Form1">
      <center>
        <asp:Table id="mainTable" Runat="server">
        </asp:Table>
      </center>
    </form>
  </body>
</HTML>
```

We will add a `TableRow` and `TableCell` to the `Table` within the C# code, rather than in the `.aspx` file. The backing C# class is called `GraphicsDemo` and looks like this:

```
1.  using System;
2.  using System.Web.UI;
3.  using System.Web.UI.WebControls;
4.  using System.Drawing;
5.  using System.Drawing.Imaging;
6.
7.  public class GraphicsDemo : Page
8.  {
9.      protected Table mainTable;
10.     protected Panel imagePanel;
11.     protected System.Web.UI.WebControls.Image tempImage;
12.     const int panelWidth = 600, panelHeight = 300;
13.
14.     protected override void OnInit(EventArgs args)
15.     {
16.         Load += new EventHandler(PageLoad);
17.     }
18.
19.     void BuildTable()
20.     {
21.         mainTable.HorizontalAlign = HorizontalAlign.Center;
22.         TableCell cell = new TableCell();
23.         TableRow row = new TableRow();
24.
25.         imagePanel = new Panel();
26.         imagePanel.Width = panelWidth;
27.         imagePanel.Height = panelHeight;
```

```
28.      imagePanel.BackColor = Color.PeachPuff;
29.      tempImage = new System.Web.UI.WebControls.Image();
30.      imagePanel.Controls.Add(tempImage);
31.      cell.Controls.Add(imagePanel);
32.
33.      Bitmap image = new Bitmap((int)imagePanel.Width.Value,
34.         (int)imagePanel.Height.Value);
35.      Graphics g = Graphics.FromImage(image);
36.      g.Clear(Color.PeachPuff);
37.      Brush brush = new SolidBrush(Color.Yellow);
38.      g.FillRectangle(brush, 5, 5, 100, 200);
39.      image.Save(@"C:\Inetpub\wwwroot\Books\CSharpBook\" +
40.         "Chap13\GraphicsDemo\imagePanel.jpg",
           ImageFormat.Jpeg);
41.      tempImage.ImageUrl =
42.         "http://growe.homeip.net/Books/CSharpBook/Chap13/" +
43.         "GraphicsDemo/imagePanel.jpg";
44.      row.Cells.Add(cell);
45.      mainTable.Rows.Add(row);
46.   }
47.
48.   void PageLoad(Object sender, EventArgs e)
49.   {
50.      BuildTable();
51.   }
52. }
```

BuildTable() (line 19) is called from PageLoad() (line 48) so the graphics are redrawn each time the page is loaded. The Table mainTable defined in the .aspx file is built up in the C# code by creating a TableRow and a TableCell (lines 22 and 23). The TableCell is populated by creating a Panel (line 25) which is inserted into it. For this simple example, we could get away with just inserting the Image directly into the TableCell, but in general, the graphics would probably be accompanied by other controls such as buttons, so using a Panel to organize the contents of the TableCell is usually a good idea.

We create the web controls Image on line 29 and add it to the Panel on line 30. This Image will be directed at the JPEG file on disk after it has been drawn and saved in the code that follows line 33. We create a blank Bitmap of the desired size on line 33, and create a Graphics to let us draw on it. In this case, the graphics we produce is just a filled yellow rectangle (lines 37 and 38), but of course you could insert code here to produce whatever graphics you want.

The key point in the procedure is that after the graphics are drawn, we save the image to disk as a JPEG file (line 39), making sure to save it in a directory accessible to the web server. The URL given on line 39 is where it is stored on my machine, but if you install this program on your own web server, the path may differ so you may need to change this line.

The final step is to point the web controls Image (tempImage) at this disk file, which we do on line 41 by setting the ImageUrl property. Finally, we add the TableCell to the TableRow (line 44) and then add the TableRow to mainTable which is created in the .aspx file (line 45).

This technique isn't quite as clean as many other programming techniques, since it requires using classes from outside the web controls library, but it works well enough. The principle can be extended to load in existing image files (such as photographs) and edit them in a similar way to the example in Chapter 10, and then show them on a web page.

13.7 ■ Interactive web pages

All the examples we have seen so far are static pages in the sense that they simply display information and do not allow the user to interact with the page in any way. ASP .NET and the Web Controls library provide a great deal of functionality for creating *interactive* web pages – pages that use the usual GUI controls to allow the user to request specific information or even change information stored in databases on the server.

Before we get into a specific example, we should get a general understanding of how interactive web pages work using ASP .NET and C#.

If we load up a web page that is based on ASP .NET and then view the source HTML that was sent to produce the page, we will find that there is no mention of any ASP .NET controls or C# code files in the listing – all the source code sent to the web browser on the client is HTML, since that is all many browsers understand.

When we access a URL based on an .aspx file, we begin by sending the server a request for this file. The server recognizes that the file is written using ASP .NET and that there is a C# class behind the file providing much of the processing code. The server will then run the code required to produce the initial version of the page, translate the output into HTML and send this HTML back to the client.

If the web page is a read-only page, as with the scores listing example in section 13.5, that ends the process since the user cannot interact with the page and so has no way of sending anything further back to the server (apart from reloading the page).

If the web page contains interactive controls, such as the example we will consider in the next section, each of these controls is capable of generating events in the same way as in a Windows Forms application. If the control has been marked with a Runat="Server" attribute, all event processing is done by submitting the form's contents to the server which runs the event handler and generates a new batch of HTML which is sent back to the client in an operation known as *postback*. The server keeps track of whether the page is generated as a result of a postback or whether the page is being generated by an initial request from the client (as when the page is first loaded into a browser). The `IsPostback` property of the `Page` class can be used in the C# 'behind-code' to tell whether the code is being run during a postback or not. This can be important, since usually initialization code should be run only when the page is first loaded. Running initialization code during a postback can erase the user's settings on the page, which can be highly irritating.

As we mentioned earlier, an ASP .NET server is stateless in that it keeps no record of the state of a client's page in between requests from the client. This information is instead stored in the long string of seemingly random characters that is sent back to the client as the `VIEWSTATE` hidden field. The viewstate contains information such as the current data stored in all the controls on the form, the current properties of the various controls (such as their colours, fonts, etc.) and any other information needed to restore the page to the state it had when the request was sent.

We will now consider an example of an interactive page that uses ASP .NET to set up the page's layout, but relegates most of the processing to the backing C# class.

13.8 ■ Case study: an item editor for the adventure game

The range of facilities in an interactive ASP .NET program is vast and far beyond the scope of this book, but we can get a good feel for what is possible by considering a substantial example. As you will know if you've been following the adventure game case study throughout the book, we have stored the parameters describing the various items and characters used in the game in an Access database. Up until now, the only way of reading or entering information from the database was to use Access's own facilities for editing database tables, either by entering the data directly into a table, or by designing an Access form to make the interface more pleasing.

Although it is possible to design a specialized form within Access for editing data, it makes an interesting exercise to create an ASP .NET/C# program which allows the data to be read and edited over the web. Doing this also has the advantage that we will have a GUI data editor which will work no matter what database we use to store the data. Since all the interaction with the database is handled within the C# code, we can easily change the database connection to link into, say, SQL Server or MySQL within the C# code without having to change the front end editor interface.

Creating a complete web site that allows all aspects of the adventure to be designed, including creation of items, rooms and characters, and the attachment of items to players and rooms would be a fairly challenging introductory project, so we'll restrict ourselves to an editor that allows existing items to be viewed and edited, and new items to be created. This program will illustrate most of the techniques that would be needed to expand the application to a complete game designer.

13.8.1 ☐ **The interface**

The interface to the item editor as it appears on a web page looks as shown in Figure 13.5.

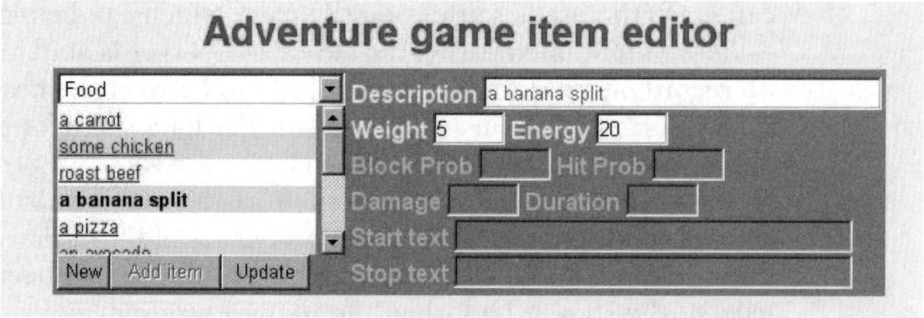

Figure 13.5 Interface to a web-based editor for items in the adventure game

On the left, a drop-down menu shows the types of items (Item, Food, Weapon, Armour, Potion, Ring and Wand) stored in the database. When the program starts, Item is selected, but the user would usually start a session with the editor by selecting one of the other types. Doing so will enable the appropriate textboxes and labels on the right. For example, if Food is selected (as in the figure above), the Description, Weight and Energy boxes are enabled since these are the only properties that a Food item can have.

Selecting a type also accesses the database to retrieve a list of items of that type that are stored already. The Description field of each of the items of that type is then displayed in a `DataList` control, as shown. Each entry in the list is shown as a `LinkButton`, which is displayed using underlined text, just like a link on a web page. Clicking one of these links displays its text in bold (like 'a banana split' in the figure) and also transforms it to ordinary text so that it is no longer an active link. The information about that item is then displayed in the text boxes on the right.

If the user wishes to edit the item's parameters, this can be done by editing the text in the text boxes (except for the Description, since this is a primary key in the database and cannot be changed – a better implementation would be to modify the database by adding a purely numerical primary key and thus allow the description of the item to be edited as well). When all changes have been made, the 'Update' button is pressed to update the record in the database back on the server.

A new item of a particular type can be added by first selecting the desired type using the drop-down menu, then pressing the 'New' button to clear the text boxes on the right. Enter the desired data and then press 'Add item' to add the new item to the database. Since a Description is required for all items in the database, we have used ASP .NET's validation feature to ensure that something is typed in the Description box when 'Add item' is pressed.

The three buttons in the lower left are enabled and disabled at appropriate times, according to what is possible at that time. In Figure 13.5 above, 'Add item' is disabled because the user has selected one of the items in the list and therefore can edit that item but not add it as a new item. Clicking 'New' deselects all items in the list, clears the text boxes and enables 'Add item'.

Obviously the layout of the components could be improved, but this is mainly a matter of adjusting the various ASP .NET settings of the controls, and is not really our main concern here. Readers who have a more comprehensive knowledge of ASP .NET may wish to experiment with the layout.

13.8.2 □ The ASP .NET code

The page requested by a web browser is stored on the server's web site in a file called `ItemEditor.aspx`. The code is concerned mainly with defining the layout of the page:

```
1.  <%@ Page Language="c#" AutoEventWireup="false"
2.    Src="ItemEditor.aspx.cs" Inherits="ItemEditor"%>
3.  <!DOCTYPE HTML PUBLIC "-//W3C//DTD HTML 4.0
    Transitional//EN">
4.  <HTML>
5.    <HEAD>
6.      <title>Scores in Adventure</title>
7.    </HEAD>
8.    <body>
9.      <form runat="server">
10.       <center>
11.       <asp:Label Runat="server" ID="headerLabel"/>
12.         <asp:Table id="mainTable" Runat="server">
13.           <asp:TableRow><asp:TableCell>
14.             <asp:Panel >
15.               <asp:DropDownList ID="typeList"
                  runat="server"
16.                 width=200 height=24 />
17.
18.             <DIV style="OVERFLOW: auto; WIDTH: 200;
19.               HEIGHT: 100" >
20.               <asp:DataList ID="itemList"
                  Runat="server"
21.                 Width=180 Height=0>
22.                 <ItemStyle BackColor = "LightYellow"/>
23.                 <AlternatingItemStyle BackColor =
                    "Khaki"/>
24.                 <ItemTemplate>
25.                   <asp:LinkButton Runat="server"
26.                     CommandName="Select"
```

```
27.                            Forecolor="Red"  ID="Linkbutton1"
28.                            NAME="Linkbutton1">
29.                            <%# DataBinder.Eval(Container.
                               DataItem,
30.                               "Description") %>
31.                         </asp:LinkButton>
32.                      </ItemTemplate>
33.                      <SelectedItemTemplate>
34.                         <B>
35.                            <%# DataBinder.Eval(Container.
                               DataItem,
36.                               "Description") %>
37.                         </B>
38.                      </SelectedItemTemplate>
39.                   </asp:DataList>
40.                </DIV>
41.
42.             <asp:Button
43.                ID="newButton" Text="New" Runat="server">
44.             </asp:Button>
45.             <asp:Button
46.                ID="addButton" Text="Add item"
                   Runat="server">
47.             </asp:Button>
48.             <asp:Button
49.                ID="updateButton" Text="Update"
                   Runat="server">
50.             </asp:Button>
51.          </asp:Panel>
52.          </asp:TableCell>
53.
54.          <asp:TableCell>
55.             <asp:Panel runat="server">
56.                <asp:Panel  runat="server"  Wrap="false">
57.                   <asp:Label ID="descLabel"
                      Text="Description"
58.                      Runat="server"/>
59.                   <asp:TextBox ID="descText"
                      Runat="server"
60.                      Width=275/>
61.                   <asp:RequiredFieldValidator
62.                      ID="requiredDescription"
63.                      Runat="server"
64.                      ErrorMessage="You must enter a
                      description."
65.                      ControlToValidate="descText"
```

```
66.                          Display="None"/>
67.                 </asp:Panel>
68.                 <asp:Panel runat="server">
69.                    <asp:Label ID="weightLabel"
                       Text="Weight"
70.                       Runat="server"/>
71.                    <asp:TextBox ID="weightText"
                       Runat="server"
72.                       Width= 50/>
73.                    <asp:Label ID="energyLabel"
                       Text="Energy"
74.                       Runat="server"/>
75.                    <asp:TextBox ID="energyText"
                       Runat="server"
76.                       Width= 50/>
77.                 </asp:Panel>
78.                 <asp:Panel runat="server">
79.                    <asp:Label ID="blockProbLabel"
80.                       Text="Block Prob" Runat="server"/>
81.                    <asp:TextBox ID="blockProbText"
                       Runat="server"
82.                       Width= 50/>
83.                    <asp:Label ID="hitProbLabel"
                       Text="Hit Prob"
84.                       Runat="server"/>
85.                    <asp:TextBox ID="hitProbText"
                       Runat="server"
86.                       Width= 50/>
87.                 </asp:Panel>
88.                 <asp:Panel runat="server">
89.                    <asp:Label ID="damageLabel"
                       Text="Damage"
90.                       Runat="server"/>
91.                    <asp:TextBox ID="damageText"
                       Runat="server"
92.                       Width= 50/>
93.                    <asp:Label ID="durationLabel"
                       Text="Duration"
94.                       Runat="server"/>
95.                    <asp:TextBox ID="durationText"
                       Runat="server"
96.                       Width= 50/>
97.                 </asp:Panel>
98.                 <asp:Panel runat="server">
99.                    <asp:Label ID="startLabel"
                       Text="Start text"
```

```
100.                        Runat="server"/>
101.                    <asp:TextBox ID="startText" ⮌
                        Runat="server"
102.                        Width=275/>
103.                    </asp:Panel>
104.                    <asp:Panel runat="server">
105.                        <asp:Label ID="stopLabel" Text="Stop ⮌
                        text"
106.                        Runat="server"/>
107.                        <asp:TextBox ID="stopText" ⮌
                        Runat="server"
108.                        Width= 275/>
109.                        </asp:Panel>
110.                    </asp:Panel>
111.                </asp:TableCell>
112.            </asp:TableRow>
113.        </asp:Table>
114.        <asp:ValidationSummary Runat="server"
115.          ID="validationSummary"
116.          HeaderText="Error:"/>
117.        </center>
118.    </form>
119.    <h2>Instructions</h2>
120.    Select an item type from the drop-down menu.
121.    A list of items of that type
122.    currently in the database will appear on the left.
123.    <P>
124.    If you want to modify
125.    an existing item, select it and its stats will ⮌
        appear on the
126.    right. Modify the stats as required and then click ⮌
        'Update'.
127.    (Note that you cannot
128.    change the item's description since this
129.    is used as the primary key in the database.)
130.    <P>
131.    To create a new item, select the item type and ⮌
        press 'New'
132.    to clear the text boxes,
133.    then enter its stats in the boxes on the right,
134.    then click 'Add item'.
135.    </body>
136. </HTML>
```

Since much of this code is concerned with layout of the components on the page, it is quite repetitive so we need not consider it all in detail. One of the problems in writing web pages is that often we need a mix of features from several different languages. In this example, we need fragments of HTML to define the overall page sections, ASP .NET to define the controls we are using, and C# to provide the code behind it all. An unfortunate feature of this sort of programming is that often all three of these languages provide features which are also available in the other two, but have different ways of specifying properties of objects and so on.

Since this is a book on C# (primarily!), the code has been written in an attempt to place as much of the actual processing in the C# code, but we do need some of the less trivial features of ASP .NET to get this example to work.

The `AutoEventWireup` property has been set to `false` (line 1) which requires us to connect the `Load` event for the web page manually. This will be done in the C# code later. After some HTML preliminaries, we add a `Label` (line 11) to display the title 'Adventure game item editor'.

After this, we begin the layout of the controls. There are various ways this can be done, but usually a layout involves using a table to provide the overall structure and panels within the various table cells to organize controls on a lower level. The ASP .NET `Table` is composed of a number of `TableRows`, each of which can contain a number of `TableCells`. It is not possible to nest `Tables` directly (that is, a `TableCell` cannot contain a `Table` unless that `Table` is enclosed within another control such as a `Panel`), so if we want to create some lower-level structure within a particular `TableCell`, we need to use other methods.

One possibility is to use the `RowSpan` and `ColumnSpan` properties of a `TableCell` to define the number of rows and columns a particular cell should span. Working out these values can be tricky, however, so we will use a different approach.

The `Panel` control is just an empty container which can be used to group together other controls. `Panels` can also be nested directly, unlike `Tables`, so we can use them to form hierarchical structures within a single `TableCell`.

The top-level design of the layout uses a `Table` with a single `TableRow`, which in turn contains two `TableCells`. The first cell contains a `Panel` which in turn contains the drop-down list, the data list and the three buttons on the left. The second cell contains another `Panel` which contains all the labels and text boxes on the right.

The `DropDownList` (the Web Controls version of a `ComboBox` in Windows Forms but bizarrely given a different name) is defined on lines 15 and 16. This definition illustrates a useful point about placing and sizing controls. Many ASP .NET controls have a default size or else size themselves to their contents. A `DropDownList`, for example, will adjust its width to fit the longest string it contains. This can be fine if the control's contents are constant, but if the contents, and hence the size, of the control changes as the page is used, the overall layout can jump around haphazardly, which is usually annoying and confusing to the user.

It is usually better to specify the size of a control so that it remains fixed in place on the layout. This can be done by explicitly setting the `Width` and `Height` properties, as we've done on line 16 for the `DropDownList` and elsewhere for some of the other controls.

Each of the text boxes used for entering or editing data is accompanied by a label. The label's text remains constant during the program, but its colour changes to reflect the state of the accompanying text box. An active text box is matched by a yellow label, while a disabled text box has a grey label. These settings are all managed within the C# code which we will examine shortly. The label is implemented using an ASP `Label` control and the textbox by `TextBox`.

13.8.3 ☐ Validation of data

Since the Description field is the primary key in the database, it is essential that the user enters a description for any new item (no matter what type). ASP .NET provides a simple validation feature which allows individual controls on an ASP form to be tested for correct values when the form is submitted to the server. On line 61, we have added a `RequiredFieldValidator` to check that the description text box has something in it. The attributes of the validator show that an `ErrorMessage` can be associated with it. `ControlToValidate` connects the validator with the control that it is to check. The last attribute sets `Display` to None. By default, if a control's validation check fails, the `ErrorMessage` is displayed beside the control on the form. Although this gives immediate feedback to the user, it also usually destroys the layout of the controls on the form, so is not usually the best way of providing feedback, unless the form is designed to have a space available for the error message.

A better way of displaying any validation error messages is to use a `ValidationSummary` control, which we have added at the end of the form (line 114). When enabled in the C# code, a `ValidationSummary` prints out all error messages from all validation controls in the form in one place. Although we've used the default version here, the control's appearance can be customized in the same way as any other web control.

The `RequiredFieldValidator` is only one of several validator classes. Others allow a field to be tested to see if its numerical value is in the correct range, or if a string value matches a regular expression. It is also possible to define a custom validator which allows the programmer to define a condition to use for validation. For details, see the documentation under 'validation server controls'.

Although validators are easy enough to insert in the ASP code, they do have a few subtleties related to when they should be active which we will consider when we study the C# code below.

13.8.4 ☐ **Interactive data display**

In our previous example showing the scores table, we used a `DataGrid` to display the data. `DataGrid`s are flexible controls for non-interactive displays, but when the user needs to be able to select items in the list, we need to use a different control that allows some interaction. ASP .NET does have a `ListBox` which allows items in the list to be selected and for this application it would have been suitable. However, the `DataList` control is a powerful class in the Web Controls library, so we have used it here to provide an introduction to its features.

The `DataList`, along with the `DataGrid` and another data display control called a `Repeater` all support the idea of a *display template*. Since these controls are designed to display data from an external source, they may all be *bound* to the data source. The data source can be as simple as an array, but whenever we are dealing with data extracted from a database, it is more usual to load the data into a `DataSet` and then bind the data display control to the `DataSet`. This is the method that we used in the previous example with the scores table, and we shall do the same thing here.

The `TableCell` containing the `DataList` is defined on lines 20 to 39. `DataList`s (in fact, all the data display controls) suffer from a slight deficiency in that they do not support scrolling if the list gets longer than the space in the table allocated for it. Rather, they tend to expand in size and force the `TableCell` containing them to expand with them, thus distorting the overall layout.

The reason for this is that, since all ASP controls must be translated into HTML by the server, all the table-like controls such as `DataList` are translated into HTML tables, which do not support scrolling. They rely instead on the web browser's main window scrolling to accommodate them, which only works if the table is on its own in the display.

Another problem with the `DataList` is that if the list contains too few items to fill up the container which holds it, the list items tend to space themselves out so that all the space is used, resulting in large gaps between neighbouring items in the list. This does not distort the table layout, but it does look quite ugly.

The `DataList` used here solves both these problems, although not in a particularly elegant way. To solve the problem of scrolling a large list, we have resorted to an HTML DIV element (line 18). A DIV acts as a container of a specified size (as given by the WIDTH and HEIGHT parameters on lines 18 and 19) that *is* recognized by HTML (and therefore can be sent to a client unmodified). It also has an OVERFLOW parameter which specifies the behaviour of the container if its contents overflow the boundaries. Using the 'auto' setting for OVERFLOW causes the container to generate scrollbars if needed, so it is just what we need. We have therefore enclosed the ASP .NET `DataList` control within a DIV.

The `DataList` itself begins on line 20. We can define a width and height for it as well, but if we set the height to be the same as that of the DIV container, the problem with short lists expanding to fill the available space detracts from the appearance of the list. One trick that seems to fool the DataList into behaving properly is to set the Height parameter to 0 (line 21). Since a control expands if its contents require more space than that allowed by its parameter settings, the control's height is made to fit the number of items in the list exactly. When the DataList's height exceeds the height of the enclosing DIV, the DIV produces scrollbars, so everything seems to work well. As we said, not the prettiest of solutions, but sometimes we need to improvise.

There is one slight problem with this setup, however. If the DataList contains a long list so that a scrollbar is produced when it is displayed, and the user scrolls down to select an item near the bottom of the list, then submits the form for processing by the server, the position of the scrollbar is not remembered by the viewstate so when the reply comes back from the server, the scrollbar is reset to the top of the list again. Since the scrollbar is a property of the DIV and not the DataList there does not seem any easy way around this problem, since the C# code cannot access anything that is not an ASP control.

Using an ASP ListBox avoids this latter problem, since HTML has a list box of its own which does contain a scrollbar. If we had used a ListBox in this example, we would not need the DIV element to contain it, and the position of the scrollbar would be remembered between visits to the page. However, a ListBox does not support the display features that are available in a DataList, to which we now turn.

13.8.5 □ Templates

As mentioned above, the three main data display controls, DataGrid, DataList and Repeater, all support the idea of templates for specifying how various parts of the list should be displayed. We have already seen the specification of display styles in the earlier example of the adventure game score table, and we have added an ItemStyle and AlternatingItemStyle to the DataList here as well (lines 22 and 23).

However, we can now extend this idea by defining templates for how the data displayed in each of these areas should be formatted. There are several templates available, but all data display controls require at least an ItemTemplate to be defined.

Our ItemTemplate is on lines 24 to 32. If the ItemTemplate is the only template defined for the DataList, it will be applied to every item in the list. The template should contain instructions as to the type of control that is used to display the data, which in turn contains an expression giving the actual data to display.

On line 25, we create a LinkButton to display the data within an ItemTemplate. A LinkButton displays text like a hyperlink on a web page – the text is underlined and will generate an event when clicked with the mouse. The event can be used to update information in the rest of the form, as we will see below.

The actual text that is displayed could be specified as an ordinary string written directly into the code, but since it is more usual for a `DataList` to be bound to a data source, we need a better way of determining the information to display.

The most commonly used method of extracting information from a data source is to use the `DataBinder.Eval()` method, as we have done on lines 29 to 30. The code given in this example may be copied verbatim into any situation where data needs to be extracted from a data source:

```
<%# DataBinder.Eval(Container.DataItem, column-name) %>
```

The only parameter that needs to be changed from one call of this method to another is the 'column-name', which specifies the column in the data source from which the data should be drawn. In this case, the data source is a `DataSet` (defined in the C# code below), and we wish to display only the Description field from this set. We could combine data from several columns in the data source by using a separate `DataBinder.Eval()` call for each one and linking them by ordinary text. For example we could say:

```
<asp:LinkButton Runat="server"
   CommandName="Select" Forecolor="Red">
   <%# DataBinder.Eval(Container.DataItem,
       "Description")
   %>
   (<%# DataBinder.Eval(Container.DataItem, "Weight") %>)
</asp:LinkButton>
```

Each line in the `DataList` would then contain the item's description followed by the weight in parentheses. Note that any text outside the `<% … %>` delimiters (such as the parentheses in the example above) is treated as text that should be inserted into the string that is displayed, and is not interpreted as an ASP command. The banana split that is shown in Figure 13.5 would then appear in the list like this:

```
a banana split (5)
```

A `DataList` supports selection of its `LinkButton` elements using the mouse and provides a `SelectedItemTemplate` to allow the programmer to define how selected items should be displayed. On lines 33 to 38 we have provided this template. A selected item displays the same information as an ordinary item, but this time it is displayed as ordinary text (there is no enclosing `LinkButton` control). We have added the HTML `<B>` tag (lines 34 and 37) which displays text in boldface. The 'banana split' item in the illustration above shows the effect of this template.

There are several other templates available for the `DataList` – further details can be found in the documentation for `DataList`.

The remainder of the ASP .NET code just inserts the various buttons, labels and text boxes. None of these controls has any functionality or event handlers defined in the ASP file – this is all done in the C# code. At the end of the ASP file we've added some plain text that gives instructions on how to use the web page to edit the database.

13.8.6 ☐ C# code for item editor

The C# behind-code is fairly lengthy for this example, so we will take it in stages. First, we can have a look at the class field declarations, most of which just provide identities for the corresponding controls in the ASP file:

```
using System;
using System.Web.UI;
using System.Web.UI.WebControls;
using System.Data;
using System.Data.OleDb;
using System.Drawing;

public class ItemEditor : Page
{
    protected DataGrid adventureScores;
    protected DataSet dataSet;
    protected OleDbDataAdapter command;
    protected OleDbConnection oleConn;
    protected Label headerLabel;
    protected Table mainTable;
    protected DropDownList typeList;
    protected DataList itemList;
    protected ValidationSummary validationSummary;
    protected TextBox descText, typeText,
        weightText, energyText,
        blockProbText, hitProbText,
        damageText, durationText,
        startText, stopText;
    protected Label descLabel, typeLabel,
        weightLabel, energyLabel,
        blockProbLabel, hitProbLabel,
        damageLabel, durationLabel,
        startLabel, stopLabel;
    protected Button newButton, updateButton, addButton;
    protected int numTextBoxes = 10;
    protected TextBox[] textArray;
    protected Label[] labelArray;
    protected bool[] quoteDBField;
```

All these declarations except for the last few just provide the objects that are inherited by the ASP file for its various controls. The last three lines define some arrays that are useful in updating the states (enabled or disabled) of the text boxes and labels, and a `bool` array that is used in constructing SQL statements for adding or updating records in the database.

The `OnInit()` method is called when the page is first loaded:

```
1.  protected override void OnInit(EventArgs args)
2.  {
3.    Load += new EventHandler(PageLoad);
4.    typeText = new TextBox();
5.    typeLabel = new Label();
6.    textArray = new TextBox[] {
7.      descText, typeText, weightText, energyText,
8.      blockProbText, hitProbText, damageText, durationText,
9.      startText, stopText
10.   };
11.   labelArray = new Label[] {
12.     descLabel, typeLabel, weightLabel, energyLabel,
13.     blockProbLabel, hitProbLabel, damageLabel,
        durationLabel,
14.     startLabel, stopLabel
15.   };
16.   quoteDBField = new bool[] { true, true, false, false,
        false,
17.       false, false, false, true, true };
18.
19.   headerLabel.Text = "Adventure game item editor";
20.   headerLabel.Height = 40;
21.   headerLabel.ForeColor = Color.Red;
22.   headerLabel.Font.Name = "Arial";
23.   headerLabel.Font.Size = 20;
24.   headerLabel.Font.Bold = true;
25.
26.   BuildTable();
27.   BuildTypeList();
28.   itemList.ItemStyle.Font.Name = "Arial";
29.   itemList.ItemStyle.Font.Size = 10;
30.   itemList.SelectedIndexChanged +=
31.     new EventHandler(itemList_SelectedIndexChanged);
32.   SetupButtons();
33. }
```

Since `AutoEventWireup` was set to `false` in the ASP file, we need to provide an explicit handler for the `Load` event (line 3). This causes the method `PageLoad()` to be called whenever the page is loaded, which happens not only when the web page itself is first accessed by the browser, but also every time a postback is made from the server in response to a client request.

`PageLoad()` performs only one function at the moment unless the page is being loaded for the first time: it turns off validation:

```
void PageLoad(Object sender, EventArgs e)
{
  validationSummary.Enabled = false;
  EnableValidation(false);
```

```
        if (!IsPostBack)
        {
            typeList_SelectedIndexChanged(null, null);
        }
    }
```

The reason for doing this is that leaving validation on all the time can cause irritating error messages to appear at inappropriate times.

Note that we have used the `IsPostBack` property to test whether the page is being loaded for the first time or as a result of a postback from the server. If the page is being loaded initially, we call the event handler for `typeList` (the drop-down menu that displays the item types) to initialize the display. We will discuss this handler later.

The variables `typeText` and `typeLabel` are a dummy `TextBox` and `Label` that are not displayed on the form, but are there to allow us to treat the entire set of `TextBox`es as an array that matches the data fields in the Item table in the database. If you glance back at the structure of this table as it was defined in Chapter 11, you will see that the first field is Description, followed by Type which stores the type of item (food, weapon, armour and so on). (Although this may look ugly, the other option would be to restructure the database so that the fields are in an order that makes it more convenient for this program, which is much more difficult to do. 'Kludges' such as this are, unfortunately, common in industrial programming.)

Lines 6 to 15 set up the arrays of text boxes and labels that we will use later when updating the states of these controls.

Line 16 sets up `quoteDBField` which is an array of `bool`s that specify whether or not a particular field in the database is a string, and will therefore require quotes around its value when it is included in an SQL statement. This makes it easier to build the INSERT and UPDATE statements in the button event handlers we consider later.

Lines 19 to 24 set up the page title. The remaining lines of this method call some other methods to set up the form and also initialize some properties of the `DataList` `itemList`, including setting up the event handler for `SelectedIndexChanged` which is generated when the user selects an item in the list.

We'll now have a look at the other methods involved in initializing the form. First, the code for `BuildTable()`:

```
void BuildTable()
{
    mainTable.BackColor = Color.DarkGray;
    mainTable.ForeColor = Color.White;
    mainTable.Font.Name = "Arial";
    mainTable.Font.Size = 12;
    mainTable.Font.Bold = true;
    mainTable.GridLines = GridLines.None;
    mainTable.HorizontalAlign = HorizontalAlign.Center;
}
```

This just sets up some default properties for the main table that holds all the controls.

Next, we build up the `DropDownMenu` that lists the available item types in `BuildTypeList()`:

```
void BuildTypeList()
{
   typeList.BackColor = Color.White;
   typeList.Items.Add(new ListItem("Item", "Item"));
   typeList.Items.Add(new ListItem("Food", "Food"));
   typeList.Items.Add(new ListItem("Weapon", "Weapon"));
   typeList.Items.Add(new ListItem("Armour", "Armour"));
   typeList.Items.Add(new ListItem("Potion", "Potion"));
   typeList.Items.Add(new ListItem("Ring", "Ring"));
   typeList.Items.Add(new ListItem("Wand", "Wand"));

   typeList.AutoPostBack = true;
   typeList.SelectedIndexChanged +=
      new EventHandler(typeList_SelectedIndexChanged);
}
```

After adding the `ListItem`s, we set `AutoPostPack` to `true`. This means that when the user selects an item in the list, the server automatically posts back the result of the event. It is a common error in ASP programming to forget to set this property – failure to do so results in the control mysteriously not doing anything when it is clicked.

Finally, we add the event handler for selecting one of the items in `typeList`. This handler populates the `DataList` with items of the chosen type, as we will see below.

The last bit of initialization adds event handlers to the three buttons:

```
void SetupButtons()
{
   newButton.Click +=new EventHandler(newButton_Click);
   addButton.Click +=new EventHandler(addButton_Click);
   updateButton.Click +=new EventHandler(updateButton_Click);
   addButton.Enabled = false;
   updateButton.Enabled = false;
}
```

We also disable the 'Add item' and 'Update' buttons since these are not usable when the page is just loaded.

With the initialization done, the form will be displayed on the web page and will await user interaction, so the next code we shall examine contains the event handlers for the controls. There are five controls that have customized event handlers provided in the C# class: the drop-down menu `typeList` which contains the list of item types, the `DataList` `itemList` which displays the items of whatever type was chosen in `typeList`, and the three buttons. We will examine the handlers in the order they must be invoked by the user.

First, an item type must be chosen, so the event handler for `typeList` is called:

```
protected void typeList_SelectedIndexChanged(
  object sender, EventArgs e)
{
  FillDataSet();
  itemList.SelectedIndex = -1;
  itemList.DataSource = dataSet.Tables["Item"];
  itemList.DataBind();
  SetStatsControls(typeList.SelectedValue, null);
  oleConn.Close();
  addButton.Enabled = false;
  updateButton.Enabled = false;
}
```

This method calls `FillDataSet()` to load the data from the database, then binds the `DataSet` to `itemList` (the `DataList` control), and then calls `SetStatsControls()` which updates the text boxes and labels so that only those that correspond to valid data fields for the selected type are enabled. The last two lines disable the 'Add item' and 'Update' buttons since these cannot be used until other selections are made.

`FillDataSet()` uses standard techniques for loading items of the selected type from the data base:

```
protected void FillDataSet()
{
  OpenDatabase();
  string sql = "SELECT * FROM Item WHERE Type='" +
    typeList.SelectedValue + "'";
  command = new OleDbDataAdapter(sql, oleConn);
  command.Fill(dataSet, "Item");
}
```

`OpenDatabase()` is called to open the database and create the `DataSet`:

```
protected void OpenDatabase()
{
  string source = "Provider=Microsoft.Jet.OLEDB.4.0;" +
    @"Data Source=C:\Books\MyBooks\CSharpBook\Programs\Chap13
    \Adventure\Adventure.mdb";
  oleConn = new OleDbConnection(source);
  dataSet = new DataSet();
  try
  {
    oleConn.Open();
```

```
  }
  catch (Exception ex)
  {
    oleConn.Close();
  }
}
```

Back in `FillDataSet()`, an SQL statement is constructed to select only those items whose Type match that selected in `typeList` and the data set is filled with the results of the query.

Back in the `typeList` event handler, after the data has been loaded and the `itemList` bound to the `DataSet`, we call `SetStatsControls()` to enable or disable each of the text boxes and labels according to the type of item that was chosen. In order to do this without writing out an enormous number of individual statements for each text box and each label for each possible type of item, we define an auxiliary class called `EditBox`, which stores the lists of properties that each type of item can have. This class is added to the bottom of the `ItemEditor.aspx.cs` file and looks like this:

```
public class EditBox
{
  bool[] textBoxEnabled;

  public EditBox(string type)
  {
    if (type.Equals("Item"))
    {
      textBoxEnabled =
        new bool[]
          {
              true, false, true, false, false, false,
              false, false, false, false };
    }
    else if (type.Equals("Food"))
    {
      textBoxEnabled =
        new bool[]
          {
              true, false, true, true, false, false,
              false, false, false, false };
    }
    else if (type.Equals("Weapon"))
    {
      textBoxEnabled =
        new bool[]
          {
              true, false, true, false, false, true,
```

```
                    true, false, false, false };
      }
      else if (type.Equals("Armour"))
      {
        textBoxEnabled =
          new bool[]
            {
              true, false, true, false, true, false,
              false, false, false, false };
      }
      else if (type.Equals("Potion"))
      {
        textBoxEnabled =
          new bool[]
            {
              true, false, true, true, true, true,
              true, true, true, true };
      }
      else if (type.Equals("Ring"))
      {
        textBoxEnabled =
          new bool[]
            {
              true, false, true, true, true, true,
              true, false, true, true };
      }
      else if (type.Equals("Wand"))
      {
        textBoxEnabled =
          new bool[]
            {
              true, false, true, true, false, true,
              true, true, true, false };
      }
    }

    public bool this [int index]
    {
      get
      { return textBoxEnabled[index]; }
    }
  }
```

The class contains a single data field called `textBoxEnabled`, which is a
`bool` array. The elements in this array are to be matched with the corresponding elements in `textArray` and `labelArray` that were declared back
in `ItemEditor`. The value in an element of `textBoxEnabled` states whether

or not the corresponding text box in `textArray` is enabled, and therefore how it should be displayed. An indexer has been added at the bottom of the class to make it easier to access the `textBoxEnabled` elements.

This class is used in `SetStatsControls()` as follows:

```
protected void SetStatsControls(string type, DataRow itemRow)
{
   EditBox editBox = new EditBox(type);
   for (int i = 0; i < textArray.Length; i++)
   {
      if (editBox[i])
      {
         textArray[i].Enabled = true;
         textArray[i].BackColor = Color.White;
         textArray[i].Text =
            itemRow == null ? "" : itemRow[i].ToString();
         labelArray[i].ForeColor = Color.Yellow;
      }
      else
      {
         textArray[i].Enabled = false;
         textArray[i].BackColor = Color.DarkGray;
         textArray[i].Text = "";
         labelArray[i].ForeColor = Color.LightGray;
      }
   }
}
```

We create an `EditBox` that is tailored to the item type that has been chosen and then loop through the elements in `textArray` and `labelArray`, setting each one according to the value of the corresponding `editBox` element. Enabled text boxes have a white background and a yellow label, while disabled text boxes have a dark grey background and light grey label. This lets the user know which text boxes will accept data for a given item type.

`SetStatsControls()` has a second parameter which is a `DataRow` from the `DataSet`. However, this is only used when filling the text boxes with data for an item that has been selected from the `DataList`, so when `SetStatsControls()` is called from `typeList`'s event handler, a `null` is passed in for the `DataRow`. This results in all the text boxes having their text cleared.

After selecting an item type, the display will show a list of items in the `DataList` (`itemList`) and the text boxes and labels will be correctly enabled. At this point, the user has a choice of selecting an item from `itemList` or pressing the 'New' button to create a new item. We'll consider the case of selecting an existing item first.

Clicking one of the `LinkButtons` in `itemList` calls the event handler for `itemList`, which is:

```
protected void itemList_SelectedIndexChanged(
  object sender, EventArgs e)
{
  FillDataSet();
  itemList.DataSource = dataSet.Tables["Item"];
  itemList.DataBind();
  DataRow itemRow =
    dataSet.Tables["Item"].Rows[itemList.SelectedIndex];
  SetStatsControls(typeList.SelectedValue, itemRow);
  textArray[0].Enabled = false;
  addButton.Enabled = false;
  updateButton.Enabled = true;
  validationSummary.Enabled = false;
}
```

`FillDataSet()` is called again to refresh the data in `dataSet`. We then retrieve the `DataRow` from `dataSet` that corresponds to the `SelectedIndex` in `itemList`. This works since the items in `itemList` are listed in the same order as they were retrieved from `dataSet`, so the index of an item in `itemList` will match the location of that item in `dataSet`.

The `DataRow` that is retrieved contains all the information about the selected item, so it is passed to `SetStatsControls()` to display the information in the correct text boxes. We then disable the Description text box (`textArray[0]`) since the user is not allowed to change the Description of an item, due to its being the primary key in the database.

The 'Add item' button is disabled, since it is not possible to add a second item with the same name as an existing item. The 'Update' button is enabled since the user is allowed to change the data in any non-Description text box and then update the database.

The last line disables `validationSummary` which turns off any error messages produced by a previous validation failure – more on this later.

This completes the event handlers for `typeList` and `itemList`. The remaining event handlers manage the three buttons.

If the user presses the 'New' button, the form should be prepared to accept data that describes a new item of the type currently showing in `typeList` (the drop-down menu). This means that the various text boxes should be enabled or disabled as appropriate, and all text should be cleared from them. This is exactly what happens in the event handler for `typeList`, so we can just call that when the 'New' button is pressed as well. The event handler for the 'New' button is therefore very simple:

```
protected void newButton_Click(object sender, EventArgs e)
{
  typeList_SelectedIndexChanged(null, null);
  addButton.Enabled = true;
}
```

The only other action is the enabling of the 'Add item' button, since after the user has entered the data, they must be able to add it to the database.

The handler for 'Add item' is a bit more complex. In fact, the version presented here contains only a single error check, so there is some room for improvement. Let us consider what must happen when an attempt is made to add an item to the database.

First, we need to ensure that the user has entered a Description field for the new item, since Description is the primary key in the database and must be present. We can use the validation control we inserted in the ASP code to do this, as we will see.

Several other checks could also be made here, although we have not implemented them. For example, we should check that the description entered by the user does not duplicate any existing description in the database, since duplicate primary keys are not allowed. We may also wish to check that data has been entered in the other text boxes, as appropriate for the item type, and that the data in these boxes makes sense. For example, we might wish to check that the weight is a positive number and so on.

Adding these checks is not difficult, but it is tedious and would greatly expand the code, so we leave them as exercises for the reader.

Assuming we get past all the checks, we then need to construct an SQL statement from the data in the text boxes and add the result to the database. The code for the addButton event handler is as follows:

```
1. protected void addButton_Click(object sender, EventArgs e)
2. {
3.    EnableValidation(true);
4.    Validate();
5.    if (!IsValid)
6.    {
7.      validationSummary.Enabled = true;
8.      typeList_SelectedIndexChanged(null, null);
9.      addButton.Enabled = true;
10.      return;
11.    }
12.    EnableValidation(false);
13.    EditBox editBox = new EditBox(typeList.SelectedValue);
14.    typeText.Text = typeList.SelectedValue;
15.    string sql = "INSERT INTO Item VALUES(";
16.    for (int i = 0; i < numTextBoxes; i++)
17.    {
18.      if (i == 1 || editBox[i])
19.      {
20.        if (quoteDBField[i])
21.          sql += textArray[i].Text.Length > 0 ?
22.            "'" + EscapeQuotes(textArray[i].Text) + "'" :
23.            "NULL";
```

```
24.        else
25.          sql += textArray[i].Text.Length > 0 ?
26.            textArray[i].Text : "0";
27.      }
28.      else
29.      {
30.        if (quoteDBField[i])
31.          sql += "NULL";
32.        else
33.          sql += "0";
34.      }
35.      if (i < numTextBoxes - 1)
36.        sql += ",";
37.    }
38.    sql += ")";
39.    try
40.    {
41.      OpenDatabase();
42.      OleDbCommand insert = new OleDbCommand(sql, oleConn);
43.      insert.ExecuteNonQuery();
44.      oleConn.Close();
45.    }
46.    catch (Exception ex)
47.    {
48.      headerLabel.Text = ex.ToString() + ": " + sql;
49.    }
50.    typeList_SelectedIndexChanged(null, null);
51. }
```

Since the only validation we have in the program is the check on the Description text box, we only enable validation when addButton is pressed. Leaving validation enabled at all times can cause irritating behaviour by constantly demanding that the user input something in the Description box and locking other controls until this is done. We therefore only enable validation after addButton has been pressed. A little method called Enable Validation() has been written for this purpose:

```
void EnableValidation(bool enable)
{
  foreach (WebControl validator in Validators)
  {
    validator.Enabled = enable;
  }
}
```

This method will work for any number of validators in the class, even though we only have one in this particular case.

After enabling validation, we call `Validate()` (line 4) to perform the validation check. The result of this check sets or clears the `IsValid` property of the main form, so we can check this on line 5 to decide what to do. If the validation check is failed, we turn on `validationSummary` which prints an error message below the form (since that is where it was placed back in the ASP file – see line 114 on page 628). We then refresh the display by calling `typeList`'s handler again and return from the method.

If validation is successful, we switch it off (line 12) and then proceed to add the new entry to the database. This is done using standard methods. We use an `EditBox` object (line 13) to determine which text boxes are enabled, and therefore which ones we should try to retrieve data from.

The SQL statement is built up by looping through the text boxes using `editBox[i]` as a guide to see if we should read a value or just enter a NULL or 0 instead. Note that `quoteDBField` is used to determine which fields are strings and therefore require quotes around them.

Finally, since a text field containing an apostrophe cannot be placed in an SQL string without doubling the apostrophe, we have a little routine called `EscapeQuotes()` which filters each text string and doubles any apostrophes that it finds:

```
protected static string EscapeQuotes(string text)
{
   string escaped = "";
   char[] textChars = text.ToCharArray();
   for (int i = 0; i < textChars.Length; i++)
   {
     if (textChars[i] == '\'')
       escaped += "'";
     escaped += textChars[i];
   }
   return escaped;
}
```

This is an immensely useful method to have in any program that requires building SQL statements from user input.

The only remaining event handler is for the 'Update' button. Its functionality is very similar to 'Add item' except that we need not validate the Description box (since only existing items can be updated, and these must have a Description since they are already in the database). Its code is:

```
protected void updateButton_Click(object sender, EventArgs e)
{
   EditBox editBox = new EditBox(typeList.SelectedValue);
   OpenDatabase();
   FillDataSet();
   string sql = "UPDATE Item SET ";
   for (int i = 2; i < numTextBoxes; i++)
```

```
    {
      if (editBox[i])
      {
        if (i > 2)
          sql += ",";
        sql +=
          dataSet.Tables["Item"].Columns[i].ColumnName + " = ";
        if (quoteDBField[i])
          sql += "'" + EscapeQuotes(textArray[i].Text) + "'";
        else
          sql += textArray[i].Text;
      }
    }
    sql += " WHERE Description = '" +
      EscapeQuotes(textArray[0].Text) + "'";
    try
    {
      OleDbCommand insert = new OleDbCommand(sql, oleConn);
      insert.ExecuteNonQuery();
      oleConn.Close();
      typeList_SelectedIndexChanged(null, null);
    }
    catch (Exception ex)
    {
      headerLabel.Text = ex.ToString() + "," + sql;
    }
    finally
    {
      oleConn.close();
    }
}
```

As with `addButton`'s handler, we use an `EditBox` to determine which text boxes to read data from. To update an existing item in the database however, we need the exact column name as used in the database in order to set each data field's value in the SQL statement. We therefore refresh the `DataSet` with a copy of the database and then set about building the UPDATE statement in SQL.

The code for doing this is similar to that for `addButton` so we won't go into details. After building the command, `ExecuteNonQuery()` is called to send it to the database and `typeList`'s handler is called again to refresh the display.

The code in the `catch` block changes the page's title to display the exception error message and the SQL statement if anything goes wrong, since in the development stages the problem is most often due to faulty SQL syntax.

13.9 ■ Web services

A *web service* provides methods on a remote web site which can be called by local programs. .NET and Java both provide comprehensive support for web services.

It is important to understand at the outset that a web service is *not* just a software package which is downloaded once and then integrated into a new program on the local machine. Rather, the methods that are called by the local program remain on the remote site and are called dynamically each time the program is run.

This configuration has several important ramifications. First, of course, a program that uses methods provided by a web service must be connected to the web when it is run.

From the client's point of view, probably a more worrying possibility is that the service may not remain available forever, or that the provider may change the service in some way that affects its use in the client program. The provider of a web service should feel a heavy sense of responsibility to continue to provide the service and not change it without due notification being made. Having said that, however, the web service setup does allow the provider to fix bugs and propagate these fixes to all clients without any explicit notification, since all bug fixes will automatically appear in any client program the next time the service is called.

Your first reaction to the idea of a web service might be 'what's the point'? If the main point of a web service is to provide software for programmers to use in their code, it would seem safer and easier to provide this software as a library which could be downloaded and then used locally, without subsequent recourse to the Internet. Requiring a remote call to a method every time that method is needed seems rather slow and clumsy by comparison.

This argument is valid if our main use of a web service is to access code that just does some simple calculation, which could be done more quickly on the local machine. The main power of a web service, however, lies in allowing access to a remote network in a secure way. For example, a company may provide information in its databases to clients by means of a web service. Since the data in such databases is often sensitive, the owner of the databases needs to control the access so that clients cannot read or write areas of the database for which they should not have security clearance. A web service shields the database by providing methods with all the appropriate security checks built in. In this sense, a web service acts much like an interface method in a class, in that it provides regulated access to private data.

As you might imagine, the technology that drives the ability to make a method call over a network, possibly between methods written in different languages and (ultimately) running on different operating systems is quite sophisticated. The idea of making remote method calls is not new, however. For many years, Windows programs used COM (Component Object Model) and DCOM (Distributed COM) to achieve the same ends. Anyone who has attempted to learn COM, however, will appreciate that it was far from easy.

Fortunately, programming web services in .NET is a much more approachable proposition.

The reason for the new ease of use is that .NET uses a different communication method to set up and consume web services. The new technology is called SOAP (Simple Object Access Protocol), and is an XML-based communication language that allows clients and servers to exchange method calls in a transparent way.

Understanding SOAP itself, however, *can* be challenging, but the enormous improvement from our point of view as C# programmers is that, unlike COM, we do not need to understand how SOAP works to be able to use it. For that reason, we will not delve any further into it here. Interested readers can find many books and web sites that give more details about SOAP and the associated WSDL (Web Service Definition Language). A good place to start is the W3C web site (www.w3c.org).

As C# programmers, there are two aspects of web services we need to understand: writing and *exposing* web services for other programmers to use, and using or *consuming* web services provided by others. Both of these are very simple to implement in C#.

13.9.1 ☐ Writing a web service in C#

If you have access to Visual Studio .NET, you can use its New Project dialog to create a web services project. To do this, select the File menu, choose New and then Project to open the dialog. Select Visual C# Projects in the Project Types list and then ASP .NET Web Service in the Templates list.

As usual, however, since we want to make this book accessible to those readers who do not have Visual Studio .NET, we will write our code without using it, which is actually very simple to do.

Since pretty well any C# method can be provided as a web service, we will restrict ourselves to writing only a simple service here so you can get the idea of how it is done. Once you understand the technique, it is straightforward to apply the other programming techniques described elsewhere in this book to provide more complex services.

To create a web service, all that is required is a single file with an .asmx extension. Here is a simple file called HelloWorld.asmx:

```
<%@ WebService Language="c#" Class="HelloWebService" %>
using System.Web.Services;

[WebService(Namespace="http://GroweCSBook.ac.uk")]
public class HelloWebService : System.Web.Services.WebService
{
    public HelloWebService()
    {}

    [WebMethod]
```

```
public string HelloWeb()
{
   return "Welcome to growe's web service!";
}

[WebMethod]
public int Square(int x)
{
   return x*x;
}
}
```

The first line is an ASP-style directive, stating that the file contains a web service in a class called `HelloWebService` written in C#. The remainder of the file is written in ordinary C#.

The next line includes the `System.Web.Services` namespace which is needed for writing web services.

The class itself is preceded by an attribute in square brackets labelling it as a `WebService`. The `Namespace` in parentheses within this attribute is optional, but is recommended since it helps give the class a unique identity. If you create a web service class in Visual Studio, the class is given a default namespace of http://tempuri.org/, which is not particularly informative, so it is a good idea to change it.

The namespace is usually given as a URL or URI, but this doesn't mean that the URL has be a 'real' URL in the sense of being an actual web address (the URL given in this example is not real). The namespace is not used by the web service to look up anything – it is merely a label to keep the service distinct from other services on the web that could have the same names for their classes or methods.

The class itself inherits `System.Web.Services.WebService`, which provides all the background methods needed to convert this class into a web service.

The remainder of the class is standard C#, except that those methods that are to be exposed as web services (that is, made available to other users on the web) must be prefixed by the `[WebMethod]` attribute. It is therefore possible to write other methods within the class that are needed for calculations but should not be exposed – just omit the `[WebMethod]` attribute from these methods.

The two methods given here are very simple, but illustrate a method (`HelloWeb()`) that takes no parameters and simply returns a `string`, and another (`Square()`) that takes a parameter `x` and returns an `int` which is the square of the parameter.

In order to make this class available as a web service on your machine's web server, all that is required is that this file is placed within a folder that is accessible to the web server. If you are running a standard installation of IIS, for example, the file can be placed anywhere in the `C:\Inetpub\wwwroot` directory. That is really all there is to providing a web service.

To test the code that we have just written, we could write a client as described in the next section, but usually the code can be tested by using an ordinary web browser such as Internet Explorer. To do this, load up the URL of the .asmx file that contains the C# class shown above. For example, if the file HelloWorld.asmx was stored on the server at http://www.fakeurl.com/WebServices/HelloWorld.asmx (a fictitious address, but just substitute your own server's address for 'www.fakeurl.com' and store the file in the folder C:\Inetpub\wwwroot\WebServices if IIS is installed normally), just enter this link in the web browser.

The browser should display a page that looks something like Figure 13.6.

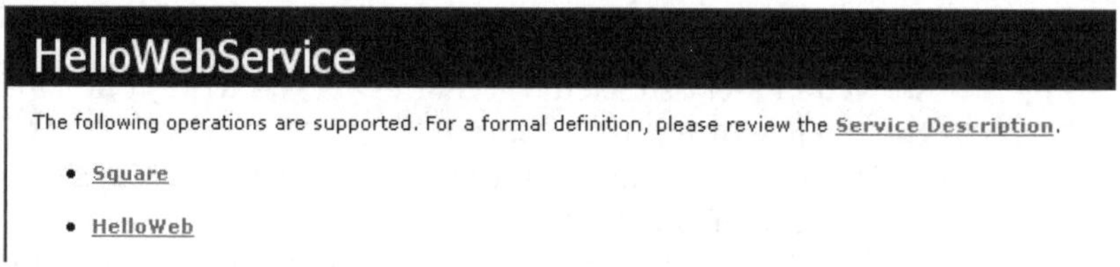

Figure 13.6 Web page showing web services available

A link is provided on this page for each method that has been exposed. Clicking on the link displays a new page that allows us to test the method by entering values for the parameters (if any) and then clicking an Invoke button to try out the method. The result of the test is a page that displays the value returned by the method, although it will be encased in XML. For example, testing the Square method by entering the value 12 for the parameter x produces the XML page:

```
<?xml version="1.0" encoding="utf-8" ?>
<int xmlns="http://GroweCSBook.ac.uk">144</int>
```

It is also possible to return instances of classes from web services. For example, we could add a simple method that takes two ints and returns a Point (from the System.Drawing package) to the HelloWebService class above:

```
[WebMethod]
public Point MakePoint(int x, int y)
{
   return new Point(x,y);
}
```

Running a test on this method produces the XML:

```
<?xml version="1.0" encoding="utf-8" ?>
<Point xmlns:xsd="http://www.w3.org/2001/XMLSchema"
xmlns:xsi=http://www.w3.org/2001/XMLSchema-instance
xmlns="http://GroweCSBook.ac.uk">
<X>12</X>
<Y>45</Y>
</Point>
```

The `Point` data structure has been converted to XML, with each of its data fields given as an XML element.

Fortunately, we do not need to concern ourselves with the details of the XML since it serves merely as a vehicle for transmitting the information back to a consumer of the web service. .NET provides all the machinery needed to convert this information back into a form that may be used within a C# program.

13.9.2 ☐ Consuming a web service

Writing a C# program that uses or consumes an existing web service is slightly more complicated than writing the original service, but not much. The key step is in locating the service we want to use and linking it with the program. The procedure for doing this varies depending on whether we are using Visual Studio or not.

A program that uses a web service need not be created in any special location. In fact, the machine on which it runs need not even have a web server running, although a connection to the Internet is, of course, required.

In the example we are about to give, we will connect to the web service that we wrote in the last section, but in general, we will need to know the URL of a service that we wish to use. There are several ways of discovering where services have been published. A good starting point is Microsoft's search engine for web services, available at http://uddi.microsoft.com/visualstudio/. In our case, we will just use the HelloWorld.asmx file we built earlier, and assume that it is available at the URL http://www.fakeurl.com/WebServices/HelloWorld.asmx as before.

Having found the web service, the next step is to connect it with the C# program we are writing. This requires a bit of work (most of which is done for us by .NET) since we must remember that the web service we are accessing may not have been written in C#. Any .NET-compliant language such as Visual Basic .NET or a non-.NET language such as Java could have been used to create the service, so it is not simply a matter of downloading the source code and adding it to our project.

It is this stage that depends most heavily on whether we are using Visual Studio to write our C# project. If we are, then in order to access the web service, we need to add a web reference for the service. To do this, open Solution Explorer (use the View menu if it's not immediately visible) and open the node for the current project. Find the References icon and right-click on it, then select Add Web Reference. This brings up the Add Web Reference dialog which contains features for searching for web services on the local machine or further afield on the web.

Assuming that we already know the address of the service we require, just type this in the URL text field near the top of the dialog and then press the Add Reference button on the right. Back in Solution Explorer, a new Web References icon should appear, within which will be the reference we just added. The name of this reference is important since we will need to use it in the code as part of the namespace for the web service methods we are invoking. (If you don't like the name given to the reference by Visual Studio, you can rename it by right-clicking on the icon and selecting Rename.) This completes the procedure for adding a web reference in Visual Studio, and we can proceed to write the C# code that uses any of the methods that are provided as services at that URL.

The process of adding a web reference actually creates a C# class that links your client program to the methods provided by the web service. To see this, look in Windows Explorer and find the directory in which your project is stored. You should find a folder called Web References within this directory, and within the Web References folder is another folder for the namespace name of the reference you just added. Within that folder are several files, one of which is called `Reference.cs`. If you have a look in this file in Visual Studio or Notepad, you will see that it contains a C# class with some rather cryptic links to the methods provided by the web service.

There is no need to understand this code in detail since we never need to edit it, but one key point that is worth noting is that the URL of the `.asmx` file containing the code for the service is used in the constructor of the C# class in `Reference.cs`. This provides the link between your program and the services you are using, and will cause your program to call the remote method(s) from the service each time it is run.

If we are *not* using Visual Studio, we still need to create a C# class that contains essentially the same code as that in `Reference.cs` that is produced by adding a web reference in Visual Studio. This can be done by using a stand-alone program called `wsdl.exe` that comes as part of the .NET SDK. This is a command-line program so you will need to open a console window to run it. (If the command is not recognized at the command prompt, use the Windows Search facility from within Windows Explorer to find it – it should be located in the Visual Studio directory if you have Visual Studio installed, or in the .NET SDK directory if you don't.)

To use `wsdl.exe`, change directory to the main folder of the project you are working on (the folder that contains the source code for the project). Then run `wsdl.exe` giving as a command-line argument the URL of the web service you wish to use, such as:

```
wsdl http://www.fakeurl.com/WebServices/HelloWorld.asmx
```

Running `wsdl.exe` produces a file containing a C# class that is almost identical to that provided by Visual Studio, except that it is not part of a namespace. Also, the file's name will be derived from the name of the class in the web service, so in our case the file is called `HelloWebService.cs`.

The last step is to compile this file into a library (DLL), which can be done using the command-line C# compiler as follows:

```
csc /t:library HelloWebService.cs
```

Then, after you've written the client application (which we will call `WebConsume.cs` in what follows), compile the whole lot together to produce an executable file:

```
csc /t:winexe /r:HelloWebService.dll WebConsume.cs
```

Assuming you don't change `WebConsume.cs` you do not need to recompile the client file even if the code in the web services changes (although you will need to recompile the client if more methods are added to the web services that you want to use, as can happen during development).

With that out of the way, all that remains is to write the client program that is to use the web services. This is just standard C#, so no more surprises await us. Here is a simple C# application that tests the two methods provided in `HelloWebService`:

```
using System;
// Required only in Visual Studio
using WebConsumeTest01.GroweNamespace;

public class WebConsume
{
  public static void Main(string[] args)
  {
    HelloWebService service = new HelloWebService();
    Console.WriteLine(service.HelloWeb());
    Console.WriteLine("Enter an integer: ");
    int number = int.Parse(Console.ReadLine());
    Console.WriteLine("The square of " + number + " is " +
      service.Square(number));
  }
}
```

The second `using` statement in this program is required only when the web reference is added to the project using Visual Studio's Add Web Reference feature. The namespace to use in this statement can be found most easily by looking in the `Reference.cs` file mentioned above – it is the namespace defined in the first line of code in this file. If you used `wsdl.exe` to create the C# class, omit this line.

The remainder of the program just creates an ordinary C# class. We can create an instance of `HelloWebService` in the usual way, even though it is only defined on the remote server. We then call `HelloWeb()` which is one of the two methods included in the service, and print out the welcome message. We then request an integer from the user and call `Square()` to calculate its square. The output from the program is:

```
Welcome to growe's web service!
Enter an integer:
12
The square of 12 is 144
```

The `.exe` file produced after compiling the client can be distributed on its own to anyone else (provided they have .NET installed on their machine). If the code in the web service methods is changed, running the program again will call the new version of the service methods, since the compilation of the service source code is done on the server, not the client, in much the same way as an ASP .NET request is processed on the server instead of the client.

Although the example we have presented here is very simple in terms of its functionality, it should be clear that web services can be used with any level of complexity in a C# program. It would be fairly straightforward, for example, to convert the ASP examples earlier in this chapter so that the database access is done using web services instead of directly.

13.10 ■ Accessing the Internet

Although we've seen some impressive methods for using the Internet together with .NET and C#, sometimes it is convenient to be able to just download a file from the web and save it to disk or use it for various purposes within the program.

.NET provides several classes that make accessing the Internet quite simple. We'll examine a few of them in this section.

13.10.1 □ Downloading files

Perhaps the simplest thing we can do in .NET is to download a file over the web. To see just how simple this can be, here is the entire program that allows a web page's HTML source to be downloaded and saved to disk on the local machine:

```
using System.Net;

public class DownloadFile
{
  public static void Main(string[] args)
  {
    WebClient client = new WebClient();
    client.DownloadFile("http://www.computing.dundee.ac.uk/",
      "dundee.html");
  }
}
```

The `WebClient` class provides several methods for accessing data over the net. The simplest is `DownloadFile()` which takes two parameters. The first is the URI of the file to be downloaded and the second is the name of the file on the local machine to which the downloaded data should be stored. Here we access the home page of the Department of Applied Computing at the University of Dundee in Scotland (where I happen to work).

It is probably more likely that we would want to save the HTML source of a web page for further processing within the program, however. `WebClient` provides an `OpenRead()` method which allows an input stream to be opened on the file being downloaded, allowing us to save the data in an object within the program rather than directly writing it to disk.

It is easiest to see how this works by presenting another example. The following program downloads a web page's source code and attempts to find all links to images embedded within the page. It then tries to download all the images and store them locally into files with the same name as they had on the original web site.

Before we delve into the code, it is worth pointing out that writing programs such as this which attempt to extract information from the HTML source code of a web page are always fraught with peril. There are a great many ways that web page code can be written, and the resulting HTML source code for any reasonably involved page is usually very messy. Attempting to extract information from such pages is difficult because we must search for obscure combinations of symbols in an attempt to isolate the information we want, and the result is rarely perfect. This should serve as a warning that programs that do attempt to extract bits of information from web pages should not be relied on too heavily.

For readers not familiar with HTML, the most common syntax for embedding an image in a web page looks something like this:

```
<img src="link to image file">
```

HTML has a special `img` tag which signals that an image is to be loaded, and the source file for the image is given as the value of the `src` attribute. The `img` tag can take many other attributes as well, which can define such things as the width and height of the image, the message that should appear as a tooltip when the mouse hovers over the image and so on.

The `src` attribute can take several forms as well. If the image file is stored in the same directory as the web page which refers to it, the file may be given simply as a bare file name, such as `src="picture.jpg"`. Sometimes a web site stores its images in a special subdirectory contained in the main directory where the web page itself is found. In this case, the `src` tag can specify the image file using a relative path name, such as `src="images/picture.jpg"`. Finally, the image could be on a completely different web server, so that a full URI might be used, as in `src=http://www.somewhere.com/ images/picture.jpg`.

Since we want to extract the actual file name from the URI in order to determine the file name we should use to store the image locally after it has been downloaded, we need to do a bit of string parsing. The regular expression library mentioned in Chapter 3 is very useful in this regard.

The following program is an initial attempt at an image extractor. It is far from perfect but does manage to extract images from a number of web pages and more to the point, illustrates several useful techniques for accessing information from web pages.

```
1. using System;
2. using System.Net;
3. using System.IO;
4. using System.Text.RegularExpressions;
5.
6. public class ExtractImages
7. {
8.   public static void Main(string[] args)
9.   {
10.     Console.WriteLine("Enter URI: ");
11.     string uri = Console.ReadLine();
12.     if (!uri.StartsWith("http"))
13.     {
14.       uri = "http://" + uri;
15.     }
16.     WebClient client = new WebClient();
17.     Stream clientStream = client.OpenRead(uri);
18.     StreamReader clientRead = new StreamReader
          (clientStream);
19.     string line, clientText = "";
20.     while ((line = clientRead.ReadLine()) != null)
21.     {
22.       clientText += line;
23.     }
24.     string uriPattern = "src=\"[^\"]*[jpg|gif]\"";
25.     MatchCollection images = Regex.Matches(clientText,
26.       uriPattern, RegexOptions.IgnoreCase);
27.     Console.WriteLine("Images found: " + images.Count);
28.     foreach (Match image in images)
29.     {
30.       string imageUri = image.ToString();
31.
32.       imageUri = imageUri.Substring(5, imageUri.Length - 6);
33.       Uri uriObj;
34.       if (!imageUri.StartsWith("http"))
35.       {
36.         imageUri = uri.Substring(0, uri.LastIndexOf('/')
            + 1) +
37.           imageUri;
38.       }
39.       uriObj = new Uri(imageUri);
40.       string fileName = uriObj.LocalPath;
41.       int lastSeparator = fileName.LastIndexOf('/');
42.       if (lastSeparator >= 0)
43.         fileName = fileName.Substring(lastSeparator + 1);
44.       try
```

```
45.          {
46.              client.DownloadFile(imageUri, fileName);
47.              Console.WriteLine("Downloaded " + fileName);
48.          }
49.          catch
50.          {
51.              Console.WriteLine("Couldn't access: " + imageUri);
52.          }
53.      }
54.  }
55. }
```

The `System.Net` namespace (line 2) is required for using `WebClient` and `System.IO` for using streams.

The program is console-based, since it just prints out information on the files that have been downloaded. It begins by asking the user to enter the URI of the web page to be scanned for images (line 10). In order to avoid the necessity of typing in the leading 'http://', we test the input string to see if it begins with 'http' (line 12) and, if not, prepend this string to the URI that was entered.

A `WebClient` is created (line 16) and then a stream is opened on the web page using `OpenRead()` (line 17). A `StreamReader` is created from the stream, since this makes reading files easier. Line 19 prepares a couple of `string`s that are used in downloading and storing the HTML. The loop on line 20 reads the HTML from the web page and appends it to `clientText` until all the file has been read.

The search for images begins on line 24, where we define the search pattern using a regular expression (admittedly hideous). The search pattern looks for a string that begins with `src="`, then contains any number of characters that does *not* include the quote character `"` and finally ends either with `jpg"` or `gif"`. This should find most JPEG or GIF files that are embedded within a page.

Line 25 then builds the `MatchCollection` by searching `clientText` (the downloaded HTML source). The third parameter in the call to `Regex.Matches()` ignores the case, since HTML is not case-sensitive. Line 27 then prints the number of images found.

Now that we have a list of image files, we need to isolate the file name for each one and attempt to download it. The loop on line 28 tries to do this. First, we extract the `string` from each `Match` object (line 30) and then strip off the leading `src="` and trailing `"` characters using the `Substring()` method from the `String` class (line 32).

Line 33 introduces the `Uri` class which is somewhat bizarrely contained in the `System` namespace (not `System.Net`). `Uri` allows us to break up a full URI into its component parts, so we can extract the host name, the local path of the file, and other components commonly found in URIs. `Uri` is a read-only class, however, so it cannot be used for building a URI, only for analyzing an existing one. (There is another class called `UriBuilder` which will construct URIs from their components.)

The limited analysis we do on the image's URI will catch some, but not all, image files found on web pages. We first check to see if the image's URI is absolute (that is, whether it begins with `http://`) on line 34. If not, the URI should be relative to the URI that was entered by the user back on line 11. For example, if the URI isolated from the `src` attribute is `images/picture.jpg`, then it is reasonable to assume that the full URI is `http://www.somewhere.com/images/picture.jpg`, assuming that the user entered `http://www.somewhere.com/` on line 11.

After patching up the URI of the image, we create a `Uri` object (line 39) so that we can try to isolate the file name. The `LocalPath` (line 40) isolates that part of the URI that contains the path to the file that is being loaded. For the full URI given in the last paragraph, `LocalPath` would be `images/picture.jpg`, for example.

All we really want, however, is the file name at the end of the local path, and unfortunately `Uri` does not have a property that gives us this, so we need to do a bit more string manipulation. We can use `LastIndexOf()` from the `String` class to find the last occurrence of the separator character `/`. If this does not occur at all, then this method returns -1, which indicates that the `LocalPath` consists of a bare file name and may be used as is. If a separator is present, we extract the bare file name as the substring that follows this last separator (line 43).

When we finally have the file name, we can call `DownloadFile()` to retrieve the image file and store it locally using the correct name (line 46), and then write a message to the console (line 47).

If the image could not be found, some type of exception will usually be thrown so we can catch these and display a message to the user.

Running this program on several sites produces varying results, since the analysis of the image file name does not consider all possibilities and can fail to download some images.

Running the program on the Applied Computing web site used earlier in this section gives the following output:

```
Enter URI:
www.computing.dundee.ac.uk/
Images found: 2
Downloaded logo.jpg
Downloaded newsicon.gif
```

Note that if we give a URI that is just a host name (that is, does not contain the name of the actual file and thus relies on the web server to unearth the home page for that site), we need to add a separator character at the end of the URI. Again, we could add some more code to the program to test for this and add the character if it is missing, but this would complicate things.

In this case, two images are found successfully, and they are both downloaded to the directory containing the `.exe` file for the program. Although this program works with most general web sites, it will not work (not surprisingly) with sites that require authorization, such as sites where a username and password are required for entry.

`WebClient` is suitable for applications that simply need to download the source code from an HTML file for further processing in the program, but lacks the flexibility needed for more involved interaction with the web site. .NET provides another pair of classes called `WebRequest` and `WebResponse` which are slightly more complicated to use but which provide many more features, including the ability to send authentication information along with a request to access a web site. Further information on these classes can be obtained in the MSDN documentation.

■ Summary

This final chapter provides an introduction to the use of C# as a language providing the power behind ASP .NET-based web pages. Although ASP .NET can be used on its own to write web pages, a powerful technique is to use only skeleton ASP .NET files to provide the controls and layout of the page, and to relegate all the code for producing the data displayed on the page and handling user interactions to a C# 'behind' file, which provides a base class for the ASP .NET page.

We examine several techniques that can be used to retrieve, display and edit information from a database by linking the database to ASP .NET controls.

Finally, we briefly describe how .NET can be used to produce and consume web services, and how C# can be used to access the Internet directly, without the use of a web browser.

Exercises

13.1 Write a simple ASP .NET file which specifies a web page containing a label, a text box and a button. The label's initial text should say 'Enter your name:' and the text box should initially be blank. Write a C# behind-code file which handles the event from clicking the button by reading whatever name the user has typed into the text box and setting the label's text to 'Hello' followed by the user's name.

Examine the source of the web page before and after pressing the button to see the HTML that is produced by the server. Note the change in the VIEWSTATE string.

13.2 Examine the MSDN documentation to see what web controls are available for insertion into ASP .NET pages. These controls are all in the `System.Web. UI.WebControls` namespace. A complete list of the available web controls can be found by clicking 'Derived classes' from the `System.Web.UI. WebControls.WebControl` documentation page.

Try out some of the simpler controls, such as CheckBox, RadioButton, DropDownList, ListBox and so on. Compare the web control to its Windows Forms counterpart (which in most cases has the same name). For each control you try, read the documentation to see what events can be generated by it, then try inserting the control in an ASP .NET page and adding handlers for some of the events in the C# behind-code. Since no output to a console is possible for an ASP .NET project, you can print out test messages in event handlers by setting the text of a label on the web page.

For the exercises involving databases, we will refer to the Books database used as an example in Chapter 11, but if you have your own database, the exercises can be done using that as well.

13.3 Using the Books database from Chapter 11, write an ASP .NET/C# program which reads the names of all the authors from the Author table and displays them using an unadorned DataGrid on the web page.

13.4 Refer back to Chapter 11 and construct an SQL statement that will retrieve the list of books in the database and display each book with its first author in a DataGrid.

13.5 Investigate the properties available in a DataGrid for customizing the appearance of rows and columns in the grid and modify the grid used to display the data in Exercises 13.3 and 13.4 to make it more attractive. You should consider changing the font used to display the text, adjusting the column widths so they fit the data, spacing out the cells, and designing a pleasing colour scheme for the rows and/or columns.

13.6 Add a search facility to the page in Exercise 13.5. This could consist of a text box into which the user types a search string and a button which when pressed searches the database for all books whose title contains that string. These books should then be displayed in the DataGrid.

13.7 Enhance the interface to Exercise 13.6 by allowing individual books in the grid to be selected. Add a number of labels and text boxes so that, for each selected book, the details of that book (author, number of pages, etc) can be displayed in the text boxes. Allow the user to edit the data in the text boxes and provide another button that will 'update' the data in the database. Ensure that the text boxes and buttons are enabled and disabled at the correct times.

13.8 In the ItemEditor example in section 13.8, we defined the entire layout of the web page in the .aspx file by using an ASP .NET Table containing Panels. It is also possible to create an ASP .NET Table (or parts of it) within the C# code. For example, the code in ItemEditor.aspx (lines 54 to 111) that defines the right table cell (the one containing the text boxes displaying the parameters for a selected item) can be replaced by C# code that builds the table programmatically. To do this, replace lines 54 to 111 in the .aspx file with the single line:

```
<asp:TableCell runat="server" ID="rightCell"/>
```

Then define a `TableCell` field in the `ItemEditor` class in the C# file and create (using the `new` operator) and add the controls to `rightCell` in the `BuildTable()` method within the C# code. You will need to set the properties of each control (such as `Text`, `Width` and so on) with C# statements, but you do not need to specify 'Runat = "server"' since any code in the C# file is automatically run at the server end.

Make sure that `BuildTable()` is called *before* `textArray` and `labelArray` are defined in the `OnInit()` method, since you are now creating the controls (using `new`) within the C# code rather than relying on the ASP .NET page to do it for you.

Although it is questionable whether creating this particular table cell in C# is preferable to doing it in the ASP .NET file, the ability to create tables dynamically in the C# code can be very useful if the table size changes from one 'page load' event to the next.

13.9 As a simple exercise in providing a web service, write a method that returns a clever quote at random from a repository of such quotes. The quotes can be hard-coded into the method as an array of `strings`, or if you are more ambitious, you might store them in a database.

For example, the repository of quotes might contain strings such as "A penny saved is pointless", "Cleanliness is next to impossible" and "A bird in the hand is a mess". Write a C# class that contains a method called `Quote()` which returns one of the strings at random, and expose this method as a web service. Use the procedures described in the text to ensure that the service is working properly, and then write another C# program that consumes this web service and prints out a random quote whenever it is run.

13.10 Many web browsers such as Internet Explorer provide an 'off-line viewing' feature which allows you to download a web page and store it locally on your computer so you can view it later after disconnecting from the Internet. Write a C# program that requests a URI and then downloads the HTML for that URI and saves it locally as a separate file.

13.11 More advanced off-line viewing features allow you to specify the 'depth' of links you want to store, starting from a particular web page. For example, a depth of 0 means to store only the starting page, a depth of 1 means to store the starting page and all pages to which that page is linked by hyperlinks somewhere on the page. A depth of 2 follows all links found on the pages linked to from the starting page and so on.

Add a depth feature to the program in Exercise 13.9. To do this, you will need to identify hyperlinks embedded in the HTML, most of which are specified by a `<a href="www.link.com" ... /a>` type link. You will need to extract the URI from the `href` attribute and then make a link to that site to download its content, and then repeat the process from that page, and so on, until the full depth has been saved. (Be careful with this program, however, since a depth greater than 1 can lead to an enormous number of links to save!)

Index

abstract 224–7
Access 473, 483, 486
accessing base classes from derived classes 198–9
accessors 19–20
ActiveX technology 483
adapter classes 507
Add () method 498–9
addition (+) operator 39, 49–50
   overloading 153, 155–6
addresses 81
ADO.NET 483
adventure class 260–78
affine transformations 391–2
aliases 174
alpha value of colours 373–4
alternating fill algorithm 387–8
anchors 322–4
AND operator 52–3
animation 421–8
  and threads 422–8
API (Application Programming Interface) 483
apostrophes 645
applets 619
area calculations 226
arrays 93–7
  bounds checking 95
  declaration 93–4
  initialization lists 96–7, 102
  jagged arrays 101–4
  length property 94
  multidimensional 98–108
  null rows 103–4
  parameter passing 104–8
  rectangular 98–100
  of reference data types 94–5
  subscripts 93
  two-dimensional 98–100
  of value data types 94
as keyword 221–2
ASCII character set 36

ASP.NET 603, 604–10
assembly files 315
assignment operator 56, 58–9
  overloading 157–8
associativity rules 58–9
ATTLIST 551, 552
attributes in XML 539–40
automatic garbage collection 122, 126–7

backslash 37
base classes 195, 198–9
base keyword 202
binary operator 47, 58
bit shift operator 54–5
bitmap files 351–2
bitwise operators 52–3
  overloading 161
Boolean data types 36, 47
bounds checking 95
boxing 216–18
  structs 218–20
break statement 71–2
browsers 541
brushes 376–84
Build menu 8–9
buttons 295–6, 322
  mnemonic keys 330
  non-rectangular 441–7
  radio buttons 335–41, 347
  on toolbars 351–3
byte 29
byte addresses 81

C#, definition 1–3
C++ 13
calculator program 326–31
callback functions 296
calling method 146
candidates 22
casting 31, 45–7, 162–7

explicit 163
  implicit 163, 166
  misuse of 167
  user-defined 164
catch blocks 281, 283–6
CDATA 553
chained statements 56
character classes 247–56
character data types 36–8
checkboxes 335–41
checked keyword 32–3, 46, 166
checkers game 410–17
class data fields 115–16, 202
Class View 8
classes 11, 13, 14–19
  adapter 507
  adventure 260–78
  base 195, 198–9
  candidates 22
  character 247–56
  derived 195–6, 198–9
  design 430–1
  diagrams 21–2, 234
  item 238–47
  language-independent 313
  Object class 211–15
  protection levels 197
  room 256–9
  URI 657–8
  utility 410, 416
  wrapper 88, 216–17
client area of forms 330–1
clock program 342–8, 362
code generation systems 314
colours 330, 373–4
COM (Component Object Model) 647
combat sequences 237–8
ComboBox 367
command line compiler 3–5, 6
commands 188–9, 236
  command builder 508–9
comments 17, 540
Common Runtime Language (CRL) 1
comparing memory addresses 212–13, 214
comparison operator 55
  overloading 157
compatibility of data types 220–1
compound statements 113

concatenating strings 39, 50
conditional operators 57–8
  overloading 158–9
conditional statements 61–6
connecting to a database 483–91
consoles 317
Console.Writeline () method 38, 40
const keyword 149
constructors 19, 84, 137–41, 320
  and inheritance 201–2
  static 147–8
continue statement 71–2
controls see GUI (graphical user interface)
    programming; web controls
convenience assignment operator 56–7, 59
conversion of data types 31–2, 44–7
coordinate system 375
COUNT () 493
creating objects 18–19, 84, 145, 149–50
CRL (Common Runtime Language) 1
.cs files 6
cse.exe 4
currency
  calculations 35
  symbols 41
customizing DataGrids 614–19

data carried by exceptions 289–90
data fields 14, 17
  accessing base classes from derived classes
      198–9
  initializing 19
  instance fields 145, 151
  ordinary 144–5
  static 144–6
data overflow 32–3
Data Source Names (DSN) 489
data types 17, 474
  Boolean 36, 47
  character 36–8
  compatibility of 220–1
  conversions 31–2, 44–7
  decimal 35
  floating-point 33–4
  integer 29–31
  overflow checking 32–3, 46
  reference data types 81–8, 117, 127–8
    in arrays 94–5

data types (*continued*)
   round-off errors 34
   structs 127–30
   see also strings; value data types; variables
data validation *see* validation
databases 469–535
   Access 473, 483, 486
   API (Application Programming Interface) 483
   connecting to 483–91
   `DataGrids` 504–10, 511–25, 612–19
   `DataSets` 500–3, 510, 511–25
   filters 518
   many-to-many relationships 472
   MySQL 484, 487–90, 490–1
   namespaces 483, 490–1
   numerical keys 471, 472
   ODBC (Open Database Connectivity) 483, 484, 488
   one-to-many relationships 471–2
   primary keys 472–3, 475, 497–8, 509, 518
   queries 469–70, 476–8, 492–6
   referential integrity 482
   SQL Server 483, 486
   tables 470–3
   and web controls 610
   see also SQL (Structured Query Language)
`DataGrids` 504–10, 511–25, 612–19
   customizing 614–19
`DataSets` 500–3, 510, 511–25
date and time formatting 41–2
DCOM (Distributed COM) 647
debugging, Start without debugging 9
decimal data type 35
declaration
   of arrays 93–4
   of delegates 297–8
   of objects 14, 18
   of variables 14–15, 81–3, 87, 114
      and memory management 117–27
decrement (--) operator 50–2
   overloading 157
default values 139
delegates 296–300
   declaration 297–8
   and entry point of threads 310
   multicast 301–3
deleting records 482, 524
derived classes 195–6, 198–9

design of classes 430–1
diagrams
   of classes 21–2, 234
   of inheritance 233
dialog boxes 348–50
Distributed COM (DCOM) 647
division operator 50
DNS (domain name servers) 603
docks 322–4
DOCTYPE statements 553–4, 567
documentation 2, 9, 21, 324–6
   in XML 585–8
DOM (Document Object Model) 542, 558–62
domain name servers (DNS) 603
double data type 33–4
`do...while` 67–8
downloading files 654–9
drawing on images 405–7
drawing shapes 374–6
`DrawLine ()` method 375–6
DSN (Data Source Names) 489
DTD (Document Type Definitions) 550–8, 589–90
   DOCTYPE statements 553–4, 567
   writing 551–3
dynamic binding 204–6

elements in XML 539–40, 551, 552
encapsulation 14–19, 198
ENTITY 551
entry points 5, 18
   of threads 310
`enum` (enumeration) keyword 17–18, 108–12
enumerated lists 553
equality testing operator 55
`Equals ()` method 212–15
error handling 331–5
   see also exceptions
escaped characters 37, 39–40
event handling 227, 295–6, 303–7, 321–2, 454–65
   in Java 295–6
   keyboard events 418–21
   mouse events 407–18
   and toolbars 352–3
   validating event 332–4
   see also delegates

exceptions 281–93
    data carried by 289–90
    handling 283–6
    and inheritance 286–8
    throwing 288–9
    use of 292–3
    user-defined 290–2
ExecuteNonQuery () method 496–7, 499
ExecuteReader () method 492, 494–6
ExecuteScalar () method 492–3
explicit casts 163
explicit keyword 165
explicit type conversions 45–7
exponent 34
expressions
    conditional 57–8
    initialization 68
    regular 42–3
    update 68, 69, 70
Extensible Markup Language see XML
Extensible Stylesheet Language (XSLT) 542,
        578–84

false operator 57
    overloading 158–9
filename filter 362
files
    downloading files 654–9
    extensions 6
filling shapes 376–84, 387–90
filters
    in databases 518
    for filenames 362
flickering of images 417, 422
floating-point data types 33–4
focus 330, 332
fonts 329, 400–3, 618
for loop 68–70
foreach loop 97–8, 100, 102–3
Form Editor 318–19
format transformations in XML 542, 578–84
formatting
    colours 330, 373–4
    date and time 41–2
    fonts 329, 400–3, 618
    layout manager 322–3
    strings 40–2
FromFile () method 378

functions 12, 14
    callback functions 296
    see also methods

garbage collection 122, 126–7
GDI+ (Graphics Device Interface) 372
GetHashCode () method 213
GIF graphics 404
goto 72–4
gradient fills 379
graphics 371–465
    animation 421–8
    filling shapes 376–84, 387–90
    flickering of images 417, 422
    GraphicsPath 385–7, 392–3
    in Java 371–3
    keyboard events 418–21
    Matrix class 391–400
    mouse events 407–18
    raster graphics 372, 404–7
    text production 372–3, 400–3
    transformations 373, 391–400
    vector graphics 372, 373–85
    in web pages 619–22
Graphics Device Interface (GDI+) 372
GraphicsPath 385–7, 392–3
GUI (graphical user interface) programming
        313–68
    anchors 322–4
    calculator program 326–31
    checkboxes 335–41
    ComboBox 367
    dialog boxes 348–50
    docks 322–4
    environment choice 313–15
    error handling 331–5
    event handlers 321–2
    Form Editor 318–19
    ListBox 367–8, 519
    menus 342–8
    radio buttons 335–41, 347
    status bars 350, 354, 361
    toolbars 351–3
    TreeView 368
    see also buttons

handling exceptions 283–6
HatchBrush 378–9

heap 120–6, 127
HTML 537–8, 542, 580, 581, 583–4, 605, 608–10, 622

icons 351
if...else statement 61–3
image files 404–5
immutable variables 39
implicit casts 163, 166
implicit keyword 165
implicit type conversions 31–2, 44–5
import statement 314
increment (++) operator 50–2
    overloading 157
indexers 167–70
infinite loops 67
inheritance 14, 195–278
    and abstract classes 224–7
    accessing base classes from derived classes 198–9
    and boxing 216–18
        structs 218–20
    concept 195–6
    and constructors 201–2
    diagrams 233
    and exceptions 286–8
    and interfaces 227–31
    of methods 200–1
        sealed methods 222–4
        static methods 209–210
        virtual methods 204–6
    and name hiding 201, 202–3, 209
    and sealed classes 222–4
    and structs 218–20
    syntax 196–7
    and unboxing 218
    and value variables 216–18
    and versioning 207–9
    see also polymorphism
initialization 260–3, 431–41
    of data fields 19
    expressions 68
    lists 96–7, 102
    of variables 91
inserting new records 475–9
instance methods 145, 151
integer data types 29–31
interactive web pages 622–3, 631–2

interfaces 385, 429–30, 624–5
    and inheritance 227–31
    listener interfaces 227, 295–6
    see also GUI (graphical user interface) programming
Internet
    ASP.NET 603, 604–10
    downloading files 654–9
    servers 603
    see also web pages
Internet Service Providers (ISPs) 603
is 220–1
is-a-type-of relationships 196
item classes 238–47
item editor 623–46
    data validation 630, 635–6
    interactive data display 631–2
    interface 624–5
    templates 631, 632–3

jagged arrays 101–4
Java
    applets 619
    event handling 295–6
    graphics 371–3
    import statement 314
    JDK (Java Development Kit) 585
    JSP (Java Server Pages) 603
    JVM (Java Virtual Machine) 371
    layout manager 322–3
    libraries 2
    platform independence 1
    Shape interface 385
    threads 307–8
joins 478–81
JPEG graphics 404, 619

keyboard events 418–21
    modifier keys 421
keyboard mapping 9
keywords
    abstract 224–7
    as 221–2
    base 202
    checked 32–3, 46, 166
    const 149
    enum (enumeration) 17–18, 108–12
    explicit 165

implicit 165
new 209, 210
null 83
operator 165
out 91–2
override 205, 207–8, 209, 223
params 106–8
private 14
protected 199
readonly 150
ref 88–91
sealed 222–4
static 144–8
super 201
this 151–3
throw 288–9
using 5, 172–4, 314–15
virtual 204–6
see also operators

language independence 1, 313
layout manager 322–3
left-associative operators 58–9
length property 94
libraries 2, 314–15
    see also documentation
line segments 386
LinearGradientBrush 379
ListBox 367–8, 519
listener interfaces 227, 295–6
loading saved files 594–9
local variables 112–15, 116
logical operators 54
    overloading 159–61
long 30, 31, 162
loops 66–70
    do...while 67–8
    for 68–70
    foreach 97–8, 100, 102–3
    infinite 67
    nested 73–4
    while 66–7

Main () method 18, 25–6
managed heaps 127
mantissa 34
many-to-many relationships 472
maps for adventure games 447–51

matching characters 42–3
matrices 154, 391–2
Matrix class 391–400
memory 117–27
    automatic garbage collection 122, 126–7
    comparing addresses 212–13, 214
    heap 120–6, 127
    stack 120
    storage of variables 81–2, 120
menus 342–8
methods 14
    abstract 224
    Add () 498–9
    calling 146
    Console.Writeline () 38, 40
    DrawLine () 375–6
    Equals () 212–15
    ExecuteNonQuery () 496–7, 499
    ExecuteReader () 492, 494–6
    ExecuteScalar () 492–3
    FromFile () 378
    GetHashCode () 213
    implementation in running code 151
    and inheritance 200–1
        sealed 222–4
        static 209–210
        virtual 204–6
    instance 145, 151
    Main () 18, 25–6
    OnPaint () 374–5, 393
    overloaded 141, 142–4
    PlayGame () 26
    PrintDescription () 197, 200
    ReferenceEquals () 212–15
    sealed 222–4
    side effects 88
    signatures 142, 297
    static 146–7, 151, 209–210
    ToString () 23–6, 211–12
    virtual 204–6
    see also constructors; functions; parameter
        passing
MFC (Microsoft Foundation Classes) 372, 404
mnemonic keys 330
modal dialog 349–50
modifier keys 421
modulus operator 50
Mono project 1

mouse events 407–18
MSDN documentation 2, 324–6, 368
multi-tasking systems 307
multi-word commands 189
multicast delegates 301–3
multidimensional arrays 98–108
multiplication operator 50
    overloading 153
MySQL 484, 487–90, 490–1

name hiding 201, 202–3, 209
namespaces 5, 8, 170–4
    aliases 174
    for databases 483, 490–1
    defining 170–2
    motivation for 171
    nesting 173
    SqlClient 490–1
    System namespace 315
    using statement 5, 172–4, 314–15
naming variables 108
nested loops 73–4
nesting namespaces 173
.NET xiii
    ADO.NET 483
    ASP.NET 603, 604–10
    definition 1–3
    language independence 1, 313
    Visual Basic .NET 2, 13, 313
    Visual Studio .NET xv, 3, 6–9, 314, 315–17
new keyword 209, 210
new operator 84, 122
newline characters 39
nodes 540
non-modal dialog 349–50
non-printing characters 37
non-rectangular buttons 441–7
NOTATION 551
Notepad 3–4, 364–7
null keyword 83
null rows 103–4
numerical keys 471, 472

Object class 211–15
object-oriented programming 11, 12–13
    creating objects 18–19, 84, 145, 149–50
    declaring objects 14, 18
ODBC (Open Database Connectivity) 483, 484, 488

OleDB 483, 484
one-to-many relationships 471–2
OnPaint () method 374–5, 393
operands 47–8, 153
operating systems 307
operator keyword 165
operators 47–61
    addition (+) 39, 49–50
    as 221–2
    assignment 56, 58–9
    associativity rules 58–9
    binary 47, 58
    bit shift 54–5
    bitwise 52–3
    comparison 55
    conditional 57–8
    convenience assignment 56–7, 59
    decrement (—) 50–2
    division 50
    equality testing 55
    false 57
    increment (++) 50–2
    is 220–1
    logical operators 54
    modulus 50
    multiplication 50
    new 84, 122
    overloading 153–62
        rules for 161–2
    precedence 59–61
    ternary 47, 57
    true 57
    unitary 47
    XOR 52–3
    see also keywords
OR operator 52–3
ORDER BY 481
ordinary data fields 144–5
orthogonal arrays see jagged arrays
out keyword 91–2
overflow checking 32–3, 46
overloading 153–62
    addition (+) operator 153, 155–6
    assignment operators 157–8
    bitwise operators 161
    decrement (—) operator 157
    false operator 158–9
    increment (++) operator 157

logical operators 159–61
methods 141, 142–4
multiplication 153
rules for 161–2
override keyword 205, 207–8, 209, 223

paint 371, 374–5
parameter passing 86–91, 115
in arrays 104–8
out keyword 91–2
and polymorphism 207
ref keyword 88–91
scope 115
params keyword 106–8
parsing 542, 550, 554–8
Pascal 11
PathGradientBrush 380–3
pathnames 4–5
pattern matching 42–3
pens 374–6, 384
perimeter calculations 226, 229–30
pixel coordinates 375
placeholders 40
platform independence 1
PlayGame () method 26
pointers xiv
polymorphism 14, 201, 203–4, 206
and compatibility of data types 220–1
and parameter passing 207
and references to abstract classes 227
popup menus 342
postback 622–3
precedence operator 59–61
prepared statements 497–9, 508
primary keys 472–3, 475, 497–8, 509, 518
primitive data types see data types
PrintDescription () method 197, 200
private keyword 14
procedural languages 11–12
procedures 12
projects 6–7
properties 13–14, 19–21
protected keyword 199
protection levels 197
providers 486
pseudo-random numbers 274

queries 469–70, 476–8, 492–6

radio buttons 335–41, 347
random numbers 274
raster graphics 372, 404–7
drawing on images 405–7
image files 404–5
rays 389
reading 543–50
readonly keyword 150
rectangles 225–6, 228–31
rectangular arrays 98–100
ref keyword 88–91
reference data types 81–8, 117, 127–8
in arrays 94–5
ReferenceEquals () method 212–15
references to abstract classes 227
referential integrity 482
regular expressions 42–3
rendering 386
requirements documents 21
RGB colour model 373
right-associative operators 58–9
room class 256–9
rotation actions 373, 391, 396–8
round-off errors 34

saving files 589–94
SAX (Simple API for XML) 542
sbyte 29
scaling actions 373, 391, 398
schemas 543, 550–1
scope rules 112–16
SDK (Software Development Kit) 3, 6
sealed 222–4
searching with XPath see XPath
SELECT 476–9, 492–3
servers 603
set accessor 20
Shape interface 385
shearing actions 373, 391, 398–400
short 30
shortcut keys 346
shortcuts 9
side effects 88
signatures 142, 297
signed integers 29–30
Simple API for XML (SAX) 542
Simula 13
single-word commands 188

Smalltalk 13
SOAP (Simple Object Access Protocol) 648
Software Development Kit (SDK) 3, 6
SolidBrush 377
Solution Explorer 6, 8, 316, 587
special characters 39–40
specification of programmes 13
SQL Server 483, 486
SQL (Structured Query Language) 473–82
   apostrophes 645
   COUNT () 493
   data types 474
   deleting records 482, 524
   inserting new records 475–9
   joins 478–81
   ORDER BY 481
   prepared statements 497–9, 508
   queries 476–8, 492–6
   running SQL commands 487, 491–9
   SELECT 476–9, 492–3
   UPDATE 482
SqlClient 490–1
square bracket [] notation 167
stack 120
stack trace 281, 289
stateless pages 609, 623
statements
   break 71–2
   chained 56
   conditional 61–6
   continue 71–2
   goto 72–4
   if...else 61–3
   switch 63–6
   using 5, 172–4, 314–15
states 371, 372
static constructors 147–8
static data fields 144–6
static keyword 144–8
static methods 146–7, 151, 209–210
statistic displays 451–4
status bars 350, 354, 361
storage of variables 81–2, 120
strings 38–42, 177
   concatenating 39, 50
   formatting 40–2
   inserting special characters 39–40
   matching characters 42–3

stroke 371
structs 127–30
   boxing 218–20
   and inheritance 218–20
sub-menus 346
subpaths 386–7
subscripts in arrays 93
super keyword 201
switch statement 63–6
System namespace 315
System.Object class 211–15

tab sequences 330
TabControl 511–12
tables in databases 470–3
   joins 478–81
tags 537–9, 541
templates 578–9, 631, 632–3
ternary operator 47, 57
test code 18
text editors 313–14
text production 372–3, 400–3
TextureBrush 377–8
this keyword 151–3
threads 307–11
   and animation 422–8
   entry point 310
   in Java 307–8
throw keyword 288–9
tiling 383–4
time and date formatting 41–2
toolbars 351–3
top-down design 12
ToString () method 23–6, 211–12
transformations 373, 391–400
   affine 391–2
   matrix representation 391–2
   rotation 373, 391, 396–8
   scaling 373, 391, 398
   shearing 373, 391, 398–400
   translation 373, 391, 393–6
   in XML 542, 578–84
translation actions 373, 391, 393–6
tree structure 540, 550
TreeView 368
triangular brush 380–4
true operator 57
   overloading 158–9

`try...catch` block 281, 283–6
turn-based combat sequences 237
two-dimensional arrays 98–100

`uint` 30
`ulong` 30, 31
UML (Universal Modelling Language) 234
unboxing 218
Unicode system 36–8
unitary operator 47
unmanaged heaps 127
unsafe code xiv
unsigned integers 29–30
UPDATE 482
update expressions 68, 69, 70
`URI` class 657–8
URL (Uniform Resource Locator) 603
use cases 21–2
user interaction 295
user-defined casts 164
user-defined exceptions 290–2
`ushort` 30
`using` 5, 172–4, 314–15
utility classes 410, 416

validation 332–4, 543, 550–8, 630, 635–6
value data types 81–8, 117, 127–8
  in arrays 94
  and inheritance 216–18
  structs 127–30, 218–20
variables
  class data fields 115–16, 202
  declaring 14–15, 81–3, 87, 114
    and memory management 117–27
  initializing 91
  local 112–15, 116
  naming 108
  passing as parameters 86–91
  scope rules 112–16
  storage in memory 81–2, 120
  see also data types
vector graphics 372, 373–85
  brushes 376–84
  colours 373–4
  drawing shapes 374–6
  filling shapes 376–84, 387–90
  pens 374–6, 384

vectors 154, 391
versioning 207–9
`virtual` 204–6
Visual Basic .NET 2, 13, 313
Visual Studio .NET xv, 3, 6–9, 314, 315–17

web controls 606, 608, 610, 621–2
web pages 603–4
  ASP.NET 603, 604–10
  downloading files 654–9
  graphics 619–22
  interactive 622–3, 631–2
  postback 622–3
  stateless pages 609, 623
web servers 603
Web Service Definition Language (WSDL) 648
web services 647–54
  consuming 651–4
well-formed files 550
`while` loop 66–7, 67–8
whitespace characters 37
winding filling mode 389–90
Windows programs 315–19
  see also GUI (graphical user interface)
    programming
`WrapMode` 379
wrapper classes 88, 216–17
WSDL (Web Service Definition Language) 648

XML (Extensible Markup Language) 537–99
  attributes 539–40
  comment lines 540
  documentation 585–8
  DOM (Document Object Model) 542, 558–62
  DTD (Document Type Definitions) 550–8,
    589–90
  editing 566–78
  elements 539–40
  format transformations 542, 578–84
  loading saved files 594–9
  nodes 540
  parsing 542, 550, 554–8
  reading 543–50
  saving files 589–94
  schemas 543, 550–1
  searching with XPath 542, 562–6
  tags 537–9, 541
  tree structure 540, 550

XML (Extensible Markup Language)
    (*continued*)
  using 541–3
  validation 543, 550–8
  well-formed files 550
  writing 566–78
XmlDocument 568–78

XMLTextReader 543–50
XmlTextWriter 566, 567–8
XOR operator 52–3
XPath 542, 562–6
XSLT (Extensible Stylesheet Language) 542, 578–84
  templates 578–9